BUILDING THE E-SERVICE SOCIETY
E-Commerce, E-Business, and E-Government

IFIP – The International Federation for Information Processing

IFIP was founded in 1960 under the auspices of UNESCO, following the First World Computer Congress held in Paris the previous year. An umbrella organization for societies working in information processing, IFIP's aim is two-fold: to support information processing within its member countries and to encourage technology transfer to developing nations. As its mission statement clearly states,

> *IFIP's mission is to be the leading, truly international, apolitical organization which encourages and assists in the development, exploitation and application of information technology for the benefit of all people.*

IFIP is a non-profit making organization, run almost solely by 2500 volunteers. It operates through a number of technical committees, which organize events and publications. IFIP's events range from an international congress to local seminars, but the most important are:

- The IFIP World Computer Congress, held every second year;
- Open conferences;
- Working conferences.

The flagship event is the IFIP World Computer Congress, at which both invited and contributed papers are presented. Contributed papers are rigorously refereed and the rejection rate is high.

As with the Congress, participation in the open conferences is open to all and papers may be invited or submitted. Again, submitted papers are stringently refereed.

The working conferences are structured differently. They are usually run by a working group and attendance is small and by invitation only. Their purpose is to create an atmosphere conducive to innovation and development. Refereeing is less rigorous and papers are subjected to extensive group discussion.

Publications arising from IFIP events vary. The papers presented at the IFIP World Computer Congress and at open conferences are published as conference proceedings, while the results of the working conferences are often published as collections of selected and edited papers.

Any national society whose primary activity is in information may apply to become a full member of IFIP, although full membership is restricted to one society per country. Full members are entitled to vote at the annual General Assembly, National societies preferring a less committed involvement may apply for associate or corresponding membership. Associate members enjoy the same benefits as full members, but without voting rights. Corresponding members are not represented in IFIP bodies. Affiliated membership is open to non-national societies, and individual and honorary membership schemes are also offered.

BUILDING THE E-SERVICE SOCIETY

E-Commerce, E-Business, and E-Government

IFIP 18th World Computer Congress
TC6 / TC8 / TC11 4th International Conference on
E-Commerce, E-Business, E-Government (I3E 2004)
22–27 August 2004
Toulouse, France

Edited by

Winfried Lamersdorf
Hamburg University, Germany

Volker Tschammer
Fraunhofer FOKUS, Germany

Stéphane Amarger
Hitachi Europe SAS, France

KLUWER ACADEMIC PUBLISHERS
BOSTON / DORDRECHT / LONDON

Distributors for North, Central and South America:
Kluwer Academic Publishers
101 Philip Drive
Assinippi Park
Norwell, Massachusetts 02061 USA
Telephone (781) 871-6600
Fax (781) 681-9045
E-Mail <kluwer@wkap.com>

Distributors for all other countries:
Kluwer Academic Publishers Group
Post Office Box 322
3300 AH Dordrecht, THE NETHERLANDS
Telephone 31 78 6576 000
Fax 31 78 6576 254
E-Mail <services@wkap.nl>

Electronic Services <http://www.wkap.nl>

Library of Congress Cataloging-in-Publication Data

A C.I.P. Catalogue record for this book is available from the Library of Congress.

Building the E-Service Society: E-Commerce, E-Business, and E-Government
Edited by Winfried Lamersdorf, Volker Tschammer, and Stéphane Amarger

ISBN 978-1-4419-5488-6

Printed on acid-free paper.

Contents

E-GOVERNANCE

M-COMMERCE

SERVICE PROVISIONING

VALUE CHAIN MANAGEMENT

E-BUSINESS MODELS

Conference Committees

General Chair
Stéphane Amarger

Programme Co-Chairs
Volker Tschammer and Winfried Lamersdorf

International Programme Committee

N. Bjørn-Andersen, Denmark
W. Cellary, Poland
D. Deschoolmester, Belgium
A. Dogac, Turkey
T. M. van Engers, Netherlands
M. Funabashi, Japan
T. F. Gordon, Germany
S. Gusmeroli, Italy
A. Iyengar, USA
F. Kamoun, Tunisia
B. R. Katzy, Netherlands
R. M. Lee, USA
M. J. Mendes, Brazil
M. Merz, Germany
Z. Milosevic, Australia
M. Pallot, France
C. Passos, Brazil
G. Piccinelli, United Kingdom
D. Polemi, Greece
J. Posegga, Germany
R. Riedl, Switzerland
N. Ritter, Germany
M. Schoop, Germany
S. Shrivastava, United Kingdom
K. Stanoevska-Slabeva, Switzerland
R. Suomi, Finland
R. Traunmüller, Austria
A. Tsalgatidou, Greece
V. Wade, Ireland
F. Weber, Germany
H. Weigand, Netherlands
R. Wigand, USA
M. A. Wimmer, Austria
H. D. Zimmermann, Switzerland
K. Zielinski, Poland

I3E Steering Comittee

K. Bauknecht, Switzerland
C. Glasson, Australia
D. Khakhar, Sweden
J. Miettinen, Finland
M. Mendes, Brazil
H. Rudin, Switzerland
S. Teufel, Switzerland
V. Tschammer, Germany

Additional Reviewers

Introduction

Computer applications like e-commerce, e-business, and e-government provide efficient means to offer, access, and use many kinds of services electronically for still increasing numbers of users. Despite economic ups and downs of "e-services" offerings in distributed "open service" computing environments, many such services have now become an important and integral part of modern society's computer network applications.

The technical basis for e-services is built by distributed computer applications supporting increasingly complex electronic interactions ("transactions") between heterogeneous partners in their respective roles as consumers, businesses and/or government agencies (in all possible combinations). However, the resulting distributed communication systems can not be employed successfully without additional contributions addressing both information system as well as security aspects.

Therefore, following its initial conference on "Trends in Electronic Commerce" 1998 in Hamburg, IFIP set up a series of conferences on "E-Commerce, E-Business, and E-Government" as a joint effort by the three technical committees TC6 (Communication), TC8 (Information Systems), and TC11 (Security). Previous conferences took place in Zürich, Switzerland (2001), Lisbon, Portugal (2002), and Sao Paolo, Brazil (2003) providing a forum for users, engineers, and researchers to present their latest findings in e-commerce, e-business, and e-government applications and the underlying technologies which support those applications.

This year (for the first time), I3E is co-located with the IFIP World Computer Congress providing additional information opportunities on a broad spectrum of challenges and solutions that enable the emerging paradigm of ambient intelligence to support the future knowledge society.

The I3E2004 conference programme comprises nine sessions – three for each of its main programmatic areas:

E-Government:	E-Government Models and Processes E-Governance Service Provisioning
E-Business:	Infrastructures and Marketplaces M-Commerce Purchase and Payment
E-Commerce:	Value Chain Management E-Business Architectures and Processes E-Business Models

In addition, two keynote speakers address aspects of the knowledge-based economy as well as European e-government, and a panel discusses the question whether e-Business provides only chances without risks.

For the scientific programme, a total of 26 papers have been accepted for presentation and are published in this proceedings. They were selected out of 81 submissions in a rigorous review process by the International Programme Committee with an acceptance rate of just 32%.

Contributions came from all five continents supporting IFIP's mission of encouraging and assisting people from all over the world in the development, exploitation, and application of information technology. Authors contribute to a debate about issues ranging from rather philosophical issues, like trust and governance, organisational subjects, like business models and job chances, to specific issues of communication and information technology.

Finally, we would like to thank the many people who have contributed to the success of this conference: the keynote speakers, the panel organisers and panellist as well as the members of the international programme committee and all reviewers for writing up some 250 reviews and for assistance in organising the conference programme. Special thanks go to the IFIP secretariat and the organisers of the WCC2004 for their very efficient support and assistance w.r.t. publicity and organisation of the conference and, last but note least, to all those who helped produce these proceedings including those at our own local sites.

Winfried Lamersdorf, Volker Tschammer, Stéphane Amarger
Hamburg, Berlin, Sophia Antipolis

E-GOVERNMENT MODELS AND PROCESSES

TOWARDS KEY BUSINESS PROCESS FOR E-GOVERNMENT

Amauri Marques da Cunha and Paulo Mendez Costa
Núcleo de Computação Eletrônica - Universidade Federal do Rio de Janeiro

Abstract: Since 1994, when started the commercial use of the Internet, several manners of doing business emerged around the world. Following this trend, governments started using new tools from the Information and Communication Technologies (ICT), giving raise to the e-government area. In this paper, recent evaluation reports about government portals from all over the world are summarized. They show that there are still much work to be done to attain a high-level of integration and quality of services. Then, a new approach is proposed to e-government initiatives, introducing the concept of Governmental Key Business Processes (G-KBP) that is based on process modeling techniques and modern public administration concepts. This proposal may be used as a guideline to the construction and maintenance of highly integrated e-government environments.

Key words: e-government, business process, public services, process modeling

1. INTRODUCTION

The emergence of Internet enabled a low cost of information sharing and dissemination, independent of the existing distance between the producer and the consumer of the information. This new environment allowed access of a growing number of citizens and customers to new kinds of businesses that has been continuously revealed. This novelty is changing the environment where corporations, governments and communities interact. The changes are, especially, in the way information is received, processed, sent and stored. In this new environment, speed, flexibility and innovation are essential.

Since the middle of the 1990s, governments from all over the world have been adopting initiatives of using the Internet potential to improve public services. The Internet, as the personal computer, became an essential tool in the day-to-day of public administration.

The main objective of those initiatives is to take into account the public opinion trends, which are the reduction of public spending and the improvement of public services [14]. Citizens tend to behave the same way as private companies customers, that is, they are continuously requiring more for less. They can (and must) realize that the adoption of new technologies can increase productivity in the public sector, as can be observed in the private sector.

Therefore, the e-government is a vision of the future as much as a reality in our daily life. It can transform and improve the quality of the managerial actions and the political activities. E-government should be used as an instrument of public administration to better serve the citizens. Governments should consider the point of view of citizens and firms – as a commitment. Thus, the central point is: how to do it without simply transfer the governmental bureaucracy to the Internet?

Motivated by the importance of this issue, we found that despite of the significant work already done in this area, there is no structured methodology to the development of an e-government environment. Using a process approach, we introduce the Key Business Process (KBP) concept and its extension to the government environment, named Government Key Business Process (G-KBP). From these concepts, it is possible to build a framework to e-government initiatives, in a way that leads to a complete integration of the delivered services. That is the goal of this work.

The paper is organized as follows. Section 2 presents the evolution of the public administration as a foundation for e-government implementation. Section 3 shows evaluation initiatives of e-government environments around the world. Section 4 presents new approaches to government and e-government areas. Section 5 describes the Business Process Engineering and its analogy to the public sector. Section 6 presents the Governmental Business Process Engineering and the benefits of its approach. The last section concludes and suggests some future work.

2. FOUNDATIONS TO E-GOVERNMENT IMPLEMENTATION

During the 20th century, successive significant advancements have occurred in the Information and Communication Technology (ICT) area, as well as in the administration science. The governmental sector has been affected by these facts. The governmental bureaucratic model – also known as Weberian – has suffered theoretic and practical contestation. The public management model – also known as managerialism – has been proposed for governmental actions all around the world [1], [3].

2.1 The Evolution of Public Administration

The pre-capitalist and pre-democratic societies did not make clear distinction between public and private property. During the so-called "Patrimonialism" age, the government was unable or reluctant in distinguishing public from private property.

As capitalism emerged, came to light the need to differentiate these two kinds of properties, producing changes in the way nations were administered. Thus, the concept of an administration that protects public interests from the nepotism and corruption associated with patrimonialism appeared, laying down the foundation for the modern "Bureaucracy". According to Bresser-Pereira [3], this type of public administration is based on "the principles of a professional civil service and of an impersonal, formal, and rational administrative system". Max Weber was the most important theorist that showed the advantages of bureaucracy over patrimonialism in its classical book called "Economy and Society" edited in 1922 [3]. Some authors name these ideas about public administration as "Weberian".

However, the significant development that has occurred during the 20th century has increased the responsibilities of states, even in capitalist societies, to face new challenges. In this new scenery, some advantages of the bureaucratic administration – such as the rigid hierarchy and the formalism in the procedures – became to be perceived as obstacles in achieving the agility and the effectiveness required by the governments.

In this context, the managerial public administration emerges in the second half of the 20th century, as an answer, amongst other things, to the fiscal crisis of the state, which therefore needed to administer its resources more efficiently in order to satisfy the expectations of its citizens in regards to the services provided, and to the technological development and the globalization of the world economy. According to this set of ideas, called managerialism [3], the state should be mainly oriented by efficiency and effectiveness values when offering public services, and therefore, it should adopt a (new) management culture.

Managerialism in public administration cannot be considered as a single way of thinking and acting. At theoretical as well as at practical level, it was composed (and still it is) by an aggregation of elements that can vary according to the author and the country where it was implemented. It is interesting to mention the attempt made by Abrucio [1] to categorize managerialism. He has studied several state reforms tries made in the 20th century last decades. This author recognizes that it is impossible to classify every occurrence, and that the three types of managerialism that have been identified, still present an overlapping of features. However, it is worthwhile to detach the following general ideas employed by managerialism:

- Administrative decentralization;
- Privatization of some activities;
- Performance evaluation of public services expenditures;
- Looking for efficiency and productivity through cost reductions;
- Focus on effectiveness of governmental actions;
- Use of management contracts to achieve prefixed goals;
- Attempts to adopt some private administration ideas, like:
  - Consider users as clients and/or consumers;
  - Establish "competition" among public organizations,
  - Total Quality Management (TQM).

This list is not a structured framework, it is only a set of ideas that can inspire good practices, and it cannot be accepted as a theory or a technique of public administration. Nevertheless, many of these ideas were used in different reforms of public sectors in many countries.

In addiction, we would like to emphasize two other factors that seem to be fundamental in this way of thinking. The first one is the big influence of private sector theories and techniques, probably due to the significant success achieved by the corporations that have adopted them. The second is the increasing use of ICT to enable many of the performed changes. In our opinion, the correct understanding of these two factors will enable relevant propositions towards public sector improvements. Consequently, e-government initiatives should benefit from these ideas.

However, before discussing and proposing some new approaches, some recent studies concerning governmental portals evaluations are presented in the following Section.

3. E-GOVERNMENT INITIATIVES EVALUATIONS

The e-government topic became part of governmental agendas with big visibility, because the societies have realized the importance of using ICT within public administration. In 2002, the United Nations (UN) made a study about the initiatives and the commitment of part of its 190 members in the e-government area [14]. At the same time, in Brazil, the Industries Federation of Rio de Janeiro State (FIRJAN) developed research projects with the purpose of measuring the achievements of Brazilian states and municipalities in this area [6], [7]. The methodologies used and some conclusions reached by these works are briefly described in the next Sections.

3.1 The UN Evaluation [14]

The aim of this study was to discover the commitment level of UN members with the e-government area, and their ability to support on-line solutions. The final measures of this research, called E-government Index, were calculated using three indicators: Web Presence, ICT Infrastructure and Human Capital of the country.

The Web Presence Measure indicates the on-line development stage of each country. The stage of development was organized in 5 levels from the emerging (the basic level) till the seamless (the most advanced), according to Table 1. For this indicator, the target governmental sectors considered were: health, education, labor and employment, social welfare, and finance.

Table 1. Stages of E-government [14]

Stage of Development	Description
Emerging	An official government online presence is established.
Enhanced	Government sites increase; information becomes more dynamic.
Interactive	Users can download forms, e-mail officials and interact through the web.
Transactional	Users can actually pay for services and other transactions online.
Seamless	Full integration of e-services across administrative boundaries.

The ICT Infrastructure Measure was calculated using six primary indicators, as for example: PCs per 100 individuals, percentage of a nation's population online and quantity of telephone lines per 100 individuals. The Human Capital has tried to measure, from the analysis of social indicators, the country's and its citizens' facilities and opportunities to use on-line government.

The result was that only 35 countries (25%) - among the 144 evaluated - presented an E-government Index above 2.00 points, which was considered a high capability in e-government area. On the other hand, 71 countries (49.3%) presented an E-government Index considered minimal or deficient. The e-government programs of these countries reflect their limited capability in infrastructure area and in human capital.

According to this evaluation, USA was considered the global leader in the e-government area, and the only country to reach an E-government Index above 3.00 points. The report concludes that this is due to several factors, such as: tradition and leadership in ICT area, high schooling level of the population and the economic power. However, despite of these factors, it is pointed out that the USA e-government became successful only after the launching of www.firstgov.gov, the official portal of the federal government.

We can find a low quality grade in the majority of the e-government initiatives explored by the UN. It is interesting to mention that none of the initiatives described in this report has reached the highest stage of development: the seamless one. In this stage, it should occur a total integration of all the support functions for the available electronic services through the departmental and administrative boundaries.

In this UN report, Brazil was distinguished as the South America regional leader with an E-government Index of 2.24 points, thanks to the grade 4.0 acquired in the Web Presence Measure indicator. According to the report, various countries, including Brazil, are capable to overcome theirs infrastructure limitations to develop a complete e-government program.

3.2 FIRJAN Evaluations [6], [7]

This work addressed the e-government initiatives implemented by the Rio de Janeiro State's Municipalities and by the Brazilian States' administrations. It has considered three indicators: Website Development Stage, Extensiveness of Subjects and Technical Level.

The Website Development Stage corresponds to the quantity of on-line services available, classified by the evolution grade reached by its transactions. This evolutional rating was classified in four levels, from the most basic – the informative level – till the most advanced – the integrative level – according to Table 2.

Table 2. Stages of E-government [6], [7]

Stage of Development	Description
Informative	Publishes information about diverse governmental departments.
Interactive	Includes information and data received from citizens.
Transactional	In addition to information exchange, values can be exchanged too.
Integrative	Convergence of all governmental services rendered in one unique portal.

The Extensiveness of Subjects was defined as the quantity of subjects found in each portal, which belong to a reference list of 25 subjects. Selecting all the relevant services that were present in at least one of the researched websites created this reference list. Finally, the Technical Level corresponds to the usability and graphical design evaluations according to Nielsen and Tahir [10].

The outcome of this report is a consolidation of the indicators presented above. With respect to the Website Development Stage, none of the States or Municipalities was in the integrative development stage, considered the ideal in e-government applications. In the Extensiveness of Subjects criterion, where the grades were assigned regarding the set of subjects found in all sites, the evaluation was unfair by the absence of an external quality factor. The Technical Level rates stayed between 5.6 and 5.8 points with relation to 10 possible points. It can be considered a bad result taking into account that this area has been studied for a long time.

There is much work to be done to establish a solid e-government environment in Brazil. The development of an effective e-government environment seems to be complex and involves other questions that will be discussed forward in this article.

Nevertheless, how to reach this high level, named integrative or seamless for e-government applications? We believe the answer may be found using new approaches to this issue.

4. SOME NEW APPROACHES TO E-GOVERNMENT

This Section presents some new approaches to government administration, and particularly to e-government, which were considered interesting to induce new initiatives. They are: the USA Federal Government portal, Traunmüller's point of view, and the Bresser-Pereira proposal for a Brazilian State reform.

4.1 The USA Federal Government Portal

According to the UN evaluation introduced in Section 3.1, the best country's portal was the USA Federal Government. A plausible reason is that this country is the principal in generating new ideas and concepts for the business world. Something similar occurs in the e-government area.

Along with several published documents in the last years, the Osborne & Gaebler [12] book seems to be the most notable and the most popular in USA. As many other subsequent publications, this book claims for the necessity of innovation and entrepreneurship to revamp government. Moreover, Osborne & Gaebler propose that the government should work more as catalyst than operator within society.

Because of Osborne & Gaebler and many other authors' ideas, and some local government reports, we met in [11] the implementation strategy of the USA e-government environment, consisting of three basic principles:

- Citizen-centered, not bureaucracy-centered;
- Results-oriented; and
- Market-based, actively promoting innovation.

This document identifies four user / services groups (Table 3) that should be focused when delivering governmental on-line services.

Table 3. USA Federal E-government Services [11]

E-government Service	Description
Individuals/Citizens: Government-to-Citizens (G2C)	Build one-stop points-of-service that make it easy for citizens to access high-quality government services.
Businesses: Government-to-Business (G2B)	Reduce government's burden on businesses by eliminating redundant collection of data and better leveraging E-business technologies for communication.
Intergovernmental: Government-to-Government (G2G)	Make it easier for states and localities to meet reporting requirements and participate as full partners with the federal government in citizen services, while enabling better performance measurement, especially for grants.
Intra-governmental: Internal Efficiency and Effectiveness (IEE)	Make better use of modern technology to reduce costs and improve quality of federal government agency administration. Agencies will be able to improve effectiveness and efficiency, eliminating delays in processing and improving employee satisfaction and retention.

Table 3 presents the four high-level options at USA Federal Government portal. The services are organized in line with the user (client) type. We believe the fact that the two first types of users (individuals and firms) can be considered as "clients" of the services, it is not a coincidence, since they are taxpayers. It probably reflects the priority assigned to satisfy the client's needs.

The other two types of users described in Table 3 may be considered "internals" for the government. The first one is oriented to other government instances, like states and municipalities, while the last one is clearly aimed to federal government employees.

4.2 Traunmüller's Point of View

In Europe, it also happened a proliferation of ideas concerning government reforms and e-government. The European Community (EC) has succeeded, thanks to a considerable number of published ideas about countries integrations. The same occurred in ICT area to support this integration.

There are also many reports about local administrations accomplishments. However, the integration level reached by USA has not yet been achieved, due to administrative, cultural and financial issues. Despite of this, there are proposals to establish a general framework to arrange new initiatives. One of these suggestions is Traunmüller's [13] point of view, where four perspectives are stated concerning e-government:

1. The Citizen Perspective – to offer public services to citizens, which are the taxpayers. In this perspective, the portals could be tools for delivering services. The services should take into account the citizens' and suppliers' points-of-view. The absence of the citizens' viewpoint when developing the solutions has been the biggest cause of failure. Users cannot cope with the logic of administrative thinking and they cannot be forced to understand administrative jargons.
2. The Process Perspective – to reconsider the government productive processes at all levels. This means that the external structures of the services should be adequately mapped to the internal processes. Hence, the customer perspectives have to be complemented by a restructuring of the business processes. Process reorganization in the public sector may often result in the rethinking the institutional structures of government.
3. The Cooperation Perspective – to integrate the distinct governmental institutions, and these with private and non-governmental organizations. Thus, the decision process could be accelerated without loosing quality as preventing fragmentations and redundancies that may exist in these relationships between several actors.
4. The Knowledge Management Perspective – to allow the government to create, to manage and to make available in appropriate repositories, the knowledge generated and accumulated by several government institutions.

This proposal emphasizes, in the first and in the second items (and probably the most significant), an interesting progress when compared to the USA portal. Although the item 1 mentions only the citizens, when it refers to the taxpayer role, we can also include companies. However, the most interesting thing is stressing the need of processes identification - made in the second item of the proposal - clarifying the interdependence between the productive processes and the delivery of services to the citizens. This idea seems to be very powerful in the direction of improving the performance of the governmental processes.

The last two items call attention to "internal" aspects of the administration. The Cooperation Perspective does it explicitly, while the Knowledge Management Perspective should be understood as "internal operations oriented", since only the needful knowledge must be managed.

4.3 Bresser-Pereira Proposal for a Brazilian State Reform

The so-called "emergent" countries suffered intensely the 70's and 80's crisis in the 20th century. In addition to proposals made by international organisms to deal with the problems, it also came out local suggestions in many countries. Brazil was one of these countries, where Bresser-Pereira, an Economy and Administration professor, was in charge of the Ministry of the Administration and Reform of the Brazilian State.

The Bresser-Pereira's proposals were summarized in [3]. In this report we can find out the interesting point of view that the crisis of the countries were a governance crisis, as occurred in many big private corporations at the same time. Therefore, there was a necessity to reform the state in order to "come again to be effective" and to face its (new) responsibilities.

Bresser-Pereira, a follower of the managerialism mentioned in Section 2, has formulated and has partly performed a reform of the Brazilian State, based on the next concepts concerning the major functions that should be performed by a modern state [3]:

1. Strategic core – "is where law and policies are defined and their enforcement is in the last instance assured";
2. Exclusive activities – "are the ones that involve state power. They are the activities that directly guarantee that laws and public policies are followed and financed. The armed forces, the police, the tax collection agency - the traditional functions of the state - and also the regulatory agencies, the agencies that finance, foment and control social services and social security are part of this sector";
3. Non-exclusive services – "are the services that the state provides, but, as they do not involve the use of the extroverse power of the state, the private and the public non-state ("non-governmental") sectors may also provide. This sector comprises the educational, health, culture and scientific research services"; and
4. Production of goods and services sector – "is formed by the state-owned enterprises".

One interesting aspect must be emphasized in this proposal. In spite of having a clear functional inspiration, it was built from a high level of generality regarding the state functions. So, one can deduce the "products" that should be delivered by each sector of the state to its "customers". The existence of this proposal means a hope that the state services can be characterized, providing more objectivity in the discussions about how to increase government effectiveness and efficiency in delivering its "products".

4.4 A Short Discussion

With the presentation of these new approaches in e-government we point out some different ways to answer one of the most significant challenges of the modern society. In our opinion, the use of ICT is mandatory when planning solutions to this question. On the other hand, the appropriate use of ICT requires a correct identification of opportunities. As they are support tools to human activities, we should understand the true nature of the government functions, in order to decide where and how to plan the use of these technologies.

An organization is characterized by the objectives and goals that were assigned to it at the moment of its creation. Therefore, the ideas about evaluation and reform of the state are so important. New objectives and goals may arise too. These are the signs we want to study in order to make new propositions.

We believe the new approaches presented have some general attributes that are shared with many existing proposals in private business, which are:

- To understand and satisfy the customer;
- To understand and characterize the deliverables (products or services);
- From the knowledge of the preceding items, create the organization structures and procedures.

An example of a new possible approach to e-government that goes after these requirements is what we call Business Process Engineering, which is outlined in the following.

5. BUSINESS PROCESS ENGINEERING

First, it is necessary to state a concept of process. Davenport in [5] defined a process as a "structured, measured set of activities designed to produce a specific output for a particular customer or market. It implies a strong emphasis on how work is done within an organization, in contrast to a product focus's emphasis on what. A process is thus a specific ordering of work activities across time and place, with a beginning, an end, and clearly identified inputs and outputs: a structure for action". Further, he complements: "Taking a process approach implies adopting the customer's point of view.

Processes are the structure by which an organization does what is necessary to produce value to its customer. Consequently, an important measure of a process is customer satisfaction with the output of the process".

This concept of process is central for the Business Process Engineering, which has originated from Business Process Reengineering (BPR) studies made by Davenport [5], Jacobson [8] and others. Nowadays, many authors and organizations work with the expression BPM – Business Process Management [2], which seems to be the successor of BPR. In our research work [9], we prefer to use the expression Business Process Engineering, which was introduced by Jacobson in his seminal book [8].

The process perspective implies a horizontal view of the business that may involve many parts of the organization. Consequently, it demands that the interfaces between functional units be either improved or eliminated, which means to de-emphasize the functional structure of the business. Thus, the process approach generates, necessarily, a conflict with the (functional units oriented) hierarchical structure of the organization. For this reason, it is even now very difficult to find a completely process-oriented organization, which is the ultimate aspiration of the Business Process Engineering.

The core tool for Business Process Engineering is business process modeling, which aims to represent the processes in a simple and formal manner at different levels of abstraction. The availability of complete process models allows a critical analysis of the existing activities to make improvements in the processes, and to decide the more adequate use of ICT in each activity.

Many organizations have revised their business processes, using modeling techniques, before developing information systems. The main results reported are an increase of the quality of products and services and in customers' satisfaction [4].

However, business process modeling is not a completely established field. Large theoretical and practical difficulties have to be overcome. The first one: there are a huge number of available approaches and techniques. Another important one is how to choose the most suitable abstraction level of the business.

Since the early reengineering works, it is known that extraordinary and innovative benefits can only be achieved when processes are broadly identified [5], thus requiring a high level view of the business. Narrow processes, when reformed, may cause just few improvements that usually have limited impacts on the organization. In the latter case, where the abstraction level is low, we have the so-called "continuous improvement" or "total quality" approaches, leading to significant advantages in long time only.

In order to obtain a considerable amount of innovation, Davenport pointed out that leading companies have identified a few number of major (and broad) processes, which he has named "key business processes". Inspired by this idea, we have called the same way, the broad and complete processes that are responsible for the construction of the product or service that is delivered to the customer of an organization.

In a more precise way, we define the concept Key Business Process (KBP) of a company, as the complete set of activities that are executed to: receive the customer order, build the product and/or service, deliver the product and/or service, and receive the payment corresponding to this business [9]. That way, it is possible to ally a high abstraction level of the most important processes with a clear characterization of these processes' boundaries.

As an example of the KBP concept, let us consider a household appliance store selling a refrigerator. This KBP should comprise the entire possible steps such as: receiving customer order, product delivery, installation service, product warranty, credit line offer, and customer payment. Each instance of the KBP is an execution of a set of steps chosen by a specific customer.

We added to this KBP concept, the Jacobson's proposal that considers the information systems as a part of the business system [8]. Jacobson has proposed the extension of the "Use Case" concept to business processes. It allowed the following adaptation of the existing graphical representation of "Use Cases": the actor that previously represented the role performed by a user of the information system, in this new context represents the role of a business process customer. The role of the business process is to accomplish the result demanded by the customer. The next diagram illustrates a generic KBP [9].

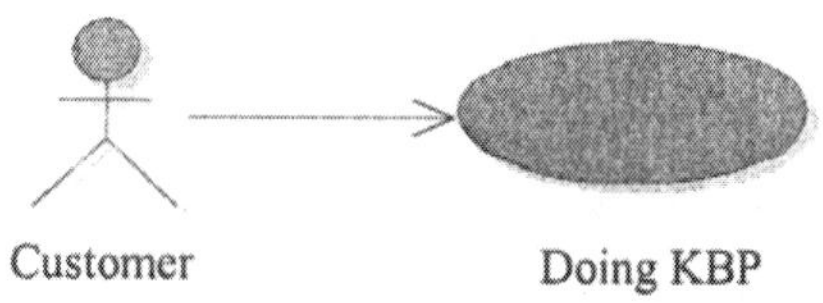

Figure 1. A Generic KBP

Obviously, even with this extensive definition, the KBPs are not the unique processes that can be identified in a firm. However, we are convinced that they are the first and foremost processes to be identified when pursuing the full advantages of any process approach.

If this idea is relevant to the private sector, how could it be used in the public sector? Which would be the possible adaptations to be done?

5.1 A Brief Discussion about the Public Sector

Government operates in a large variety of sectors. Some of its activities are similar to those of the private sector, while others are completely different. Some singular properties of public services should be emphasized when thinking about e-government:

- The government is a bigger and more complex organization than any private firm;
- Legal standards must be used in communications with society and with other governmental entities;
- It is necessary to ensure equity of access to public services.

A main difference between governmental and private businesses is that governments only deliver services. Even when delivering some product to the "customer", it is made within some service of wider scope. An example is the provision of a medicament during the execution of a medical assistance service.

Another important difference is related to the payment of the governmental services. This payment is done by taxation and, in general, it is not the counterpart of a specific service. Therefore, the governmental services may be considered "paid in advance", within an existing "contract" between the citizen and the state. This "contract" may be represented by the set of laws and regulations of an independent state.

It is worthwhile to stress the distinction between the penalty payments made in some governmental sub-processes and the payment for the governmental service execution, which is made by taxation. Penalties should not be considered as payment for a delivered service, but a punishment regarding a fault. In this case, the real customer of this process is not the penalty payer but the society.

Then, keeping these ideas in mind when modeling a governmental environment may ensure the design of e-government applications that are aligned with customers' necessities, where all the services would be well characterized. The desired integrative or seamless levels, described in Sections 3.1 and 3.2 would be reached, with this approach, in a planned, gradual and objective way. The mistake of simply transposing the governmental bureaucracy to the Internet, mentioned in Section 1, would be minimized.

However, to make these ideas come true, the basis for Governmental Business Process Engineering is suggested in the following.

6. GOVERNMENTAL BUSINESS PROCESS ENGINEERING

Here the fundamental concept is the Governmental Key Business Process (G-KBP). It can be represented by the complete set of activities that government executes to: receive the customer demand, realize the service and deliver the complete service to the customer. This concept has two "simplifications" when compared to private organizations' KBP: it does not include the payment, and the result delivered to the customer is always a service.

In governmental environment, the service represented by the G-KBP is always very large and it is realized in many stages. One can identify inside G-KBP processes, as in some private sector processes, several partial deliveries and several partial requests. Generally, a partial request corresponds to one or more partial deliveries, and conversely, one partial delivery may correspond to several partial requests. It is worthwhile to state that even the private sector has enormous difficulties to achieve good performance with such complex services.

Therefore, the critical issue on G-KBP is the appropriate description of the complete service to be delivered. It is also hard to identify the "customer" of a G-KBP. Frequently, the one who does the request of a governmental service is not the same person who receives the service. Hence, it is advisable to discriminate the two roles. We call Applicant the first, and User the latter. Therefore, the following diagram can graphically represent a generic G-KBP.

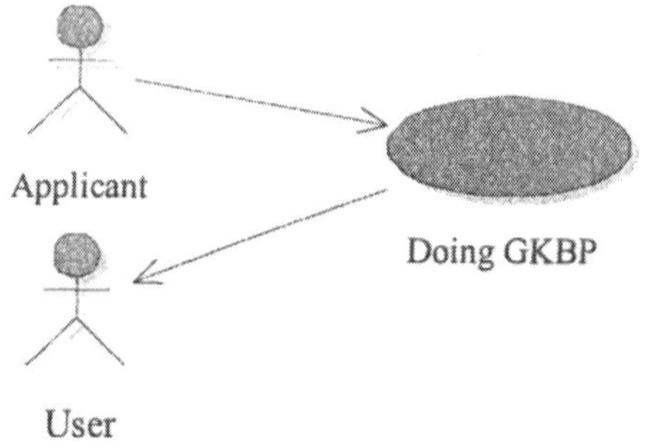

Figure 2. A Generic G-KBP

6.1 Identifying Governmental Key Business Processes

The big challenge of this approach is to identify the existing G-KBPs. In our opinion, the innovative ideas presented in Section 4 point towards enabling this approach.

We suppose that the USA leadership in the UN report presented in Section 3.1 is a consequence of its portal structure shown in Table 3. This structure seems to approximate to the G-KBP concept in practice. The Traunmüller [13] proposal discussed in Section 4.2 also tends to come near to the G-KBP concept when recommending the adoption of the "Citizen Perspective" and the "Process Perspective" for e-government initiatives. Nevertheless, we believe that the Bresser-Pereira [3] proposal, presented in Section 4.3, is the most promising to truthfully concretize the G-KBP idea.

When classifying the state functions in: Strategic Core (to make laws and regulations), Exclusive Activities and Non-exclusive Services, Bresser-Pereira shows a plausible manner of organizing, from the highest level of abstraction, "all" services delivered by the states. For example, one can visualize a law as a neat outcome (product) from a G-KBP of the Strategic Core. The main client of this kind of service is the citizen. Thus, the "Making Laws" G-KBP could be graphically represented by the diagram bellow.

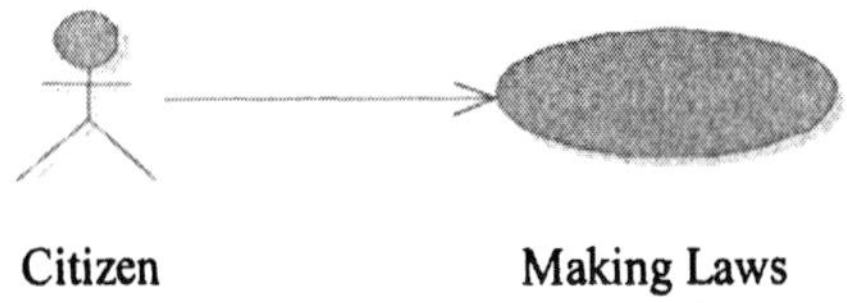

Figure 3. "Making Laws" G-KBP

Other actors could be added as clients of this G-KBP, such as syndicates, associations, and so on. We presume it is possible to do similar reasoning to identify specific G-KBPs from the Exclusive Activities and Non-exclusive Services, completing the identification of the essential services the state should offer.

We cannot minimize the immense theoretical and practical challenges that have to be surpassed to reach a G-KBP. It requires much work in multiple human knowledge areas, such as Political Science, Public Administration, Philosophy and many others. The theory and practice of Business Process Modeling also need great development to deal with the size of this area. Despite the obstacles, the introduced approach copes with the e-government matter in a very clear and objective way.

In the following are delineated some gains that can be obtained with this approach.

6.2 Some Benefits of the G-KBP Approach

6.2.1 Identification of a G-KBP and characterization of its "product"

An obvious advantage of the characterization of a G-KBP is an increase of governance, once the public administration would be able to measure the process performance and its "product" in order to improve both. The quality of the public administration will increase as long as the number of G-KBPs identified and managed increases too.

If the G-KBPs and their products are well characterized, this information may be publicized, and they can reach the potential customers of these processes. It can generate the following good consequences:

- Each "customer" could promptly identify the services that are applicable to him;
- "Customers" could struggle to improve the processes and their "products";
- The "complete" services delivered by the G-KBPs will be much more effective than the current fragmented ones.

6.2.2 Characterization of the "customer" of a G-KBP

The immediate consequence of a right characterization of the customer of a business process is the appropriate representation of such a customer in the organization internal files. In case of a government, these files are the basic tools for the G-KBP execution, and to ensure equity in accessing its services.

After every one of potential G-KBP's "customers" have been filed, it arises the following benefits:

- Reduction of the "customer" effort in applying to the service;
- Quality improvement in the great number of required interactions between the "customer" and the process;
- Increasing universalization of services;
- Enabling public agents to attract the "customers" of the G-KBP, which is especially important in social services;

6.2.3 Specification of the interactions between the "customer" and the G-KBP

This critical question is rarely taken into account in the business process area. It is not sufficient to identify the process, its "product", and its "customer" to succeed using a processes approach. It is necessary to complement this knowledge with the specification of the flow of interactions between the "customer" and the process. In the case of a G-KBP, the "customer" frequently does several requests and several partial deliveries are made until the service is completed.

These interactions involve much information, not only due to the quantity of G-KBP stages, but also due to the large amount of information exchanged. Let us take as example a simple health service fulfilled in some stages. Each step needs at least the following interactions between the "customer" and the process:

- The "customer" performs the request and sends some specific information;
- The process interacts with the "customer" to schedule the execution of the step, which in general involves the "customer" attendance and the allocation of several other process' resources;
- The process sends the result of the step to the "customer", and occasionally communicates the need for scheduling the next step.

As can be observed, these interactions are substantially informational. Then, there is an opportunity of intense utilization of ICT, in order to improve the processes and to reduce interactions costs. However, the appropriate use of ICT will only be achieved if all factors mentioned in this Section are considered.

7. CONCLUSIONS

We believe there is a long road to reach the G-KBPs, but we also believe it is worthwhile to try because the return can largely pay the investments.

First, we should not lose track of establishing the G-KBPs in a top-down way. As far as we can see, the Bresser-Pereira's work [3] has shown a possible starting point. Much work and reflection from many other human knowledge areas are needed to achieve such result.

However, we do not need to wait the conclusion of these works. If we take into consideration the concepts and recommendations presented in Sections 5 and 6 concerning processes, we can begin identifying small governmental processes that deliver partial and/or fragmented services. Then, using a bottom-up approach, it will be possible to continuously aggregate these small processes, creating repeatedly other bigger processes without loosing the goal of attaining the G-KBP level.

This working method may be used as a fundamental guideline to the construction and maintenance of e-government portals. It seems to be a way to reach the highest levels of governmental portals presented in Sections 3.1 and 3.2 – the integrative and the seamless - respectively.

Finally, we state that the adequate use of ICT in addition to the G-KBP - Government Key Business Process concept may be important enablers of enhancing e-government environments.

REFERENCES

[1] ABRUCIO, F. L. "O impacto do modelo gerencial na administração pública - Um breve estudo sobre a experiência internacional recente", Cadernos ENAP; n. 10, p.52, Brasília, 1997.

[2] BPMI.ORG "The Business Process Management Initiative", Retrieved January/2004 from: http://www.bpmi.org/.

[3] BRESSER-PEREIRA, L. C. "Managerial Public Administration: Strategy and Structure for a New State", Journal of Post Keynesian Economics, 20(1) – 1997.

[4] CASTANO, S., De ANTONELLIS, V., MELCHIORI, M. "A methodology and tool environment for process analysis and reengineering", Data & Knowledge Engineering, vol. 31, issue 3, November/1999.

[5] DAVENPORT, T. H. "Process Innovation: Reengineering Work through Information Technology", Harvard Business School Press, Boston, October/1992.

[6] FIRJAN - Federação das Indústrias do Estado do Rio de Janeiro. "Desburocratização Eletrônica nos Municípios do Estado do Rio de Janeiro", Rio de Janeiro, June/2002.

[7] ____________________. "Desburocratização Eletrônica nos Estados Brasileiros", Rio de Janeiro, November/2002.

[8] JACOBSON, I., ERICSSON, M., JACOBSON, A. "The Object Advantage: Business Process Reengineering with Object Technology", Addison-Wesley, September/1994.

[9] MARTINS, L. G., CUNHA, A. M., Lecture Notes from "Fundamentals of Object Oriented Business Modeling", Graduate Program on Informatics, NCE/IM-UFRJ, 2003.

[10] NIELSEN, J., TAHIR, M. "Homepage Usability: 50 Websites Deconstructed", New Riders, November/2001.

[11] OFFICE OF MANAGEMENT AND BUDGET. "E-Government Strategy - Simplified Delivery of Services to Citizens", February/2002, Retrieved January/2004 from: http://www.whitehouse.gov/omb/inforeg/egovstrategy.pdf.

[12] OSBORNE, D. E., GAEBLER, T. "Reinventing Government: How the Entrepreneurial Spirit Is Transforming the Public Sector", Addison-Wesley, 1992.

[13] TRAUNMÜLLER, R. "E-Government – A Roadmap for Progress", 3rd IFIP Conference on e-Commerce, e-Business, and e-Government, Guarujá, September/2003.

[14] UN – United Nations. "Benchmarking E-government: A Global Perspective", May/2002, Retrieved January/2004 from: http://www.unpan.org/e-government/Benchmarking E-gov 2001.pdf.

AN INTELLIGENT SEARCH ENGINE FOR ELECTRONIC GOVERNMENT APPLICATIONS FOR THE RESOLUTIONS OF THE UNITED NATIONS SECURITY COUNCIL

Hugo C. Hoeschl, Tânia Cristina D. Bueno, Andre Bortolon, Eduardo S. Mattos, Marcelo S. Ribeiro, Irineu Theiss and Ricardo Miranda Barcia
E-Gov, Juridical Intelligence and Systems Institute – Ijuris, Florianópolis, Santa Catarina - Brasil, tania@ijuris.org, digesto@digesto.net, bortolon@wbsa.com.br, mattos@wbsa.com.br; marcelo@wbsa.com.br, irineu@wbsa.com.br, rbarcia@eps.ufsc.br, http://www.ijuris.org

Abstract: The paper describes the Olimpo System, a knowledge-based system that enables the user to access textual files and to retrieve information that is similar to the search context described by the user in natural language. The paper is focused on the innovation recently implemented on the system and its new features. It is included an explanation about the UN Security Council itself and how it works, as well as a detailed analysis of the format of the resolutions and its main characteristics. A detailed description is presented about the search level and the similarity metrics used by the system. The methodology applied to the Olimpo system emphasises the use of information retrieval methods combined with the Artificial Intelligence technique named SCS (Structured Contextual Search).

Key words: UN Security Council's Resolutions, Dynamically Contextualised Knowledge Representation (DCKR), Structured Contextual Search – SCS, Information of Technology, Data retrieve

1. INTRODUCTION

Some complex and specific domains require an information retrieval system that is more than just a great technology to search for documents in large text databases. A good knowledge representation is also required.

The present approach enables to retrieve textual information that is similar to the search text described by the user using natural language. Through the extraction of relevant information using DCKR technology (Dynamically Contextualised Knowledge Representation) [8] [9], new documents are automatically included in the knowledge database. Concepts of Case-Based Reasoning (CBR) [1] [2] and information retrieval techniques were applied to obtain a better performance of the system, leading to the technology named Structured Contextual Search – SCS.

The following items 2 and 3 of this paper address the UN Security Council and the Resolution document; in item 4 the knowledge representation methodology is presented; in items 5 and 6 the Olimpo system is described and its performance is analysed; in items 7 to 9 characteristics and new features of the system are described; and item 10 is the conclusion of the paper.

2. ABOUT THE UN SECURITY COUNCIL

As a consequence of the current world context, the UN Security Council is at the highest evidence. The international media is proving that. Taking as an example the date 18th of September 2002, the Security Council was on the front page of some of the most important newspapers worldwide:

- The Washington Post: "U.N. Questions Need for New Resolution on Iraq";
- Le Monde:"Irak: Division au sein du Conseil de sécurité";
- Independent: "UN split over Iraqi offer";
- El Pais: "Bush desprecia la oferta de Irak e insiste en que la ONU debe actuar";
- The Times: "Saddam offer tests fragile alliance";
- Clarín: "Bush ignora la oferta de Irak: 'Es hora de actuar'".

The importance of the UN body becomes noticeable when one follows the main global means of communication and no further arguments are required. Being the source of the documents handled by the Olimpo system, it is useful to give more details about the Security Council and its document base.

According to its Charter (Article 7-1), the United Nations Organization (UNO) is comprised of six special bodies, as shown on Figure 1. All of them issue relevant documentation and it is highly important to have an adequate tool to retrieve those documents.

Given its characteristics and aspects related to the Resolutions, the Security Council was chosen as application field of the Olimpo system.

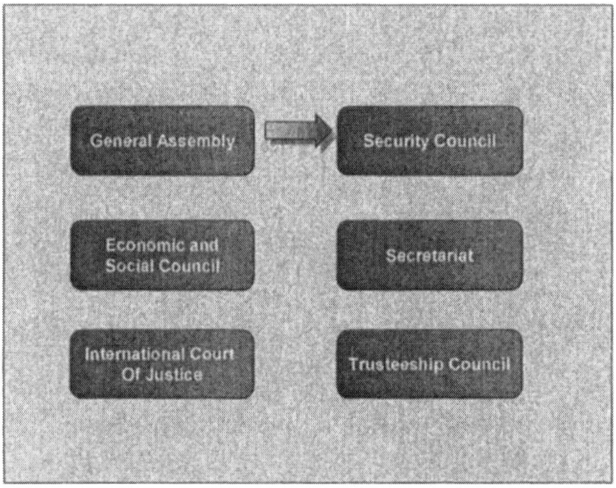

Figure 1. UNO main bodies issuing resolutions (Source: www.un.org/documents/index.html)

The Security Council is described by Article 7-1 of UNO's Charter, where it is referred to as a special body of the United Nations. The Security Council is specifically addressed in Chapter V, Articles 23 to 32. As per Article 24-1, its central function is to assume "*the main responsibility in maintaining international peace and security.*"

It should be emphasized that the Security Council has a juridical and an executive profile. According to Kelsen (apud Steinfus [11]), it is juridical because it holds the monopoly of legitimate violence at the international scope and judges the existence of facts, determines sanctions on them and who will enforce these sanctions. That turns it a juridical body. And this profile enables a good application of the technology of juridical information, especially SCS and its particular method of rhetoric structure analysis of a given jurisdictional context, based on the knowledge structure involving the body, which maximizes the task of intelligent retrieval of documents when adequate modelling is used.

The Security Council has also political characteristics and it has discritionary power to establish violations, according to Steinfus [11]; therefore the Security Council holds an executive characteristic, turning it a juridical-executive body.

The Security Council presents some peculiarities. One of them is to be currently the most powerful jurisdictional body on the planet. Another one is the existence of internal, informal instances, named "P 3" (Western permanent member countries) and "P 5" (all permanent member countries), according to Steinfus [11]. Another peculiarity is the existence of internal bodies with specific power delegation to perform certain tasks, on a permanent or "ad hoc" level, like the sanctions committee, as shown on Figure 2.

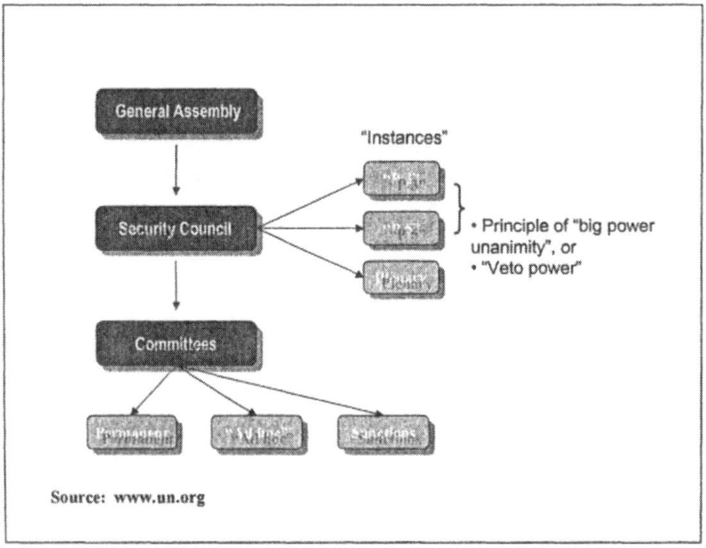

Figure 2. Position of the Security Council

Among the documents issued by the Security Council, six of them have greater relevance, as shown on Figure 3. Based on their structure and relevance, the Resolutions were chosen for the application of the Olimpo system.

As per the structure of the document, the Resolutions have some characteristics that make it easier to apply the technology referred to herein.

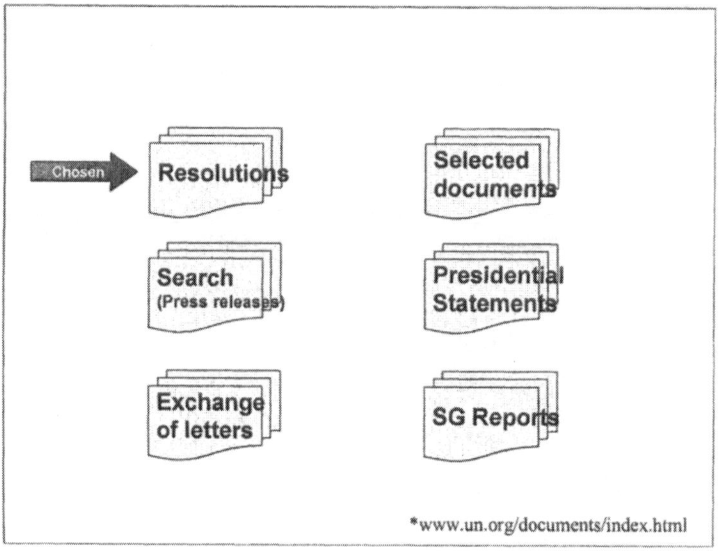

Figure 3. Types of documents issued by the Security Council

3. ABOUT THE RESOLUTIONS

Many different aspects surround the current debate on the Iraqi crisis, but one is definitely important: the document that will support the decision on the issue will be a Resolution of the Security Council. It is necessary to learn how these documents look like and which is their writing format.

As shown on Figure 4, the official UNO's site shows a specific section about documents designated as Documentation Centre, which maintains up-dated documents of UNO's bodies, including the Security Council.

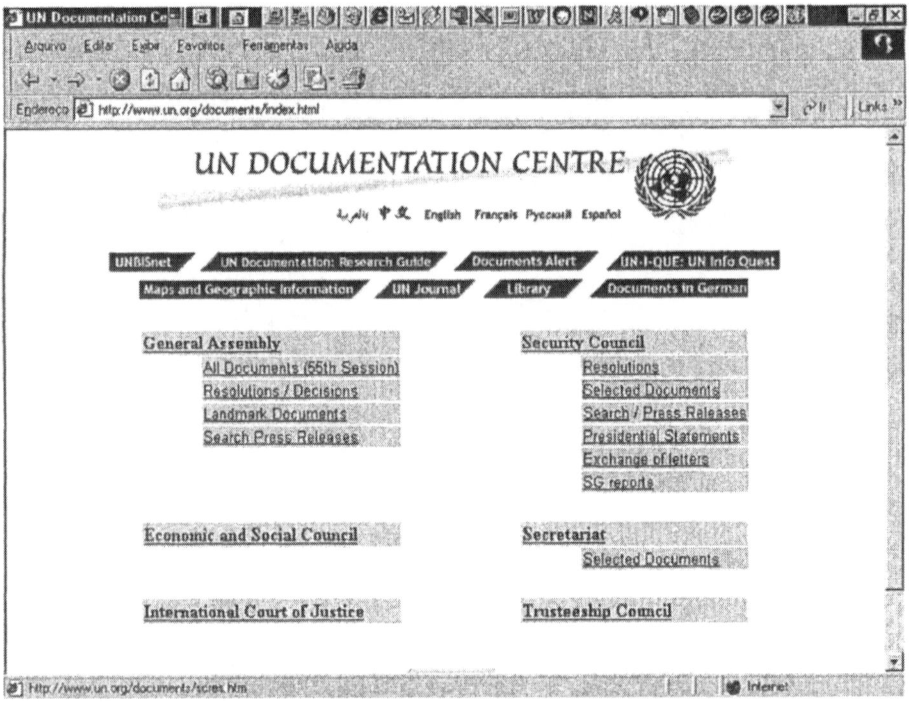

Figure 4. UN Documentation Centre

It was interesting to notice that the Security Council had the largest variety of documents among the different UN bodies and this confirmed the relevance of structuring the information belonging to that body.

Once the source of documents was selected, it started the process of capturing the documents on the web to build the knowledge base of the system.

To get a better understanding of the structure of a Resolution, it is useful to take a look at one of these documents (or part of it). It is shown below part of the text of Resolution number 1244, issued in 1999. This Resolution was chosen because it presented a high number of indicative expressions (a total of 137 expressions).

"Security Council resolution 1244 (1999) on situation relating to Kosovo

United Nations

S/RES/1244 (1999)

10 June 1999

RESOLUTION 1244 (1999)

Adopted by the Security Council at its **4011th meeting**,
on 10 June 1999

The Security Council,
Bearing in mind the purposes and principles of the Charter of the United Nations, and the primary responsibility of the Security Council for the maintenance of **international peace** and security,
Recalling its resolutions 1160 (1998) of 31 March 1998, 1199 (1998) of 23 September 1998, 1203 (1998) of 24 October 1998 and 1239 (1999) of 14 May 1999,
Regretting that there has not been full compliance with the requirements of these resolutions,
Determined to resolve the grave **humanitarian situation** in Kosovo, **Federal Republic of Yugoslavia,** and to provide for the safe and free **return of all refugees** and **displaced persons** to their homes,
Condemning all **acts of violence** against the Kosovo population as well as all **terrorist acts** by any party,
Recalling the statement made by the **Secretary-General** on 9 April 1999, expressing concern at the humanitarian tragedy taking place in Kosovo,
Reaffirming the right of all refugees and displaced persons to return to their homes in safety,

(..........)

10. Suspension of **military** activity will require acceptance of the principles set forth above in addition to **agreement** to other, previously identified, required elements, which are specified in the footnote below.1 A **military-technical agreement** will then be rapidly concluded that would, among other things, specify additional modalities, including the roles and functions of Yugoslav/Serb personnel in Kosovo:
Withdrawal
- Procedures for withdrawals, including the phased, detailed schedule and delineation of a buffer area in Serbia beyond which forces will be withdrawn;

Returning personnel
- Equipment associated with returning personnel;
- Terms of reference for their functional responsibilities;
- **Timetable** for their return;
- Delineation of their geographical areas of operation;
- Rules governing their relationship to the international security presence and the **international civil** mission.

The arrows indicate, respectively, the subject, number of the Resolution, issue date, and the beginning of the text from which the indicative expressions (in bold) were extracted.

4. DYNAMICALLY CONTEXTUALISED KNOWLEDGE REPRESENTATION

Olimpo´s performance is centred around the combination of aspects derived from CBR and text information retrieval, in addition to an adequate organisation of the knowledge related to the subject the system is focused on (in the present case, the UN Security Council´s Resolutions). The aforementioned knowledge organisation is what enables the DCKR technology, which is a methodology that provides the possibility of comparing the contexts described in the documents and not only a comparison between words or attributes.

In general, the system works in a way similar to other case-based systems [3] [5] (see Figure 5), where a manual entry passes through an adjustment and is then submitted to a comparison with the documents contained in the database, from which the most suitable ones are selected based on similarity calculations.

After a refined modelling of the database, the Resolutions are stored by Olimpo system, according to their characteristics and central attributes (main topics, related subjects, countries involved); peripheral attributes (other related Resolutions, other UNO´s organisms referred to); and superficial attributes (dates, numbers and names). This kind of structure allows to give (variable) weights to attributes, enabling a more precise, contextualised search.

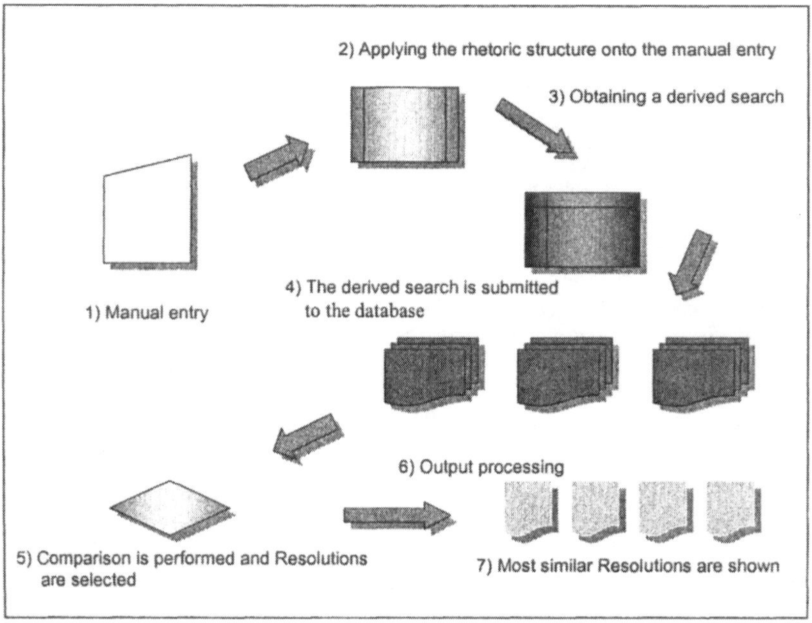

Figure 5. Searching Process

5. ANALYSIS OF THE RHETORIC STRUCTURE

The rhetoric structure of the system is comprised of indicative expressions used for comparison means and it was, first time ever, dynamically prepared. Up to then it was usual to choose a list of index pointers from a source external to the research group (for example, Court library indexes). Little work was done on the list of index pointers and its selection was based on its similarity with the context of the system under development. For the Olimpo system it was decided to build a particular and specific list, which should be aligned with the issues effectively treated by the Resolutions and, on the other hand, should be coherent with the documentation context of the managing entity of the database. In this view, in order to collect a list of expressions a detailed reading of the Resolutions was performed, searching onto UNO's database on the Internet was done and debating with research groups was used. Those expressions were then tested and subject to statistic analysis in order to evaluate their function as reference elements for the indexation and retrieval of documents. A set of expressions with high significance was selected, eliminating those ones with very high or very low frequency of occurrence because they were not very much helpful for establishing a context.

This process had a dynamic characteristic because it was done several times and expressions were included or excluded according to their statistic performance. The routine described by Figure 6 shows how it worked to obtain a final list containing a set of expressions that could efficiently reflect the generic, rhetoric structure of the Resolutions, which gave the material form to the dynamically contextualised knowledge representation.

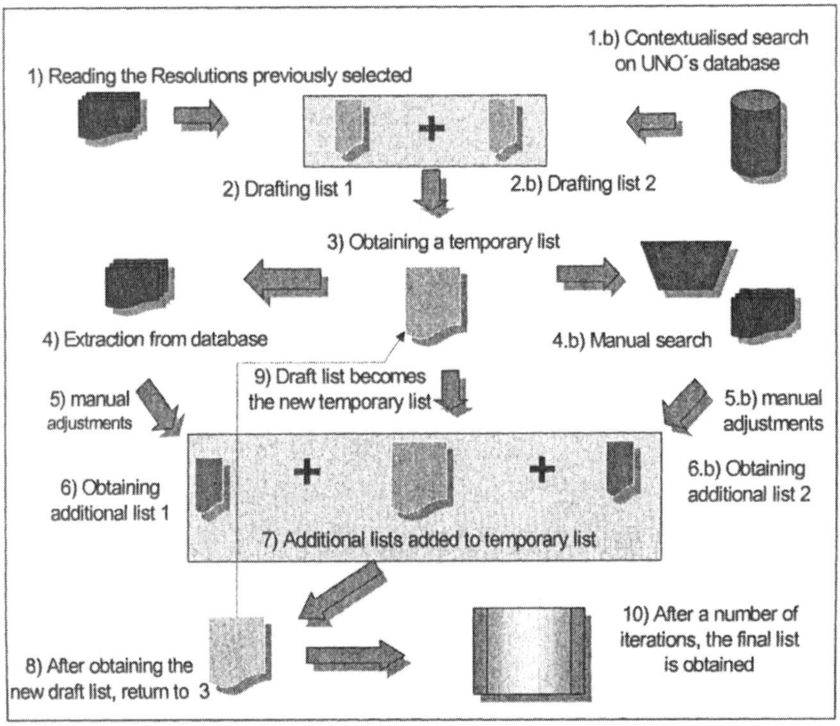

Figure 6. Analysis of the Rhetoric Structure

6. CHARACTERISTICS OF THE DOCUMENTS

As to the structure of the document, UNO's Security Council Resolutions have some characteristics that facilitate the application of the technology presented in this paper. They are the following:

- Text written in homogeneous format – standard format used for all the documents;
- Standardised rhetoric structure – the domain vocabulary is quite specific and restrict, defined by Organisation's attributions as stated in the United Nations Charter;

- The language of the domain needs to be simplified to turn it more usual – the Resolutions are public, official documents (they need to have an usual language so that information can be retrieved when accessed by people).

7. STRUCTURED CONTEXTUAL SEARCH – SCS

The searching process being described is said to be "contextual" and "structured" due to the following reasons:

- • For building the rhetoric structure of the system, it is taken into consideration the context of the stored documents;
- • This context is the basis for the input adjustment process, as well as for the comparison and selection of documents;
- • When writing the search text, the input is not limited to a set of words or attributes, but it can take the format of a long text, including the possibility of setting specific attributes, which work as filters and function as a preliminary selection of documents to be searched.

Furthermore, the control of depth of search enables a selection of documents according to a higher or lower occurrence of indicative expressions within the text of the Resolution, before starting to compare the documents. This process provides a more efficient way of reducing the search field; it is not a mere pre-selection of documents based on their superficial characteristics, but a preliminary comparison oriented by the context related to the search input.

After completing the process, the result is a list of indicative expressions referring to the Resolutions, producing an individual record of the occurrence of each one of the expressions within the text of each Resolution. These records allow the system to make the comparison and to apply the global similarity metrics.

In addition to the indicative expressions, the process of automatic extraction of attributes was prepared to detect and extract the subject, date, number of the Resolution, acronyms, country names, and parts of the text that contain the expressions with higher occurrence.

8. OPERATION AND PERFORMANCE OF THE OLIMPO SYSTEM

The main features of the Olimpo system are the simultaneous use of textual information retrieving techniques based on CBR and the possibility of an extensive textual input. That makes the system to reach a differentiated performance in terms of information retrieval.

However, considering that the comparisons are based on a rhetoric structure previously prepared, the better working of the system is linked to a description of the search entry closer to that rhetoric structure. So, the system performance becomes gradually more consistent as the search entry language gets closer to the structure identified in the documents that generated the knowledge base of the system.

It has to be mentioned that all the Resolutions were monitored all the time with respect to the number of indicative expressions they presented during the structuring phase of the Resolutions knowledge base.

9. THE OLIMPO SYSTEM

Information contained in the documents is represented in the form of a case, consisting of the original document and a set of eight indexes in the form of pairs of attribute-value: subject, date, number of the Resolution, meeting, country, acronyms, decisions, and indicative expressions. These indexes are part of the system interface (see Figure 7).

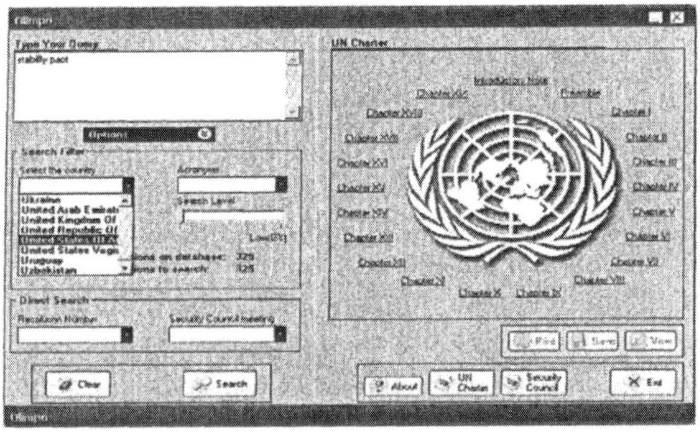

Figure 7. Olimpo Interface

10. SIMILARITY METRICS

The similarity metrics was structured to consider the indicative expressions present in the case and in the search, after applying the rhetoric structure on the textual entry and producing the derived search. This derived search is actually the reference to work out the similarity metrics.

Taking as an example the case where a derived search with a total of 50 expressions is obtained after applying the rhetoric structure on a given search text: this set of expressions is compared to the records in the database and the similarity percentage is calculated based on the number of similar expressions found within each individual record. If 43 expressions are found, for instance, then the similarity will be 86%; it will be 72%, if 36 expressions are found, or 56% in the case of finding just 28 expressions, and so on.

This type of metrics is quite simple, one of the most simple that could be used in this situation, but it works in a quite stable way and can be improved in the future by incorporating new mechanisms like trigrams or applying internal weights to the most frequent words found in the text of the Resolution.

In fact, what is the strong feature of the system is not the similarity metrics, but the way how the indicative expressions are organized so that the metrics provides a better performance.

A clear example of this particularity of the system is an expression formed by two words like "United Nations". A simple similarity based on counting individual words will show a 100% index when both words are found within the text, regardless their position, or 50% in the case just one of the words is found. However, if a differentiated indexation is used, by which "United Nations" (the two exact words appearing together) is one expression, "United" is another expression, and "Nations" is a third one (all with the same weight, for the time being), this configures a different situation. In this case, it is not enough finding the two words within the text, even when separated; they should appear together and having the exact meaning. Based on these criteria, the similarity index will be 33.33% when only one of the two words is found, or 66.66%, when both words are found in separate location, and it will reach 100% only when both words are present and appear together.

11. COMPOSING THE RECORDS

Besides searching for indicative expressions, the process of automatic extraction of attributes was prepared to detect and extract the subject, date, number of the Resolution, acronyms, name of countries, number of decisions, as well as parts of the text containing the expressions with higher ocurrence within the text, as shown on Table 1

Table 1. Automatic extraction of attributes

Index	Description	Importance of retrieval
Subject	Short description about the most important situation discussed in the Resolution	Used to know the Resolution subject
Date	Year of issuance of the Resolution	Determine a specific year of interest
Resolution Number	States the number supplied by de UN Security Council	Used to identify the Resolution
Meeting	States de number of the meeting when the Resolution was issued	Can be used to retrieve the Resolution by refering to the meeting
Countries	States the countries involved in the issue	Used to know the countries involved in the conflict/subject
Decisions	Number of different decisions in the Resolution	Can be used to understand the extension and complexity of the Resolution
Acronyms	Acronyms of official and unofficial institutions	Can be used to retrieve the institutions related to the Resolution. E. g.: OTAN
Indicative Expressions	Determines the most relevant information in the Resolution and its redefinitions	Used to retrieve the Resolutions based on similar topics

The analysis taking into consideration all these information enables the documents to be compared, in a precise way, among themselves, with other texts, or with the text of the query entered by the user.

12. COMPARATIVE ANALYSIS: DATABASE SEARCH TOOL VERSUS OLIMPO

When a random input is typed, the chance of an effective retrieval is lower than in the case of an input based on a text written in a language coincident with that already identified, for example, the text of a Security Council's Resolution. For random inputs, the conventional database presents a superior performance; but this changes as the search text becomes closer to the language used in the documents contained in the system database.

The possibility of having an input with higher volume of text (2,300 words, 15,000 characters or 270 lines of text) becomes an important differential factor for the Olimpo system. The output obtained with the traditional database tool is quite limited when compared with the output produced by Olimpo.

As illustrated on Figure 8, Olimpo's efficiency increases as the number of words in the input text increases. On the other hand, the efficiency of the database search tool decreases sharply as the volume of input text increases.

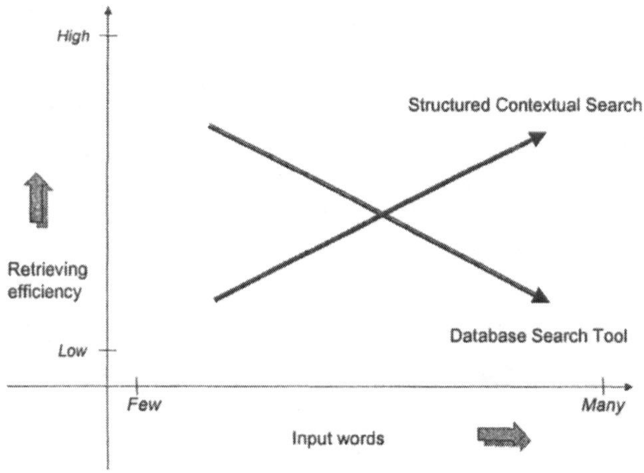

Figure 8. Olimpo System Retrieving Efficiency

13. SEARCH LEVEL

An important feature of the Olimpo system is the possibility of previously filtering the documents to be included in the similarity metrics.

The filtering process, designated as search level, is described by Figure 9. It reduces the amount of records to be searched, but it is not a simple partition of the database. It is not a question of format, but is based on "merit" issues, enabling a preliminar look at the searching universe even before starting the search.

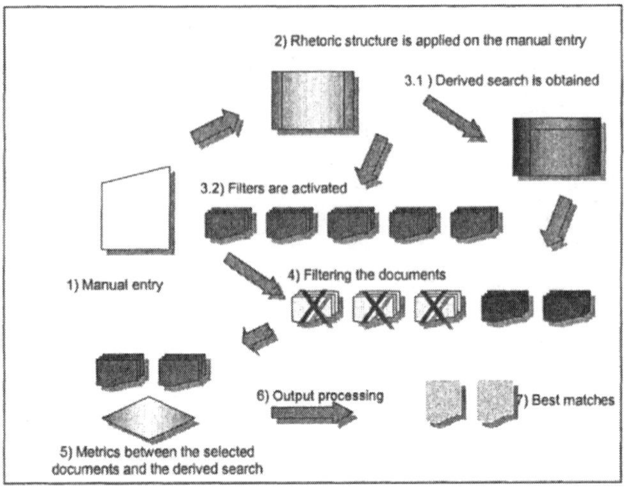

Figure 9. Searching process (with filters and pre-search)

By controlling the depth of the search level it is possible to select documents based on the number of indicative expressions found within each document before starting to compare them. This process is described by Figure 10 and it provides a reduction of the searching universe in a more efficient way. It is not about simply selecting documents according to superficial characteristics, but it makes possible to have a preliminary comparison oriented by the context related to the query entered by the user. This process enables a significant improvement of the system performance.

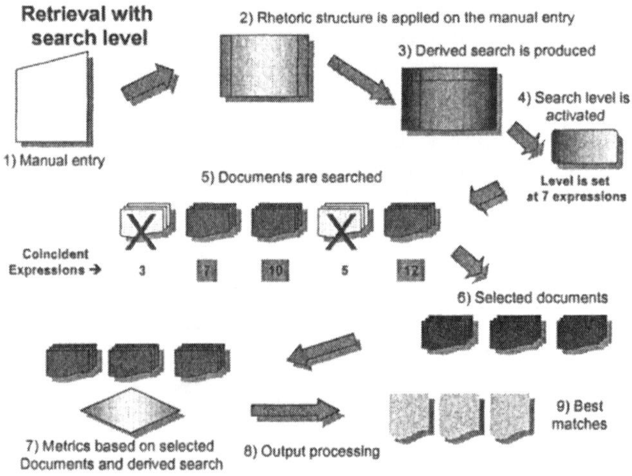

Figure 10. Retrieval with search level

14. SYSTEM STATISTICS

The statistical analysis of the relationship between concepts and Resolutions provides relevant conclusions. The average of indicative expressions per Resolution is 55.18, which is an impressive number when considering that this average would never be over 10 using the former methodology. That average should increase significantly after completing the development of the system and including all the Resolutions in the system database.

Among the Resolutions with the best performance, 12 of them were selected showing over 100 indicative expressions found (Table 2).

Table 2. Occurrence of indicative expressions

Order	*Resolution number*	*Ocurrences*
1	1244	137
2	1075	124
3	1265	123
4	1234	120
5	1087	119
6	1247	113
7	1199	112
8	1124	111
9	1174	111
10	1072	106
11	1284	106
12	1203	100

The usual language of the Security Council includes the frequent ocurrence of acronyms. The different number of acronyms occuring within the text of a Resolution is counted; Table 3 shows the 10 Resolutions with the highest number of acronyms.

The meaning of this information is linked to the institutional context of a Resolution. Probably the one making reference to a higher number of acronyms (among those commonly used by the Security Council) involves a subject with stronger relation to different institutions.

Table 3. Occurrence of acronyms

Resolution	**Acronyms**
1075	6
1045	5
1063	5
1087	5
1118	5

1035	4
1048	4
1124	4
1127	4
1195	4

15. NEW FEATURES OF THE OLIMPO SYSTEM

The Olimpo system was the subject of a paper presented at ICAIL 2001, in St. Louis [10]. Since then significant changes have been implemented as described above. Besides them a number of minor features have been implemented, turning the system more complete, more user-friendly and more dynamic. These new features help to improve the general performance of the system and include the following:

- • A new interface allowing the user to visualize, at the same time, the search query and the result produced by the system;
- • The use of text mining to generate statistics from texts shown in a graphical form;
- • More Resolutions were added to the system database, including the whole set issued in 2002 and the most recent ones issued in 2003;
- • The United Nations Charter was added as a document available for direct searching;
- • The Provisional Rules of Procedure of the Security Council were also added to the document base for direct searching purposes.

16. CONCLUSION

The Olimpo system is a clear example of an innovative approach to the issue of information retrieval from complex text databases. Based on SCS technology (Structured Contextual Search, the system reaches a higher performance using DCKR technique for knowledge representation.

The innovation and new features implemented represent an upgrade of the Olimpo system, improving its overall performance and usability.

REFERENCES

1. AMONDT, A.; PLAZA, E. "Case-Based Reasoning: Fundamental Issues, Methodological Variations, and System Approaches". AI Communications 17(1), 1994.

2. Bench-Capon, T. J. M. Some observations on modelling case based reasoning with formal argument models. In: Proceedings of the Seventh International Conference on Artificial Intelligence and Law, p. 36-42, Oslo: Norway, June 14-18, 1999. 220 p.
3. Bruninghaus, Stefanie; ASHLEY, Kevin D. Toward adding knowledge to learning algorithms for indexing legal cases. In: Proceedings of the Seventh International Conference on Artificial Intelligence and Law, p. 9-17, Oslo: Norway, June 14-18, 1999. 220 p.
4. Bueno, Tânia Cristina D'Agostini. The use of juridical theory for retrieval from large juridical textual databases. Master Dissertation, PPGEP/UFSC. Florianópolis (Brazil): 1999. Original title: O uso da teoria jurídica para recuperação em amplas bases de textos jurídicos.
5. Bueno, Tania Cristina D'Agostini; Hoeschl, Hugo Cesar; Mattos, Eduardo da Silva; Barcia, Ricardo Miranda; Wangenheim, Christiane Gresse Von. JurisConsulto: Retrieval in Jurisprudencial Text Bases using Juridical Terminology. In: The Seventh International Conference on Artificial Intelligence And Law, 1999, Oslo. Proceedings of the Conference. New York: ACM, 1999. v.1. p.147-155.
6. Bueno, Tania Cristina D'Agostini; Hoeschl, Hugo Cesar; Mattos, Eduardo da Silva; Wangenheim, Christiane Gresse Von; Barcia, Ricardo Miranda. The use of juridical theory for retrieval from large juridical textual databases. In: Encontro Nacional de Inteligência Artificial, 1999, Rio de Janeiro. Anais do XIX Congresso Nacional da Sociedade Brasileira de Computação. Rio de Janeiro: Edições EntreLugar, 1999. v.4. p.107-120. Original title: Uso da teoria jurídica para recuperação em amplas bases de textos jurídicos.
7. Bueno, Tania Cristina D'Agostini; Hoeschl, Hugo Cesar; Mattos, Eduardo da Silva; Barcia, Ricardo Miranda; Bortolon, André; Wangenheim, Christiane Gresse Von. JurisConsulto. Florianópolis (Brazil): 1999. Software rights registered.
8. Hoeschl, Hugo Cesar. Olimpo System: Juridical Information Technology for UNO's Security Council. Florianópolis (Brazil): UFSC, 2002. Doctorate Thesis. Original title: Sistema Olimpo: Tecnologia da Informação Jurídica para o Conselho de Segurança da ONU.
9. Hoeschl, Hugo Cesar; Barcia, Ricardo Miranda; Bueno, Tânia Cristina D'Agostini; Mattos, Eduardo da Silva; Bortolon, Andre; Donatti, Fabrício Tadeu. Olimpo System. Florianópolis (Brazil), 2000. Software rights registered.
10. Hoeschl, Hugo Cesar; Bueno, Tânia Cristina D'Agostini; Mattos, Eduardo da Silva; Bortolon, Andre; Barcia, Ricardo Miranda. Olimpo: Contextual Structured Search to improve the representation of UN Security Council Resolutions with information extraction methods. In: The 8th International Conference on Artificial Intelligence and Law, 2001, St.Louis, MO, USA. Proceedings of the Conference. New York: ACM, 2001. v.1. p. 271-218.
11. STEINFUS, Ricardo. Handbook of International Organizations. Porto Alegre (Brazil), 1997, 352p. Original title: Manual de organizações internacionais.

KNOWLEDGE IN E-GOVERNMENT

Enhancing Administrative Processes with Knowledge

Maria Wimmer and Roland Traunmüller

Institute of Informatics in Business and Government, Johannes Kepler University of Linz, Altenbergerstr. 69, 4040 Linz, Austria

Abstract: With the emergence of e-government and a novel concept of governance the role of knowledge has become dominant. Building a modern administration with new patterns of cooperation means that the redistribution of knowledge has to be designed and orchestrated carefully. This corresponds to the concept of "knowledge enhanced Government". In the public realm there is cosmos of knowledge repositories and a plenitude of diverse processes. Thus, understanding the knowledge part in administrative processes is a must. This contribution investigates knowledge aspects in e-government and gives a survey on relevant knowledge issues in the public sector. Based on the comprehension of public sector knowledge, examples are considered where administrative work is enhanced with knowledge. Examples of such intelligent e-government processes are given in the second part of the paper: data interchange in routine processes, policy making and citizen advice. Next step of knowledge enhancement in e-government is to seamlessly interweave human and software expertise.

Key words: e-government, knowledge management, frameworks, e-governance, public services

1. KNOWLEDGE IN GOVERNMENT AND PUBLIC GOVERNANCE

1.1 Integrating Government and Public Governance

The issue of public governance draws more and more attention. Also the views about Government become broader and comprise legislature, executive and judiciary as well as sustaining democratic deliberations. The notion includes democratic policy formulation, citizen involvement, the execution of policies and the evaluation of their results so as to improve future policy making. In the same line goes the growing interest in e-democracy and e-voting. This has led to a broader scope regarding the whole governance cycle.

Further, the standpoint of governance is a necessary counter-position to the service view. The State is to be considered as one of the largest organizations to be managed and governed. Yet all too long, administration's activities have been subsumed under the header of public service provision respectively. This is surely not the case when the State collects taxes and when traffic wards issue parking fines. One has to recall the principal rationale: the activities of diverse branches of government (legislature and the judiciary included) contribute to the balancing of societal interests and maintaining the stability of patterns of societal life. This is reached often by using authority and by the state monopoly of legitimate use of physical coercion. Public governance is the underlying principle guiding and ruling government activity in general.

1.2 Knowledge is key in Government and Governance

Exerting authority and control can be understood as cycle. Viewing governing as cybernetic model has been widely used as it is a good means for explaining control in government and administration. Control loops can be visualized in the following way: starting with observing a specific domain and gathering of administrative data, then comparing incoming data with values provided from norms set, and subsequently turning to appropriate actions in order to control the events in the domain.

In reality, countless cycles exist - in parallel, nested, on diverse levels. But one fact is in common: for every cycle, informational input is the key for action. In this connection, one has to recall the breadth of Government and Governance to imagine maze of cybernetic feedback. And all these loops have one goal - ensuring social stability. Government has to guarantee (and enforce) a well-organized, structured and safe society as well as standards of quality of life within a common culture and society. Basic goals of its action include: proper functioning of legislation and jurisdiction; promotion of economic development; protection of principles of civic rights; preservation of nature; emergency management, etc.

The goals to be attained are set politically and they are partly rooted in the national constitution. Managing the implementation of these goals and the assessment of success thereof is a responsibility and activity of public governance. As such, public governance can be understood as governing and managing a society via the instrument of government, i.e. the implementation of goals. Sometimes, goals are ambiguous and even in contradiction with other goals, yet public governance has to cope with that.

As a matter of fact, Government and Governance as a whole can be understood as a large knowledge-intensive organization. Public agencies host a particularly high percentage of professionals and special staff who command important domains of knowledge-based activities, especially in ministerial departments, in the judiciary, and in regulatory agencies. Many public organizations are chiefly "intelligence organizations" and officials can be considered as knowledge workers par excellence. Complex decisions are particularly knowledge demanding. Decision making is a public official's daily bread. For any agency, its specific domain knowledge is an asset of key importance.

2. MAKING KNOWLEDGE WORK

2.1 A must from the point of demand

From the point of demand prospects for knowledge management in e-government are remarkable. Ultimately, a better management of knowledge will lead to forms of "smart government": Knowledge derived from previous action or gained through policy evaluation will be fed back into policy making in an attempt to improve and better target policies.

Knowledge Management aims at managing knowledge distributed within and outside an organization with the purpose to establish an organizational memory. This is done in a systematic way according to a lifecycle of knowledge production, integration and validation. In praxis, the development process is an ongoing and adaptive interaction with the instrument of a knowledge base. Moreover, an organized transfer of know-how, skills and expertise has to be arranged in a proactive way; a learning organization is the goal which one has in mind. Technical means for that are KMS (Knowledge

Management Systems) which integrate diverse concepts and tools. For more on Knowledge Management and KMS we refer to the literature (Borghoff and Pareschi, 1998; Macintosh et al, 1999; Probst et al, 1996; van Engers, 2001, Wimmer, 2003).

2.2 The praxis: Managing knowledge is still underrated

Turning to the public sector as application domain, one has to say that public administrations are not yet mentally prepared to that development. Crucial as it is – knowledge management is underrated in this field. There are several reasons that dealing with knowledge finds little regard: not many administrations will evaluate "their knowledge" in financial terms, others see themselves not responsible for that issue. Sometimes even a high esteem may be the cause: knowledge is seen as so high appreciated and so complicated that only someone in the higher ranks can cope with. So administrators have to become conscious that, in their agencies, respectable and extensive riches of knowledge – a real bounty of worth and benefit - is hoarded. More, administrators have to conceive themselves as knowledge workers and so, they must have concern for knowledge as an asset.

2.3 The goal: knowledge enhanced administrative processes

Building a modern administration means novel patterns of cooperation. Thereby, changing the distribution of knowledge is tantamount. In a novel concept governance and service provision have to become more intelligent. Redistribution of knowledge has to be designed and orchestrated carefully. All these facts point to the concept "knowledge enhanced Government".

Such a new direction will engender considerable progress. In the main, the focus of attention is shifted away from a discussion of structures and processes towards issues of content. It reaches the very heart of administrative work: making decisions. The management of legal and administrative domain knowledge is becoming a critical factor in governance. Seeing governance as cybernetic model dates back to the Sixties (Luhman, 1966) and has been widely used for explaining control in government and administration. A comprehensive recent governance model can be found in (Palmirani, 2003). A deeper understanding of the connections between processes and knowledge becomes important for building of the system and design of the user interface. The next two sections dig deeper into the analysis of knowledge in e-government.

3. THE BREADTH OF ADMINISTRATIVE KNOWLEDGE: A COSMOS OF KNOWLEDGE TYPES AND REPOSITORIES

3.1 Knowledge types in administrative action

Considering the dynamics of administrative work, one may discern the environment, the own action of an administration, potential addressees, states concerning the administration itself, and the boundaries of the own action. The handling of information in the public sector deserves great care and has to be characterized through remarkable consideration. At a first glance, governmental work involves manifold types of knowledge:

- Knowledge about legal regulations and their use in administrative decision processes.
- Knowledge concerning the cases to which the actions of the administration are directed.
- Knowledge about the potential effects that the communication of an administrative act entails on the environment of the administrative body.
- This includes also the knowledge about the own resources and abilities in order to influence this environment as well as to enforce the law.
- Knowledge about the internals of the administrative system in general. This is approximately in the sense of an internal accounting and evaluation.
- Expertise knowledge when applying the general knowledge to particular cases.
- Knowledge how to protect basic citizen rights.

3.2 Knowledge in repositories

One may regard the plethora of knowledge residing in long-known procedures and existing data collections. For the latter, three clusters of repositories can be distinguish:

- *Registers*: A big amount of administrative data is stored in traditional registers covering information on persons, land, real estate, property rights, entitlements, and geographical data. Also repositories on income tax, corporate tax, tariffs, duties, excise etc. are registers that have always been basic to authorities.
- *Legal databases*: Another big realm is the legal one. The traditional way of implementing political decisions and – at the same time - of observing standards of rule of law and public safety is legislation. The legal struc-

turing of administrative work has several functions. It can be seen both as a restricting and as a guiding force. In the concept of the rule of law, norms serve to protect basic freedom of the citizenry from public interference. At the same time, legal norms are a standard vehicle of communication between government and executive agencies. Especially in continental Europe, public administrations are highly regulated by legislation which is enacted on European, national, regional and local levels. This leads to a multitude of legal databases storing a huge bunch of governmental knowledge.

- *Management information*: A further area to mention are the plentitude of repositories containing controlling and management information. Such data are mainly financial in nature; yet the traditional controlling is changing and a broader view arises. Only in coupling with other data, new planning systems are possible that cover the full domain "citizen-politics-administration". Departing point for the development are the existing systems with major numbers of the budget, from which - over traditional procedures of the accounting - key numbers are derived. What is necessary is a connection to other tiers and the creation of new key numbers. To give an example, further data may be added to a controlling system from the environment, geographic information or also soft data from opinion polls.

3.3 Knowledge embodied in Governance

Legislation is managed and enacted on various layers. Governance on a *strategic-political layer* defines and assesses the strategic decisions using the law and regulatory instruments in the realm of politics. So the repositories of this layer comprise legal databases as well as socio-economic planning data. Implementation at the *tactical layer* is given in the way of policies (policy formulation and the managerial part of policy implementation). In concrete, it means applying the framework of law. At the tactical layer of the administrative bodies, the procedural workflow is being defined specifying (and enforcing) work processes to be performed at the executive layer. It should be mentioned that - in defining a workflow - often some de facto changes with regard to the wording of the law may occur. So in design, categories are specified and indefinite law terms are defined; hence the room for discretion becomes restricted (e.g. grades of fines are being defined, but no continuum is allowed; etc).

In public agencies, the executive staff exerts diverse actions in order to carry out the policies of the administrative bodies. The *executive layer* is the world of action and a plenitude of knowledge types is involved: laws and regulations, organization models, process models (workflow), information objects of all kind, human resources with their skills, competencies and experiences. At the execution level, process knowledge is central and the motto is best practice.

3.4 Knowledge management in Government

Bringing together afore mentioned types of knowledge leads to rethinking knowledge distribution in a systematic way. Knowledge management in Government has to be understood as a continuous work and several tasks have to be completed such as categorizing knowledge, integration of content and planning ways of dissemination. Questions about the various knowledge sources, structures and containers are central. For domain ontology, a rich kit of methods for knowledge representation exists: taxonomies, semantic nets, semantic data models, hyper links, knowledge based reasoning, time models and process graphs. Regarding Public Administration the problem is that sizeable formalized ontologies are scarce. Administrative work, in general, lacks such precise descriptions. As an auspicious sign such activities are under way, so to mention the Power system (Boer and Van Engers, 2002) leading to MetaLex[1] and CEN activities on metadata[2].

Content integration has to follow meaning the tough task of connecting the countless existing data collections. Mostly a collection of rather heterogeneous data repositories is entailed that contains data of diverse type formats that are originated from different sources. Content integration engages all sorts of conventional ways of keeping data: files, databases, legacy information systems. Efforts for content integration are rather high and the basis is a sophisticated content management. Minor or major obstacles are common just as to mention rendering information visible by use of one browser for all diverse data types and formats involved. Rather problematic becomes the question of joining different content - as the semantics of data in a particular application often have been defined long time ago. Such problems accrue in automatic such as in data mining, when semantic inconsistencies in data may lead to statistical artifacts causing misinterpretations.

Disseminating knowledge means orientation towards the addressee; information on actual and potential users is necessary for a matching of offers and demands. It is a pro-active approach that is needed ensuring a sufficient flow from sources to demand. To promote this idea, the somehow placard-style notion of a knowledge pump (Borghoff and Pareschi, 1998) has been invented. For administrative data some additional questions arise: How to

[1] http://www.metalex.nl/pages/welcome.html

[2] http://www.cenorm.be/cenorm/aboutus/information/cenproducts/index.asp

prepare knowledge for public display? How to ensure data protection? How best present geographical databases and environmental information?

4. APPROACHING THE KNOWLEDGE PART IN ADMINISTRATIVE PROCESSES

4.1 Interweaving knowledge and processes

Administrative decision-making exhibits characteristics which depart from well-structured bureaucratic production processes. In the latter, interpretation of the law plays only a minor role whilst in a typical decision process, legal premises and knowledge holdings are brought together in ways which often defy their structuring beforehand. The legal premises are themselves objects of knowledge which apply to both, the decision content and the process structure in which the decision-making processes evolve. There is a hard-to-define relationship between law, facts of the case, knowledge about law & facts, and decision-making. This relationship has to be clarified either by a single decision-maker or in a co-operative act: Knowledge and law strongly shape the decision and the process in which the decision is reached. Also, co-operative patterns may be of importance if the decision is not taken by a single actor.

4.2 Categories of administrative processes

Administrative processes are different – so when comparing them with the common view on production processes several distinctions become visible. First of all, a huge variety of different processes can be encountered. Then, a tension exists between fully structured production processes and complex decision processes. Most actual processes fall in between these two extremes. Numerous cases exist where at the moment when a process starts, it is far from clear how complex it will eventually become. Although many ways exist in which different agencies make their distinct interventions into the social fabric. So there is a necessity for major revisions compared to conventional processes: In the case of well-structured recurrent processes an extension to open decision processes is necessary. Also negotiation and consensus building of the administrative process need a blending of procedural and collaborative work modes. In public services additional views of customers have to be added. A very coarse-grained distinction may differentiate four basic categories of administrative processes (Wimmer et al, 2001) a shown in table 1.

The various process types identified exhibit certain characteristics with regard to the knowledge required in carrying them out. We will not deal exhaustively with all types of knowledge of some relevance for service provision and for administrative and democratic decision-making. Rather, we highlight some typical coincidences. The use of knowledge depends on the type of process. In an earlier publication (Lenk et al, 2002) we have treated typical problems arising for diverse types of processes in the context of knowledge management.

Table 1: Categories of administrative processes and related knowledge aspects

Process type	Issues in Information and Knowledge Management
Routine processes	Knowledge from interaction, citizen information; interchange
Individualized decision making	Knowledge of law and "process memory"
Negotiations	Knowledge-enhancing platforms for group decision-making
Democratic deliberation	Basic civic information / structuring debates

4.3 The dynamics of legal knowledge

From the standpoint of knowledge, the picture of influences and transformations is amazing. In closer regarding one may start with the point that in administrative decision-making both, legal norms and a predefined schedule guiding the course of administrative processes, play an essential part. With respect to law this may be seen evident, as it is the basis concretizing administrative decisions; concerning the process the workflow is dominant. But both influence each other and one sees an interwoven fabric of regulation, process and knowledge. Legal knowledge exerts multiple and dynamic influence in administrative processes. In several ways, e.g. consensus seeking or using earlier decisions as precedence for later ones, even feedback loops are created; thus legal knowledge is both, influencing and becoming influenced. The influences occur in multiple forms – sometimes stamping, sometimes subtle: yet their comprehension is necessary for the sake of achieving a good design. Some interdependencies between processes, regulations and knowledge are sketched next in outlining some influences (Lenk et al, 2002):

- Almost all processes are shaped by legal rules; in the regulations there are parts defining the (workflow) routing of documents and the course of decisions within the workflow systems.

- Consequently, the external structuring of the flow is derived from the legal regulations in general as well from the particular procedural rules valid for a certain agency.
- Forms intertwine processes and data and so exert a substantial influence. Part of the influence is effected by stating, which pieces of information are in and which are out (quod non est in actis non est in mundo).
- In some cases, also the material contents of the legal norms might determine the flow prescribing, which particular expert persons or agencies are to be involved.
- Such demands make the process open leading to the creation of a "process memory" (which later on might influence the course of the process).
- Also general legal requirements such as data privacy or the request for transparency may have a specific influence on the definition of the workflow.
- The mutual influence between process and law can be very subtle. With the modeling of an administrative process, inevitable ambiguities in regulations must be cleared.
- In establishing a workflow, discretion rooms are limited in multiple ways: giving categories, declaring default variables, encircling indefinite law terms; substituting them by defined types.
- An additional mutual interdependence is given by the fact that every agency tries to edit decisions that are in some way consistent.
- In that way, former decisions influence later and discretion rooms are limited. Such limitations may be given in a direct form by guidelines, yet, may also occur when glancing at former decisions.
- It is a mark of consensual procedures that collaboration is high. So in an actual procedure, convergence of opinions will come through an internal discussion of the civil servants.

4.4 Decision taking - the essence of the procedure

Decision taking is what knowledge is aimed at. Generally speaking, administrative decisions are the result of combining factual and legal information in more or less well structured processes. Here the ambiguity of the term "decision" should be mentioned denoting choosing particular options per se as well as processes of such choice acts. A decision can be seen as the result of using different pieces and different types of knowledge. The focus on decision making determines the whole process.

In administrative decision-making, formal and material factors combine: formal structures depend on administrative procedures whereas the content of the decision is influenced by legal norms applicable to the specific problem domain. In addition to legal interpretation, handling individual cases is characterized by a higher degree of communication with certain dynamics. Taking building permits as examples: On the whole, there is no routine: much legal interpretation becomes necessary and communication becomes intense. The big difference to the recurring and well structured processes is that, at the beginning, the process sequence is not always foreseeable.

One has to discriminate the single steps within the process and one has be well aware that decisions are made at the very steps of the process. Some may be trivial or automatic in nature, other need enormous effort: steering the process, gathering pieces of information that are required, knowledge exchange in collaborative modes, the decision taking part per se. These different steps are also reflected in the use of diverse tools: tools may sustain the decision taking part by itself by modeling (expert systems, software agents etc.), other tools necessary managing knowledge repositories (e.g. databases and document management systems) or support collaborative problem solving (argumentation systems such as Issue-Based Information Systems (IBIS)). Further tools are still in their infancies yet will become important such as to mention support for categorizing, retrieval and navigation with advanced systems for categorization, fuzzy retrieval and case based search.

4.5 Decision taking seen as knowledge interaction

In an attempt to develop a comprehensive concept for understanding the various kinds of knowledge in the public sector, the authors suggest a three-layers concept as depicted in Figure 1. This view on e-government reflects many knowledge aspects which are combined to reach the intended goals.

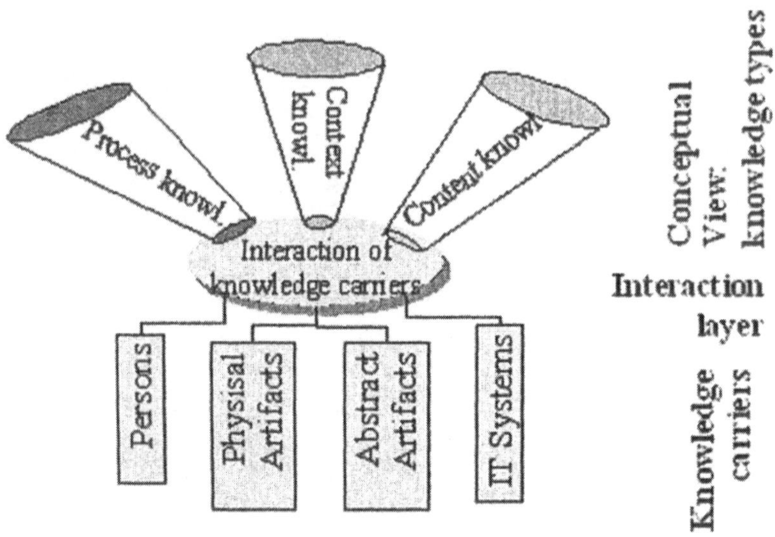

Figure 1. Three-layers concept of knowledge identification

The conceptual layer (knowledge types) provides a general distinction on three different categories of knowledge: process, context and object knowledge. The interaction layer discusses the combination of different knowledge categories according to the systemic view on a productive process. We understand that knowledge is embodied in different types of artifacts that interact to perform a specific process. The representation layer treats aspects of knowledge reflected in different knowledge carriers and how these components are interwoven. Such knowledge carriers may be IT systems, where knowledge is embodied in workflow systems, information systems, specific application systems, databases, controlling systems, management information systems, etc. Equally to knowledge in IT systems, knowledge is available in people's minds and in physical and abstract artifacts belonging to the system. From the people's point of view the third layer of Figure 1 comprises specific know-how, expertise, skills intuition and information. Putting focus on material and ideal artifacts, manuals, equipment, formal rules and laws etc. would be reflected. In a holistic view, the layered concept can be considered as a three-dimensional space addressing on one axe the three different layers, on the second axe the different types of knowledge and on the third one the different knowledge stakeholders: people, IT systems and other material and ideal artifacts belonging to the productive system.

It is the interchange between the conceptual layer of knowledge types and the knowledge representations that attracts our attention, because an adequate mapping of knowledge concepts and flow of knowledge is a prerequisite for attaining a proper functionality of the system. Key traits of knowledge types and knowledge stakeholders mark and emboss the interaction in the interaction layer. In that way, a determining influence is exerted with broad effect: on the particular tool, on the interoperability of tools and on the way tools are used in co-operation. A further strong influence between the layers is that a highly achieved functionality has always a history of adapting and tuning, i.e. a dynamic evolution of knowledge is an important matter.

Exemplification of knowledge embodiment in administrative action will ease the understanding of knowledge in e-government. Three examples are provided in the next sections: routine processes, policy making and citizen advice.

5. MODELLING LEGAL KNOWLEDGE FOR DATA INTERCHANGE

5.1 Turning to particular examples illustrating knowledge enhancement

Now we turn on discussing three particular points where legal/administrative knowledge comes in. First example shows that even for rather apparently unglamorous routine processes modeling knowledge is a prerequisite because data interchange of administrative information is far from being trivial. Further examples treat the knowledge part in processes of planning and policy making and show how knowledge enriched public services may improve citizen information.

The first example focuses on the embedding of legal/administrative knowledge for automatic data interchange. The way towards standards is via legal ontologies. If one compares the public and the commercial domain one can see both, differences as well as commonalities (Wimmer, Traunmüller, Lenk, 2001). The later ones occur at the technical level; at the application level, the complexity may significantly surmount the private sector. All in all, standardization has to be seen with a broad focus including several issues: establishing a common understanding of processes, while building on widespread administrative concepts, ensuring interoperable platforms, having a workable administrative domain ontology, defining formats for data interchange. Standardization is an enormous task yet from its accomplishment, all partners involved will gain

The core of the problem is not on the technical level, it is at the conceptual level as one has to capture the semantics of legal-administrative concept and norms. It is the characteristics of a web that data that formerly have been used locally before these have become used globally. It becomes necessary that data carry along their specific legal-administrative context. So there occurs a lot of automatic data interchange when regarding a case (e.g. civil marriage) handled via online one-stop Government.

5.2 Standards for data interchange

So for the life situation of a civil marriage, many transactions and numbers of repositories are involved. They may be dispersed over many locations under the competencies of diverse agencies and residing on several systems. Before the event takes place, several documents located in different agencies have to be checked; afterwards, a lot of updates have to be sent (change of name, civil status, common domicile) to documents that are also distributed on diverse locations. Interstate e-government makes the example even more complicated. One may imagine the case of two persons with different citizenship marrying in a third country. For the aim of maintaining a smooth running of system, interchange has to be done automatically. Such an automatism is only possible if both, semantics and rules, are in the systems.

On closer inspection, one can see that standards are not a technical problem only; moreover it is an issue of accountability and privacy as well. In some way releasing data can be seen similar to opening Pandora's box. As often the data are sensitive releasing data in the custody of an agency has to be founded trust in a reliable system preventing misuse. To say it frankly: standards are a core issue from many aspects. In fact, the initiatives and projects of the European Union have spurred a lot of discussion on this topic and one can be proud on the progress already achieved; nevertheless – it is still unfinished business.

5.3 Defining standards – an exercise in knowledge engineering

Standardization has to be seen with a broad focus. Ensuring interoperable platforms and defining formats for data interchange are one part; establishing a common understanding of administrative concepts and processes is another. Standards at the technical level are often common to the public and the commercial domain, but vexing problems are posed by standards for a multitude of applications which imply forms of interaction between human actors and software which are extremely manifold. Standardization is an enormous task and sophisticated domain knowledge is indispensable for their development. From its accomplishment, all partners involved (public agencies, software industry, private companies) will gain in the long run.

There is a long history of data interchange with EDI as most renowned pioneer. It has enabled smooth computer-to-computer exchange of standardized information items and of transactions, yet demands on description have grown. So current interest points at other exchange features such as extensible markup languages together with resource description facilities (XML and RDF). With them it is possible to build standards for rather complex structured concepts. So it becomes the basis for a Governmental Markup Language (GovML)[3], i.e. a language for defining administration specific content. Such a language has to provide a common, flexible and extensible syntax for administration-specific content. Other attempts such as the standardization activities from MetaLEX and CEN are cited in section 4.3.

However, defining legal concepts is not easy due to the inherent intricacy and complexity of law. So troubles start on the basis with legal terms themselves that all too often are not adequately defined. This is due to several reasons: vagueness that may be on purpose, genuine inconsistencies and fuzziness, dynamics in law, planned discretionary power of street level bureaucrats etc. Further, mapping administrative semantics is full of more or less inhibiting difficulties: profound differences in legal systems, adequate meaning of terms, different connotations of terms and non-existence of counterparts.

6. PLANNING, POLICY MAKING AND ADMINISTRATIVE KNOWLEDGE

6.1 Planning and policy making

Policymaking is normally taking place through multiple processes of negotiation, ranging from cooperative search for acceptable solutions to outright clashes in interests. Decision making in public policy is a process

[3] GovML has been defined in an EC-cofunded Project called eGOV (an integrated platform for realizing online one-stop government), http://www.egovproject.org/, the Governmental Markup Language is described in Deliverable D231

which more often than not is characterized by a mix of commonality in interest and struggle. It is rarely abiding to well-behaved teamwork.

The amount of negotiations, their length, as well as the amount of parties they involve seem to be constantly increasing. Many negotiations in public policy span organization boundaries. The classical policy triangles involving parliamentarians, administrators and field representatives has emerged to a net. The negotiated character of policymaking becomes apparent in all phases of the policy process, even in as early phases like information collection and analysis.

Mostly taking decision is characterized by a mix of commonality in interest and struggle. One type may resemble a litigation process with clear-cut roles of opponents acting in a quasi zero sum game. Labor relations and international conflict are often of this type as are many judicial processes. In other cases, positions may seem contradicting at first glance, but a skilful mediation process might lead to an acceptable compromise. Town and regional planning provides ample evidence for conflicts, which may be resolved in that way. Related to this is enhancing democratic participation in planning processes and other decision making which can be achieved in reasonable time frames through better support. Parliamentary commissions are another case in point. Other types of negotiations have the goal of achieving a common strategy such as it may be the case in a board meeting. At the implementation level, policy negotiation may also occur, although strategies are given. Also discretionary behavior of street level bureaucrats is normally accompanied by negotiation with clients.

6.2 Knowledge used in planning

Supporting the most various settings in which planning and policy deliberations take place is a must. It goes in two directions, bringing in the knowledge and sustaining the cooperation. The amount of knowledge used in a concrete planning decision is mostly extensive. There is a high dependence on organizational goals and on the situation. Some aspects are listed below:

- Pending tasks and general expectations about them
- Situation of the institution and the world outside
- Key numbers from controlling and result of evaluation and inquiries
- Expertise gathered from operating processes and handling citizen contacts
- Stakeholder in decisions (institutions and persons) and their interests
- Discretion for actions given by legal rules
- Familiarity with the organization, its structures, personal compositions and traits

- Possible procedures and directives, grip on resources
- Control of effectiveness and monitoring of directives
- Anticipating the effects of decision options
- There is a rich collection of instruments for support:
- First and foremost, tools should sustain the decision taking part by itself by modeling (expert systems, software agents etc.).
- Other tools necessary in decision taking manage knowledge repositories (e.g. databases and document management systems)
- Important is the support of collaborative problem solving (argumentation systems such as Issue-Based Information Systems (IBIS)). Mindmaps and semantic nets are graphical means to be used as well.
- Further tools are still in their infancies yet will become important such as to mention support for categorizing, retrieval and navigation with advanced systems for categorization, fuzzy retrieval and case based search.

6.3 Sustaining cooperative decision making

What has to be sustained is cooperation in the broad. Support of computer-mediated cooperation in a comprehensive sense means sophisticated tools, multi media and video-contact become a must. First, the meeting activity per se may be performed via video techniques – so economizing on travel costs and time. Next, many activities associated with meetings can be largely improved by tools using multimedia. Examples are plentiful: clarifying procedural questions; scheduling of meetings and implied sub-activities; supporting the agenda setting and spotting experts. Special software may assist in brainstorming sessions and structuring issues as well as bringing material such as geographical information. Many attempts can be found under the label of computer supported cooperated work (CSCW) as well as E-Democracy applications using group decision and mediation systems (Gordon and Märker, 2001, Märker and Trénel, 2002, Paralic et al, 2003, Richter and Gordon, 2004).

7. IMPROVING INFORMATION FOR THE CITIZEN

7.1 Poor usability means poor uptake

Common experiences show deficiencies in usability of public services. The typical interaction process on the Web revealed harsh insufficiencies.

Users were unable to cope with the logic of administrative thinking and did not comprehend the legal language. What the users lack in particular is a customized assistance, i.e. help that meets the individual situation and competence. Giving mere textual information does not suffice, information has to be "palatable" for citizens. A priority request is to translate the demand for a service from the citizen's life-world to administrative terminology. This is part of a very common conflict situation: an urgency of a citizen's request and the limited explanatory capabilities of the system to provide the necessary in-depth explanations in an unambiguous way.

7.2 Knowledge enhancement

Thus usability becomes a main concern and improvements go several ways. Some are less spectacular as building on past experience and applying common sense. So even plain rules will contribute to usability such as "Less is more" and "Keep it straight and simple". But there are complicated interaction processes needing a deeper analysis. So design may use several means, mostly it means putting more intelligence in the application. Such knowledge enhancement is particularly necessary when legal information is presented. There are too many users who are neither familiar with concepts of law nor with the logic of administrative thinking. They need active help in finding the information items they are searching for. This means translating demands of the everyday-world in the legal-administrative jargon and vice versa. Legal information touches some matters of principle, as the law as a citizen right has to be promoted as a matter of principle. Further, an active participation of the citizens in democracy can only be achieved on the basis of knowledge.

In praxis, several modes are viable for improvement. One would construct clarifying dialogues, and describe illustrative scenarios. Also detailed knowledge (on both, on the field in question and on the interaction) can be embodied in software agents. All this works in actively helping users in accomplishing their tasks. Finally, very advanced future design will result in intelligent multi-lingual and multi-cultural personal assistants being integrated in electronic public services portals. So we will consider several task with high potential for improvement.

7.3 Offering an integrated access management

An integrated access management has to adapt to diverse preferences: some persons may stick to writing letters; others might transfer the dominant written mode from mail to Internet; numerous citizens want to personally expose a problem to an official; some do it during an actual visit and others via a multimedia linkage. No wonder that the following become crucial points: how is the actual access point arranged in its physical setting and how is the organizational framework. So the delivery of services may be provided in various forms such as:

- Municipal neighbourhood one-stop offices functioning like miniature town halls;
- Multifunctional service centres working like a travel agency (offering public services as well as commercial services like insurance or banking);
- Virtual offices, where several formally independent agencies are made to appear as a single one. Citizen entering would get immediate access to the services of all agencies.

7.4 Taking care of the routing part

One of the first steps is to route automatically to relevant knowledge repositories or to the agency with competencies in the legal sense. The concrete target may be diverse: a plain database, a sophisticated software, a staffed service center or an official in a particular agency. An annotation should be made that demands of the agencies have to be considered as well: offering access options and rights, indexing and profiling, providing assistance in tracking etc. From a technical point of view various means are possible such as comparing keywords of requests or evolving scenarios of life situations. Also avatars should be mentioned with their capability for guiding user. Further meta-dialogues aiming at structuring tasks and artifacts in communication are important. A core problem of routing is that formalized ontologies are scarce.

7.5 Adequate interaction in public services

Citizen services have to be viewed in as an interaction between agencies and citizens someway resembling the world of Commerce. Schmid (1999) has defined a Business Media Reference Model pointing out the different phases of transaction in both, e-commerce and e-government. It has been adopted by adding an aftercare phase:

- Information: This phase deals with providing necessary information to customers. This includes push- and pull-services, adequate representation on the web, search mechanisms etc.
- Intention: This phase covers the representation of supply and demand. In the case of e-government, this means that it should be easily possible for the customers to map their intentions to the offered services.

- Contracting: The agreements taken in this phase have to be in a form that it is clear for both parties, what they want and what they are obliged to do. Since the contact that is signed here is obligatory, this phase includes the problems of the identification of persons and the authenticity of documents.
- Settlement: In this phase the agreements of the contract are realized. This includes exchange of goods, money, documents and/or information.
- Aftercare: Claims-management, caring for the client as well as a feed-back on the quality of service deserve special attention.

7.6 Invoking human expertise

After the routing of the demand according to administrative competencies as next step advice capability comes in focus. A lot of improvement is possible with minor resources and in small steps: working on better comments, drawing clearer scenarios, adding help-functions. Giving the complexity of the field, there is need for substantial improvements as well. So intelligent pieces of software may act in performing clarifying dialogues. One could also envisage service portals which comprise intelligent multi-lingual and multi-cultural personal assistants.

Given the complexity of cases, a purely software driven solution for advice is not an ideal option. Indeed in the public sector, many situations exist that require the intervention of a human mediator:

- Mediating persons at the counter of public one-stop-service shops improve their capability for advice by using the system. For the designer, this means not only to focus on the citizen but to regard also the people behind the counter.
- Remote expert know-how is accessible when needed for a specific case. Such expert dialogues may be enabled via advanced multimedia technology.
- With mediating persons and remote experts themselves using knowledge repositories ultimately human and machine expertise become totally interwoven. This is knowledge enhancement at its best.

8. OUTLOOK: CONFIDENCE AND CAVEATS

Closing a tour d'horizon on the enabling capabilities of Knowledge Management one comes back to the point of departure: Will Government use the potentials offered by concepts and technology? Let us mention some of the plentiful opportunities:

- providing proper information for planning and achieving better decisions;

- better information and services for citizens;
- civil servants empowered to improved work;
- surmounting organizational boundaries of public agencies;
- tailor-made service delivery for citizens or companies;
- citizen feedback as part of quality-oriented policies;
- measurable effectiveness and quality of public interventions;
- stakeholder participation in zoning and planning processes.

The crucial point in this question is not the state of technology; it is the state of awareness and concern of the leading administrators, of those who have to blaze the trail in the right direction. They have to be convinced: it is knowledge that they need for accomplishing their professional task. At the moment mixed signals are coming in. There are encouraging pilot applications, yet for administrative practice change is slow. Thus knowledge and change management become the keys to success. Only so the public sector will make a leap in innovation.

REFERENCES

Boer, A., Van Engers, T. 2003. A Knowledge Engineering Approach to Comparing legislation, in: Wimmer, M. (ed). Knowledge Management in Electronic Government, Springer-Verlag, Heidelberg.

Borghoff, U.M. and Pareschi R. (Eds.). 1998. Information Technology for Knowledge Management, Springer Verlag

Gordon, T. and Märker, O. 2001. Mediation Systems. in: Hilty, L. and Gilgen, P. (eds.). Sustainability in the Information Society, Metropolis Verlag, Zürich,

Lenk, K., Traunmüller, R., Wimmer, M. A. 2002. "The Significance of Law and Knowledge for Electronic Government", in Grönlund (ed.), Electronic Government - Design, Applications and Management, Idea Group Publishing, Hershey, pp. 61-77

Luhmann, N., Recht und Automation in der öffentlichen Verwaltung, Berlin: Duncker und Humblot, 1966.

Macintosh, A., I. Filby and J. Kingston 1999. Knowledge Management Techniques: Teaching & Dissemination Concepts. International Journal of Human Computer Studies (Special Issue on Organizational Memories & Knowledge Management), vol. 51, no. 3, Academic Press.

Märker, O. and M. Trénel, (eds.) 2002. Online-Mediation. Neue Medien in der Konfliktvermittlung - mit Beispielen aus Politik und Wirtschaft. Berlin, Edition Sigma.

Palmirani, M. 2003. Role of the legal knowledge from e-Government to e-Governance. in: Palmirani, M. and Traunmüller, R. (eds.). E-Government: Modelling Norms and Concepts as Key Issues. CIRSFID, Bologna.

Paralic,J., Sabol, T., Mach, M. 2003. First Trials in Webocracy. in: Traunmüller, R. (ed.). Electromic Government. Springer-Verlag, Heidelberg.

Probst, G.J.B., Raub, S. and Romhardt, K. (Eds.) 1996. Wissen managen: wie Unternehmen ihre wertvollste Ressource optimal nutzen (2nd Ed.), Gabler Verlag, Wiesbaden

Richter, G. and Gordon, T. 2003. DEMOS – Delphi Mediation Online System, ERCIM News No.48, January 2002

Schmid, B. 1999. Elektronische Märkte - Merkmale, Organisation, Potentiale. In Hermanns, A; Sauter, M. (Eds.), Management-Handbuch Electronic Commerce, München: Vahlen

Van Engers, T. 2001. Knowledge Management.Belastingsdienst. SIKS, Amsterdam.

Wimmer, M. (ed.). 2003. Knowledge Management in e-government. Proceedings KMGov 2003. Springer Lecture Notes #2645, Heidelberg et al.

Wimmer, M., Traunmüller, R., Lenk, K. 2001. Prozesse der öffentlichen Verwaltung: Besonderheiten in der Gestaltung von e-Government. In Horster (Hrsg.). Elektronische Geschäftsprozesse: Grundlagen, Sicherheitsaspekte, Realisierungen, Anwendungen. it Verlag (IT Security & IT Management), Höhenkirchen, pp. 436 – 445

Wimmer, M., Traunmüller, R., Lenk, K. 2001. Electronic Business Invading the Public Sector: Considerations on Change and Design. Proceedings of the 34th Hawaii International Conference on System Sciences (HICSS-34), Hawaii

E-GOVERNANCE

DEMOCRACY IN THE ELECTRONIC GOVERNMENT ERA

Thais Garcia, Claudia Pomar and Hugo Cesar Hoeschl
E-Gov, Juridical Intelligence and Systems Institute – IJURIS Florianópolis, Santa Catarina - Brasil

Abstract: This article describes Electronic Democracy as an emergent statecraft model. Electronic Democracy is analyzed from a theoretical perspective that proposes edemocracy as the new millennium democratic system. In order to achieve this goal, an e-government concept was required. It is proposed that Electronic Government is presented as the appropriate environment to originate a new role model for managing the public engine: e-democracy. In this particular case, the analyzes focuses on the most important democracy theories – Classic Democracy and Radical Democracy – intending to demonstrate that Electronic Government contains the democracy ideals from both of these theories. Although E-democracy is shown to provide solutions to many social problems, some drawbacks are also discussed. Finally, as a result of this analysis, the ways in which Electronic Government can help the Information Society to become more and more democratic is described.

1. INTRODUCTION

The Information Technology and Cybernetic society brings new ways to manage a republic and the institutions that determine the path of society must change appropriately. Due to the social transformations that are occurring, electronic government – or e-gov – is presented as the best option for government administration in the Information Society.

From Brazil to Singapore, countries are developing policies to implement e-gov, which is becoming an ever more present reality in the daily routine of citizens by the day.

E-gov is presented as one of the most important institutions to appear in the new millennium, bringing a new form of thinking with public participa-

tion in issues which concern them, an emergent and genuine democratic system, contrary to all predictions regarding the future of democracy.
This paper describes an analysis of this new democratic reality that is arising. The target of this study is to demonstrate that electronic democracy – e-democracy – reveals itself as the present and the future of world democracy, a true option for rethinking all democracy theories.

2. ELECTRONIC GOVERNMENT

In order to enable a global vision of the new emergent democratic phenomenon, is required a panoramic analysis of the governmental reality that provided the springboard for electronic democracy.

Historically, the fusion of knowledge centred on a relevant and determined objective results in a new concept, which tends to become a referential. In this way, the convergence of information technology with government administration resulted in the birth of e-gov, in order to fulfil the need for the public administration presence in cyberspace, with the intention of reinforcing citizenship and invigorating public administration.

The domination models that characterized the state structures are being standardized with the advent of e-gov, modifying society from the individual level, up to the power bases of worldwide organization. The joining of technology and power, virtual environment and government, brings about a rebirth of concepts, essentially in relation to power and information, which can be assimilated in harmony with the citizenship ideal.

The domination culture is rearranging, as a result of the importance that the virtual environment is earning, as the perfect environment for government - citizen interaction.

This new decentralized and flexible government architecture enables the elaboration of horizontal nets between the actors in society, allowing that e-gov opposes itself to the centralized and oppressive government. It seems to be the end of the current concept of power. E-gov is born under the sign of democratization.

E-gov is based on complementation – as opposed to a single unit. It appears as a juxtaposition of techniques, processes and structures of governmental management and technology. Juxtaposition because the result is a disconnected fusion that can be divided into two closed subgroups, however, if they return to their original state, there won't be a single common point.

Through this explanation, it is concluded that e-gov – in summary – is the result of an adjusted act: a frenzy of specificities and primary concepts, from which a new attribute is created. E-gov means a reinterpretation of, and also a revolution in, the management of public power, supported by information technology, with the intention of supporting the governmental changes.

Zweers & Planquéii define Electronic Government as an emergent concept that aims to supply or to provide information, services or products, through an electronic environment, starting with public agencies, at any time or place, in order to add value to all stakeholders in the public sphere. [1]

Hoeschl defined the starting objects: "government" is characterized as the public power management with its three powers or spheres (municipal, state and federal), and "electronic" in the sense of digital qualification, or, a digitally qualified government in terms of tools, media and procedures.

In a subsequent work, the author introduces the concept of "Digital Government" and asserts: prepare ourselves to the government forms biggest revolution in History. It is very close, generated by the technology enforce, and it will sprout from the relation between the ' government ' and ' connectivity ' concepts. [2]

Then, Electronic Government can be defined as the public power management invigorated by the introduction of information technology in its scope, aiming to extend the context of citizenship, due to the possibility of making institutional and internal management faster and more transparent; as it also enables a better integration between society, the government and the marketplace.

3. A MINIMUM CONCEPT OF DEMOCRACY

During human history, society has deliberated, incessantly, about government models, as well as has discussed popular participation in public issues and its decision procedures. It is known that many of these discussions are prophecies and exercises to foresee how the government will be conceived in the future. However, there is no doubt that the majority of these forecasts have democracy as a premise. Today, there are few who glimpse the future of humanity far from the democratic ideals. The new theories that appear – especially at universities – are, mostly, rearrangements of past democratic theories or junctions of concepts from diverse theories.

The politic society – meaning a collective life organization – has many ways to determine its organization, according to the place and the time. [3] The proposal of this article is to identify and analyze the new government forms worldwide trend: the electronic democracy.

In this paper, it was opted to discuss some of the most recent and recognized diagnosis of classic democratic theory and also radical democracy, intending to demonstrate that, in both the theories, the electronic democracy can be presented as future trend.

With didactic purposes, it was opted to detaching aspects of Norberto Bobbio's theory – chosen as defender of classic theory – and John Dewey – as the precursory of democratic radical modern theory.

3.1 Bobbio's Classic Democracy Theory

Bobbio characterizes a minimum concept of democracy by setting a group of rules (primary or basic) that establish who is authorized to make collective decisions and with which are its procedures. [4]

The author quotes minimum requirements to validate democracy, which are: a high number of the members of the group with power attribution to make collective decisions; the rule of majority taking these decisions and, finally, the intrinsic necessity of those who have the power to decide with true possibilities for choosing.

The rights of freedom, opinion and expression are also viewed as estimated presuppositions necessary to a real democratic system. [5]

Bobbio also presents a systematic regarding about the main forms of democracy: direct and representative democracy. In direct democracy, all governmental decisions involve citizens' participation. [6] A representative State, however, is a state in which political deliberations are taken by elected representatives. [7]

In the next topic, we will expose a brief summary of the radical democratic theory view.

3.2 Dewey´s Radical Democracy

Currently, the main discussion on radical democratic theory is oriented toward the dispute between republicanism and procedimentalism. The reconstruction of the theory of John Dewey presents, nowadays, a third option, in which the author tries to understand democracy as a reflexive means of continuous cooperation. [8]

According to this theory, reducing the idea of democratic formation of the public desires to the numerical principle – the rule of the majority – means to understand the society as a disorganized mass of isolated individual purposes which are so incongruous that the intention or the opinion held by the majority must be discovered arithmetically. [9] Hence, Dewey starts to explore the democracy that emerges from society, presented as a social organism in which each individual contributes with its own activity for the reproduction of all.

From this contribution, the concept of complete individual sovereignty emerges, which appears to support the democratic ideal of reciprocal trust. Society being seen as sovereign implies an unlimited development of its personality, in which each individual can find its own appropriate function in the society cooperation complex.

For Dewey, the State function, in this context, is to be the political institution that executes this common will through the social cooperation function. This is why the government must be an "alive expression" of the agreed effort to attempt to implement the cooperatively desired wishes.

This concept of State, meaning experimental resolution of problems, is bonded to the cooperative society needs of aiming [10]. To the author, the communicative character of rational resolution of problems can only be achieved where the debate methods of individual certainties assume institutional form, represented by the State.

The State would be a secondary form of association in which the associated public will try to rationally solve unexpected social coordination problems. On the other hand, the State has the duty to assure social conditions under which all citizens can articulate their own interests, without constraints, and with equal chances, which is driven by the law system [11].

According to this point of view, it would be possible for the unlimited opinion formation processes to take on a more important role in real democracy, in order to introduce the concept of "public" as a way to discuss cooperative solutions to society's problems.

This democratic formation of the public statecraft, according to Dewey, would only be possible with the social division of work [12], which would, consequently, allow the creation of a cooperative conscience and responsibility of sharing – in turn making it possible that each individual becomes an active participant in the cooperative society.

4. THE NEW EMERGENT DEMOCRACY

Having presented the fundamental base of the most important democratic theories, electronic democracy, known as e-democracy, can now be analyzed, as the most recent perspective on democratic regimes.

Electronic democracy is conceived as emergent political and social reality, resulting from the implementation of electronic government throughout the world. Its fundamental principle is the possibility to extend, significantly, the effective popular participation in government decisions.

It is certain that this new democratic reality brings new perspectives regarding the democratic regimes discussed above.

From the classic democratic theory, e-democracy brings the possibility that e-gov will extend the number of individuals endued with the power of taking decisions for the collective welfare. In this approach, spreading the power to decide on public issues is the main landmark of e-democracy.

From the radical theory, resurges the self management idea. By the time citizens could, due to the electronic vote, for instance, represent itself in the political decisions, the Internet becomes a mechanism of extinguishing political representation.

Either with a radical perspective or the classic one, it is a fact that e-gov allows the creation of a new relationship between citizen and State, much more interactive than ever, in which the citizen has the real opportunity to acquire a differentiated status in the social organization: the status of active citizen.

Information services – one of the fundamental elements of e-gov– enables the dissemination of information about the government, which contributes to stimulating the critical exercise of the population and also to foment the indirect control of the government actions through the InterNet.

In the Information Society Era, it is known that knowledge is a factor in political and social development. In this Society, knowledge can analogously be compared with what oil meant to the Industrial Revolution, in another words, knowledge is the master mechanism of this new cycle of history.

To publicize the governmental acts – and all other information related to the statecraft – enables the citizen to have a real knowledge of the state machine functioning. Even though that are still researchers who argue that information about public issues always existed, it is the first time in History that society has had such a powerful medium as the Internet. An informed citizen is capable of forming judgments of value and opinions on society matters. Spreading governmental information via e-gov enables much more knowledge generation. And knowledge, nowadays, is power. Spreading knowledge implies spreading the political power, in order to decentralize the power of decision in society.

Although the digital divide is accepted as a barrier to the successful implementation of the e-gov policy, there is also a possibility that the number of conscientious citizens gradually increases. These Citizens can contribute decisively to solving society's problems.

With all the respect, we disagree. It seems that the heart of the quarrel is the fact the critics do not glimpse citizens as protagonist of the electronic government policy, by seeing them as merely participants of the process.

The politics' banalization – pointed by the criticals as one of e-gov problematic aspects – as it will lose part of its typical procedures is an argument constructed under the unconscious will to maintain the status quo.

Banalize is to become banal, common, ordinary. And that's the e-democracy major aim: enable the democratic exercise to become simple to everyone. Perhaps some people can not face it so positively, because to simplify procedures implies the possibility to widen, considerably, the number of active participants in the statecraft. The more simple integration between State and society becomes, the more solid will be the democracy.

The electronic democracy does not face the massive population participation as "banalization of politics", but it sees this as an efficient instrument to enhance the exercise of citizenship. The " typical procedures lost" is nothing else than a rethink of the citizenship exercise mechanisms.

The end of bureaucracy does not denote the lost of legislative process' legitimacy, in the opposite, it enables that a huge amount of the population that is in apathyc political situation became active citizens again.

To simplify political participation procedures implies to bring actors who are far distant from the public administration back to the political arena. And if the "politics' banalization" is a consequence of this, it has to be worth.

If the new technologies the responsables for the procedural simplification, it is inevitable to recognize that the solutions employed today – and also the ones being developed – have as focus bringing the citizen back to the political and governamental arena.

There are innumerable e-gov solutions developed especially for the public who is unaware of the technological advances, as, for instance, the Brazilian electronic ballot box.

On this issue, let's discuss the critical of SABBATINI[13]:

The author's concern about the predominance of individualism when taking decisions is extremely pertinent. We agree that the decisions taken, in favor of the common wealth have more legitimacy that the decisions based in particular interests.

However, even if we admitt that a human being is fully capable to separate to its conceptions and its individual yearnings to take decisions aiming exclusively the common wealth, it is not the decision maturation time of the decision that assures the certainty that it was the most adequate choice.

SABBATINI places the emotional factor, said as easily manipulable, as factor of risk to the politicals decisions, almost considered as an unadvised decision. It is evident that imagine that the information cannot be manipulated is a naivety, but to face this as undoubtful truth implies to recognize that we are all government or media marionettes.

Taking decisions politics, in this proposal, is a way to adapt the popular participation procedures to the speedness of nowadays social transformations.

If the biggest difficulty of the Brazilian Legislative is to keep the legislation updated –in accord with the social transformations –, the electronic democracy enables that this legislation can be modified more easily, in order to follow the changes that are to occurring in a short period of time.

Let imagine, for example, if to each significant change of the legislation a popular countersignature was made. This democratic institute, presented in

Brazilian's Federal Constitution of 1988, in article 14, II, is the simplest alternative available to consult the popular in the present time.

And even if the simplest alternative of popular consultation demands a huge mobilization from the public administration and from the civil society, why can't we create simpler alternatives?

With electronic government, the popular consultation can have its concept extended. And it is not possible to see the rapidity and the agility of this process as a negative factor, because these are its greatest attractives. The Internet revolution gives the possibility of a governmental performance finally updated to the social trends by the time they occur.

As the number of well-enable electronic citizens increases, the greater will be the legitimacy of the consultation or the vote. However, the illusion of that the universal suffrage by itself would guarantee the freedom of the people was already fought by innumerable philosophers, detaching BAKUNIN. [14]

This quarrel retraces to the ideals of Dewey, ideals of sovereign cooperative society, in which – as it was said in the 4.2.2 chapter – the State is an instrument through which the individuals cooperates between itself with the purpose to solve the society problems.

Dewey considered that the social division of the work stimulated the social conscience in the individuals, indispensable the successful functioning of the cooperative society. However, we consider a small change in its theory: the electronic government will be capable to create the political and social conscience so desired by the radical democrats, either by means of disseminating the knowledge, either for magnifying the social participation in the political decisions.

As we can see, electronic government is retaking lots of the democratic ideals forgotten ahead the impossibility of applying them in the practical.

Electronic democracy is only starting its first steps. Digital inclusion programs and the reduction of electronic equipment prices are indispensable for its existence. However, we can not deny this democratic reality while there are still people without access to the Internet.

We have to keep in mind that electronic government is also an environment where the community can its problems and solution. Who knows, maybe from the proper electronic government, does not appear excellent a proposal of inclusion, as a result of the citizen's interaction with government, research groups, organizations and many others State actors?

5. FINAL CONSIDERATIONS

Even the arduous critical of the electronic democracy do not resist to a strong analysis. Perhaps due to the some researchers exaggerated pessimism, that say that is impossible to accept electronic democracy nowadays.

Pessimism this that is, in our opinion, fear of the stranger, a fear that devastates the humanity since its begging. As well as the wheel scared the prehistoric ones and the healers had been burned in the Average Age, defending electronic democracy is not an easy job.

Lots of issues can be argued in the theorical and ideological sphere, but, the electronic democracy is already part of our daily reality, even if we didn't have faced it yet.

Too precious time is lost by arguing on the e-democracy's plausibility, when the fact is that electronic government in makes us gain time and efficiency while citizens. The electronic democracy is simply a direct reflex of what occurs in the political and social sphere. It is impossible to conceive the Information Society – fulled of knowledgement and for cybernetics – that can not accept that a new model of democratic system had appeared, "electronically".

The democracy based on bureaucracy and extreme organiscism is inapt to answer to the current society yearnings. If all the segments of human life – either science or the intersubjective relations – are is a constant process of transformation, why can't we think that the governmental model does not require any modernization?

Electronic democracy allows the development of many kinds of technological solutions that aim to approach the citizen of the state apparatus and its political decisions.

In the electronic democracy era, technology will finally have the possibility to "redeem" itself from the society. Technological solutions can be responsible, for example, to promote the digital inclusion.

There are innumerable ways in which this new form of democracy can be exerted and managed. We, as citizens of the future, have the power to became part of this process, and to start searching for the best alternatives of exerting the democratical ideal in this new political and governmental arena.

REFERENCES

1. Zweers K & Planqué K. Electronic Government. From a Organizational Based Perspective Towards a Client Oriented Approach", In: *Designing E-Government*, Prins J.E.J. (ed.), Kluwer Law International: 2001, pp. 92

2. HOESCHL, H. C. *Quarta instância: Os principais aspectos do Governo Eletrônico.* Consultor Jurídico Magazine, October, 7th, 2002.
3. BOBBIO, Norberto. . *A teoria das formas de governo.* Trad. de Sérgio Bath, 4ª ed. Brasília: Editora Universidade de Brasília, 1985, p. 31.
4. BOBBIO, Norberto. ***O futuro da democracia: uma defesa das regras do jogo.*** Trad. de Marco Aurélio Nogueira. Rio de Janeiro: Paz e Terra, 1986, p. 18.
5. ______________. Op. cit., p. 19-20.
6. ______________. Op. cit., p.42.
7. ______________. Op. cit., p. 44.
8. HONNETH, Axel *in Democracia hoje: novos desafios para a teoria democrática contemporânea.* Jesse de Souza (org). Brasília: Editora Universidade de Brasília, 2001, p. 65.
9. ______________. Op. cit., p. 66-67.
10. DEWEY, John. *Ethics of Democracy* in The Early Works of John Dewey, 1882-1898, vol. 1, ed. Jo Ann Boydston, Carbondale: Southern Illinois Universtity Press, 1969, pp. 227-249.
11. ______________. Op. cit., p. 71.
12. DEWEY *apud* HONNETH, op. cit., p. 72.
13. SABBATINI, Renato M. E. *Democracia Eletrônica.* Campinas: Jornal Correio Popular, 30/7/92. Disponível em http://www.nib.unicamp.br/sabbatin.htm. Acesso em 19 de novembro de 2002.
14. BAKUNIN, Mikahil. *A ilusão do sufrágio universal.* Avaible in http://www.phoenix-library.org. Access in February, 15th, 2003.

USABILITY EVALUATION AS QUALITY ASSURANCE OF E-GOVERNMENT SERVICES
The E-Poupatempo Case

Lucia Filgueiras[1], Plinio Aquino Jr.[1], Vera Tokairim[2], Carlos Torres[2] and Iara Barbarian[2]
[1]Escola Politécnica, University of São Paulo. Av. Prof Luciano Gualberto, t3 -158 São Paulo, SP Brazil; [2]Prodesp, Poupatempo. Rua Florêncio de Abreu 848, São Paulo, SP Brazil

Abstract: This paper describes the role of usability evaluation as quality assurance of e-government services. Usability evaluation intends to identify difficulties experienced by a user when interacting with a computer interface. Usability evaluation is a key issue in assessing the return from investment in government sites, as it can measure how the services impact the citizen and is a significant source of requirements for design reviews of present services. This paper describes the creation of a Laboratory for Human-Computer Interaction (LabIHC) devoted to assess Sao Paulo State, Brazil, government services usability. This Laboratory evaluates about 250 users per day using different e-government services and can produce accurate reports on usability problems. The paper describes LabIHC's pluralistic evaluation methodology, composed of four different techniques, as well as the set of recommendations that were derived from LabIHC results for e-government services.

Key words: e-government; usability; universal usability; usability evaluation.

1. INTRODUCTION

Several initiatives demonstrate the Brazilian government effort to use Information Technology as an effective means of bringing together citizens and government, by making available information of public interest and enhancing services efficiency.

Usability is a main issue in e-government applications. Any interactive system must be checked for human usage suitability, but in e-government applications, usability is more than a design goal: it is a tool for democracy. If a bad design in e-commerce, for example, can drive away a customer definitely, a bad design in e-government can result in a citizen being alienated from important information or from a necessary service.

However, there is no simple way to define usability in e-government applications. Many nations are presently facing the challenge of developing interfaces for user groups that are diverse in their needs and in their knowledge of computer technology[1]. In developing countries, e-government application designers have an additional challenge of designing for citizenship education and social inclusion.

This paper proposes a methodological approach to the usability-in-e-government problem. It presents the initiative of São Paulo State government in Brazil to install a Usability Laboratory (LabIHC - Laboratory for Human-Computer Interaction) for monitoring usability of present e-government services so that designers can objectively remove barriers to effective use of those services. Section 2 in this paper presents usability concepts applied to e-government applications.

Usability evaluation helps assure appropriateness of governmental investments. A reliable evaluation process closes the quality cycle through monitoring of how citizens actually use the services.

Being in charge of observing the real use of government services and identifying difficulties citizens may be facing when interacting with these services, LabIHC acts as a prototype for an e-government Quality Assurance service, conforming to recent directives of the São Paulo State Committee for Quality in Public Management. Section 3 presents the institutional environment for LabIHC.

A single usability evaluation technique is not effective in identifying usability problems. Section 4 presents LabIHC's pluralistic methodology for usability evaluation, composed of four different techniques.

Usability problems resulting of LabIHC evaluation are reported to service designers. In order to help them avoid common usability problems, a set of guidelines was developed and resulted in the e-poupatempo usability standard (eUS) for evaluating e-government transactional services. A discussion of these guidelines is presented in Section 5.

2. USABILITY FOR E-GOVERNMENT SERVICES

Even though Usability Engineering is an over 10-year old discipline, only recently the Internet pressure for better interaction with non-technical users has led to a more significant and systematic concern about human-computer interface.

Usability is defined as the ability of a human-computer interface to be easily and efficiently used by humans. ISO/IEC 9126[2] defines usability as composed by attributes of learnability, understandability and operability. Subjective and emotional aspects such as helpfulness and satisfaction also play an important role in usability.

Designers must employ user-centered development processes in order to produce a computer application that can be used efficiently and comfortably by different users. Usability evaluation techniques play an important role in this process. A Usability Laboratory is an environment where computer application usage is observed, monitored, experimented and analyzed, in order to identify obstacles faced by users. Different e-government services have different audiences. Sometimes, obstacles are due to human behavior. Many times, though, errors and difficulties arise from design. More than often, obstacles are different for different user profiles.

A recent research published by Accenture[3] identified that governments are simultaneously tailoring service delivery to meet citizens' needs and demanding that projects to deliver Return on Investment. Usability evaluation can report on changes needed to make a service suitable to a user population. Quantitative data can help a more controlled use of project budget. Also, by establishing the present usability level of an application, monitoring usability level improvement is a valuable proof of the return from government investment.

3. ENVIRONMENT FOR THE USABILITY EVALUATION: LABIHC AND THE E-POUPATEMPO PROJECT

São Paulo State in Brazil has a population of about 40 million people, in a 250.000-square-kilometers territory, meaning a need for access comparable to many countries in Europe. E-government challenges for SP are to provide updated and universally accessible government information. This is a key challenge in Brazil, where the rate of computers per inhabitants is still low. Besides increasing the availability of computers, through programs of distribution of equipment in schools and in needy communities, SP State program for e-government is strongly oriented towards educating the citizen to be an autonomous, proactive user of e-government services.

Poupatempo ("*save time*", in Portuguese) is a successful project of the Sao Paulo state government that provides a single locale wherein several public services are available to citizens. E-poupatempo is the virtual version of this project and is a portal where public services are gathered for easy access. Presently, public service processes are being integrated and optimized in order to free citizens from displacement and bureaucracy[4].

Considering that lack of access to computers is a major obstacle to universal usability in Brazil, a special place for e-government services was created in one of the Poupatempo stations as a prototype. In this location, citizens can access any government or public interest internet site, aided (if necessary) by trained personnel that assist the user both in completing the intended use and in manipulating the computer.

LabIHC, Laboratory for Human-Computer Interaction, is part of e-poupatempo project. LabIHC was set by a joint effort of the Sao Paulo State Secretaria da Casa Civil, Prodesp (the State IT company) and Poupatempo Superintendence, technically assisted by the Software Technology Laboratory at Escola Politécnica, University of São Paulo.

LabIHC is responsible for identifying barriers posed to citizens in the service usage. The innovation of LabIHC compared to other usability labs is its ability to observe hundreds of real users per day. LabIHC benefits from the fact that about 250 citizens per day go spontaneously to the e-poupatempo station. To date, this database amounts to more than 60.000 usage records, which lead to quantitative results with statistical significance. Also, specific experiments are developed for testing more rare usage conditions and prototypes, thus contributing towards improving quality in G2C relationship.

4. LABIHC PLURALISTIC APPROACH TO USABILITY EVALUATION

Combined evaluation techniques are known to be more effective than one single method[5]. LabIHC employs a set of techniques to deliver more comprehensive results to e-government service designers.

Some of the difficulties captured in LabIHC evaluations are quite obvious to an expert eye; others are rare exceptions that only real usage could have raised. Due to the diverse nature of these difficulties, one single approach to Usability Laboratory would not capture a significant amount of usability problems.

LabIHC, thus, evaluates usability through a pluralistic approach, in which user profile and usage experience are collected by four different techniques:

- Direct observation. Attendants observe usage and keep a record of every user experience with computers and user profile.
- Questionnaires answered by a sample of the population, in order to map subjective expectation and satisfaction.

- Formal experiments, which address rare cases or alternative designs.
- Usability expert inspections based on usability criteria.

LabIHC delivers usability evaluation results as Usability Evaluation Reports (UERs) that are sent to the service providers upon request. UERs contain data about user profile and a detailed description of difficulties experienced by the users. UERs are intended to be used for design reviews.

4.1 Role of attendants

A key success factor for LabIHC methodology is the role played by e-poupatempo attendants. Their main duty is to help citizens with whatever need they have while performing the e-government services. Because of their close contact with citizens' needs and difficulties, they were assigned the task of collecting usability information. As public workers, their observation does not violate citizens' privacy. No information about the user identity is collected.

Attendants work as agents for universal usability, as they "bridge the gap between what users know and what they need to know"[6]. Answering citizens' questions, they gather a valuable knowledge of each site weaknesses. They encourage citizens to use the computer service by themselves in order to raise doubts and difficulties[7]. Even though the citizen has never used a computer before, he or she is invited to try and is frequently successful.

The traditional usability approach of having usability experts to monitor usage had to be discarded because the citizen cannot be constrained or embarrassed while using a public service that may require personal and confidential data. Video recording was also discarded because it would depend on each citizen's personal authorization, and this would not be feasible in a 250-user-per-day basis, besides generating a prohibitive amount of data that would be very difficult to analyze.

Success of attendants as usability observers depends heavily on training in usability concepts and methodology. As users ask for help, if there is a usability problem, the question is classified and registered. While this procedure makes the process independent of attendants' observation accuracy, the process is still dependent on his or her ability to classify questions as usability problems.

4.2 Usability variables

LabIHC evaluation methodology addresses a set of variables that describe the user and his/her usage experience. Independent variables describe citizen profile and can be conditioners of use: age, socio-economical situation, declared experience with computers and frequency of Internet access.

Dependent variables characterize usage profile and express usability parameters:

- User performance, measured by the service duration
- User proactivity, as the reaction of the user to the autonomous use of the computer, judged as a proactive or passive behavior
- Usage difficulties and their nature
- User expectancy and satisfaction

4.3 Direct observation

Direct observation protocol is computed for 100% of services performed and transferred to databases. This instrument collects variables that can be obtained by attendants, by observation or simple questions. Objective information collected this way contributes to evaluate the efficiency usability goal. Some important information that can be easily extracted from direct observation database is:

- Service time
- User profile for declared experience with computers and the Internet
- Difficulties profile for the service
- Users' proactivity profile
- Required assistance index

This technique has the advantage of resulting in statistically significant, quantitative data.

4.4 Expectation and Subjective Satisfaction Assessment

Questionnaires are distributed to a sample of the population, intending to collect information on data that cannot be observed directly by attendants such as age and income and also information of subjective nature, like perceived security, duration of service, ease of use and suitability of human assistance.

User satisfaction is traditionally evaluated in usability studies. However, first applications of questionnaires had to be discarded, because they resulted in a positive biased return. This was explained by the citizens' extremely negative expectation of public services quality. LabIHC team now collects subjective data of expectation for the subjective variables thus representing more reliably citizens' emotions towards the service.

Satisfaction evaluation can return information on whether the user will be inclined to perform the service by him/herself, in a future occasion. This technique has the advantage of resulting in subjective data, yet in a statistically significant, quantitative way.

4.5 Usability experiments

Usability experiments are used either to rehearse special conditions that do not frequently occur or to evaluate prototypes. Usage scenario image and sound are recorded for late review. Subjects for the test are recruited by invitation. LabIHC is especially conscious of ethical aspects of testing and recording humans.

One of the advantages of this technique is the ability to document difficulties and communicate them to designers.

4.6 Expert evaluation

In an expert evaluation technique, the usability expert can determine if a certain aspects of a specific product or web site follows recognized usability principles and guidelines.

There are many different kinds of expert evaluation techniques. The process is best done by someone who is knowledgeable in usability issues and/or has some familiarity with the product domain. LabIHC evaluates a service by both usability experts and also by attendants. Together, they can list a large number of usability problems.

This technique has the advantage of being fast and in finding an important quantity of usability problems. Yet, it is a qualitative technique.

5. THE E-POUPATEMPO USABILITY STANDARD

LabIHC evaluation experience has led to a set of recommendations intended to avoid most frequent difficulties faced by citizens.

These recommendations represent the e-poupatempo Usability Standard (eUS) for transactional e-government services. Those issues sometimes go beyond ISO/IEC 9126 definition of Usability and should be interpreted broadly as a framework for Quality Assurance in citizen-computer interaction. By following these recommendations, a transactional service is expected to meet the e-poupatempo usability goals, defined as:

- Citizens must be able to complete the service (success)
- Citizens must want to do it again by themselves (proactivity)

eUS recommendations are intended to be used complimentarily to the many more general guidelines of human-computer interaction and web design available in literature (for example, see work by Nielsen[8], the FAA Human Factors Design Standard[9] and Microsoft web guidelines[10]) and in e-government publications[11]. Specifically, eUS is complimentary to the Brazilian Federal Government recommendation for Internet sites[12].

Table 1 summarizes eUS issues, grouped by usability aspects.

5.1 Content

Content recommendations ensure that information is suitably oriented to citizen needs. **Relevance** is how much information is meaningful to the user.

Table 1. Usability aspects for eUS (e-poupatempo Usability Standard)

Aspect	Definition	Issues
Content	Information quality, independent of media	Relevance Coverage Sequence of service Content management
Presentation	How the content is exhibited	Aesthetics Structure Navigability Error management Accessibility
Credibility	Ability to support and preserve citizens' confidence in the service	Timeliness Updating Reliability Security Monitoring
Relationship	Communication between citizens and services	Language suitability Community involvement Customization Promotion

A citizen accessing an e-government service is frequently solving a problem or looking for necessary information on rights and duties, motivated by a compulsory need instead of looking for entertainment or pure knowledge. Also, content must have **coverage** of alternative means of performing the same service, depending on user needs. Also, citizens should find information on situations that cannot be handled electronically.

Lack of understanding of service **sequence** has been one of the major reasons for difficulties. Services should present a clear sequence for their performance. Interruptions in the service flow due to the lack of a document or information cause serious trouble to citizens, so citizens should be clearly informed on all prerequisites for service. In the service end, a clear result must be presented to the user, as well as recommendations of how to proceed in his problem-solving – for instance, mailing a document to some government office.

Content management guidelines address the need for establishing responsibility for the content as well as references to other government branches or third-party information providers.

5.2 Presentation

Presentation guidelines refer to look and feel aspects of the site service. Aesthetics guidelines address the equilibrium of multimedia usage to convey a feeling of modernity and professionalism and stimulate predisposition to interaction success. **Structure** guidelines intend to ensure an error-free, predictable navigation. **Navigability** guidelines address reachability through URL and visibility by other public portals and search engines.

Error management guidelines intend to reduce the observed feeling of uncertainty experienced by occasional e-government users, keeping the citizen informed about results. **Accessibility** guidelines ensure that content is not image or sound dependant and that handicapped users can access service appropriately.

5.3 Credibility

The concept of credibility is associated to mechanisms that stimulate and keep the confidence assigned by a citizen to the website. In e-government services, trustworthiness in an e-government site is generally extended to the Government and to the branch responsible for the service. The same will happen if the site is not dependable.

Timeliness is frequently associated to response time and thus affected by communication bandwidth. In e-government services, response time requirements are less restrictive than in e-business applications, for the alternative is the personal service usually far more complicated and time consuming. In spite of that, timeliness guidelines must be associated to usefulness of results, mainly for those services that require manual intervention by some government officer. Site credibility is much impaired by obsolescence. Outdated information can lead the citizen to monetary and time loss and – even more difficult to recover from – to a state of error in concepts or procedures. eUS guidelines for **updating** issues care for information on change dates and frequency of updates.

Reliability guidelines state the need for correct and valid information, while **security** guidelines state recommendations for interface tools for informing citizens on policies for protecting their privacy, mainly in public computers. **Monitoring** guidelines assert requirements for informing the citizen on user and service performance data.

5.4 Relationship

Relationship aspect covers the usability of the communication channel between citizen and government, through the e-government service.

Language suitability is one of the most difficult issues of relationship for e-government services, even though Brazil, unlike many other countries, benefits from a single language speaking population. However, there is a significant disparity in education and literacy levels. Popular names given to documents and services represent today a barrier for many people in finding correspondence between their problem and the e-government service solution. Also, present e-government services are polluted by "legalese" and bureaucratic language often incomprehensible to users. eUS guidelines require a terminology balance to be achieved, so that the citizen can be guided into in recognizing the correct wording but can be directed to it by his or her known alias term. Language suitability also addresses the minimalist use of interaction widgets that are recognized as barriers for some populations.

Citizens' questions and suggestions result in continuous improvement of services. **Communication** guidelines help designers define usable communication channels for diverse user profiles. For instance, only a small parcel of the population have email address, so guidelines require alternative means of communication, such as telephone or regular mail

From the citizen's point of view, service quality is also measured by its ability to recognize him or her as an individual, as well as recalling her or his usage history and adapt to it. **Customization** is issued by eUS guidelines in an evolutionary set of requirements that will help designers to implement CRM features in a near future.

Finally, **promotion** of e-government services is another important usability issue. Many services are not used only because citizens have never heard about their rights. Promotion guidelines help not only an easier access to the services but more than that, aim to be a factor for citizenship education.

6. CONCLUSION

Usability is a complex issue, yet essential for e-government services. Huge amounts of money will be spent in the next years in order to change citizen-to-government to a modern, improved new paradigm of electronic services.

Different government services have different target audiences, each with their peculiar difficulties. One government service may have children who use computers at school as a target population; rural population that seldom has access to computers may access another one. Therefore, there is no simple answer to usability issues in e-government. This paper addressed the establishment of a governmental usability monitoring and quality assurance service as an answer to the need of knowledge about people and their true difficulties. e-poupatempo LabIHC can act effectively because of closeness to true usage in a unique environment.

Usability evaluation can act as a compass to aid managers in the always-difficult task of allocating project budget. More than that, usability evaluation is the only way to prove that this effort is reaching the citizen.

REFERENCES

1. ACM *Interactions* Special Issue 2003 HCI in Developing World, March-April 2003.
2. International Organization for Standardization, International Electrotechnical Commission, International Standard ISO/IEC9126 Information Technology – Software product evaluation – Quality characteristics and guidelines for their use. Geneva, 1991.
3. Accenture, eGovernment – More customer focused than ever before (April 29, 2004) digitalforum.accenture.com/DigitalForum/Global/CurrentEdition/Features/egov_more_cust_focused.htm
4. Governo do Estado de São Paulo, *Projeto e-poupatempo*, 2002 (in Portuguese)
5. F.B.Wood et alii, A practical approach to e-government web evaluation, *IEEE IT Pro*, May-June, 2003.
6. B. Shneiderman, Universal usability, *ACM Comm.* 43, 5.
7. L.V.L Filgueiras, C.Torres and I. Barbarian, Next time I'll do it all by myself: enforcing proactivity of novice e-government users (April 29, 2004); www.acm.org/sigs/sigchi/cuu2003/Next time Ill do it all by myself.pdf
8. J. Nielsen, *Designing Web Usability*, New Riders, 2000
9. V. Ahlstrom, K. Longo, Human Factors Design Standard, Report Number DOT/FAA/CT-03/05 - HF-STD-001, 2003
10. K. Keeker, Improving web site usability and appeal (April 29, 2004); http://msdn.microsoft.com/library/en-us/dnsiteplan/html/improvingsiteusa.asp
11. Online Office of the e-Envoy, Web guidelines (April 29, 2004); http://www.e-envoy.gov.uk/Resources/WebGuidelines/fs/en
12. Brasil, Comitê Executivo do Governo Eletrônico, Resolução no. 7 de 29 de julho de 2002 (in Portuguese), (April 29, 2004); http://federativo.bndes.gov.br/destaques/egov/docs/resolucao7_egov.pdf

RETHINKING TRUST AND CONFIDENCE IN EUROPEAN E-GOVERNMENT
LINKING THE PUBLIC SECTOR WITH POST-MODERN SOCIETY

Reinhard Riedl
University of Zurich

Abstract: In this paper, we shall discuss the meaning and the relevance of trust for e-government. First, we shall identify trust concepts from philosophy, which might be important for trust engineering in e-government. Then we shall look at trust models for e-commerce, and we shall discuss how they may be transferred to e-government. Afterwards, we shall present the results of two empirical studies among young people. The theoretical and the empirical results will be used to derive recommendations for trust engineering in practice. Finally, we shall have a second look at philosophy, discussing the implications of post-modern reality for the design requirements for e-government solutions, and we shall derive a research agenda based on recent results in applied cryptography.

Key words: trust and confidence, digital identity, anonymity, e-government, e-voting, credential technology

1. INTRODUCTION

Many experts on information and communication technology have provided educated speculations about the importance of trust and confidence, including the author of this paper. However little can be found in the literature on this topic. In many cases trust and confidence is mixed with security, although it is evident that trust and confidence rather relates to *perceived security* than to *security* itself.

In late 2000, the FASME IST project (http://www.fasme.org) has analysed the heterogeneity among 7 European municipalities. One of the results was that the attitudes of citizens towards authentication technology and data protection were differing severely, and that the opinions of civil servants were rather diametrically opposite to each other. For example, while in one municipality the administration fully accepted the right of citizens to stay anonymous, the administration of another municipality was strongly interested to implement DNA-based authentication. Public opinions on digital ID cards were controversial, and the Italian role concept of the head of family turned out to be rather unique. At that time it seemed rather impossible that the European Union could agree on a joint concept for the use of trust and confidence technology in e-government.

Little convergence has been achieved since then. Several countries have issued electronic identity cards or have identity card projects running: Finland (FinEID), Austria (Bürgerkarte), Belgium (Electronische Identiteitskaart), Estonia (Estonian eID card), Italy (Cartà d'Identita Elettronica), Spain (pilot project with civil servants), and France (Titre Fondateur project). Further, the Swiss Federal Department of Justice and Police has published plans for a digital identity card, in Spain and Norway, local municipalities have issued citizen cards, and the European Union is funding the demonstration project eEpoch, which is supposed to propose solutions for the harmonisation of smart card infrastructure. However, the public enthusiasm for digital identity cards has been modest so far. Estonia had the biggest relative success with approximately 130 000 cards issued.

The cards in use and the card concepts in development differ with respect to the personal data set they carry (protected or unprotected), the ability to store digital documents and multiple applets on the card, and the nature of the CA running the PKI (government or private sector). See chapter 4.6 in [Auerbach 2004] for a detailed comparison. What we are observing is the emergence of increasingly mature identity management technologies, both in e-business and in e-commerce, which will eventually lead to lots of smaller and bigger islands, with very different trust and confidence technologies and data storing principles in use. It might seem a natural attempt to look for interoperable, European-wide scaling solutions, but we shall not pursue that approach. Instead, we shall suggest to fundamentally rethink the concept of trust and confidence in e-government. Is it really so strongly correlated with security and digital identity? And if it is: with which security and identity technologies?

We shall first review several philosophical discussions of trust as well as the historical development of trust in society. Then we shall review trust models for e-commerce and discuss, how they map to e-government. Next we shall present the results of two small empirical investigations among young people, which have been carried out, in our research group, and we shall shortly discuss the perspectives of civil servants. Integrating these perspectives, we shall deduce several recommendations for action to increase the trust in e-government.

After having thus analysed trust issues from a conventional point of view, we shall have a look at the meaning of role structures in the public sector and in post-modern society. This will lead us to a novel concept for trust and confidence, based on previous work by several experts from cryptography. Finally, we shall derive an R&D agenda to deal with the resulting open questions.

2. THE PHILOSOPHY OF TRUST

In [Bailey], Tom Bailey sketches a short history of trust in philosophy: "*Trust is as elusive in philosophy as in practice. Philosophers often simply ignore or presuppose it, and when they do consider it, they often struggle to explain it or confuse it with other things. Nonetheless, by considering some major philosophers' thoughts on trust and related matters, we can reveal certain important features of it, and see why it might be so elusive, in both philosophy and practice.*" He then surveys the most important theories on trust according to his judgement, opposing Glaucon (Socrates' brother), Machiavelli and Hobbes with Hume, Locke, Kant and Marx. The first group argues that self-interest will always cause a human being to be evil unless fear of detection and punishment threaten him. Machiavelli draws the conclusion that the Medici should commit any cruelty to maintain power. Thomas Hobbes (compare [Hobbes 1994] justifies the existence of the state. He believes that trust makes life simpler and safer and is a precondition for many co-operative activities, but he doubts its rationality in most situations. On the contrary David Hume (compare [Hume 1978]) believes in the good in mankind, as the behaviour of human beings is governed by their remarkable desire for company. John Locke and others even presuppose a shared sense of morality, which may be cultivated to overcome self-interest. Tom Bailey concludes his paper with the thesis, that – different from the opinions of both groups of philosophers – "*my reliance on others can be ensured simply by their taking responsibility for how their behaviour will influence my decisions about how to act in a particular regard*". He then gives examples such as medical doctors, who take some responsibility for our health.

While Bailey's concept reads rather elusively by itself, we think that its main point is the following: Trust means that we believe that someone else will take responsibility for us according to the social role in which she is performing in a particular context. Such a definition fits well with the concept of an independent third party in electronic commerce.

In [Luhmann 2000], Niklas Luhmann describes trust as a means to reduce the social complexity. He highlightens the necessity of trust by stating that no one would be strong enough to leave his bed in the morning without trust: "*Solch eine unvermittelte Konfrontierung mit der äussersten Komplexität der Welt hält kein Mensch aus.*"

Luhmann says that trust is mostly irrational and used to deal with situations where there is a deficit of information or knowledge. Thus, trust arises in conditions where Herbert Simon's *bounded rationality* governs human behaviour, but it is characteristic only for those situations with a considerable risk and a clear orientation towards the future, for which predictions based on trust rather then on information are made. Furthermore, Luhmann notes that familiarity is an important precondition for trust as well as for distrust.

Contrary to Luhmann, in [Coleman 1990] James Coleman describes trust as a rational behaviour related to the calculation of the quotient of two expectation values, which has strong similarities with ROI, namely the expected gain divided by the expected loss. He states that trust increases the bandwidth of possible gains and losses. He stresses the importance of collecting information in order to increase the reliability of the individual estimate of the quotient, which again rephrases the situation of bounded rationality. And he emphasises the role of time in the development of trust towards a person.

Integrating all these partially contradictory views we may say

- Trust relates to risk, caused by incomplete information and/or principal unpredictability
- Trust is needed due to the impossibility to deal with the world in its full complexity, the impossibility to avoid this complexity completely, and the impossibility to protect oneself completely against all risks of evil behaviour from others
- Trust is further motivated by the benefits of co-operation with others, and by the possibility to increase the bandwidth of possible gains
- Trust may be justified in several ways, such as institutional security, the establishment of global moral and role-based, social standards for right behaviour, and the collecting of experience in a relationship
- Trust may (and should) be partially replaced by the collecting of information, thus increasing the rationality of trust.

3. THE HISTORY OF TRUST

Government comprises all activities, which are set up to serve res publica. It has always been a goal of good governance to create trust and confidence for the citizens as a basis for economic behaviour. However, in recent history, the necessity of open exchange with others for the economic success of a society has been understood. Thus government now intends to create trust without creating too many dependencies and other constraints to freedom. A lack of trust prevents co-operative activities and destroys the markets for exchanging goods and services. It thus hinders the success of economy significantly. However, if the price for trust is dependency, this will have similar negative effects as distrust.

Historically, trust was first bound to the family and the tribe. Later on, there were three competing institutions: family, religious organisations (e.g. the Catholic Church), and the government. Ironically, the concept of love, which has been used by Hume and others to explain the human inclination, is a rather modern quality of family, which was attributed to magic rather than to the nature of mankind in earlier times. The concept of friendship may be considered as a much older artificial conceptual extension of family.

In recent centuries, non-profit organisations were formed to support welfare, which implicitly contributes to trust in society. The trust in professional roles of knowledge workers is nowadays a central foundation of trust. Thereby, the trust in a person performing in a particular role is no longer necessarily causally related with the trust in her performing in other roles. Furthermore, in the 20th century the average amount of trust in society has become strongly positively correlated with the health of economy.

Thus we are now facing a much more scattered trust landscape than in earlier times. Religious beliefs are fading. Cultural guarantees (like the handshake in the Alps) are dying out and are increasingly replaced by law technology. On the opposite, economic theory is focussing on trust issues, e.g. when it compares the principal agent theory and the shareholder value concept with the stakeholder concept and the team production model offering a trust dividend. Further, the post-communist period in Eastern Europe has demonstrated that the trust in institutions and the effectiveness of G2B administrative procedures is a key success factor for economy. And the success of digital information and communication technology has created new possibilities and challenges, like biometry for truly secure authentication and Internet business without synchronous interaction.

The complexity of the situation may be one of the reasons why a globally unique and interoperable, digital identity seems to be the silver bullet for trust and confidence as well as for the security of the state. While in earlier times, balanced power among the trust providing institutions (competing for power) provided a maximum of trust and freedom to the people, these days many people are calling for a joining of the forces of all institutions to fight the evil. The capabilities for data networking of digital information and communication technologies may help that this vision becomes reality (compare [Popp 2004]). However, our empirical investigations have indicated that the networking of trustworthy institutions is perceived as untrustworthy and dangerous.

4. THEORETICAL TRUST MODELS

Most authors discussing trust issues in e-commerce name some or all of the following trust building elements: technical security, protection of privacy, trustworthiness (trust property, trusting beliefs) of the supplier, public reputation of the supplier, certification by a trusted third party, quality of the Web-design, quality of products, and the individual skills of the customer. In particular, they consider trustworthiness of e-commerce to be positively correlated with public reputation. For example, in [Papadopoulou 2001], the following trust properties are given: benevolence, integrity, predictability, competence, ability, credibility, reliability, goodwill, fairness, etc.

There are several models for trust in e-commerce, which describe the interplay of trust building factors, among them [McKnight 2002] and [Egger 2000] (see also [Zachar 2002]. McKnight considers in his model the dependencies among trust building levers (perceived vendor reputation, perceived site quality), trust in vendor (trusting beliefs, trusting intention / willingness), institutional and structural factors (structural assurance of the Web, perceived Web risk), and the behavioural intentions of the customer (intention to follow vendor advice, intention to share personal information with vendor, intention to purchase from site). Egger partitions his trust model into tiers: pre-interactional filters (general intention to trust, general attitude towards e-commerce, reputation, and transference of opinions from others), interface properties (appeal, overview, usability), and information content (products and services, company, security, privacy, communication).

Both models consider site quality, security, reputation, individual skills, and the development of trust as rather important, although they describe these features differently. For example, in [Egger 2003] trust development is implicitly represented by the relationship management for the interaction process, as he stresses the importance of communication. In addition, Egger integrates products and services and privacy into his trust model.

The basic concepts of these models can be transferred to e-government, but we have to consider the differences between e-commerce and e-government when trying to draw up a trust model for e-government. First, the citizen interacts with government in a much richer set of different contexts and life episodes than with a single e-commerce vendor. She has less freedom to choose the interaction and the data collected are often of an especially sensitive nature, e.g. religious belief or personal income. Usually, she is also aware that data mining is an important technique for government to fight crime and terrorism. Consequently, the networking of these data threatens her more than the networking of e-commerce data, which is why privacy will play a more dominant role in e-government. Second, while in the last years e-commerce customers have learned to distinguish between different providers, e-government is perceived and advertised as one strategic mission of the state. It is thus rather the structural assurance of e-government than that of the Web in general, which counts. Third, in many countries trusting beliefs with respect to government institutions are stronger than with respect to business companies, despite of the fact that public reputation may be lower ("e-government is slow, civil servants are expert sleepers"), while in some countries with a short democratic history they are weaker. Depending on the country, reputation may be little of a problem or a big problem, which has to be handled on a more global scale. However, independent of the reputation, privacy concerns towards government play a major role in most European countries due to history. Fourth, the trust and confidence technology currently considered for e-government is much higher developed than that used in e-commerce. This suggests that e-government could be advertised by stressing its technological advantage with respect to security over e-commerce. Fifth, we conjecture, that e-government is much less known than e-commerce, as it has been appearing more rarely and for a short period of time in the media, which implies that user acceptance is low simply for the fact the a majority of citizens do not know the offers yet. Sixth, since the interaction in e-government is mostly defined by Law, and because in many cases it is perceived as an unpleasant duty, it is not the nature of products, which plays a significant role, but the degree of reduction of interaction efforts. Finally, legal principles require an equal treatment of all citizens. Although that does not explicitly imply equal efforts to establish trust and confidence from all parts of society, there are strong arguments in favour of an equality of trust winning efforts, which pays particular attention to elderly people.

We conclude that the pre-interactional filters in e-government are available information, Internet skills, assumed privacy and security risks, the attitude towards e-government as a whole – and in some countries the lack of reputation. The usability is part of the product/service, and it may dominate the general distrust in the Internet or e-government services. This is particularly true, if the time spent on the unpopular interaction with public administration is significantly shortened. Further, rich communication facilities will increase the trust-worthiness of the e-government services. Thus, [McKnight 2002] and [Egger 2000] partially apply to e-government, but the priorities there are rather different and they depend on the country.

5. EMPIRICAL INVESTIGATIONS

The target group for the empirical investigations in our research group was young people in Zurich. We did not intend to obtain representative numbers, but rather we wanted to identify trends among young people since they are opinion leaders with respect to the use of Internet technology. Due to the globalisation of youth culture, these trends are likely to generalise to the whole of Europe. However, the impact of the long and special tradition of direct democracy in Switzerland should be taken into account. Although voting is much more complex in Switzerland than in most other democratic countries, young people are very well informed about the traditional voting procedures.

In the fist study (see [Pfleghart 2003]) 166 pupils in the canton of Zurich, between 17 and 21 years of age, answered a questionnaire on e-voting. In the second study (see [Zumsteg 2004] 371 students of the University of Zurich answered a more complete questionnaire on e-government as a whole.

5.1 E-Democracy and the 80-20 Law

Based on the assumption that only people searching for political information on the Web would use e-voting, in [Lindner 2001] it was estimated that the overall increase of participation in votings could be at most 3.5%. The results of the first study exhibit a typical 80-20 law with respect to e-democracy other than e-voting and they strongly question the above type of reasoning. About 80% had no interest to discuss on politics via the Internet and did not use the Internet to access political information, although they were collecting political information from newspapers and the Bundesbüchlein. However, 60% said they wanted Internet voting using the web-browser, although half of them had strong doubts that electronic voting was safe from manipulation, two third were somewhat or strongly concerned that electronic votes could be lost, and half of them were concerned about possible violations of anonymity. Thus, the pupils between 17 and 21 years had strong interests in web-based e-voting, despite of the fact that they distrusted its security, but they had little interest in other forms of democracy.

5.2 Contradicting Opinions and Lack of Information

The second study among students at the University of Zurich has shown that 70% are using the Internet on a daily basis. When asked whether they would have a stronger trust in government or in commercial companies, half of them preferred government and one eighth preferred business. A more detailed analysis showed, that trust in Justice was strongest, followed by trust in the national government, which was better trusted than public administration and the Houses of Parliament.

Internet voting was nearly equally popular as voting by mail (75%), and twice as popular as ballot box voting (40%). Half of the students had serious security concerns, but nearly 80% said that they would use e-voting despite of their concerns. Nevertheless, only 10% had a considerable knowledge about the first Swiss e-voting trial!

The situation was similar for the electronic submission of tax declarations: 60% wanted to submit the tax declaration electronically, but 50% noted that they had privacy and security concerns, although 80% considered the technology itself to be trustworthy. Further, more than 50% said they would not use e-assistance services if they had to provide personal data.

Among the measures to reduce fears, the use of digital ID Cards and the declaration on data protection on the Web-site were considered most important, followed by the information provided by family and friends. Furthermore, the possibilities to contact the administration by e-mail or phone, information about security on the Web-site, the use of biometric authentication, easy navigation on the site, cost reductions (e.g. for e-taxes), information from the media, and help-buttons on the Web-site were considered as useful, in the order they are cited here.

Part of these observations might seem to constitute a contradiction in itself, but we think that they reflect three important facts

- trust and confidence are emotionally perceived, not intellectually (which is why contradictions may occur)
- the Swiss government has failed to properly inform about e-government and e-democracy initiatives (which is why contradictions are likely as many citizens have not much thought about the issues they are concerned about)
- the benefits of e-services are considered higher than the risks by young people in Switzerland (which is why significant concerns do not hinder user acceptance)

Finally, we asked which of the e-government Web-sites were known. The result was remarkable: Nearly 80% did not know the Swiss national e-government portal www.ch.ch at all and only 6% had visited it.

5.2.1 Summary

There was no statistically relevant correlation between experience and attitudes. E-voting via Web-browsers and electronic submission of tax-declarations enjoy a high acceptance. Indeed, the benefits of e-voting are considered to be more important than the strong concerns about it. On the contrary, e-assistance earns user acceptance only if users do not have to provide personal data. The most important concerns are privacy and lack of security. The biggest deficit so far is the failure of PR activities for e-government. Students all make extensive use of the Internet, but they simply do not know about high profile activities. Remarkably enough, the less direct contacts students have with forms of e-government, the better they trust them. However, there is also a strong concern that privacy might be in danger when one uses e-government services.

These results confirm our conclusions in section 4, drawn from previous trust models for e-commerce. Furthermore, James Coleman's definition of trust is confirmed: It is the quotient of gain (multiplied by its likelihood, compare the results on e-assistance) and risk which determines trust. On the contrary, Niklas Luhmann's assumption that familiarity is a precondition for trust or distrust does not seem to hold in this context.

6. CIVIL SERVANT PERSPECTIVES

The views from civil servants somewhat differ from those of citizens. For example, in [Knörri 2003], security for the e-voting in Zurich is depicted as made up of four elements: technical security (30%), security through organisation (40%), security through threatened punishment (20%), and security through user handling (10%). We may observe the combination of traditional concepts (Glaucon and Hobbes, although in the absence of Machiavelli) with modern concepts of effective government, inspired by the management concepts in [Drucker 2001]. In two personal interviews, Knörri who is a civil servant himself has confirmed the importance of organisational security, usability, and pilot projects. However he was much less enthusiastic towards an early integration of users and an early information of the public. Furthermore, he said that the use of open source software for e-voting projects was an academic idea, which was no option for e-voting in practice.

This clearly shows that there is a strong distrust in transparency among civil servants. Other studies carried out in our research group have confirmed this observation (see [Sidler 2003]. Rather than protecting data, it is data protection, which is highly protected and kept secret by the civil servants implementing new data pools.

7. RECOMMENDATIONS FOR ACTION

The following recommendations try to combine the theoretical and the empirical findings above with the opinions observed in interviews and e-mail communication with civil servants. They address current development of e-government solutions rather than R&D issues.

1. Develop a risk-sensitive integrated road map for all national e-government initiatives. One failure of a high risk application might block all activities
2. Use state of the art security technology – and do advertise that fact!
3. Consider the introduction of digital identity cards[4] - or a similar solution with corresponding functionality but improved privacy.
4. Respect data protection carefully and talk about it. Clear and easy to understand declarations of pursued privacy policies are a must.
5. Design easy-to-navigate Web-sites for all and keep in mind that usability is part of the value of an e-government service. People want to use e-government services because they expect that the time spent on them will be much less than with traditional government services.
6. Start to advertise the e-government services. The attitude to keep pilot projects secret points in the direction of failure. The time has come to really talk with the citizens about e-government.
7. Consider the needs of the citizens and perform empirical studies!

Our investigations obviously do not generalise to all sectors of society in Switzerland, the less to Europe as a whole. However, they demonstrate that folklore is wrong. For example, trust is not always a precondition for user acceptance. Or rather, it is trust in the sense of Coleman, which counts, not trust in general. In depth empirical studies are needed for a better understanding of the reasons for trust and the impact of trust.

8. RETHINKING IDENTITY

We have seen that data protection is a key issue for trust in e-government services. Rather than patching violations of privacy wherever they occur, we suggest to completely rethink digital identity as a whole in order to develop sustainable solutions for the future.

8.1 Privacy, Government, and Post-Modern Reality

Electronic Government, or e-Government, comprises all aspects of *the use of digital information and communication technology in the public sector* including the resulting structural *change*. Technological developments,

[4] Unfortunately, biometric technology is not ready yet for a use which confirms to the European guidelines on the protection of biometric data.

information, and productivity are not at the heart of e-government, as they are not a primary concern of modern society. It is the managed institution being an instrument of society, which creates results (compare [Drucker 2001].

But how do these institutions, how does the public sector work? It is based on a clear role structure. There is a long tradition, dating back thousands of years, that the role is more important than its performer. The structural design of e-government solutions must implement these role structures.

E-government creates a new, virtual public space, but how do the role structures in real public space develop? Since several decades, the public space is increasingly being invaded by private life. This means, that the distributed context structure of public space is much more scattered and heterogeneous as it used to be. Social rules for behaviour in public are less stringent but also more difficult to understand. The virtual public space of e-government has to be designed according to the needs of the citizen. It must not ignore cultural trends of the presence, and thus, it must admit a rich mix of role-structures and context definitions.

We are living in post-modern society. What are the consequences for our communication habits in private and in public? The coupling of the roles we play in different communication channels gets looser and looser. We focus more on the context, as we have been taught that the message is created at the receiver. Our statements are usually made with explicit or implicit reference to a context. If that context is removed, our words are more contradictory than it would have been socially accepted a hundred years ago. Western communication style thus approaches African traditions of personal relationship management. As a consequence, the real threat to our identity is not, that privacy is violated in a known context, but that personal data are stripped their context and combined for a context unknown to their producers.

Our identity is more open and fragmented than it used to be hundred years ago. It consists of all the roles in which we are performing in different contexts. Thus it is made up of situated identities. Our interaction with the Internet creates personal data, the sum of which constitutes our digital identity. However, these situated data are valid for a particular context only. Combining digital from different strongly roles violates our privacy. This observation is represented by the context principle in European data protection principles[5]. Personal data created and stored for one context must not automatically be reused in another context.

[5] Directive 95/46/EC

We thus conclude that the public sector and post-modern reality are both furnished with rich role structures, which are becoming increasingly complex. The design of e-government solutions must support these role structures and their management by the citizens and the government agencies (although organisational measures have to take care that no definition of roles for the sake of the exploitation of technology takes place). Further care has to be taken that only productive role structures and role structures with productive side-effects on the institutional culture are designed and implemented. These considerations lead us to a new concept of digital identity, where the certificates of identity do not necessarily provide the name of the certified citizen, but only some of her attributes.

8.2 A Holistic Concept for Identity

In its broadest sense, digital identity may be understood as the set of all personal data of a person (compare [Köhntopp 2001]). Subsets of these data represent partial identities. Any certified subset of these data constitutes a trustworthy digital identity. We usually use the term "credential" for such a certificate. If it is impossible to identify the represented person from the partial digital identity given, we may call it an anonymous digital identity. Depending on the existence of certificates this anonymous digital identity may be trustworthy or not. If there is a means to provide evidence that one owns a trustworthy digital identity (i.e. that a set of personal data is a valid description of oneself) without creating an identifiable digital trace, this constitutes an untraceable trustworthy digital identity, which by its very definition is anonymous.

Trustworthy partial digital identities may be used to access digital services based on a role concept. The latter means that authorisation to access a service is based on an access control list made up of pairs of roles and trust levels. A role consists of attributes, i.e. it is an anonymous partial digital identity, and a trust level defines the rules to accept a certification of a role, that is the credential. If credentials are non-traceable, then it is impossible to violate the privacy of the credential holder without his notice: Citizens performing in different roles cannot be traced across roles. In fact, even more is true: In general, it is impossible to deduce how many persons are personifying a role.

Several mathematical concepts for such credential systems have been developed, e.g. [Chaum 1987], [Brands 2000], and [Camenisch 1999]. The last one presents to the best of our knowledge the up to date most advanced credential technology. It has the following properties (among others): The user has control over her data and her transactions are not linkable. Organisations do not know the identity of the user, but only her pseudonym. The revocation of credentials in case of fraud is possible. And based on the credential protocol alone, co-operating users are not able to receive credentials which they would not receive without co-operation.

IT architectures have been designed and prototypically evaluated which use this credential technology for real world scenarios. In particular, it has been shown that it is possible to anonymously access different e-government services through a single-window e-government broker ([Király 2003]) as long as now tracing based on lower level protocols is possible (see [Roduner 2003]). We may conclude from these results that a system of digital identities is technically feasible, although lots of technical problems exist to be solved yet. Thus, for the future our suggestion number 3 in chapter 7 should be rewritten: Make use of credential technology for the implementation of trustworthy digital identity!

This statement is supported by the fact that European data protection principles require that the storage of personal data has to comply with the context needs in size and quality. It is not admissible that more data are stored than needed. This implies in particular, that any transaction, which can be carried out anonymously, must be carried out anonymously. Trustworthy anonymity guarantees data quality and widens the range of e-government transactions which do not require the name of an involved citizen to be given- It thus strengthens privacy protection and it provides a most elegant implementation of the data protection principles.

8.3 Time for Decisions

Any holistic concept of digital identity should exhibit the following three properties

1. It should support role structures and digital interaction based on these role structures.
2. It should enable the citizen to control her privacy and her relationships with organisations offering digital services to a maximal extent, which requires that she controls the distribution of her personal data
3. The risk of identity theft and of any crime through the manipulation of the relationships between a citizen and organisations offering digital services should be kept to a minimum.

Credential technology fulfils requirements 2 and 3 to a large extent. Since there is a one-to-one correspondence between credentials and roles, credential technology is the natural candidate for the implementation of the role concept in future IT solutions for e-government.

The next steps in e-government will be concerned with GAI – government application integration. In [Leitner 2003], chapter 4 of part 1, the vision of future integrated e-government is depicted. Its implementation will decide what digital identity will be like in the next decades. Integrated e-government requires G2G integration, which in turn requires a clear concept of identity. Once this concept has been coded in expensive software it will persist for a long time. We have to decide now, if we want to implement a full protection of privacy or not.

9. RESEARCH AGENDA

As we have argued above, there is a strong need for both a better protection of privacy and a better digital support of post-modern role structures. This puts the following issues on our R&D agenda:

User acceptance for anonymous digital identity & usability of credential management systems. Trustworthy anonymous digital identity is not a trivial concept. It provides a means for risk avoidance, but not an affordance by itself, which should be communicated clearly. Keeping control over all personal data, which we have spread in the world, is impossible so far. But even if technology, service provider acceptance and the support from government would provide us with the technical capabilities to track and control our lots of partial digital identities, this would be an enormous cognitive challenge. Therefore, credential management systems are needed, which are easy to understand and use for all and which enable users to effectively manage privacy risks rather than to track their individual relationships with service providers in detail and to control all their partial identities one by one.

Process analysis with respect to the legal needs to use fully identifiable personal data. From a technological point of view, it seems to be possible to design e-tax services based on anonymous credentials. For example, based on the credential system presented in [Camenisch 1999], the extended digital identity concept in [Auerbach 2004] and the IT architecture for anonymous service access in [Király 2003], this could be achieved by the following type of script (see [Riedl 2004]), where the root-CA (root credential authority) controls whether a citizen has paid her taxes or not:

1. Root-CA sends a request to each registered citizen to fill in his tax declaration form. 2. Each citizen requests and obtains wages credentials from her employer and expenses credentials for all expenses she may subtract from her income before taxation. She then submits her tax declaration form together with all credentials to the tax office. 3. The tax office requests and gets transcripts for all citizen credentials from a revocation manager. It delivers theses transcripts to the root-CA, which does a global revocation and checks whether all credentials belong to the same main secret, and then reports ok or not ok to the tax office. 4. Based on the answer of the root-CA,

the tax office creates a 'taxes paid' credential and sends it to the citizen, who may thus prove to the root-CA that she has paid her taxes.

This protocol would prevent any linking of the actual contents of the tax file with the name of the citizen. However, it is unclear whether the implementation of such a protocol is legally admissible and organisationally feasible. Likewise a wide range of traditional e-government services could be implemented with trustworthy anonymous digital identity and similar scripts. Therefore, an extensive investigation on the legal and organisational constraints for administrative processes with unidentified citizens seems to be worthwhile. Clearly, most e-assistance services will be within the practical application domain for trustworthy anonymous digital identity, but in other cases the situation is unclear.

Development of design principles for balancing the complexity of role structures in an information society. The more complex the role structures are and the more advanced e-government services are, the more difficult it will be to control one's personal data affiliated with particular roles and the more difficult the implementation of security infrastructure is – in particular when the need for delegation of rights comes into play. What we need is a new discipline of transparency engineering. In distributed systems terminology, transparency has a double meaning, namely "single system image" as a technical design goal and "visibility of crucial activities" as an organisational design goal. From the user perspective, digital identity management should provide a balanced transparency that allows her to handle technical and organisational complexity in a way, which is optimal for her abilities and life contexts. This implies that customised user interfaces with differing degrees of complexity must be provided by the digital identity management system and that the role structure and the application structure are designed appropriately. The latter is a conditio sine qua non for the success of holistic identity concepts in a highly heterogeneous and cognitively challenging world. Therefore, research on useful role structures for the public sector is needed, which should be performed jointly with research on transparency engineering for IT architectures.

Development of a PCI (public credential infrastructure) concept analogous to PKI & development of standardised ontologies to achieve European-wide interoperability of future credential architectures. The deployment of credential technology on a larger scale in practice requires the development of a PCI, which is an extension of the well-known PKI (compare e.g. [Austin 2001]), as it has to deal with richer forms of revocation. Thereby, the analogues of the CP (certification policy) and the CPS (certification practice statement) play an important role. One of the critical issues is the scalability of revocation mechanisms; another is the lack of ontologies to write credentials, which can be used throughout Europe.

The famous example for the likely conceptual failure of cross-border use of credentials is the statement "Mr X is married." issued by a Dutch government agency. The statement does not declare the gender of the marriage partner of Mr X and thus will not be accepted by countries where same sex marriage is not admissible, even if that statement itself is accepted as his marriage partner is a woman. The famous example for the likely practical failure is the proverbial English power bill used to prove evidence of living place, but probably not understood as such by a German authority. Other examples for conceptual and/or practical problems are the unique Italian concept of auto-certification or the German 'unwillingness' to issue any digital certificates (as we could observe it in the eMayor project: http://www.emayor.org). Thus, the two key problems that may hinder a European-wide use of identity management based on credential technology are identical terms describing similar but different concepts and differences in certification cultures.

Empirical studies differentiating target groups according to age, social position, and cultural identity. The bottom line of any research agenda on trust and confidence should be that it addresses the fears and cultural traditions of the people. This requires extensive empirical studies in order to understand the security concerns of citizens

9.1 Roadmap for Research

Summing up, we conclude that a lot of transdisciplinary co-operation is required due to the complex interplay of very different issues, which have to be handled by experts from different disciplines. The roadmap for R&D should be as follows

1. Building a set of trust models for e-government, which depict the full heterogeneity of Europe and which are based on empirical investigations (on a much broader scale than those presented in this paper)
2. Designing a new social and organisational 'architecture' for the future public sector, which is based on a role structure and new co-operation models (which reflect dissolving boundaries and trust structures as well as the growing self-responsibility of citizens and the growing importance of trusted non-profit organisations)
3. Rethinking and renegotiating legal requirements for IT-architectures providing global digital identity management and (nearly) ubiquitous, cross-organisational and cross-border access to e-government services (based on a flexible concept for the interface between Law and IT architecture)
4. Developing a PCI and ontologies for European-wide e-government and developing a security framework architecture for government

application integration, for government-to-government co-operation and for (the thus enabled) secure, borderless one-stop e-government services for citizens

5. Developing user-friendly and barrier-free digital identity management systems, which enable users to control their 'digital identity' in a complex information society (and which are part of a general concept for the presentation tier in government application integration)

These R&D activities should be accompanied by two transversal activities

- Basic research on transparency engineering, which addresses the citizen to e-government/e-business/e-commerce applications interaction
- Public discussion of emerging e-government solutions to gain democratic support for the future reorganisation of the public sector

In order for such a roadmap to become reality, significant efforts are needed to nurture interdisciplinary co-operation and the convergence of existing expertises.

9.2 Looking Beyond European Borders

The quality of e-government has to be measured with respect to several different yardsticks, probably the most important of which is the joint existence of trust and confidence and of freedom in society. Some of the issues discussed in this paper, e.g. the heterogeneity of Europe, are typically European. But is the whole world less complex than its part? Is data protection only a need of young Swiss people, young Europeans, the European society? Are Swiss or European people special and more critical of data misuse? Is post-modern reality only a European phenomenon? We suggest that the research vision pursued targets the development of holistic IT solutions for digital identity, which scale to a world-wise usage both in the public and the private sector.

ACKNOWLEDGEMENTS

This paper is in parts based on the theses written by several students of our research group: Niklas Auerbach, András Király, Michael Pfleghart, Christof Roduner, Andreas Sidler, and Franziska Zumsteg.

REFERENCES

[Auerbach 2004] N. Auerbach, Anonymous Digital Identity in e-Government, Thesis, University of Zurich (to appear)

[Austin 2001] T. Austin, PKI – A Wiley Tech Brief, John Wiley & Sons, 2001

[Bayley 2002] T. Bailey, On Trust and Philosophy http://www.open2.net/trust/downloads/docs/ontrust.pdf

[Brands 2000] S. A. Brands, Rethinking Public Key Infrastructures and Digital Certificates, MIT Press, Cambridge, Mass., USA, August 2000

[Camenisch 1999| J. Camenisch and A. Lysyanskaya, An Efficient System for Non-Transferable Anonymous Credentials with Optional Anonymity Revocation, vol 2045 of Lecture Notes in Computer Science, 93-118, Springer Verlag, January 1999

[Coleman 1990] J.S. Coleman, Foundations of Social Theory, Cambridge, Mass. USA 1990.

[Chaum 1985] D. Chaum, Security without Identification: Transaction Systems to Make Big Brother Obsolete, Communications of the ACM, 28(10), 1030-1044, October 1985

[Drucker 2001] P. Drucker, Management for the 21st Century, Chapter 1, Harper Business 2001

[Egger 2000] F.N. Egger, Towards a Model of Trust for E-Commerce System Design, http://www.zurich.ibm.com/~mrs/chi2000/contributions/egger.html

[Hobbes 1994] T, Hobbes, Leviathan, with Selected Variants From the Latin Edition of 1668, edited by E. Curley, Hackett, 1994.

[Hume 1994] D. Hume, A Treatise of Human Nature, edited by L.A. Selby-Bigge, revised by P.H. Nidditch, Oxford University Press, 1978

[Király 2003] A. Király, Credential-Based Implementations of Digital Indentity for Non-Traceable Access to E-Government-Services (in German), http://www.ifi.unizh.ch/egov/Diplom_Kiraly.pdf, Master's Thesis, November 2003.

[Köhntopp 2001] M. Köhntopp, A. Pfitzmann, Identity Management and ist Support of Multi-lateral Security, Computer Networks, 37: 205-219, 2001

[Knöri 2003] D. Knöri, e-Voting des Kantons Zürich, http://www.statistik.ch/projekte/evoting/e-Voting.ppt

[Leitner 2003] C. Leitner (editor), J.-M. Eymeri, K. Lenk, M.M. Nielsen, R. Traunmüller (authors), F. Heinderyckx, A. Moussalli, M.A. Wimmer (contributors), eGovernment in Europe: The State of affairs, European Institute of Public Administration, 2003.

[Luhmann 2000] N. Luhmann, Vertrauen: ein Mechanismus der Reduktion sozialer Komplexität., 4. Auflage. Stuttgart: Lucius und Lucius, 2000.

[McKnight 2002] D.H. McKnight, V. Choudhury, and C. Kacmar, The Impact of Initial Consumer Trust on Intentions to Transact with Web Sites: A Trust Building Model, Journal of Strategic Information Systems 11, 297 – 323, 2002.

[Papadopoulou 2001] P. Papadopoulou, A. Andreou, P. Kanellis, D. Matakos, Trust and Relationship in Electronic Commerce, Internet Research: Electronic Networking Applications and Policy, Vol 11, No 4, 322 – 332, 2001

[Pfleghart 2003] M. Pfleghart, E-Voting im Kanton Zürich aus der Perspektive junger Bürgerinnen, http://www.ifi.unizh.ch/egov/Diplom_Roduner.pdf, Master's Thesis, January 2003.

[Popp 2004] R. Popp, T. Armour, T. Senator, and K. Numtych, Contering Terrorism through Information Technology, Communications of the ACM, Vol 47, No 3, 36-43, 2004

[Riedl 2004] R. Riedl, A. Király, Anonyme digitale Identität im E-Commerce and E-Government, in preparation for Tagungsband des Rechtsinformatiksymposiums IRIS 2004

[Roduner 2003] C. Roduner, Citizen Controlled Data Protection in a Smart World, http://www.ifi.unizh.ch/egov/Diplom_Roduner.pdf, Master's Thesis, November 2003.

[Sidler 2003] A. Sidler, Datenschutz im E-Government, http://www.ifi.unizh.ch/egov/Diplom_Sidler.pdf, Master's Thesis, December 2003

[Zachar 2002] T. Zachar Antropomorhe Agenten in kommerziellen Webseiten und ihr Einfluss auf das Nutzervertrauen, http://www.cmr.fu-berlin.de/research/diplom/documents/zachar.pdf, Master's Thesis, 2002,

[Zumsteg 2004] F. Zumsteg, Die Bedeutung von Vertrauen f!ur den Erfolg von E-Government, http://www.ifi.unizh.ch/egov/Diplom_Zumsteg.pdf, Master's Thesis, January 2004

M-COMMERCE

EXPLORING THE RELATIONSHIP BETWEEN MOBILE DATA SERVICES BUSINESS MODELS AND END-USER ADOPTION

Per E. Pedersen[1] and Leif B. Methlie[2]
[1] *Agder University College, Grooseveien 36, 4896 Grimstad, Norway;* [2] *Norwegian School oj Economics and Business Administration, Breiviksveien 40, 5045 Bergen, Norway*

Abstract: Adoption of mobile data services may be analyzed within the framework of two-sided markets. Service or content providers should adopt platforms for developing, integrating and distributing mobile services and end-users should adopt the offered services as well as the user platform offered. These two markets are often analyzed separately using different theoretical perspectives and models. In this article, we propose a model for integrating the two sides of the mobile data services market. The model is used to propose relationships between dominant actors' choice of business models for individual services and the end-users' perceived value of these services.

Key words: business models; mobile data services; adoption; user acceptance; strategy; governance form; customer value; network effects.

1. INTRODUCTION

Recent analyst reports and academic papers suggest that open, collaborative business models are required to obtain variety in service offerings and consequently adoption of service platforms as well as end-user services. The authors most often refer to the Nordic experience with the so called CPA-models (Content Provider Access) for SMS and MMS services (Strand Consult, 2002, Northstream, 2002). However, this open model has not been equally successful in providing WAP services in these countries. Furthermore, recent examples suggest that closed, vertically integrated business models have been successful when introducing the more advanced mobile data services likely to be expected in 3G networks. Examples are the semi-walled garden model of DoCoMo's I-mode services in Japan and the model applied by Vodafone to provide their "Live!" services. Thus, it seems that examples of both successful and less successful service introductions may be found applying both closed and open business models.

While the conceptual dimensions of business models have recently obtained considerable attention (Camponovo and Pigneur, 2003; Faber et al., 2003, Bouwman, 2003), dominant actors' choice of specific business models and the relationship between these decisions and firm or service performance have been less attended to. End-users perception of intrinsic service attributes has also obtained considerable attention in resent research on the adoption of mobile data services. However, research on the perception of extrinsic service attributes, such as end-user network size and complementary service variety has mainly been focused in contexts of professional end-users and traditional computer contexts, such as operating systems.

The purpose of this paper is to extend research on the conceptual dimensions of mobile services business models into explorations of the relationship between business model dimensions and performance. In this paper, performance is discussed in the context of the perceived and anticipated value of the services offered. In the next section, we review some of the literature and recent empirical studies on mobile services business models, mobile services attributes and end-user adoption. In section 3, a model of the relationship between these elements is presented. In section 4, we present a set of propositions that emerge from this model, and in section 5 we conclude and discuss how to use this model for service analysis and empirical research.

2. THEORY

Explanations of mobile data services success span from focusing specific factors, such as the lack of an appropriate revenue model (Foros et al., 2001) to suggesting general systemic explanations, such as the dynamics of industry ecosystems (Vesa, 2003). The most common approach, however, is to combine a set of technological, business strategic and behavioral or cultural factors. For example, Henten et al. (2003) suggest technology, economy, market development and structure, marketing, socio-cultural, policy intervention and regulation as the relevant explanatory factors. Pedersen (2001) suggested three general requirements for successful adoption of mobile data services; technology-, business strategic-, and behavioral requirements. Some authors apply a comparative perspective analyzing differences in adoption between Asian and European markets. For example, Bohlin et al. (2003) compare the developments of mobile data services in Japan and Europe and oppose popular assumptions that differences in adoption rates may be explained by differences in technology, regulatory regimes, cultural differences, Internet penetration and differences in consumer segments focused in marketing. Instead, they suggest the important differences are the coordinated and vertically integrated service concepts and the revenue models offered by Japanese operators. Our focus is on the integrating role of business models and behavioral factors. We suggest that the choice of specific business models by dominant actors is one of the most important explanations of mobile data services success.

2.1 Business models

The term business model has been used mostly in traditional electronic commerce. One of the first contributions came from Timmers (1998) suggesting that a business model describes the architecture for the product, service and information flows, including a description of various business actors and their roles, a description of potential benefits for the various actors, and a description of the sources of revenue. Thus, it includes infrastructure, value proposition and financial dimensions. Similarly, Weil and Vitale suggest that a business model is the "*description of the roles and relationships among a firm's consumers, customers, allies and suppliers that identifies the major flows of products, information and money, and the major benefits to participants*" (Weill & Vitale, 2001, p. 34). Methlie and Pedersen (2002) included three operational dimensions in their business model concept; integration model, collaboration model and revenue model. They focus that individual providers' business model options are restricted by structural determinants and value network considerations because value creation in both traditional and mobile electronic commerce requires a shared understanding of the business model of each network member. In some industries the business models options of each value network member are indirectly determined by the business model of the dominant members (e.g. operators in some mobile services industries and operating system developers in the software industry). Recently, several authors have applied the business model concept to mobile commerce and mobile data services contexts (Camponovo and Pigneur, 2003; Faber et al., 2003, Bouwman, 2003). With some variations in propositions, these authors mainly suggest four dimensions of business models; the product innovation, the customer relationship, the infrastructure and the financial dimensions, covering the product related value proposition, the customer related value proposition, the structural dimension and the revenue dimension, respectively (e.g. Camponovo and

Pigneur, 2003). However, the choice between specific options along these dimensions and the performance effects of choosing specific options under different structural conditions have been given less attention in this literature. Instead, performance effects of the choice of options for product-, customer-, financial- and infrastructural business model dimensions are treated separately in individual research areas such as product innovation, industrial organization and strategic marketing. Thus, integration is necessary to apply this research to a specific industry like the mobile data services industry. It is beyond the scope of this paper to integrate and apply the vast literature on the performance effects of business model options to the mobile data services industry. However, it is well documented in this literature that the choice of a specific business model affects the intrinsic and extrinsic attributes of the product developed or produced (Nicholls-Nixon and Woo, 2003; Zahra and Nielsen, 2002; Sengupta, 1998; Stuart, 2000).

2.2 Customer value

Service attributes emerge from two different sources. Intrinsic attributes refer to the inherent attributes of the service itself, whereas for network goods, extrinsic attributes emerge from the networks that provide and use the service. This involves an extension of the traditional typology of intrinsic and extrinsic sources of value suggested by Holbrook (1996), and underlines how network services are different from traditional products and services where extrinsic attributes often originate from supplier services and consumer investments (Mathwick, Malhotra and Rigdon, 2001). The two types of attributes represent the sources of intrinsic and extrinsic value unique to network effects products as suggested by Lee and O'Connor: "*extrinsic value... is unique to network effects products... is the set of benefits derived from outside the product itself, such as the size of the installed base and the availability of compatible and complementary products...*" (Lee and O'Connor, 2003, p. 244).

Many unique intrinsic attributes have been mentioned characterizing mobile services. One of the most obvious characteristics of mobile services is the lack of constraints related to time and space (Balasubramanian, Peterson, and Jarvenpaa, 2002). Watson, Pitt, Berthon, and Zinkhan (2002) suggest the "U-commerce" construct to describe services characterized by ubiquitous-, universal-, and unison access as well as uniqueness. Doyle (2001) suggests the following key characteristics of SMS: personal, real time delivery, unobtrusive, low price, simple, supports two way communication, can be forwarded, and location based potential. Thus, being personal seems to be an additional intrinsic attribute of mobile data services (Siau, Lim, and Shen, 2001). This corresponds well to the suggestions by Kannan, Mei Chand, and

Whinston (2001). They argue that wireless devices are accessible, personal and location aware, and thus, that these attributes are unique to mobile services.

A problem with considering accessibility and "being personal" as unique attributes of mobile services is that these attributes are general and unrelated to the content of the mobile service. Even though the lack of constraints related to time and space of mobile services has been suggested as the basis for their usefulness (Pedersen and Nysveen, 2003), usefulness is mainly determined by the content of the service – its functionality. Often, the usefulness of mobile services depends on other users using it rather than the accessibility or personalization attributes of the service. This is particularly true for communication or person-interactive services, where extrinsic attributes are more important for creating customer value than the intrinsic attributes of the service. Still, for information or machine-interactive services, the usefulness of the service is an important intrinsic attribute (Pedersen and Nysveen, 2003). A unique intrinsic attribute found important in six studies of mobile service adoption by Nysveen, Pedersen and Thorbjørnsen (in press) was enjoyment. Even for services with functionality that in principle was unrelated to enjoyment, such as mobile payment services, enjoyment was found to be an important intrinsic attribute (Pedersen and Nysveen, 2003). This finding corresponds well to studies of mobile services in uses and gratification research suggesting that gratifications of "relaxation" (Leung and Wei, 2000) and "nutz-spaz" (Höflich and Rössler, 2001) are important to the adoption and use of mobile services. Intrinsic attributes of a service may also be described by technical specifications, for example related to speed and capacity. It is difficult to determine such attributes for services in general, and mobile services are no exception. Still, attributes such as network bandwidth, dial-up speed, coverage and signal strength have been suggested. For example, in a service quality framework for mobile services, Nordman and Liljander (2003) suggested dial-up speed and configuration settings as important components of service quality.

A study by Ling (2001) shows that mobile phones are used to express fashion and social identity. Other results also indicate that mobile devices and services are used to express and confirm the users' personal identity (Pedersen and Nysveen, 2003). These symbolic and expressive attributes of mobile services are mainly extrinsic attributes because they result from the service being used in a network context. The two most often mentioned extrinsic attributes of network goods are direct and indirect network effects. Direct network effects are the effects related to increasing value of a service as the size of the network increases (Liebowitz and Margolis, 1999). Network effects are typical of all communication and person-interactive mobile services and have been the basis for understanding value propositions and the choice of governance forms in telecommunication networks. In their study of 125 value added services, Brosseau and Quelin (1996) found that communication and information services were provided applying systematically different governance forms.

While direct network effects are important extrinsic attributes of communication services, indirect network effects are more often focused in information, transaction or machine-interactive services. Indirect network effects originate from direct network effects when the networked good is a platform for complementary services and products (Gupta, Jain and Sawhney, 1999). Mobile data services differ with respect to their potential as a platform for complementary services. For example for information and machine-interactive services like premium SMS, mobile Internet access or game services, the potential for generating indirect network effects is great. From indirect network, a set of operational extrinsic service attributes, such as complementary service variety, speed of complementary service development and complementary service quality may be identified. As for direct network effects, considerable attention has been given to the importance of indirect network effects in consumers' assessment of service or product value. For example, researchers in economics, marketing and information systems have concluded that the availability of complementary goods affects the prices that can be obtained for networked goods (Gandal, Kende and Rob, 2000; Basu et al., 2003; Brynjolfsson and Kemerer, 1996).

Recently, end-users perception of network effects has been given considerable attention. Studies of innovation adoption take sensitivity to network effects into consideration and argue that network size is more important when the network is small than when it is large. This suggests that adoption likelihood is sensitive to critical mass and anticipation of future network size (Shapiro and Varian, 1999). For example, the use of pre-announcement and commitment announcements are examples of strategies used to convince end-users that future network size is expected to be large and that it will increase quickly (Lee and O'Connor, 2003; Montaguti, Kuester and Robertson, 2002). Perceptions and anticipation of direct network effects have also recently achieved considerable attention in information systems, strategy and marketing literature (Gallaugher and Wang, 2002; Schilling, 2003; Frels, Shervani and Srivastava, 2003). Most of these studies have been conducted in professional end-user markets suggesting that direct network effects are taken into consideration in professional end-users' value assessment process. We are unable to identify similar research in traditional consumer markets. However, economic theory on network effects assumes that consumers are somehow able to make such assessments and includes network size elements in consumers' utility functions (e.g. Katz and Shapiro, 1992; Foros, 2003). For indirect network effects, end-users' appreciation of complementary service variety and innovativeness may also vary across user segments. For professional consumers, it is likely that complementary service variety is assessed and appreciated (Frels et al., 2003). For simple consumer network goods where the complementary goods are content goods delivered on a content distribution platform such as a video game platform, this is also very likely (Schilling, 2003). However, for complex or radically new network goods like mobile data services, the assessment and valuation of indirect network effects are much more difficult. In this case, consumers will often also have to assess the value of future indirect network effects as a consequence of adopting the network goods platform. This is an even more difficult task requiring considerable experience or cognitive capacity.

From this selective and brief review of some of the recent research on business models, service attributes and service adoption in mobile services markets we suggest that the relationships between these elements may be explained by a research model where options along specific business model dimensions are operational, relevant intrinsic and extrinsic service attributes are specified, and knowledge of end-users' perceptions of service attributes are moderated.

3. MODEL

The proposed model follows the structure-conduct –performance (SCP) framework often applied in empirical industrial organization (Kadiyali, Sudhir and Rao, 2001). Structural determinants, however, have been focused elsewhere (Gressgård, Methlie and Stensaker, 2003) and the conduct-performance relationship is focused here. The model is illustrated in figure 1. In the model, we propose that specific business model dimension options affect the intrinsic and extrinsic service attributes as well as end-user characteristics. Furthermore, we propose that the relationship between service attributes and perceived and anticipated value is moderated by end-user characteristics. While the literature cited in section 2 was general with respect to business model dimensions, service attributes and end-user value perceptions, a research model will have to be more operational for these concepts to be useful in hypothesis development.

The business model concept has been operationalized along three dimensions. For the financial arrangement dimension found in the business model ontology literature we focus on the *revenue model* including revenue valuation and sharing. Content based valuation means that end-users pay per unit of the service content delivered, whereas transport based valuation means that end-users pay for the amount of time online, packet charge or similar volume units. The revenue share element may have a complex option structure, but we simplify this to revenue shares favoring content rather than transport. A content oriented revenue share involves a relatively larger proportion of revenue is redistributed to content providers, whereas a transport oriented revenue share involves a relatively larger proportion of revenue is redistributed or retained by network or transport providers. In almost all practical settings, the objects of revenue valuation and sharing are equivalent. Consequently, we apply the dichotomy of content versus transport oriented revenue models here.

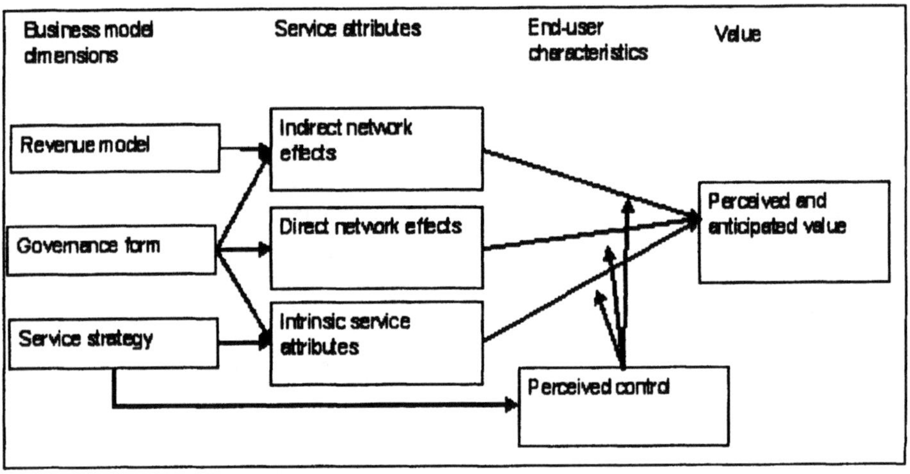

Figure 1. Research model

For the infrastructural arrangement dimension, we focus on *governance form* corresponding to governance form or mode as treated in new institutional economics and organization theory. Providers' options further correspond to the traditional categorization of governance forms as market, relational and hierarchy modes or forms (e.g. Ghosh and John, 1999). However, governance form is a complex element, and it may include several options. We have previously suggested that the relational form of governance includes so many options that it may be treated as a separate element in the infrastructure dimension of a providers' business model (Pedersen, 2001). For example both network forms and alliance forms are relational forms, but there is little doubt that these forms may have quite distinct and different effects on service attributes and thus, performance.

The product innovation and customer relationship dimensions may be treated under the common term *service strategy* with two elements including service value proposition[6] and market focus elements corresponding to Porter's (1985) generic strategy elements. The options for the service value proposition element are service dependent and related to the specific gratifications of the mobile data service investigated applying the model. We have discussed some of these gratifications above but here we focus two important option issues. The first is to what degree the value proposition focuses the unique attributes of mobile services. Examples are accessibility that only may be obtained through the mobile device or personalization that is unique due to identification of the end-user. The second option issue is that of breadth in service attribute offerings. Examples are services that cover a large set of mobile service gratifications versus services that cover a focused set of gratification as part of their value proposition. Thus, we suggest the two options of mobile-specificity (uniqueness) and proposition breadth (scope). For the market focus element we apply the focused versus undifferentiated options of Porter (1985).

In principle, all these options may be treated as continuous. For example, the choice of governance form is not a discrete choice between market, relational and hierarchy forms. Instead, the options vary with respect to the degree that hierarchical, relational and market oriented governance mechanisms or processes are included (Heide, 1994). Thus, closed business models include governance mechanisms of the hierarchical form whereas open models include governance mechanisms of the relational and market forms. Similarly, revenue share options involve a choice of the revenue share redistributed to content provider rather than an absolute value above or below 50% indicating a content versus transport oriented model.

As suggested in section 2, mobile data services attributes are categorized as intrinsic reflecting inherent attributes of the service itself, or extrinsic reflecting direct and indirect network effects. For *indirect network effects* we suggest that the attributes of the complementary services network include complementary service variety, -quality and speed of development. For *direct network effects* we suggest that the attributes are related to end-user network size and speed of diffusion. While several *intrinsic attributes* were discussed in section 2, we suggest mobile specific usefulness, service quality, ease of use and interoperability[7]. Intrinsic attributes may also be specific to the service category being investigated, and thus, other intrinsic service attributes may be focused for example for goal-oriented versus experiential

[6] The terms "positioning" and "positioning option" are often used in marketing strategy literature (e.g. Ghosh and John, 1999)

[7] Ease of use and interoperability may be included in the service quality concept if applying a framework similar to SERVQUAL for mobile services (Nordman and Liljander, 2003).

service categories. For the moderating factor termed end-user characteristics in figure 1, we focus *perceived control*. The term is often used in information systems adoption literature (e.g. Taylor and Todd, 1995) to reflect the combination of end-users perceptions of their own resources (e.g. skills, experience, financial) and facilitation of the service provider. The model is based on rationalistic assumptions suggesting that end-users adopt mobile data services with high *perceived and anticipated value*. Value perceptions reflect the value assessments that are made from current intrinsic and extrinsic service attributes whereas anticipated value reflects expectations of further development of these attributes. In figure 1, intrinsic and extrinsic attributes are unrelated, but for many mobile services these attributes are related. Still, because such relationships are service specific, the *general* model in figure 1 initially propose that service attributes are unrelated. However, this proposition may be modified for service specific versions of the model.

The relationships in the model illustrate the main influences from the choice of business model options on service attributes and the main and moderated influences from these attributes on perceived and anticipated value. We suggest that the choice of revenue model primarily influences the complementary service attributes of mobile data services, in particular if the mobile data services offered represent service platforms (e.g. SMS, MMS or WAP). Governance form is expected to influence both extrinsic and intrinsic attributes. For example, hierarchical governance forms are likely to give service developers full control of the intrinsic attributes of a service and the attributes of its complementary services. Furthermore, if the firm applying this form is large, it may utilize its installed base to obtain speed of diffusion in new service domains. The choice of a particular service value proposition is the most influential factor determining the intrinsic attributes of a service, whereas the choice between a focused or an undifferentiated market strategy is likely to affect whether end-users have the necessary experience or skills to perceive behavioral control of the mobile service being used.

The relationship between service attributes and end-user value includes two sets of influences. The first set is the main effects of service attributes on perceived and anticipated value. In the second set, we assume that these relationships are moderated by the perceived behavioral control of end-users. For example, one may propose that complementary service variety leads to high perceived value for all users, but one may also propose that this is only true for experienced end-users being able to utilize and choose among these services. Less experienced end-users may be confused by a great variety of complementary service offerings.

4. PROPOSITIONS

As can be seen from figure 1, two sets of propositions may be suggested: A) Propositions on the relationship between business model options and service attributes, and B) propositions on the relationship between service attributes and perceived and anticipated value. In section 3, we suggested the two most relevant financial dimension elements of the business model to be revenue share and valuation object. In almost all empirical settings, the objects of revenue valuation and sharing are equivalent. Thus, the same theoretical arguments may be given for both elements of the revenue model dimension. We suggest that revenue share models may be categorized according to their implicit appreciation of content versus transport. Because the value network for mobile data services involves complementary services, we assume that complementary service variety, quality and speed of development will be obtained by stimulating the providers of these services. Consequently, pricing and revenue sharing become parts of the innovation process of network and platform providers (Jonasson, 2001). There are many ways to design the revenue models that stimulate the providers of complementary services. For example, economists have discussed the use of different forms of subsidizing in two-sided markets to obtain profit in the base (e.g. platform) market and stimulate competition in the other (e.g. content provider) market (see e.g. Armstrong, 2002). However, complementary service providers will be able to assess the degree of competition in the complementary service market making them reluctant to innovate if this strategy is used aggressively by the network or platform providers to obtain monopoly profits. Another issue is that network or platform providers may use access costs as an instrument in regulating service providers' access to the network or platform (Rochet and Tirole, 2002; Foros, Kind and Sørgard, 2002). We assume that mobile data services markets have a two sided structure where platform or network providers recognize the need to stimulate innovation in complementary services and that revenue sharing in some form contributes to this. Thus, we suggest that regardless of the use of subsidizing, access pricing or other strategy for regulating content or service providers access to the network or platform, complementary service providers will be stimulated better if platform providers' offer transparent and content/service based revenue models. For example, if a mobile operator uses a content based revenue object, the revenue sharing model will be based upon this revenue object and providers of complementary services will have a simple model that makes it easer for them to assess the potential revenue from accepting operators' business model and adopting their service provisioning platform. Thus, we propose:

A1a-c: Using content oriented revenue models increases complementary service variety, quality and speed of development.

The element of the infrastructure dimension that we have focused is governance form. We suggested categorizing the governance form in market, relational and hierarchy forms. We also suggested that the hierarchy versus relational and market forms represent a continuum rather than a discrete categorization of governance forms. Still, we maintain the original option categorization here and propose:

A2a-b: Using relational and market governance forms increases complementary service variety and speed of development.

The arguments behind this proposition were discussed in section 2. In particular, literature on governance forms in network markets as well as resource based theory suggest that complementary service variety and diversity is better obtained using open forms of collaboration (e.g. Schilling, 2003). Zahra and Nielsen (2002) found that relational forms increased development speed. In addition, when involvement and formal coordination were included as moderators, market forms of governance also increased development speed. Service quality on the other hand, may come out of the service integrator's control or service quality may not be related to perceived quality elements when governance is left to market or relational forms (Dyer and Singh, 1998; Ghosh and John, 1999, p. 137). Thus, we propose:

A2c: Using hierarchical governance forms increases complementary service quality.

Governance form is also expected to influence direct network effects. For example, Frels et al. (2003) found that professional consumers where able to assess direct network effects through the strength of the user network of operating systems. Gallaugher and Wang (2002) suggested mindshare was an important proxy used by professional consumers to assess future direct and indirect network effects. We suggest that firm size is a moderating variable in the relationship between governance form and direct network effects in that size is required to make the hierarchical governance forms trigger direct network effects in the form of end-user network size and speed of diffusion. Thus, we propose:

A3a-b: For larger firms hierarchical governance forms increase end-user network size and speed of diffusion.

Finally, governance form is expected to influence intrinsic attributes of the individual service offered through a provider's business model. From the product innovation literature cited in section 2 we also suggest that innovativeness is promoted both in the complements and platform markets through the use of relational and market governance forms. Also, a study by Srinvasan, Lillien and Rangaswarny (2002) found that a hierarchy culture was negative related to technological opportunism whereas an adhocracy culture was positively related to technological opportunism[8]. Because these culture forms were derived from governance forms, the findings support the following proposition:

A4a: Using relational and market governance forms make providers able to offer more innovative, useful services.

On the other hand, relying on relational and market forms of governance may make platform providers and individual service providers lose control of the production and distribution process of their service. Furthermore, internal interoperability and intrinsic quality may not be obtained by relying on standards that may be interpreted differently by different providers collaborating using relational and market forms of governance. For example, Sahay and Riley (2003) found that vertical integration lead to increased focus on customer interface standards, but they found no support for their proposition that vertical integration lead to less focus on compatibility standards. Thus, relying on transaction cost theory, we suggest:

A5a-b: Using hierarchical governance form increases the ease of use, interoperability and intrinsic service quality.

In section 3, we suggested two elements of relevance to value proposition; service value proposition and market focus. For the service value proposition element we suggested the issue of mobile specificity (uniqueness) and breadth (scope) of offerings to be important. We suggest that the potential for creating higher value among end-users is greater when the service offerings are mobile specific. This means that the services are designed to meet the unique gratifications expected from mobile services. Thus, we propose that this will be reflected in the potential ease of use, usefulness and quality of the service. Thus, we propose:

A6a-c: Mobile-specific value propositions increase ease of use, usefulness and intrinsic service quality.

Mobile specificity may require focusing the service offering, but research shows that a variety of gratifications is expected from mobile data services (Leung and Wei, 2000; Nysveen, Pedersen and Thorbjørnsen, in press). However, trying to fulfill a variety of gratifications may result in more complex services with less mobile specific usefulness and service quality. Thus, we suggest:

A6b-c: Value propositions with greater breadth reduce intrinsic service quality, ease of use and usefulness.

[8] For opposite arguments, see the discussion on new product development in integrated firms and responsiveness (e.g. Richardson, 1996) and the "incumbent's curse" discussion (Chandy and Tellis, 2000)

For market focus, we suggested applying the traditional categorization of focused versus undifferentiated strategies from Porter (1985). In general, a focused strategy makes it easier for the provider to adapt their services to the requirements and qualifications of end-users. We suggest that the successful adaptation is reflected in the perceived control of end-users. Perceived control is assumed to be influenced by experience, resources and end-users' self-efficacy. In general, we suggest that due to a better adaptation of services to experience, resources and skills:

A7a: Using focused market strategies increases perceived control.

The next set of relationships in the model illustrated in figure 1 is the set of relationships between service attributes and perceived and anticipated value of end-users. We first suggest a set of propositions on these direct relationships. Next, we suggest how perceived control is likely to moderate these relationships. While research in economics indirectly assumes network effects are perceived and anticipated, behavioral research in marketing and strategy is not so conclusive on this matter. While several studies have shown that the availability of complementary goods increases the perceived value of the platform good (e.g. Basu, Mazumdar and Raj, 2003), Cottrell and Kaput (1998) also showed that the variety of complementary goods increase platform value. However, research suggests that consumers appreciate variety and quality differently, and that there may be product and service differences in the appreciation of variety versus quality. For example, Bohlman, Goldman and Mitra (2002) investigated the survival of pioneers and found that pioneers did better in product categories where variety was important and worse in categories where product quality was important. Still, for the complementary service attributes variety, quality and speed of development, we suggest:

B1a-b: Complementary service variety, quality and speed of development increase perceived value.

and

B1c: Complementary service speed of development increases anticipated value.

Direct network effects attributes are service dependent, complicating the assessment of the end-user value of these attributes. However, we assume a minimum degree of direct network effects and focus on attributes reflecting direct network effects that are not specific to any particular mobile data service category. In general, the rate of which a networked service is adopted by users is expected to increase end-user value because critical mass will be reached earlier. Also, when anticipating future value, end-users process information under the assumptions of bounded rationality. Using heuristic judgment, it is likely that current network size is used as a proxy for future network size (Tversky and Kahneman, 1974). Thus, we suggest:

B2a-b: Increasing speed of diffusion and network size increase perceived and anticipated value.

Our proposed relationships between intrinsic attributes of mobile data services and perceived value focus the specificity and variety of gratifications sought by end-users. We argue that gratifications obtained should be mobile specific and because end-users seek a variety of gratifications from mobile services, richness in service attributes is also appreciated. Thus, we suggest the following propositions:

B3a-d: Mobile-specific usefulness, ease of use, interoperability and greater service quality increase perceived value.

While it may be argued that there are direct effects of service attributes on perceived and anticipated value of mobile data services, it is even more likely that this relationship is moderated by the perceived control of end-users. For example, resources in the form of both monetary resources and skills make it more likely that end-users having these resources have explored and tested a variety of data services, and that they are better qualified in making assessments of value based upon such trials. For example, Herpen and Pieters (2002) found that both preference awareness (negatively) and expertise (positively) moderated the relationship between assortment variety and preference. Thus, we suggest three propositions where perceived control positively moderates the relationship between service attributes and perceived and anticipated value.

B5a-c: Perceived control positively moderates the effect of complementary service variety, speed of development and speed of diffusion on value.

The other propositions on moderating effects assume that the relationship between service attributes and value is moderated negatively by perceived control. For example, users with little experience in using mobile data services will appreciate ease of use more than experienced users. The moderated influence of network size, on the other hand, is difficult to decide. Users with considerable perceived control are likely to be sensitive to network size, but these users may use other measures of current and future network size than currently observed size. Thus, we suggest five propositions on the moderated relationship between service attributes and value:

B6a-e: Perceived control negatively moderates the effect of complementary service quality, network size, ease of use interoperability, and intrinsic service quality on value.

In an empirical study it is impractical to investigate the large number of propositions suggested here. From this exploratory investigation, the number of relevant propositions needs to be reduced and directions for empirical research must be further specified.

5. CONCLUSIONS AND FURTHER RESEARCH

We have presented a model suggesting that business model decisions influence end-users' perceived and anticipated service value through the intrinsic and extrinsic service attributes they promote. From the model, a set of propositions emerges that may be investigated empirically. However, the model may also be used for analytical and normative purposes if it is validated empirically.

From our experience with using the model for analytical purposes, we suggest that many studies of mobile data services success investigate services at an insufficient level of detail. We may illustrate this by applying the model to an analysis of the mobile payment service of Telenor, the largest Norwegian mobile operator. Its payment service, Mobilhandel™, may be used to pay for a variety of services, content and products. Still, mobile payment services are often analyzed as one service category with one set of service attributes without discussing their richness of functionality. In the case of Mobilhandel™, the service may be used to pay for products and services at the point-of-sales, to pay money to other users, or to recharge users' prepaid phone cards. It is obvious that the intrinsic and extrinsic attributes of these service functionalities are very different. At the point-of-sales, end-users will appreciate that a large number of merchants accept the payment solution. Thus, the variety of the complementary service network is the most important attribute of this functionality. To pay other people, the size of the network of Mobilhandel™ users is of most importance, so that end-users can pay anyone using the service just as they use cash. Finally, the most successful functionality of the service, representing more than 80% of current transaction volume, is recharging end-users' own or other mobile phone users' prepaid card. This is a functionality that is unrelated to network size and its perceived value is only influenced by whether it is considered useful and easy to use. The conclusions that may be drawn from this example are that the three functionalities of the service may be offered to end-users applying three different business models promoting indirect network effects in the first case, direct network effects in the second, and controlling intrinsic service attributes in the final case. This also corresponds well to the suggestions of Brousseau and Quelin (1996) concluding that "*the success of an information-intensive service is based on its intrinsic quality... there are no network externalities ... therefore, when possible, a single firm should seek to become a core firm*" (Brousseau and Quelin, 1996, p. 1223.

To validate the model, empirical research is required. Because the model uses service attributes as the key intermediary concepts linking business model decisions and end-user value, empirical investigations should investigate the business models and end-users' perceived value of services with contrasting intrinsic and extrinsic service attributes. For example, communication services appreciated for their end-user network size should be compared to content services appreciated for their complementary service variety along two dimensions. The first is how business model decisions promote appreciated service attributes in each case, and the other is how end-users assess the value of these attributes. Other examples of such comparative service categories are gaming versus dating services. Both services are appreciated for their intrinsic attribute of enjoyment, but the value of dating services depend directly on network size whereas the perceived value of gaming services only indirectly depend on end-user network size through indirect network effects. These examples illustrate the two directions our future research will take. First, we survey mobile data services offerings to categorize services according to intrinsic and extrinsic service attributes. Second, we design two sets of empirical studies investigating, 1) the business models applied to promote the unique intrinsic and extrinsic service attributes believed to be important for each of these service categories, and 2) the valuation process of end-users explaining how these unique attributes affect perceived and anticipated value as well as how this process is moderated by behavioral control.

REFERENCES

Armstrong, M., 2002, Competition in two-sided markets. *Proceedings of the 57th European Meeting of the Econometric Society*, Venice, Italy, August 25.28.

Balasubramanian, S., Peterson, R. A., and Jarvenpaa, S. L., 2002, Exploring the implications of M-commerce for markets and marketing. Journal *of the Academy of Marketing Science*, **30**: 348-361.

Basu, A., Mazumdar, T. and Raj, S.P., 2003, Indirect network effects on product attributes. *Marketing Science*, **22**: 209-221.

Bohlin, E., Bjorkdahl, J. and Lindmark, S., 2003, Strategies for making mobile communications work for europe: Implications from a comparative study. Presented at the European Ploci Research Conference (EuroCPR), Barcelona, Spain, March 23-25.

Bohlman, J.D., Golder, P.N. and Mitra, D., 2002, Deconstructing the pioneer's advantage: examining vintage effects and consumer valuations of quality and variety. *Management Science*, **48**, 1175-1195.

Bouwman, H., 2003, Designing metrics for business models describing mobile services delivered by networked organizations. Presented at the16th Bled Electronic Commerce Conference, Bled, Slovenia, June 9-11.

Brousseau, E. and Quelin, B., 1996, Asset specificity and organizational arrangements : the case of the new telecommunications services markets. *Industrial and Corporate Change*, **5**: 1205-1230.

Brynjolfsson, E. and Kemerer, C.F., 1996, Network externalities in microcomputer software: An econometric analysis of the spreadsheet market. *Management Science*, **42**: 1627-1647.

Camponovo, G. and Pigneur, Y., 2003, Business model analysis applied to mobile business. Presented at the 5th International Conference on Enterprise Information Systems, Angers, France, April 23-26.

Chandy, R.K. and Tellis, G.J., 2000, The incumbents curse? Incumbency, size and radical product innovation. *Journal of Marketing*, **64**: 1-17.

Doyle, S., 2001, Software review: Using short message services as a marketing tool, *Journal of Database Marketing*, **8**: 273-277.

Dyer, J.H. and Singh, H., 1998, The relational view: Cooperative strategy and sources of interorganizational competitive advantage, *Academy of Management Review*, 23: 660-679.

Faber, E., Ballon, P., Bouwman, H., Haaker, T., Rietkerk, O. and Stern, M., 2003, Designing business models for mobile ICT services. Presented at the16th Bled Electronic Commerce Conference, Bled, Slovenia, June 9-11.

Foros, Ø., Kind, H.J. and Sørgard, L., 2001, Hvem vinner når tele og media motes? Aksessleverandørenes strategiske utfordringer. In Ulset, S. (ed.) *Fra summetone til informasjonsportal*, pp. 93-112, Fagbokforlaget, Bergen, Norway. (In Norwegian)

Foros, Ø., Kind, H.J. and Sørgard, L., 2002, Access Pricing, quality degradation, and foreclosure in the Internet. *Journal of Regulatory Economics*, **22**: 59-83.

Foros, Ø., 2003, Price strategy and compatibility in digital networks. SNF Working Paper no. 39/03, Foundation for Research in Economics and Business Administration, Bergen, Norway.

Frels, J.K., Shervani, T. and Srivastave, R.K., 2003, The integrated networks model: Explaining resource allocations in network markets. *Journal of Marketing*, **67**: 29-45.

Gandal, N., Kende, M, and Rob, R., 2000, The dynamics of technological adoption in hardware/software systems: the case of compact disc players. *RAND Journal of Economics*, **31**: 43-61.

Gallaugher, J.M. and Wang. Y.M., 2002, Understanding network effects in software markets: Evidence from web server pricing. *MIS Quarterly*, **26**: 303-327.

Ghosh, M. and John, G., 1999, Governance value analysis and marketing strategy. *Journal of Marketing*, **63**: 131-145.

Gressgård, L.J., Methlie, L.B. and Stensaker, I., 2003, Mobile Internet services: Integration models and structural determinants, SNF-report no. 36/03, Foundation for Research in Economics and Business Administration, Bergen, Norway.

Gupta, S., Jain, D.C., Sawhney, M.B., 1999, Modeling the evolution of markets with indirect network externalities: An application to digital television. *Marketing Science*, **18**: 396-416.

Heide, J.B., 1994, Interorganizational governance in marketing channels, *Journal of Marketing*, **58**: 71.85.

Henten, A., Olesen, H., Saugstrup, D. and Tan, S.E., 2003, New mobile systems and services inEurope, Japan and South-Korea. Presented at the Stockholm Mobility Roundtable, Stockholm, Sweden, May 22-23.

Herpen, E. van, Pieters,R., 2002, The influence of expertise on preference for assortment variety: when less variety is better. *Advances in Consumer Research*, 29: 438-439.

Holbrook, M.B., 1996, Customer value – A framework for analysis and research. *Advances in Consumer Research*, **23**: 138-142.

Höflich J.R. and Rössler, P., 2001, Mobile schriftliche Kommunikation oder: E-Mail für das Handy. *Medien & Kommunikationswissenschaft*, **49**: 437-461.

Jonasson, A., 2001, Innovative pricing effects: theory and practice in mobile Internet networks. Presented at the Nelson and Winter Conference, Aalborg, Denmark, June 12-15.

Kadiyali, V., Sudhir, K. and Rao, V.R., 2001, Structural analysis of competitive behavior: New empirical industrial organization methods in marketing. *International Journal of Research in Marketing*, **18**: 161.186.

Kannan, P. K., Mei Chang, A.-M., and Whinston, A. B., 2001, Wireless commerce: Marketing issues and possibilities, *Proceedings of the 34th Hawaii International Conference on System Sciences*, Computer Society Press, Washington, pp. 1-6.

Katz, M.L. and Shapiro, C., 1992, Product introduction with network externalities. *The Journal of Industrial Economics*, **40**: 55-83.

Lee, Y. and O'Connor, G.C., 2003, New product launch strategy for network effects products. *Journal of the Academy of Marketing Science*, **31**: 241-255.

Leung, L. and Wei, R., 2000, More than just talk on the move: Uses and gratifications of the cellular phone, *Journalism & Mass Communication Quarterly*, **77**: 308-320.

Liebowitz, S. and Margolis, S., 1998, Network Externality. In *The New Palgraves Dictionary of Economics and the Law*, MacMillan, UK.

Ling, R., 2001): It is in. It doesn't matter if you need it or not, just that you have it. Fashion and the domestication of the mobile telephone among teens in Norway, Working Paper, Telenor R&D, Oslo, Norway.

Ling, R., Julsrud, T. and Yttri, B., in press, Nascent communication genres within SMS and MMS." in Harper, R., Taylor, A. and Palen, L (eds.), *The Inside Text: Social perspectives on SMS in the mobile age*, Kluwer London.

Mathwick, C., Malhotra, N. and Rigdon, E., 2001, Experiential value: conceptualization, measurement and application in the catalog and Internet shopping environment. *Journal of Retailing*, **77**: 39-56.

Methlie, L.B. and Pedersen, P.E., 2002, A taxonomy of intermediary integration strategies in online markets. Presented at the15th Bled Electronic Commerce Conference, Bled, Slovenia, June 17-19.

Montaguti, E., Kuester, S. and Robertson, T.S., 2002, Entry strategy for radical product innovations: A conceptual model and propositional inventory. *International Journal of Research in Marketing*, **19**: 21-42.

Nicholls-Nixon, C.L. and Wood, C., 2003, Technology sourcing and output of established firms in a regime of encompassing technological change. *Strategic Management Journal*, **24**: 651-666.

Nordman, J. and Liljander, V., 2003, Mobile service quality – a study of contributing factors. Working Paper, Marketing Dep., Hanken Swedish School of Economics and Business Administration, Helsinki, Finland.

Northstream, 2002, Den norska SMS-marknaden. Analyst Report, Northstream AB, Stockholm, Sverige (in Swedish).

Nysveen, H., Pedersen, P.E. and Thorbjørnsen, H., in press, Antecedents of intention to use mobile services: Model development and cross-service comparisons. To appear in *Journal of Academy of Marketing Science*.

Pedersen, P.E., 2001, An adoption framework for mobile commerce. In Schmid, B., Stanoevska-Slabeva, K and Tschammer, V. (eds.). *Towards the E-Society*. Kluwer Academic Publishers, Ma., pp. 643-656

Pedersen, P.E. and Nysveen, H., 2003, Usefulness and self-expressiveness: extending TAM to explain the adoption of a mobile parking service. Presented at the 16th Electronic Commerce Conference, Bled, Slovenia, June 9-11.

Porter, M.E., 1985): *Competitive Advantage: Creating and Sustaining Superior Performance*, The Free Press, NY.

Richardson, J., 1996, Vertical integration and rapid response in fashion apparel. *Organization Science*, **7**: 202-212.

Rochet, J.C. and Tirole, J., 2002, Cooperation among competitors: some economics of payment card associations. *RAND Journal of Economics*, **33**: 549-570.

Sahay, A. and Riley, D., 2003, The role of resource access, market considerations, and the nature of innovation in the pursuit of standards in the new product development process. *Journal of Product Innovation Management*, **20**: 338-355.

Schilling, M.A., 2003, Technological Leapfrogging: Lessons from the U.S. Video Game Console Industry. *California Management Review*, 45: 6-32.

Sengupta, S., 1998, Some approaches to complementary product strategy. *Journal of Product Innovation Management*, **15**: 352-367.

Shapiro, C. and Varian, H.R., 1999, *Information Rules: A Strategic Guide to the Network Economy*, Harvard Business School Press, Boston, Ma.

Siau, K., Lim E.P. and Shen, Z., 2001, Mobile commerce: Promises, challenges, and research agenda. *Journal of Database Management*, **14**: 4-13.

Srinivasan, R., Lillien, G. and Rangaswamy, A., 2002, Technological opportunism and radical technology adoption: An application to e-business. *Journal of Marketing*, **66**: 47-60.

Strand Consult, 2001, Show me the money: Revenue models on the mobile Internet. Analyst Report, Strand Consult, Copenhagen, Denmark.

Stuart, T.E., 2000, Interorganizational alliances and the performance of firms: A study of growth and innovation rates in a high-technology industry". *Strategic Management Journal*, **21**: 791 – 811

Taylor, S. and Todd, P.A., 1995, Understanding information technology usage: A test of competing models. *Information Systems Research*, **6**: 144-176.

Timmers, P., 1998, Business models for E-commerce. *Electronic Markets*, **8**: 3-7.

Tversky, A. and Kahneman, D., 1974, Judgment under uncertainty: Heuristics and biases. *Science*, **211**: 1124-1130.

Vesa, J., 2003, The impact of industry structure, product architecture, and ecosystems on the success of mobile data services: a comparison between European and Japanese markets. Presented at ITS 14th European Regional Conference, Helsinki, Finland, August 23-24.

Watson, R. T., Pitt, L. F., Berthon, P., and Zinkhan, G. M., 2002, U-commerce: Expanding the universe of marketing, *Journal of the Academy of Marketing Science*, **30**: 333-347.

Weill, P. and Vitale M.R., 2001, Place to Space. Migrating to E-business Models. Harvard Business School Press, Boston, Ma.

Zahra, S.A. and Nielsen, A.P., 2002, Sources of capabilities, integration and technology commercialization. *Strategic Management Journal*, **23**: 377-398.

EXPLOITATION OF PUBLIC AND PRIVATE WIFI COVERAGE FOR NEW BUSINESS MODELS

Thomas Lindner, Lothar Fritsch, Kilian Plank and Kai Rannenberg
Chair for Mobile Commerce & Multilateral Security, Johann Wolfgang Goethe University.
{ThomasLindner|Lothar.Fritsch|Kilian.Plank|Kai.Rannenberg@M-Lehrstuhl.de}
Gräfstraße 78, D-60054 Frankfurt am Main, Germany

Abstract: The expected boom in wireless networking and the rapidly increasing number of private and public access points prepare the ground for additional – initially unintended – usage possibilities of this fast growing infrastructure.

A first example is 'Location Based Services'. Since access points constantly broadcast unique, identifiable information like the MAC address, this data could be exploited for additional services. Because of the narrow broadcasting range of a WLAN (Wireless Local Area Network) cell, precise location information can be obtained at low cost. This could be used i.e. as a basis for LBS (push), or navigational services (pull).

Since WLAN chips are integrated into more and more devices like PDAs (Personal Digital Assistant) and mobile telephones, WLANs could be used for access to simple classic internet services like WWW or email as well as more sophisticated services like VoIP (Voice over Internet Protocol).

This paper describes four exemplary possibilities of exploiting the WLAN infrastructure for additional services, provided that WLAN is almost ubiquitous in a coherent area.

Key words: WLAN, WiFi, Business Model, LBS, UMTS, VOIP

1. INTRODUCTION

WLAN is an intensely discussed topic not only at professional trade conferences (it was the main theme of the 2003 Cebit computer fair), in trade journals, and even in mass media from television to newspapers. A rapidly increasing number of access points can be observed. For example, the largest German mobile network operator T-Mobile recently announced plans to operate 10,000 hotspots worldwide by the end of the year (T-Mobile 2004). In the same way, the equipment of all Intel notebook CPUs with WLAN functionality fuels the diffusion of this network access technology. This accelerating wireless network spread already led to the speculative question whether WLAN is a competitor or even the undertaker of UMTS (Universal Mobile Telecommunication System).

At present the WLAN infrastructure is based on three columns:
- private (non-consenting, possibly consenting in future)
- corporate (non-consenting)
- commercial (consenting and non-consenting)

The notion "consenting" denotes the hotspot operator's consent to use his infrastructure within a business model. Today, WLAN technology is just used as (internet) network access technology with the advantage of no need for wires.

The existing business models of commercial hotspots providing wireless internet access are insufficient from a financial perspective as they have to compete in terms of price with the comparatively inexpensive wire based internet access the customers are used to. Today's target group of commercial hotspots, offering the business traveler mobile access to corporate mail and network is rather limited. Nevertheless, comparing capacity with actual usage reveals an obvious lack. This lack seems to offer opportunities in economic terms for both providers as well as customers.
Further business possibilities for premium services could be i.e.:
- inner city navigation
- promotional and/or informational messaging
- synergistic business models by mobile operators
- private bandwidth sharing

Since WLAN has been unconsidered in economics research so far, there are hardly any empirical examinations. Hence, this paper tries a tentative approach in this direction. Since wide coverage is a precondition for further exploitation, we examine in a first step the WLAN coverage in a large German city representative for other congestion areas. In a second step, we present four exemplary business models trying to reveal the particularities of decentralized mobile network infrastructures. The application of a business model ontology is to provide for structure and comparability. Finally, we discuss our findings and give advice for successive research steps.

2. EMPIRICAL EXAMINATION

We evaluated the WLAN infrastructure in Frankfurt am Main / Germany selecting business and residential districts to investigate the coverage in a representative urban area.

Using the following hard- and software we drove through the selected districts and located and mapped existing WLANs:

Hardware	Software
• Sony Vaio notebook PCG-GR214EP • D-Link WLAN adapter DWL-650+ • Garmin Etrex GPS personal navigator	• Winows XP Version 2002 Service Pack 1 • NetStumbler Version 0.3.30 • StumbVerter MapPoint 2002 Edition Version 1.0.0 Beta 5 • Microsoft MapPoint Europe 2002

Windows XP was necessary for the usage of the D-Link DWL-650+ in order for it to work with NetStumbler. Using NetStumbler on the drive we detected the available WLANs and mapped them with the exact positioning coordinates downloaded via NMEA protocol from the Garmin Etrex. A summary of the log-file created by NetStumbler was plotted on MapPoint Europe 2002 maps using StumbVerter.

3. RESULTS

A screenshot of NetStumbler is presented in figure 1.

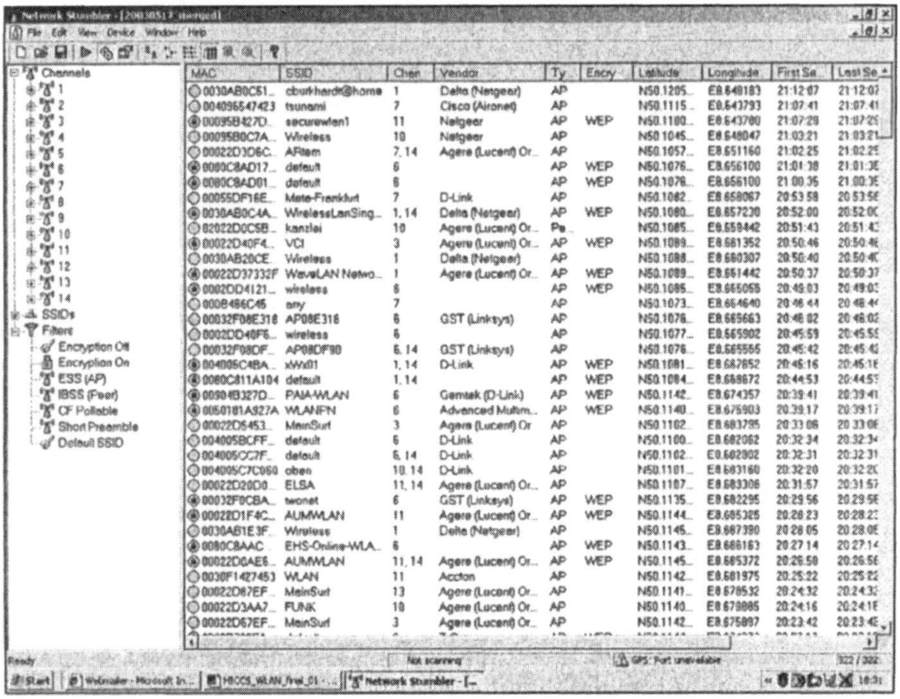

Figure 1. NetStumbler screenshot of log-file data

The collected information was then transferred into a graphical presentation using StumbVerter and Microsoft MapPoint as shown in the following pictures.

Figure 2 demonstrates an overview of the studied Frankfurt city area in a large scale.

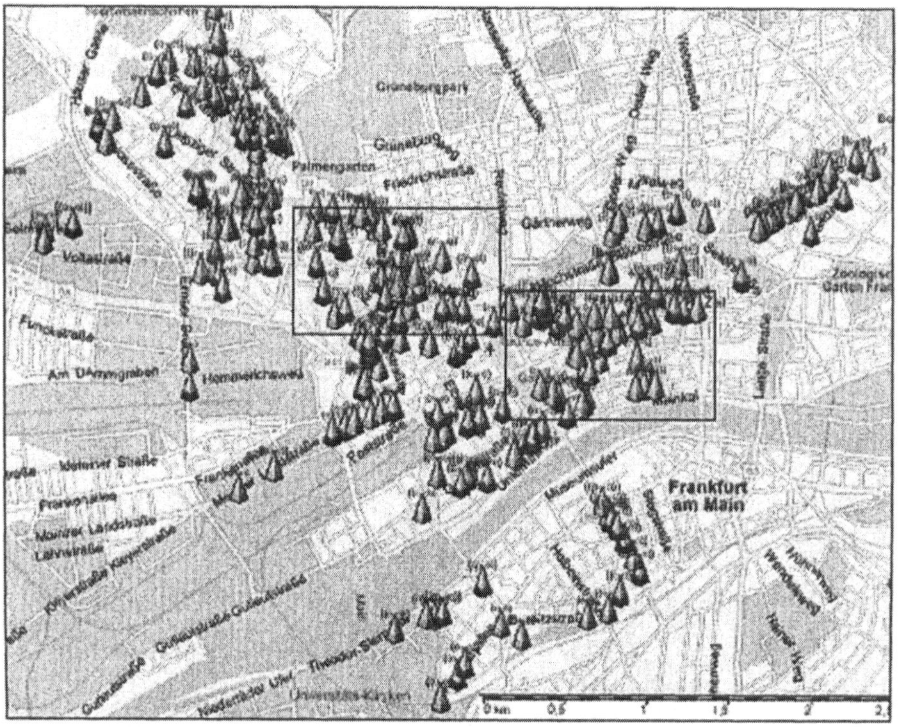

Figure 2. Overview of evaluated areas of Frankfurt

In Figures 3 (residential area – left box) and 4 (commercial area – right box) selected residential and commercial districts are shown in smaller scales in order to give a better impression of the WLAN availability in specific areas.

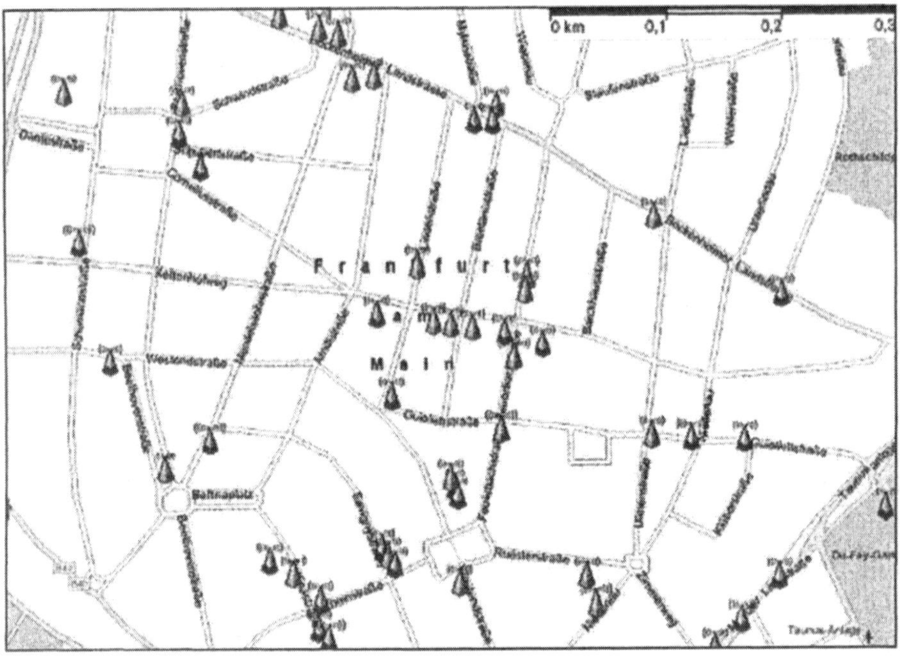

Figure 3. A selected residential area (Westend)

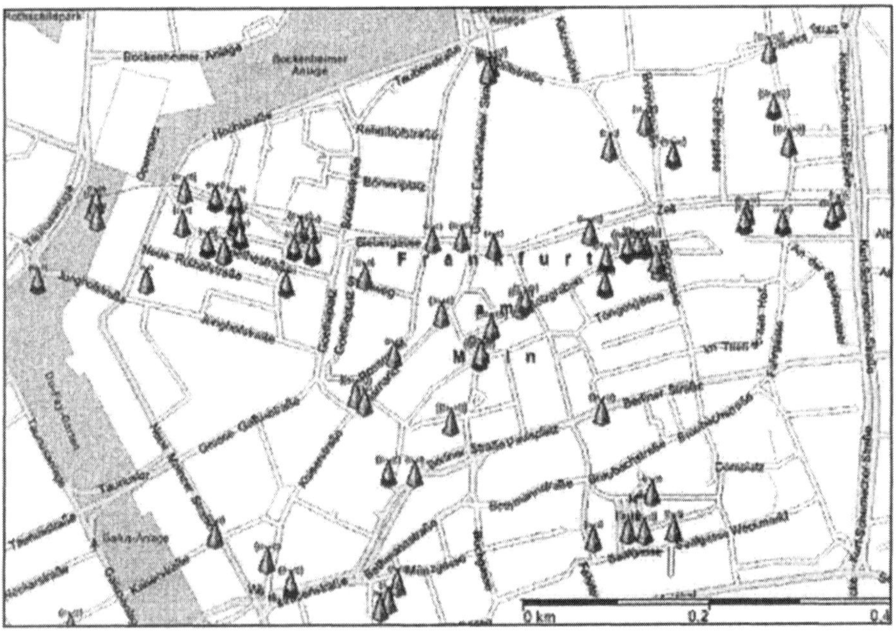

Figure 4. A selected commercial area (Zeil – Fressgass – Römer)

A total of 322 WLANs were detected and mapped in the researched areas. With only 139 (43.17%) access points being protected through web equivalent encryption (WEP) the majority of 56.83% (183) was not protected using WEP. While 39 access points did not broadcast an SSID, 40 access points sent the manufacturer's default SSID. 9 WLAN access points could be identified as being commercial hotspots.

4. BUSINESS MODELS

We will analyze four possible business models making use of WLAN access points. These models are either in consent with the respective access point provider or non-consenting. For comparative purposes we summarized the key elements of each business model according to the business model ontology suggested by (Pigneur 2002) at the end of each paragraph.

4.1 Business Model 1 – Inner City Navigation by Non-Consenting Use of Broadcasted Access Point Signals

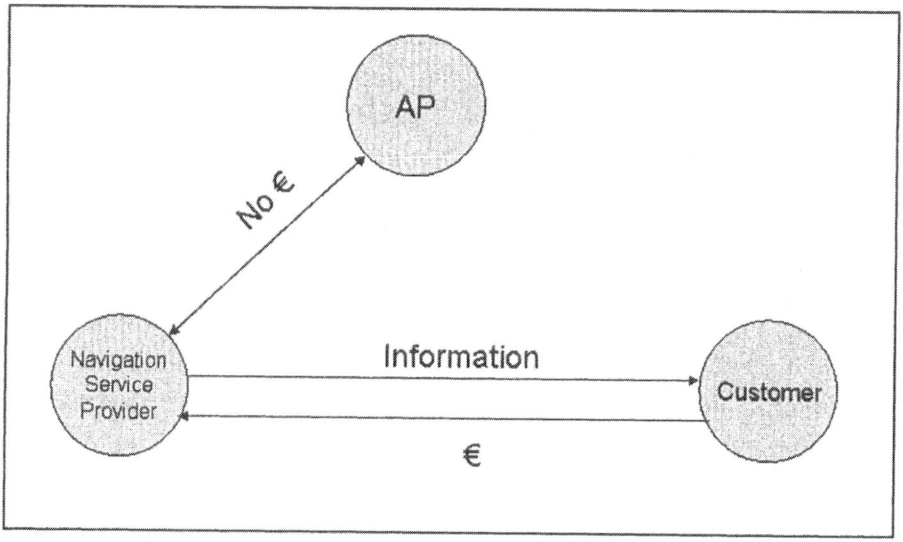

Figure 5. Non-consenting business model – inner city navigation

Today geographical location systems using GPS are limited in their accuracy in inner city areas due to their dependence on at least 4 visible satellites to triangulate the exact position. In cities this is not always achievable as buildings sometimes block the line of sight. As a consequence, information cannot always be accurate. This deficit is overcome by mobile navigation systems in automobiles by incorporating driving distance and directional changes of the car into the geographical location information calculating the position in reference to the last known triangulation point. For non-motorized users of GPS based navigation systems these supplementary and additional calculatory procedures are not available. Aggravating the situation for the non-mobile customer is the fact that GPS devices require constant energy supply.

A mobile device using the information as broadcasted by WLANs could overcome these shortfalls. Since the energy requirements a far less WLAN based location devices could be incorporated into existing mobile communication devices i.e. mobile phones, handhelds, notebooks etc. Available on today's market is the PDA Compaq iPaq 5400 which is equipped with WLAN technology including antenna and could therefore make use of the broadcasted signals without further hardware investment.

In this non-consenting business model it will be the obligation of the provider of the geographical information services to locate the available access points and map them to their geographical location. These data of access points and their geographical positioning have to be maintained on a regular basis and could be sold as a product allowing geographical location determination for motorized and non-motorized customers as well.

The product to be sold could be only the program to access the database – software solution - or comprise hardware and software as well.

Potential customers for these services could be either ad-hoc customers like business travelers or tourists coming into cities renting the hard- and software for a limited period of time to be able to navigate in the unknown environment, or customers who could be on a regular program update scheme receiving periodically updated information. Further interested customers could be tourist boards of the cities offering visitors the possibility to discover the points of interest in a city via a guided, WLAN supported tours, receiving additional information on selected points of interest in their own language.

In this model consent exists only between the database provider and their customers. The supplier of the basic information – WLAN hotspot – is not a part of the active business process and will therefore have no particular interest in assuring continuity and accuracy of the broadcasted data. One possibility of involvement for the access point provider could be that the database provider enters into a business relationship with the owners of the access points thereby ensuring accuracy of the database and revenue possibilities to the information provider (WLAN access point). This however might be a next step into a consenting model but at present using the WLAN data is to be regarded as non-consenting since a business relationship would only exist between location device users and database provider.

Value Proposition	- service provider takes advantage of a low-cost infrastructure, probably leading to lower prices for customers - WLAN enabled device is cheaper for customers than GPS equipped device
Infrastructure	- relies on high urban density of WLAN hotspots - requires accurate maintenance of hotspot location database - can provide navigation on-board or off-board dependant on the availability of mobile communications
Financials	- less infrastructure investment for the provider of the navigation service
Customer Relationship Management	- customers must be acquired and serviced by the service provider

4.2 Business Model 2 – Consenting, Target Group Oriented, and Situation Based Use of Information

The flow of information and the users of such become ever more mobile. The internet has opened the possibilities of companies addressing their customers independently of time and location – anytime, anywhere, always. One could say that the interaction between company and potential customer is always "one click away". This "click" is often farther away than one might think. Additionally it is very difficult for the information provider to specifically address their potential customers' needs due to the anonymity of the internet. This has led to the consequence of unwanted and annoying pop up ads, spam mails etc.. WebSite owners thought in the past that they finance their businesses by selling advertising space to companies on the basis of costs per thousand appearances. A possible shortfall of these models might have been that the information was distributed indiscriminately and only reached few potential customers. Decreasing click-through rates led to a change of the concepts by the advertising companies. The new business model of the advertising industry is to honor only qualified contacts. WLAN offers, due to its narrow broadcasting range, a possibility from the "one click away" in the internet to a "one step away" in real-time and real space.

This consent-type business model combines the advantages of electronic communication with the geographical accessibility. It is suggested that access point providers offer their users at the moment of connection to the platform information about services and products in the near vicinity (one step away). This platform could a be a 3rd party logon portal which supplies general interest information as well as specific, customer oriented information about nearby services i.e. theater, restaurants and of retailers with special offers. To enable the advertiser to pinpoint their offered services or products to very narrowly selected target groups will require that the customers, in using the access portal, allow an interest profiling. This profiling could be portal driven, resulting in the storage of the submitted data in a centrally located database, which could be accessed from various geographically diverse access points offering the possibility for the customer to use the personalized WLAN driven services not only at his original point of profiling but in other areas as well. The access point providers could either be a cooperation of locally active service providers or one provider with a multitude of national or even international access points.

A further possibility to store profiling data is using identity management where the profile is device driven and stored in the device itself as a standard part of the initial mobile device personalization. This identity management profiling will assure security and protection of personal information, avoiding possible conflicts with internationally different laws for personal data storage. This would require however a world wide accepted standard for multi-purpose profile data structure and transmission to enable global WLAN services usage.

The range of customer specific offers could be as widespread as from offering culturally interested persons sitting in a cafe close to the opera information about still available tickets for today's event to a nearby book seller informing a book lover next table about the latest arrivals. These examples base on an informational push model. Further on information could be offered on a pull basis as well in which a customer can access information on available services through a portal specific search engine. This pull-on-demand information can range from available activities like cinema schedules, nearby restaurants, special events, and special offers on selected products to public transportation departure times at the nearest station.

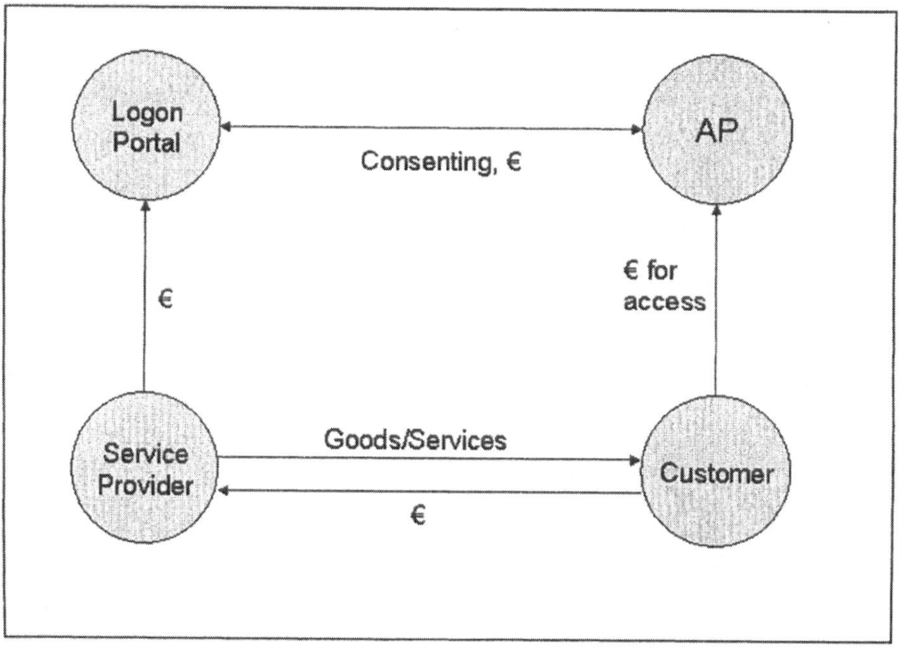

Figure 6. Consenting business model – logon portal

The narrow broadcasting range of a WLAN access point offers the possibility that the advertised offer is always just one step away. The use of modern content management systems enables the portal provider to adapt the submitted content to a wide variety of mobile communication devices i.e. smart phones, handhelds, notebooks and thereby to multiple display sizes.

Once the customer profile is consentingly stored in a database the specifically directed information messages are not limited to one geographical area or city but can be applied on a broad geographical range. In the example of a business traveler sitting on a business trip in different cities and connecting through WLAN access points offering the logon portal, will receive messages from interested parties in a reachable vicinity of the new site.

Value Proposition	- service provider can use WLAN location as an input to create localized information portal content
	- customer receives localized information for the exact hot-spot's environment he is in
	- cost of distribution channel is low compared to GSM/UMTS

Infrastructure	- requires hotspot operation in large scale or many contracts with small hotspot networks - a payment solution for access billing needs to be developed - customers can use standard WiFi enabled terminals
Financials	- additional costs result from administrative work and content acquisition - service provider receives payment either explicitly or by way of the hotspot operator
Customer Relationship Management	- customers are acquired by hotspot operators and/or service providers - customer's portal usage can be analyzed for better customer care

4.3 Business Model 3 – Synergetic Use of WLAN by a Telco

As mentioned in the introduction WLAN technology might be competing against UMTS, predicting even that WLAN could make the substantial investments in the licenses and start up costs for installing the UMTS network in Europe obsolete. We suggest that the combined use of WLAN and UMTS could lead to a better return on investment for the Telcos and by the same token offer an added value benefit for customers. In the first step of building up the UMTS networks, where upfront investments are high and the available bandwidth will be limited, WLAN could supplement these networks. From the expected standard bandwidth of 2Mbit/s only 384Kbit/s will be available in the initial phase making this a bottleneck for UMTS customers. The installation of WLAN access points in strategic locations, like airport lounges, railway stations, hotels etc. could alleviate this potential stumbling block. Telcos could offer their UMTS customers free or low cost internet access for their computers via WLAN, thereby leaving bandwidth free for multimedia mobile phone based applications. (Spinney 2003) suggests a similar symbiotic approach including a location based service with cellular-to-WiFi-handoff whenever high bandwidth is required.

In the competition amongst the telcos for UMTS customers a well positioned and well built up WLAN infrastructure could amount to a competitive advantage. Figure 7 depicts the relationships between the various actors. A UMTS or GSM customer can connect to an access point whenever possible and necessary. He is not billed separately for this services. Rather all access technologies like GSM, GPRS, UMTS and WLAN are covered by one product.

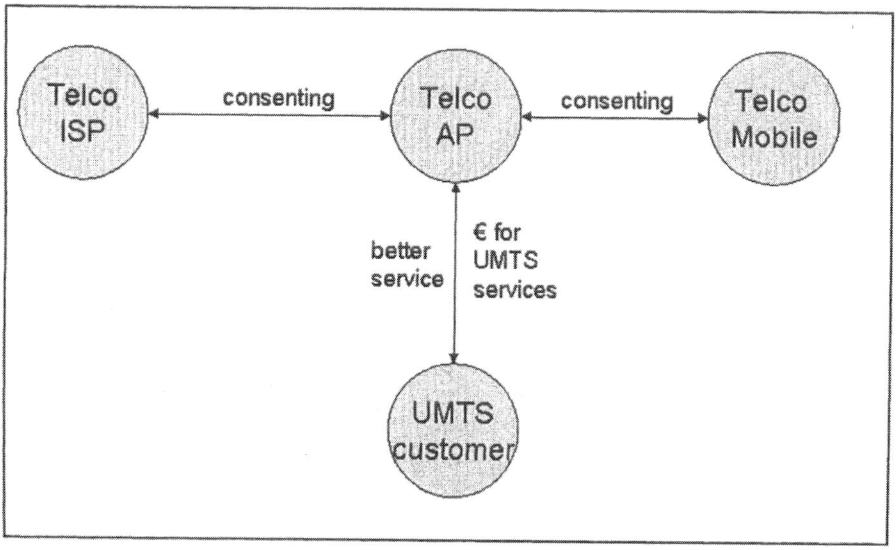

Figure 7. Consenting business model – synergistic use of WLAN and UMTS

Research has to be conducted in the areas of adoption and diffusion. Thus, empirical evidence has to be gathered regarding the effects of more product and price simplicity as well as technology and network integration on adoption and usage. Furthermore, possible implications on diffusion theory have to be considered.

Value Proposition	- customer automatically connects with the most appropriate access technology according to the situation - more simplicity, e.g. of configuration
Infrastructure	- infrastructure consists of UMTS, GSM and WLAN cells and the corresponding client technologies at the customer's side
Financials	- less infrastructure investments
Customer Relationship Management	- customer acquisition, retention and service by the service provider

4.4 Business Model 4 – Private Access Point Provision

Besides the hybrid business model 3, in which coexistence between UMTS and WLAN is suggested, an exclusive WLAN model is also imaginable. In this scenario a full coverage of wireless LANs is available in congested areas. These WLANs are to be used by any mobile device, like mobile telephones, PDAs, notebooks, etc., for any service that is also accessible on the internet, like www, email or VoIP. The main advantages in comparison with classic cellular broadband telecommunication networks are among other things lesser start up and running costs, higher user acceptance and most likely faster time to market. In case of VoIP via mobile (also called "Voice over WLAN") the announcements of many mobile device manufacturers regarding market ready WLAN enabled mobile phones in the course of 2004 underlines the increasing convergence of IT and telecommunications. However, it has to be admitted that these mobile phone manufacturers chiefly focus on indoor usage scenarios for the WLAN part of their devices. In order to build a network of WLANs there are several options. One possibility is to build a completely separate own network of wireless access points that covers a whole area (e.g. a city). This way, the whole infrastructure remains under the service provider's control. The other possibility is to include the existing infrastructure of privately owned access points and add own ones in areas with lacking coverage. However, this requires a broadband connection of the private access points to the internet or the service provider's network respectively. Currently, the most widespread broadband internet access technology in Germany is DSL, which offers a minimum download speed of 768 kbit/s. Furthermore, private persons have to be convinced and enticed to share a part of their bandwidth with others. In order to further reduce the own investments and additionally enforce the spread of broadband internet access DSL could be bundled with WLAN technology and subsidized in sale, possibly in connection with a multilevel marketing model. Furthermore, private persons could be refunded or rewarded according to the shared bandwidth.

Still, there are several major problems that have to be resolved. First, there are questions of security, trust and availability. Current research in the area of peer to peer networks and reputation systems could offer helpful approaches here. Availability is also achievable by provision of technical redundancy with the access provider and also by a network structure that constantly provides for two alternative wireless access points within reach for each customer device. Furthermore, contracts with private access point providers should include penalties in case of unavailability.

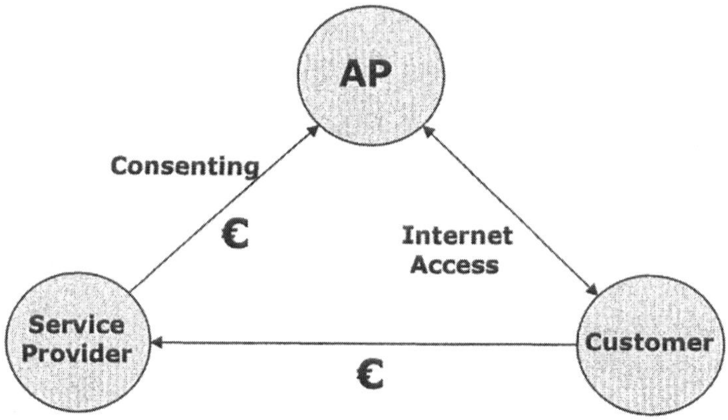

Figure 8. Consenting business model – private bandwidth sharing

Furthermore, the above described field tests have to be supplemented by further empirical examinations. Currently, we are planning studies on the evolvement of the private and public WLAN densities in major German cities. Additionally, we examine the bandwidth of associated (internet) network connections. Several field tests have to be carried out regarding necessary minimum coverage, network capacity, quality of services, performance and quality of WIFI enabled mobile phones as well as roaming. Finally, administration and management systems (e.g. billing systems, user registry) which allow for the particularities of an only partially owned infrastructure have to be developed.

Figure 8 depicts the various participants and their relationships in business model 4. The access point provider offers wireless internet access to the customer. The customer is equipped with a WLAN enabled device. He is charged by the service provider who himself rewards the access point provider.

Value Proposition	- customer simultaneously business partner
	- ubiquitous broadband voice and data services
	- better utilization of the WLAN infrastructure leads to lower costs and consequently to lower prices
	- less capital requirements for initial investments lowers market entry barriers and increases competition that in turn results in lower prices
Infrastructure	- parts of the infrastructure are provided by indi-

	viduals (wireless access point and broadband core network access) - parts of the infrastructure are provided by the provider (network access in areas that are not covered by private access points, (virtual) core network, network and user management, billing systems).
Financials	- less initial infrastructure investments - lower operator margins
Customer Relationship Management	- incentives for private access point operators to become customers

5. DISCUSSION

In this paper, we have presented various business models which aim at exploiting currently evolving private and public WLAN infrastructures for new purposes. As is often the case, many applications emerge only after some period of usage and experience.

In the navigational model, the use of broadcasted signals does not require consent with the access point operator, whereas models two, three and four require consent. Models 1 and 2 benefit from the narrow broadcasting range of the WLAN cell ranging from geographical location information to the closeness of information sender and receiver (seller and customer).

The relative density of WLAN access points as shown in figure 2 would suggest that the presented models could be easily implemented. However when analyzing the data in detail one sees that the WLAN access point density, as shown in figures 3 and 4 of residential and commercial areas is as yet insufficient. We intend to follow the development of WLAN access point availability in further studies.

Even if at first impression the existing scarcity of accessibility is perceived as contradictory to our suggested business models, it could be regarded as an advantage for commercial hotspot providers. The inexpensive installation of WLAN hotspots in commercially interesting areas requires, especially in comparison to UMTS, little investment for complete coverage, making up-front investment minimal. As a consequence the cost of the offered services could be held at a lower level and thereby assuring easier market penetration and market acceptance and lowering business risks.

The presented model one, the inner city satellite independent WLAN navigational system, should not only be regarded as a stand-alone application but could be seen as a complementary product to the automobile based GPS navigational system, enabling continuation of geographical information independently of the car. The customer parking the car, not yet having reached the final destination, could be guided via mobile WLAN based device to the end point of the journey.

The idea behind the second, portal driven, consenting model is the use of the narrow broadcasting range of the WLAN access points to bring customer and merchant together (one step away). We presented the model predominantly as an informational push model where the customer, logging on to an access point, will receive either general information or information tailored to a possibly existing profile. This geographically narrow communication concept could be offered on a pull basis as well, enabling a customer to specifically search for information. We predict that a pull model, with an active search capability, would even increase the acceptance of WLAN services and the usage of modern mobile communication devices. Identity management using the device for storage of personal data as part of the mobile communication flow will be a protective shield for the customers assuring anonymity resulting in higher acceptance rates.

The third model presented the synergistic potential of UMTS and WLAN enabling telcos to offer added services to increase the usage value of their UMTS investment. Especially in the initial introduction phase this might protect the still narrow UMTS bandwidth by transmitting larger amounts of mainly internet based data on a parallel WLAN, reserving the UMTS bandwidth primarily for multimedia smart phone based application traffic. For the customer the parallel use of UMTS and WLAN connection capability could be a decisive factor in selecting their UMTS provider. For telcos the installation of a network of WLAN hotspots could support the UMTS license and infrastructure investments by acquiring new customers and offering additional services resulting in a win-win situation.

The individually presented business models could and should not only be regarded as independent products but as supportive and possibly integrated services, making better use of the required investment in the WLAN infrastructure for the provider, and enabling the customers to seamlessly use more and better adapted services.

6. CONCLUSION AND OUTLOOK

Based on the present brisk expansion of the WLAN infrastructure the presented visions and business models might come to the market a lot faster than expected as of today. Consent between access point provider and service provider is imperative to drive the development of the commercial exploitation of the WLAN infrastructure. Only commercially viable, consent driven business models will assure a uniform and world wide accessible WLAN infrastructure.

As stated in the introduction, this paper is just a first step towards an economic analysis of decentralized and partly client owned networks. There are a lot of future research topics. First, several empirical examinations have to be conducted, in order to validate the premises, such as model-specific density requirements, access point provider acceptance or technical feasibility. Second, there are questions from a marketing point of view, e.g. pricing models and prosumer aspects. Another area of research is the examination of emerging value networks. These peer-to-peer reminiscent networks include so-called prosumers, that is customers who also act as producers or rather service providers. This leads to a couple of strategic questions for the incumbent service providers and operators. Finally, all the aforementioned phenomena are to be analyzed by microeconomics regarding possible implications or consequences.

REFERENCES

Ekahau, 2003, *Ekahau Positioning Engine for WLAN based navigation*; http://www.ekahau.com/products/positioningengine/features.html; (June 4, 2003)

Pigneur, Y. ,2002, *An Ontology for m-business models*, in S. Spaccapietra et al. (Eds.) Conceptual Modeling - ER 2002, Tampere, Lecture Notes in Computer Science, 2503, October 2002

Spinney, J., 2003, *Cellular-to-WiFi Handoff, Micro-LBS and the Symbiotic power of Location*, in "Java Location Services"; http://www.jlocationservices.com/; (June 3, 2003)

T-Mobile, 2004. *3GSM World Congress: T-Mobile announces broadband mobile launch*; www.t-mobile.net/CDA/integrated_network_set_to_launch,20,,newsid-2685,en.html?w=890&h=577; (April 29, 2004)

SUPPORTING SALESPERSONS THROUGH LOCATION BASED MOBILE APPLICATIONS AND SERVICES

Chihab BenMoussa
Institute for Advanced Management System Research, Turku Centre for Computer Science, Lemminkäisenkatu 14 A, FIN-20520 TURKU, FINLAND

Abstract: The paper aims at assessing how mobile location applications and services can support salespersons, for greater performance when they are operating within a mobile work environment. After briefly discussing the state of the art issues associated with mobile location technologies, the paper conceptualises key dimensions of location-based mobile support. The paper then suggests a categorization of salespersons tasks based on both properties of location-based mobile support and the areas of salespersons tasks that may be affected by mobile location technologies. A third section suggests potential mobile location services and applications that can support salespersons in performing effectively their everyday tasks and links such applications to the determinant of salespersons' performance. The paper concludes with a discussion of a number of critical issues such as salespersons privacy, risk of information overload, autonomy and some core areas of further research.

Key words: Mobile location technologies, Salespersons tasks, salespersons performance, knowledge-mobilisation

1. INTRODUCTION

It has been argued that the marketing department is the last organizational function to adopt information technologies (IT) in order to enhance its contribution to the overall corporate performance (Rivers et al. 1999). However despite such a laggard behaviour, the amount of IT investment the marketing department has received particularly in the form of sales force automation (SFA) is heavy compared to its counterparts functions within the organization. It was estimated that in USA alone 2.2 million salespeople were using SFA systems with a yearly growth rate of 40% (Engel et al.2000). Industry experts estimate that three-quarter of American large and medium-seized organizations have been implementing some degree of SFA. As a result, SFA market has been booming. In 1996, revenues from SFA industry reached US$ 1.5 billion (River et al.1999).

Companies have invested in sales force technologies such as sales force automation (SFA), knowledge management technologies and customer relationship management in order to take benefit from what such technologies promise in terms of decreasing costs (Taylor 1993), reducing cycle time (Thetgy, 2000), improving organization and access to information (Leifer, 1999). Some authors went too far as to claim that investments in sales force technologies are a sine qua non condition for an organization to remain competitive (Taylor, 1996; Good and Schultz 1997; Peppers and Rogers, 1998).

However, the expected benefits of such investments in terms of productivity do not seem to be realized. Studies show that for every two successful implementation of sales force support systems, there are three failures (Schafer, 1997). And given the costs in terms of both dollars and time associated with the implementation of such systems, some authors start questioning even the utility to engage in such investments. For instance, Thetgyi, 2000 believes that SFA has brought many companies pain rather than profit. Similarly Petersen, 1997 claims that the "jury is still out" regarding the true pay-back of sales force support systems. Indeed, it has been reported that the cost of implementing an SFA system can reach $ 3500 per salesperson (Girard 1998,Taylor, 1994,).

One possible cause of the gap separating sales force support systems investments and their impact in terms of salesperson ′ productivity is that such systems have been designed with insufficient attention to the tasks and the social context of salespersons′ work in general. For instance, many companies have invested in knowledge management systems such as knowledge repositories and intranets in order to support their salespeople for greater productivity. However, it has been found that most of such systems lack the customers (P. Keen et al, 2001). This is due to the fact that such knowledge management systems have been designed with stationary work setting in mind (BenMoussa, 2003). In order to benefit from their support, the sales person often has to be in a specific place (typically the office) use a specific tool (his/her personnel computer) and adapts to how the knowledge is stored and organized. However, salespersons spend a considerable portion of their time on the move. And during their extensive geographical movement, they are often away from their desktop computers, which contain most of the information they need and impose rigid constraints on how and where they can be used. The use of laptops by salespersons has contributed in reducing this gap separating salespersons on the move and their access to critical corporate resources. However, laptops still impose limitations in terms of arming salespersons with instant updates at the moment of relevance that can enable them to perform effectively their various sales activities. For instance, in order to receive instant updates using a laptop, a salesperson has to connect to the Internet or through corporate dialup, which in many cases requires them to be tied to a physical location (Rodina et al., 2003).

Mobile (or wireless) applications, despite being different in their nature, they share a common characteristic that distinguishes them from their wireline counterpart: They put the user at the centre of information and communication by enabling him/her to both receive and get access to information support anytime and despite their constant move. Location identification has become a critical component of mobile applications as it opens the door to a world of applications and services that were unthinkable only a few years ago (May, 2001). The term mobile location services (MLS) refers to a group of applications and services that utilize information related to geographical position of their users in order to provide adding value services to them (Gialias, 2003). MLS as new entrants to the mobile application world have received to date limited focus with regard to their real potential and value adding impact in terms of performance enhancement especially to workers on constant move facing the uncertainties and constraints associated with their mobility. The phenomenon is indeed simply too novel for a proper debate to be emerged. The aim of the paper is therefore to analyse how MLS can support salespersons, for greater performance when they are operating within a mobile work environment. After briefly discussing the state of the art issues associated with mobile location technologies, the paper conceptualises key dimensions of location-based mobile support. The paper then suggests a categorization of salespersons tasks based on both the properties of location-based mobile support and the areas of salespersons tasks that may be affected by mobile location technologies. A third section suggests potential mobile location services and applications that can support salespersons in performing effectively their everyday tasks and links such applications to the determinant of their performance. The paper discusses and systemises examples of location based mobile application and services in terms of the four functional types: the time saver, the relationship enhancer, the proactiveness enabler and the morale booster location-based mobile applications and services. The paper concludes with a discussion of a number of critical issues such as salespersons privacy, risk of information overload and some areas of further research.

2. TECHNOLOGY FOR MOBILE LOCATION ERVICES AND APPLICATIONS

Location technologies can be divided into two main categories: core positioning and supporting technologies. Core positioning technologies refer to the technologies that allow the determination of the location of mobile users. Facilitating technologies refer to the complementary technologies that provide the contextual and /or infrastructural environment within which mobile location services can be implemented in a value added fashion (Giaglis et al.2003).

2.1 Core Positioning Technologies

There are several positioning technologies with their own advantages and drawbacks. The most popular positioning technologies are Global Positioning System (GPS) and non-GPS positioning technologies.

2.1.1 GPS Technologies

The Global Positioning System is a satellite based navigation system developed and operated by the US. Department of Defence. GPS ´s operations rely mainly on 24 satellites that transmit signals. GPS receivers process the signals to compute positions in 3 D latitude, longitude, and altitude with accuracy of 10 meters or less. Therefore one of the main advantages of GPS technique is its high accuracy, when operational conditions are favourable. However in order for GPS technique to achieve high level of accuracy in determining the location of a mobile user, the handset must be visible at least to three satellites all the times. As a result, GPS cannot be used in indoors and it may not work in "urban canyons" area. In order to overcome the problem of positioning in weak signals environments (i.e. indoor environment, tunnels); assisted GPS method (A-GPS) has been developed. A-GPS uses the assistance of the mobile network that directs the handsets to look for specific satellites or collects data from the handset to perform location identification calculations.

2.1.2 Cellular Positioning Technologies

The most common cellular techniques for mobile positioning are cell or origin, time of arrival, Angle of Arrival and Observed Time Difference. Cell of Origin (COO) method is the most basic solution and uses the cell identification information within the mobile telephony network to identify the approximate location of the caller. The COO method identifies the approximate location of the user by knowing which cell site the device is using at a particular time. The accuracy of COO method depends on cell radius, which can be very large especially in rural areas. Therefore the accuracy of this method is higher in dense urban areas and much lower in rural areas. Time of Arrival (TOA) method determines the position of a mobile device by measuring the time of arrival of the signal from a user's mobile device to at least three cell sites. The TOA offers better accuracy (10-100 meters). Its main drawback is the additional investments network operators should undertake in order to equip cell sites with location measurement units (LMU). The Angle of Arrival (AOA) method seeks to determine the location of the mobile device based on the angle at which signals transmitted from the mobile device reach the cell site (s). The AOA technique requires line of sight between the cell sites and the mobile device in order to achieve accurate positioning results. Therefore it is not a suitable location method in dense urban areas where line of sights of two cell sites may not be possible. Observed time difference (OTD) technique determines the location of a mobile device by using location receivers, which are geographically dispersed across wide areas. OTD method determines a user's location by calculating the time it takes for a signal from at least three cell sites equipped with LMU to reach the mobile device. The main drawback of OTD method is that it requires additional investment in terms of both equipping network cell sites with LMU and the required modification of the mobile's device software in order to enable it to perform the necessary position calculation.

2.2 Supporting Location Technologies

Mobile location supporting technologies include standards, protocols and other technological capabilities that contribute to the added value mechanism stemming from the ability of determining users′ location. Supporting location technologies include mobile communication protocols such as Wireless Application Protocols (WAP), Standard technologies such as General Packet Radio Service (GPRS) or Universal Mobile Telecommunication Systems (UMTS) and other supporting capabilities such as Geographic Information Systems (GIS) (see Geaglis 2003, Smith et al. 2002,Tarasewich et al.2002 for discussion of those technologies).

3. KEY PROPERTIES OF LOCATION BASED MOBILE SUPPORT

3.1 Relevance

The application of location-based mobile support has the potential of eliminating the spatial dimension of business processes. This is of particular importance for mobile knowledge workers who work at various locations: in their own office, at clients' offices, at other members' offices, at work sites, on train, plane and car, in a hotel room, and so on. Such modalities of mobility impose challenges on mobile workers in general, particularly in terms of achieving adaptability, to the different work environments resulting from their extensive move, which can enable them to keep themselves well informed in order to work more effectively. Location-based mobile support can enhance the ability of mobile workers to adapt to the spatial constraints resulting from their extensive move by been able, thanks to the knowledge of their geographic location by the service provider, to receive relevant information and targeted support that can fit the adaptability requirements raised by their spatial position. The user's spatial position can therefore become a key element in providing relevant and adding value support to the mobile worker. For instance, the knowledge of the location of salesperson can be used as one criterion in assessing whether or not an alert is relevant and has the potential to add value to the salesperson or in the opposite it may expose him/her to information overload. Similarly, the knowledge of the salesperson ′s location and thus the nature of the working environment within which the he/she is located (i.e. face to face meeting with a client, in the train or in restaurant) can enable the service provider to select the appropriate message form (voice versus text) that fits the working environment within which the salesperson is located. For instance, the service provider can push an alert to the salesperson's smart phone in the form of text message if the salesperson is in face-to-face meeting and thus enabling him/her to read the alert and potentially exploit it during his/her interaction with the client.

3.2 Convenience

The ability of the service provider to know the geographical position of the mobile user can make it faster and simpler for such user to be provided the targeted support he/she needs. Indeed it will suffice the mobile user to notify its request to the service provider to get the service he /she is seeking as the service provider can know where the user is located. For instance, a salesperson seeking road directions to get in time to a meeting with a potential client can just notify to the service provider "how can I get to address x?" then by locating his/her position the service provider can provide him/her by the requested directions that can take into account potential traffic jams. This constitutes a unique feature of location-based mobile support as the question "how can I get to address x" without mentioning the current location is unanswerable within a wireline context.

3.3 Timeliness

Another key characteristic of location-based mobile support is the timeliness of the support that service providers can provide users with based on the knowledge of their locations. The timeliness of location-based mobile support refers to the ability of the service provider to provide the user with support at the moment of value. The moment of value can be defined as "the moment when I a service provider can do something for you where you are and regardless of where I am or what time it is"(Keen, 2001). An example of a location based service occurring at the user's moment value is when the service provider, based on its knowledge of a user's location, push to him/her an alert about a traffic jam he/she is about to approach together with proposals of alternative paths. In the absence of this traffic alert at this specific moment (before approaching the traffic jam), the user would not be able to avoid the traffic jam and thus may experience the resulting consequences in terms of time wasting and meeting delays. Another example of timely location-based support is when a salesperson, during or just before his/her interaction with a major client, receives a useful alert about this client, pushed by his/her market research department based on awareness of his/her location. The salesperson can then reflect this latest update about his client during his/her sales presentation and thus practice adaptive selling.

4. SALESPERSONS TASKS CATEGORIZATION

Perhaps the most rigorous study of the activities that salespersons perform during the course of their everyday work life is the one conducted by

Moncrief (1986). Moncrief found 121 activities that were factor analysed into ten activity dimensions: selling functions, working with others, servicing the products, information management, servicing the account, conferences and meeting, training and recruiting, entreating the clients, travel and working with distributors. Other authors (i.e. Copett 1995) categorise salespersons′ tasks into five categories: planning the sales call, approaching the prospect, making the sales presentations, negotiating resistance, confirming and closing the sale, follow up and servicing the account. More recent academic researches (i.e. Colombo, 1994, Parathasarathy, 1997, Petersen, 1997) have focused on salespersons tasks when discussing the potential impact of SFA systems on salespersons.

By combining both the information contained in the personnel selling literature about salespersons′ tasks and the proprieties of location-based mobile support in terms of relevance, convenience and timeliness, the paper creates taxonomy of salespersons tasks based on the areas that can be affected by mobile location technologies. In this structure the paper discusses three categories of salespersons tasks: Information gathering tasks, planning tasks, and interaction tasks. Each of these categories is discussed in the following section.

4.1 Information Gathering Tasks

Salespersons spend a considerable portion of their time on information gathering tasks such as prospecting, seeding and customers analysis. Prospecting is the label attached to the activity involved in generating sales leads and prospects. A sale lead is basically the name and address or telephone number of persons or organisations that may have a need for the company's products or services. Prospects are leads that are screened and qualified by salespersons to be worthy of further attention. Seeding is an agricultural metaphor frequently used by salespersons to describe prospects-focused activities. Theses activities are intended to "sow" the seeds of potential sales "harvest" and involve the gathering of such information as prospects′ industries characteristics, return on investment, profit and product quality.

Customer analysis tasks refer to activities undertaken by salespersons in order to stay at the top of new developments in their current customers operations (Coppett, 1990).

Location-based mobile support can help salesperson in their information gathering tasks through enabling them to receive useful leads, competitive or customer information, despite their constant move at the moment of relevance and without been obliged to gather such information themselves. The ability to know their geographical position together with other element such as their activity agenda would provide more specialized parties (i.e. market research department, customer support centre, external consulting firms and so on) with relevance criteria against which they may assess both the spatial and temporal relevance of the information they intend to provide salespersons with. This has the potential to enable salespersons to spend more time in revenue generating activities such as selling and still staying alerted about any development in their clients′ businesses or competitive environment.

4.2 Planning Tasks

Salespersons planning tasks include sales call planning and route planning. Sales call planning involve identifying and selecting profitable customers (Kotler 1994). Often called the "80-20", the concentration principle says that most of salesperson's sales, costs and profits come from a relatively small proportion of customers and products. That's why salespersons spend a considerable portion of their time classifying and analysing potential accounts so that they can devote the largest portion of their time to accounts with the highest buying potential.

The purpose of route planning is to minimize travel time and maximize time in front of customers and prospects (Colombo, 1994). In most companies, individual salespersons still route themselves because they know their territories and their customers best.

Location-based mobile support can affect salesperson planning tasks through relevant and timely location-based real time alerts associated with the orders of salespersons′ clients, their buying potential as well as their profitability so that the salesperson can adjust his /her call schedule and thus devote his/her time to clients with the highest profitability potential. For instance, the market research department can use its knowledge of the salesperson's location to provide him/her with alerts about the changes in the buying potential of the clients located in the geographical location where he/she is located, together with the urgency level of making sales visit to such clients. The market research department can determine such urgency of sales visits based on such information as real time client's profitability, competitors' moves or any press release that can affect the buying potential of the salesperson's clients.

Salespersons route planning can be supported by the different location based navigation services the operator can provide them with based on its knowledge of their geographical position. Such services may include location based alerts about traffic congestion or road-blocking accidents, driving direction and the provision of travel pattern based on the salesperson's current location, the list of clients he /she plan to visit and traffic conditions.

4.3 Interaction Tasks

Interactions tasks involve interactions of salespersons with both customers and co-workers within the organisation. Interaction tasks with customer are the core of salespersons′ daily work and include such activities as making sales presentations, answer clients′ questions, handle shipment problems, take the client out to lunch and calls on potential account (Moncrief, 1986).

Location-based mobile support can affect salespersons′ interaction tasks through its ability to mobilize relevant knowledge to salespersons despite their constant move and at the moment of relevance. For instance, a salesperson can get, based on his/her location, notifications about the client he/she is about to visit and thus adjust his/her sales presentation accordingly. Likewise, location-based support can reduce the time it takes to salesperson to address customer problems associated with orders or products through empowering the salespersons to deal with customer problems without referring to the head office. For instance with the ability to track the product locations, the salesperson can answer to order related questions without referring to the logistics department.

Interaction tasks with co-workers include cooperation between salespersons and other functions in the organization including marketing research, customer service, logistics, finance and engineering. Examples of interaction tasks with co-workers include reporting sales calls information to the sales managers and to the competitive intelligence department, providing sales information to other salespersons, keeping track of invoices with the finance department and handling shipment problems with logistics department. Location-based mobile support can affect salespersons′ interaction with co-worker by enabling them to locate the geographical position among each other and cooperate accordingly. For instance, based on his/her location, the salesperson can receive relevant alerts about his or her clients. Example of such alerts are "the client X you are about to visit has just paid its last invoice", "there will be a delay in delivering the order of client Y situated in the nearby ". Furthermore, salespersons can locate each other and exchange, based on their location, useful information that may enable them to exploit cross-selling opportunities that may arise.

5. LINKING SALESPERSONS MOBILE LOCATION APPLICATION AND SERVICES TO THE DETERMINANTS OF THEIR PERFORMANCE

After discussing a taxonomy of salespersons tasks, which is based on both mobile location-based support key properties and the areas of salespersons tasks that may be affected by mobile location technologies, the paper now presents potential mobile location applications and services (MLS) to support salespersons tasks for greater performance. The paper categorises such mobile location applications and services as time-savers, customer relationship-enhancers, proactiveness-enablers and morale-boosters. The paper shows how each category of such mobile location services and applications can support salesperson tasks and enhance their overall performance through its impact on a number of mediator variables that constitute salespersons′ performance determinants. Indeed, several authors (Mooney et al. 1996; Huber, 1990; Davenport 1999) have proposed that in order to uncover the added value mechanisms and the impact of information technology on productivity, studies should include intermediate benefits of information technology. For instance according to the theory of the effects of advanced information technology (Huber's 1990), the benefits in individual and organizational effectiveness occur" indirectly "through the positive impact the technology has on information and communication processes. Figure 1 depicts a framework linking location-based mobile support with salespersons′ performance.

5.1 Time-Saver MLS

The purpose of time savers mobile location services and application is to enable salespersons to achieve a better use of their time by avoiding daily time traps and thus spending their time in value generating activities such as selling. Salespersons′ time traps can be result form such factors as traffic conditions, emergency situations, poor tasks planning and occurrence of dead time.

The ability of salespersons to effectively manage their working time so that they can get the most out of each working hour is well recognized in the personnel selling literature as a key determinant of their performance (Green, 1987, Weeks, 1990, Henry, 1975). For instance Green (1987) stresses , "how a salesperson allocates his or her time across activities directly affects his or her performance and therefore impacts a firm's sales and profits."

Time-savers mobile location services and application include location-based emergency services, navigation services and location based travel pattern update.

Emergency Services

Location-based emergency services can provide salespersons with emergency support in such situations as car breakdown, accident, injury and so on. As typical road-users, location-based emergency services can enable salesperson to save a considerable amount of their time because of their ability to be provided with emergency services even in the case when they are unaware of their exact location or not able to reveal it due to the emergency situation (Geaglis, 2003).

Navigation services

Location-based navigation service can allow salespersons to receive, based on their location, point to point driving directions in order to get to a desirable destination. The salesperson Navigation services can also provide them with location aware alerts about traffic conditions (i.e. traffic congestion or a road blocking accident) and suggest alternative routes to salespersons.

Furthermore, navigation services can enable salespersons to update, irrespective of their location, their daily travel pattern based on their location and changes in their call schedule resulting form the occurrence of dead time. The salesperson can select his/her current location as a starting point; send it to the service providers together with the list of addresses he/she has to visit. The service provider can then suggest an appropriate travel pattern t together with driving directions.

Mobile yellow pages

Mobile yellow pages services can enable salespersons to receive upon request and based on their current location and preferences, information regarding nearby facilities such as the nearest restaurant, hotels or gas station. Receiving such location-based alerts would enable salespersons to save time when travelling to visit customers or taking clients out for lunch.

5.2 Customer Relationship-Enhancer MLS

Customer relationship-enhancers mobile location services and application would support salespersons during their daily interactions with customers through enabling them to practice adaptive selling, enhance their customer orientation and customer's perceptions of their expertise. Salespeople's adaptive selling is one of the main determinants of their performance. Adaptive selling behaviours are characterized by altering sales approach across and during customer contacts (Weitz et all, 1986; Sipro and Weitz 1990; Sujan 1986). Through the practice of adaptive selling, salespeople exploit the unique opportunities of personal selling. The personal selling literature proposes that adaptive selling can be improved by providing salespeople with the necessary market information and resources such that they can link insights from other sales situations to the customer contacts in which they are currently engaged (Weitz et al.1986).

Customer orientation can be viewed as the practice of the marketing concept at the level of individual salesperson. The marketing concept calls for an integrated, company wide approach in which all the firm's activities are directed toward providing customer satisfaction and establishing mutual beneficial relationship (Saxe and weitz, 1982). Reducing the time it takes to deal with a client's concern or difficulty may have a positive impact on customer orientation. Indeed, customer orientation is a key enabler of buyer-seller relationship developments (Lawler, 1992). Keeping promises is indeed a main determinant of trust, which is in turn a major factor affecting long-term relationship.

Salespersons expertise has been investigated as a crucial determinant of salespersons′ performance (Grosby et al.1990). Beatty et al. (1996) have noted that a customer who is initially attracted to a knowledgeable salesperson will feel positive about the salesperson.

Customer relationship-enhancers mobile location and services include product tracking, customer support staff locators and location based customer analysis alerts.

Products tracking applications

Product tracking application consist of enabling salespersons, irrespective of their locations, to track the delivery status of products ordered by customers, either by connecting wirelessly to smart tags incorporated in the products or through receiving location based alerts about the order status of clients situated in the same geographical location where the salesperson is located. This would enhance salespersons′ ability to answer rapidly, accurately and irrespective of their locations to customer order related inquiries, which their customer orientation. Furthermore, receiving location based alert about customers′ orders status would enable salespersons to react to eventual shipment problems that may result in a delivery delay to customers.

Customer support staff locator applications

Customer support staff locator applications would enable salespersons to locate the nearest customer support staff in order to address a client's problem. The salesperson can send a request to locate customer support staff, display their locations on a map and forward the client ′s request for service to the nearest field worker. Upon receiving confirmation to perform the service by the field worker, the salesperson can then be able to provide his/her client with accurate personnel arrival time. Dispatching the nearest customer support field employee has the potential to reduce the time needed to provide support to customers, and would enhance the customer's perception of the salesperson′ empathy.

Location-based customer analysis applications

Location based customer analysis applications consist of linking corporate customer analysis database with the salespersons calendar and exploiting his/her geographical location in order to provide them with actionable alerts about their clients which situated in the same geographical location where he/she located. Alerts may be associated with products, customer information or service delivery that salespersons can both exploit in both adapting their sales presentations and increasing their customers′ perception of their expertise.

5.3 Proactiveness -Enabler MLS and Applications

The purpose of proactiveness-enabler MLS and applications is to enable salespersons to continuously search for market opportunities and experiment with potential responses to changing environment. (Venkattraman, 1989)

Proactiveness-enablers mobile location services and applications include location-based lead alerts and location-based intelligence alerts.

Location-based leads alerts

Location based leads alert consist of alerting the salesperson about qualified leads that are situated in the same geographical location where the salesperson is locates. By identifying the salesperson ′s geographical location, the telemarketing support centre can provide a real time alert to the salesperson about high-quality leads that are in the same area where the salesperson is located. Depending on the quality of the lead (that is, sales versus no sales) and the salesperson's sales calls schedule, the salesperson can accept or deny making face-to-face sales visit to the sales call identified by the telemarketing support centre. If the salesperson accepts to make the sales visit then additional information from the marketing research department can be pushed to his/her mobile terminal about the lead including a rebuttal to prepare him/her for question that the prospect may raise. Location-based leads information would enable salespersons to adjust their sales call schedules in order to exploit sales opportunities and thus practice target selling. Target selling is defined as a salesperson's ability to identify, select, and call on profitable customers (Kotler 1994). Target selling is recognized in many selling textbooks (e.g. Stanton and Sirpo, 1999) as a determinant of salespersons performance.

Location-based intelligence alerts

Location based intelligence applications can let salespersons receive alerts about possible competitors′ threats and how such threats would affect the clients situated in the same geographical location where the salesperson is located. The salesperson can use the alert both to assess the urgency of visiting the clients and to adapt of his /her selling approach so that it can take into consideration such potential competitors move.

5.4 Morale booster MLS

Morale-booster mobile location service and applications intends to enhance salespersons′ morale by adding some fun to their job and enabling them to keep touch with their family members despite their constant move. Indeed, the unique nature of selling with its time demand, psychological strain, work-related role stress and performance orientation can put unusual pressure on the salespersons (Dubinsky et al., 1986). Organizational psychologist have pointed out that sales managers, who concentrate on creating intrinsic rewards in selling among salespersons-through setting the job up to be fun and work rewarding in itself- are likely to be more successful at encouraging adaptive selling and improving the productivity of sales force (Amabil, 1983 Sujan et all, 1988,).

Morale booster mobile location service and applications include children tracking and location-based entertainment services.

Children tracking services

Children trucking can enable salespersons to locate anytime and anywhere the location of their children. With this service the salesperson can be able to receive upon request a graphical map displaying the location of his/her children. Additionally an alarm system can notify them when their children are closed by.

Such a service has the potential to provide salespersons with assurance about their ability to react in time in dealing with problems that their teenagers especially problematic ones may experience, which would enable them to concentrate more on their selling activities.

Location-based entertainment services

Location-based entertainment services consist of providing salespersons, based on their location, with such entertainment services as games, songs and videos. For instance by identifying the position of the salesperson (i.e. in the train, airport) the operator can push an

Message suggesting to salesperson alternative entertainment services that fit his/her preferences. Then it is up to the salesperson to accept such services and have some fun or elect to focus on other activities.

6. CONCLUSION

The paper explored the area of mobile location technologies within salespersons′ work environment. More specifically, the paper discussed potential location-based mobile application and services to support salespersons tasks and linked them to the determinants of salespersons performance. The paper aims at assisting stakeholders including sales managers in understanding the potential added value that mobile location technologies can provide salespersons with and that takes into consideration the nature of their tasks and the determinants of their performance.

It is worth mentioning that mobilizing location-based application and services to support salespersons for greater performance may raise a number of critical issues. One issue associated with the use of location based mobile services and application is the protection of salespersons′ privacy. Salespersons may show a concern about having their location revealed by other parties such as network operator and market research companies. Furthermore, the lack of a unified regulatory body pertaining to location-based application and services may impede the ability of salespersons to benefit form location based support when they are visiting countries that impose regularatory constraints on such applications. Another issue associated with providing salespersons with location based mobile services and applications is the functional deficiency of information overload, where the amount of alerts the salesperson receives extends his or her cognitive capacity (Ljungberg and Sorensen, 2000). For instance if the service provider only knows about the location of the client and not for example the speed and direction in which the user is travelling, the service provider may overload the user with information. This may be the case of a user driving along a motorway and rapidly crossing the borderlines between three locations, and as a consequence being bombarded with notifications from each location (Sorensen et al., 2002).

Finally a subtle but powerful potential inhibitor to the acceptance of location-based application and services by salespersons is the "big brother issue". Big brother issue may rise if salespersons feel that location-based mobile applications services that their company provide them with reduce their freedom on the field and turn their mangers into cops (Falvely, 1994).

As the analysis of the impact of the above issues on both the added value mechanisms and the potential acceptance of location-based mobile application and services by salespersons goes beyond the scope of this paper, future research is needed to address the above-mentioned issues together with the integration of the continuous progress of mobile location technologies with the evolution of salespersons tasks and activities to generate new innovative applications that match their needs and requirements.

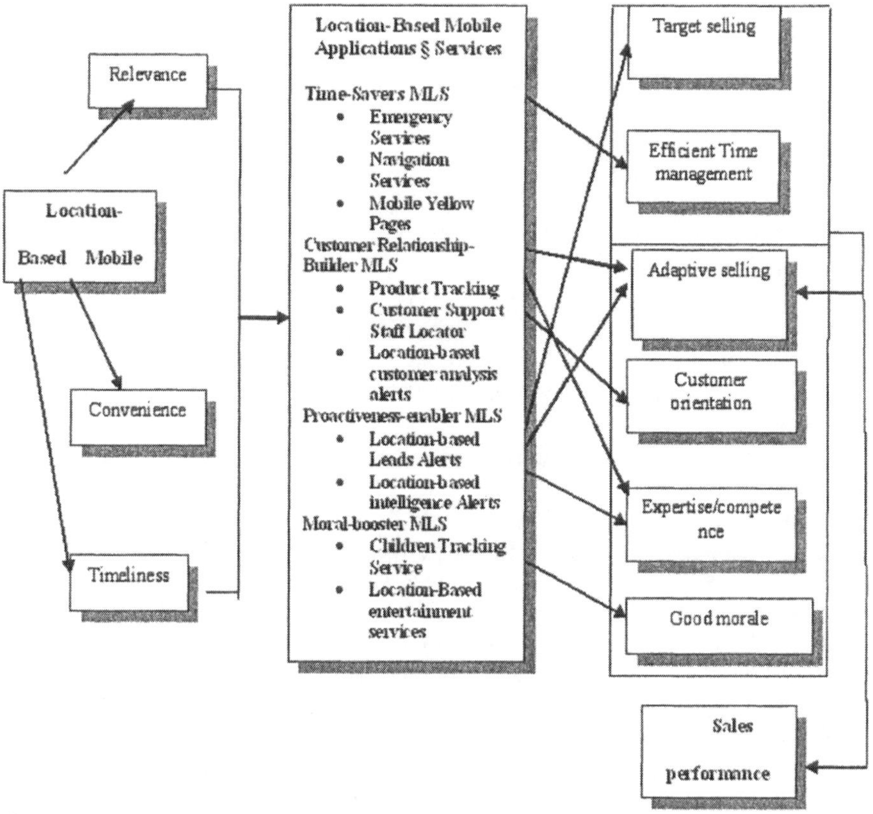

Figure 1. A model linking location-based mobile support to salespersons performance

REFERENCES

Amabile, Teressa (1983). The social Psychology of Creativity: A componential conceptualisation ". Journal of Personality and Social Psychology, 45 (August) 357-376.

Anderson R, (1995). Essential of personal selling: the new professionalism. Prentice Hall, NJ

BenMoussa.C, 2003."Effects of mobile commerce on salespersons performance. The second international conference on m-business.

Behrman D, Perreault W (1984). The role stress model of the performance and satisfaction of industrial salespersons. Journal of marketing. Vol.48 (Fall 1984), 9-12-

Boles, Johnston, Hair (1997). Role Stress, Work-Family Conflict and Emotional Exhaustion: inter-relationships and effects on some work-related situations. Journal of personal selling &sales management. Volume XVII, number 1 (winter 1997, Pages 17-28)

Boles.J, Barksdale.C and Julie.T (1997). Business Relationships: An Examination of The Effects of Buyer-Salespersons relationships on Customer Retention and Willingness to Refer and Recommend. Journal of Business and Industrial Marketing. Vol 12. No, ¾ 1997

Dar. A. (2002). Control and autonomy among Knowledge workers in sales: an employee perspective. Employee relations. Vol. 25. No 1, 2003.

Davenport C (1999). Performance Measures for knowledge management. Knowledge management handbook. Edited by Jay Liebowitz

Davenport T, (1993). Process innovation: Reengineering work through information technology. Harvard business school press. Boston, USA.

Daft R and R.h Lengel (1986) "organizational Information Requirements, Media Richness, and structural design "Management Science 36 (6), 689- 703

Drucker, P. Knowledge-worker productivity: The Biggest challenge", California Management Review 41 (Winter 1999): 79-94.

Dubinsky, Alane J., Roy D. Howell, Thomas N, Ingram, and Danny N.Bellenger (1986)"Salesforce Socialization" Journal of Marketing, 50 (October), 192-207

Jones. E, Sundaram.S and Chine.W (2002). Factors Leading to Sales Force Automation Use: A Longitudinal Analysis. Journal of personnel selling and sales management. Vol XXII, no3. pp 145-156.

Geaglis. G, 2003. Toward a classification framework for mobile location services. Idea Group Publishing.

Kakihara M & Sørensen C. (2002). Mobility: An Extended Perspective. Proceedings of the Hawaii International Conference on System Sciences Big Island, Hawaii, January 7-10.

Girard, K (1998) "Stats not good for sales technology" Computer world 32, 14 (April 6), 29

Good D. J and R.J Schultz (1997) "Technological Teaming as a marketing strategy" Industrial marketing management 26, 5 (September) 413-412

Falvely, Jack 1994, "On Guard", Sales and marketing management, 146 (January) 41

J. L. Funk "Key Technological Trajectories and the Expansion of Mobile Internet Applications" proceeding of Stockholm mobility Roundtable 2003

Kakihara & Sørensen. Post-Modern' Professional Work and Mobile Technology. The 25th Information Systems Research Seminar in Scandinavia. Copenhagen, Denmark.

Keen P.et al, 1991, (2001). The Freedom Economy, Osborne/ McGrew-Hill, USA.

Krestoffersen, s. and lijungberg, F. 1999. Making place to make IT work: Empirical explorations of HCI for Mobile CSCW. In GROUP'99: Proceedings of the International ACM SIGGROUP Conference on Supporting Group Work (Phoenix, AZ, Nov. 14–17), ACM Press, New York, NY, 276–285.

Leijfer, SC (1999) "Bringing Business Intelligence to sale Force Automation" American Salesman, 44, 5 (May) 26-30

May, P, (2001). Mobile Commerce, Cambridge University Press.

McMuurry RN. The mystique of super salesmanship. Harvard business review 1961;113-22 (March-April).

Churchil, G., Ford, N., Hartley, S., Walker, O. (1985), The Determinants of Salesperson Performance:

A Meta-Analysis, Journal of Marketing Research, 12, May, 130-118.

Huber, G. (1990), A Theory of the Effects of Advanced Information Technologies or Organizational

Design, Intelligence, and Decision Making, Academy of Management Review, 15, 1, 47-71.

Paul Markovits (1988), "Direct selling is alive and well", sales and marketing management, August PP 76-79

Kotler, Philip (1994), Marketing Management: Analysis, Planning, Implementation and Control, 8

ed., Prentice Hall, NJ.

Marshall, Greg W., Moncrief, William C. and Felicia G. Lassk (1999), The Current State of Sales

Force Activities, Industrial Marketing Management, 28, 87-98.
Robert F.Vizza and T.E,. Chambers, (1971) Time and Territorial Management for the Salesman, The sales executive club of NewYork), p 97
Ruekert.R and Walker. O (1987). Marketing Interactions With Other Functional Units: A Conceptual Framework and Empirical Evidence. Journal of Marketing Vol. 51.
Rodina,.E, Zeimpekis. V, Fouskas.K, (2003). Remote Workforce Business Process Integration through Real-Time Mobile Communication, the second international conference on mobile business, Vienna 2003.
Thayer Taylor, (1987) " Hewlett- Packard gives sales reps a competitive edge" Sales and marketing management, pp 36-37
Mooney, John G., Gurbaxani, Vijay and Kenneth L. Kraemer (1996), A Process Oriented Framework for Assessing the Business Value of Information Technology, The DATA BASE for Advances in Information Systems, Spring, 27, 2, 68-81.
Peterson, G,S (1997) High impact sales force automation. St Lucie press, Boca Raton Fl
Sager. J, Wilson. P(1995). Clarification of the Meaning of Job Stress In The Context of Sales Force Research. Journal of Personnel Selling and Sales Management.
Shipley. D and Kiley. J (2001). Motivations and Dissatisfaction of Industrial Salespeople-How Relevant is Hertzberg's Theory?. European Journal of Marketing. Vol 22,1.
Sichel, DE, (1997). The computer Revolution, Brookings Institute, New York, NY.
Sorensen C.,Mathiassen. L and Kakihara. M (2002). Mobile Services: Functional diversity and overload. In proceedings of New perspectives on 21st Century communication. Institute for philosophical research of the Hungarian academy science.
Smith H.A, N.Kulatilkay §Vankatraman (2002). "Development in IS practice III: Riding the wave :Extracting value from mobile technology, comments of AIS 8, pp 467-481
Sujan, H., Weitz, B., Kumar, N. (1994), Learning Orientation, Working Smart, and Effective Selling, Journal of Marketing, 58, July, 39-52.
Sujan, H., Weitz, B.A., and M. Sujan (1988), Increasing Sales Productivity by Getting Salespeople to Work Smarter, Journal of Personal Selling and Sales Management, August, 9 19.
Sulek, J., Maruchek, A. (1992), A Study of the Impact of an Integrated Information Technology on the Time Utilization of Information Workers, Decision Sciences, 23, 1174-1191.
Tarasewich,.P, R.Nickerson and M. Warkenten (2002). "Issues in mobile e.commerce", comments of AIS, PP 41-64
Taylor, TC (1993) "Getting in Step with computer age" Sales and marketing managemen, 145, 3 (March), 52-59.
Thetyi, O (2000) "Radical Makeovers: How three companies use strategic planning, Training, and Support to Implement Technology on a Grand Scale" Sales and Marketing Management 152, 4 8April) 78- 88
Weitz, B., Sujan, H, Sujan, M. (1986), Knowledge, Motivation and Adaptive Behavior: A Framework for Improving Selling Effectiveness, Journal of Marketing, 50, 174-191.

SERVICE PROVISIONING

APPLICATION SERVICE PROVISIONING AS A STRATEGIC NETWORK

Evaluation of a Failed ASP Project

Henry Nordström and Markku Sääksjärvi
Helsinki School Of Economics, Department of Management, P.O. Box 1210, FI-00101 Helsinki, Finland

Abstract: In this paper, we analyse Application Service Provisioning (ASP) by means of a framework derived from the strategic network approach presented in the management strategy literature. Our ex-post analysis focuses on a failed ASP project, in which a small software company and a large telecommunications operator formed an alliance in order to launch an innovative ASP software offering in the market. The objective of the paper is to operationalize the new strategic network oriented concepts in order to better understand and manage problems in developing integrated ASP offerings.

Our results from both conceptual and empirical work indicate that several important new issues can be raised if the ASP integration is examined as a strategic network (a kind of software ecosystem). We propose a framework that identifies these factors and test its power to predict success or failure in our case. On the basis of our analyses, we propose practical guidelines to be followed when moving from the management of products and services to the management of an ASP partnership network.

Key words: Application Service Provisioning, Strategic Networks; Evaluation.

1. INTRODUCTION

In the late 1990s, many industry analysts forecasted explosive growth for the Application Service Provider (ASP) market. So far the ASP market has not lived up to these expectations. A recent study on ASPs (Desai and Currie, 2003, pp.177) showed that out of the 424 companies reviewed, 203 have failed, 40 have been acquired and 8 have merged. Only 173 companies out of 424 are surviving. However, there are also ASPs that are doing profitable business. It has been suggested that the ASP industry is following the chasm model (Moore, 1991) and that it is still in the middle of the dividing chasm between the early adopter group and the majority market (Aberdeen Group, 2001).

ITAA and ASPIC have jointly defined ASP as "any company that delivers and manages applications and computer services to subscribers/clients remotely via the Internet or a private network." (ITAA press release, 2001). Some authors argue that the ASP model can be seen as an extension to IT outsourcing (Currie, 2000; Currie & Seltsikas, 2000; Heart & Pliskin, 2001, pp.34). The ASP model has also been compared to the service bureau model that was common in the 1960s and 1970s (Walsh, 2003, pp.103; Kakabadse & Kakabadse, 2002, pp.206; Toigo, 2002, pp.101). Timesharing bears similarity to the ASP model in that applications are hosted centrally at the service provider's site and rented out to a multitude of users. In addition to technological advances, the difference between the ASP model and timesharing is that ASPs offer a one-to-many business model. Technology plays a significant role as an enabler in the ASP model, as the ASP technology platform (infrastructure) is built to sustain a large number of clients, with "any time" access, using high processing power and bandwidth (Kakabadse & Kakabadse, 2002, pp.206).

An application service is an integrated bundle of elements from different domains such as network connectivity, technology platform (hardware, operating system, middleware, etc.), operations (hosting and facilities management), end services (implementation, deployment, customization, integration) and applications. (Apfel, 2000; Legg Mason Wood Walker, 1999; Klemenhagen, 1999; Giotto Perspectives, 1999). Each of these elements requires different sets of skills that are seldom mastered by a single company. Typically the application service provider has to partner with other firms to leverage expertise in all required skill domains (Sharma & Gupta, 2002, pp.164). This tendency is also illustrated by Currie and Seltsikas' ASP ecosystem model (2000, pp.5) that depicts typical partnering arrangements and various stakeholders that comprise the ASP offering. A similar idea is presented in Messerschmitt and Szyperski's (2000, pp. 23) value chain model for the software industry as well as in the ASP value chain model presented by Hoch et al. (2000, pp.6). In the "Software as a Service" strategic backgrounder of Software & Information Industry Association (Hoch et al, 2001), the ASP value chain is proposed to consist of five different expertise areas to be integrated by the provider of the customer service. These are *hardware and operations services*, *infrastructure software development and integration*, *network service providing*, *innovative application development* and *customer service provisioning.* It is evident that successful management and integration of this variety of competencies will need more complex collaboration among firms than before.

Desai and Currie (2003, pp.179) have indicated the need for research on ASP business models. They suggest that the existing research should be extended by doing case studies on ASPs to investigate how the different vendors have structured their business models and why some vendors failed while others succeeded. A relevant basis for sophisticated analyses of ASP business models could be a general model of e-commerce (e.g. Amit and Zott, 2001). Another and a more focused way could be to evaluate ASP cases using strategic network models proposed in the management strategy literature.

1.1 Objective and outline of the paper

In this paper, our aim is to operationalize the concepts and ideas presented by Gulati et al. (2000) in their strategic network model in order to better understand the complex ASP value chain or ASP business ecosystem. Based on this model, we identify a set of key factors that will be used as a tool of inquiry in the case study, covering not only the single companies involved but also important network issues proposed. Our research questions are:

1. What are the new key factors (issues) affecting the ASP-partnership when a strategic network model is applied instead of an single company view? Will these factors help us to better understand the reasons for ASP failures in real life?
2. Which principles can be derived from the network approach for the better management of new ASP offerings?

In the first section above, we have discussed the ASP model as it is presented in the existing literature. In the next section, we will review the strategic network model (Gulati et al, 2000) and generate a research framework for analyzing our case. In the following Section 3, we shortly discuss the methodology used in the case study. Section 4 presents the case study, an innovative collaborative development project between a small software company and a large operator. In Section 5, we analyze the case using the research framework proposed, and finally in Section 6 we discuss our findings and present our conclusions.

2. DEVELOPING A FRAMEWORK FOR ASP EVALUATION

2.1 The Strategic Network Approach

Traditionally, firms have often been seen in the literature as atomistic actors competing for profits against each other in an impersonal marketplace. In this article, we will use the term *atomistic view* to refer to this traditional point of view. Gulati et al. (2000) argue that the conduct and performance of firms can be more fully understood by examining the *network of relationships* in which firms are embedded. Their strategic network model challenges the atomistic view by suggesting that firms are more properly viewed as connected to each other in multiple networks of resources and other flows. These linkages bind them in complex relationships that are simultaneously competitive and cooperative.

2.2 Key Factors Generated from the Strategic Network Model

In order to answer our first research question, we generated a research framework for analysis based on the strategic network model. According to the above-mentioned strategic network model (Gulati et al 2000), the following five issues were identified:

1. Industry structure.
2. Positioning within an industry.
3. Inimitable firm resources and capabilities.
4. Contracting and coordination costs.
5. Dynamic network constraints and benefits.

These five issues are called relationship dimensions in Table 1. For each dimension, we collected from Gulati et al. (2000) a typical set of a few concrete key factors characterising each dimension and being hopefully concrete enough to be applied in an empirical study. These factors, which are mentioned in Table 1, will be applied in our ex-post analysis of the case. After the analyses, we will reduce this theoretical list into a more compact checklist of important issues to be considered when developing a partnership-based ASP service integration.

Table 1. The Five Relationship Dimensions generated from the Strategic Network Model

Relationship Dimensions	Key Factors
A) Industry Structure	- Network structure (density, holes, equivalence) - Network membership (status of industries, limits on firms' entry) - Tie modality (strength of connections, rules and norms, opportunism)
B) Positioning within an industry	- Intra-industry strategic groups or 'cliques' - Positions of the participants (core vs. peripheral) - Mobility barriers
C) Inimitable firm resources and capabilities	- Key resources and capabilities of the participants - Network resources - Capability of managing the alliance and extracting value
D) Contracting and coordination costs	- Motivation of the participants - Available alternatives for the participants - Trust and reputation effects
E) Dynamic network constraints and benefits	- Lock-in and lock-out effects - Alliance portfolios of the participants - Exogenous or endogenous changes in the network

3. RESEARCH METHODOLOGY

The research was conducted using an exploratory single-case study design. Since it is often very hard to get detailed information about failed projects, the case can be seen as an extreme case and as a revelatory case. An embedded approach was used. First, the causes of failure were determined on the basis of interviews of representatives of both companies involved. Then, the sets of key factors presented in Table 1 were considered and a new list of potential causes was developed. Comparing these two outcomes, conclusions were made regarding the important new issues proposed by the network model applied. Finally, a general checklist of important relationship-based issues was built based on the findings.

3.1 Data Collection

According to Yin (1994, p.91), a major strength of case study data collection is the opportunity to use many different sources of evidence. In this case study, three different sources of evidence were used: documents, interviews and participant observation.

The documents included a comprehensive archive of official agendas, presentations and minutes from project team meetings. They also included two co-operation contracts that were signed between the companies. Additionally, the material available to the authors included other unofficial documentation produced by both companies. One of the authors worked as a project manager for the project in the software company for the whole course of the project. During this period, he had participated in dozens of official and unofficial project meetings.

Both authors carried out interviews in the companies. The independent author interviewed in open-ended 2-hour interviews, two representatives of the strategic and development management of Softco to better understand the background history and competencies of the company. The interviews were documented and checked by the interviewees. The other author, on his side, carried out a 2-hour interview of the telecommunications operator's responsible project leader and made a few verifying interviews with the software company's specialists. Also these interviews were documented.

The last phase was the reconstruction of the case according to the factors listed in the five dimensions of our framework and then the compression of these into final recommendations. Both researchers made their evaluations independently, and the outcome is presented as our conclusion.

4. CASE DESCRIPTION: THE DELTA PROJECT

4.1 Background Information of the Participating Companies

SoftCo was established in 1990 as an in-house supplier of IT services for a regional, mid-sized industry corporation. During the first ten years, it concentrated on system integration and IT consultation services. In 2000, SoftCo separated from its parent corporation and bought two smaller companies specializing in Internet-based software. The company wanted to move from the area of traditional IT services into the more lucrative software product business. In 2000, SoftCo had 20 employees and a turnover of about

2 million euros. The company aimed to multiply its turnover during the following three years.

TelCo was a major Scandinavian national telecommunications operator with an aim to become a global player in the market. TelCo had decentralized its operations into several independent business units. In this way TelCo hoped to promote the development of new business models and leverage the convergence of telecommunications and information technology in the form of new products and services. At least two different business units of TelCo were experimenting with new ASP services.

4.2 The Delta Project

The aim of the Delta project was to create an ASP concept targeted at very small companies (typically with 1-10 workstations). The service would cover the most essential business applications that a small enterprise needs. The customer would have access to the service via the Internet for a monthly per-user fee.

In the beginning of the project, the contents of the package were based on the modules that SoftCo had already developed: sales force automation, invoice processing, project management and hour reporting applications. However, the ultimate target was to build a much more comprehensive and tightly integrated package that would cover also i.a. accounting and material management. Two important points were identified when the selected target segment was analysed:

- Because the chosen target segment consists of companies that typically do not have their own IT organization and have limited computer abilities, the service must be very simple to use.
- The target segment is very cost-sensitive, so the service must be aggressively priced. A monthly per-user fee is preferred, as the pricing policy must be easy to comprehend.

The customers would only need a web browser to use the applications. The service should perform well even with modest communication lines (modem or ISDN). The software would have to utilize the hardware resources effectively: one server should be able to serve hundreds of simultaneous users. Because of these requirements, the project team ruled out the possibility of using streaming technologies such as Citrix Metaframe. The opinion of the project team was that streaming technologies waste considerable amounts of both server and communications capacity compared with well-constructed web-native solutions. Because of the cost-effectiveness requirement, it was also decided that the process of adding a new customer to the system should be partly automated and not take longer than 15 minutes. This caused strict requirements for the administration processes and tools.

The project aimed at cost-effectiveness through high customer volumes. Even with aggressive pricing, the service would be very profitable if there were enough users. The idea was to deliver the service to thousands of users from one standardized environment. The software would not be customized at all for individual customers.

4.3 The Onset of the Project

Because SoftCo was developing browser-based software that could be delivered over the Internet, they identified ASP as a possible business model for reaching their expected growth rates. The alternative of partnering with a company that already had an extensive sales force seemed inviting. Telecom operators seemed a good choice for a partner because of their experience in producing and selling high-volume network services and also because of their administrative infrastructure regarding, e.g., small customer invoicing. SoftCo also thought that the strong brands and the massive customer bases of the telecommunications operators would help in reaching high volumes of sales for the service.

In early 2001, SoftCo found out that TelCo - one of the biggest operators in the region - had a suitable project going on. The project team had already invested in the required service infrastructure consisting of server hardware and middleware applications. They had experimented with simple application solutions such as web-based email and calendar services. Now they were looking for more serious business applications. After a few meetings and demonstrations, the teams decided to establish an alliance for the project.

The software developed by SoftCo seemed to fit the architecture in which TelCo had invested. The applications were written in Java, and standard SQL was used for database support. However, the software modules that SoftCo had developed were not integrated with each other. It was then decided that the applications must be integrated on both database level and user interface level so that they would appear to the user as different parts of a single application.

4.4 Responsibilities Between the Parties

TelCo agreed to take responsibility for the hosting infrastructure, marketing and sales operations, customer invoicing and primary customer support. SoftCo would be responsible for developing the new software as well as taking care of secondary customer support, in other words problem situations caused by the software. Both parties would be operating at their own risk. Revenues from the new service would be divided on a 50/50 basis among the parties.

4.5 The Development Project

A cooperation agreement was signed between the companies in August 2001. Thus the work commenced in SoftCo regarding both integrating the existing pieces of stand-alone software into each other and adapting the software to the platform of TelCo. A pilot installation with two of the applications running in TelCo's environment was completed in September 2001. It soon turned out that the integration task was much more demanding than initially foreseen. Nevertheless, the teams were getting along very well and their cooperation seemed almost seamless.

In early 2002, with the first phase of the project still underway, the companies started planning the next phase of the project. This new phase would include more features, including financial package functionalities. The idea was to have accounting companies integrate Delta into their own services and thus act as a sales channel for the software. The customers would use Delta for processing their sales and purchase invoices, but the accounting company would do the actual accounting. At that time, the target was set to have the first phase of the project completed and released into production by the summer.

4.6 Preparing for Production

After several re-schedulings, the first phase of the project was finally completed six months late from schedule. SoftCo's time estimate regarding the integration of the stand-alone applications turned out to be overoptimistic. The delay was increased by problems in the J2EE application server environment of TelCo. Some of the features of the application server (among others, session management and proxy features) did not fully conform to J2EE standards. This non-conformance had to be circumvented by writing lots of additional code.

In November 2002, the system was finally ready for production. By that time, more than 120,000 lines of new code had been written. According to one estimate made by an external consultant based on the COCOMO-model (Pressman, 2000, pp.135), this would represent 34 person-years of development. After a rigorous testing procedure, TelCo confirmed that the system was robust and scalable enough to accommodate hundreds of simultaneous users from a single server. The first meetings between SoftCo and the sales organization of TelCo were held in October. Although the sales organization wanted some time to get things up and running, both teams believed that the following year would be a breakthrough for Delta.

4.7 The End

In late 2002, TelCo was going through major changes in its organization. TelCo's representatives initially convinced SoftCo that the Delta project would actually benefit from the new situation. However, in a project managerial team meeting that was held in January 2003, TelCo announced that the situation in the company had changed dramatically. The company would retire from all its ASP activities, including the Delta project. TelCo explained that this was because the corporation as a whole had decided to withdraw from all projects that did not belong to its strategic focus area and had negative cashflow.

4.8 The Aftermath

For SoftCo, the premature ending of the project had a shocking effect. For more than a year, almost half of the personnel in the company had been allocated to the Delta project. The turnover of the company was considerably lower as there was no invoicing for the work done in this project. All the expectations had been placed on the future, as SoftCo expected that sales of Delta would start in 2003. SoftCo was forced to refocus its operations. Luckily, the company was financially solid. It had not completely abandoned the integration and consultation services, which became once again their focal business. In early 2003, SoftCo signed a channel partner contract with one of the leading global Enterprise Resource Planning software companies. The intellectual rights for the software created in the Delta project were owned by SoftCo, but it decided not to market this software via the ASP channel on their own. Instead, some of the applications found a new life as add-on products for the ERP system. In 2003, SoftCo sued TelCo for breach of contract. The legal proceedings ended one year later as SoftCo won the case against TelCo.

According to its new, curtailed strategy, TelCo has returned to its roots as a telecommunications operator. TelCo's project team was quickly disassembled: some of the employees were relocated internally, others left TelCo.

5. ANALYSIS OF THE CASE

5.1 Single Company (Atomistic) View

SoftCo seemed to select a really high-risk approach in the Delta project as it devoted the major part of the software development resources to this single project, especially as the first income would have been their part of the revenue generated. Before this revenue could be collected, the partners would have to complete the development project, get the online service up and running as well as find the customers for the service. However, should the planned ASP approach have succeeded, this new business area would have become very profitable for SoftCo. For TelCo, both the risk level and the expected rewards were much less significant compared with the size of the company.

Regarding the delays in the project schedule, SoftCo seemed not to have sufficient resources to complete the project on time. The management should have understood the disparity between the schedule and the amount of work, on the one hand, and their existing development resources, on the other. While SoftCo had experience in developing professional tailor-made software, it had no previous track record in developing standardized software packages. However, the software system was eventually shipped and approved by TelCo for production use before it withdrew from the project. Thus the delay as such cannot be taken as the main explanation for the failure.

The functionality of the application software was not selected on the basis of any kind of market research or other reliable indication of the actual customer needs. Rather, the applications were selected because they happened to be there. It seems that a major weakness in the execution of the project was that the companies were developing the product without having any 'real' end customer representative of the target market participate in the project.

When a project fails, it is not uncommon for the participants to start blaming each other for the failure. Quite as often, the participants fail to see that maybe they themselves could have done some critical activities better. Project Delta was no exception. After being sued by SoftCo for breach of contract, TelCo claimed that SoftCo had miserably and maybe intentionally failed in fulfilling their part of the contract. SoftCo's managing director was equally bitter:

> "The TelCo guys were constantly adding new features to the requirement catalogue while demanding us to keep the previously agreed schedule. Their testing procedure was so scrupulous that probably none of the

shrink-wrapped software products in the market would have passed those tests. What comes to the marketing efforts they promised us, we never saw anything realized."

5.2 Case Analysis Based on the Research Framework

a) *Network structure.* In fact, there was no structural equivalence in this mainly bilateral partnership. One of the partners (TelCo) was clearly the real core company, having the possibility to establish and maintain similar partnerships with other software developers. TelCo had several other partnerships that did not help SoftCo at all. SoftCo was in the position of an almost peripheral company, and had believed too much in the core company's market brand and competency in marketing. Unintentionally, the network was missing a key member: the customer for the new software. Regarding the tie modality, obviously the strength of the coalition was not the best possible as the partners were in an opportunistic relationship and could not benefit from their earlier interactions with their existing industry partners. These had been very important for SoftCo's earlier success as a business software application developer in its special industry domain. Also, the set of working rules and norms were very different as TelCo and SoftCo represented two different cultures, software innovator versus technical operator.

b) *Positioning within an industry.* Obviously, there was an asymmetry in the positions of the partners, with TelCo being the owner of the delivery infrastructure, administrative routines, and key customer contacts. On the other hand, TelCo was entering into new competition with large global players; this was a very new situation for a well-doing technology company. Even in the home market, there was another similar new coalition (strategic group) establishing ASP services.

c) *Inimitable firm resources and capabilities.* SoftCo's traditional key expertise areas had focused on delivery of professional software development and IT maintenance services, mostly for companies in a certain special industry, based on a business-to-business relation. SoftCo was unable to leverage this industrial knowledge in the Delta project, because the focus changed from customer service into mass products. This area was completely new for SoftCo. Mass production of even simple and small software packages is very different from the service and consultation business. In the ASP service business, there are elements that are closer to the consumer business rather than the B2B business. This was not well understood by either of the companies, and there were no investments into knowledge transfer and development of common knowledge of the partners. The benefits from the partnership were in fact not synergetic enough. On the other hand, TelCo had no expertise in selling software. Its large customer base could not be benefited from as the main focus of the new software, small enterprises and their business applications, was outside the earlier focus of TelCo.

d) *Contracting and coordination costs.* It is well known that in the case of innovative software development, the transaction costs may be very high and therefore, a hierarchical ownership-based control is required. In a partnership arrangement, hierarchical control of the other innovation partner is not possible: it will easily spoil the trust. It is very likely that extra costs were caused by TelCo, and this may have resulted in a negative incentive for both partners. Despite of the different backgrounds of the teams and the short history of Delta, the local social networks between the development teams of Telco and SoftCo were working in a feasible way. The problem was that at the executive level of TelCo management, there was no real trust in this cooperation. The contractual formalities (compensations and penalties) had been left open and therefore, the parties could not seriously solve problems as soon as they occurred.

e) *Dynamic network constraints and benefits.* Typically, lock-in and lock-out effects are the most important factors affecting the shaping of the strategic networks in the longer run. Because of the evolving stage of development, nothing serious can be said about the lock-in effects in the Delta case. However, from the ex-post perspective it was not very smart from SoftCo (and probably from the whole partnership point of view) to sign an exclusive alliance with TelCo. A sub-coalition approach to develop an integrated software package as fast as possible might have been a better strategy.

The above analysis according to our framework revealed several viewpoints that could – and should – have been taken into account before the alliance contract was signed. Most of the five dimensions (especially a and c) were relevant to produce concrete factors that could have reduced the risk associated if taken seriously into account before signing the alliance. We think that both partners of our Delta case were not sufficiently aware of the new complexities involved in the integration process required to offer online ASP software services. The complexities seemed to be caused partially by the new ASP offering itself (integration of software development, operations, and customer service businesses), partially because of the more complex management of the network arrangement required to integrate the competencies needed. Many of the factors listed seem to be potential general success factors in any business based on ASP integration. Therefore, in the final section we will summarise our experience with the case study into a more general evaluation of a few key management issues for building ASP services.

5.3 Limitations of the Study

The selection of the case was based on the exceptional access that the authors had to the data. The fact that one of the authors was in a central position in the project being studied and is at the time of this writing employed by the company that participated in the project may have caused some bias of his view. This was eliminated from the results by our arrangement in which both authors as independent researchers generated their lists of factors on the basis of the research framework.

The issue of construct validity was addressed by triangulation of data sources: multiple sources of evidence were used to provide multiple measures of the same phenomenon (Yin 1994, pp.92). To improve the reliability of the study, the material collected for the study was stored in a study archive.

6. DISCUSSION AND CONCLUSIONS

The ASP literature suggests that a multitude of different technologies and competencies are required in order to integrate successful ASP offerings. The more recent proposal to turn the ASP concept into "Software as a Service" (Hoch et al, 2001) makes it even more clear that successful management of online applications from one single point and as online transaction services to mass customers can only be based on a specific network structure (or software ecosystem) where the palette of all required competencies are economically available. Therefore, the tendency to form alliances and strategic networks in the ASP industry is clear. The networked nature of the ASP industry makes it an interesting candidate for being studied through a network-theoretical lens.

In our particular case, the new insights and evaluation factors drawn from the general strategic network model turned out to be useful and opened important new perspectives on the ASP market. The five dimensions proposed and the prototypal factors generated accordingly as predictors of success or failure offered interesting and useful concepts not only to objectively evaluate the potential problems caused, but also to better plan and manage any ASP ecosystem.

On the basis of the literature review and our framework we propose that companies planning establish ASP services should learn from the strategic network issues discussed. In addition to management of both product and service, it is important to pay attention to the management of the network of competent partners. This will require design of incentives that work, creation of effective governance mechanisms, investments in the development of knowledge sharing routines, and formal contracting and other lock-in mechanisms for crisis situations. Finally, attention should be paid to the generation of customer value and to the role of the customer as an important member of the network.

REFERENCES

Aberdeen Group (2001). The Evolving CRM-ASP Model – An Executive White Paper. Aberdeen Group, Inc; http://www.salesforce.com/us/pdf/analysts/aberdeen-010301.pdf

Amit, R. and Zott, C. (2001). Value Creation in E-Business, Strategic Management Journal, Vol. 22, pp. 493-520 (2001).

Apfel, A (2000). *ASP Six-Layer Model.* Research Note. Gartner Group RAS Services, 6.November, 2000; http://archive.quadratic.net/docs/ASP6LayerModel_00093846.pdf

Currie, W.L (2000). *Expanding IS Outsourcing Services Through Application Service Providers.* 8th European Conference on Information Systems, Vienna, Austria, 3-5 July

Currie, W.L & Seltsikas, P. (2000). *Evaluating the Application Service Provider (ASP) Business Model.* Centre for Strategic Information Systems Executive Publication Series CSIS 2000/004.

Desai, B. and Currie, W. (2003). *Application Service Providers: A model in Evolution.* 5th International Conference on Electronic Commerce(ICEC), Pittsburgh, PA Sept 30 - Oct 3 2003, pp174-180.

Giotto Perspectives (1999). *How ASPs deliver Value: Next-Generation Portals for Business Applications.* In ASP – Application Service Providing – The Ultimate Guide to Hiring Rather than Buying Applications. Friedrich Vieweg & Sohn Verlagsgesellschaft mbH., pp. 233-240; http://www.giotto.nu/services/samples/citrix_E9.pdf

Gulati, R., N. Nohria, N. and Zaheer, A. (2000). *Strategic Networks*, Strategic Management Journal, Vol.21 No.3, pp. 203-215; http://www.ranjaygulati.com/new/research/stratnet.pdf

Heart, T. and Pliskin, N. (2001). *Is e-Commerce of Application Services (ASP) Alive and Well?* Journal of Information Technology Theory and Application, Vol.3 No.4

Hoch, F. et al. (2001). *Software as a Service: Strategic Backgrounder.* Software & Information Industry Association, 2001.

ITAA (2001). ITAA, ASPIC *Collaborate on Joint Defintion of ASP.* ITAA Press Release May 22, 2001; http://www.itaa.org/news/pr/PressRelease.cfm?ReleaseID=990568087

Kakabadse, A. & Kakabadse, N. (2002). *Application Service Providers (ASPs): New Impetus for Transformational Change.* Knowledge and Process Management, Vol.9 No.4, pp.205-218.

Klemenhagen, B. (1999). *Application Service Providers (ASP) Spotlight Report.* Cherry Tree & Co; http://www.webharbor.com/download/ct_whppr.pdf

Legg Mason Wood Walker, Inc. (1999). *Application Hosting Market.* In ASP – Application Service Providing – The Ultimate Guide to Hiring Rather than Buying Applications. Friedrich Vieweg & Sohn Verlagsgesellschaft mbH. pp. 93-106.

Messerschmitt, D.G. and Szyperski, C. (2000). *Industrial and Economic Properties of Software – Technology, Processes and Value*; http://www.eecs.berkeley.edu/~messer/PAPERS/01/Software-econ/

Moore, G. (1991). *Crossing the Chasm - Marketing and Selling Technology Products to Mainstream Customers.* Harper Collins Publishers Inc.

Pressman, R.S.(2000). *Software Engineering - A Practitioner's Approach.* Fifth Edition. McGraw-Hill Publishing Company.

Sharma, S.K. and Gupta, J.N.D. (2002). *Application Service Providers: Issues and Challenges.* Logistics Information Management Vol.15 No.3, pp.160-169.

Toigo, J.W. (2002). *The Essential Guide to Application Service Providers.* Prentice Hall PTR.

Walsh, K.R. (2003). *Analyzing the Application ASP Concept: Technologies, Economies, and Strategies.* Communications of the ACM, August 2003/Vol.46 No.8

Yin, R.K. (1994). *Case Study Research - Design and methods.* SAGE Publications, Inc.

ELECTRONIC TRANSMISSION OF PRESCRIPTIONS

An Evaluation of the Technical Models Used in the English ETP Pilots 2002

Bob Sugden[1] and Rob Wilson[2]

[1]Centre for Software Reliability, School of Computing Science, University of Newcastle 11th Floor, Claremont Tower, Newcastle upon Tyne, NE1 7RU, UK, +44 191 222 8007, Bob.Sugden@ncl.ac.uk; [2]Centre for Social and Business Informatics, Institute of Policy and Practice, University of Newcastle, Claremont Bridge, Newcastle upon Tyne NE1 7RU, UK, +44 191 222 5502, Rob.Wilson@ncl.ac.uk

Abstract: This paper reflects on the evaluation of three different technical models of ETP piloted in England in 2002. ETP architectures, message sets, message content, message volume, security and privacy issues, functionality, integration with local legacy systems, and usability were examined. The authors conclude that the technical implementation may be the lesser of the problems confronting successful adoption of such systems, with the critical success factors more closely related to the ways in which ETP models are instantiated in local systems used by prescribers and pharmacists, and their consequent impact on the business practices of those users. Other barriers to successful adoption of ETP were observed, including the requirement for changes in legislation to facilitate electronic communication with digital signatures, and the need to gain patient consent to use of ETP.

Key words: Electronic Transmission of Prescriptions (ETP), Integrated Care Record Service (ICRS), Electronic Health Record (EHR), B2B, B2C, G2B, G2C, Electronic Services for Citizens and Enterprises, Inter-organizational Systems, Informatics Evaluation

1. INTRODUCTION

The development of a system of Electronic Transmission of Prescriptions (ETP) in England is closely related to key strands of UK Government policy in the National Health Service (NHS), described in *Delivering 21st Century IT Support for the NHS*[i] and *Pharmacy in the Future*[ii], which will be supported by the NHS National Programme for IT (NPfIT). It is expected that, as well as being more convenient for the patient, ETP will improve safety by reducing prescription errors and providing better information at the point of prescribing. It will also ensure that prescription information forms part of each citizen's NHS Care Record.

In addition, ETP is expected to deliver important administrative improvements[iii]. Current arrangements require prescription data to be manually entered into different systems on three separate occasions: by the prescriber, the pharmacy, and the Prescription Pricing Authority (PPA). With ETP in place, data will only need to be entered once and then passed between the collaborating systems. With over 624 million prescription items issued in 2002-3 and volumes growing by around four to five and a half per cent annually, ETP is seen as essential to meet increased demand whilst saving staff time and costs.

The overall objective is to implement a National Electronic Prescriptions Service by 2005 for 50 per cent of transactions, with full implementation by 2007. In 2001 the Department of Health (DH) commissioned three ETP pilots in different areas of England, covering acute and repeat prescribing by General Practitioners (GPs), but excluding repeat dispensing, nurse prescribing, dispensing doctors, community dentist prescribing, or the prescribing of controlled drugs. They commenced operation in mid-2002 and were closed in June 2003. The pilots were financed and implemented by private sector consortia: *Flexiscript*, *Pharmacy2U*, and *TransScript*[iv].

Each pilot offered a different ETP business process model, using a different technical approach. The intention was to explore the technical effectiveness of each model, to develop technical standards for implementation and associated electronic messages, to explore the socio-technical context of ETP, and to assess the change management issues inherent in introducing ETP.

To this end, a formative evaluation exercise was commissioned to run in tandem with the pilots, the key findings of which are summarised in a report to DH[v]. The purpose of this paper is to discuss the technical issues which emerged as key factors in the ETP pilots, and the implications for development of a single implementation model; other themes of the evaluation are not reported here except where they were observed to be a direct consequence of technical factors. A description of the evaluation framework and process, together with a summary of the business process and change management issues observed, is to be published in the UK Journal of Health Informatics[vi].

Table 1 shows the topics covered by the evaluation. The issues discussed in this paper are in plain font; other issues addressed in the evaluation are in italic font.

Table 1. Evaluation topics addressed

Topic	Scope
1 Dependability of communication	Reliability, availability, speed, security and safety of ETP architecture, messages and systems
2 Content of information	Clarity and persistence of information passing between systems *Errors, irregularities and changes to risks of fraud*
3 Changes in processes of communication	GP practice procedures for ordering, checking, authorising, producing, and collecting prescriptions *Pharmacy receiving, checking, dispensing and endorsing prescriptions* *Potential change in PPA procedures for assessing and paying dispensing claims for prescriptions* *Ways that patients and carers order and collect their prescriptions* *Changes in advice given to patients and carers* *Changes in communications between stakeholders*
4 Service and quality of care	*Patient satisfaction with ETP service including convenience and willingness to participate* *Pharmacy and GP practice assessment of ETP service and quality*
5 Workload and work practices of stakeholders	*Potential change to PPA workload and work practices* *Change to pharmacy workload and work practices* *Change to GP practice workload and work practices*
6 Stakeholders attitudes to ETP and beliefs about ETP	*Attitudes and beliefs of GPs, GP practice managers, and administrators* *Attitudes and beliefs of pharmacy staff* *Attitudes and beliefs of patients and carers*
7 Use of ETP	*Barriers and drivers for use of ETP* Usability and functionality of the pilot ETP systems System 'work around' strategies employed by users *Training and education issues*
8 Implications for roll-out	*NHS strategy and policy issues* *Analysis of the costs involved with aspects of ETP* *Legal and regulatory issues* *Ethical and professional practice issues* *Patient confidentiality and recruitment issues* Most appropriate technical and infrastructure (including network and security analysis) Most appropriate message design (including standard and solution-specific/proprietary messages) Most appropriate public key and digital signature infrastructure (including analysis of potential future technical developments) *Barriers and drivers for national implementation*

Prior to this evaluation, there has been little published research worldwide on experience of the implementation of ETP. Although there is a considerable body of literature on electronic prescribing (in excess of 90 articles were identified during a literature review), few of these actually refer to a process by which prescriptions are transmitted electronically from GP practice to pharmacy, and none to any subsequent transmission to an equivalent body to the NHS Prescription Pricing Authority (PPA). The majority of UK literature on this topic has not been published in peer-reviewed journals but has been undertaken by market research companies for an organisation contracted to deliver one of the ETP pilots. Studies of ETP implementation in Denmark suggest that ETP confers benefits for GPs, pharmacists, and patients[vii viii], whilst studies from the USA have explored technical issues with a view to future implementation of ETP[ix x].

2. THE ETP MODELS

Whilst there are many differences in the technical approaches adopted by the three consortia, it should also be recognised that the architectures adopted in the pilots are not the only ones possible. Two of the pilots used a point-to-point connection between GP and pharmacy, whilst the third used a centralised messaging service ('relay' model) where the pharmacy called down the prescriptions when dispensing was requested by the patient.

The data flows in prescribing between GP, patient, pharmacy and the PPA are shown in figure 1. The minimum flows include GP to pharmacy and pharmacy to PPA (data flow Y), mirroring the flow of the current paper-based system. In addition there are two other possible flows between GP and pharmacy: query resolution between the pharmacy and the GP (data flow 'β'), and confirmation of dispensing to the GP (data flow Z). For the pilots, a copy of all prescribing messages (known as the '*gold script*') was forwarded to the PPA directly from the GP practice. All three pilots facilitated electronic claims for payment by sending 'endorsed' prescription messages from the pharmacy to the PPA, and messages could also be sent from the PPA to the pharmacy if any claims for payment were rejected.

A paper form signed by the patient was required for initial registration for any of the ETP services. Similarly, in accordance with current legislation, the patient (or patient's representative) was required to sign to verify prescription charge exemption status if appropriate (either a paper copy of the prescription, or a special-purpose 'exemption declaration form, depending on the pilot).

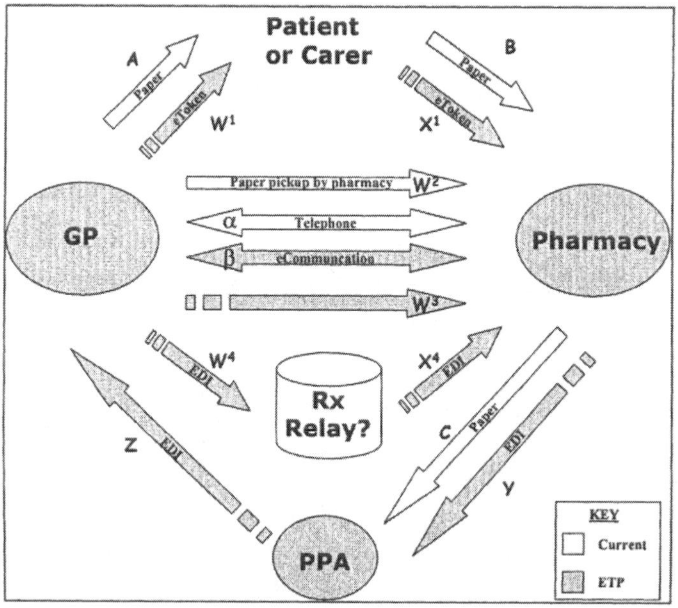

Figure 1. Current and ETP Prescribing and Dispensing Process Messaging

Table 2. Explanation of data flows depicted in Figure 1

Flow	*Description*
A	Paper FP10 prescription form (GP to patient)
B	Paper FP10 prescription form (patient to pharmacy)
C	Paper FP10 prescription form with pharmacy endorsements and exemption status information (pharmacy to PPA: used as claim for payment)
W^2	Prescription collection service (GP to pharmacy)
W^1	Information flow analogous to 'A' with prescription information or method of accessing prescription information using a token (e.g. bar-coded FP10) (GP to patient)
X^1	Information flown analogous to 'B' with prescription information or method of accessing prescription information using a token (e.g. bar-coded FP10) (Patient to pharmacy)
α	Telephone communication (between GP and pharmacy)
β	Electronic communication (between GP and pharmacy)
W^3	Electronic prescription (GP to nominated pharmacy)
W^4	Electronic prescription (GP to relay)
X^4	Electronic prescription (forwarded by relay to nominated pharmacy or called down by pharmacy)
Y	Information flow analogous to 'C' or paired with 'C' (prescription with pharmacy endorsements and exemption status information (pharmacy to PPA: used as claim for payment)
Z	Confirmation of dispensing (primary compliance feedback) from PPA to GP

The term 'acute prescription' is used in this paper to describe those for which it is not anticipated there will be a repeat request, and also those that initiate medication for which a repeat prescription is possible. Repeat prescriptions are usually requested by patients using the practice administration staff as an intermediary, but can also be made via a pharmacy 'prescription collection service', or direct to the GP in a face-to-face consultation.

2.1 Pharmacy2U

This model uses point-to-point messaging between GP practice and pharmacy to replicate the existing processes for acute and repeat prescribing.

For acute prescribing a prescription message is sent from the GP direct to the pharmacy. For a repeat prescription request made directly to the GP, the GP initiates a prescription message to the pharmacy. For a repeat prescription request via GP practice reception, administration staff generate a repeat prescription which is sent to the GP for approval, who then either applies a digital signature for authorisation and forwards the message to the pharmacy, or rejects the request. Where a repeat prescription is requested via a pharmacy the pharmacy sends a request message to the GP practice. The GP can then generate a digitally signed prescription message to the pharmacy in response, or a message to communicate any reason for rejecting the request.

As the prescribe message is received in the absence of the patient, the pharmacy can pre-dispense medication before the patient arrives to collect it. When collecting the prescription items, the patient is identified verbally, in line with current practice where prescription collection services are used. With the current paper system, it is estimated that up to 20% of all prescriptions are never presented by patients for dispensing, and automatic direction in this way may lead to an increase in the proportion of prescriptions actually dispensed. Note that the pharmacy should not claim for dispensing unless the patient actually collects the prescribed items, even though the pharmacy has automatically received the prescription and may have dispensed the items in anticipation of collection.

Patient registration for the service is initiated at the pharmacy, which then sends a registration message to the GP practice, with the practice system returning an acknowledgement. De-registration is initiated at the GP practice, which then sends a message to the pharmacy. Patient feedback indicated that they liked the ability to de-register or change their preferred pharmacy at the GP practice rather than at the pharmacy.

In this model, 'current medication' information is sent with every prescription message, and also with the initial registration confirmation message. This facilitates intervention by the pharmacist, e.g. drug interaction checking; reminders to the patient of repeat medication they may need. A unique mail-order home delivery service was operated by one of the pharmacies involved in this pilot (confusingly named 'Pharmacy2U Ltd'). This service also telephoned patients (with their prior permission) to remind them to request repeat prescriptions. This feature was well-liked by those patients who took advantage of the mail-order service.

2.2 TransScript

This model also uses point-to-point messaging between GP practice and pharmacy to replicate the existing process for repeat prescribing. For acute prescribing, the GP issues a bar-coded paper prescription form to the patient to carry the prescribing information to the pharmacy, rather than an electronic message. The use of a bar-coded acute prescription allows the patient complete flexibility in choice of pharmacy, and as the information is also in printed form, a non-ETP pharmacy can also be used. For the patient, there is no difference from the current paper system for acute prescriptions. For repeat prescriptions the prescribing, dispensing and collection processes are similar to those for *Pharmacy2U.*

Patient registration for the service is initiated at the pharmacy, which then sends a registration message to the GP practice, with the practice system returning an acknowledgement. De-registration is initiated either at the GP practice or pharmacy, initiating a message to the other party informing them of de-registration.

2.3 Flexiscript

This model uses a centralised messaging service or 'relay' between GP practice and pharmacy to replicate the existing processes for acute and repeat prescribing. Communication between GP practices and the PPA, and between pharmacies and the PPA, was by point-to-point messaging.

For acute prescribing a prescription message is sent from the GP to the relay. A bar-coded paper prescription is also printed and issued to the patient with a Unique Prescription Identifier (UPN). The patient takes the printed prescription (as a token of identification) to the pharmacy, which then connects to the relay and requests the prescription details electronically using the UPN.

For a repeat prescription request made directly to the GP, the process is as for acute prescriptions. For a repeat prescription request via GP practice reception, administration staff generate a repeat prescription which is sent to the GP for approval, who then either applies a digital signature for authorisation and forwards the message to the relay, or rejects the request. A bar-coded paper prescription with UPN is also printed and collected by the patient or passed on their behalf to a pharmacy of their choice.

Where a repeat prescription is requested via a pharmacy the pharmacy sends a request message to the GP practice, via the relay. The GP can then generate a digitally signed prescription message to the relay in response, or a message to communicate any reason for rejecting the request. A bar-coded paper prescription is also printed and collected by the patient or collected on their behalf by the pharmacy. If the pharmacy collects the prescription, it can then contact the relay and dispense the medication prior to collection by the patient.

The use of a relay allows the patient flexibility in final choice of pharmacy for both acute and repeat prescriptions, and as the bar-coded prescription information is also in printed form, a non-ETP pharmacy can also be used. The prescribe message is received only when the patient contacts the pharmacy, so the pharmacy can only pre-dispense medication if the patient has contacted them prior to collection. This can be done by telephoning the pharmacy and quoting the UPN to allow the pharmacy to access the prescription information.

Patient registration for the service is initiated at the pharmacy, which then sends a registration message to the relay, for which an acknowledgment is returned. When a GP practice connects to the service, a list of all current ETP-registered patients for that practice is downloaded to the practice system. De-registration is also initiated at the pharmacy, which then sends a message to the relay, for which an acknowledgment is returned.

In this model, 'current medication' information is sent to the relay with every prescription message, and also with the initial registration confirmation message. This could be retained on the relay to form the basis of an electronic health record, although for the purposes of this evaluation this feature was not implemented.

3. EVALUATION FINDINGS

As noted above, this paper describes the technical issues which emerged as key factors in the evaluation; other themes are not reported here except where they are observed to be a consequence of technical factors.

3.1 Implementation and Trends in Use

The pilots demonstrated that ETP is technically viable, and all three consortia successfully implemented ETP based on three different models and using three different message sets, all of which eventually operated as expected. Many of the performance and usability shortcomings identified appeared to be caused by system designs which conflicted with existing user business processes, or were poorly integrated with existing local systems. The consortia identified and overcame a number of these problems before closure of the pilots. For the majority of GP practice and pharmacy systems ETP was implemented on existing hardware, with bar-code readers and suitable printers being added where required. In all systems, software changes were required to support ETP.

When the evaluation was designed it was anticipated that observation and data collection would take place over a period of six months of live processing in the three pilots, and that during this time there would be at least 100,000 electronic prescribe/dispense messages. Initial methods used to recruit patients resulted in a very slow take up of ETP, and additional recruitment methods were eventually employed to increase the numbers of patients using ETP. Specific constraints on functionality were imposed by the Department of Health for policy reasons, which required some re-engineering of the initial models developed by the consortia. This had to be taken into account when evaluating certain aspects of the pilots.

Final commissioning of the pilots was also delayed by problems encountered during a rigorous programme of technical testing for each site connected, devised by the PPA. The volume of messages was therefore lower than expected, although in the last two months of 2002 it reached significant figures (an aggregate of nearly 15,000 dispensed prescriptions from 34 GP practices and 23 pharmacies) and continued this upward trend in the early part of 2003, after the evaluation had ended.

It is estimated that by 2007 NHSNet (and its successor, N3) could need an additional annual capacity of up to 193TB (Terabytes) to carry sufficient message traffic to support 100% of all prescriptions issued. Between 26TB & 61TB could be required in 2005 to support transmission of 50% of prescriptions, depending on the architecture employed. Although there may be some advantages in adopting a 'relay' approach to message forwarding, this could as a consequence generate more message traffic. A compression algorithm for messages could be implemented, and should that be specific to ETP messages, could also offer additional security.

3.2 System Architectures

Of the three architectures implemented, the 'relay server' architecture is the most technically complex, although on the other hand it offers a more flexible service to patients. The relay implemented by *Flexiscript* is an 'unknowing' or 'un-trusted' relay, which was a constraint imposed by the Department of Health. This required additional encryption with a consequent impact on data volumes due to increased message sizes.

Implementing a 'trusted' relay with closer integration between the relay and the PPA would remove the need for the 'gold script' original copy of the prescription message which is matched with the dispense claim message from the pharmacy, and thus reduce data volumes and the number of messages required.

Closer integration between a relay and the PPA would also facilitate additional functionality such as checking prescription charge exemption status, information on which is held on PPA systems. This could remove the need for a patient signature to declare exemption status, and would facilitate a further reduction in the amount of manual processing at the PPA. Automated exemption status checks could also be implemented through dialogue between pharmacy and PPA systems.

A hybrid model could be envisaged, whereby the majority of prescriptions could be 'pushed' immediately to a pre-determined pharmacy, with the remainder held in a 'relay' server awaiting a pharmacy request to 'pull' it down on behalf of a patient. It has been estimated that 'push' would accommodate 70% of all prescriptions without difficulty, with 10% of patients requesting a deferred decision on choice of pharmacy. The remaining 20% of prescriptions would continue to require use of the existing paper forms for various reasons until policy, legislation and practice are changed to facilitate extended use of ETP, including mobile use.

3.3 Electronic Messaging

A standard message set was designed by an independent group prior to pilot implementation. In practice this did not fully support the pilot implementations. Some additions to the message set were required to support the full scope of the ETP business process, and some amendments were proposed as a more complete understanding of the business processes emerged from the evaluation.

For example, an addition to the message set was required to enable a GP to inform a pharmacy that a repeat prescription request made by a patient via the pharmacy had been refused. Another proposed amendment arising from observation that the actual process of repeat prescribing is more complex than envisioned in the original message set design is where the prescriber handling a repeat request is not necessarily the prescriber that authorised the previous issue of the medication. Also administration personnel are often involved in processing requests for repeat medication. As such there is a requirement for ETP to allow messages to be routed securely via administration personnel, who can then direct the messages to an appropriate prescriber as in the current paper based system.

The NHS has adopted XML as a messaging standard, and this was used for the ETP pilots. It is proposed that any future message developments will also accommodate standards such as HL7[xi], and frameworks such as eGIF[xii]. It is also proposed that XML schemas (in preference to DTDs) should be used in future implementations as they minimise the management required for version control, can express shared vocabularies, and can offer more constraint on the type and form of message content (e.g.. constrain quantities to be expressed only as integers).

Message acknowledgement was not effectively implemented initially, operating only at the transport level (TLA), and it was agreed that the receipt of all messages should be acknowledged at the application level (ALA) as well. TLA alone only confirms that the message has 'arrived', not that it has been successfully accepted for processing. To communicate the receipt of a usable or useful message the recipient application should validate the structure of the message, and acknowledge only messages with valid structures. An important issue is whether the sending of an ALA is dependent on the content of the message as well as the structure. If data that is required is not present or invalid in a message does an ALA get sent or not? One approach is to send an ALA if a message has an acceptable structure. If the content is in any way unacceptable then a separate query message could be sent to request re-issue or a re-send with any required amendments. It was not possible to experiment with the practical use of these alternatives in the pilots.

Other message content issues include the need for a common drug dictionary, as currently the pharmacy may spend time searching for the item which most closely matches what has apparently been prescribed. Prescription item and quantity fields can also be populated in different formats on different clinical systems. The NHS Primary Care Drug Dictionary (PCDD) will be used in future implementations of ETP, and clinical terminology will ultimately migrate to a common form via SNOMED-CT, to ensure that messages between systems are not misinterpreted by a recipient system using a different coding scheme.

There was insufficient evidence from the pilots to indicate any patterns in message sending. However it is imperative that patients gain access to prescribed medication without delay. Therefore prescription messages and prescription requests are unlikely to be suitable for batching, but administrative messages (e.g. claims for payment for dispensing) not associated with the patient getting medication may be suitable for batching.

3.4 Bar Codes

Electronic messaging has been shown to work by *Pharmacy2U* without the need for paper or bar-coding, although this solution does limit patient choice to those dispensers that are ETP-enabled. Where a bar-code solution was adopted, appropriate bar-code readers were required at pharmacies, with upgraded printers at GP practices. A two dimensional bar-code could contain the actual prescription item information as well as a unique prescription identifier, as in the *TransScript* pilot. Patients may prefer the prescription information to be printed in human-readable form as well as bar-coded, and this also allows processing during times of system unavailability, or by pharmacies not using ETP.

3.5 Security and Privacy

All three pilots achieved integrity and confidentiality of the electronic prescriptions by using variants of Public Key Cryptography (PKC). Lack of a single standard for all three pilots caused additional difficulties in integration with existing GP practice, pharmacy and PPA systems. There were no major concerns with the security provided by the pilots, although theoretical security compromises were identified, caused by poor physical security of the installation and networks, incorrect software behaviour, and insecure user behaviour such as leaving systems unattended whilst logged in.

Security compromise was deemed most likely to occur through lack of protection of the stored private key and by people being irresponsible with their passwords. If a private key is compromised then it will be possible to create messages as if they came from the person issued with the private key, to alter messages signed by the private keys owner without detection by using the private key to resign the altered message, and to decrypt messages intended for the private keys owners' eyes only. To ensure that private keys are not compromised both electronic and physical safe guards must be in place, such as encrypting a private key, keeping passwords safe and controlling computer access.

Only authorised users of ETP should be allocated with keys, requiring adequate user identification mechanisms. The pilots used either documentation or face to face recognition to identify people for authorization as ETP users. It was not a requirement of the ETP pilots to provide pharmacists with individual keys, and consequently, all of the solutions only provided keys to a pharmacy as a whole. If there is more than one pharmacist at a pharmacy then it is not possible to distinguish who has sent an ETP message, and if fraudulent activity is detected at a pharmacy it would not be possible to identify who is involved.

Security analysis also proposed that improved methods are needed for the secure identification of patients when collecting medication from pharmacies, to replace presentation of the paper prescription. When addressing these concerns, it is important to compare the proposals to current practice. For example a pharmacy dispensing repeat medication to a patient using a pharmacy collection service commonly uses only verbal identification of the patient. Identification token methods based on paper prescriptions, barcoded paper prescriptions, and 'unique prescription numbers' were successfully used in the pilots. Other possible solutions, such as patient entitlement or 'smart' cards, were not used in the pilots.

3.6 User Business Processes

Several changes in business processes were observed as a consequence of the technical models implemented, affecting all participants in the process. It was immediately apparent that the point of contact between pharmacy and GP practice had shifted from practice administration staff (via prescription collection services and telephone calls from pharmacies) to individual doctors (via electronic requests for repeat prescriptions and electronic messaging to resolve queries on prescriptions). This was partly responsible for a reported shift in workload from administration staff to GPs, and also caused problems when the original prescriber was unavailable for any reason. A system design which more closely mirrors existing collaborative workflow for repeat prescribing in GP practices[xiii] would probably be more acceptable, which would require routing of messages from pharmacies (and to a lesser extent from the PPA) to the GP via practice administration staff.

Current legislation requires a handwritten signature from the prescriber on issue of the prescription, and also from the patient or the patient's representative on collection of dispensed items, when prescription charge exemption status is declared. A number of alternative methods were used in the pilots to replace this: digital signature of electronic messages by GPs, and the printing of prescription charge payment exemption forms at pharmacies for patient signature. In two of the pilots, the prescriber still had to sign paper prescriptions as well as electronically signing each prescription message. The electronic signing of repeat prescriptions was facilitated by a 'bulk signing' option. This may be a useful option to save time, but the implementation observed in the pilots raised questions about user attention to individual patient circumstance, and the majority of users avoided using this facility for this reason.

4. CONCLUSION

Evaluations of healthcare IT applications are by necessity multi-perspective and multi-disciplinary. In order to understand the mechanisms which cause new systems and procedures to succeed or fail, it is necessary to take account of the social and work environment within which they are being introduced, as well as the technology adopted for implementation. The advantages of this holistic or multi-method approach to evaluating interventions and the social systems, or context, within which the intervention exists, have been described and demonstrated by others[xiv xv xvi].

Whilst the three models described here offer some differences in the service offered, the majority of patients perceived little or no difference from the existing paper system, apart from those who opted to use the mail-order pharmacy. There was some concern by pharmacies that where the model required patients to pre-select a pharmacy, the prescriber might unduly influence the 'direction' of prescriptions to a particular pharmacy. Otherwise, users in practice found little difference between the models offered apart from detailed implementation issues.

This evaluation, and research elsewhere[xvii], indicates that the continuing use of paper prescriptions will feature regardless of the introduction of ETP, for reasons including patient comfort (being able to read what was prescribed), GP/patient interaction (issue of a prescription is the prime signal that the consultation is over), staged implementation, and back up in case of failure of the overall message-handling system or a participant local system.

The critical success factors for users of ETP were the poor fit to their existing business processes, and initial difficulties experienced with software bugs. These problems were compounded by variations from agreed messaging formats and the different application program interfaces (API's) offered by each model, causing difficulty in successful integration with existing GP practice, pharmacy and PPA systems. Consequential impacts resulted in clumsy work-around solutions and shifts in workloads between different classes of user.

ACKNOWLEDGEMENTS

The evaluation was a collaborative project between the Sowerby Centre for Health Informatics at Newcastle; the School of Pharmacy and Pharmaceutical Sciences (University of Manchester); the Industrial Statistics Research Unit (University of Newcastle) and QinetiQ. The Principal Investigator was Professor Ian Purves of SCHIN.

REFERENCES

[i] Department of Health, 2002, UK, *Delivering 21st Century IT Support for the NHS* (April 2004) www.dh.gov.uk/assetRoot/04/07/16/76/04071676.pdf

[ii] Department of Health, 2000, UK, *Pharmacy in the Future* (April 2004) www.dh.gov.uk/assetRoot/04/06/82/04/04068204.pdf

[iii] Strange, M., March 2004, *Why should the National Programme for IT include the electronic transmission of prescriptions?*, British Journal of Healthcare Computing 21, No2, 30-32

[iv] Prescription Pricing Authority, ETP Pilot Consortia, (April 2004) http://www.ppa.org.uk/news/consortia.htm

[v] Sugden, B., 2003, *Report on the Evaluation of Pilots for Electronic Transmission of Prescriptions* (April 2004) www.dh.gov.uk/PolicyAndGuidance/Medicines PharmacyAndIndustryServices/Prescriptions/ElectronicTransmissionOfPrescriptions/fs/en

[vi] Sugden, B. and Wilson, R., Integrated Care and Electronic Transmission of Prescriptions: Experience of the Evaluation of ETP Pilots, Health Informatics Journal, Sage Publications, ISSN: 1460-4582 (to be published 2004)

[vii] Moorman PW, Bernstein K, eds. Regional Health Care Networks in Europe, *The CoCo Project Report*, Deliverable 4.2, CoCo Project, HC 1074/ HC 1008, 1999, ISBN 87-90839-00-5

[viii] W.J. van der Kam, P.W. Moorman, M.J. Koppejan-Mulder, *Effects of Electronic Communications in General Practice*, International Journal of Medical Informatics, 2000; 60: 59-70

[ix] *Secure System for Transmitting Prescriptions and Related Patient Information Between Prescribers and Pharmacists*, 2000, Study for the National Association of Pharmacy Regulatory Authorities (NAPRA), (April 2004) www.napra.org/practice/information/calian.pdf

[x] *A Proposal for Electronic Prescription Security Standards*, 2001, National Association of Pharmacy Regulatory Authorities (NAPRA), (April 2004) www.napra.ca/pdfs/practice/erx_security.pdf

[xi] Shafarman, M., March 2004, *HL7 Version 3: Developed Globally, Implemented Locally*, (April 2004) www.hl7.org.uk/version3group/downloads/MS_HL7v3_masterclass.ppt

[xii] (April 2004) www.govtalk.gov.uk/schemasstandards/xmlschema.asp

[xiii] Wilson, R., Sugden, R. and Jones, N. *Responsibility in GP Repeat Prescribing*, DIRC Workshop on Dependability in Healthcare Informatics, Edinburgh, UK, 22-23 March 2001, DIRC workshop proceedings, pp - 10-14

[xiv] Heathfield, H.A., 2001, *Evaluating clinical systems: the social programme perspective*, Health Informatics Journal 7, 8-12

[xv] Heathfield, H., Pitty, D., and Hanka, R., 1998, *Evaluating information technology in health care: barriers and challenges*, British Medical Journal 316, 1959-1961

[xvi] Anderson, J.G., Aydin, C.E., and Jay, S.J., 1994, *Evaluating health care information systems: methods and applications*, London: Sage Publications

[xvii] Mundy, D., Chadwick, D., and Ball E., March 2004, *Some Expectations and Perceptions of Electronic Transfer of Prescription Systems*, British Journal of Healthcare Computing 21, No2, 34-36

ON LOCATIONS OF CALL CENTRES

An Illustration from Two Rural Regions in Sweden and Finland

Anna Moberg[1], Birger Rapp[1], Charlotte Stoltz[1] and Reima Suomi[2]
[1]Economic Information Systems, Department of Computer and Information Science, Linköping University, S-581 83 Linköping, Sweden; [2]Turku School of Economics and Business Administration, FIN-20520 Turku, Finland

Abstract: Call centres are a key business form in the modern information society. Call centres, based on e-work, allow flexibility in space concerning organisational locations. The long-term aim of our study is to understand factors behind establishments, locations and continued existence of call centres, and this paper is one step in this process. The paper illustrates call centre locations in two rural regions, Ljusdal in Sweden and Kuusamo in Finland. In the analysis we use a model for call centre location, based on our earlier studies in the field. The model consists of five factors that affect call centre location, or relocation, in a specific region; Business Environment and Community Related Factors, Communications and Organisation Related Considerations, Market Existence and Access, Resource Availability and Entrepreneurship. The paper illustrates how two regions give different prerequisites for call centre location.

Key words: call centre, contact centre, cluster, location, regional development, outsourcing.

1. INTRODUCTION

As infrastructure for information and communication technology develops and for strategic purposes or in order to reduce costs, organisations organise around smaller units and workplaces geographically distant from a main workplace, i.e. distance work or e-work. An increased application of e-work, i.e. an information based activity which use information and communication technology, leads to an increased mobility and geographically independent organisations emerge. A call centre is here regarded a cost effective organisational form for certain types of e-work services. An increased mobility means at first hand that competition increases within a specific country regarding call centre locations. Nationally there is a tension between urban and rural districts. Often a political agreement prevails concerning job creation and regional development and here peripheral or less favourable areas are especially targeted. Today, an international competition for call centre locations is also emerging. The national tension may therefore be extended to also include cross-border tensions between different nations in the world. From this background it is important to understand why organisations chose a specific location and why establishments remain in this chosen location. The long-term aim of our research is to understand factors behind the establishment, location, and continued existence of call centres. This paper is a step towards a comprehensive understanding of call centres that have a high viability and how that is related to their location in a certain region. We use our earlier studies as a basis for our analysis and a model for call centre location is applied to two rural regions - Ljusdal in Sweden and Kuusamo in Finland. We use the model to illustrate call centre locations in a specific region. Then we point at some results from call centre locations and call centre development in our regions.

In this paper we will use the concept call centre and we will not distinguish it from contact centres. It is defined as:

> "an organisation or a unit, located at a geographical distance from its customers and/or principals, that handles inbound or outbound calls in order to answer questions from customers or clients or in order to gather information for a certain activity. Communication with customers includes the use of telephones as well as modern communication media, such as e-mail and chat. Further, call centre activities can be performed either inhouse, which refers to services that are provided internally within an organisation, or outsourced, which means that the call centre attends to other organisation's tasks." *(Stoltz, 2004 and Moberg et al., 2004).*

2. METHOD

The Swedish illustration is mainly based on the case of Ljusdal, closer reported in our earlier studies (Moberg et al., 2001a, Moberg et al., 2001b and Stoltz, 2004). The study is based on visits and contacts made during the time period 2001 to 2004. During spring 2001 we conducted 17 face-to-face interviews with 18 different interviewees - mainly managers of Ljusdal's call centre organisations. These interviews were semi-structured with open questions where the respondents were encouraged to talk freely about their organisation and especially its history and development. Elements of the study are also a part of a larger European Union project, EMERGENCE[9]. Continuous contacts from 2001 to 2004 with representatives for Ljusdal's call centres and the municipality has provided us with further information and it also means that we have kept ourselves updated with the development in the region.

The case of Ljusdal forms the empirical basis for our development of the model for call centre location (Moberg et al., 2004) that we use in this paper. In order to explore regional as well as nation differences we have chosen to complement our study with one further region - Kuusamo in Finland. We wanted to study a region located in a country with similar information and communication technology maturity as Sweden, a region that has similar demographical characteristics as Ljusdal in terms of number of inhabitants and classification as a rural region and also is a region that hosts a relatively high share of call centre work opportunities. The case of Kuusamo is based on three telephone interviews conducted in November 2001, two telephone interviews conducted in April 2004 and one official report (Tikkanen and Korpela, 2001) on call centres located in the region. Both cases have also benefited from use of secondary data in the form of statistics, www-sites, newspaper articles and other research papers. For the general discussion about Sweden, we have for instance used our previous research regarded geographically dispersed organisations (cf. Moberg, 1993 and NUTEK, 1993).

3. A MODEL FOR CALL CENTRE LOCATION

In our earlier paper (Moberg et al., 2004) we introduce a model to structure the complex patterns with many interactions affecting call centre location, or relocation, in a specific region. We classified these factors according to five overall factors, i.e. Market Existence and Access, Communication and Organisation Related Considerations, Business Environment and Community Related Factors, Resource Availability and Entrepreneurship, that act on society level, municipal level, organisational level as well as individual level. A brief description follows below. For a detailed presentation see Moberg et al. (2004).

Market Existence and Access concerns the existence of a sales market and where that market is geographically located in relation to a specific call

[9] Estimation and Mapping of Employment Relocation in a Global Economy in the New Communications Environment. More information about this project can be obtained at <www.emergence.nu>.

centre establishment. Geographically independent work, or e-work, means different business circumstances compared to many manufacturing organisations and also compared to more traditional service organisations such as hairdressers, restaurants and repair shops. The most important difference is that e-work organisations such as call centres are not dependent on a local market in the same way as their products and services can relatively easily and quickly be transported at a low cost over long distances. The factor also concerns aspects related to access to customers, niche development, innovations and market conditions (i.e. boom or slump).

Possibilities for changing organisational structures in the form of relocation of or outsourcing of business activities due to development of communication infrastructure for both physical and information based transportation is dealt with in *Communications and Organisation Related Considerations*. Along with increased use of information and communication technology it is not unusual that (larger) organisations, for purposes of rationalisation, relocate or outsource parts of their business activities from city areas to more peripheral areas. Non-traditional ways of structuring and organising businesses will have an affect on the establishment potential, of geographically independent operations such as call centres, in smaller localities and sparsely populated areas.

Business Environment and Community Related Factors emphasises the local business environment and existence of social networks as a basis for stimulating new business establishments and location, or relocation, of call centre activities to a specific area. Actions taken by different regional actors to develop the local business climate for call centre businesses are also included. The factor involves many different aspects related to the local business environment in a delimited region; *demography* - number of inhabitants, population density, age structure etc., *industry structure* - shifts in the local industry, percentage of total work opportunities in the region etc., *the local business climate* and *political support* - especially from public or semi-public agents. Also, *tradition and predecessors* tend to have an important effect on the extent of new business formation in and location, or relocation, to a specific region. Different s*upport services* for small organisations can also positively stimulate the local business environment. Other business environment and community related factors are *education and training programmes* and *living environment*, i.e. housing, child-care, travelling time to work, safety, closeness to nature etc, in the region.

Resource availability concerns access to various resources determining the prospects of establishing and locating, or relocating, call centres to a specific region. The resources are of various kinds. They can be material, such as available *premises* and access to *equipment* such as computers and information and communication network. They can also be *financial* such as access to start-up capital/risk capital or possibilities to get subsidies. Another type of resource is *competence*, i.e. available competent workforce, expert knowledge, language skills, social skills, personal contact network etc. Low entry barriers to new business formation for call centres in terms of capital, premises and other requirements, facilitate locations and relocations of call centres to a much greater compared to the manufacturing sector. Information based business services provide intangible products, often embodied in experienced individuals. The expertise is not tied strongly to that of the organisation and knowledge is therefore highly mobile. Coupled with low entry barriers this enables individuals to leave established organisations to set up new operations. With access to resources such as laid-off competent personnel and available premises with certain equipment, a new call centre organisation can be started up relatively quickly.

Individual initiatives taken by people working in or who are on their way to start up call centre activities as well as people from local authorities, so-called social entrepreneurs, are considered in *Entrepreneurship*. Many researchers emphasise individual's intrinsic motives and abilities as an explanatory criterion for new business formation and location, or relocation, of business activities in a specific region. The motives can be characterised as career or coercion. Career involves the entrepreneur's own ambitions as a driving force, i.e. he or she wants to make a career, but also his or her attachment to a certain region, for example in the form of investments, networks and predecessors. The basis for coercion is that external circumstances force people to start up their own business in order to make some kind of livelihood in a specific locality. Coercion and career are different sides of the same coin where the first is a push factor while the second is a pull factor. Both stimulate business dynamics in a specific region in form of location or relocation. A high level of business dynamics within a delimited geographical area facilitates enterprise of call centres.

4. CALL CENTRE LOCATIONS IN SWEDEN AND FINLAND

In the service sector call centres have asserted themselves as con the market and expanding. As far as Sweden and Finland is concerned, there is a lack of reliable statistics on the number of job opportunities offered in call centres. In a government-instigated study in 1999 ISA[10] estimated that there were about 33,000 full-time jobs in Swedish call centres (SOU, 1999). Of these about 8,000 people worked in call centre organisations dealing with outsourced assignments from other organisations. The number of job opportunities in Swedish call centre was estimated to have grown to 50,000 by the end of 2001 and to 60,000 by the end of 2002.[11] We have no corresponding figures for Finland. An investigation by Federation of European Direct Marketing estimated the total number of employees in Finnish call centres to be between 6,600 and 8,000 or about 0.4 percent of the active population by the end of 2000 (Eurocallcentre, 2001). Another indication of the number of call centre jobs in Finland could be the number of members in the Help Desk Nordic Institute. Finland had in 2001 some 90 members whereas Sweden had 200 and Norway had 100.[12] Using these figures to calculate call centre employees in each country gives that Finland had about 22,500 employees in relation to Sweden's 50,000 by the end of 2001. If Finland then continued their call centre development during 2002 at the same pace as Sweden, they had about 27,000 call centre work opportunities compared to Sweden's 60,000 by the end of 2002. Using these figures of call centre job opportunities in respectively country to calculate the percentage of all work opportunities, call centre jobs represent 1.4 percent in Sweden and 1.0 percent in Finland.[13] These figures can be compared to 2.2 percent in United Kingdom, which is the largest call centre market in Europe, and an European Union average of 1.2 percent (Datamonitor, 2002). There seems to be a significant variation in the definition of call centre activities in both Sweden and Finland (compare Stoltz and Moberg, 2004). Regardless of the exact number of work opportunities offered, call centres are important business activities in both Sweden and Finland and this is especially valid for peripheral or rural areas.

Sweden has during the last years seen a growing demand from the *market* for call centre activities. According to ISA (2001, 2002a) there are several reasons to invest in call centre activities in Sweden. Sweden has a central

[10] Invest in Sweden Agency is a government agency providing business and economic data, contacts, solutions and procedural assistance free of charge for foreign companies considering establishment or expansion of business operations in Sweden.

[11] Interviews with ISA (Invest in Sweden Agency) representatives, January 29, 2002 and March 12, 2003. Statistics for 2003 are not available (April, 2004).

[12] Telephone interview with Aale Roos, Help Desk Institute Nordic Oy, November 28, 2001.

[13] These figures have been calculated from official statistics by December 31, 2002, from Sweden's and Finland's statistical databases, on total employment in each country. Statistics for 2003 are not available (by April, 2004).

geographic position in Scandinavia and the Baltic Sea Region. People here have good language skills in, for instance, English, German and French. Sweden has, compared to the other Nordic countries, also the highest share of people speaking the other northern languages. Internationally Sweden is regarded as a favourable location among the Nordic countries and there is evidence in form of a relatively considerable share of foreign investments in the country. Out of 41 of Fortune 100 organisations that have established Scandinavian headquarters and/or Baltic Sea Region headquarters for at least one business division, 35 chose Sweden, 2 Norway and 4 Denmark (ISA, 2002b). Some of these investments are made regarding call centre activities. There are also a number of call centres that have started up on small scale and then have been acquitted by foreign investors who wanted to expand their business to include the Nordic countries. These well established international call centres act as references, or models, for further call centre locations in Sweden. Another reason to invest in call centres in Sweden is Sweden's high ranking, together with Finland and Norway, as an information economy (ISA, 2001). Sweden has a deregulated telecom market with low telecom rates, reliable telecommunications and information technology infrastructure. Penetration of Internet access, mobile phones, and personal computers are among the highest in the world and Sweden has the highest volume of e-commerce in Europe. Sweden is also regarded as an internationally favourable choice for location with low corporate taxes, competitive wage costs, access to a knowledgeable, service-oriented workforce and a relatively low employee turnover. Besides foreign investments made in Sweden, there also exist Swedish owned call centres which tend to expand their market reach to include more than the Swedish market.

The general feasibility of Finland as a place to run businesses is regarded to be of high quality. In the World Competitiveness Yearbook 2001, Finland was rated the third best place for organisations to settle down after the United States and Singapore (IMD, 2001). According to the ministry of foreign affairs (Virtual Finland, 2001 and 2004), reasons to invest in Finland include a leading position in the development of electronic commerce, in terms of cellular mobile phone subscribers per 1,000 inhabitants, in organisations' ability to self-finance (i.e. generating enough cash-flow), in fitness between the educational system including university education and the needs of a competitive economy as well as regarding globalisation and credibility of managers. Finland also has a high ranking concerning computers per capita, infrastructure maintenance and development, organisations' usage of information technology to create value-added as well as in terms of sustainable development. The country also has a relatively high ranking in terms of real GDP growth for European countries. Looking at details, some quite visible differences compared to Sweden can be found. First, Finland has a long tradition of trade with the Soviet Union and currently Russia. The country is keen to act as a gateway to the Russian and Baltic Markets and many organisations have settled down in Finland with this in mind. This also applies for call centres where Finland is regarded as a good location for call centres that serve the Russian and Baltic market (Eurocallcentre, 2001). However, there is, due to language similarities in combination with low personnel costs, a growing tendency for call centres serving the Finnish market to locate in Estonia. The importance of call centre activities in Finland has generally increased during the last years and this especially applies to peripheral areas in the country. Another difference is that Finland is officially bilingual having both Finnish and Swedish as official languages. This secures capability to give high quality service also in the Swedish language. Third, the telephone market was early deregulated and this has lead to a competitive situation and a service orientation among teleoperators that compared to Sweden has been going on for a longer period of time.

A substantial difference in Finland as compared to Sweden is that the local national market is considerable smaller in Finland. Demand for call centres must be related to the population size, around 9 million inhabitants in Sweden and 5 million inhabitants in Finland. Another difference is that large, traditional export-oriented organisations such as Volvo, SKF and Alfa-Laval are few in Finland. Even Nokia's success is of quite recent history. Organisations were for a long period of time more directed towards domestic or Russian markets and thus the marketing functions were not so developed in Finland. In general, Finnish organisations have tended to focus more on manufacturing and therefore external networking and service activities have lacked in scope.

Swedish organisations are known to be non-bureaucratic and to have non-hierarchical business cultures (ISA, 2001). Together with the high penetration of information and communication technology, mentioned above, Sweden is often regarded as a country keen on adapting new technology and trying out *new organisational forms*. We can see that organisations focusing on their core operations make it possible to start up businesses activities in order to offer complementary services and one such emerging business form is so-called outsourced call centres. In general there are only a few organisations offering *outsourcing services* in Finland, but outsourced call centres are slowly emerging also in Finland (Eurocallcentre, 2001). In total for call centre activities in Finland, we see three parties. First, there is the traditional teleoperators that run massive call centre activities for themselves and for customer organisations. Then there are large organisations running their own call centres or outsource this type of business activity. Finally, there are also some small independent call centre operators on the market.

In both Sweden and Finland, political agreement prevails that *decentralisation of businesses* to sparsely populated areas is positive, both for the individual regions and for the country as a whole. Direct investments are made in the form of different types of grants for establishment and investments within certain prioritised geographical areas. Organisations that have geographically decentralised parts of their activity have often had major problems with high staff turnover in major cities as one of the main reasons behind their decision to relocate (cf. Moberg, 1993 and Stoltz, 2004). In Sweden, which has compared to Finland experienced a relocation trend from urban to rural areas for a longer period of time (cf. SOU, 1989), we see a growing range of geographically independent organisations such as call centres. We believe that this trend will continue to be important for call centre location, or relocation, in urban as well as rural areas.

5. CALL CENTRE LOCATIONS IN LJUSDAL, SWEDEN

Ljusdal, which is described in Moberg et al. (2001a), Moberg et al. (2001b), Stoltz and Moberg (2003) and Stoltz (2004), is the name of both the municipality and the central locality. Ljusdal is geographically located in more or less the middle of Sweden. The region has in total 19,771 inhabitants and there are about 4 inhabitants per square kilometre, which is among the lowest population density figures in Europe.[14] Even if the municipality is wide in geographical terms, the population is concentrated to some main localities, the built up areas of Ljusdal, Järvsö and Färila, i.e. people do not live far apart in Ljusdal. The total recruitment area however also comprises neighbouring municipalities.

Ljusdal is a region of interest because it is classified as a sparsely populated area in northern[15] Sweden and rural regions often has problems creating jobs. These types of regions are often characterised by a high rate of people migrating from the area and thus a loss of local manpower. Traditionally, Ljusdal has been characterised as a municipality with a high rate of traditional base industries such as forestry and timber, as well as some tourism. But during the last 5-10 years a thorough restructuring has taken place and the local labour market has undergone major changes. Ljusdal has managed to attract internationally competitive organisations with a considerable share of geographically independent business activities such as call centre activities. In Ljusdal there is a cluster of call centres and the municipality has

[14] According to official statistics by December 31, 2003, from the municipality of Ljusdal, on total population

[15] Geographically Ljusdal is located in the middle of Sweden but when considering population and number of work opportunities the municipality is classified as belonging to northern Sweden.

about 40 organisations that form this cluster. Examples of business areas are information management and brokering, booking and transport, advertisement and media as well as information technology development and support. The total number of jobs in the region is 8,250 and 850, or 10.3 percent, of these are found in call centres.[16]

Ljusdal has been actively engaged to compensate for their geographically disadvantageous location in Sweden. The municipality was early in investing in new *information and communication technology infrastructure* and this has been further developed during the years. Representatives of Ljusdal's call centres consider that the infrastructure as well suited for their needs. Ljusdal also has good *physical communications* in terms of road and railway networks. They do however not have any air connections and the nearest airport, which is located 56 kilometres away, is relatively small. In order to be close to the market and/or to clients, some organisations have chosen to complement their call centre activities located in Ljusdal with marketing and sales offices located in major cities such as Stockholm, Gothenburg and Malmö.

At municipal level, three important players appear in Ljusdal. These are the municipality, the industrial foundation (Närljus) and the job centre. *The municipality* has laid the basis for a positive development and growth of call centres in the region. A political decision taken already in the beginning of the 1970s to guide the municipality's industry towards new branches of industry such as geographically independent service activities in combination with active investments in suitable training programmes and infrastructure has played an important role in the development of Ljusdal's call centre organisations. A "call centre spirit", which is nationally known, has during the years been created and the region. In Ljusdal, people are proud of their call centres.

In 1986 the municipality created a political *foundation for trade and industry*, Närljus, which is jointly owned by the municipality and industry. Närljus gathers all activities for future business development within the district through an active partnership between the organisations and the local authorities. For instance, Närljus act as a regional contact coordinator for potential establishers and they have taken initiative and formed a group for co-operation among the call centre organisations and the local authorities. Our interviews with representatives from Ljusdal's call centres show satisfaction with both how the municipality's and Närljus' representatives act. The representative for Närljus is seen as a very committed person with a

[16] According to official statistics from Ljusdal's municipality by December 31, 2002 on daytime population and call centre employees. Statistics for 2003 are not available (by April , 2004).

sensitive ear and with good knowledge of the local businesses and their needs. Local authorities are characterised as forward looking, market oriented, proactive and helpful.

Ljusdal also has a very active *job centre*, which attends to manpower needs in the local trade and industry. According to our interviews the job centre is very sensitive to the entrepreneurs' needs. They have a management group that monitors training needs, communication solutions and employees' needs. Some opinions on the job centre are that they respond quickly, work effectively and professionally and find flexible solutions. We feel that without the commitment from the municipality and the local authorities a number of locations and relocations in Ljusdal would never have been implemented.

Ljusdal hosted by the end of 2003 about 40 *call centre organisations*, see table 1 for some examples. Ljusdal's structural change towards call centre organisations began already at the beginning of the 1970s with the start of Byggfakta. Several of the people interviewed feel that Byggfakta has been a model for the town and acted as a "door-opener" for other organisations. Byggfakta showed that work at a distance, i.e. activities outside urban areas such as Stockholm, with the help of telephony, was possible for information based organisations.

Ljusdal's call centres co-operate closely with each other. They meet regularly and arrange seminars or study visits with the aim of catalysing the spread of information and knowledge between the organisations. Almost all the interviewees consider the network as important for the region. There is a great sense of affinity between the organisations and even if they compete for the same personnel, this is not experienced as a problem. The call centre cluster gives employees a relatively high possibility of choosing their workplace and the region is able to retain competent personnel who otherwise would have sought career options elsewhere. There is a considerable rotation of personnel and managers between the organisations and we judge that this has contributed to an important spread of competence, which in turn creates strong ties within the network and strengthens the local identity. Our opinion is that this *social capital in form of a network of contacts* is an important factor for Ljusdal's successful development of call centres.

At the same time as the first call centre organisation began to set up in Ljusdal, the municipality made a political decision and started up an upper secondary school programme aimed at office work and distribution. Over the years, this training has profiled itself towards the region's call centres and this has lead to availability of a *skilled workforce* in Ljusdal. Inhabitants are in general familiar with the use of information and communication technology. Employees have long experience from using different forms of communication media for taking care of customer service activities on distance. Ljusdal's call centre cluster contains a number of organisations that act on a

Nordic market and this means that a workforce who speaks Nordic languages is available in the region. Rotation of personnel between organisations means synergy effects as it contributes to knowledge creation and spreading in the region. Access to motivated and competent personnel, with relevant training and professional experience for call centres, is an attraction factor for Ljusdal.

Table 1. Examples of call centre organisations in Ljusdal with regard to type of activity (i.e. type of business and the principal's organisational belonging), number of employees (December 31, 2003) and year of establishment in Ljusdal. Type of activity is based on the following division: II = In-house and Inbound, IO = In-house and Outbound, OI = Outsourced and Inbound respectively OO = Outsourced and Outbound. Source: Ljusdal's industrial foundation Närljus. A more comprehensive table is given in Stoltz (2004).

Organisation	Type of activity	Number of employees	Established in Ljusdal	Comments
Byggfakta	IO	48	1971	
Svenska Media	IO & OO	8	2003	Taken over from Byggfakta by employees in 2003
Annonskraft	IO & OO	6	2000	Spin-off from Svenska Media
ByggIndex	IO	Sold	2000	Subsidiary of Byggfakta - re-merged in 2002
MarknadsData	IO	14	1991	Spin-off from Byggfakta
Callcentermedia	IO	Relocated	1999	Spin-off from Byggfakta - relocated from the region in 2003
Q Survey AB	IO	12	1999	Conducts quality studies of Swedish call centres
DHL International	II	117	1992	
JKW Servicecenter	OI	-	1999	Taken over by Manpower Outsourcing AB in 2000
PPM	II	Sold	1999	Acquired by Manpower Outsourcing AB in 2001
Manpower Outsourcing	OI & OO	-	2001	Closed down in 2003
Alfakassan	II	29	1990	
Datasvar	OI	Relocated	1992	Relocated from the region in 1997
Twenty4Help	OI	340	1997	Result from the relocation of Datasvar
Solvus Support	OI	70	1997	Result from the relocation of Datasvar
Proffice	OI & OO	11	2003	

Call centres have relatively low entry barriers in terms of *capital required for investments*. Since most of the call centres located in Ljusdal have started up on small scale and then worked up some capital, they have managed to take on investments on their own. Financial help for investments have in some cases also come from some stakeholders who believed in a specific business. Another type of external capital is subsidies or grants. Ljusdal is located in one of the most highly prioritised support areas in Sweden and business establishments are entitled to various forms of grants. Received grants have not been a prerequisite for bringing about the establishments, but they have been of importance in the sense that they have constituted a push-factor for a number of the establishments.

In Ljusdal, suitable *premises* are available in general for call centre businesses. More specifically vacant premises and unused *equipment* after call centre closures have in at least three cases contributed to new business start-ups. Some of the interviewees felt that in principle they have started up their activity over a weekend. In these cases free capacity together with personal networks have governed the choice of localisation.

In Ljusdal about 1,000 inhabitants or 5 percent of the population is self-employed. This is a figure that points to *entrepreneurship* and individual initiative. In 1999 Ljusdal was ranked as Sweden's fifth most prominent region with a percentage growth of 6.2 percent (Affärsvärlden, 2001). For call centres we have identified a number of entrepreneurs who have contributed, either directly or indirectly, to business start-ups. There are management personnel and company founders who have been locally recruited from other organisations within the cluster. Some of them have had career as a motive since they have seen new business opportunities and acted upon them. Movements among management personnel and local spin-off establishments are regarded as an important factor contributing to the region's development. Other entrepreneurs have been driven by more coercive factors. In order to make a livelihood in the region, individuals have in these cases been more or less forced to become self-employed.

6. CALL CENTRE LOCATIONS IN KUUSAMO, FINLAND

The Finnish case is the locality Kuusamo in the northern part of Finland. Kuusamo, which is located in the Koillismaa area close to the Russian Border, is regarded as a sparsely populated area. In total, the region has 17,300 inhabitants or 3,7 inhabitants per square kilometre, but even if there is a low population density figure, the population is mainly concentrated to the central town Kuusamo where about 11,000 people live.[17] This means that as in the case of Ljusdal, people do not live far apart in the region.

Kuusamo suffers from migration problems, i.e. decline in population. However, the region is one of the most renowned and attractive tourist areas in Finland (Ruka, 2004), especially for winter sports, and this has lessened the migration problems. The unemployment figure for 2003 is 16,6 percent in Kuusamo and 9,0 percent for the whole of Finland.[18]

The main industries in Kuusamo are distributed as follows: Primary production 14 percent, processing industries 16 percent, services 64 percent (private 32 percent and public 32 percent) and unclassified 6 percent.[19] In total, Kuusamo offers 5,900[20] work opportunities and a share of 64 percent means that almost 3,800 work opportunities are offered within service businesses. Tourism and travelling is Kuusamo's main industry sector and the region has a long tradition of service orientation. More recently this has been extended to also include call centre activities as some establishments have taken place in the region. Kuusamo had by the end of 2003 eight call centre organisations established in the region (see table 2). The total number of work opportunities offered in call centres amount to 168 or 2,8 percent of the active population.[21]

Table 2. Examples of call centre organisations in Kuusamo with regard to type of activity (i.e. type of business and the principal's organisational belonging), number of employees (December 31, 2003) and year of establishment in Kuusamo. Type of activity is based on the following division: II = In-house and Inbound, IO = In-house and Outbound, OI = Outsourced and Inbound respectively OO = Outsourced and Outbound. Source: Kuusamo vocational institute.

Organisation	Type of activity	Number of employees	Established in Kuusamo
TeliaSonera	II & IO	82	1998
Pfizer/Invespo	OO	15	2001
Sentraali	IO	23	2000
FinFun	II & IO	15	1989
Econet	II	13	1998
Mawell	OI	5	2004

[17] According to official statistics by December 31, 2003, from the municipality of Kuusamo, on total population

18 According to official statistics by December 31, 2003 from the county of Oulu and from Finland's statistical databases.

19 According to statistics from the Naturpolis Kuusamo development programme.

20 According to interview with a represenatative for Kuusamo vocational institute April 23, 2004.

21 Ibid.

Diverse tourism call centers	-	15	-

Among Kuusamo's call centres, teleoperators who have set up a remote call centre for handling customer service predominate. Besides this are some examples of smaller call centres with connections to the tourism sector and a newly started call centre for health care advice given over the phone.

Kuusamo, which belongs to the Koillismaa area, has together with three neighbouring municipalities Kuusamo built up an area network with optical cabling. The network offers access points with ATM, ISDN and modems and there are continuous investments made to this *information and communication technology infrastructure*. Data communications and information network infrastructure are maintained at peak level in Kuusamo. Kuusamo enjoys the privilege of having its own *airport* with daily connections to and from Helsinki. From the nearest large city, Oulu, there is a drive of some 3 hours to Kuusamo. The fast *road connections* from Oulu as well as direct air traffic from Helsinki means that there are favourable links between the Kuusamo outlet and other parts of the country and the rest of the world. Further, Kuusamo eagerly waits to get its own international border station to Russia, which is due in a few years. This would mean a major growth in traffic in the region and probably also increased cross-border trade with Russia. Kuusamo does not have any rail connections.

The municipality of Kuusamo decided in 1987 to embark on developing telematics systems and services in the community. In 1996 actors realised that it was important to find job opportunities for people with educational degrees and they learned from Sweden that call centre activities was a promising option. Kuusamo is located peripherally in Finland but technology infrastructure was regarded as well developed and it was also affordable for this type of business. The municipality set up a goal to attract two employees to establish call centre activities in Kuusamo and employ 40 people by 1998 and 100 by 2000. The first call centre to establish was a so-called Help Desk for locally developed software. They started up September 1, 1997 and had 4 employees from the start. The following year Sonera trained employees for performing in-house support activities for the organisations end customers. The development continued and the target of 100 call centre job opportunities in the region was reached in 2000. Today the region offers 168 work opportunities in call centres.[22]

An important cornerstone for the development in Kuusamo is the *Naturpolis Kuusamo development program*, targeted at years 2001-2006. The program contains activities in areas such as competencies, information industry, tourism, local area services and rural development. Telephone services or

[22] This part is mainly based on Tikkanen and Korpela (2001).

call centre activities is one prioritised area in the Naturpolis Kuusamo development program. For more information on this program, see Naturpolis (2004).

A development project of Kuusamo Town and 6 organisations called *TVC24-project* (TeleVoiceCenter 24h) started up in 1997. This project is especially targeted towards call centre operations in the region. The project received partly foundation in 1999 by the European Union DGV/Atricle6. The main goal of the project is to train skilled personnel for the partner enterprises and to create permanent work opportunities for the recruited employees. Training programs are offered to people and most of the participants receive a work in a call centre after they have finished the program. The aim is also to develop the call centre - know-how within the sectors of information industry and travel services. The model has also been implemented in the neighbouring municipality Taivalkoski where there are further 70 call centre job opportunities.

The development of call centres in Kuusamo has lead to a decrease in the unemployment rate by 2 percentage points and the number of unemployed people in Kuusamo has been reduced by 10 percent (Tikkanen and Korpela, 2001). The call centre development has also been profitable from the community standpoint since each new work opportunity in the region means a tax income for the municipality. In total, the development has been of importance for the region as an employment creator and it has also brought capital to the region.

Kuusamo is entitled to the highest *EU-supports* available in Finland, i.e. they are a so-called Tavoite 1-region. Several national and local initiatives have added to the feasibility of the area for information industries. The initiatives have supported mainly education and infrastructure building, and their support to individual organisations has not been decisive.

When it comes to a *skilled workforce* for call centre activities, Kuusamo has a sufficient number of job applicants available who have received commercial and information and communication technology-related training. Major emphasis has been in the fight against unemployment, and preventing educated people to move from the region. Connections with the tourism industry equip the local people with a natural service attitude and this is also needed for call centre operations. Availability of workforce is seen as a key resource factor for Kuusamo. In addition, the good telecommunication infrastructure helps the situation. Kuusamo lacks their own higher education, but intellectual resources are collected from a close co-operation with the University of Oulu. The municipality also offers organisations operational facilities, for instance - on reasonable terms, if they decide to establish in the region.

The so-called new economy organisations tend to settle down in metropolitan areas such as Helsinki or other university cities, whereas traditional *entrepreneurship* has traditionally been strongest in the Botnia region. However, we can see no direct correlation between the establishment of call centres and existence of an entrepreneurship environment in Kuusamo. As it comes to individuals, there is not yet any visible call centre entrepreneur to be seen. Mainly the development has been within large teleoperating organisations. They have several motives to start up call centres and this includes; to find new traffic for their networks, to expand their business portfolio with value-adding activities, to establish themselves as socially responsible organisations in their environment or to put services to the call centre mode in order to decrease costs, educate customers in new forms of services as well as maintaining professionalism and quality of service. As it comes to organisation managers, no one has gained any major good reputation or fame for their call centre establishment activities in Finland. A telecommunications manager focusing at career advancements is more to focus on mobile services at the time being.

7. CONCLUDING REMARKS

In this paper we have illustrated call centre locations in two regions in Sweden and Finland. For the analysis we use our model for call centre location (Moberg et. al. 2004).

Both regions are classified as rural districts and this means that the local *market* is not enough to support businesses located in the regions. They are directly dependent on a national and/or an international market. Both countries have one of the world's highest information technology maturities and this is a prerequisite for e-work and geographically independent organisations such as call centres. As the national market is somewhat larger in Sweden as compared to Finland and that there are a considerable higher share of people who talk foreign languages in Sweden, we see that Market Existence and Access has a somewhat higher influence in Ljusdal, Sweden as compared to Kuusamo, Finland. Sweden sometimes acts a gateway to the other Nordic countries and Finland is often regarded as a gateway to Russia.

The *communication infrastructure* in both Sweden and Finland has a high standard. Networks for both physical and information-based transportation connect the whole countries. We can also see that there is a trend toward relocation and outsourcing of business activities. In order to gain competitive advantage organisations try to find cost effective solutions. This could involve a call centre located in a rural district or abroad. Sweden has a long tradition from the 1970s of supporting relocation of business activities from urban to rural areas. Today more than 11 percent of the total workforce in

Ljusdal work within call centres and the corresponding figure for Kuusamo is about 2 percent.

Ljusdal has a very positive *business environment*. Here we find active local actors and a positive call centre spirit due to co-operation and networks among the call centres located in the region. In Kuusamo, there is a high service attitude stemming from tourism and leisure activities. This means that there is a high potential for call centre activities. Both regions have regional actors who have developed the local call centre business climate. For instance large investments are made to the region's information and communication infrastructures and in the regions' educational and vocational training programs. In this respect the differences between Ljusdal and Kuusamo are relatively small.

In both countries we have seen a political support in form of grants. However the level of support is decreasing and in total the supply of risk capital is not the same in Finland as in Sweden. Capital is however not a scarce resource in neither country. *Resources* in form of a well educated workforce with language skills have traditionally been readily available in Ljusdal. This means, in combination with the business dynamics, that call centre organisations have been able to start up relatively quickly. We have identified the availability of a motivated and skilled workforce in the region. However the workforce is now becoming a scarce resource and call centres have recently started to move their operations and establish complementing activities in neighbouring regions. Kuusamo has a high unemployment rate. However they are probably not directly suitable for work in call centres even if the tourism and service tradition in Kuusamo indicates a high potential for call centres. Today the share of call centre work opportunities is 2 percent and the unemployment rate is 16,6 percent in the region.

Entrepreneurship and individual initiatives have a strong influence on business start-ups and location of call centres in a specific region. Both the studied regions have a high proportion of self-employed people - 1,000 out of 19,771 in Ljusdal and 1,000 out of 17,300 in Kuusamo. However none of the regions can be classified as an entrepreneurial region. In Kuusamo, call centres are mainly run by large organisations that have their head offices located in urban districts or abroad. In Ljusdal we can see a considerable rotation among call centre management personnel. We interpret this as an important factor for the call centre development in Ljusdal. It has contributed to the dynamics in the region and thereby also to a total positive development over the years. Ljusdal also shows, in relation to Kuusamo, a higher share of important social entrepreneurs that have acted to develop call centre business in the region.

To sum up the discussion we have drawn table 3. It compares the different factors influence on the climate for call centres establishments and location, or relocation, in a specific region. We have here illustrated that the two regions give different prerequisites for call centre locations depending on different market conditions and organisation related consideration in each country and region. There is also different business environmental and community related factors in each of the regions that affect call centre locations, or relocations, in these specific areas.

Table 3. A comparison between the two regions. (Key: + = major positive effect, 0 = no effect or no major positive or negative effect, - = negative effect).

Factor	Ljusdal, Sweden	Kuusamo, Finland
Market Existence and Access	+	0
Communications and Organisation Related Considerations	+	0
Business Environment and Community Related Factors	+	+
Resource Availability	0 (+)	0 (+)
Entrepreneurship	+	0

ACKNOWLEDGEMENTS

We wish to thank the Knowledge foundation and Vinnova for financial support.

REFERENCES

Affärsvärlden (2001). Regioner och kommuner - företagandet lyfter Stockholm (Regions and municipalities - entrepreneurship lifts Stockholm, In Swedish). Affärsvärlden January 10 2001.

Eurocallcentre (2001): *Knowledge centre on Call centres - Report Finland.* Downloaded from Federation of European Direct Marketing <http://www.eurocallcentre.com/> November 30, 2001 and April 23, 2004.

Finland's Statistical Databases. Accessed November 27, 2001 and April 23-29, 2004 through Statistics Finland's homepage <http://www.stat.fi/ or http://www.tilastokeskus.fi/>.

IMD (2001). *The World Competitiveness Yearbook 2001.* Lausanne: International Institute for Management Development (IMD).

ISA (2001). *Invest in Sweden - Report 2001.* Roglar, S. (eds.). Stockholm: Invest in Sweden Agency.

ISA (2002a). *Invest in Sweden - Contact Centres. Sweden - the natural location for contact centre operations in Scandinavia and the Baltic Sea region.* Stockholm: Invest in Sweden Agency.

ISA (2002b). *Invest in Sweden - Shared Services. Sweden - centre for support and infrastructure services in Scandinavia and the Baltic Sea region.* Stockholm: Invest in Sweden Agency.

Lorentzon, S. (1998). The Role of ICT as a Locational Factor in Peripheral Regions - examples from "IT-active" local authority areas in Sweden. *Netcom*, Vol. 12, No 1-2-3, pp. 303-331.

Moberg, A. (1993). *Satellitkontor - En studie av kommunikationsmönster vid arbete på distans* (Satellite Work Centres - A Study of the Communication Patterns As Pertains to Distance Work, in Swedish). Lic.-dissertation, No. 406, Economic Information Systems, Department of Computer and information Science, Linköping University, Linköping, Sweden.

Moberg, A., Rapp, B., Stoltz, C. (2001a). Ljusdal - the happy family? An example of a growing cluster of e-business companies in a rural district in Sweden. In *Proceedings of the 6th International ITF Workshop and Business Conference*, Amsterdam, Netherlands, August 26-30 2001.

Moberg, A., Rapp, B., Stoltz, C., Petri, C.-J. (2001b). How can one minus one equal three? The dynamics in an e-work district in Sweden, In *Proceedings of the 8th International Assembly on Telework: t-world 2001*, Helsinki, Finland, September 12-14 2001.

Moberg, A., Rapp. B., Stoltz, C. (2004). *Towards a Model for Call Centre Location*. Paper submitted to Regional Studies.

Naturpolis (November 27, 2001 and April 23, 2004): Homepage accessed November 27, 2001 and April 23, 2004 through <http://www.naturpolis.fi/>.

NUTEK (1993). *Utlokalisering av tjänsteföretag - En konsultstudie* (Relocation of service companies - a consultancy study, In Swedish). NUTEK Rapport 1993:52. Stockholm: NUTEK-analys.

Ruka (April 2003, 2004). Homepage <http://www.ruka.fi/ > accessed April 23, 2004.

SOU (1989). *Omlokalisering av statlig verksamhet - utvärdering av utflyttningen på 70-talet* (Relocation of government activities - evaluation of the moving out during the 1970s, In Swedish). Huvudrapport SOU 1989:8A. Stockholm: Statskontorets publikationsservice.

SOU (1999). *Från callcenter till kontaktcenter - Trender, möjligheter och problem* (From call centre to contact centre - Trends, possibilities and problems, In Swedish). IT-kommissionens rapport 99:3, Statens offentliga utredningar 1999:38, IT-kommissionen. Stockholm: Fakta info direkt.

Stoltz, C. (2004). *Calling for Call Centres - A study of Call Centre Locations in a Swedish Rural Region*. Lic.-dissertation, No. 1084, Economic Information Systems, Department of Computer and information Science, Linköping University, Linköping, Sweden.

Stoltz, C., Moberg, A. (2003). *The Importance of Proximity for Geographically Dispersed Organisations - Indications from a Call Centre Cluster in Sweden*. Paper presented in the proceedings of the 17th Nordic Conference on Business Studies in Reykjavik, Iceland, August 14-16 2003.

Stoltz, C., Moberg, A. (2004). Call Centre, a concept full of Nuance - On definitions of Call Centres. In Stoltz, C. (2004). *Calling for Call Centres - A study of Call Centre Locations in a Swedish Rural Region*. Lic.-dissertation, No. 1084, Economic Information Systems, Department of Computer and information Science, Linköping University, Linköping, Sweden.

Sweden's Statistical Databases. Accessed June 2001 - April 2004 through Statistics Sweden's homepage <http://www.scb.se/>.

The municipality of Kuusamo (November 27, 2004). Homepage <http://www.kuusamo.fi/yleistietoa/index.htm> accessed November 27, 2001.

Tikkanen, H., Korpela, T. (2001): Development of Local Telematics Know-How and Business in Kuusamo. Paper presented at the e-työn alueelliset ulottuvuudet-seminaari, Tampere, September 4-5 2002. Downloaded April 23, 2004 from <http://www.ework.fi/materiaali/seminaari/TaunoK.doc>.

Virtual Finland (December 3, 2001 and April 23, 2004). Homepage <http://www.finland.fi/finfo/english/competitiviness.html> accessed December 3, 2001 and April 23, 2004.

PURCHASE AND PAYMENT

FAIR PAYMENT PROTOCOLS FOR E-COMMERCE

Hao Wang and Heqing Guo
School of Computer Science & Engineering, South China University of Technology, Guangzhou, China 510641.

Abstract: It has been widely accepted that fairness is a critical property for electronic commerce. Fair payment protocol is designed to guarantee fairness in a payment process over asynchronous network. Fairness means that when the protocol terminates, either both parties get their expected items, or neither does. In this paper we first present a new generic offline fair payment protocol with fairness, timeliness and invisibility of TTP. Then we introduce the property of abuse-freeness into electronic payment and implement a fair abuse-free payment protocol.

Key words: Electronic commerce, Offline payment, Fairness, Abuse-freeness

1. INTRODUCTION

Electronic payment system is the most important building block for electronic commerce. As classified by Asokan et al. [1], there are two types of electronic payment system: *cash-like* payment and *check-like* payment. In cash-like payment system, payer first withdraws a certain amount of money (e.g. electronic coins) for the payment process, when payee received the money, s/he can deposit those coins into the bank. But in check-like payment system, payer sends some certified document (e.g. electronic check) so that the payee can have the check paid through direct bank transfer. When these two types of payment systems are to be migrated into asynchronous network, the issue of fairness has to be well studied. Fairness means that when the electronic transfer terminates, either both parties get their expected items (e.g. electronic check and its receipt), or neither does. Fair payment protocol is designed to guarantee fairness in electronic payment system on asynchronous network.

As suggested by Louridas in [16], fair protocol and requirements of its application domains should match, which means assumptions of the protocol must be rooted in the protocol's application scenario. For this reason, we first set up the application scenario for our fair payment protocols: company B (the client, denoted as Bob) is going to buy some electronic goods from company A (the merchant, denoted as Alice) and they have settled on the goods and the price. Now they need to finish the exchange of Bob's check with Alice's goods on a relative insecure and asynchronous network. Bob's check is composed of his bank-certified account information, payment information and can be validated only after signed by his signature. With that signed check, Alice can get her money paid from Bob's bank. Note that *anonymity* is not considered in this scenario and it will be discussed as a possible extension in Section 5. With this scenario set, we can make our protocols' assumptions explicitly stated (see Section 2).

To achieve fairness, Alice must send to Bob a non-repudiation evidence of origin (**NRO**) proving she has sent the goods. And Bob's check can be used as a non-repudiation evidence of receipt (**NRR**) proving he has received the goods. In addition, a trusted third party (TTP) must be involved when an error occurs. Because it is widely accepted that no deterministic fairness can be achieved without any third party exists. To achieve timeliness, a party (say Alice) can initiate the resolve or abort sub-protocol to terminate the exchange (success or failure). Resolve means to let the TTP decide whether the exchange can be succeeded. Alice run the abort protocol to prevent Bob from resolving at a later time she will not wait.

1.1 Related Work

In 1996, Asokan et al. [2] introduce the idea of optimistic approach and presents fair protocols with offline TTP, in which TTP intervenes only when an error occurs (network error or malicious party's cheating). Ever since then, subsequent efforts in this approach resulted in efficient and fair protocols (Asokan et al. [3], S. Kremer and O. Markowitch [14], we call them as *AK protocol*) that can guarantee that both parties can terminate the protocol timely while assuring fairness (called property of *timeliness*). Although they were attacked for some designing details (see [12]), their messages & rounds optimality (see [23] for detailed discussions) and basic building blocks (main protocol, resolve and abort sub-protocols) are well analyzed and widely accepted.

Offline TTP generates evidences different from those produced by the sender or the recipient, which make the protocol suffer from *bad publicity* [17]: "intervention of the TTP can be due to a network failure rather than a cheating party", and it may cause doubt on either party's honesty. *Invisible TTP* is first introduced by Micali [20] to solve this problem. The TTP can generate exactly the same evidences as the sender or the recipient. In this way, judging the outcome evidences and received items cannot decide whether the TTP has been involved. There are two way of thinking:

The first one is to use *verifiable signature encryption* (VSE). It means to send the signature's cipher encrypted with TTP's public key before sending the signature itself. And try to convince the recipient that it is the right signature and it can be recovered (decrypted) by TTP in case of errors. Asokan et al. [3], Bao et al. [6] and Ateniese [5] make use of this approach to realize invisibility of the TTP. But as Boyd and Foo [7] has pointed out, verifiable encryption is computationally expensive.

The other approach is to use *convertible signatures* (CS) and it is recently focused approach. It means to firstly send a partial committed signature (verifiable by the recipient) that can be converted into a full signature (that is a normal signature) by both the TTP and the signer. Protocols proposed by Boyd and Foo [7] and Markowitch and Kremer [17] are early efforts to use this approach to construct fair protocols. But the former protocol is not efficient computationally and suffers from relatively heavy communication burden (for its interactive verifying process); the latter one cannot generate standard signatures as final evidences. In particular, the CS scheme proposed by Boyd and Foo is to split multiplicatively the secret key of a standard RSA signature. Recently, Park et al. [22] propose a CS scheme which splits the key additively, and based on that, present a very efficient protocol in which the partial signature is non-interactively verifiable. But unfortunately, Dodis and Reyzin [10] break the scheme by proving the TTP can obtain Alice's entire secret key with only her registration information. Dodis and Reyzin also propose an efficient CS scheme based on GDH signature, but this scheme cannot directly be applied efficient enough to construct an abuse-free protocol (further discussed in Section 5).

Abuse-freeness, as a new requirement of fair protocols, is first mentioned by Boyd and Foo [7], and formally presented by Garay et al. [11]. And Garay et al. have also realized an abuse-free contract signing protocol. Based on the Jakobsson-Sako-Impagliazzo designated verifier signature [13], they introduce a new signature scheme called *Private Contract Signature* to realize this property. The protocol has been formally analyzed by Kremer and Raskin [15], Chadha et al. [9][8]. And based on their intensely formalized study, Chadha et al. present improved definition of abuse-freeness. Briefly, abuse-freeness means that before the malicious party (say Alice) gets her full evidence, she cannot convince any outside party that Bob has participated in the protocol. This property is quite important, especially for critical scenarios like contract signing and fair payment (further discussed in Section 4).

Previous efforts studying the fairness issue in payment systems include Asokan et al. [2] and Boyd and Foo [7]. As discussed earlier, these two protocols are not efficient and practical enough as to recent advances in area of fair exchange.

1.2 Our Work

In this paper we first present a generic fair payment protocol based on AK generic protocol and an adaptation of the convertible signature scheme proposed by Mao et al. [19] (*MP signature*). The original CS scheme uses an interactive verification protocol that is not practical for fair protocols. So we propose the use of secure non-interactive zero-knowledge proof method. And we prove that the general payment protocol satisfies the three main desired properties: fairness, timeliness and invisible TTP.

But as the normal zero-knowledge proof is universally verifiable, which may introduce defects in abuse-freeness. To solve this problem, we use a non-interactive *designated verifier proof* method to implement a fair abuse-free payment protocol. Briefly, designated verifier proof means that the proofs can convince nobody except the designated verifier (say Bob) and its underlying statement is "Either θ is true or I can sign as Bob". In this way, outside parties will not believe θ is true as Bob can simulate this proof himself.

When implementing the protocols, we have incorporated the label and message construction design principles proposed by Gurgens et al. [12].

Finally, we discuss several possible extensions to our protocols, including: possibility of using other cryptographic tools, protecting privacy in the fair payment protocol, using our results to construct a new fair abuse-free contract signing protocol and other implementation options.

The remainder of the paper is structured as follows. In Section 2, we state our protocols' assumptions and their requirements. Section 3 presents the general fair payment protocol framework. Section 4 discusses the abuse-freeness and presents the fair abuse-free protocol. In Section 5, we give some remarks and outline the possible extensions. Some concluding remarks presented in Section 6.

2. PROTOCOL REQUIREMENTS AND ASSUMPTIONS

2.1 Requirement on Fair Payment Protocols

Five requirements for fair exchange has formulated by Asokan et al. in [4] and further discussed in [25]. But their requirement definitions haven't presumed new advances in recent years. And in [18] Markowitch et al. study many former fairness definitions and present a well-knitted definition. Based on these former works, we present a complete set of requirement definitions for fair payment protocols.

Definition 1 Effectiveness
A fair payment protocol is *effective* if (the communication channels quality being fixed) there exists a successful payment exchange for the payer and the payee.

Definition 2 Fairness
A fair payment protocol is *fair* if (the communication channels quality being fixed) when the protocol run ends, either the payer gets his/her expected goods and the payee gets the payment or neither of them gets anything useful.

Definition 3 Timeliness
A fair payment protocol is *timely* if (the communication channels quality being fixed) the protocol can be completed in a finite amount of time while preserving fairness for both payer and payee.

Definition 4 Non-repudiability
A fair payment protocol is *non-repudiable* if when the exchange succeeds, either payer or payee cannot deny (partially or totally) his/her participation.

Definition 5 Invisibility of TTP
A fair payment protocol is *TTP-invisible* if after a successful exchange, the result evidences of origin/receipt and exchanged items are indistinguishable in respect to whether TTP has been involved.

2.2 Protocol Assumptions

With the application scenario set, we state our protocol's assumptions as following:

- **No Self-mutilation** Either Alice or Bob will not take any action that would hurt his/her own benefit. This assumption is quite plain and is omitted in our later analysis.
- **Communication Channel** As many fair protocols do, we assume the resilient channels between exchangers (Alice/Bob) and TTP, and unreliable channel between Alice and Bob. Messages in a resilient channel can be delayed but will eventually arrive. On the contrary, messages in unreliable channel may be lost. We also assume that both kinds of channels cannot be eavesdropped by any third party.
- **Cryptographic Tools** Encryption tools, including symmetric encryption, asymmetric encryption and normal signature scheme, are secure. In addition, the adopted signature scheme is message recovery.
- **Honest TTP** The TTP should send a valid and honest reply to every request, which means that when the TTP is involved, if a resolve decision is made, Alice gets the payment and Bob gets the goods; if a abort decision is made, Alice and Bob get the abort confirmation and they cannot resolve the exchange in any future time.

3. A GENERIC FAIR PAYMENT PROTOCOL

In this section, we present a generic fair payment protocol which is used to implement the fair abuse-free payment protocol. This generic protocol includes 4 parts: the main protocol, the resolve sub-protocol, the abort sub-protocol and the register sub-protocol. The register protocol is new as to the origin AK protocol with offline TTP. It is presented because both parties must negotiate with TTP on some common parameters like shared secret keys. The registration protocol between the Alice/Bob and TTP needs to be run only once. And the resulting common parameters can be used for any number of transactions.

Notation To describe the protocol, we need to use several notations:

- $E_k()$: a symmetric-key encryption function under key k
- $D_k()$: a symmetric-key decryption function under key k
- $E_X()$: a public-key encryption function under pk_X
- $D_X()$: a public-key decryption function under sk_X
- $S_X()$: ordinary signature function of X
- k: the key used to cipher goods
- pk_X: public key of X
- sk_X: secret key of X
- $cipher = E_k(\text{goods})$: the cipher of goods under k
- l: a label that uniquely identifies a protocol run

- *f*: a flag indicating the purpose of a message
- *h*: a secure one way hash fuction

Our protocol uses the adapted MP signature as a basic building block. So we first briefly describe this signature scheme. Then the four parts of the protocol is presented.

3.1 Adapted Mao-Paterson Convertible Signature Scheme

Let n be the Alice's RSA modulus. n is a composite integer relatively prime to $\phi(n)$. Alice chooses three integers denoted by c, d and e satisfying:

$$cde \equiv 1(\mathrm{mod}\, \phi(n)n)$$

and

$$de \neq 1(\mathrm{mod}(\phi(n)))$$

Her public key is the pair (e,n) and private key is d. c is the secret key shared between Alice and TTP, and will be used to convert the partial signature to a final one. c,d,e also satisfy:

$$\forall m < n^2 : m^{cde} \equiv m(\mathrm{mod}\, n^2)$$

and

$$\forall m < n : m^{cde} \equiv m(\mathrm{mod}\, n)$$

The signature scheme contains one register procedure and several signing/verifying algorithms.

- **Register Procedure** Signer (say Alice) requests for key registration by sending her public key pair (e, n) and c to the TTP (for security, c is encrypted by the TTP's public key, $E_{TTP}(c)$). TTP checks the validity of n (using the function denoted by *checkn*()), if passes, he sends a random number $\omega < n$ as the reference message. ω satisfies $gcd(\omega, n) = 1$ and $gcd(\omega \pm 1, n) = 1$. Alice then computes $PS(\omega) = \omega^d$ and send it to the TTP. After TTP checks (using the function denoted by $check\omega$()) whether
$$\omega \equiv PS(\omega)^{ce}(\mathrm{mod}\, n^2)$$
If it holds, the TTP will send a certificate $cert_A = S_{TTP}(A, E_{TTP}(c), n, \omega, PS(\omega))$ to Alice.
- **Signing/Verifying Algorithms of Full Signature** They are just normal signing/verifying algorithms of RSA signature: in the MP signature scheme, the complete secret key is dc. So the signing algorithm is $FS(m) = m^{dc}$, and the verifying algorithm $Ver(FS(m), m)$ is to check whether $FS(m)^e = m(\mathrm{mod}\, n)$ (outputting **true** means yes).

- **Signing/Verifying Algorithms of Partial Signature** The signing algorithm is $PS(m) = m^d$. The verifying algorithm *PVer(PS(m), m)* needs to check whether *PS(m)* and *m* have a common exponent *d* with respect to $PS(\omega)$ and ω (outputting **true** means being yes). And that is what zero-knowledge proof can do.
- **Converting Algorithm** The TTP run this algorithm *Convert(PS(m), c)* to convert *PS(m)* to *FS(m)*: $FS(m) = PS(m)^c (\bmod n)$. If the result *FS(m)* is a valid RSA signature on *m*, it implies that *PS(m)* is a valid partial signature. So the TTP needs not running the *PVer(PS(m), m)* to check validity of *PS(m)*.

3.2 The Protocol

3.2.1 Registration Sub-protocol

To participate in a fair payment protocol, both Alice and Bob need to run the register procedure with the TTP as required by MP signature. Note that it will not affect the security if they share a same reference message ω.

3.2.2 Main Protocol

After Alice and Bob settle the price and the goods, they can follow the main protocol:

- *Step 1*, Alice sends encrypted *goods* (*cipher*) with the key *k* encrypted by the TTP's public key ($E_{TTP}(k)$), her partial signature on them (a=(*cipher*, $E_{TTP}(k)$), $PS_A(a)$) to initiate the payment process.
- *Step 2*, if Bob decides to give up or he doesn't receive Alice's message in time, he can simply quit and retain fairness. When he receives the message, he will first run $PVer(PS_A(a), a)$, if it equals **true,** he will send his *check* and his partial signature on it ($PS_B(check)$) to Alice. Otherwise, he quits the protocol.
- *Step 3*, if Alice decides to give up or she doesn't receive Bob's message in time, she can invoke the *abort* sub-protocol to prevent a later resolution by the TTP. When she receive the message, she will first run $PVer(PS_B(check), check)$, if it equals **true**, she will send *k* and her full signature on *a* ($FS_A(a)$ as the **NRO**) to Bob. Otherwise, she also invokes the *abort* sub-protocol.
- *Step 4*, if Bob doesn't receive the message in time, he can invoke the *resolve* sub-protocol. When he receive the message, he will check whether *k* can decrypt the *cipher* and the *goods* is satisfactory, also he will

run $Ver(FS_A(a), a)$, if all these checking pass, he will send his *check* and his full signature on it ($FS_A(check)$) to Alice. Otherwise, he will invokes the *resolve* sub-protocol.

- *Step 5*, if Alice doesn't receive the message in time, she can invoke the *resolve* sub-protocol. When she receives the message, she will run $Ver(FS_B(check), check)$, if it equals **true**, she will accept the check. Otherwise, she will invoke the *resolve* sub-protocol.

3.2.3 Resolve Sub-protocol

Whenever necessary, Alice/Bob (noted by *X*) will invoke the *resolve* protocol to let the TTP decide whether finish or abort the payment process.

- *Step 1*, *X* sends to the TTP $E_{TTP}(k)$, PS_A(a), *check*, $PS_B(check)$ to initiate a resolve process. Because of the resilient channel between *X* and the TTP, this message will eventually arrives the TTP.
- *Step 2*, when the TTP receive the message, it will first check whether the protocol has already been resolved or aborted, if so, it will stop because it is sure that both parties have got the resolved items or the abort confirmation. Then it will decrypt $E_{TTP}(k)$ with its secret key sk_{TTP}, if succeeds, it will run $PVer(PS_A(a), a)$ and $PVer(PS_B(check), check)$. If both equals **true**, the TTP will run $Convert(PS_A(a), c_A)$ and $Convert(PS_B(check), c_B)$, send the $FS_A(check)$ to Alice and FS_A(a) & *k* to Bob. If any checking fails, it will abort the protocol and send confirmations to Alice and Bob.

3.2.4 Abort Sub-protocol

In step 2 of the main protocol, Alice can invoke this sub-protocol to make the TTP abort this payment protocol run.

- *Step 1*, Alice sends an abort request to the TTP. Because of the resilient channel between *X* and the TTP, this message will eventually arrives the TTP.
- *Step 2*, if the protocol has not been resolved or aborted, the TTP will abort the protocol and send confirmations to both parties.

3.3 Analysis of the Protocol

Following is the analysis with respect to requirement definitions in Section 2.1.

CLAIM 1 *Assuming the channel between Alice and Bob is unreliable and adopted cryptographic tools are secure, the protocol satisfies the effectiveness requirement.*

PROOF: When both Alice and Bob are honest, thus they will follow the protocol to send messages. If the probability of successful transmission in the unreliable channel is δ, then the probability of successful execution of one main protocol run will roughly be δ^4. Even it's small, but it means that successful execution without TTP's involvement is still possible. Thus the protocol satisfies the effectiveness requirement.

CLAIM 2 *Assuming the channels between the TTP and exchangers (Alice and Bob) are resilient, adopted cryptographic tools are secure and the TTP is honest, the protocol satisfies the fairness requirement.*

PROOF: The first part of fairness requirement implies two aspects: fairness for Alice and fairness for Bob.

- *Fairness for Alice* Assuming Alice is honest, then risks she may face include:

  1) She did not receive any message or the message is invalid in step 3. She can request abort to prevent that Bob may call a recovery later. If Bob's recovery request arrives to the TTP before her abort request, the TTP still will send the recovered item and evidence to her. Thus will not affect her benefit.

  2) She did not receive any message or the message is invalid in step 5. She can submit a recovery request, because the TTP is honest, the exchange will be forced to complete. If Bob sent a recovery request during this period, the result will be the same; if Bob sent an abort request which arrived before Alice's recovery request, the exchange will be aborted by the TTP, and no party can gain advantage.

- *Fairness for Bob* Assuming Bob is honest, then risks he may face include:

  1) He did not receive any message or the message is invalid in step 2. He can simply stop without any risk. And at this time, Alice cannot call recovery.

  2) He did not receive any message or the message is invalid in step 4. He can request recovery and the exchange will be forced to complete. If Alice request recovery at the same time, the result will be the same.

CLAIM 3 *Assuming the channels between the TTP and exchangers (Alice and Bob) are resilient, adopted cryptographic tools are secure and the TTP is honest, the protocol satisfies timeliness requirement.*

PROOF: Alice can conclude the protocol in one of the two ways:

- requesting abort before sending the message of step 3.
- requesting recovery in any other time.

Bob can conclude the protocol in one of the three ways:

- stopping at any time before sending the message of step 2.
- requesting recovery in any other time.

With the channel assumption, the abort confirmation or the recovered information will arrive to both parties in a finite amount of time. And all these conclusions, as discussed in the proof of claim 2, will not hurt either party's interests. So the timeliness is guaranteed.

CLAIM 4 *Assuming the channels between the TTP and exchangers (Alice and Bob) are resilient, adopted cryptographic tools (including the adopted zero-knowledge proof method) are secure, the TTP is honest, the protocol satisfies non-repudiation requirement.*
PROOF: When the exchange succeeds, either by following the main protocol or resolved by the TTP, Alice will get $FS_B(check)$, and Bob will get $FS_A(a)$ & k. If a payment protocol succeeds, by showing $FS_B(check)$, Alice can convince outside parties that Bob has received *goods* and claim her money from Bob's bank. Similarly, Bob can prove that Alice has sent *goods*. In this way, the non-repudiation requirement is satisfied.

CLAIM 5 *Assuming the channels between the TTP and exchangers (Alice and Bob) are resilient, adopted cryptographic tools (including the adopted zero-knowledge proof method) are secure, the TTP is honest, the protocol guarantees invisibility of the TTP.*
PROOF: Either the TTP is involved or not, the resulting signatures ($FS_B(check)$, $FS_A(a)$) are just the same, so the TTP is invisible.

4. IMPLEMENTING A FAIR PAYMENT PROTOCOL TO PROVIDE ABUSE-FREENESS

As discussed in Section 3, applying a secure non-interactive zero-knowledge proof method to the MP signature scheme can achieve an efficient fair payment protocol. But this kind of protocol may result in undesirable circumstances: because the partial signature's proof is universally verifiable, a not-so-honest Alice can present Bob's partial signature to an outside company proving that Bob has purchased something, and in this way to affect the company's purchasing decision.

Abuse-freeness, defined by Garay et al. [11], means that before the protocol ends, no party can prove to an outside party that he can choose whether to complete or to abort the transaction. Recently, Chadha et al. [8] propose a more precise definition of this property. They say that one party cannot prove to an outside party that the other party has participated in the protocol (for more discussion, see [8] Section 5)

To achieve the feature of abuse-freeness, we need a non-interactive designated verifier proof to replace the normal zero-knowledge proof. The non-interactive designated verifier proof presented by Jakobsson et al. and strengthened by [27][24] just satisfies all those requirements and they can be easily adapted to fit in. As described in Section 1, this kind of proof can convince nobody except the signature's designated verifier. In this way, the partial signature can only be verified by two parties: the signature recipient (the designated verifier, who can be convinced by the proof) and the TTP (who can convert the partial signature to check whether the result is a valid full signature).

4.1 Non-interactive Designated Verifier Proof

The original designated verifier proof by Jakobsson et al. works for an ElGamal-like public-key encryption scheme. So we replace the public generator g with ω in our protocol. And we assume that Alice knows $PS_B(\omega)$ and Bob knows $PS_A(\omega)$. This proof can convince only the designated verifier because proof sender (say Alice) generates the proof using $PS_B(\omega)$ and Bob can simulate a second proof that can pass the same verification process.

Generating Proofs Alice selects randomly $\alpha, \beta, u \in Z_q$, where q is large enough and it is publicly accessible) and calculates

$$\begin{cases} s = \omega^{\alpha} PS_B(\omega)^{\beta} \bmod n^2 \\ \Omega = \omega^{u} \bmod n^2 \\ M = m^{u} \bmod n^2 \\ v = h(s, \Omega, M, PS_A(m)) \\ r = u + d_A(v + \alpha) \bmod q \end{cases}$$

The proof of the $PS_A(m)$, denoted by $pf(PS_A(m))$, is $(\alpha, \beta, \Omega, M, r)$.

Verifying Proofs When Bob gets the $PS_A(m)$ and $pf(PS_A(m))$, he will calculate

$$\begin{cases} s = \omega^{\alpha} PS_B(\omega)^{\beta} \bmod n^2 \\ v = h(s, \Omega, M, PS_A(m)) \end{cases}$$

and verifies

$$\begin{cases} \Omega PS_A(\omega)^{v+\alpha} = \omega^r \bmod n^2 \\ MPS_A(m)^{v+\alpha} = m^r \bmod n^2 \end{cases}$$

The verifying operations *PVer*($PS_A(m)$,*m*) is instantiated as $verify\_des(pf(PS_A(m)), m, PS_A(m), \omega, PS_A(\omega))$. If the verification fails, the function returns **false**.

Simulating transcripts Bob can simulate correct transcripts by selecting $t, \gamma, \eta \in Z_q$ and calculate

$$\begin{cases} s = \omega^\gamma \bmod n^2 \\ \Omega = \omega^t PS_A(\omega)^{-\eta} \bmod n^2 \\ M = m^t PS_A(m)^{-\eta} \bmod n^2 \\ v = h(s, \Omega, M, PS_A(m)) \\ \mu = \eta - v \bmod q \\ r = (\gamma - \mu) d_B^{-1} \bmod q \end{cases}$$

4.2 Implementation of the Protocol

When implementing the protocol, we follow the principles proposed by Gurgens et al. [12] as briefly described here:

- Label Design Principles
  - **Verifiability** The creation of a label should be verifiable by anybody;
  - **Uniqueness** The label should be able to uniquely identify a protocol run;
  - **Secrecy** The values that are used to compute the label must not reveal any useful information about the exchange items (i.e. the goods).
- Message Construction Principles
  - **Authenticity** All message parts should be included in the respective signature (in plaintext or as hash);
  - **Verifiability** Every recipient should be able to verify this message;
  - **Context of Message** It should be possible for the recipient of a message to identify the protocol run to which its parts belong.

The protocol is described in form of program modules (similar with Vogt et al. [25]) and the notation *<event>*:*<description>* to describe the steps of every module. The *<event>* can be sending a message from *X* to *Y* (denoted by $X \rightarrow Y$) or some local operations of a participant (denoted by his/her name, i.e. *A*, *B*, or *TTP*). The <*description*> is a brief explanation of contents of the message being sent or operations performed locally.

4.2.1 Register Module

This module is a direct instantiation of the register procedure described in Section 3.1.

Registration Module

$X \rightarrow TTP: f_{\mathbf{Reg}}, pk_X, E_{TTP}(c)$
TTP: **if not** *checkn*(*n*) **then** stop
$TTP \rightarrow X: f_{\mathbf{Ref}}, X, \omega$
$X \rightarrow TTP: f_{\mathbf{Ref}}, PS_X(\omega)$
TTP: **if not** $check\omega$ () **then** stop
$TTP \rightarrow X: f_{\mathbf{cert}}, X, cert_X$

4.2.2 Main Module

The label for a protocol run is computed by Alice: $l=h(A, B, TTP, h(cipher), h(k))$. And $E_{TTP}(k)$ is replaced by $E_{TTP}(l, k)$ to ensure this encrypted key can not be decrypted in a different protocol run. In our protocol, we denote the content to be signed by Alice for **NRO** as $a=(f_{\mathbf{NRO}}, B, l, h(k), cipher, E_{TTP}(k))$. Bob's check is signed with *A* and *l* ($b=(A, l, check)$), so the signed check will be $PS_B(b)$ and $FS_B(b)$. With this construction, the signed check can only be used by Alice to claim the money.

Main Module

$A \rightarrow B: f_{\mathbf{EOO}}, B, l, h(k), cipher, E_{TTP}(l, k), PS_A(a), pf(PS_A(a))$
B: **if not** $verify\_des(pf(PS_A(a)), a, PS_A(a), \omega, PS_A(\omega))$ **then** stop
$B \rightarrow A$□$f_{\mathbf{EOR}}, A, l, PS_B(b), pf(PS_A(b))$
A: **if** times out **then abort**
elseif not $verify\_des(pf(PS_B(b)), b, PS_B(b), \omega, PS_B(\omega))$ **then abort**
$A \rightarrow B$□$f_{\mathbf{NRO}}, B, l, k, FS_A(a)$
B: **if** times out **then** call **resolve**[$X{:=}B, Y{:=}A$]
$B \rightarrow A$□$f_{\mathbf{NRR}}, A, l, FS_B(b)$
A: **if** *A* times out **then** call **resolve**[$X{:=}A, Y{:=}B$]

4.2.3 Resolve Module

The resolve protocol is similar with the one in AK protocol. It is executed when an error happens, one party needs TTP's help to decrypt the key k and generate the final evidences for him/her. Assume the TTP keeps a record on whether the protocol has been resolved or aborted (denoted by two variables: *aborted* and *resolved*)

Resolve Module

$X \rightarrow TTP$: $f_{\text{RecX}}, f_{\text{Sub}}, Y, l, h(cipher)$, h($k$), $E_{TTP}(k)$, $\mathbf{Rec_X}$, $PS_A(a)$, $PS_B(b)$
    TTP: **if** $h(k) \neq h(D_{TTP}(E_{TTP}(k)))$ **or** *aborted* **or** *resolved* **then** stop
            else *resolved*=true
            $Convert(PS_A(a), c_A)$ and $Convert(PS_B(check), c_B)$
$TTP \rightarrow A$: $f_{\text{NRR}}, A, l, FS_A(a)$
$TTP \rightarrow B$: $f_{\text{NRO}}, B, l, k, FS_B(b)$

4.2.4 Abort Module

Alice submits an abort request using abort module, i.e. set the aborted=**true**, preventing Bob may recover in a future time which she will not wait. $\mathbf{Con}_a$ denotes the abort confirmation.

Abort Module

$X \rightarrow TTP$: f_{Abort}, l, B, **abort**
    TTP: **if** *aborted* **or** *recovered* **then** stop
            else *recovered*=true
$TTP \rightarrow A$: $f_{\text{Cona}}, A, B, l, \mathbf{Con}_a$
$TTP \rightarrow B$: $f_{\text{Cona}}, A, B, l, \mathbf{Con}_a$

---

5. DISCUSSIONS

In this section, we give some remarks on the cryptographic tools and implementation, resulting an outline of possible extensions.

5.1 The Dodis-Reyzin CS signature

This CS signature is quite efficient for it additively split the secret key and preserve security. But this signature is based on the GDH signature (see [10] section 4), whose verification needs zero-knowledge proofs and the partial signatures are to be verified both by the recipient (in main protocol) and the TTP (in resolve sub-protocol). When realizing abuse-freeness, if directly applied with the designated verifier proofs, the TTP will NOT be convinced of the validity of the partial signature. As a result, a different proof method should be adopted to make both the recipient and the TTP convinced. Recently, Wang [26] has proposed a new proof method call Restrictive Confirmation Signature Scheme (RCSS) that fulfills this requirement. But the outcome is quite complicated and adds computation burdens. So we choose the RSA-based CS signature scheme, which splits the secret key multiplicatively similarly with the one in Boyd and Foo protocol. But our protocols are more efficient in that they use non-interactive partial signature verification and more importantly, our protocol assures timeliness.

5.2 The Saeednia-Kremer-Markowitch Designated Verifier Scheme

Recently, Saeednia et al. [24] has proposed a stronger and more efficient designated verifier scheme, which can be easily adapted to our abuse-free protocol if stronger requirements are assumed.

5.3 Protecting the Payer's Privacy

Anonymity is an important issue in payment system because normally customers are not willingly to have his purchase exposed (especially in a open network, that is why we assume two companies in our scenario for they can afford more secure channels and honest TTP). We propose two variations considering our protocol: 1) Not including any goods information in Bob's check. It will weaken the property of non-repudiation, as Alice won't get a signed list of purchased goods by Bob. 2) Applying anonymous but traceable e-cash into the protocol (see Wang [26]).

5.4 Extending Our Results to Contract Signing

Abuse-freeness is first introduced in context of contract signing, and our protocol can be easily transformed into fair exchange of two signatures. So constructing a new abuse-free contract signing protocol is a useful extension of our protocol.

6. IMPLEMENTING THE PROTOCOL USING AGENT MECHANISMS

The agent mechanism has been widely used in electronic commerce applications. Pagnia et al. [21] have presented implementation of fair protocol using mobile agents.

7. CONCLUSIONS

In this paper, we produce an efficient generic fair payment protocol with RSA-based convertible signature. Based on that, we implement a fair abuse-free payment protocol using non-interactive designated verifier proof as a new proposal on the issue of abuse-freeness.

We have shown that the protocol are practical because their standardized evidences and high efficiency. Our future work will be focused on the application of the fair payment protocols to real electronic commerce systems like SCM and CRM.

ACKNOWLEDGEMENTS

The authors would like to thank Steve Kremer for helpful discussions on the issues of abuse-freeness and designated verifier proof. Furthermore, we would like to thank the anonymous reviewers of I3E for valuable comments.

REFERENCES

[1] N. Asokan, Philippe A. Janson, Michael Steiner, and Michael Waidner, "The State of the Art in Electronic Payment Systems", IEEE Computer, September 1997, pp. 28-35.

[2] N. Asokan, M. Schunter, and M. Waidner, "Optimistic protocols for fair exchange", in Proceedings of the fourh ACM Conference on Computer and Communications Security, Zurich, Switzerland, April 1997, pp. 6, 8-17.

[3] N. Asokan and V. Shoup, "Optimistic fair exchange of digital signatures", in Advances in Cryptology -- EUROCRYPT '98, volume 1403 of Lecture Notes in Computer Science, Springer-Verlag, 1998, pp. 591-606.

[4] N. Asokan, V. Shoup, and M. Waidner, "Asynchronous protocols for optimistic fair exchange", in Proceedings of IEEE Symposium on Research in Security and Privacy, 1998, pp. 86-99. (Printed version contains some errors. Errata sheet is distributed together with the electronic version).

[5] G. Ateniese, "Efficient verifiable encryption (and fair exchange) of digital signatures", in Proceedings of the 6th ACM conference on Computer and communications security, Nov. 1999.

[6] F. Bao, R. Deng and W. Mao, "Efficient and practical fair exchange protocols with off-line TTP", in Proceedings of IEEE Symposium on Security and Privacy, Oakland, May 1998, pp. 77-85.
[7] C. Boyd, E. Foo. "Off-line Fair Payment Protocols using Convertible Signatures", in Advances in Cryptology---ASIA CRYPT'98, 1998.
[8] R. Chadha, J. Mitchell, A. Scedrov and V. Shmatikov, "Contract signing, optimism and advantage", in CONCUR 2003 - Concurrency Theory, 14-th International Conference, Marseille, France, September 2003. Volume 2761 of Lecture Notes in Computer Science, Springer-Verlag, 2003, pp. 366-382
[9] R. Chadha, M. Kanovich and A. Scedrov, "Inductive methods and contract-signing protocols", in Proceedings of 8th ACM confererence on Computer and Communications Security(CCS-8). Philadelphia, Pennsylvania, ACM Press, November 7, 2001, pp. 176-185.
[10] Y. Dodis and L. Reyzin, "Breaking and repairing optimistic fair exchange from PODC 2003", in Proceedings of the 2003 ACM workshop on Digital rights management, Oct. 2003.
[11] J. Garay, M. Jakobsson and P. MacKenzie. "Abuse-free optimistic contract signing", in Advances in Cryptology - CRYPTO '99, volume 1666 of Lecture Notes in Computer Science, SpringerVerlag, 1999, pp. 449-466.
[12] S. Gurgens, C. Rudolph and H. Vogt, "On the Security of Fair Non-repudiation Protocols", in Proceedings of 2003 Information Security Conference, volume 2851 of Lecture Notes in Computer Science, Bristol, UK, Oct. 2003, pp. 193--207.
[13] M. Jakobsson, K. Sako, R. Impagliazzo, "Designated verifier proofs and their applications", in Eurocrypt'96, volume 1070 of Lecture Notes in Computer Science, Springer Verlag, 1996, pp. 143-154.
[14] S. Kremer and O. Markowitch, "Optimistic non-repudiable information exchange", in 21th Symposium on Information Theory in the Benelux, Werkgemeenschap Informatie- en Communicatietheorie, Enschede, may 2000, pp. 139-146.
[15] S. Kremer and J.F. Raskin, "Game Analysis of Abuse-free Contract Signing", in 15th Computer Security Foundations Workshop (CSFW 2002), IEEE Computer Society. Cape Breton, Nova Scotia, Canada, 2002.
[16] P. Louridas, "Some guidelines for non-repudiation protocols", ACM SIGCOMM Computer Communication Review, Oct. 2000.
[17] O. Markowitch and S. Kremer, "An optimistic non-repudiation protocol with transparent trusted third party", in Information Security: ISC 2001, volume 2200 of Lecture Notes in Computer Science, Malaga, Spain. Springer-Verlag, Oct. 2001, pp. 363-378.
[18] O. Markowitch, S. Kremer and D. Gollmann, "On Fairness in Exchange Protocols", in Information Security and Cryptology - ICISC 2002, volume 2587 of Lecture Notes in Computer Science. Springer-Verlag, 2002.
[19] W. Mao and K. Paterson, "Convertible Undeniable Standard RSA Signatures", 2000; http://citeseer.ist.psu.edu/mao00convertible.html.
[20] S. Micali, "Certified e-mail with invisible post offices", Available from author: an invited presentation at the RSA'97 conference, 1997.
[21] H. Pagnia, H. Vogt, F.C. Gatner, and U.G. Wilhelm, "Solving Fair Exchange with Mobile Agents", Volume 1882 of Lecture Notes in Computer science, Springer, September 2000, pp. 57-72.
[22] J.M. Park, Edwin K. P. Chong and H. J. Siegel, "Constructing fair-exchange protocols for E-commerce via distributed computation of RSA signatures", in Proceedings of the twenty-second annual symposium on Principles of distributed computing, July 2003.

[23] B. Pfitzmann, M. Schunter and M. Waidner, "Optimal efficiency of optimistic contract signing", in Proceedings of the seventeenth annual ACM symposium on Principles of distributed computing, June 1998.

[24] S. Saeednia, S. Kremer and O. Markowitch, "An efficient strong designated verifier scheme", in 6th International Conference on Information Security and Cryptology (ICISC 2003), Lecture Notes in Computer Sciences, Springer-Verlag. Seoul, Korea, Nov. 2003.

[25] H. Vogt, H. Pagnia, and F.C. Gartner, "Modular Fair Exchange Protocols for Electronic Commerce", In Proceedings of the 15th Annual Computer Security Applications Conference, Phoenix, Arizona. IEEE, Dec. 1999.

[26] C.H. Wang, "Untraceable Fair Network Payment Protocols with Off-Line TTP", in Advances in Cryptology - ASIACRYPT 2003: 9th International Conference on the Theory and Application of Cryptology and Information Security, volume 2894 of Lecture Notes in Computer Science, Spring-Verlag, 2003, pp. 173 - 187

[27] G. Wang, "An Attack on Not-interactive Designated Verifier Proofs for Undeniable Signatures", Cryptology ePrint Archive, Report 2003/243, 2003; http://eprint.iacr.org/2003/243/.

SEMOPS: PAYING WITH MOBILE PERSONAL DEVICES

Antonis Ramfos [a], Stamatis Karnouskos [b], András Vilmos [c], Balázs Csik [d], Petra Hoepner [b] and Nikolaos Venetakis [a]

[a]Intrasoft International, Athens, Greece, www.intrasoft-intl.com

[b]Fraunhofer Institute FOKUS, Berlin, Germany, www.fokus.fraunhofer.de

[c]SafePay Systems, Budapest, Hungary, www.safepaysys.com

[d]Profitrade, Budapest, Hungary, www.profitrade.hu

Abstract: The growth of mobile commerce is directly related to the increase of ownership and use of mobile personal, programmable communication devices, including mobile phones and PDAs. These devices provide effective authorisation and management of payment and banking transactions since they are capable of offering security and convenience advantages compared with existing methods, such as credit/debit card transactions and online payments through a PC. Some of these advantages are part of the existing devices' functionality while others require modest, inexpensive enhancements likely to be incorporated in the mobile devices to come. It is expected that the use of secure and convenient mobile personal devices can revolutionise the payment, banking and investment industries worldwide. This paper presents SEMOPS, a secure mobile payment service implemented on innovative technological solutions and introducing a competitive business enabler of mobile commerce. SEMOPS intends to exploit the business opportunities inherent in the billing, customer-service, technical relationships and banking services among mobile customers, mobile operators and banks in order to offer a competitive solution to existing payment services.

Key words: e-commerce; m-commerce; e-payment; m-payment; security

1. INTRODUCTION

The increasingly popular ownership of mobile personal, programmable communication devices worldwide promises an extended use of them in the purchase of goods and services in the years to come [3]. Security in payment transactions and user convenience are the two main motivations for using mobile devices for payments.

Authorisation in existing electronic payment systems, including ATM and credit/debit card transactions as well as on-line payments through a PC, is based on account-holder authentication. Account-holder authentication, however, can fail in multiple ways, including the compromise of the bank's computers or, in the case of online banking, the compromise of the user's computer, which is, typically, protected with minimal security mechanisms and processes. Moreover, existing payment networks do not always distinguish among user fraud, compromise of the user's computer, or compromise of the bank's computer. For example, in most countries, if the user claims not to have authorised a credit card transaction, the transaction has to be cancelled and the bank cannot prove that the user is not cheating. In such cases, responsibility is not necessarily allocated fairly, and non-corrupted, innocent parties may find themselves responsible for somebody else's fraudulent activity or security breach. The lack of a technical solution for preventing and resolving fraud creates substantial risk and expense for users, merchants and banks alike.

It is now well understood that a secure electronic payment transaction can only be ensured through a device that offers its own I/O interface to the user, so that the initiator of the payment transaction is clearly identifiable [5]. Mobile personal devices provide a technical solution for personalised I/O interface to payment transactions since the transaction initiator is the owner of the mobile device also. Security in payment transactions through a mobile device, therefore, is ensured by the authentication mechanisms of existing mobile devices, as a way to prevent call theft. Moreover, additional built-in mechanisms to ensure secure transaction authorisation and execution are relatively easy and inexpensive to be incorporated by device manufacturers. Therefore, payment through mobile devices benefits merchants and banks by supporting transactions where most fraud is prevented and responsibility for the remaining fraud is fairly allocated. As far as the end customer is concerned, the value of secure transactions far outweighs their possible cost.

Convenience is the other reason people are expected to use mobile personal devices for payments. Convenience can result from people using their mobile personal device when paying for goods and services, while on foot, in cars, planes, or trains, and when authorising payment transactions at remote servers of banks, brokerages, and merchants. Payments through mobile devices will enable validation of the customer's consent to the transaction during online, by telephone or by post purchases, since the merchant and the customer are at separate locations and the merchant cannot get the customer to sign in order to authorise the payment. In addition, payment through mobile devices will enable the secured purchase of content and services delivered via the network, as well as person-to-person payments and money transfer.

Several mobile payment systems have been realised as prototypes or even as commercial products, however none of them managed to establish itself as a global mobile payment service. There have been several criteria on the technology side and on the business model that have restricted the capabilities of such procedures. SEMOPS features an extensible business model that takes advantage of the legacy infrastructure and its trust relationships, and also tackles privacy. Furthermore, most existing payment procedures today can satisfy a limited number of scenarios such as Top-Ups, mTicketing or P2P payments, but with sometimes complex procedures, not cost-effective solutions and limited applicability. The SEMOPS approach is more general, can be easily extended to integrate any third party financial service provider and is suitable for any payment scenario, even for cross-border ones. This paper will provide an insight on some design and implementation decisions of SEMOPS and we will balance this with the commercial viewpoint of the approach.

2. MOBILE PAYMENT SOLUTIONS

Figure 1 outlines a typical mobile payment transaction. This modular transaction architecture can be used for multiple applications and scenarios. The simplest scenario involves only the user, the device and a single payment processor, such as a mobile operator, bank, credit card organisation, broker or an insurance company. The user identifies to the mobile device through secure identification mechanisms, including physical possession and password or even via biometric methods; the device then authorises the transaction to the payment processor for money transfer. More complex transactions involve at least one additional party, the merchant. In this case, the merchant may be affiliated with a different payment processor, and, then, the two payment processors have to be able to interoperate.

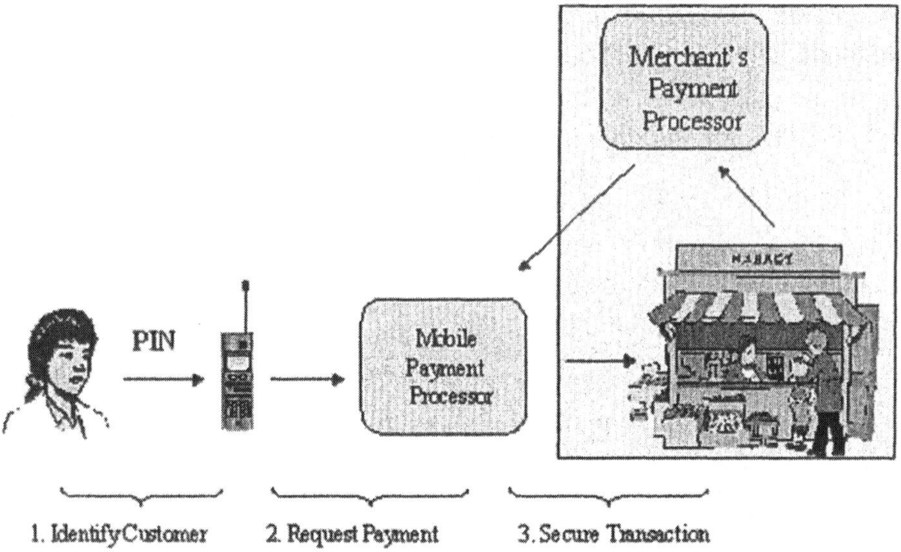

Figure 1. Mobile Payment Transaction

Most of the existing mobile payment solutions assume that a mobile payment service is offered to the customers of a particular mobile network operator (MNO), as shown in Figure 2. These payment solutions allow customers of a particular mobile operator to perform payment transactions with merchants who are contracted by the same MNO. In these payment solutions, no cross-over to other operators is foreseen, no direct involvement of trusted organisations, such as banks, takes place and, hence, payment transactions are limited to micro-payment transactions only, typically under 2€. Although a limited number of existing payment solutions have the capability to reach the critical mass for the adoption of mobile commerce, they offer limited transaction potential and limited accelerator effect of mobile commerce [2].

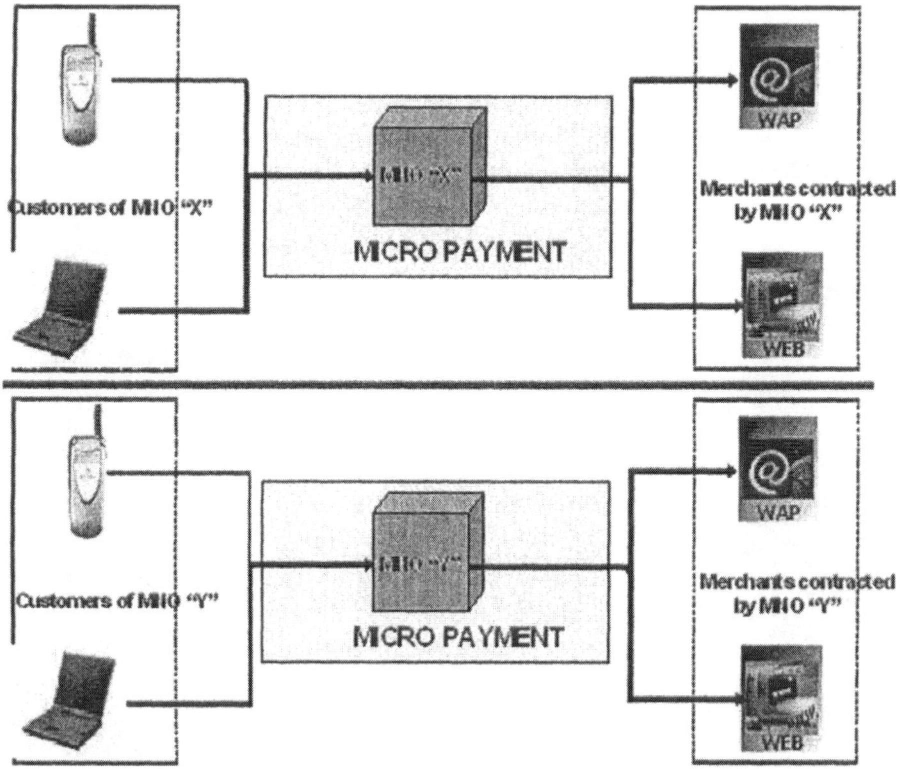

Figure 2. Existing m-payment solutions

In this paper, we present SEMOPS [1] a mobile payment solution that is capable of supporting micro, mini (e.g., between 2 € and 20 €), as well as macro payment (e.g., over 20 €) transactions. It is a universal solution, being able to function in any channel, including mobile, Internet and POS; it can support any transaction type, including P2P, B2C, B2B and P2M (person to machine), with a domestic and/or international geographic coverage. As shown in Figure 3, SEMOPS enables the realisation of a mobile payment network that combines different payment processors, and, hence, it can realise a payment service with huge transaction potential, lower user fees and large turnover [4].

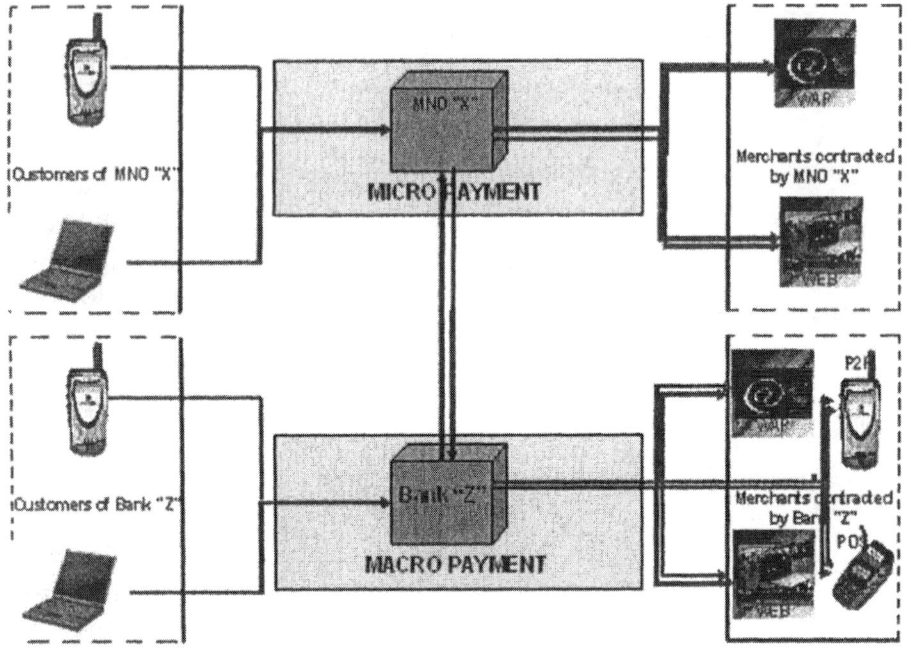

Figure 3. SEMOPS m-payment solution

As shown in Figure 3, the SEMOPS payment solution allows both, mobile operators and banks to become payment processors in a mobile payment service. There can be different combinations, depending on whether the user uses his bank or MNO account and whether the merchant accepts the payment on his bank or MNO account. Furthermore, the SEMOPS model is versatile and any trusted service provider that can offer the customer an account (e.g. credit card, financial service provider) can also easily take the role of the SEMOPS payment processor.

3. SEMOPS TRANSACTION ARCHITECTURE AND FLOW

As in every payment system, the aim of SEMOPS is to transfer funds from the customer to the merchant, or, in more general terms, from the payer to the payee. The SEMOPS payment solution, however, is novel in that it establishes a process flow that allows cooperation between banks and mobile operators. Figure 4 gives a view of the modular architecture of the SEMOPS payment solution in which the payer and the payee exchange transaction data, while the fund transfer is done via trusted payment processors, the customer and merchant banks, respectively. Each user (payer or payee) connects with his home bank/MNO only. The banks exchange messages between them via the Data Center (DC). The legacy systems of the bank and of the merchant are integrated in the SEMOPS infrastructure and are used as usual. Note that, the payers can authorise payments by both mobile devices and web browsers, whereas payees can participate with any sale outlet, including WAP, POS, vending machines, or web. Moreover, SEMOPS can support mobile Person-to-Person (P2P) transactions with the same convenience as any other payment transaction.

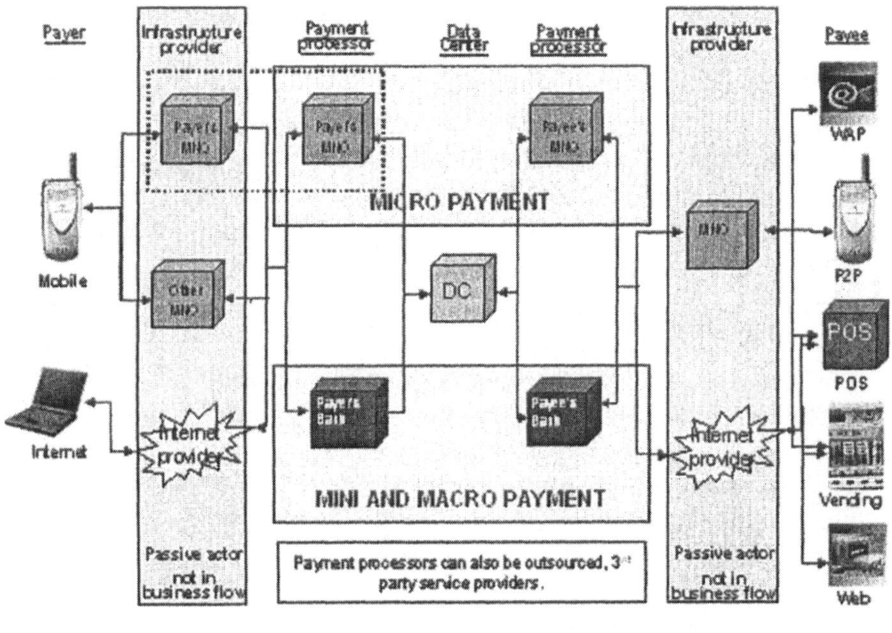

Figure 4. Overview of SEMOPS payment network architecture

The transaction flow, which is completely controlled by the payer, follows a simple credit push model. A typical SEMOPS transaction flow for a prompt payment from a customer to a merchant is presented in the following, (see Figure 5):

- The merchant (in general, any POS/VirtualPOS) provides to the customer the necessary transaction details (e.g. via IrDA, Bluetooth or even Instant Messaging), (Step 1). This data includes certain static and dynamic elements that identify the merchant and the individual transaction. During the whole payment process, the customer does not identify herself to the merchant, nor does she provides any information about herself, her bank, or any other sensitive data.

- The customer receives the transaction data from the merchant. (Step 2). A standard format payment request is prepared to be sent to the selected payment processor who is the trusted partner of the customer – either her bank or her mobile network operator. When the payment request is ready for transfer, the customer checks its content, authorises it (via PIN and/or PKI), and sends the payment request to the selected payment processor.
- The customer's payment processor receives the payment request, identifies the customer and processes the payment request, (Step 3). Processing includes the verification of the availability of the necessary funds, and reservation of the required amount. When the processing is completed a payment notice is prepared by the payment processor and is forwarded to the Data Center of the SEMOPS service. The Data Center identifies the addressee bank of the payment notice and forwards the message to the merchant's trusted payment processor, who again can be either its bank or mobile operator. The Data Center handles the message delivery among the payment processors. We assume that at least one Data Center per country will exist, and in case of an international transaction a second Data Center is also involved, namely the local Data Center of the foreign merchant's country. The two Data Centers cooperate and the transaction is routed accordingly.
- The merchant's payment processor receives the payment notice and identifies the merchant. The payment processor advises the merchant in real time about the payment by forwarding the payment notice (Step 4). The merchant has the chance to control the content of the payment notice and can decide, whether to approve or reject the transaction. By confirming the transaction to its payment processor, (Step 5), a confirmation through the Data Center to customer's payment processor is forwarded (Step 6).
- When customer's payment processor receives the positive confirmation, it initiates a regular bank transfer to merchant's bank. This transfer is based on the regular well-established inter-banking procedures. In case of successful money transfer, the merchant's bank sends a notification to the merchant, and the customer's payment processor sends a notification to the customer. If for whatever reason the merchant rejects the transaction, the customer's payment processor releases the funds it has reserved for the purchase.

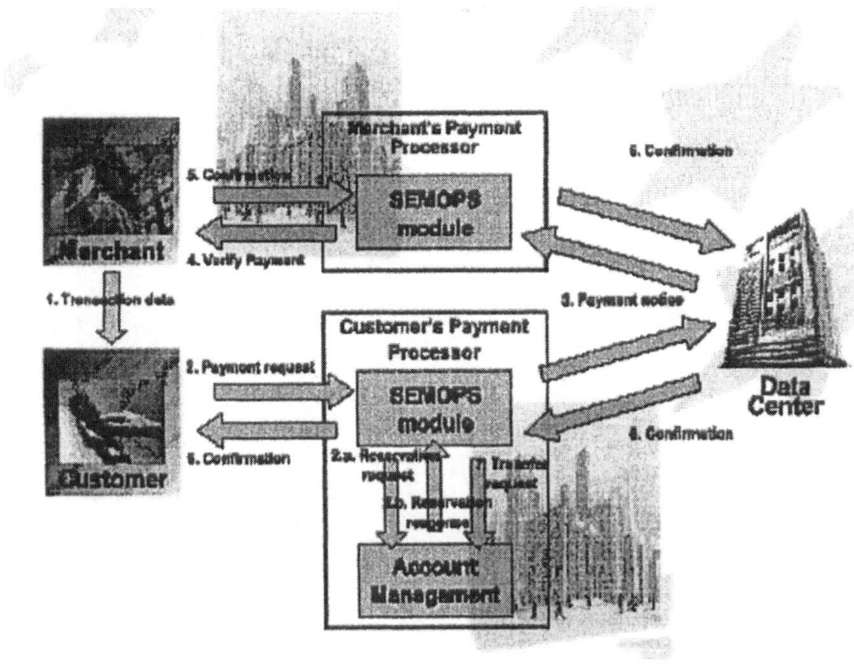

Figure 5. SEMOPS Transaction Architecture

The above-mentioned description refers to a prompt payment. However, the SEMOPS solution is more versatile and allows also deferred, value date and recurring transactions. SEMOPS supports a refund feature as well, and in case of cross border transactions conversion between currencies is also possible.

Should for whatever reason the transaction is not completed, , the customer's payment processor releases the funds it has reserved for the purchase. The following reasons could cause disruption to a transaction:

- The customer may use a wrong PIN while requesting payment
- Not enough funds are available on the customer's account
- The merchant may reject the transaction
- Communication problem

4. SEMOPS SYSTEM TECHNICAL INFRASTRUCTURE

Unlike the PC environment, the mobile environment presents the challenge of supporting multiple data channels and platforms. Mobile communications are characterised by the variety of data technologies, device capabilities, and standards. Shopping and payment may take place on separate channels. For example, a customer may shop with WAP or receive an actionable alert, and carry out the payment over SMS, USSD, raw GPRS or WAP to the payment processor. Therefore, in defining mobile solutions, it is important to recognise that multiple technologies coexist, and will continue to do so.

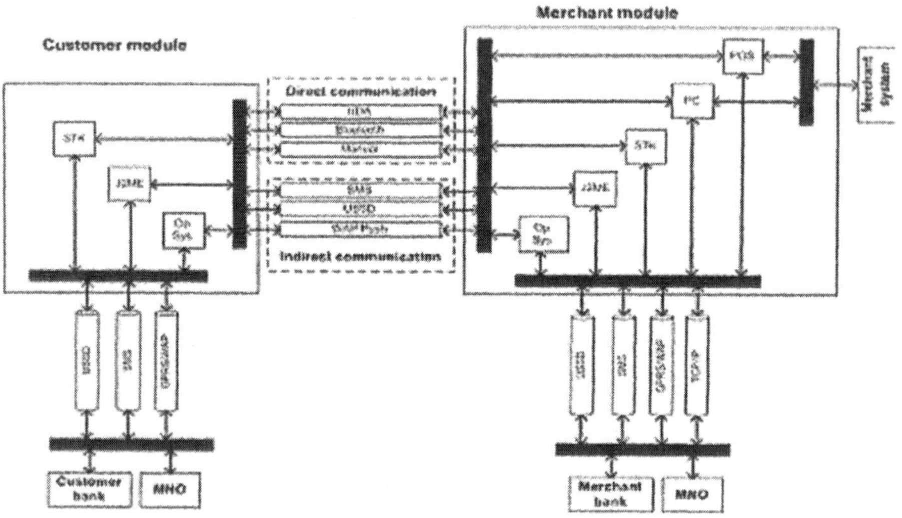

Figure 6. Base Technologies of Front-End Modules

The main modules in the SEMOPS solution are the front-end modules, namely, the customer and the merchant modules. These are designed to have extended functionality, security, openness, usability and a versatile application-executing environment. The back-end modules comprise of transaction management applications that reside in the payment processors' premises and interact with their accounting systems, as well as the Data Centre modules, which is responsible for the communication and reconciliation of transactions between involved payment processors.

As shown in Figure 6, the SEMOPS front-end modules are very versatile from the mobile technology point of view and combine all viable implementation possibilities in user-process and client technologies.

4.1.1.1 Customer Module

The customer module has two basic forms, the mobile and the Internet one. A variety of implementations exists in the mobile form, namely, a SIM toolkit (STK) based, a Java based and an operating system (OS) based module. The customer module assists the customer to carry out a payment transaction using the service. There are three basic features in all types of customer modules, i.e., personalisation, payment processing and transaction management. The personalisation features allow high-level usability and convenience for the users. The module can be downloaded and updated over the air or from the Internet, thus, avoiding the usual hassle one has to go through, when subscribing for a service. The module allows storing of all user related, non-sensitive information that is frequently used. It also enables storing multiple user and payment processor profiles, in order to let the user choose her preferred payment processor for each individual transaction. All information can be password-protected, and the protection level is also adjustable by the customer. The actual payment functions include communication with the merchant's systems, preparation of payment request, communication with the selected payment processor, administration of the transaction details, and notification of the user about a transaction status. Transaction management includes a wide variety of functions that are related to the handling of the stored transaction information. Besides providing historical information about past purchases, certain manual transaction types, refund requests and synchronization commands can also be launched using the administrative functions.

4.1.1.2 Merchant Module

The merchant module is the bridge between the payee's sales outlet and the payer, and also between the payee and the payee's payment processor. For this reason, the merchant modules include an Internet and a POS version, along with multiple mobile versions (STK, Java, OS). The merchant module receives the necessary transaction information from the merchant's sale system and transfers it to the customer. Similarly to the customer module, all permanent information can be safely stored, minimising the data amount that needs to be transferred between systems or input manually. During the payment transaction the merchant module communicates with the customer and transfers all the information necessary for completing the payment. An important function of the merchant module is the approval of the transaction. The merchant's payment processor advises the merchant about the payment and the module either approves or rejects the transaction automatically based on the information it has. The merchant module features also extensive administrative functions e.g. report generation, refund initiation etc.

It can be clearly seen from Figure 6 that the SEMOPS solution achieves the widest technology coverage in terms of:

- The platform of the customer module
- The platform of the merchant module

- The merchant – customer communication channel
- The customer – customer Bank communication channel
- The merchant – merchant Bank communication channel

5. DESIGN AND IMPLEMENTATION CONSIDERATIONS IN SEMOPS

The design of the system is open and flexible for future integration of hardware and software modules, as well as cooperation with other applications and services.

In order to accommodate the heterogeneity of supported mobile platform in SEMOPS front-end modules (STK, J2ME, other platforms), all front-end modules' design share common UML Use Case models and Activity Diagrams. After achieving this common design base for all front-end modules, operating platform-specific designs were produced, (depicted in Figure 7).

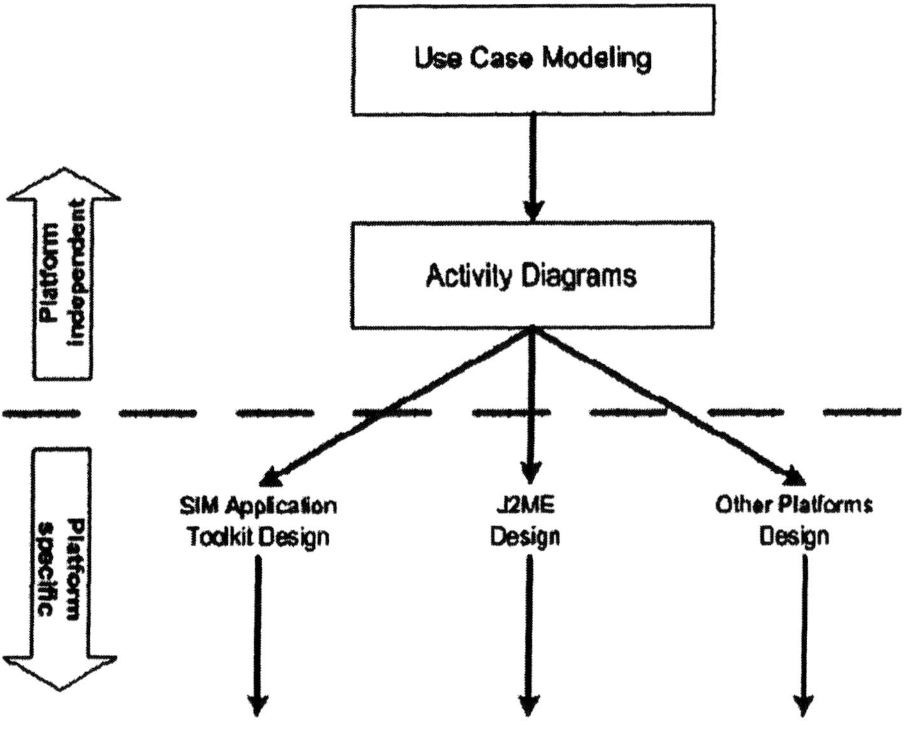

Figure 7. Overview of the mobile module designs

From these operating platform-specific designs, the SIM Application Toolkit one is the most unique, since the design steps are a mixture of the

RUP/UML methodology and the procedural system design. Due to the limited storage and process capabilities of SIM cards, the application was decomposed into re-usable components in order to achieve an efficient storage management within the inherent SIM cards storage limitations.

The software implementation environment of the SEMOPS solution consisted of: Java2 (J2EE/J2ME), XML, ORACLE9i, and WebSphere v5.1

6. SECURITY IN SEMOPS

SEMOPS provides a strong end-to-end encryption for transferred data and allows the usage of different authentication techniques embedded into this encryption. SEMOPS built up its security framework with the following considerations:

- Banks do not allow encrypted information into the Intranet: Decryption must be done in the Demilitarised Zone (DMZ).
- Banks usually have their own authentication system already: SEMOPS must co-operate with existing authentication facilities.
- SEMOPS uses heterogeneous channels, e.g., TCP/IP, GPRS, SMS, USSD: SSL cannot be used as encrypted channel.
- Different country regulations prohibit the usage of the same keys for encryption and signing: SEMOPS works with multiple key pairs.

Based on these considerations, SEMOPS utilises the security model depicted in Figure 8. The termination of the physical channels and the decryption of the messages occur in the DMZ. The decrypted information reaches the SEMOPS Bank Module (residing on the Intranet of the bank and implementing the core business logic) through the bank's standard authentication system, which is already used for applications, like home banking. Currently SEMOPS uses 1024 bit RSA encrypted XML with 3DES message keys, and also uses 1024 bit RSA digital signatures on the messages, but with a different key pair. The security modules execute all the cryptographic operations in the system, resulting in the split security operations depicted in Figure 8.

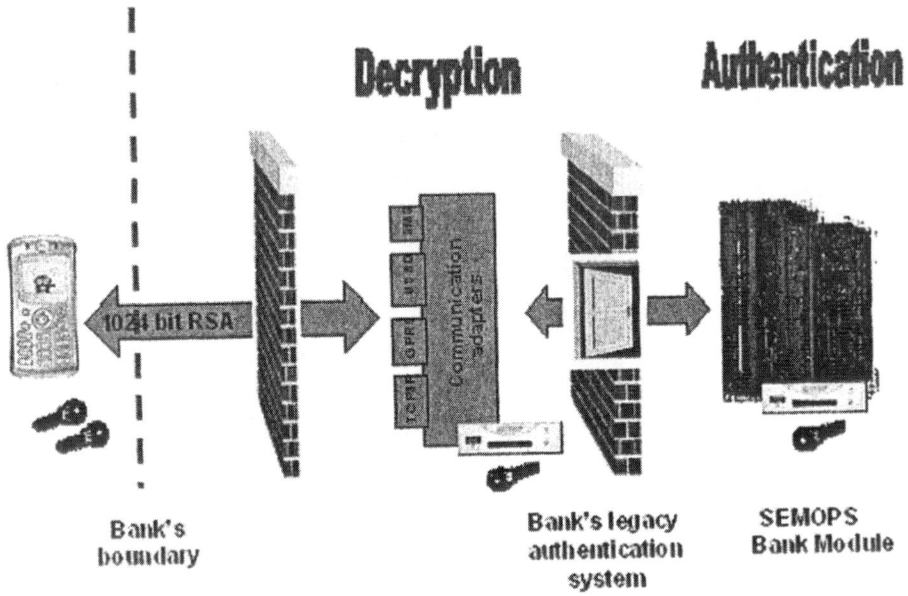

Figure 8. SEMOPS Security Infrastructure at Payment Processors Site

7. CONCLUSIONS

SEMOPS realises a secure mobile payment solution, which is capable of electronic and mobile commerce scenarios. The SEMOPS approach can also accommodate anonymous payments, which is something that can be done only with cash today and limited prepaid money-token cards. Both, modules that interact with payers and payees (front-end modules) and modules that interact with payment processors' systems (back-end modules) are designed to have extended functionality, security, openness, usability and a versatile application-executing environment. In particular, SEMOPS front-end modules are very versatile from the mobile technology point of view and combine all viable implementation possibilities in user-processes and mobile/Internet technologies. Its design enables the cooperation of banks and MNOs in providing a trusted and convenient mobile payment service. The payment processors in the SEMOPS service can be any combination of banks and MNOs, and each actor in the service, either payer or payee transacts only with his trusted bank or MNO. SEMOPS covers both mobile and Internet transactions, addresses domestic and cross border payments, and can accommodate various transaction types, irrespective of value, function, time, currency etc. It is worth noting that SEMOPS features a distributed approach where banks and MNOs can dynamically join the system with their customer base, something that will allow SEMOPS to grow fast and reach a critical mass that may establish it as a global payment service. Trial SEMOPS services have been deployed in Hungary and Greece. Future plans include extensive cross-border trials and tests, as well as the deployment of a pan-European pilot until 2005.

ACKNOWLEDGEMENT

This paper describes work undertaken and in progress in the context of the SEMOPS (IST-2001-37055) [1], a two-year project (2002-2004), which is partially funded by the Commission of the European Union. The authors would like to acknowledge all SEMOPS partners.

REFERENCES

[1] Secure Mobile Payment Service (SEMOPS), http://www.semops.com

[2] "Mobile Payment: The German and European Perspective", Joachim Henkel, G. Silberer (ed.): Mobile Commerce, Gabler Publishing, Wiesbaden (2001).

[3] Mobey Forum White Paper on Mobile Financial Services, June 2003, http://www.mobeyforum.org/public/material/

[4] "Standardized Payment Procedures as Key Enabling Factor for Mobile Commerce", Kreyer, N.; Pousttchi, K.; Turowski, K. In: Bauknecht, K.; Quirchmayr, G.; Tjoa, A M. (Hrsg.): Proceedings of the EC-WEB 2002, Aix-en-Provence, 2002.

[5] "Trustworthy user devices", Pfitzmann, A., et al: Multilateral Security in Communications, G. Muller and K. Rannenberg, Eds., Addison-Wesley, 1999, pp 137-156

E-BUSINESS ARCHITECTURES AND PROCESSES

VM-FLOW:

Using Web Services Orchestration and Choreography to Implement a Policy-based Virtual Marketplace

Ivo J. G. dos Santos and Edmundo R. M. Madeira
Institute of Computing - UNICAMP – University of Campinas
13083-970 - Campinas, SP, Brazil
{ivo, edmundo}@ic.unicamp.br

Abstract: Companies are daily trying to find new ways to cope with the increasing competitive pressures imposed by the global economy. Static and huge enterprises are being replaced by dynamic business networks where each participant offers to the others specialized services. *Service-Oriented Computing* (SOC) is being considered by many as a very interesting technological solution to the new B2B interactions introduced by this economical scenario. This paper presents a Virtual Marketplace infrastructure, called VM-Flow, which supports Dynamic Virtual Enterprises, is workflow-based and introduces a series of interaction policies that treat aspects like autonomy and privacy. Also, Service Composition is shown as a suitable solution to implement these policy-based interorganizational interactions. Some issues on the developed prototype are discussed and an application built over it is described.

Key words: Service-Oriented Computing; Orchestration and Choreography; Virtual Enterprises; Marketplaces; e-Business; Workflow; Interaction Policies.

1. INTRODUCTION

The digital and global economy represents a daily challenge to companies. They need to find new ways to cope with increasing competitive pressures imposed by the market. One of the main goals is to reduce costs, and, therefore, increase sales, always maintaining (or even improving) the quality of the products and services [OT01].

Static and huge enterprises are being replaced by dynamic business networks where each participant offers to the others specialized services. Traditional technological infrastructures previously managed and owned by a single enterprise are giving way to networks of applications, whose control is distributed among many business partners [CKMT03]. On this context, *Service-Oriented Computing* is being applied by many as one good technological solution, mainly because of the way SOC treats the heterogeneity introduced by these new business networks. Services become then the basic building blocks for the construction of applications through the use of *Service Composition.*

On the e-Business/e-Commerce field, concepts like Virtual Enterprises (VE) and Virtual Marketplaces (VM) have already been applied for some years as a way to improve the quality and efficiency of the Business-to-Business (B2B) interactions. The VEs in particular allow the distribution of the business processes among different partners, trying to reduce the time-to-market and operational costs. They also permit companies that in the past could only reach local markets to operate, sometimes, on global scale [OT01].

We put together these two approaches, Service-Oriented Computing and Virtual Enterprises/Marketplaces, and propose a model for a *Dynamic Virtual Marketplace* (called *VM-Flow*) that offers supporting mechanisms for all phases of an e-Business process (including both inter- and intra-organizational aspects). The VM-Flow is workflow-based and its control is decentralized – the process instance (a *case*) carries the execution plan and moves with it from host to host [SWME00] (respecting some privacy issues that will be later discussed), what brings scalability to the infrastructure. Also, all basic services needed for the creation and maintenance of the Dynamic Virtual Enterprises (DVEs) are offered by the VM-Flow.

The main contribution of this work is the proposal of a set of interaction policies between the marketplace and its business partners (the DVE members – "real world" companies). Also, differently from other works in the area [BBS98, OT01], our infrastructure is implemented through the use of *Orchestration* and *Choreography* of Web Services.

This article is organized as follows: Section 2 presents some concepts related to our work; Section 3 introduces and discusses the VM-Flow model, the Interaction Policies and also shows how the Orchestration and Choreography are performed; in Section 4 some infrastructure issues are presented; an application built over the platform is shown in Section 5; Section 6 presents the final considerations and suggests some extensions to this work.

2. BASIC CONCEPTS

In this section we present the Virtual Enterprises, the Marketplaces and also how Service Composition is achieved using Orchestration and Choreography.

2.1 Virtual Enterprises and Marketplaces

The Virtual Enterprises (VEs) represent a set of entities geographically distributed, probably functionally and culturally different, and linked through Information Technology (IT) mechanisms. They share competencies, infrastructure and business processes and have as main goal to fulfill some specific market necessity. The VEs may be classified in two groups [Ouz01]:

- *Static Virtual Enterprises* (SVEs): in this category the relationships between partners are static, pre-configured and can't be easily changed.
- *Dynamic Virtual Enterprises* (DVEs): this category is an evolution of the SVEs. The DVEs take advantage of the opportunities offered by the Internet and by the global economy. They may have short lifecycles, dynamic business relationships between partners and a flexible and autonomous behavior.

A more recent approach to automate the creation and management process of a VE is the use of a Virtual Marketplace (VM). The potential members register their resources and business processes on the VM. The marketplaces are very important to keep the competitiveness of the VEs [OT01]. These centers offer, besides the basic infrastructure, different types of services to the VEs, increasing their flexibility and scalability; examples are search and mediation functions for the customers and the support for business partner selection. These services can be complemented by more advanced ones, like automated negotiation and electronic contracts.

2.2 Services and Composition

Service-Oriented Computing (SOC) is a computational paradigm that considers services as fundamental elements to the development of applications. In this context, services can be defined as open, self-described components that support a fast and low cost development of distributed applications [PG03]. The application of SOC on the web is manifested through the *Web Services* technology.

A *Web Service* can be defined as an interface (or a port) to some functionality performed by an application behind it (note that the way the application implements this functionality is not important at all to a service client). This interface is described and accessed through some Internet standards and protocols, like XML, HTTP, SOAP and WSDL.

A description of a service is used to publish what the service offers, its interface, behavior and quality. Service clients (organizations that act as final users) and service aggregators (organizations that compose multiple services into new ones) use these descriptions to achieve their objectives [PG03]. On the *Web Services* world, descriptions are based on WSDL (*Web Services Description Language*) [W3C04a], an XML-based language proposed by the W3C (*World Wide Web Consortium*).

To build a composition, services are combined following a certain pattern, in order to achieve a business goal, solve a scientific problem, or provide new service functions in general. These compositions may themselves become new services, what makes composition a recursive operation [CKMT03].

When composing *Web Services*, two approaches are usually considered: *orchestration* and *choreography*. The difference between these concepts is, sometimes, not so clear [Pel03], but there are some characteristics that may help this differentiation:

- In the *orchestration* approach, all interactions that are part of a business process (including the sequence of activities, conditional events etc) must be described, like on a traditional workflow system. This description is then executed by an orchestration engine, which has control of the overall composition;
- The *choreography* approach is more collaborative and less centralized in nature. Only the public message exchanges are considered relevant – and more, each service only knows about its own interactions and behavior. Differently from Orchestration, there is not an entity that has a global view/control of the composition.

While at the first moment the choreography approach seems to be more interesting because of its collaborative advantages, there are some scenarios where a global view of the process being performed by the composition is necessary (or even mandatory) - that's where orchestration comes as an affordable solution.

Regardless of the nature of the composition (orchestration or choreography), some questions should be considered when building a composite service:

- Can the interactions happen in any order?
- If no, which rules govern the sequence of interactions?
- Is there any relationship between messages sent and/or received?
- Are there a "beginning" and an "end" on a given sequence of interactions?
- Can a given sequence of interactions be undone?

- Is it possible/necessary to draw a global view of all message exchanges?

Two important specifications in the area of *Web Services* composition are BPEL4WS [BIM+03] and WSCI [BIS+02].

BPEL4WS (*Business Process Execution Language for Web Services*), or simply BPEL, is a specification published by IBM, Microsoft and BEA that models the behavior of Web Services inside a business process applying workflow concepts. It defines a language based on XML that describes the control logic required to coordinate the participant Web Services on a process flow. This description can then be interpreted and executed by an orchestration engine, controlled by one of the participants. This engine coordinates the different process activities and takes care of compensation mechanisms when errors happen. BPEL is, essentially, a layer over WSDL.

WSCI (*Web Services Choreography Interface*) is a specification from SUN, SAP, BEA and INTALIO that defines an XML-based language to describe Web Services choreography. An important aspect of WSCI is that only the visible behavior is described – WSCI does not treat the definition of executable private processes like BPEL. A WSCI-based choreography includes a set of WSCI documents, one for each partner. There is no process controlling the composition globally.

There is also an on-going effort being held by the W3C to establish a choreography standard language: WS-CDL (*Web Services Choreography Description Language*) [W3C04b]. Its first working draft has been published by the end of April 2004. WS-CDL, like BPEL and WSCI, is an XML-based language that describes peer-to-peer collaborations of *Web Services* by defining, from a global viewpoint, their common and complementary observable behavior; where ordered message exchanges result in accomplishing a common business goal. WS-CDL does not treat executable processes (like BPEL), but only the choreography aspects of a composition.

3. INFRASTRUCTURE MODEL

The VM-Flow model, its facilities and the set of Interaction Policies we propose are presented next on this section.

3.1 The Virtual Marketplace

The VM-Flow is composed of a set of facilities, each one responsible for specific tasks that are necessary to support the DVEs and their interactions [SM03]. The infrastructure scheme is shown in Figure 1. The facilities that are part of the infrastructure are:

- *MPCI* (Marketplace Customer Interface): it is the interface between the VM-Flow and the customers that wish to acquire some product or service;
- *MPRS* (Marketplace Repository Set): consists of a set of repositories and services, responsible for the storage of different data sets (product and service catalogs, contracts, infrastructure information, history and backup data, auditing information, among others);
- *VBM* (Virtual Business Manager): the VBMs are the coordinators of a determined business process. They are responsible for tasks such as building a proposal, writing an execution plan and also the selection (or creation) of a DVE to a give process. The VBMs are grouped into agencies. There can be different kinds of VBMs, derived accordingly to the necessities of a specific business sector. A VBM can manage various business process instances, but given an instance, there is only one VBM associated to it;
- *DVEC* (Dynamic Virtual Enterprise Coordinator): each DVE has one (and only one) DVEC associated to it during its whole lifecycle. The DVEC is responsible for: 1. Selecting members ("real" enterprises) to a DVE; 2. Managing the contracts among those members; 3. Coordinating the interactions between the members and the VM-Flow; 4. Applying the execution plan prepared by the VBM; 5. Managing the entries and exits of DVE members; 6. Renegotiating dynamic plan changes when necessary.

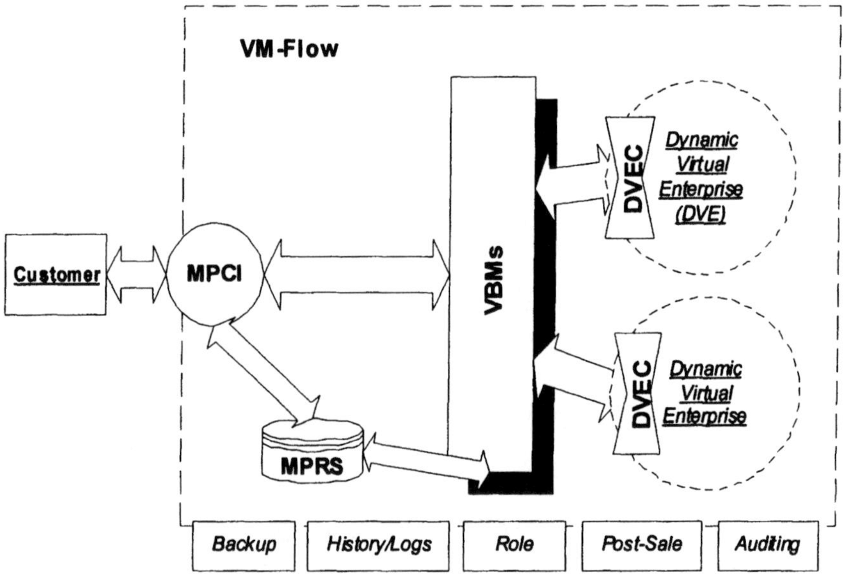

Figure 1. VM-Flow general infrastructure scheme

3.1.1 Supporting Services

The VM-Flow also offers some additional services:

- *Backup Service*: responsible for keeping security copies of the operations held on the hosts of the platform, in order to guarantee a safe recovery in case of faults;
- *History/Log Service*: together with the backup service, it is part of the fault recovery system;
- *Auditing Service (External and Internal)*: used to evaluate the efficiency and integrity of the business processes executed by the VM-Flow and by the DVE partners;
- *Role Coordinator*: responsible for the resource allocation (services or people) in order to execute a determined task that is part of an execution plan;
- *Post-Sale Coordinator*: responsible to contact the customers to discover their opinion about the products/services acquired and also to manage warranty issues imposed by regional laws.

3.2 Interaction Policies

In order to guarantee a greater level of flexibility, autonomy, privacy and support different kinds of collaboration between the DVE members and the VM-Flow, our model defines two orthogonal Interaction Policy Categories: *Partner Autonomy Policies* (VM-Flow x DVE) and *Partner Cooperation Policies* (DVE member x DVE member).

3.2.1 Partner Autonomy Policies

This category defines the interaction level between the DVEC and each member of the DVE. At the moment a (real) company candidates to participate on a DVE, a negotiation takes place to define what kind of interaction it wishes to have with the VM-Flow. The DVEC then acts in one of the following manners:

- *Supervisor*: interaction through a well-defined interface with the company's private workflow – the VM-Flow does not act on the partner's inside domain. The following kinds of interaction are supported for a Supervisor DVEC:
  - <u>Consulting-only</u>: the DVE can only ask for status information of a process instance;
  - <u>Selective</u>: the DVEC and the partner negotiate in which points of the execution plan interactions will be allowed;

- Participative: the DVEC can interact with all activities of the execution plan (start, pause, resume, cancel, send/receive data, check status).
- *Coordinator*: the DVEC (through a Proxy shown later) has total control over the tasks being executed by the partner's internal workflow, which becomes an extension of the VM-Flow.

The DVEC is the responsible for determining the different policy combinations that could exist inside a DVE, based on the necessities imposed by the business process, by the execution plan and by each one of the partners.

3.2.2 Partner Cooperation Policies

The main question regarding the interaction between partners (real companies that are part of a DVE) is, usually, how to treat the privacy and integrity of data that are part of a business process instance. Through this perspective, we identify three classes of partner-partner cooperation:

- *Total Cooperation*: the two partners fully trust each other. When a process instance leaves one partner and moves to another one, it is not necessary to hide neither the plan nor the data from the previous stage;
- *Controlled Cooperation*: there is a pre-established set of information that should be passed to the next partner and another set that should be hidden by the DVEC (actually by its Proxy);
- *Total Privacy*: there is no interaction between the partners. All information is returned to the DVEC, which has access to the plan and then decides what to do next, hiding from the following partner the activities and data from the previous stage.

3.2.3 Policies and the "Real" World

As mentioned before, the two policy categories previously presented are fully orthogonal. Their selection and combination inside a DVE depend both on business questions (confidentiality of data, for example) as well as on technological limitations (compatibility level among the different partner's workflow systems, for example).

We could, for instance, associate a *Supervisor DVEC + Controlled Cooperation Policy* with an e-Business Service Provider scenario – this provider would be a third entity, independent, that offers its infrastructure and services to other companies that wish to participate on a virtual marketplace.

In another example, an automobile industry supply chain [MZ02, SRKT00] could apply a policy with a *Coordinator DVEC + Total Privacy*. In this scenario, the car manufacturer could be, for instance, the owner of the marketplace, controlling the production processes of its suppliers.

3.3 DVEC x DVE Interaction

In order to present how the composition of the activities that are part of an execution plan is achieved it is necessary to take a deeper look at the DVEC x DVE interaction.

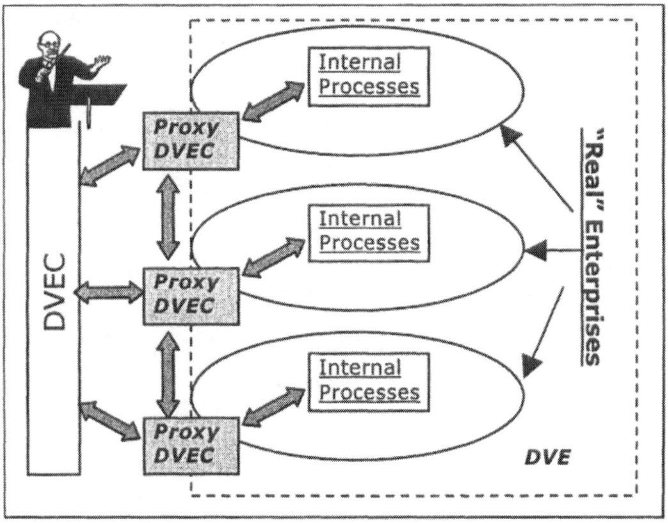

Figure 2. DVEC, DVE and the Proxies

A new element is introduced in Figure 2: the *DVEC's Proxy*. It is the responsible for implementing the interaction between the VM-Flow and a partner, executing the local portion of the plan, always according to the *Autonomy Policy* selected. This proxy must also "talk", when applicable, to the next partner (respecting the execution plan and the selected Cooperation Policy). The DVEC becomes then responsible to orchestrate the process globally through the various proxies (each one of them coordinating the orchestration/choreography of the local plan).

The DVEC and its proxies participate on two different levels of service composition:

1. The DVEC orchestrates its Proxies. The global execution plan consists of the composition of all partner proxies' Web Services;
2. Each Proxy is responsible to orchestrate (or simply participate on a choreography) of the local execution plan – according to each partner's Autonomy Policy.

3.4 Related Work

The area surrounding *e-Business*, *Marketplaces* and *Interorganizational Business-to-Business Interactions* is, although relatively new (pushed by the advent of the Internet), already broad and with much research being done. Due to this broadness, and in order to situate our work in the field, on this section we decided to present only the works that are closely related to our platform.

3.4.1 Marketplaces and Virtual Enterprises

DIVE. The DIVE project (*Agent-based Life Cycle Management for Dynamic Virtual Enterprises*) [OT01] proposes an infrastructure for DVEs based on mobile agents and introduces a life cycle model for the DVEs. On Table 1, a comparison between the VM-Flow and DIVE is presented.

Table 1. DIVE x VM-Flow

----	DIVE	VM-Flow
Marketplace Management	Mobile Agents	Mobile Cases + Workflow
DVEs Management	Mobile Agents / Life Cycle	Service Compos. / Life Cycle
Scalability	Yes	Yes
Interaction Policies	No	Yes
Interorganizational Aspects	Partially	Yes
Implementation	FIPA / XML / Java	Web Services / XML / Java

Even though DIVE and VM-Flow propose different approaches to implement a marketplace, the life cycle model proposed by DIVE guided the definition of VM-Flow's DVE behavior.

Other works in the VE area not directly related to VM-Flow but that present interesting solutions are [APC02, BBS98, TBV02].

3.4.2 Interorganizational System Integration

BPFA. The interorganizational system integration is discussed by [SO01], including privacy issues. It presents a classification of the business processes into *private* and *shared*. The private processes expose interaction points where the shared processes connect to, in such a way that a business process can be part of two or more organizations. A framework to support these two categories of processes, BPFA (*Business Process Framework Architecture*) is also introduced by [SO01]. The BPFA consists of a set of components that execute instances of an interorganizational process model, extending a company's workflow infrastructure and allowing process-oriented communication among partners and customers. Table 2 presents a comparison between the VM-Flow platform and the BPFA framework.

Table 2. BPFA x VM-Flow

----	BPFA	VM-Flow
VE Support	Partial	Yes
DVE Support	No	Yes
Core	Workflow-based	Workflow-based
Interorganizational Interact.	WfMS[23] Responsibility	Orchestration / Choreography
Privacy and Autonomy	Private and Shared Processes	Interaction Policies

The Interaction Policies proposed in the VM-Flow platform complement the solution given by [SO01], offering, to the context of Virtual Marketplaces, more flexibility on the definition of privacy and collaboration levels between partners.

Public-To-Private. The approach proposed by van der Aalst on [AW01], called Public-To-Private (P2P), is based on the notion of inheritance. It consists of three main steps:

1. The specification of a shared public workflow;
2. The partition of this public workflow over the participant organizations;
3. The creation, for each organization, of a private workflow. This private workflow is a subclass of its respective part on the public workflow.

The P2P solution is very elegant and surrounded by a formalism called *WF-Nets* [Aal98] (derived from *Petri nets*). We believe that as P2P is an approach to model interorganizational workflows (regardless of the technology used to implement it), we could apply a Service-Oriented implementation to a P2P based workflow model (an interesting solution would be to apply *orchestration* on the private workflows and *choreography* on the public workflows).

3.4.3 Workflow Management

Table 3. WONDER x VM-Flow

----	WONDER	VM-Flow
Main Goal	Large Scale WfMS	Virtual Marketplace
Core	Workflow-based	Workflow-based
Distributed Objects Techn.	CORBA	Java/RMI
Interorganizational Interact.	No	Yes
Decentralized Control	Yes (Mobile Cases)	Yes (Mobile Cases)

[23] WfMS: *Workflow Management System*

WONDER. Traditional *Workflow Management Systems* have an intrinsic scalability limitation, the central server. It represents a performance bottleneck and a point of failure on systems where a great number of processes is executed simultaneously [SWME00]. To solve this limitation, the WONDER [SWME00] architecture proposes a *Large Scale WfMS* that introduces the use of *mobile cases* (business processes instances) that migrate over the system nodes, following an execution plan that they carry with themselves. VM-Flow's decentralized management model was inspired by the ideas presented by the WONDER platform. Although having different goals, a comparison between WONDER and VM-Flow is shown on Table 3.

3.4.4 Service Composition

In the area of Service Composition, [Pel03] presents a survey about Orchestration, Choreography and their main specifications and tools. On [VDDTR03] the FUSION system, a framework for dynamic composition and automatic execution of *Web Services* is analyzed.

4. IMPLEMENTATION ISSUES

We built a prototype of the VM-Flow platform that implements the main functionalities described on the model (Section 3). Our choice was to implement it on an object-oriented language – more specifically Java because of its platform independence characteristics. The access to the MPCI and to the partners' internal systems is achieved through Web Services. The orchestration is implemented based on BPEL4WS - the engine used was BPWS4J [IBM03]. Next we discuss in more details the implementation.

4.1 Platform Core

The Figure 3 presents a snapshot of the main interfaces that are part of the platform core. Besides *MPCI_I*, *VBM_I*, *VBMAgency_I*, *DVE_I*, *DVEC_I* and *DVECProxy_I*, related to the facilities previously presented in the model, there some other relevant interfaces:

- *BusinessProposal_I*: a business proposal, when approved, becomes the base for the construction of the execution plan;
- *ExecutionPlan_I*: the execution plan;
- *VMData_I*, *BusinessProcess_I*, *Case_I*: all data exchanged among VM-Flow objects inherit from *VMData_I*. *BusinessProcess_I* is used to build the business process templates, while *Case_I* represents these processes' instances;

- *RealEnterprise_I*: a "real" enterprise or a partner is a member (or member candidate) of a Dynamic Virtual Enterprise.

The *case* (business process instance), represented by the class *Case* (Figure 4), migrates from one facility to the other carrying the execution plan (note that *ExecutionPlan* is one of *Case*'s attributes), what makes the control inherently decentralized. This migration is achieved through the method *ReceiveCase()*, present in many of the classes shown in Figure 4. Another important characteristic illustrated on this figure is the *DVECProxy* family class hierarchy: *DVECProxy_SP*, *DVECProxy_SC*, *DVECProxy_SS* and *DVECProxy_CC* implement the different *Autonomy Policies*. These classes are responsible for coordinating the execution of the local portion of plan, according to the selected policies, and also to coordinate the orchestration/choreography of the DVE members' internal services (note that there is one DVECProxy object associated with each DVE member).

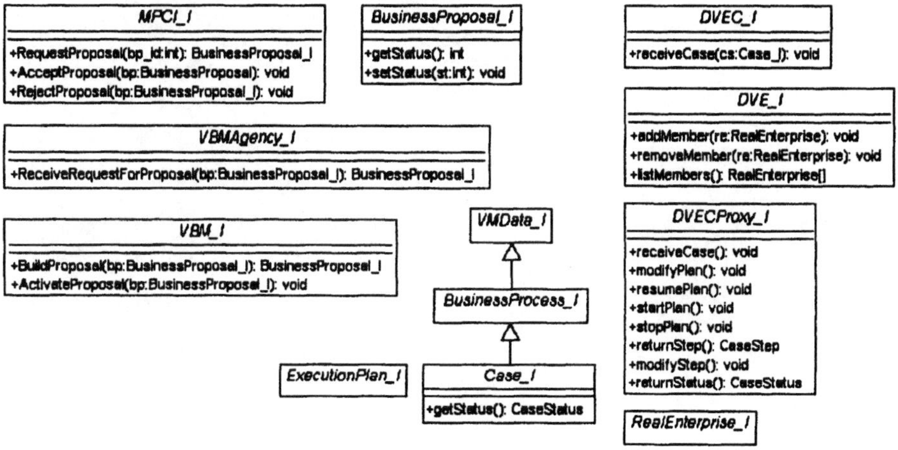

Figure 3. VM-Flow Core Interfaces

4.2 Orchestration and Choreography

Our model for orchestration and choreography is built over BPEL (Subsection 2.2). BPEL defines two business process models:

- *Executable Business Processes*: models the behavior of partners in a specific interaction, essentially like a private workflow. They are executed by an orchestration engine;
- *Abstract Business Processes*: business protocols that specify the public message exchanges between partners. The business protocols are not executable and do not treat internal process details.

Essentially, the executable processes offer support for orchestration while the abstract processes focus on the choreography of the services. As already mentioned on Subsection 3.3, the services composition is held on two levels:

1. A DVEC orchestrate its Proxies; each Proxy is implemented as a JAVA class that exports its interface as a Web Service. The global execution plan consists on the composition of those Web Services through a BPEL executable business process.
2. According to its partner's autonomy policy, each Proxy is responsible to orchestrate (via executable business processes) or simply participate on a choreography (using abstract business processes) of the local execution plan.

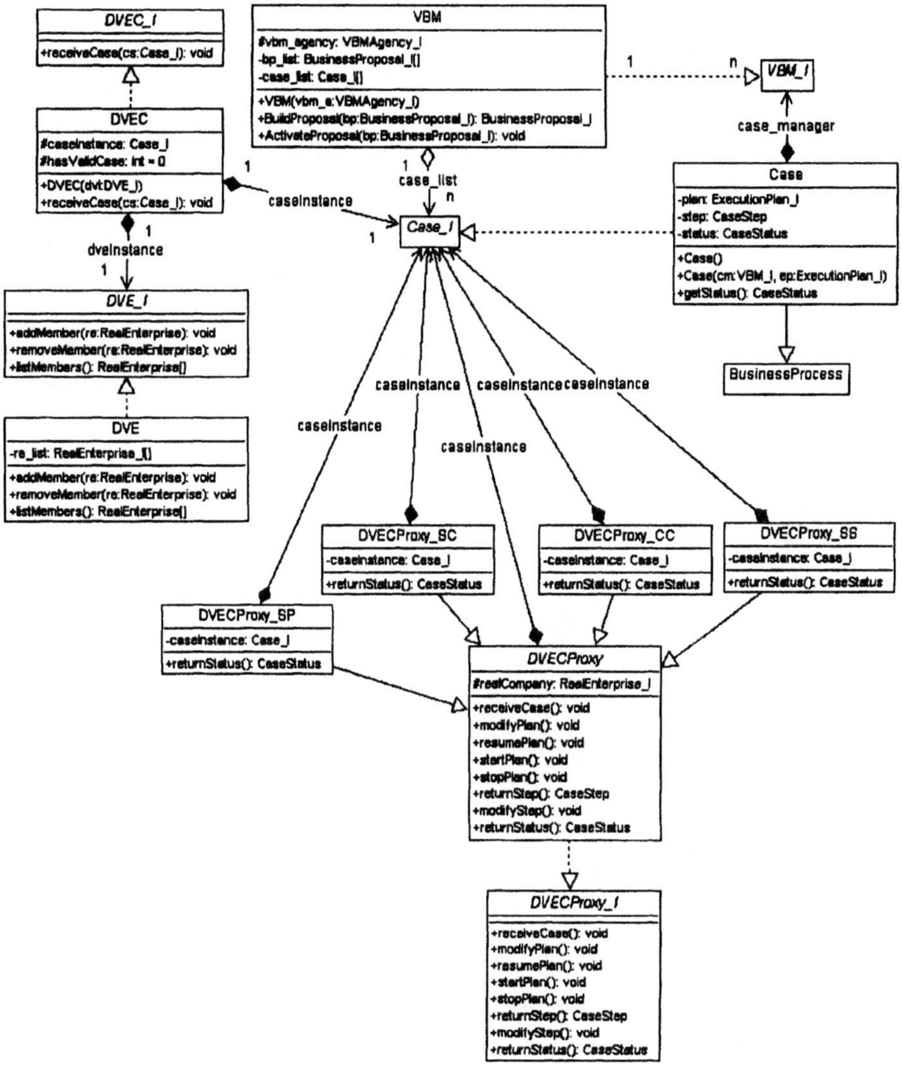

Figure 4. Platform Core Class Diagram

4.2.1 VM-Flow x Business Partners interaction

When the DVEC acts as *Coordinator*, the VM-Flow, through the DVEC's proxy, uses the BPEL's executable business process definitions to *orchestrate* the plan inside a DVE member. On the other hand, when the DVEC acts as *Supervisor*, the abstract definitions are used in a *choreography* context.

4.2.2 Partner x Partner interaction

When *Total* or *Controlled Cooperation* is the chosen policy for a partner-partner interaction, abstract business processes are useful to define the message exchanges between the proxies (*choreography* context).

4.2.3 BPEL Orchestration Example

The Figure 5 presents an example of a BPEL executable business process used by the DVEC to orchestrate its proxies. The `<sequence>` tag indicates a series of activities that should be executed one after the other, while the tag `<flow>` determines activities that should be executed in parallel; `<invoke>` presents a call to some external Web Service operation and `<receive>` prepares the BPEL process to receive a call from another Web Service. This example illustrates some migrations of case between the DVEC and its proxies (on the DVE members).

```
<sequence>
    <invoke name="sendCase_1" partnerLink="proxy_1"
operation="receiveCase" inputVariable="caseInstance" />
    <receive name="receiveCase_1" partnerLink="proxy_1"
operation="receiveCase" variable="caseInstance" /receive>
    (...)

 <flow>
      <invoke name="resumePlan_6" partnerLink="proxy_6"
operation="resumePlan"/>
      <invoke name="resumePlan_7" partnerLink="proxy_7"
operation="resumePlan"/>
    </flow>
    <receive name="receiveCase_7" partnerLink="proxy_7"
operation="receiveCase" variable="caseInstance" /receive>
</sequence>
```

Figure 5. Executable Business Process Extract

The structure of a document defining an abstract business process is similar to an executable process definition – the difference is that it is used only as a protocol to validate a given sequence of messages exchanged by other running processes instead of being executed by the engine.

5. APPLICATION EXAMPLES

In this section we present a detailed example of an application built over the VM-Flow platform. We also show other scenarios where the VM-Flow could be used.

5.1 Computer Industry

The application implemented to validate our infrastructure models one hypothetic computer industry called *LEED*. In the business model adopted, this industry is responsible only for integrating the components, not being responsible for their manufacturing. Thus, *LEED* uses the VM-Flow platform to find component suppliers that will attend its customers' needs.

In Figure 6, a general scheme of the VM-Flow use by the *LEED* industry is presented. It has the following peculiarities: the Customer can be an equipment reseller or a big corporate customer; three kinds of VBMs are defined to manage the different product categories offered by *LEED* (desktops, notebooks and servers); the Partner Candidates represent the potential component suppliers.

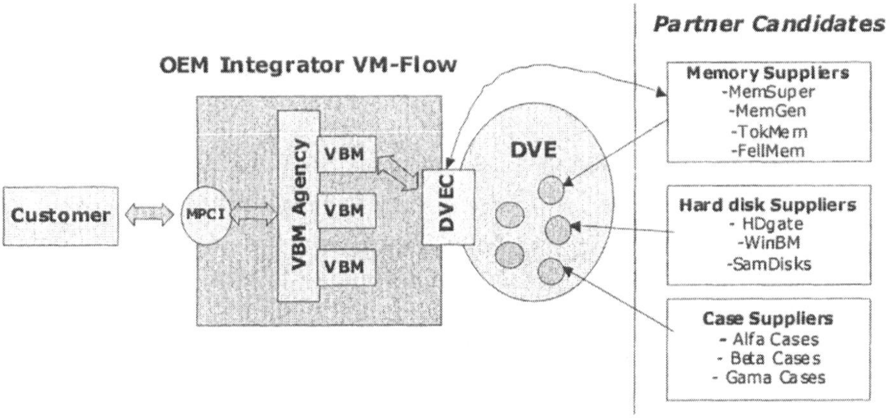

Figure 6. Application Example – *LEED* PC Industry VM-Flow

A typical *LEED* business process consists of the following steps (Figures 7 and 8 present a Sequence Diagram showing these steps):

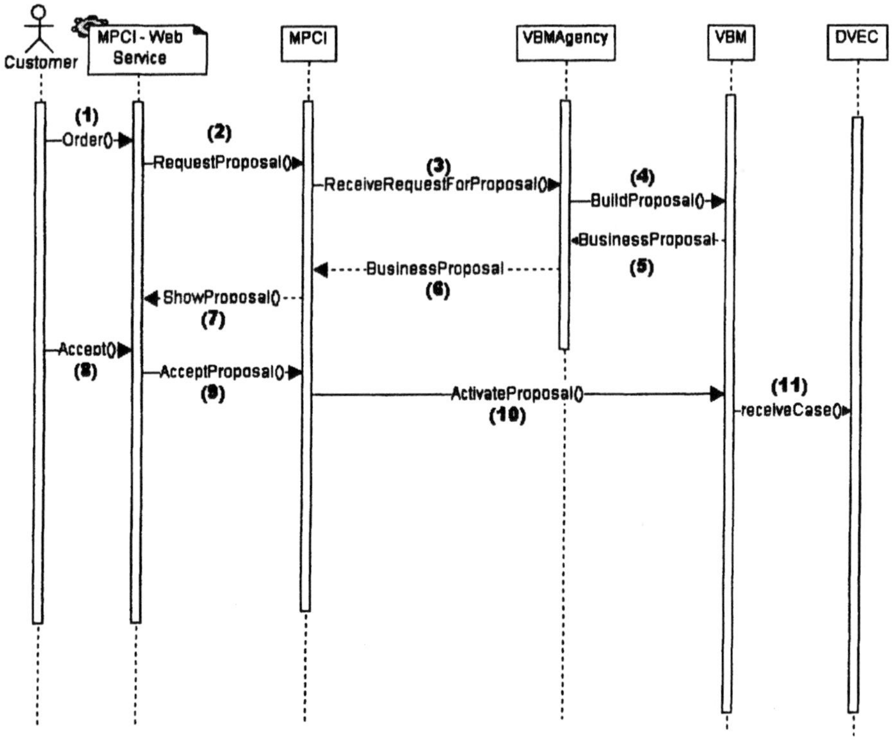

Figure 7. LEED Business Process Example – Part 1

- The *customer* interacts with the *MPCI*, consulting product information and asking for a business proposal (1,2);
- The *MPCI* contacts the *VBMAgency* (3). According to the product(s), an adequate *VBM* is allocated to handle the business proposal (4);
- The *VBM*, based on the customer needs and on the information given by the potential suppliers, builds a business proposal and a draft version of the execution plan (5,6). The proposal is then presented to the customer through the *MPCI* (7);
- In case of approval (8,9,10), the *VBM* immediately creates a *DVEC*, sending to it the draft version of the execution plan (11). This DVEC then selects the *DVE* members and finishes together with the *VBM* the execution plan definition;
- From this moment on, the *DVEC* becomes the responsible for the execution of the plan, interacting with the Proxies placed on each one of the *DVE* members (12). Note that the member associated with *DVECProxy_1* has a *Cooperative* relationship with the member associated with *DVECProxy_2*, because it sends the case directly to its partner (13). The same does not happen in the partner 2 x partner 3 relation – *DVECProxy_2* is forced to send the case back to the *DVEC*, which for-

wards it to *DVECProxy_3* (with the applicable privacy restrictions imposed by the policy between 2 and 3) (14,15,16).

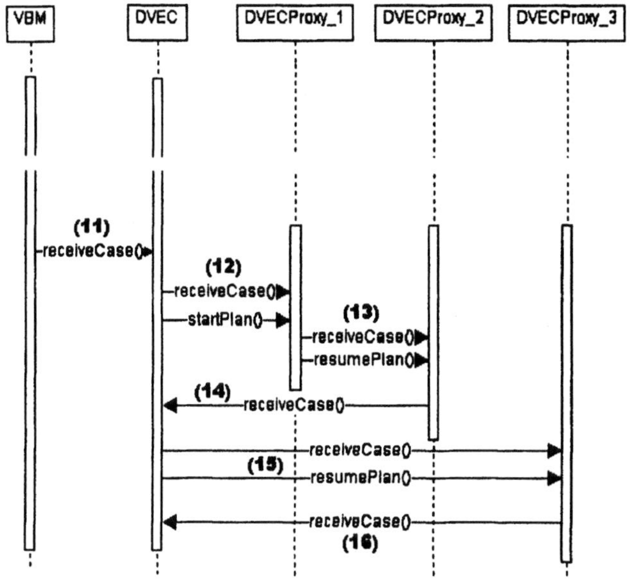

Figure 8. LEED Business Process Example – Part 2

5.2 Other Scenarios

Next we present other scenario examples in which the VM-Flow platform can be applied (besides the ones already mentioned on Subsection 3.2.3 – e-Business Service Provider and Automobilist Industry).

Tourism. The customer (or a Travel Agent on behalf of a customer) uses the VM-Flow to find hotels, air companies and car rental stores. In another example, an Agency/Operator, with the help of the VM-Flow, can build a tour that will be offered to various tourist groups. In this context, a *Consulting Supervisor DVEC* could be combined with a *Total Cooperation Policy* (on the *Hotel x Air Company x Car rental store* relationship) and *Total Privacy* (on the relationship of potentially concurrent companies – two air companies that fly to the same destinations, for example).

Civil Construction. Real-state agencies, material suppliers, entrepreneurs, engineering offices and architects can associate with a specialized VM-Flow and offer projects, building and decoration services. This scenario seems adequate for the appliance of a *Total Cooperation* policy inside a DVE (except for potentially concurrent partners – two material suppliers, for example).

Government Applications. The platform could be adapted (through VBM specialization) to offer support for public bids. Being the Government the owner of the platform, *Participative Supervisor DVECs* or even *Coordinating DVECs* could be used on this scenario.

6. CONCLUSION

This paper presents and discusses the *VM-Flow* platform, a Virtual Marketplace infrastructure that supports Dynamic Virtual Enterprises and is workflow-based. The platform offers as its main contribution different privacy and autonomy levels to its partners through various *Interaction Policies*, implemented applying resources like Orchestration and Choreography of *Web Services*. The use of BPEL4WS as a *Web Services* composition technology was successful and showed us its potentiality, even though some issues remain open and an effort to create a standard for composition and coordination of services is still in progress.

The model presented is flexible and extensible, with the goal to support different market rules and needs. Implementation aspects are discussed and also an application built over the infrastructure is presented.

Extensions to this work may include the enhancement of the infrastructure (facilities specialization and creation of new ones), adaptation of the *Interaction Policies* to specific market sectors and the proposal of new applications. Some problems introduced by dynamic discovery of partners (expressiveness and semantics, for instance) were not in the scope of this work and could be part of extension studies.

ACKNOWLEDGEMENTS

This work was funded by CAPES and CNPq.

REFERENCES

[Aal98] W.M.P. van der Aalst. The application of Petri Nets to Workflow Management. The Journal of Circuits, Systems and Computers, 8(1):21-66, 1998.

[APC02] P. Ávila, G.D. Putnik and M. M. Cunha. Brokerage function in Agile/Virtual Enterprise integration – A literature review. 3rd IFIP Working Conference on Infrastructures for Virtual Enterprises (PRO-VE'02), pp. 65-72, Portugal, 2002.

[AW01] W.M.P. van der Aalst and M. Weske. The P2P Approach to Interorganizational Workflows. In *Proceedings of the 13th International Conference on Advanced Informa-*

tion Systems Engineering (CAiSE'01), volume 2068 of Lecture Notes in Computer Science, pages 140-156. Springer-Verlag, Berlin, 2001.

[BBS98] M. Bichler, C. Beam and A. Segev. An electronic broker for business-to-business electronic commerce on the Internet. Int. Journal of Cooperative Information Systems 7, pp 315-331, 1998.

[BIM+03] BEA Systems, IBM, Microsoft, SAP AG and Siebel Systems. Business Process Execution Language for Web Services (BPEL4WS) – Version 1.1, 2003; http://www-106.ibm.com/developerworks/webservices/library/ws-bpel/.

[BIS+02] BEA Systems, Intalio, SAP and Sun Microsystems. Web Services Choreography Interface 1.0, 2002; http://www.sun.com/software/xml/developers/wsci/sci-spec-10.pdf.

[CKMT03] F. Curbera, R. Khalaf, N. Mukhi, S. Tai, and S. Weerawarana. The next step in Web Services. Communications of the ACM, 46(10):29-34, 2003.

[IBM03] IBM. Business Process Execution Language for Web Services Java Run Time, 2003; http://alphaworks.ibm.com/tech/bpws4j/

[MZ02] H. Min and G. Zhou. Supply chain modeling: past, present and future. Computers & Industrial Engineering 43, pp 231-249, 2002.

[Ouz01] V. Ouzounis. An Agent-Based Platform for the Management of Dynamic Virtual Enterprises. Doctor Thesis, TU Berlin, 2001.

[OT01] V. Ouzounis and V. Tschammer. Towards Dynamic Virtual Enterprises. Proceedings of The First IFIP Conference on e-Commerce, e-Business, e-Government (I3E 2001), pp 177-192, Zurich, Switzerland, 2001.

[Pel03] C. Peltz. Web services orchestration - a review of emerging technologies, tools, and standards. White Paper, Hewlett Packard, 2003.

[PG03] M.P. Papazoglou and D. Georgakopoulos. Service-oriented computing. Communications of the ACM, 46(10):25-28, 2003.

[SM03] I.J.G. Santos and E.R.M. Madeira. Policy-based Orchestration and Choreography of Services on Dynamic Virtual Enterprises. 3rd IFIP I3E Conference on e-Commerce, e-Business and e-Government, Research Colloquium, Brazil, 2003.

[SO01] K. Schulz and M. Orlowska. Architectural Issues for Cross-Organisational B2B Interactions. International Workshop on Distributed Dynamic Multiservice Architectures (DDMA), IEEE Computer Society Press, USA, 2001.

[SRKT00] C. Stricker, S. Riboni, M. Kradolfer and J. Taylor. Market-based Workflow Management for Supply Chains of Services, 33rd Annual Hawaii International Conference on System Sciences (HICSS-33), 2000.

[SWME00] R.S. Silva Filho, J. Wainer, E.R.M. Madeira. and C. Ellis. CORBA Based Architecture for Large Scale Workflow. IEICE Transactions on Communications, Vol. E83-B, No. 5. , pp. 988-998, 2000.

[TBV02] M. Tolle, P. Bernus and J. Vesterager. Reference Models for Virtual Enterprises. 3rd IFIP Working Conference on Infrastructures for Virtual Enterprises (PRO-VE'02), pp. 3-10, Portugal, 2002.

[VDDTR03] D. VanderMeer, A. Datta, K. Dutta, H. Thomas, K. Ramamritham and S. B. Navathe. FUSION: A System Allowing Dynamic Web Service Composition and Automatic Execution. IEEE International Conference on E-Commerce, p. 399, California, USA, 2003.

[W3C04a] World Wide Web Consortium (W3C). Web Services Description Language (WSDL) Version 2.0 – Part 1: Core Language. W3C Working Draft, http://www.w3.org/TR/wsdl20, March 2004.

[W3C04b] World Wide Web Consortium (W3C). Web Services Choreography Description Language Version 1.0 (WS-CDL). W3C Working Draft, http://www.w3.org/TR/ws-cdl-10/, April 2004.

EVOLUTION OF SERVICE PROCESSES BY RULE BASED TRANSFORMATION

Christian Zirpins[1] and Giacomo Piccinelli[2]
[1]University of Hamburg, Germany, [2]University College London, UK

Abstract: The notion of service is closely coupled with the notion of process in general and of workflow in particular. Processes capture the coordination logic for the various resources involved in the realisation of the service content. Moreover, processes drive the actual delivery of a service. Internal processes underpin the capabilities of a service provider. Delivery processes underpin contractual agreements between service providers and consumers. In both cases, the ability to adapt service processes in response to changing environmental conditions is fundamental. Change must be rapid but at the same time accurate and consistent. In this paper, we present the framework for automated process transformation developed within the context of the FRESCO (Foundational Research on Service Composition) initiative. The conceptual part of the framework builds on the standard workflow meta-model proposed by the WfMC (Workflow Management Coalition). The change logic is expressed by transformation rules that can be automatically applied to the processes underpinning a service. The technical part of the framework specifically targets Web service platforms and BPEL (Business Process Execution Language).

Key words: Inter-Organisational Integration, Cooperative Interaction Processes, Electronic Services, Process Evolution, Rule-Based Workflow Transformation

1. INTRODUCTION

Processes in general and workflow in particular are at the core of services and service-oriented computing (Papazoglou and Georgakopoulos, 2003). The realisation of a service depends on the value-added coordination of multiple resources. The coordination logic must be expressed in a way that is at the same time easy to understand for the human designer and effectively manageable by the execution infrastructure. Workflow frameworks of the type proposed by the Workflow Management Coalition (WfMC, 2004) include process models and notations, organisational and resource models, integration and execution models, development methodologies, as well as execution and management platforms.

Services in general and families of services in particular depend on a multiplicity of processes. A first categorisation of service processes is based on the distinction between internal and delivery processes. Internal processes encompass all the activities that service providers perform in order to realise the core capabilities of a service. Using the freight environment as an example, the core capabilities of a freight service revolve around the handling and transportation of goods. Delivery processes encompass all the activities that service providers perform in order for the service consumer to access and use the core capabilities of a service. In the freight example, this could be advertisement of destinations and spare capacity, contract negotiation, customer interaction or notification management. Service processes are tightly coupled, both within and across categories. As an example, the possibility to deliver progress reports to customers requires specific action (e.g. scanning) to be introduced in the design of the goods-handling processes. Changes at one level must be consistently propagated at all levels. Failing to do so may result in operational inefficiencies as well as potential breach of contractual agreements. The ability to manage change is vital for service providers.

The observation at the base of our work is that the structural change required for a process often reflects a change in overall logic of the service. For example, the scanning steps introduced in a goods-handling process probably derive from the intention of a service provider to include notification facilities in a freight service. The immediate problems with a direct change approach are time and precision. Manual analysis and change of all the processes related to a service is time consuming and error prone. Moreover, the lack of a systematic approach to process adaptation makes organic process evolution extremely difficult. The approach we propose is to capture formally the adaptation requirements for service processes in the form of pattern-based transformation rules. The approach is substantiated by a rule-definition language and related process transformation tool.

In Section 2, we outline the relations between services and processes. In section 3, we discuss the need and scope for automatic process adaptation, and we detail our proposal for a rule-based approach to change. Sections 4 and 5 provide a description of the actual rule language and process transformation tool included in the FRESCO toolkit (Zirpins et al., 2004). Related works are discussed in Section 6. Conclusions from our initial experience are reported in Section 7.

2. PROCESS BASED SERVICES

Effective and efficient support of organisational services depends on the ability to organise and structure the variety of their internal and external processes as well as the mutual interrelations between them. A consequent service model has to consider both, a conceptual part that reflects the background of organisational services as well as a precise representation that allows for automated processing.

Our *conceptual service-model* (Piccinelli et al., 2003b) defines a view on services that is provision-oriented and service-centric. There, cooperation procedures that constitute atomic, self-contained parts of a service-relationship are exposed by so-called *capabilities*. In particular, capabilities represent *purpose*, *interaction logic* and *resulting artefacts* of the cooperation between organisational *roles*. A service is made up by a set of such capabilities.

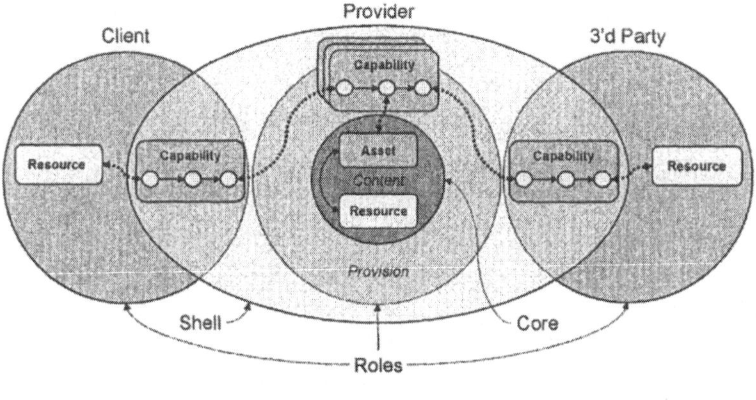

Figure 1. FRESCO service model

A distinctive characteristic of the model is a separation of capabilities in terms of service content and -provision. *Content* reflects the purpose of a service (e.g. moving goods). It is assumed that it arises from specific resources of the provider (e.g. internal processes, knowledge, people, machines, etc.). To represent service content, interactions procedures with such resources are explicitly exposed as meaningful units of content (e.g. transport tracking...) by capabilities referred to as *assets*. Assets don't contain any further cooperative interaction but resource binding (Bussler, 2002) and have to be *provided* to clients indirectly by other capabilities. Assets are grouped into a *service core* representing the complete content. *Provision* addresses procedures that drive a service and make available content (e.g. negotiating terms and conditions, incorporating assets, etc.), whereby control is exclusively and proactive. Service provision capabilities (hence called "capabilities") are grouped around core assets in a layer called *service shell.* Within a shell, capabilities are mutually interrelated and share a common view on roles and provision-relevant information. Interrelations embody the overall behaviour of provision by defining the global interplay of capabilities. A *service* is fully characterised by defining the basic core and, above all, the enabling shell (fig.1). Our focus is on the latter.

The conceptual service-notion is further substantiated by an architectural model referred to as *service-oriented architecture* (SOA). SOA uses workflow (wf) concepts to define a service as a partitioned set of interrelated components with precise interaction behaviour, where a subset C (service resources) represents interacting participants and a subset S (shell capabilities) represents their cooperation patterns.

In detail, a *role* $r \in R$ is responsible for a set of resource components C_r that are necessary to engage in a service relationship. Actually components are given by their communication endpoints $E_r = \cup e_c, c \in C_r$ that represent service interactions. Within an interaction, data artefacts $D_e \in D$ are communicated. Shell capabilities appear as *glue* between ports, representing a self-contained cooperation task.

The shell is a set of capabilities $S \subset C \times R \times P^*$ where each $s = (c, r, P_s)$ represents a component that is explicitly bound to a role and enforces a set of interaction processes. A process $p \in P_s$ defines a set of transitions $T_p \subset A_p \times A_p$ that forms a precedence graph between interaction activities $A_p \subset E_c \times R \times D^* \times \{in, out\}$. For a capability $s = (c_s, r_s, P_s)$, an activity $a_1 = (e_{cs}, r_s, D_1, in)$ represents an incoming interaction that is externally initiated and includes the communication of artefacts D_1 with endpoint e_{cs} provided by the capability's role r_s itself. An activity $a_2 = (e_x, r_y, D_2, out)$ represents an outgoing interaction where the communication of artefacts D_2 is initiated by r_s and the endpoint e_x is provided by some other role r_y. For two capabilities $s = (c_s, r_s, P_s)$, $t = (c_t, r_t, P_t)$, the interaction processes $p_1 \in P_s$, $p_2 \in P_t$ are *composed* by two activities $a_1 = (e_{ct}, r_t, D, out)$, $a_2 = (e_{ct}, r_t, D, in)$ where a_1 defines an outgoing interaction of p_1 and a_2 defines an incoming interaction of p_2.

The capability-notion from the conceptual model maps to SOA in the sense that implicit semantics of architectural elements (e.g. by ontology-associations) define the *purpose* of *interaction logic* that emerges from the flow of interaction activities and *results* in the flow of data artefacts. Furthermore, the concept of capability interrelation is achieved by composition of interaction processes.

As the SOA model is based on fundamental workflow concepts, it can be mapped to the WfMC metamodel (WfMC, 2002). Subsequently, service specifications, referred to as *service-schemata*, are represented in the XPDL workflow language.

For illustration, we will outline the example of a *compound transport service.* This logistic end-to-end service combines the transport of goods over multiple legs that are served by different carriers. Related organisational roles include FreightMixer (F) the compound service provider, various transport carriers (T_x, where x is the leg number they serve), an insurer (I) and a customer (C). A major task of F that we will look at, is the control of cooperative handover procedures between T_x and T_{x+1} serving two consecutive legs L_x and L_{x+1}. Handover control includes a standard procedure for trouble free cases as well as a procedure to resolve problems like delay or disaster happened in a leg (fig.2). The overall task is considered as a self-contained capability of the service.

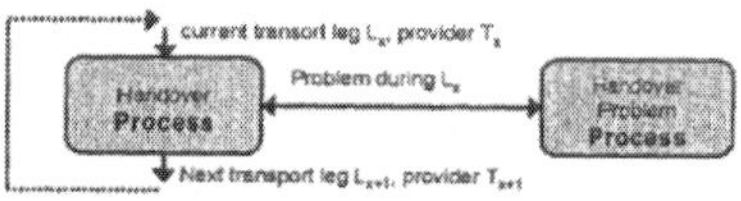

Figure 2. A compound end-to-end transport service

In more detail, the standard handover procedure between a current leg L_x and the next leg L_{x+1} starts with F waiting for a notification from T_x. In the normal case, F notifies I and C about the partial result as well as T_{x+1} about the beginning of his leg and initiates the next handover procedure (fig.3).

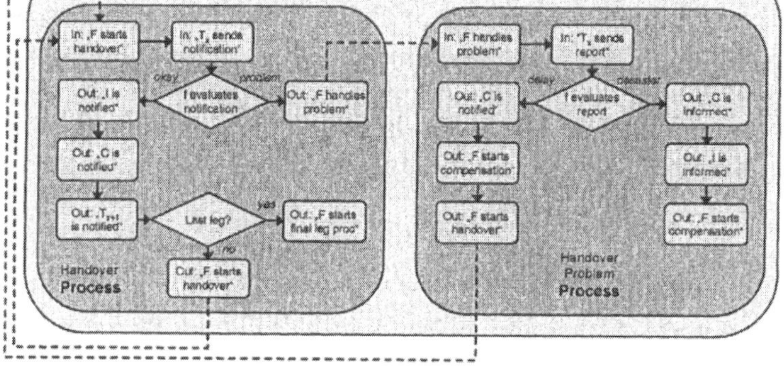

Figure 3. Handover control capability

In case of a problem, F starts a problem handling procedure that is modelled as a separate interaction process. There, F waits for a problem report from T_x. If there was a delay, F notifies C, starts some compensation and proceeds. In case of disaster, F informs C and I, starts some compensation and stops. The complete set of handover procedures forms the handover control capability. The capability is part of the transport-service shell and associated with F. All activities represent an interaction with a specific component provided by a specific role. In the figure, only (recursive) capability interrelations are shown (dotted lines). The other activities associated with F represent interactions with assets; all others embody interactions with participant resources.

3. SERVICE PROCESS EVOLUTION

Back on conceptual level, services are often required to adapt to change in terms of both the user needs and the operational conditions of service providers. To an extent, flexibility can be built into the structure of a service. An example is the ability of a freight service to support different types of packaging. Still, there are degrees of flexibility as well as operational capabilities that cannot be supported by a given realisation for a service. In the previous example, the possibility to transport perishable goods might simply not be available. Flexibility comes at a cost.

The engineering of a service is substantially based on a complex work of balancing conflicting requirements. In terms of service offer, a rich set of options is likely to attract a wider range of customers, and to provide a better fit for the needs of individual customers. The issues are complexity and cost. More options imply a more complex service design, and a more expensive service infrastructure. In the freight example, the option to transport perishable goods is likely to involve a completely different technical and normative infrastructure. The common approach is to target specific customer segments, and to prioritise the requirements coming from such customers. Still, the more a service is successful the more the need for change tends to emerge. Existing customers will demand better integration and customisation. Prospective customers will demand extensions to the basic service offer. A systematic approach to change is essential for the organic evolution of a service.

The evolution of a service essentially depends on two factors: processes and resources. New capabilities may require new types of resources. In the previous example, the transport of perishable goods requires refrigerated containers. In addition, the realisation of new capabilities requires new processes, for the coordination of new and existing resources. In the example, specific activities will be required for the setting and verification of the temperature for the containers, as well as for the hand-over of the containers at different stages of the transportation. Entirely new processes are occasionally required, but service extension and customisation are mainly based on the adaptation of existing processes. A coherent and consistent evolution of all the processes underpinning a service is essential for the service itself to be operationally efficient and meet customer expectations.

The approach we propose for the evolution of service processes is based on the concept of *transformation rule*. The change logic is captured explicitly in the form of sets of rules, which can then be applied systematically to sets of service processes. A software tool supports the automatic application of the rules to the processes. The formal specification of the rules, a description of the software tool, and an application example are presented in the following sections.

The current model for the transformation rules is based on pattern-matching and direct replacement. The service designer specifies patterns for the portions of a process that need modifications, as well as the changes to apply to the actual processes that match the pattern. The simplicity of the model reflects fundamental requirements such as usability and precision. Current practices revolve around direct changes to process specifications based on a find and replace approach. The rule-based solution we propose builds on current practices in an attempt to improve adoption. Techniques that are more complex would involve costly learning efforts for service designers. Most importantly, the simplicity of the model makes it easier for service designers to appreciate and verify the impact of change. Service designers are ultimately responsible for the result of changes and modifications. Building confidence in the change model is essential.

A direct benefit of explicit formalisation for the changes required to the service processes is consistency. A complete view of the change logic facilitates a systemic view of the impact that the changes will have on the service. Relations between different types of changes become more visible, and conflicts as well as synergies become apparent. A coherent view of the change plan enables a more direct validation of process changes with respect to the actual service evolution requirements. In particular, an explicit evolution plan provides a base for tracing service-level changes to structural changes in service processes, and ultimately to service realisation and delivery.

4. RULE BASED SERVICE TRANSFORMATION

In the SOA model, the definition of service processes is based on workflow concepts. The subsequent approach to systematic change of SOA service-schemata applies a rule based *workflow transformation language* that is described in this section. This language allows describing change strategies for general workflow configurations that can be globally enforced. Thereby the effects of change can be individually restricted to a useful context (e.g. only service processes for private-customers are to be changed but not those of business-customers). Within this context, processes containing an inappropriate configuration are identified. Changes are given as transformation instructions from the base-configuration into a desired target-configuration. These transformations are then applied to all selected processes in a complete, precise and reversible way.

Change strategies are structured into sets of individual transformation rules. Each rule contains a *process-selection-part* to restrict the application context, a *match-part* to identify the base-configuration within processes of the context and a *replacement-part* to transform the processes as desired.

Systematic change is fundamentally based on *workflow patterns* that allow reliably identifying specific structures throughout an extensive collection of processes. Generally, a pattern enumerates and names workflow elements with respect to a set of match-conditions:

```
<pattern type>
  <match condition1>,
    ...
  <match condition n>;
```

Each of the match-conditions describes requirements for a subset of workflow elements. Workflow elements that satisfy the requirements are bound to a specific name. Requirements are given in terms of type, cardinality and state:

```
<element type> {<cardinality>} : <binding name>
  <Boolean expression>;
```

Type requirements restrict elements to a specific type. Thereby, types are classes of workflow elements as specified in the XML Schema of XPDL (WfMC, 2002).

Cardinality requirements restrict a valid match to a specific number of elements. By default, exactly one element is matched. Other ranges can be specified by different modifiers. The *optional* (?) modifier makes a match condition non-obligatory. An *asterisk* (*) causes multiple bindings (including zero) of elements and results in a set that contains all matching elements except for those matched in previous parts of the pattern. *Existence* (+) is similar to asterisk, but requires the element set to be non-empty. *Exclusion* (–) acts as a guard because pattern matching fails in case any such element exists. As a special case of condition, exclusion can be defined for a conjunctive combination of sub-conditions.

State requirements are specified as a Boolean expression in terms of element attributes and associations. Within expressions, attribute values of all elements bound within the whole pattern can be accessed, evaluated and combined by various operators. In addition to standard element comparison (`==`, `!=`), numerical comparison (`<`, `>`, `<=`, `>=`), arithmetic (`+`, `-`, `*`, `/`) unary (`+`, `-`) and Boolean (`and`, `or`, `not`) operators, also string operations (`contains`, `+`) ant type castings (`str`, `int`, `bool`, `date`) are possible. *Contained elements* (specified by XPDL as parts of an XML Schema complex type) are either accessible via dot notation or by their obligatory Id attribute (e.g. `myProcess.activities["start"].name`).

In Transformation rules, the *process-selection-part* is given as a specific *selector-pattern* that consists of exactly one *selector-condition*. The *selector-condition* always prescribes the element-type `Process` together with the `+` modifier. The state-requirement allows specifying an expression that describes the process instances to be considered. In the following example, all processes are pre-selected, whose name attribute contains "handover" and who are part of a workflow package, created before 2004. Also, note that the expression includes type conversion.

```
RULE "transport: conditionally add insurer notification"
FOR_ALL_PROCESSES p
  p.name contains "Handover",
  date(p.package.packageHeader.created)
  < date("01/01/2004 00:00");
```

The *match-part* of a rule is specified by a *match-pattern*. The match-pattern prescribes a specific configuration of arbitrary workflow elements whose existence is a precondition for further processing. Additionally, it declares the binding of element enumerations that result from condition matches, referred to as *condition-match-enumerations*, for further processing. The complete match of a pattern results in a set of condition-match-enumerations referred to as *pattern-match-set*. If a condition is not unique, it can be possibly matched in multiple ways. Subsequently, a match-set is one permutation of the possible condition-match-enumerations. Here, two application semantics are possible: Either to apply the remaining rule for all match-sets individually (*match all*) or to apply it exactly once (*match once*).

The following example illustrates a pattern with match-all semantic and exclusion of two simultaneous conditions. It describes a specific single activity "compensation" that is only matched if there does not exist another specific activity "information" as well as a transition that links them together. If this configuration is found in a process multiple times, the rest of the rule will be applied for all occurrences of "compensation" activities individually.

```
MATCH_ALL
  Activity start_compensation:
    start_compensation.name == "F starts compensation";
  EXCLUSION "excludeIfInformed"
    Activity inform_insurer:
      inform_insurer.name == "I is informed";
```

```
Transition inform_compensate:
  inform_compensate.from == inform_insurer,
  inform_compensate.to == start_compensation;;
```

A rule is concluded by a *replacement-part* that defines how to transform the match-set. It consists of transformation operations for all condition-match-enumerations of a match-set. The default operation is removal so that an empty replacement-part leads to the removal of the complete match-set. To preserve a condition-match-enumeration it has to be explicitly referenced in the replacement part whereby all element attributes can be modified. Additionally, the creation of new elements can be instructed that are to be added to the process. After creation, attributes are initialised with default values that can be modified as appropriate. Syntactically, element creation consists of a type, a name and various attribute value assignments.

```
<element type> : <binding name>
  <attribute name> = <expression>,
   ...
  <attribute name> = <expression>;
```

To affect the placing of elements within a process, a special attribute called "container" is introduced that allows accessing and changing the parent of any element. When using references to optional elements of the match-set, the transformation operation has to be declared optional, too.

In the example, the match-set contains only a single activity. The exemplary replacement-part preserves this activity by referencing it initially. Additionally it instructs the creation of another activity and a transition that connects both activities.

```
REPLACE_WITH
  start_compensation;
  Activity notify_insurer:
    id = "notify_insurer",
    name = "Notify insurer",
    implementation = No();
  Transition compensation_notify:
    id = "compensation to notify",
    from = start_compensation,
    to = notify_insurer;
```

To enforce changes, specified by a number of rules, the aggregated rule set is applied to a pool of workflow processes as follows:

1. Rules are taken from the rule set one at a time. They are applied to a process pool individually as described in the next steps.
2. Initially, the selector-pattern is applied to the process pool. For each process within the pool, the pre-selection condition is evaluated exactly once. If the Boolean expression evaluates true, the process is selected for further processing.

3. In the next step, each pre-selected process is checked against the match-pattern. For each condition of the pattern, corresponding elements are collected that satisfy the type- and state-requirements. A subset of these elements is bound with respect to the cardinality requirement whereby bound elements are excluded from further matches. In terms of sequence, obligatory conditions (none or + modifier) are matched first, followed by optional single matches (?) and finally optional enumerations (*). In case of non-unique patterns, all permutations of binding combinations are considered. The pattern matching fails if a) a match condition fails or b) an exclusion condition is violated. In this case, the processing is terminated. Otherwise, the resulting matches are structured into pattern-match-sets of condition-match-enumerations, each set representing one binding permutation. Depending on the match-semantic, either all (match-all) or exactly one match-set (match-once) is further processed.
4. Finally, the sequence of match-sets is transformed one at a time as specified in the replacement part of the rule. All non-referenced condition-match-enumerations are removed from the process. All others are modified as instructed. New elements are created and added to the process. For the resulting process, a basic consistency check is done that detects obvious violations of the process structure and rolls back the transformation in case of an error. The transformation also fails in case of unbound references.

To illustrate the usage of transformation rules for changing service processes, we revisit the transport-service example. Let's assume that Freightmixer's management decides to change the business procedure. In a first change, the insurer ought to be informed after a problem compensation procedure was started. For obvious reasons, this is not necessary if the insurer was informed directly before. For this change, the rule introduced before can be used to detect and transform every such situation.

In a second change, all interaction processes of any cooperation ought to be stripped down by removing costly notifications of the customer. This can be achieved by the following rule:

```
RULE "transport: remove notifications"
FOR_ALL_PROCESSES p
  p.name contains "Handover";
MATCH_ONCE
  Activity{*} a IN notificationActivities:
    a.name contains "C is notified";
REPLACE_WITH
  FOR_EACH a IN notificationActivities:
    name = "activity without function",
    route = Route();
```

The second rule is an example of match-once semantic. This is sufficient because the match condition of the pattern is unique. Elimination of notifications is done by changing interactions into inactive routes, thereby omitting a complicated change of transitions for the sake of simplicity. After adding both rules to a combined rule set, they are applied to the service specification. The result is a change in both interaction processes of the handover control capability (fig. 4). In both processes, the notification activities disappeared. (Actually, they are changed to trivial routing activities that are simplified as single transitions in fig. 4. This is also visible in fig.6, where the associated tool shows an out/in comparison ("diff") of the change effects.) In addition, the insurer is informed after a compensation activity, but only in the case where he was not already informed before.

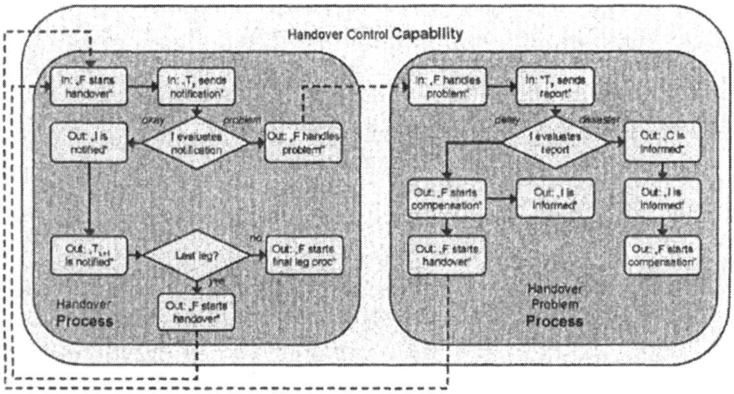

Figure 4. Changed handover control capability after rule application

5. PROTOTYPE

As proof of concept, we developed the functionality of rule based workflow transformation as part of a prototype environment referred to as *FRESCO Toolkit or FrescoTK*[24]. FrescoTK is an implementation of the FRESCO SOA. It implements a fundamental way for service realisation as well as a set of crucial service engineering mechanisms (Zirpins et al., 2004).

Major implementation technologies include the Open Grid Service Architecture OGSA (Foster et al., 2002) together with specific aspects of the more general Webservice Architecture (Tsalgatidou and Pilioura, 2002) and

[24] FrescoTK is available under academic free licence at www.servicecomposition.org

a BPEL enabled workflow management system. Fig 5 provides an architectural overview.

In the toolkit, FRESCO *services* are implemented as sets of OGSA Grid-service-components, divided in two subsets: capabilities and resources. *Resources* are implemented as conventional Gridservices, extended by a set of OGSA service-data attributes. *Capabilities* are components that can be accessed as Gridservices too, but also proactively enforce service specific behaviour.

While resources have to be realised and provided outside the scope of FrescoTK, capabilities are generated and deployed by the FrescoTK on the basis of a service-schema specification. Internally, they consist of a BPEL enabled workflow engine that drives the capability's interaction processes. As BPEL engines are based on Webservice technology, they are not originally applicable in a grid environment. Thus, capabilities feature an integration-architecture to bridge between Grid- and Webservices. This integration-architecture uses various interceptors (represented as proxies and adapters) that translate calls and convert instance management information.

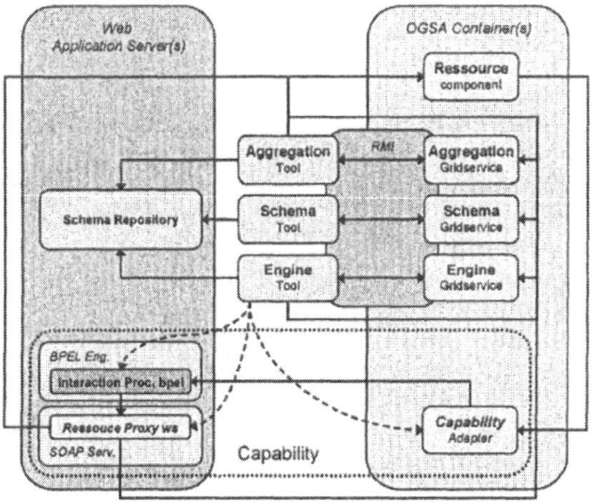

Figure 5. FRESCO Toolkit architecture

The engineering of services is based on a set of *management components*. In brief, these components provide essential functionality to plan, build and run FRESCO services by service-schema management (Schema Tool), service-instance creation and resource management (Aggregation Tool) as well as service-capability generation and control (Engine Tool). Management components are designed as tools that provide a GUI for human users. Additionally, they are designed as system support mechanisms that provide an API for programmatic use. Therefore, the components are implemented as java standalone applications and major management operations are accessible via Grid. Each component is represented as a Gridservice by a proxy, to which it is connected via Java remote method invocation.

The *Schema Tool* (fig.6) holds generic specifications of various service-schemata and makes them programmatically accessible. Its vital characteristic is the ability to apply a variety of transformations to them that allow for controlled change as well as translation into executable format. Management operations – provided via GUI and Grid – include *storage, retrieval, removal* and *browsing* of service-schemata, *translation* of service-schema into executable BPEL process-schemata as well as *change* of service-schemata by application of customised transformation rules.

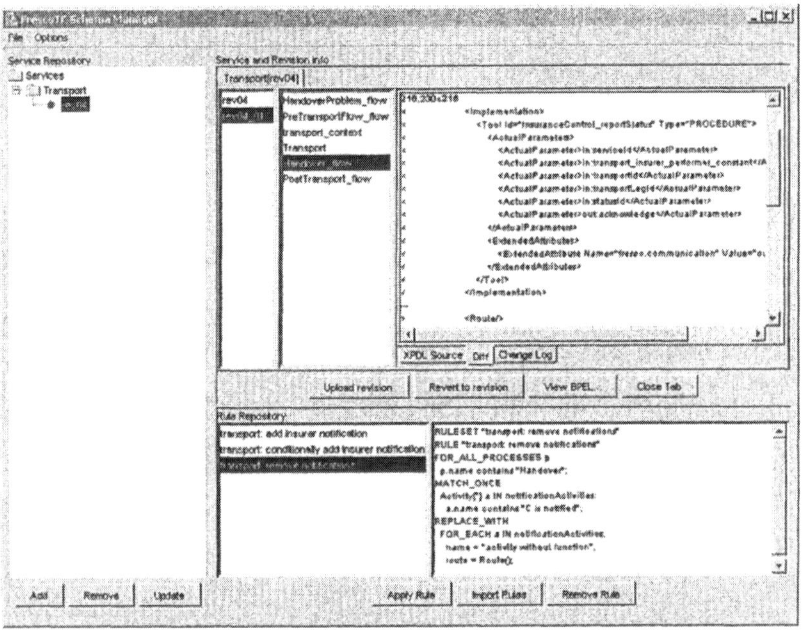

Figure 6. FrescoTK service-schema tool

Transformation rules are held in a *rule repository*. They are directly entered or imported from a file, whereby validation takes place. Then, they can be applied to service-schemata that are selected from the schema repository. Revision management allows tracking changes and doing rollbacks in case. A rule is always applied to one specific revision of a schema. If it leads to changes in any of the revision's packages, a new local revision is created. Stable revisions can be chosen to be persisted in the repository.

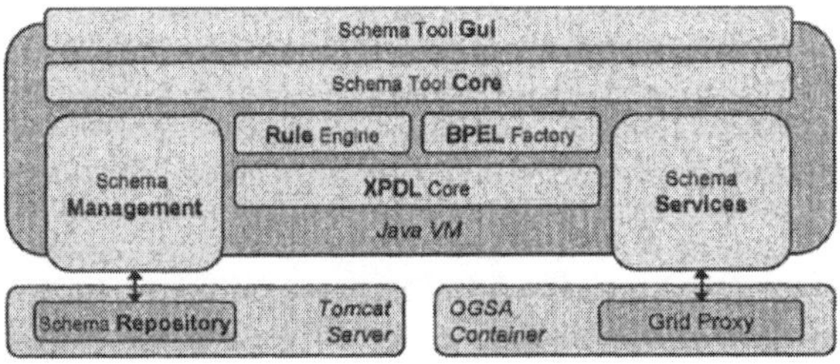

Figure 7. Schema Tool Architecture

Rules are processed by the *rule engine* that is embedded in the schema-tool architecture (fig.7). There, it is used by the *schema-tool core* to provide transformation services for GUI and Grid (via RMI-connected proxy) access. The rule engine is based on the FRESCO XPDL core; a Castor-generated XML binding API (ExoLab, 2004) that implements XPDL elements as beans, using Jakarta Beanutils (Jakarta-Project, 2004). Here, support of mapped and indexed bean properties allows for rich rule expressions; i.e. `process.activities[5]` (indexed property) or `extendedAttributes["myAttribute"]` (mapped property). Such expressions are implemented using ANTLR (Parr, 2004) and a grammar of this language is available as part of the FRESCO Toolkit's source code. The engine itself implements the change algorithm as explained in the previous section.

6. RELATED WORK

The FRESCO service model is mainly related to work from three different areas of inter-organisational process management. In *BPM (business process modelling & management)*, virtual enterprises and inter-enterprise-processes are a major concern (Bussler, 2001, Georgakopoulos et al., 1999, Perrin et al., 2003, Schuster et al., 2000, Baïna et al., 2003). The DySCo project (Piccinelli et al., 2003a) introduced a basic process-based service model and developed methods to deduce participant-related sub-processes for service control. *Inter-organisational workflow* adds concepts of distributed control structures (van der Aalst, 1999) and technology of related management systems (Mecella et al., 2001, Colombo et al., 2002). Finally, the focus of *service composition* (Papazoglou and Georgakopoulos, 2003) is on combining atomic functions of loosely coupled systems (Webservices) by processes (Casati et al., 2001, Dumas et al., 2002, Bhiri et al., 2003). The view on services adopted in FRESCO combines concepts from these areas as regards inter-organisational business processes, workflow architecture for their control and service technology for their implementation. It adds a cooperation model with novel service-oriented concepts (e.g. service capabilities with explicit separation of service content and service provision)

The issue of evolution for process specifications has been object of attention for quite a few years, both from the scientific community and the industry. *BPR (Business Process Re-engineering)* was a major area of activity in the late 1990s' (Hunt, 1996). The results produced cover extensive requirements analysis, as well as methodologies and techniques to address the various technical and organizational issues related to process change (i.e. (Sethi and King, 1998, Piccinelli et al., 2002)). BPR activities have been substantially based on direct intervention on process definitions by teams composed of process engineering and business experts. The rule-based approach we propose would complement the operational model used in BPR environments.

A second important line of activity for process evolution is based on *data mining* techniques applied to the process execution logs generated by workflow management platforms (Agrawal et al., 1998, Srinivasa and Spiliopoulou, 2000). The focus is on the identification of patterns in the execution trace of multiple process instances in order to infer areas of improvement for the specification of the process. Patterns can involve individual processes or span groups of related processes (Cook and Wolf, 1998). The patterns identified by the data mining techniques can be combined with the technical and domain expertise of process designers in order to define the evolution strategy for the processes. The rule-based approach we propose can be used to capture and execute the chance strategy.

In terms of *workflow patterns*, fundamental research has been done in the Petri-net community (van der Aalst et al., 2000). Additionally, concepts to ensure consistency of changes (e.g. *workflow inheritance*) where proposed (van der Aalst and Basten, 2002). Our approach can directly benefit from this foundation and helps transporting it to practice.

7. CONCLUSION

The capability to adapt the processes underpinning a service is essential for service evolution and customisation. The resource base of a service provider changes over time. Similarly, customer requirements change and diversify. The alignment between service logic and the underlying realisation and delivery processes of a service can become an issue for providers, and ultimately also for the consumers.

The rule-based framework we propose for the adaptation of service processes balances usability and precision against semantic and abstraction richness. The pattern-matching model used in the transformation rules is close to the find-and-replace model normally used by service designers. Rules add the benefit of a systematic approach to the specification as well as the application of the change logic. The combined use of the rule model and the tool developed for rule application reduces the risk of omissions and mistakes intrinsic in manual approaches. In addition, direct improvements can be achieved in terms of the tractability of change.

An important benefit of the approach proposed is the possibility to capture an overall change strategy, and to separate definition and application of such strategy. Future work will concentrate on support for the validation of an overall change strategy with respect to service evolution requirements as well as verification of consistency for the set of rules composing a strategy.

ACKNOWLEDGEMENTS

We would like to thank HP Labs Bristol for support of the FRESCO project. Furthermore, we want to thank the FRESCO team, especially Thomas Plümpe and Henning Brandt, for their help to achieve this work.

REFERENCES

Agrawal, R., Gunaopulos, D. and Leymann, F. (1998) *Mining Process Models from Workflow Logs,* In *Proc. Advances in Database Technology - EDBT'98, 6th International Conference on Extending Database Technology, Valencia, Spain*(Eds, Schek, H. J., Saltor, F., Ramos, I. and Alonso, G.) Springer, pp. 469-483.

Baïna, K., Tata, S. and Benali, K. (2003) *A Model for Process Service Interaction,* In *Business Process Management International Conference, BPM 2003, Eindhoven, The Netherlands, June 26-27, 2003. Proceedings*(Eds, Aalst, W. M. P. v. d., Hofstede, A. H. M. t. and Weske, M.) Springer, pp. 261 ff.

Bhiri, S., Perrin, O., Gaaloul, W. and Godart, C. (2003) *An Object Oriented Metamodel for Inter-enterprises Cooperative Processes based on Web Services,* In *Proc. Modeling and Developing Process-Centric Virt. Enterprises with Webservices (VIEWS'03), Austin, USA.*

Bussler, C. (2001) *The role of B2B protocols in inter-enterprise process execution,* In *Proc. Technologies for E Services. Second International Workshop, TES 2001.*(Eds, Casati, F., Georgakopoulos, D. and Shan, M. C.) Springer, pp. 16-29.

Bussler, C. (2002) *Behavior abstraction in semantic B2B integration,* In *Conceptual Modeling for New Information Systems Technologies. ER 2001 Workshops. HUMACS, DASWIS, ECOMO, and DAMA. Revised Papers Lecture Notes in Computer Science Vol.2465. 2002*(Eds, Arisawa, H. et al) Springer Verlag, Berlin, Germany, pp. 377-89.

Casati, F., Sayal, M. and Ming Chien Shan (2001) *Developing E-Services for Composing E-Services,* In *Proc. Advanced Information Systems Engineering. 13th International Conference, (CAiSE 2001)*(Eds, Dittrich, K. R. et al) Springer, pp. 171-86.

Colombo, E., Francalanci, C. and Pernici, B. (2002) *Modeling Coordination and Control in Cross-Organizational Workflows,* In *Proc. CoopIS/DOA/ODBASE 2002*(Eds, Meersmann, R. and Tari, Z.) Springer, pp. 91 ff.

Cook, J. E. and Wolf, A. L. (1998) *Discovering models of software processes from event-based data, ACM Transactions on Software Engineering and Methodology,* **7**.

Dumas, M., Benatallah, B. and Maamar, Z. (2002) *Definition and Execution of Composite Web Services: The SELF-SERV Project, Data Engineering Bulletin,* **25**.

ExoLab (2004) *Castor Project,* http://castor.exolab.org/, 1.2.2004

Foster, I., Kesselman, C., Nick, J. and Tuecke, S. (2002) *The Physiology of the Grid: An Open Grid Services Architecture for Distributed Systems Integration,* Open Grid Service Infrastructure WG, Global Grid Forum

Georgakopoulos, D., Schuster, H., Cichocki, A. and Baker, D. (1999) *Managing process and service fusion in virtual enterprises, Information Systems,* **24,** 429-56.

Hunt, V. D. (1996) *Process Mapping: How to Reengineer Your Business Processes,* John Wiley & Sons.

Jakarta-Project (2004) *JaKarta Commons,* http://jakarta.apache.org/commons/, 1.2.2004

Mecella, M., Pernici, B., Rossi, M. and Testi, A. (2001) *A Repository of Workflow Components for Cooperative e-Applications,* In *Proceedings of the 1st IFIP TC8 Working Conference on E-Commerce/E-Business (Salzburg, Austria, 2001)*BICE Press, pp. 73-92.

Papazoglou, M. P. and Georgakopoulos, D. (2003) *Service-oriented computing: Introduction, Communications of the ACM,* **46,** 24-28.

Parr, T. (2004) *ANTLR Translator Generator,* http://www.antlr.org/, 1.2.2004

Perrin, O., Wynen, F., Bitcheva, J. and Godart, C. (2003) *A Model to Support Collaborative Work in Virtual Enterprises,* In *Business Process Management International Conference, BPM 2003, Eindhoven, The Netherlands, June 26-27, 2003. Proceedings*(Eds, Aalst, W. M. P. v. d., Hofstede, A. H. M. t. and Weske, M.) Springer, pp. p. 104 ff.

Piccinelli, G., Emmerich, W., Zirpins, C. and Schütt, K. (2002) *Web Service Interfaces for Inter-Organisational Business Processes: An Infrastructure for Automated Reconciliation,* In *Proc. 6th International Enterprise Distributed Object Computing Conference (EDOC2002), September 17-20 2002, Lausanne, Swizerland*(Ed, Williams, A. D.) IEEE Computer Society, Los Alamos, California, pp. 285-292.

Piccinelli, G., Finkelstein, A. and Williams, S. L. (2003a) *Service-oriented work-flows: the DySCo framework,* In *Proc. 29th Euromicro Conference, Antalya, Turkey.*

Piccinelli, G., Zirpins, C. and Gryce, C. (2003b) *An Architectural Model for Electronic Services,* University College London, University of Hamburg

Schuster, H., Georgakopoulos, D., Cichocki, A. and Baker, D. (2000) *Modeling and Composing Service-Based and Reference Process-Based Multi-enterprise Processes,* In *Proc CAiSE 2000*(Eds, Wangler, B. and Bergman, L.) Springer, pp. 247-263.

Sethi, V. and King, W. (1998) *Organizational Transformation Through Business Process Reengineering.,* Prentice Hall.

Srinivasa, S. and Spiliopoulou, M. (2000) *Discerning Behavioral Properties by Analyzing Transaction Logs,* In *Proc. of the 2000 ACM symposium on Applied computing 2000, Como, Italy*(Eds, Papadopoulos, G. and Omicini, A.) ACM Press, NY, USA, pp. 281 - 282.

Tsalgatidou, A. and Pilioura, T. (2002) *An overview of standards and related technology in Web Services, Distributed and Parallel Databases,* **12,** 135-62.

van der Aalst, W. M. P. (1999) *Process-oriented architectures for electronic commerce and interorganizational workflow, Information Systems,* **24,** 639-71.

van der Aalst, W. M. P., Barros, A. P., Hofstede, A. H. M. t. and Kiepuszewski, B. (2000) *Advanced Workflow Patterns,* In *Cooperative Information Systems, 7th International Conference, CoopIS 2000, Eilat, Israel, September 6-8, 2000, Proceedings*, Vol. 1901 (Eds, Etzion, O. and Scheuermann, P.) Springer, pp. 18-29.

van der Aalst, W. M. P. and Basten, T. (2002) *Inheritance of workflows: an approach to tackling problems related to change, Theoretical Computer Science,* **270,** 125-203.

WfMC (2002) *Workflow Process Definition Interface -- XML Process Definition Language 1.0 Final Draft,* WFMC-TC-1025, Workflow Management Coalition

WfMC (2004) *Workflow Management Coalition,* http://www.wfmc.org, 20.1.2004

Zirpins, C., Lamersdorf, W. and Piccinelli, G. (2004) *A Service Oriented Approach to Interorganisational Cooperation,* In *IFIF International Conference on Digital Communities in a Networked Society: eCommerce, eBusiness, and eGovernment (I3E) 2003, Proceedings*(Eds, Mendes, M., Suomi, R. and Passos, C.) Kluwer Academic Publishers.

SERVICE COMPOSITION APPLIED TO E-GOVERNMENT

Neil Paiva Tizzo[1], José Renato Borelli[3], Manuel de Jesus Mendes[2], Luciano Lançia Damasceno[3], Aqueo Kamada[3], Adriana Figueiredo[3], Marcos Rodrigues[3] and G. Souza[3].
PUC Minas Poços de Caldas/MG, [2] Universidade Católica de Santos/SP, [3] Centro de Pesquisas Renato Archer, Campinas, Brazil

Abstract: One of the public administration big challenges is the need to integrate services in order to offer a wide variety of new services, more suitable and better designed, that can be electronically accessed in a uniform way. Recently, the Web Service technology appeared with the promise to compose services through the Internet in a simple way. Despite the Web Services advantages, minimal technology independence is desirable at the design of such compositions in order to guarantee and preserve all the efforts invested in the development of services. In this article a Service Composition Management Framework is proposed, that focuses in a technology-independent description. The referred framework is part of a more complete platform, developed for the electronic delivery of Government services.

Key words: e-Government, Web Services, Services Composition, Collaboration, MDA, MOF.

1. INTRODUCTION

The pressure to continuously cut costs and to provide broad and efficient public access to the information has driven governments all over the world to develop electronic government (*e-Gov*) initiatives. There is a convergence among the different e-Gov strategies that points out to integrated and cross-agency services. The collaboration between the several agencies, partners of an e-Gov structure, can provide more suitable services for the potential users (citizens and enterprises).

The São Paulo State Government, Brazil, is investing a great effort in this direction. As an example, it is on the way of installing public services, directly to the society, by electronic means, mainly through the Internet, improving existing presential systems (Poupatempo's). These systems have to integrate the involved databases and applications on the back-office, independent of their locality (municipal and regional), thus saving time, displacements, simplifying processes and avoiding the presentation of paper documents. A first step has been decided with the execution of a project, named eGOIA (eGOIA, 2003), to implement a demonstration system based on the development of a software infrastructure, in order to allow the access of citizens, through the Internet, to integrated public services, at several levels.

The eGOIA project intends to develop a platform to support Internet collaborative systems in the government context (Cardoso, 2004). The authors of this paper are involved in eGOIA and the examples presented come from this real experience.

The set of Web Services (*WS*) standards is a good proposal to provide such collaborative environments. Web Services, as it will better explained in other sections of the paper, are considered as high level components, configured in order to allow the composition of basic services, if possible "on-the-fly", and thus forming new complex services. In the context of e-Gov, several situations exist for an intensive use of this kind of composition tools.

In this paper, a proposal of a Service Composition Management Framework is explained. Due to the great diversity and volatility of composition solutions and standards in the field of Web Services, a technology independent collaboration tool is proposed. In order to reach this goal, the different aspects of collaboration are developed following the concepts of MDA (Model Driven Architecture): services and related metadata are first modeled independently of technology and platform, by means of UML and EDOC. Later on, these platform independent models are mapped to the specific technologies of Web Services.

The remainder of the paper is organized as follows. In section 2 we review several concepts that are to be used in the proposal. Section 3 presents the main ideas that configure the Service Composition Management Framework and discusses some results of a prototype being developed. A realistic e-Gov service composition case study is described in section 4. Section 5 describes related works and section 6 concludes this paper.

2. OVERVIEW OF CONCEPTS

In this section we present the technical foundations that guide the development of the framework, specifically regarding aspects of multi-tier architectures, Web Services stacks of standards, MDA and MOF.

2.1 Multi-tier e-Gov Architectures

Looking at the multi-tier architecture (Frankel, 2003) used in the current generation of e-Gov systems (Figure 1), there are several opportunities for the use of service composition. Such architecture has been considered for the eGOIA project.

For simplicity, three tiers are represented: the user, the business and the persistence tier. The services will be offered through a portal in the Internet, accessed by the citizen through PC-browsers, public points of access, or other type of access channels.

The persistence tier represents the government legacy system, applications and databases *("back-office")*, and is managed by the government agencies. Future evolution, with possible legacies reengineering, brings the opportunity of data services composition, in order to allow a better integration and access by applications from other tiers.

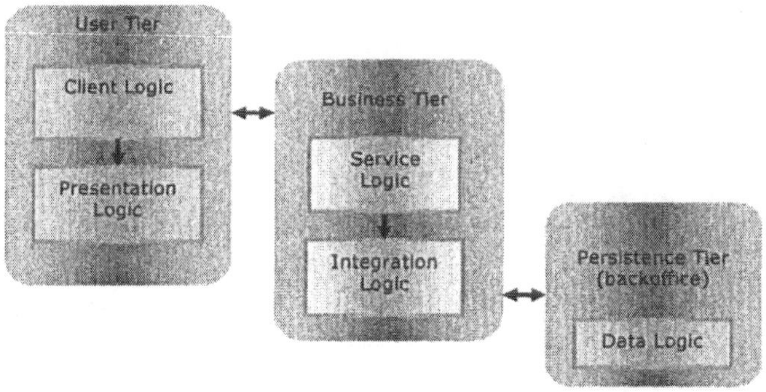

Figure 1. The multi-tiered architecture for e-Gov systems.

The business tier encloses the services and the integration logic. The integration logic is responsible for the unification of data, used by the e-Gov services, and coming from the persistence tier. Otherwise a great diversity of basic services (e.g. form server, authentication, access control, security, accountability services) will be located in it. The composition of these basic services will be used for the expansion of agency capabilities, as well as, for the support of government services.

The service logic includes a great diversity of government services (e.g. health, education services). Its deployment brings again an interesting field for the use of composition techniques, in order to offer more complex services for the users, mainly on a "one-stop" context.

2.2 Web Service Concepts, Protocols and Languages

There are three, at least, related areas speaking about interoperability and integration of applications in the internet. The correspondent standard stacks are represented in Figure 2. All of them share basic aspects (HTTP, XML) (Turner, 2003).

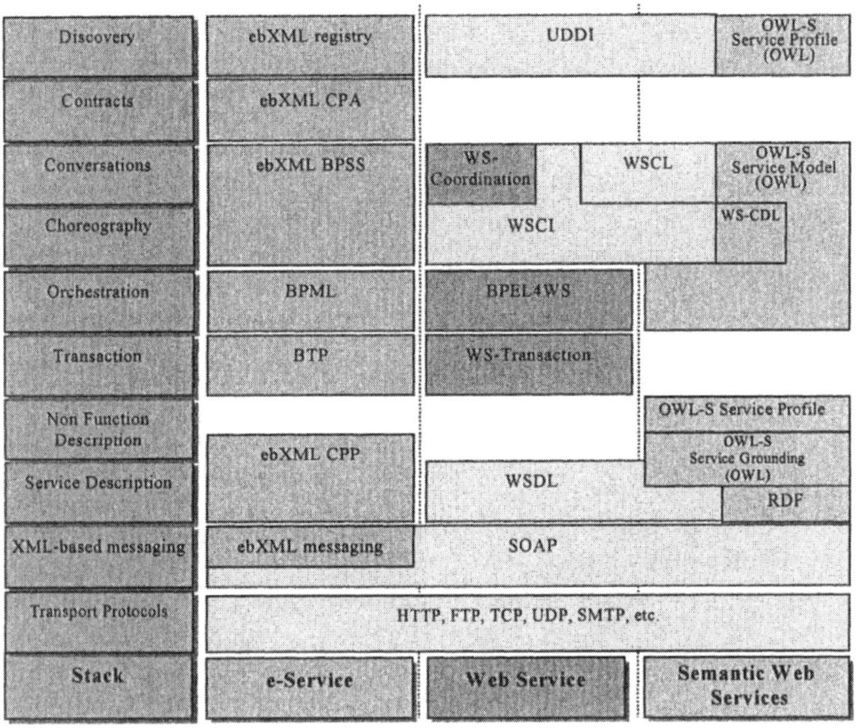

Figure 2. Related stacks of electronic services standards.

The left stack deals with *e-Services* and corresponds to the concepts being developed in the context of B2B (Medjahed, 2003a). e-Services are delivered electronically, through the Internet. Interest in e-Services has been growing continuously in the recent years. Examples of e-Services include software solutions provided by Application Service Providers, and Supply Chain information management networks. A composite e-Service is a group of several e-Services that can be seen as a workflow. A *workflow* is an automated business process that manages the sequence of work activities and the use of appropriate resources associated with the various activity steps. This kind of composition tends to be of static nature and is related to the topic of application integration (EAI). There is a large number of XML-based frameworks for B2B interactions (e.g. *eCO, cXML, RosettaNet, ebXML*). In the Figure 2 some aspects of ebXML are represented.

The right stack, *Semantic Web Services (S-WS)*, is a branch of the DAML program (DARPA, 2004) and has been integrated recently in the standards stack of the Semantic Web community. The focus is more in AI agents, and th outside the scope of this paper. Services are agents acting in the Web and the aspects of autonomy are of relevance (W3C, 2002). The correspondent standards are thus not elaborated in the same degree of detail as it happens in the other stacks. The automatic composition of Web Services is slated to play a major role in enabling the envisioned Semantic Web (Medjahed, 2003b). The semantic of Web Services is crucial to enabling automatic service composition.

The stack in the middle deals with *Web Services (WS),* main subject of this paper. WS's can be defined as applications that can be published and consumed as services, by other applications, using Internet standard technologies, such as XML, SOAP, WSDL and UDDI. WS's should be easily composed dynamically with locally developed or externally available services, irrespective of the platform, development language or object model used to implement them, configuring new complex composite services. In this sense they represent an example of SOA (Service Oriented Architecture) and are high granular components, to be joined dynamically. Each composition can involve a great number of services, each one playing a specific role in the collaboration.

Composition may involve several levels of functionality of the so called Web Services stack: conversation, choreography, orchestration and transaction (Turner, 2003). Again the literature is rather confused about these topics, for example, not distinguishing exactly the meanings of choreography and orchestration. The following concepts have been adopted in this paper. *Conversation* deals with initial activities, necessary for the finding of partners (e.g. UDDI), defining roles and, if necessary, negotiating collaboration contracts. This is a field where few standards have yet been defined. *Orchestration* (related to the concepts of workflow or business process) is the description of the flow of data and control involved in the execution of a set of services. Later on in the paper, the use of modeling languages as UML and EDOC is introduced. This will help on clearly stating orchestration as the activities similar to those of defining business processes (workflows). *Choreography* specifies the coordination of some Web Services under the aspect of protocols, defining messages and the sequence of messages exchanged between the parts. This corresponds also to the EDOC concepts of choreography. *Transactions* describe the execution of composite services in an atomic form, i.e., providing rollback mechanisms in case of local failures or service abortions.

In order to better understand this subject a brief description of existing standards is now given. SOAP (Simple Access Object Protocol) handles the transport layer of XML messages among nodes, e.g. over HTTP, SMTP, XML-RPC. WSDL (Web Service Description Language) handles the interface layer by defining the syntax of the I/O, the names of the operations, the error messages. UDDI (Universal Description, Discovery and Integration) handles the registration of services offered by businesses. WSCI (Web Service Choreography Interface) describes the flow of messages exchanged by a WS participating in choreographed interactions with other services. BPEL4WS (Business Process Execution Language for Web Services) provides a language for the formal specification of business processes and business interaction protocols. It supersedes WSFL and XLANG. CS-WS provides the conversation support framework, executing "conversations" that require a more loosely coupled, peer-to-peer, dynamic, proactive model of interaction between the messaging system and business processes. WS-Coordination describes an extensible framework for providing protocols that coordinate the actions of distributed applications. WS-Transaction describes coordination types that are used with the coordination framework in order to implement distributed (e.g. atomic) transactions.

In this paper the set of Web Services standards is considered as the right proposal to provide a collaborative environment in the context of eGovernment. There are several problems related to this architecture as, for example, the volatility of the standards stack. The current WS architecture proposes several layers of functionality, each one containing different solutions (protocols, languages) that strive to become standards. However, the adoption of a possible universal solution for each layer will never be accomplished. Furthermore, new technologies (or even layers) can appear to fill new requirements for specific WS contexts.

Finally, the three approaches (e-Services, WS and S-WS) are not necessarily mutually excluding, and situations may be visualized where they may cooperate. The basic WS standards (e.g. SOAP and WSDL) have been adopted also in the context of e-Services and S-WS.

2.3 MDA and MOF

MDA, Model Driven Architecture, (OMG, 2004) has been adopted as the modeling framework in our research project. MDA provides an open, technology independent, approach to address the problems of productivity, portability, interoperability, maintenance and documentation in software development process, building upon and leveraging the value of established modeling and metamodeling standards. It separates business logic from specific platform technology (e.g. WS standards) creating a new way of developing software in which the platform independent Models (PIM's) turn into the long-term maintainable artifacts. A PIM can be transformed in platform specific Models (PSM's) and code applications, deployed on a variety of platforms (e.g. J2EE, CORBA, .NET, Web Services and future new ones).

In the core of the MDA approach is the Meta-Object Facility (MOF), which is used to manage the models generated during modeling activities. MOF provides a model repository and an abstract language, the MOF Model, which can be used to specify and manipulate metamodels, thus providing support consistency in manipulating models in all phases of the use of MDA. Models and metamodels are *metadata*, information about data. The MOF main objective is to facilitate the access, the management, the processing and the sharing of a great collection of structured and/or non-structured metadata (Kerhervé, 1997). Using MOF is possible to define different languages for modeling different aspects of systems and to integrate models expressed in different languages.

The MOF highlight characteristics are: (i) it is self-defining, i.e., the MOF Model is used to self-describing; (ii) the MOF Model is object oriented; (iii) it uses models to define other models; and (iv) it is based on the four-layer metamodeling architecture. The lowest layer of the architecture, the Information Layer or M0, holds objects and data. The layer above, called the Model Layer (Metadata Layer) or M1 that describes the M0 data, consists of instances of M2 metamodel constructs. The M2 is the metamodel layer consisting of MOF-compliant metamodels, standardized or not. And finally, the M3 or meta-metamodel layer conceptually consists of only one model, called the "MOF Model".

As MOF is platform independent, it will allow mappings to different technologies. At the present time, there are several MOF technology mappings, like: the Java Metadata Interchange (JMI) (JMI, 2002) that defines a set of rules for mapping the elements of a MOF compliant model or metamodel to Java interfaces, allowing the metadata in the repository, represented as Java objects, to be manipulated through the use of them; the MOF-CORBA mapping that defines mapping rules to CORBA IDL enabling the manipulation of the stored models and metamodels as CORBA objects; and the MOF-XML mapping called XML Metadata Interchange (XMI) (OMG, 2004). These mappings produce XMI documents, and Java or CORBA interfaces, to manipulate the models and metamodels stored in the repository.

However, the physical format of how the metadata should be stored is not predefined.

XMI is a mechanism to be used by various tools, repositories and middleware to interchange models and metamodels serialized into XML documents and XML Document Type Definitions (DTDs)/XML Schemas respectively. The import (or export) of XMI documents is a means for exchanging metadata among repositories, living in different business domain.

Currently, OMG is working on a MOF-WSDL mapping that will make possible to expose MOF repositories for Web Services.

3. PROPOSALS FOR SERVICE COMPOSITION

The Service Composition Management Framework *(SCMF)*, proposed in this paper, has as main modules the Composition Planning (CP) module and the Composite Service Enactment (CSE) module. These two modules cooperate with two other systems that are being developed by our group, the Modeling System (MoS) and the Metadata Management System (MMS). The functionalities of the SCMF and their interaction with the others are shown in Figure 3.

The Composition Planning (CP) receives the initial request for a service composition and elaborates a plan for it. The Modeling System (MoS) generates models and metamodels and their transformations. The Metadata Management System (MMS) is a MOF based system to support the definition and management of different types of metadata (models and metamodels). The Composite Service Enactment (CSE) is responsible for running the composite service.

CP receives the service request from a client and proceeds to its identification, fetching the necessary information from MMS (step 1). If the composite service is not existent, CP, based on the MMS contents, prepares the master plan to guide the service composition and activates MoS (step 2). MoS consults MMS for the metadata of each service involved (step 3), generates the new composite service metadata and stores it (step 4) in the MMS. Finally, CP requests the service execution (step 5) by the CSE that receives the necessary information from the MMS (step 6).

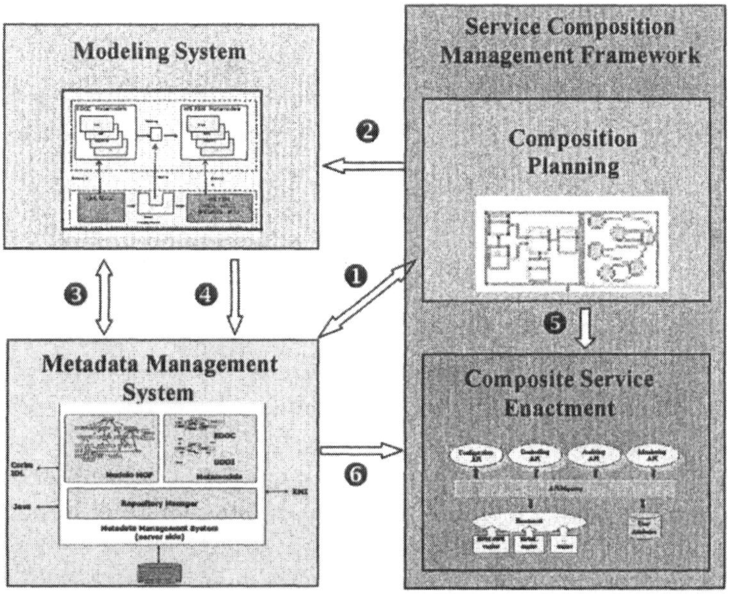

Figure 3. Interaction between the Composition components.

3.1 Composition Planning (CP)

The CP module owns the main external interface of the proposed SCMF. It is responsible to receive the initial request for a service composition, which shall describe the general characteristics and desired results. Based on the platform resources, rules and constraints, CP analyzes the viability to attend it, and elaborates a composition plan.

Initially, the analysis consists on the existence and availability verification, of the necessary basic services in the platform or elsewhere in the system. This step must obey some concepts of modularity and reusability of the services and there descriptions. Therefore, the CP identifies the units of constituent services in the MMS. Determined the existence and availability of the basic services, the CP analyzes the models, from which the basic services types are instanced, and compares their syntactic and semantic features to determine whether they may me composed. Some restrictions and legal constraints, such as service provider domains and contracts, must be verified. Aspects such as sequence of service execution and services dependencies must be evaluated. Services characteristics such as demand, time of execution, run time resources, priorities, are also considered in the analysis. Finally, as a last criterion, each service utilization weight cost may be used to decide the services selection.

Once the service composition viability is confirmed, the CP generates the contracts between the services providers, which shall define the composition and documents, and a master plan, that will guide the composition implementation by the MoS. Afterwards, the CP must generate all the necessary support and management information to the other modules, in order to promote the composition results as stated in the master plan.

3.2 Modeling System (MoS)

The independence, in respect to the technology used to compose services, is obtained through the development of PIM's (e.g. with EDOC) and their posterior mapping to the different technologies (Web Service PSM).

PIM, in this context, means that the composition will not be defined in terms of specific current languages used to do the Web Service composition (e.g. BPEL4WS, WSCI, BPML, WSTrans). As cited before, there is no settled standard in this area. For example, the functionalities expressed with BPEL4WS can be alternatively reached with the junction of the WSCI and BPML. In this context OMG has issued a RFP for UML Extensions for Workflow Process Definition (OMG, 2004) that requests, in particular, proposals for one metamodel and/or profile, which extends the UML to define workflow processes. An example of a unified metamodel proposal for workflow processes creation, expressed as a UML profile, and its supported software was developed by Soto (Soto, 2002).

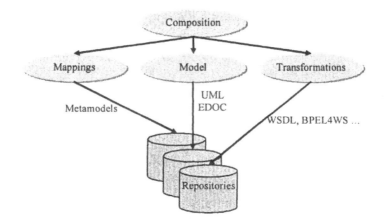

Figure 4. Service Composition Modelling

The different aspects of service composition are first modeled by means of EDOC. Different MDA tools allow, later on, the transformation of these models to technology specific models. In order to produce the model transformations it is first necessary to produce metamodels of WS standards (e.g. WSDL, SOAP, UDDI, BPEL4WS) and to map them to the correspondent EDOC Metamodels (Figure 4).

EDOC is composed of several parts assembled under the so called Enterprise Collaboration Architecture (ECA), each one well defined by a particular metamodel: the Component Collaboration Architecture (CCA), the Entities profile (ER), the events profile (EP), the Business Process Profile (BPP), and the Relationships Profile (RP) (Figure 5). A last one, the Pattern Profile, may also be used for the composition through collaboration patterns previously defined and stored in a library.

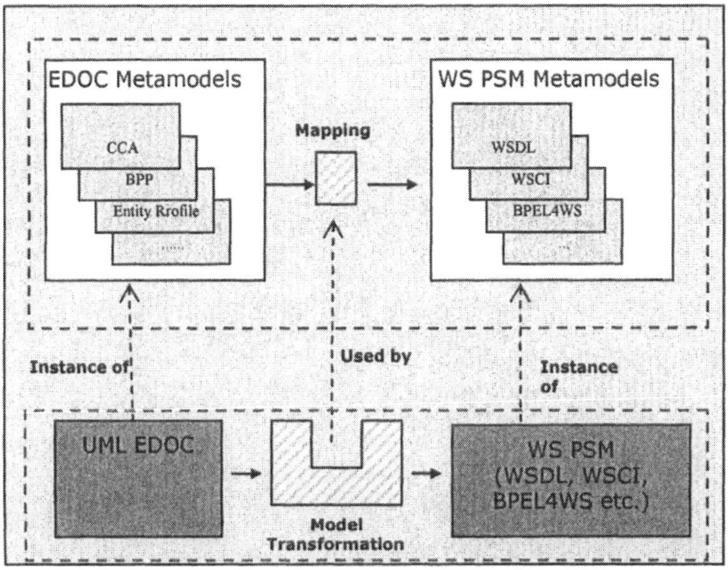

Figure 5. Mappings and transformations.

CCA represents the basic concepts of a service, including activities, ports, artifacts and process and is closely related to WSDL. Their similarities allow the mapping of their metamodels and the transformation from an CCA-PIM to WSDL documents.

CCA goes much further, explicitly defining richer collaboration metamodels, including control mechanisms of choreography and transaction. These mechanisms may be mapped to correspondent WS metamodels of SOAP, WSCI (W3C, 2002) and BPEL4WS. As stated in these specifications, WS choreography concerns the observable interactions of services with their users. A choreography description is a multi-party contract that describes the behavior across multiple WS, through the presence of messages that are exchanged and their sequence. EDOC contains a recursive component model, which in turn can express the choreography of the component's data exchange with the outside world and through recursion, with its inside world.

The Entity Profile of EDOC is used to generate new PIM Data Models, for example models of messages being exchanged in the choreographies. There is yet no similar standard proposed in the context of WS's. This could be relevant, for example, to allow the integration of existent Data Base accessed by specific basic services, which participate in the composition. Based on the concepts of CWM (CWM, 2003), proposals are discussed by the authors in another paper (Figueiredo, 2004)

The Business Process Profile (BPP) provides modelling concepts that allow the description of business processes in terms of a composition of business activities, selection criteria for the entities that carry out these activities, and their communication and coordination. These are the concepts needed for the orchestration modelling of Web Services. For example, developing a metamodel of BPEL4WS will allow later on the mapping to the BPP metamodel and though transformations of BPP models to BPEL4WS descriptions.

With these proposals we are, in reality, constructing a WS–Metamodel, formed by different metamodels, as is already the case in EDOC. Using MOF (see section below) based rules we assure a coherent construction and storage. But EDOC is very rich in its semantic and includes several modelling mechanisms not yet included in the WS standards.

3.3 Metadata Management System

A Metadata Management System (MMS), also referred as a repository system, is a key system to the support of the composition framework proposed in this work. We took the approach to develop the MMS based on the modeling framework as defined by OMG, i.e., using MOF and XMI technologies.

The motivation for defining a MOF-compliant system is to facilitate the implementation of a repository system for models and metamodels from different domains. Furthermore, XMI offers a standard way for exchanging models between our and other tools environments.

The metadata management system is a central component of an e-Gov system (Figueiredo, 2004). In that work, an extensive use of standard metamodels is proposed to promote the integration of distributed and heterogeneous legacy data.

In the context of this work we foresee the MMS being used to support the definition and management of different types of metadata:

- EDOC metamodels:
- EDOC models, instances of the EDOC metamodels;
- Transformation rules metamodel: rules models are used to map for example, a PIM to a PSM;
- WS-Metamodels, for example
  - o UDDI metamodel: the UDDI metamodel will supply details of the offered services. In order to support details of the composed services, the UDDI metamodel will be extended;
  - o WSDL metamodel: instances of the WSDL metamodel will describe simple services and composed ones.
  - o BPEL, WSCI ,etc metamodels
- WS- Models (WSDL, BPEL, WSCI,etc)

The server-side of MMS is presented in Figure 6. Its main components are the repository manager and a database mechanism to persistent metamodels and models. The repository manager provides services to modeling, retrieving and managing the artifacts in the repository. Additionally, it provides functions specific to a repository system, such as checkout/checking, version control, configuration control, notification and workflow control. A set of tools, such as a graphical editor, a compiler and a modeler viewer, in the client-side complete the MMS system.

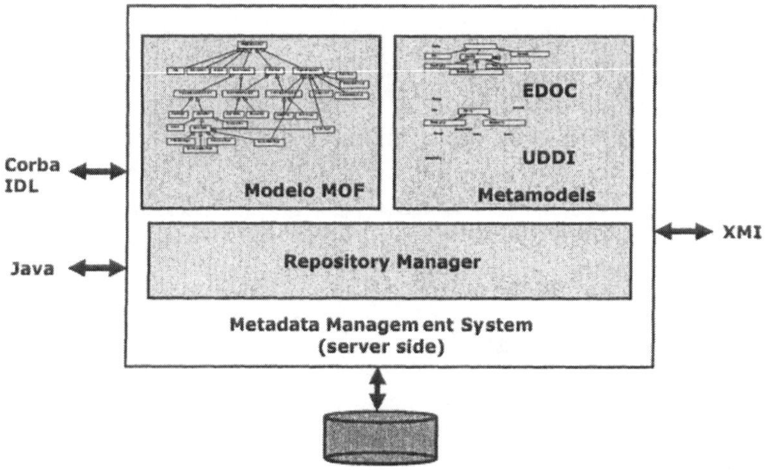

Figure 6. Metadata Management System Architecture

3.4 Composite Service Enactment

The Composite Service Enactment (CSE) is responsible to run the composed service. Depending on the language/protocol used to describe the composition, the CSE connects one specific engine for its execution. New engines can be connected to the module. This flexible architecture allows the adoption of new technologies or standards (Figure 7).The CSE is build by the following principal components: User's API, API Mapping, Enactment and User's Attributs data base.

The User's API functionality is aligned to that defined in the Workflow Reference Model described by the Workflow Management Coalition (WfMC, 2004). Below, a brief description:

- **Configuration**: defines how the Enactment component will run, i. e., the deployment configuration, as well as the service priorities and security access control;
- **Controlling**: supplies the API for administration and interaction of the work list managed by the Enactment. It allows, for example, search for work in progress, the examination of the composition execution status, initiation, pause, cancellation or stop;
- **Auditing**: the date, time, person steps etc, are recorded in a history repository. The auditing interface provides access to this data;
- **Monitoring**: reporting and analysis such as the total work accomplished.

The API Mapping receives the request from the User's API and maps it to the specific engine that is being used. So, several different engines are accessed by the same API. The transformation rules that permit the mapping are stored in the MMS. When a new engine is linked to the module, its associated transformation rules need to be processed and stored at the MMS.

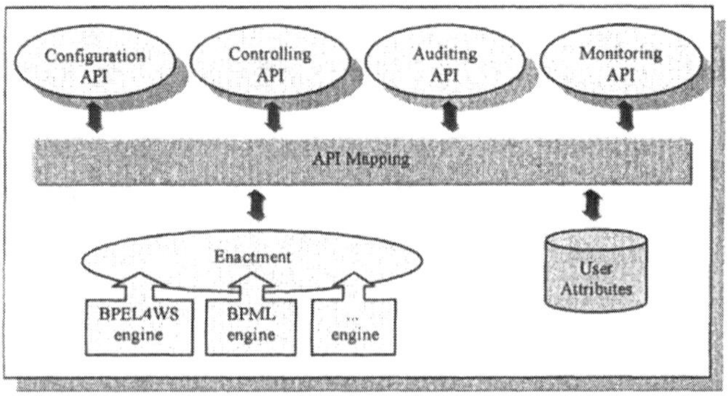

Figure 7. Composite Service Enactment Module

A User's Attributs Data Base stores the configuration for each user. When a request arrives, the API Mapping consults it to do the proper mapping for each one. The data base also stores the access policies. Depending on these policies, the user (client application) may be able to access the entire or only part set the functionalities correspondent to the controlling, auditing and monitoring API's.

The Enactment is responsible to connect and control the specific engine for each application. It does the communication between the engine and the API Mapping.

When an event is generated by one engine, it is captured by the Enactment that resends it to the API Mapping. At this time, the mapping needs to be done at reverse order, i.e., the specific engine event is mapped to the User's API. Again, the API Mapping accesses the MMS to do it.

3.5 Implementation Aspects

Figure 8 illustrates an e-Gov platform prototype being implemented in our project. The users will access the services through a portal site that will ensure an uninterrupted and easy communication with the service provider.

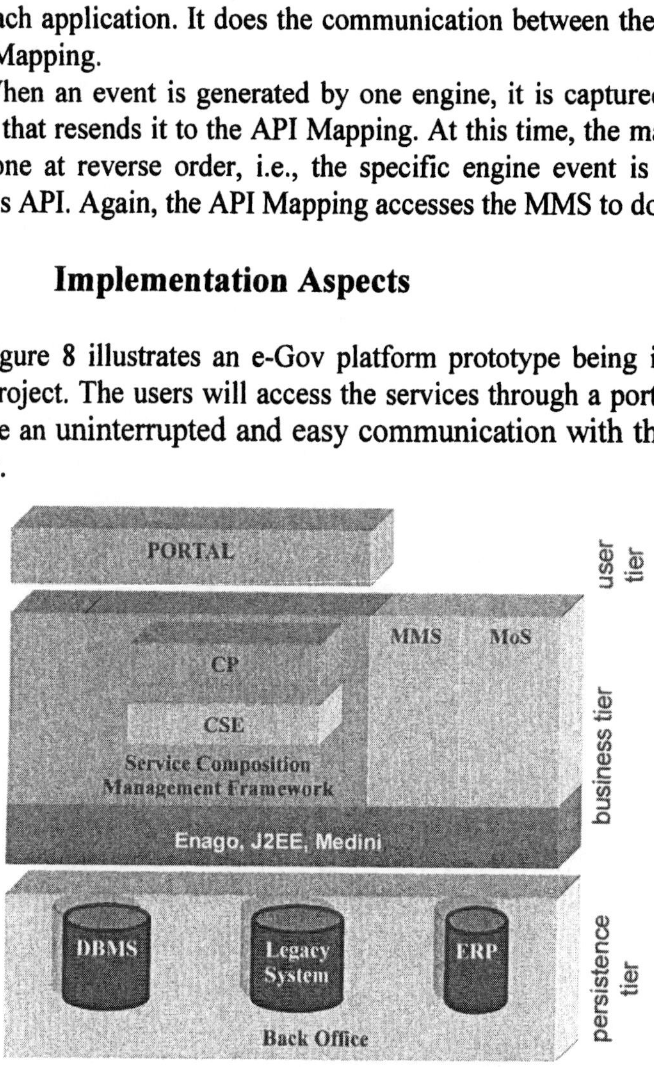

Figure 8. Implementation aspects.

In the first version of the prototype, the framework proposed will reside on top of Enago (Figure 8), an open service platform developed by the Fokus Institute (Fokus, 2004). Enago provides a secure and uniform service access and management environment, across different administrative and technological services. The main focus of Enago is to enable the integration, composition and management of existing and emerging application services based on different access technologies and different service technologies.

The Medini tool suite, also developed by Fokus Institute, is the MoS adopted in this first version. Medini provides a modeling infrastructure based on the EDOC and Enago metamodels. PIM models instantiated from the EDOC metamodel are stored in a MOF-compliant repository and, subsequently, transformed to Enago PSM models and Java code. The Medini tool suite (Kath, 2003) provides transformations tools between a PIM written in EDOC to PSMs for Enago Platform and J2EE. The transformations are supported by MoS.

The development of the Composition Planning module is still in the phase of conception. The format for the service composition request, that shall describe the characteristics and the desired results of the service composition, is still undefined and it is conceived to attend as well the general users' requisitions, through a web portal, as also the planning of e-government internal services, through an e-Gov framework.

The MoS is in an advanced stage of implementation and now the activities are focusing the metamodels development and needed mappings, in the WS context described.

The Composite Enactment Service module is under implementation. The BPWS4J (IBM, 2002) engine has been integrated in it and the next step is to connect other engines. Further, we intend that the Enactment will be able to support collaborations between WS's that use different choreography languages.

4. CASE STUDY: VEHICLE EXTRACT

As an example to show the problem, we propose a real scenario to modify a vehicle ownership. The already existing basic services in the example are the following (VID is a vehicle ID and CID is a citizen ID):

1. *Vehicle service*: supplies vehicle data;
   Interface 1: *search (in: VID, out: owner ID);*
   Interface 2: *setOwner (in: VID, CID, out: transfer certification);*
2. *Citizen service*: supplies citizen data;
   Interface 1: *search (in: CID, out: citizen data);*
3. *Tax service*: government taxes;
   Interface 1: *search (in: VID, out: tax data);*
4. *Fine service*: government penalties;
   Interface 1: *search (in: VID, out: fine data).*

In order to present to the user more suitable services, the *vehicle extract* is created. It returns an extract and is composed by the basic services above mentioned. It has the following interface: *extract (in: VID, out: report)*. It starts when the user supplies the VID. The tax, fine and vehicle basic services are accessed in parallel; the vehicle service returns the "owner ID" that is the equal to the CID code used by the citizen service. The Extract Assembler is a new service that was created to supply the need of this composition. It assembles the data returned form the other services and sends it back to the user. In this example the vehicle service interface 2 was not used (Figure 9).

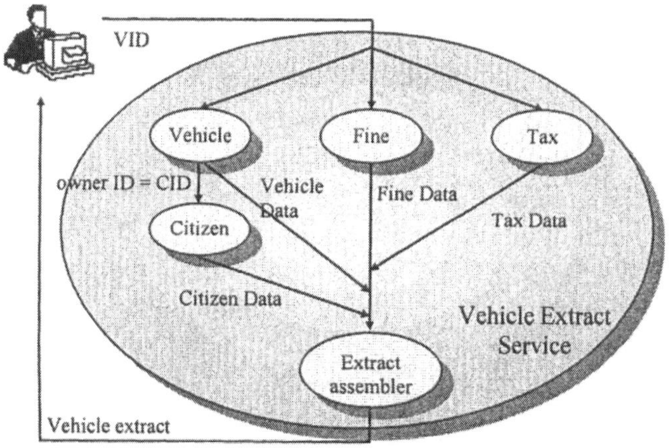

Figure 9. Case study: vehicle extract.

5. RELATED WORK

In this section, we discuss some initiatives for composition of B2B e-Services, Web services and Semantic Web Services, which related to our research.

Many software industries, such as IBM, Sun Microsystems, Microsoft, BEA systems, HP and Oracle are currently working on implementation of B2B e-Services platforms. The common key technologies for almost all of them are J2EE components, XML and the use of a workflow engine. The IBM WebSphere integrates support for Web service standards such as SOAP, UDDI, and WSDL. Additionally, it provides distributed transaction support for major database systems. The Sun ONE iPlanet is the core of Sun ONE platform. It includes a stack of products that allow the creation, deployment, and execution of B2B e-Services.. Microsoft .NET embraces the concept of Web services to enable B2B e-Services interaction. It consists of key elements, which provides the standard based tools for SOAP, WSDL, and UDDI.

In (Orriëns, 2003) a tool for service composition specification, construction and execution is presented. This tool intends to support the development and delivery of composite services in a coordinated and effectively reusable manner, turning aspects related to business process modeling languages, such as BPEL4WS, more flexible and less complicated. It also focuses on the modularity and reusability of the existent services in the platform. A Service Composition Specification Language (SCSL) is developed, where activity, binding, condition and composition type constructs are defined, among others, in order to support the web service composition.

In the Semantic Web Services area the major initiatives use ontologies and software agents to deal with Web services composition. The autonomous Semantic Web Services (Paolucci, 2003) is a mechanism that tries to bridge the gap between the Web Services infrastructure and the Semantic Web. It is based on the DARPA Agent Markup Language for Services (DAML-S), which promises capabilities for discovering, invoking, composing and monitoring Web services. The ontology-based framework for the automatic composition of Web services (Medjahed, 2003b) starts from high-level declarative descriptions and generate composite services by defining formal composition safeguards through the use of composability rules. These rules compare the syntactic and semantic features of Web services to determine whether two services are composable or not. In the agent-based multi-domain architecture (Maamar, 2003) a software agent-based approach is presented, that supports the interleaving of Web Services composition and execution.

6. CONCLUSIONS AND FUTURE WORK

In this work, which is concerned with the requirements on WS dynamic composition, we present a framework to discovery and compose WS's and to invoke and execute the new composite service. This emphasizes the coexistence and seamless interoperation on varieties of software components, which have been deployed based on legacy applications or on emerging service standards.

We propose a Framework for Web Services composition that is part of an e-Gov platform Prototype. The system uses a metamodeling infrastructure and the MDA concepts in order to be independent of composition technologies as conversation, choreography, orchestration and transaction.

The WS area is still very volatile. The great advantage of the proposed system is that it provides platform independence, avoiding the obsolescence caused by the appearance of new technologies. Otherwise, it contributes to solve the problem of applications heterogeneity and improves their portability among different platforms.

The proposed Framework is under development. Besides the proof of concepts, the prototype will be used to test performance aspects, in particular, the practical use of the framework in the context of dynamic composition. Nowadays, the more promising solutions for dynamic composition are being proposed by the community of Semantic Web Services, with strong focus on "automatic composition tools". In this context the semantic aspects are overwhelming. Our proposal goes in a similar direction for Web Services, with the use of metadata concepts.

A further issue, that needs to be addressed, is the incorporation of Business Rules, due to the need to express logical statements, e.g. preconditions and post conditions, or rules to describe dependencies between service elements. In this sense, one of the challenges is to integrate concepts, technologies and tools coming from both Semantic Web Services and Web Services worlds. There are many aspects and problems that have to be considered, such as the mapping between ontology concepts and metadata software engineering concepts, that are not always straightforward.

REFERENCES

Cardosol J. L., et al., 2004, Implementing Electronic Government: the eGoia project, EULAT Workshop on eGovernment and eDemocracy, May 2004, Chile.

CWM, 2003, Common Warehouse Metamodel (CWM) Specification - Version 1.1, Volume 1, OMG Document Number: formal/03-03-02; 2003.

DARPA, 2004, The DARPA Agent Markup Language Homepage, (February, 2004); http://www.daml.org/index.html.

EDOC, 2001, A UML Profile for Enterprise Distributed Object Computing, Joint Final Submission, Part I, Version 0.29, 18 June 2001; http://www.omg.org/.

eGOIA, 2004, Electronic Government Innovation and Access, EU-@LIS Project (September, 2003); http://www.egoia.info/.

Figueiredo, A. C., et al., 2004, Metadata Repository Support for Legacy Knowledge Discovery in Public Administrations, In: 5th Working Conf. on Knowledge Management in eGov, May 2004, Austria.

Figueiredo, A. C.. et al., 2003, Using Metamodels to Promote Data Integration in an e-Government Application Scenario, In: Third I3E IFIP Conference, September 2003, Guarujá, SP, Brazil.

Fokus, 2004, Fraunhofer Institute for Open Communication Systems (February, 2004); http://www.fokus.fraunhofer.de/.

Frankel, David S., 2003, Model Driven Architecture - Applying MDA to Enterprise Computing, Wiley Publishing, Inc, 2003.

IBM, 2002, IBM Business Process Execution Language for Web Services Java Runtime (April, 2004); http://www.alphaworks.ibm.com/aw.nsf/reqs/bpws4j.

JMI, 2002, Java Metadata Interface (JMI) Specification, version 1.0, JSR40 – Java Community Process (June/2002); http://jcp.org/aboutJava/communityprocess/final/jsr040/ index.html

Kath, O., Born, M., 2003, An Open Modeling Infrastructure, Fokus Institute. (January, 2004); http://modeldrivenarchitecture.esi.es/pdf/04-2_Born_Kath.pdf.

Kerhervé B., Gerbé O., 1997, Models for Metadata or Metamodels for Data?, Proceedings of 2nd IEEE Metadata Conference.

Medjahed, B., et al., 2003a, Business-to-business interactions: issues and enabling technologies, The VLDB Journal (2003) 12: 59–85 / Digital Object Identifier (DOI) 10.1007/s00778-003-0087.

Medjahed, B., et al., 2003b, Composing Web services on the Semantic Web, The VLDB Journal (2003) 12: 333–351 / Digital Object Identifier (DOI) 10.1007/s00778-003-0101-5.

OMG, 2000, UML Extensions for Workflow Process Definition – Request for Proposal, OMG Document Number: bom/2000-12-11; 2000.

OMG, 2004, Object Management Group, (March, 2004); http://www.omg.org/.

Orriëns, B., Yang J., Papazoloug, M. P., 2003, SerciveCom: A Tool for Service Composition Reuse and Specialization (April, 2004); http://maximus.uvt.nl/sigsoc/pub/Orriens %20et%20al%20- %20ServiceCom%20-%20A%20tool%20for% 20service% 20compo sition %20reuse%20and%20specialization.pdf

Paolucci, M., Sycara, K., 2003, Autonomous Semantic Web Services, IEEE Internet Computing (September, 2003); http://www-2.cs.cmu.edu/~softagents/papers/Internet Computing.pdf

Soto, J. A., 2002, Uma Abordagem Unificada para Modelar Processos de Workflow e seu Software de Suporte. Unicamp, Brazil, 2002.

Turner, M., Budgen, D., Brereton, P., 2003, Turning Software into a Service, In: Computer, Edited by IEEE Computer Society, October 2003, pp. 38-44.

W3C, 2002, Web Services Architecture Requirements, W3C Working Draft 29 April 2002 (April, 2004); http://www.w3.org/TR/2002/WD-wsa-reqs-20020429.

WfMC, 2004, Workflow Management Coalition (February, 2004); http://www.wfmc.org.

INFRASTRUCTURES AND MARKETPLACES

IDENTITY-ENRICHED SESSION MANAGEMENT

Tobias Baier and Christian P. Kunze
Distributed Systems Group - VSIS, Department of Informatics, University of Hamburg, Vogt-Kölln-Straße 30, 22527 Hamburg, Germany

Abstract: The Internet has become an important part in every day life for many users. It has changed from an instrument to exchange and link scientific data to an economical and social place, where people spend their working and spare time. But the underlying technology has not adapted to the newly risen demands of communication and collaboration. The user is almost isolated and anonymous when using the web, while still leaving traces threatening their data security and privacy. There is no global concept of "digital citizens" modern collaboration applications could base on. To overcome this lack, this paper introduces an approach of identity enriched session management. It offers the possibility to integrate different (and distinguishable!) users into meaningful relationships. This paper presents the essential concepts of identity enriched sessions and a prototypical realisation which have been developed in the "open net environment for Citizens" (onefC) project.

Key words: Digital Identity, Identity Management, Session Management, Self-Determination, Digital Citizen, Online Communities

1. INTRODUCTION

The management of user and session information in most distributed systems (for example web applications) is very complicated for users and likewise for service providers. Users need to manage their personal information for every single Internet service or communication application they use, including user-name and password but also preferences and further personal information. The situation is even worse with sessions, users have no information about sessions they have within applications and they have no power to change these sessions, for example add encryption or join the session with another application. Mostly users do not even realise that they are participating in a session, because it is not directly displayed in the client. On the other hand, service providers do have information about sessions, but problems arise when sessions need to be shared between multiple services or applications. Even more critical problems emerge when different service providers want to share sessions. Modern service composition models support the integration of organisational resources within cooperation processes that can be applied for changing participants [Zirpins et al., 2004]. To ensure the accuracy of mutual participant interactions, the concept relies on a secure exchange of session and user information. There are several approaches to achieve this, but so far they concentrate on user profile information exchange in a rudimentary way.

Identity management systems are used to manage and exchange user profile information in a reasonable way. Reasonable in this context means: automatically, purposeful, fine-grained and secure. Automatic data exchange is often wanted for insensible data or well known risk free connections. Concerning username and password this is called "Single Sign-On" and is already discussed and deployed in some places (see section 1.1). But users would not want to send their username and password to anyone, so it has to be considered to whom the information is sent to and why this communication partner needs it, therefore purposeful. Also, not everyone the user trusts should receive all identity information, so the granularity of data access should be as fine as possible. But in the end, no system which manages or even exchanges personal data makes sense without dealing with security and privacy concerns. Even if Scott McNealy says: "You have zero privacy anyway, get over it!" [Sprenger, 1999], an identity management system should provide as much privacy as possible.

It is obvious that identification, authentication and any exchange of personal data in most cases makes only sense when content bearing communication follows. Telling an online clothes shop that ones favourite colour is "blue" makes only sense when afterwards some personalised offers are made. Self-portrayal is only done with consecutive communication, whilst this communication is then identity enriched. The communication partners gain knowledge about the other side, which is used during the communication session. It follows that exchange of personal information makes most sense in a session based environment. Current trends show that more and more internet services are session based, as they combine all messages of a session and append further attributes to it. See subsection 2.3 for further details on what sessions are used for and how they are managed today. As a motivation for this paper it is enough to say that today's sessions are not application independent and are not structured in any way. Most notably they have no concept of participants and information about them, since HTTP "sessions" only have one participant (the requesting user) by default.

The idea of the project onefC (open net environment for Citizens) at University of Hamburg is to design and build a generic identity management system which is tightly integrated into an application and network independent session infrastructure. The identity management system will make it possible to store, manage and exchange personal user information. The session infrastructure will enable application independent multi-user sessions with an integrated concept for the representation and management of the users.

1.1 Related Work

There have already been several attempts in identity management. Most notably Microsoft deployed the .NET Passport system, which enables Single Sign-On on participating web services (of which eBay is the most prominent). Users can store an email address, first and last name as well as some personal data like date of birth, languages or region. They can choose whether to share nothing, only the email address, additionally their first and last name, or everything stored in their profile to passport enabled services, when they are "logged on passport". While this is very coarsely grained, the technology is insecure and has been broken several times already.

Another commercial initiative to enable Single Sign-On was started by Sun Inc., which was joined by many major companies not only from the IT sector. The Liberty Alliance implements federated identities, which mean that services can exchange user information directly, if the users' consents and the services are in a federation. The Liberty Alliance builds on secure standards like SAML (Security Assertion Markup Language).

There are several research projects, which attempt to build identity management systems with different emphases. Of these, the DRIM project at TU Dresden [Clauß, 2001] and the ATUS project at University of Freiburg [Jendricke et al., 2000] are the most advanced in terms of privacy support, while the IDManager of TU München [Koch, 2001] is leading in community support systems.

2. IDENTITIES AND SESSIONS

This chapter describes the concepts which have been developed for identities and sessions in the onefC infrastructure. While there has been profound research on identities, the research on sessions in this meaning is still young.

2.1 Concept of Personal Digital Identities

The question what an identity is and how it can be represented is one of the most important in identity enriched session management. As the project onefC has the aim to aid people to become someone on the net [Baier et al., 2003], a closer look on the interpersonal comprehension of identities is needed. This section shows up the complexity of the term identity by arguing aspects of philosophy, psychology and sociology. The extracted aspects build up the grounding of the used identity model.

Regarding the identity from the philosophic and mathematic point of view the ability to certainly identify an object is the focus. This is expressed by defining the identity as a binary relation which links an object just to itself. That means it is the finest relation of equivalence and can be seen as a special or marginal case of equity. This abstract definition does not help to make a precise decision about the identity of two objects. To answer this question the philosophical term of the moderate numerical identity can be used. It accepts the identity of objects if consecutive characteristics remain even while their state is changing or the object maintains in a continuous but not total change. [Brockhaus, 1989][Henrisch, 1976][Mittelstraß, 1984]

Psychology regards the identity of a person as the construction of the single individual. The creation of the identity is based on interactive experiences and relationships in adopted roles in different social contexts. The understanding of being an individual and having the control directs to the unconscious behaviour of presenting the own identity in parts of different size adapted to the actual played role and social context. Thus identity is regarded as a complex structure with multiple elements, where a subset of these is activated or deactivated depending on the actual context. For this reason an identity consists of many group, role, body or task drawn identity parts and is also called "patchwork" which expands every day automatically by inserting new parts.

The second important question next to the structure of an identity is its content. Every part of an identity represents a set of attributes. These attributes contain objective and subjective characteristics of the corresponding person. The objective attributes are similar to entries in a passport - they are more or less verifiable facts like size, age, gender or the appearance as well as achieved skills. The subjective content can cover capabilities in comparison to others, the social appearance, sentiments and moods. [Döring, 1999][Resch, 1998][Suler, 1996][Turkle, 1999]

As exposed the personal identity evolves in social interaction. This implies that identities influence each other. From this sociologists derivate a superior structure which is called group or social identity. This structure depends on an unordered set of people which have decided to become a member of a social group and share their more or less characteristic attributes. The link between personal and social identity is represented especially by the feeling of the affiliation to the group - the in-group relationship.

The characteristics and attributes of a social identity do not vary from the ones of a personal identity. That means a development in a group is always a development of the personal identity. [Abdelal and Herrera, 2001][Debatin, 1996][Döring, 1999][Donath, 1996]

2.2 Identity Management as Self-Portrayal

In addition to the private dimension of an identity there is also a public one - the aspects of the person which are presented to the public. This presentation of the identity is always an act of balance between social rules and the demand of the person itself. The content of the displayed attributes is chosen and possibly adjusted according to the actual played role and the pursued goals.

Thereby we always act in a manner which helps us to achieve our goals. This means we do not necessarily present us in a positive way - creating an unpleasant impression could be part of our strategy. This (mostly automatic) change of the presented identity and its attributes is called self-portrayal. [Döring, 1999][Fuchs, 2002][Jendricke et al., 2001]

2.3 Identity Enriched Sessions

The term "session" is widely used in computer systems. However, it rarely is defined or at least described: the meaning is implicitly given through the context or just assumed to be known. For the onefC project a clear definition is needed.

A session is an abstract construct which comprises of a set of communication acts, a representation of the participants and a set of describing attributes.

The session contains its participants to be able to associate each communication act to its originator. The participants are represented by the identities described in subsection 2.1. Furthermore, the session attributes can have an arbitrary content, for example the type of encryption or access rules for new users to join the session. As sessions are structured in a hierarchical way, a special kind of attribute is used to assign sets of super sessions. If a session is part of other sessions it inherits any attributes of them.

In particular, our notion of sessions must not be confused with the "session" from the OSI Open Systems Interconnection Layer 5. While this session layer is absent on the Internet, it would only serve for resynchronisation of sessions on a technical layer after the communication might have been interrupted by network problems. These sessions have no further notice of participants than a TCP or UDP socket from the layer below.

On the Internet, (user-) sessions are used on the service side to track user behaviour on web sites, to store information about the user's actions (like shopping cart contents) and to gain generic information about the services effectiveness. Today's web applications use a session construct which is attached to the (historically not session based) HTTP protocol. Since the session can not be found out by the HTTP-request which a user sends, it needs to be identified using cookies, HTTP-parameters or URL-encoding [Lerner, 2000]. But it is not possible to transmit sessions between application servers, be it for intra- or even inter organisational use.

On the client side the current technology successfully hides sessions from users. In some cases it is desired that users log in or log out of the service (for example web based email systems or online banking), but most sessions are invisible to the user. We consider this a problem, since the user is not aware of certain session attributes like the (amount of) data collected on either side, type of encryption or actual session participants.

To solve these problems and to enable multi-application and multi-user sessions we propose a session infrastructure with the abstract notion of a session given above. Applications should be able to initiate or join existing sessions, users should be able to directly monitor and modify sessions. With such an infrastructure, a new generation of online services will be possible. Multi-application sessions will enable users to use several applications in one session without loosing the context. This will make it possible for services to include the functionality of more than one application into their service. The possibility to use any session enabled application also creates a choice for the user to use her favourite one. All of this increases usability. Furthermore, multi-application sessions enable online services to include functionality into their services which could not easily be integrated before.

Multi-user sessions enable a new dimension in online activities as well. So far, all sessions were only for two users. There are constructs in special applications which simulate multi-user sessions, particularly in multi-user chat systems, but while the multi-user aspect of these constructs is analogue to ours, these constructs are far from being as powerful as our sessions.

Our notion of a session is heavily inspired by real world, where people meet to discuss or negotiate. The participants of real world sessions have an image of each other, since they are able to use direct or indirect self-portrayal. All which is said within a session is implicitly associated with it. Some characteristics of the session may be negotiated beforehand, like the permission to tell non-participants about the outcome of the session. This real world concept becomes applicable to Internet sessions with the introduction of Internet identities. Without these, sessions will lack their central component.

The other way around, personal identity information may be useless for communication partners, if they can not associate any substantial statements or requests with them. Identity management and exchange of personal information rarely is an end to itself, it mostly serves other needs (for example to personalise a web service or to authenticate a user, see section 4 for more extensive examples). For these needs, the identity information must be associated with the actual communication, which is done through sessions in the onefC infrastructure.

3. THE "OPEN NET ENVIRONMENT FOR CITIZENS" (ONEFC): AN APPROACH TO REALISE IDENTITY-ENRICHED SESSIONMANAGEMENT

Demands for a digital identity model can be derived from the reflection of the interpersonal comprehension of identities. One of the central aspects is the ability to identify objects distinctly and consistently as well as the assignment of the identity in time and over different contexts. The model should allow the user to create and to activate parts of his identity in accordance with the actual context, role or situation. The contained attributes should not be restricted to any predefined data to keep the model as open as possible. In addition attributes should be reusable in and adaptable to different contexts. To integrate the concept of social identities is eligible, because the influence of the identities of other members of a group holds an opportunity of manifold appliances.

3.1 The Digital Identity Model

The onefC identity model is inspired by the presented "identity patchwork" (see subsection 2.1). It maps this concept to a data tree (see figure 1, the data tree is represented by the self reference of the Identity class). Each node of the tree represents one part of the personal identity, which can be activated in one or more contexts. As a consecutive element a unique identifier ties all nodes together. This identifier makes it possible to identify the user across different contexts. Every single context represents a common and shared background of experiences in which one part of the identity is presented. It can relate to the actual role the user presents or to the situation the communication takes place in. Together with the unique identifier the context directs to the part of the identity which is activated and thus both imply the presented attributes.

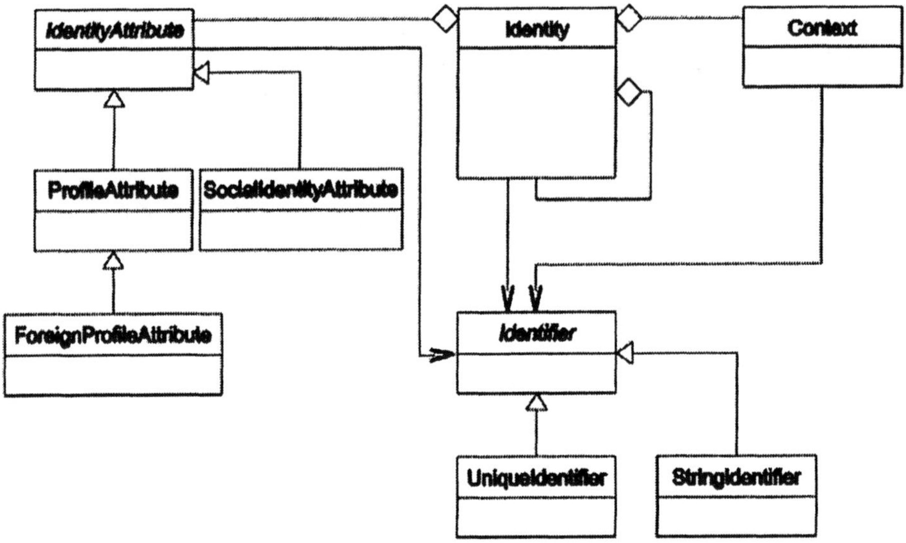

Figure 1. The onefC identity model

Using a tree as the foundation of the onefC data model has several advantages. At first the contained hierarchy is used to define an inheritance concept for the attributes of the identity. Each child node inherits all attributes from its parent. Therefore each layer of the identity tree can be seen as a refinement of the layer above. If there is a set of similar identity parts, the common attributes do not have to be defined several times. E.g. there could be a general identity part for the context "e-commerce" which contains information of the user's name, address and payment method. For each supplier this general data can easily be adapted and refined in special sub identities. A second advantage of this attribute hierarchy is the actuality of the data because every change in an attribute of higher level is passed on to the child elements.

A visibility concept is introduced to adapt attributes, which are implied by the inheritance concept to a part of the identity tree, to the actual context. This allows overwriting the value of an inherited attribute. The new local value masks the old one of the higher levels. This can be used for example if the user has several email addresses and wants to use a special one to separate the emails of single supplier.

The attribute model which is used in the identities is designed to make as little limitations to the potential content as possible. Until now there are two different basic attribute types. The first one represents the basis for all profile attributes which contain characteristics of the user. The second type stands for the "in-group" relationship of a social identity.

As mentioned above the social identity in not represented directly in the onefC model. Merely the feeling to be a member of a particular group can be expressed by the so called "SocialIdentityAttribute". To get an impression of the group identity, the attributes of the members have to be aggregated.

The second type of attributes is the profile attribute which can be used by applications to store and integrate their data. This kind of attributes is designed as a container. This container includes additional metadata about its content. Especially the information about the ontology of the data is important when sharing data between different applications.

3.2 The Identity Management Component

The social behaviour of presenting the personal identity in accordance with the actual context, role, or situation is the basis of the identity management. And therefore digital identity management can be seen as the digital equivalent of self-portrayal. While aiming mainly on digital self-portrayal, the identity manager should still be a very secure tool to increase the protection of personal data. [Berthold and Köhntopp, 2000]

The onefC identity manager which has been developed as a prototype [Kunze, 2004] provides an integrated and infrastructural service and a uniform platform to administrate own and foreign identities (see figure 2). The central management component encapsulates the access to the contained identities. It enforces the security requirements of the user. To achieve this it uses several services which are designed as modules. They are integrated into the system using defined interfaces. This allows the user to use services of his choice and trust. The most precarious service is the security service. This component performs the task to judge about the decision whether an attribute is allowed to be shared or not. It also makes a decision about using an unknown pseudonym instead of the known identifier. A prototypical sample is using the P3P[25] and APPEL[26] specification to set the rules for attribute access. Every communication about identities is done through sessions, so there is no need for identity managers to communicate directly. To keep the user track of the exchanged data the communication is logged by the monitoring service. This allows the user to inspect which data is shared and with whom. The persistence service enables the manager to store the

[25] http://www.w3.org/P3P/

[26] http://www.w3.org/TR/P3P-preferences/

identity data to arbitrary media. Especially the use of smart cards is ideal, because the user can carry the digital identity to any place and use it there.

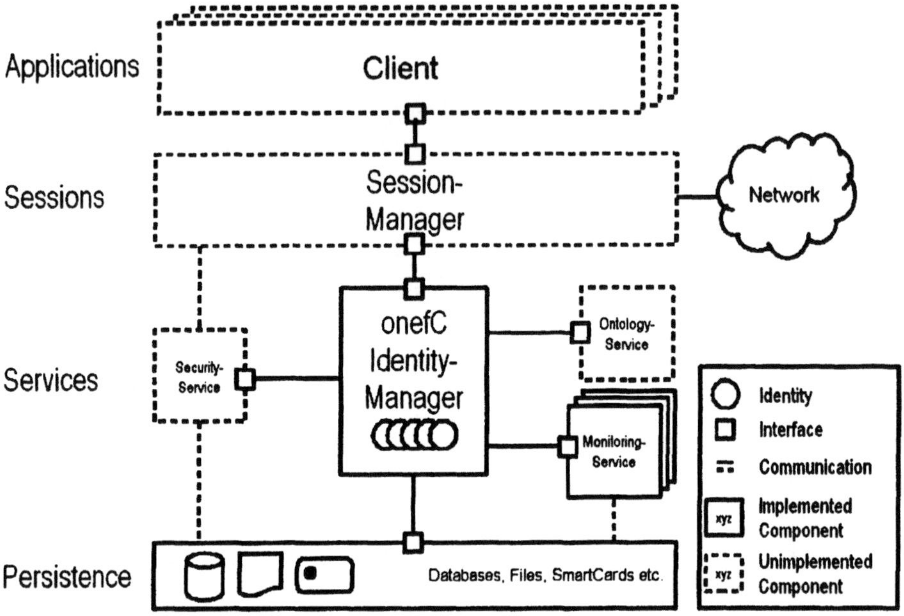

Figure 2. The components of the onefC identity manager

4. SAMPLE SCENARIOS OF ONEFC USAGE

This section presents some sample scenarios which show some of the possibilities and effects an identity enriched session infrastructure might have. As with all new technologies, it is very hard to predict what use it might be put to, just consider the World Wide Web, which ought to connect academic institutes for scientific exchange.

4.1 E-Commerce Sample Scenario

Electronic commerce transactions consist of several phases. These are often divided into information, negotiation and execution phase [Griffel et al., 1998]. During these phases different participants may join the e-commerce transaction. Also, different degrees of visibility of the participants are desired.

Figure 3. Degree of visibility during business transactions

During the information phase, anonymous browsing of the different offers might be wanted. Contrariwise, the offers might be personalised or even include privileges if the search is not done anonymously but with certain personal information given out to the partners. Negotiation then might already require some personal attributes, so that the service side can decide which conditions apply to this customer. In execution phase, it might be important to invite new participants to the e-commerce session, for example a financial institute which regulates payment issues. Implementing such a transaction is a complex matter, because not only transaction terms must be followed, but also security constraints must be carefully attended. Using the proposed onefC identity and session infrastructure, the development of complex e-commerce applications would be highly simplified.

4.2 E-Government Sample Scenario

The default example for E-Government is e-voting, since it requires a high degree of security and anonymity and therefore sets a high demand on the infrastructure. Although the onefC infrastructure might help to constitute a viable e-voting mechanism, it cannot solve the problem alone. Let us instead consider online registrations at the registry office. It must be assured that the person is not faking her identity by any means, but in contrary to e-voting anonymity is not required. Registration might require several steps: announcement of the former registry office (or signed registration information), server side check whether this information is valid, then the declaration of the new address. This scenario requires secure authentication, which can be reached through certificates which can be stored within the identity manager. The registry office can store digitally signed registration information within the users digital identity, so the user can show this address to other online services like online shops which need a delivery address.

During registration, session would be created to support further requests from the server side being associated to the original communication. This would enable a "wizard"-kind of question and answer dialogue with the online registration service.

4.3 E-Society Sample Scenario

While Single SignOn and easy of use for web services is one major goal of our infrastructure, the main target remains to install a possibility for an Internet society. Societies consist of individuals, and identity management enables Internet users to create Internet identities which make up individuality on the net. Consider the Internet user Alice, who is very active on various web boards. She checks Slashdot[27] often for new articles she could comment and has gained a high "Karma" on that site. This karma is a sign of reputation – it means that her comments were rated high by other SlashDot readers. Alice also writes comments on Tom's Hardware Guides Community Board (Tom's HGCB)[28], but less frequently, so she did not gain any reputation there yet. In the current Internet, she can only give the Tom's HGCB readers a web link to her Slashdot account stating her good karma there, but presumably few will take the time to check the link, since news enquiry must be fast for most Internet users. If Alice could use the same identity from an Identity Manager on both sites, other readers could automatically rate or sort articles on the one board based on reputation values the author gained on the other board. Also, a certain reader on Tom's HGCB (lets call him Bob) might have seen Alice's articles on Slashdot before. Bob liked Alice's articles very much and marked her as a trusted person for IT related information. Bob can unambiguously recognise Alice in Tom's HGCB, although she might post using a different pseudonym (username) there. This way, Alice can keep her personal reputation regardless to the application or service provider used. This is a major factor to build Internet societies. As long as Internet users can build their identity only in the small context of one service, communities will have no chance to interact and have influences on one another, which would be a main aspect of general Internet societies.

5. CONCLUSION

The "open network environment for Citizens" (onefC) project is still in development. It aims to combine identity management with session management. The main goal is to provide mechanisms for online society consti-

[27] http://slashdot.org
[28] http://www.community.tomshardware.com

tution. There is no society without individuals, and these individuals need a representation. There are several other projects leading to a similar goal, but they are motivated differently and have different emphases. The architecture of onefC is kept open and flexible so that outcomes may be used in other projects and contexts. Current status of onefC is an early prototype of the identity manager which has not been released for public review yet. There also exists a sample application which uses onefC to implement the user representation of collaborative filtering software. Future work will include the design and implementation of a session manager which fulfils the requirements described in this paper. The protocols for identity data exchange must be specified. Further, components for semantic integrity (ontology based) and privacy (P3P) are being developed.

REFERENCES

[Abdelal and Herrera, 2001] Abdelal, R. and Herrera, Y. M. (2001). treating identity as a variable: measuring the content, intensity, and contestation of identity. Technical report, Harvard Business School.

[Baier et al., 2003] Baier, T., Zirpins, C., and Lamersdorf, W. (2003). Digital identity: How to be someone on the net. In Proceedings of the IADIS International Conference of e-Society, volume 2, pages 815–820.

[Berthold and Köhntopp, 2000] Berthold, O. and Köhntopp, M. (2000). Identity management based on p3p. In Workshop on Design Issues in Anonymity and Unobservability.

[Brockhaus, 1989] Brockhaus, F. A. (1989). BROCKHAUS ENZYKLOPÄDIE in vierundzwanzig Bänden: Zwölfter Band Kir – LAG.

[Clauß, 2001] Clauß, S. and Köhntopp, M. (2001). Identity Management and Its Support for Multilateral Security. In Computer Networks 37 (2001), special issue on electronic business systems, Elsevier, North-Holland 2001, pages 205-219.

[Debatin, 1996] Debatin, B. (1996). Elektronische Öffentlichkeiten. Über Informationsselektion und Identität in virtuellen Gemeinschaften. web-site. http://www.unileipzig.de/~debatin/english/Articles/Fiff.htm.

[Donath, 1996] Donath, J. S. (1996). Identity and deception in virtual community. Technical report, MIT Media Lab.

[Döring, 1999] Döring, N. (1999). Sozialpsychologie des Internet. Hogrefe. Identity-Enriched Session Management 13

[Fuchs, 2002] Fuchs, T. (2002). Der Begriff der Person in der Psychiatrie. Der Nervenarzt, 73(3):239–246.

[Griffel et al., 1998] Griffel, F., Boger, M.,Weinreich, H., Lamersdorf,W., and Merz, M. (1998). Electronic contracting with cosmos - how to establish, negotiate and execute electronic contracts on the internet. In C.Kobryn, C. Atkinson, Z. M., editor, 2nd Int. Enterprise Distributed Object Computing Workshop (EDOC '98), page 10. IEEE.

[Henrisch, 1976] Henrisch, D. (1976). Identität und Objektivität: eine Untersuchung über Kants transzendentale Deduktion. In Sitzungsberichte der Heidelberger Akademie derWissenschaften – Philosophisch-Historische Klasse, volume 1, page 54 et sqq. Winter.

[Jendricke et al., 2000] Jendricke, U., Gerd tom Markotten, D. (2001). Usability meets security – the Identity Manager as your personal security assistant for the internet. In Proceedings of the 16th annual Computer Security Applications Conference, pages 344-353.

[Koch, 2001] Koch, M. and Wörndl, W (2001). Community Support and Identity Management. In: Proc. European Conf. on Computer Supported Cooperative Work (ECSCW 2001), Bonn, Germany, pages 319-338.

[Kunze, 2004] Kunze, C. P. (2004). Digitale Identität und Identitäts-Management. Informatiktage 2003.

[Lerner, 2000] Lerner, R. M. (2000). At the forge: Session management with mason. Linux Journal, 2000(76es):24.

[Mittelstraß, 1984] Mittelstraß, J. (1984). Enzyklopädie Philosophie und Wissenschaftstheorie 2. Wissenschaftsverlag.

[Resch, 1998] Resch, F. (1998). Zur präpsychotischen Persönlichkeitsentwicklung in der Adoleszenz. Psychotherapeut, 43(2):111–116.

[Sprenger, 1999] Sprenger, P. (1999). Sun on privacy: Get over it.

[Suler, 1996] Suler, J. (1996). Identity Management in Cyberspace. web-site. http://www.rider.edu/users/suler/psycyber/identitymanage.html, 06.10.2002.

[Turkle, 1999] Turkle, S. (1999). Leben im Netz: Identität in Zeiten des Internet. Rohwolt Taschenbuch Verlag.

[Zirpins et al., 2004] Zirpins, C., Lamersdorf,W., and Piccinelli, G. (2004). A service oriented approach to interorganisational cooperation. In M. Mendes, R. Suomi, C. P., editor, Digital Communities in a Networked Society: eCommerce, eBusiness, and eGovernment. Kluwer Academic Publishers.

VIRTUAL COMMUNITIES FOR SMES: A CAUTIONARY TALE OF AN ELECTRONIC MARKETPLACE

Janice M. Burn
School of MIS, Edith Cowan University, Joondalup Campus, Perth. WA.

Abstract: This paper reviews the concepts of virtual communities and electronic marketplaces and, in particular, their relevance for SMEs. A specific example of a Regional Electronic Marketplace (REM) using a Community Web model is examined within this context. The author reviews the underlying philosophy for the project and the planning which preceded implementation. A review of the case highlights the issues which are critical for successful implementation and provides a framework to guide future REM developments. The case is analysed within an e-community context and recommendations made for future portal developments. Finally the author questions the readiness of SMEs to adopt a virtual organisation model.

Key words: virtual communities, small and medium enterprises (SMEs), electronic marketplaces

1. INTRODUCTION

International reports show an increasing uptake of online activity in the Small to Medium Enterprise (SME) sector, but, there is little evidence to link this with real added value or increased levels of global business (Fariselli et al, 1999, Tetteh and Burn, 2001). Research indicates that SMEs are still confused by the myriad opportunities presented by different e-markets, the risks inherent in going online and the need for different business models with strategic national and international alliances to exploit the global marketplace (Kleindl, 2000). By nature SMEs are typically lone rangers and ill prepared for virtual organisations where the focus is on alliances and networking with collaborators and competitors (Carver, 1999; Lee et al, 2003).

SMEs represent a vast sector of the global economy (OECD, 2000). In Australia they account for 95% of companies and are the largest employer of labour in both urban and regional Australia [www.noie.gov.au]. Their combined turnover contributes substantially to the economic vitality and dynamism of the Australian economy. This is not unique to Australia but is mirrored in most economies around the world. As such there has been considerable interest in the take-up of e-business by SMEs allowing them to expand into a global marketplace. Internet-based electronic business is projected to rise from the current estimated level of US$2 trillion in world-wide revenue to between US$ 5-9 trillion by 2005 (UNCTAD, 2002). Attention is being focused on SMEs as additional sources of national and global competitiveness, market innovation and job creation. Recent research indicates however that Australian SMEs are hesitant in their approach to e-business (SBI, 2001; DCITA, 2000) and lag behind many other developed economies in exploiting the Internet. An OECD report "Enhancing the Competitiveness of SMEs in the Global Economy: Strategies and Policies" (2000) found that the penetration rate of the Internet for e-business in the Australian SME sector was only 25% compared with figures of over 60% in Europe for example. The Pacific Access Survey (2001) shows a slight increase with 31% of small businesses with a home page or dedicated Internet site and 26% using the web for procurement out of a sample of 1800 Australian SMEs.

In Australia, as in other developed countries, research studies have focused on the adoption and use of the Internet as a medium for doing business by SMEs (Poon and Swatman, 1997; Swatman, 2000; OECD, 1998; Bode and Burn, 2001). These studies point to some of the common characteristics of SMEs with respect to adoption levels, challenges, and general benefits from online infrastructures. While there appears to be much enthusiasm about electronic business, current studies show that it is the minority of SMEs who are reaping significant benefits from the Internet (Burn and Tetteh, 2001; Bode and Burn, 2001a; Levy and Powell, 2003). The majority of SMEs use the Internet only as a basic communications facility (Burn and Spadacinni, 1999). The reasons for the relatively low level of use include: the lack of technological expertise, uncertainty about benefits, low commitment of owner/manger, poor understanding of the dynamics of the electronic marketplace and their inability to devise strategies to leverage online infrastructure for profit (Standing 2001). Indeed, the ability to use IT in an effective manner is still of major concern to policymakers worldwide in respect to leveraging SMEs' productivity and global participation (Fariselli et al, 1999; Grewal et al, 2001). One of the solutions which is suggested for more effective IT penetration is the use of third party providers of IT services and the development of electronic markets specifically for SMEs (Kaplan and Sawhney, 2000; Grewal et al, 2001). This paper reports on one such development and evaluates the success within a virtual community context.

2. E-MARKETPLACES

The emergence of electronic marketplaces creating trading hubs where suppliers are matched with buyers for equipment, products and services has the potential to a play a major role in realising the potential of e-commerce for SMEs. Indeed, if SMEs are to remain competitive they need to adopt the changes that are occurring in the area of electronic commerce (Standing and Vasudavan, 1999; Bode and Burn, 2001b).

An electronic marketplace is defined as an 'inter-organisational information system that allows the participating buyers and sellers to exchange information about prices and product offerings' (Bakos, 1991, p 296). The profusion of these electronic marketplaces, the speed of transition to the electronic environment, the variety of business models and the varying requirements of different industries and service sectors cloud an already confused marketplace picture (Grewal et al, 2001). Despite this, there is immense pressure on companies to move quickly to the electronic marketplace, often without a full understanding of what benefits they can accrue from participation in them and the issues that should be considered in the selection process (Banham, 2000). It is clear that this type of e-trading is threatening the more fixed forms of virtual supply chains where an organisation is integrated electronically with its suppliers down the supply chain (Clark and Lee, 1999).

Previous studies have identified the different levels of service that are offered by e-marketplaces, developing from trading hubs that support the identification of potential trading partners to more complex models offering selection and, increasingly, execution services (Choudhury, Hartzel and Konsynski, 1998). The models that have developed offer the following methods of trading:

- Catalogues either individual vendor or multi-vendor
- Auctions buyer or seller driven
- Exchange comparable to trading exchanges with a bid and ask system
- Storefronts participants maintain an open Webpage within the marketplace
- Negotiation the marketplace acts as intermediary for transactions such as RFQs

The reported benefits to companies that are trading through e-marketplaces are compelling and suggest that cost savings being experienced by companies are considerable. Lucking-Reiley and Spulber (2000) estimate that online transactions could reduce costs by a factor of five or ten or more. Typical cost saving efficiencies are lower procurement and search costs, reduced administration costs and development time, integrated global suppliers and a strengthening of relationships with commercial partners, cuts in inventory holdings and up-to-the-minute order tracking. Non-financial benefits include access to better quality goods and services, value adding information obtained from the e-marketplace, greater choice in the buying/selling process and greater convenience for participants (Standing 2001).

The scope of the individual marketplace will determine how many of the benefits can be experienced by the participants of a particular marketplace. One of the major issues for SMEs is whether to select a "horizontal" or "vertical" portal as the market model. Horizontal markets offer an open shopping mall experience with a wide variety of goods, whereas vertical portals cluster together similar industries and will attract product specific shoppers. An SME has to make the decision as to whether they gain competitive advantage from a unique product in an open marketplace or to ally with competitors to offer a wider range of products in a discrete marketplace. The element of choice in selecting an e-marketplace is often constrained by traditional partners or the positioning of major industry players.

Our ongoing research indicates that even where SMEs have some awareness and use of e-commerce there still remain problems (Tetteh and Burn, 2001, Bode and Burn, 2001a). For example, the expectations of a positive impact from the Web are unlikely to be fully realised as only approximately one third of Web enabled SMEs have any form of a Web strategy. SME websites are primarily information sites for customers and only 20% are capable of taking an order online (Korchak andRodman, 2001). Less than a third of SMEs use the Web for procurement and there has been low penetration of e-marketplaces Although e-marketplaces are being increasingly used by large organisations, which have been quick to realise their potential, SMEs have been slow to take up their adoption as a mechanism for buying and selling.

Many of the problems relating to the failure of SMEs to address the importance of electronic marketplaces lies in a lack of understanding of the advantages and how they can benefit from them. SME understanding of the global marketplace is not good and they have little idea of the nature of the Internet and how it interacts with other methods of trading. Smaller companies do not see themselves as part of a large supply chain and they underestimate how the Web can benefit them by sharing information, buying from suppliers with no paper system, electronic fulfilment, tracking, and efficiencies in cost and time (Korchak and Rodman, 2001). If they do not understand their ability to function within the larger supply chain they will lose out to large firms in the electronic markets. The developing world markets, brought about by e-commerce and the increased ability to trade globally facilitated by electronic markets, adds to pressure on the SMEs as there are more firms with the ability to trade in each region (Said, 2000).

Increasing globalisation and a climate of more outsourcing has both increased the pressures on SMEs to perform, but also extended the opportunities for them to do so. SMEs have little control over the market so must harness the pressure and respond quickly (McAdam, 2000) utilizing the advantages of electronic markets. The main influences on e-commerce adoption are size, leadership/culture, IT experience and access to skills (Jones et al, 2000). An added complication comes from poor understanding of the participation requirements in electronic marketplaces and the motivation and activity levels necessary to achieve meaningful benefits (Kleindl, 2000; Grewal et al, 2001).SMEs require assistance to acquire the necessary skills and knowledge to make the move to the electronic environment and evidence suggests that this help needs to come from neutral sources such as government or business associations (Burn and Tetteh, 2001; Fariselli et al, 1999). As a result we are increasingly witnessing the emergence of virtual communities sustained by regional portals (Cowan et al, 1998: Burn and Zanaboni, 2003).

One such example of Government supported marketplace development can be found in the 2Cities.com regional electronic market developed for the regions of Joondalup and Wanneroo in Western Australia. The 2Cities project offers SMEs an opportunity to select their preferred business model and to develop their strategy for online business in accordance with their preferred business philosophy. This unique concept combines both horizontal and vertical marketplaces and provides the underlying business infrastructure for SMEs to take advantage of electronic trading.

3. PLANNING FOR THE REM

As early as 1999, a small group of interested parties came together to discuss whether the Internet could be used to facilitate a community portal for a regional community area north of Perth in Western Australia. The region was Joondalup, a rapidly developing suburban 'new town' area and the players were the local council, the Business Enterprise Centre and the local Business Association. These key players realised that funding support would be needed but also that they could substantially increase their bargaining power by extending the concept to their neighbouring region – Wanneroo (despite a highly competitive and sometimes acrimonious relationship). This enhanced stakeholders group included both councils and business associations and also the University with the largest campus in the area, Edith Cowan University and two local colleges in the same education precinct. The stakeholders were approximately 220,000 residents, 7000 small businesses and three Tertiary Education Facilities. This group together sought seed funding of $20,000 from State Government and in 2000 developed a demonstration site to sell the concept.

A survey of 1000 of these businesses conducted in association with Edith Cowan University comprising 600 businesses in Joondalup and 400 businesses in Wanneroo indicated that e-commerce usage in 2001 was fairly high as shown in Table 1.

	Joondalup	**Wanneroo**	**Australian Average** [1]	
			Small	**Medium**
	%	%	%	%
Internet Connection	58	60	60	89
Web Page	44	40	25	56
Purchase on Line	31	27	17	28
Sell on Line	31	N/A		
Business needs Web Page	23	20		

Table 1. e-Commerce Usage in 2Cities area

This indicated that businesses in the region were at least as well advanced as average Australian businesses, and possibly more advanced in the areas of web page and on-line transactions. The REM project was given the go-ahead by NMCOA in conjunction with business for the benefit of businesses in the region and to develop the Northern Suburbs as an attractive location in which new business can develop and grow. The initiative intended to train businesses in the skills required to buy and sell on-line and also allow easy access to the products offered by these businesses to the major consumers in the region.

Specifications were developed and budgets proposed and when the extent of funding and commitment required was fully understood the North Metro Community On-Line Association (NMCOA) was formed in March 2001. Additional funding was sought from the Department of Employment, Workplace Relations and Small Business (DEWRSB) under the Regional Assistance program (RAP) and a grant of $90,660 received. At this time, the three main players, the two councils and the university were asked to make a substantial investment in the concept and provided funding of $108,000. NMCOA would act as an independent body to manage finances and control the development of the REM.

Discussions by NMCOA's Business Development Manager (PM-A) with a wide range of businesses indicated the clear expectation that the project would assist them to accelerate entry to the on-line market place, provide them with a wider market in the regional context and allow them to use these technologies to become globally competitive.

Other factors that the businesses would be looking for in the REM included: -

- High profile.
- Secure business transactions.
- Information feedback on visits to the site.
- Support to allow them to effectively enhance web sites with reasonable cost effectiveness.
- An independant source of technical expertise and advice they could trust.

The 2Cities Gateway Project would provide, through a "Community Web" model, an official portal to be a single point of entry for individuals, communities, governments (Federal, State and Local), and business to access and interact within the Wanneroo/Joondalup region. The gateway would also provide the basis for regional online information exchange activities and encourage, support and develop awareness of the benefits and use of the Internet technology. 2Cities is about re-establishing a village community in a networked world:

> 'Our goal is "e-inclusion" - by having Residents, Community Groups and Businesses interacting online. Importantly, it's not just about technology - rather we're developing a tool for all groups within our community to interact with each other. It will also build our region as a "Smart Region" - to put us at the forefront of the information economy and reap the benefits of cost saving from effective use of the Internet'.

As a regional access point there would be a broad focus, providing a single 'official' point of entry for a range of community, business and other services and products of the region. Additionally, educational services, business products and services, institutions and services, business to business transactions, community groups needs, associations, and marketing of the region for social, economic and other development would be provided.

4. PROJECT DEVELOPMENT

The objective of the project was to develop an e-marketplace within the community (Figure 1). This would be known as the Regional Electronic Marketplace (REM).

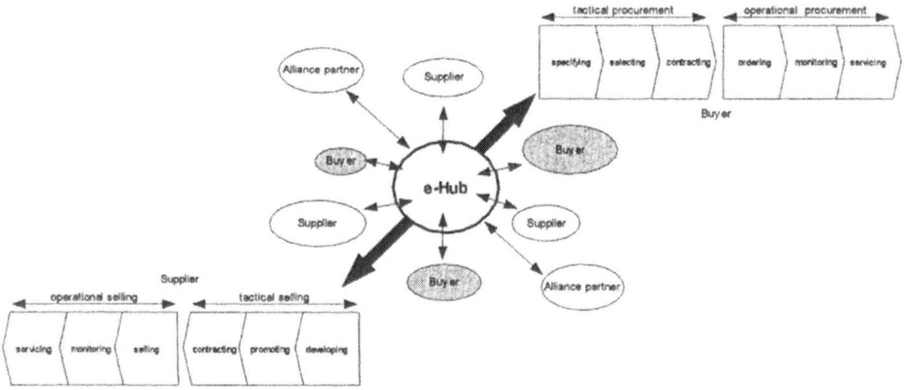

The e-Marketplace is meant to permit Joondalup and Wanneroo region based businesses to sell, but theoretically anyone worldwide to buy through the e-Marketplace once registered. This policy is intended to give to business settled inside this region an infrastructure that can be a competitive advantage, and could also encourage relocation of business. In addition, 2Cities is meant to develop the communities of Joondalup and Wanneroo and to offer a marketing service for promoting the area, through directories like: environment, sport, tourism and education. Finally there's the plan to try to foster local job recruitment, as another way to improve the attractiveness of the region.

The 2Cities supports five different types of e-business relations:

- **Business to Government (B2G)**: supporting all the procurement activities (tenders and normal purchases) of government structure (Administration, Education and Health) both inside and outside the region.
- **Government to Consumer (B2C)**: letting people both inside and outside the region obtain information from the different government structures inside the region.
- **Business to Business (B2B)**: letting business both inside and outside the region once registered to buy from registered businesses inside the region.
- **Business to Consumer (B2C)**: 2Cities will be used by consumers both inside and outside the region basically to search for a business inside the region, but the system also supports the full range of B2C eCommerce.
- **Consumer to Consumer (groups) (C2C)**: developing an active online community for social groups and social services

Organisations seeking to purchase goods or services can use the model to send RFQs, lodge orders and segregate suppliers by locality. Sellers can be notified of RFQs by e-mail, fax or SMS and orders can be placed in a similar manner. In order to sustain the market large corporate buyers have to commit to the market and support agreed from the cities of Joondalup and Wanneroo, Mindarie Regional Council and the university. This will also supply buyers with easy access to a large range of suppliers and choice of goods, and increase their ability to obtain competitive pricing. In addition it is anticipated that suppliers operating within the marketplace will use the process to purchase their own requirements, and in so doing increase the level of trade within the region. Expansion of the system to allow the regions domestic consumers to purchase on-line has the potential to result in rapid growth in transaction levels. Once familiar with e-trading and having benefited from increased regional sales, business will be in a position to expand outside the region, to state, interstate and overseas markets.

NMCOA and the Business Associations believed themselves well placed to assist companies in this type of expansion and where required arrange introductions to local companies already operating in these marketplaces. Such a mentoring process can lead to efficient entry into new markets. Training is an additional requirement and the Small Business Development Corporation provided 92,000A$ to recruit a training officer for the REM. The 'conservative' estimate used in the business model was that some 1,200 companies would be operating within the e-marketplace within five years.

5. PROBLEMS IN THE DEVELOPMENT

Table 2 shows the development timetable, some of the key players and the major milestones impacting on implementation of the portal. The problems can be summarised as follows:

- poor business plan
- low capitalisation
- project overrun
- poor project management – 3 separate project managers
- mis-timing of training requirements
- no marketing and training budgets
- 'warring' stakeholders
- limited understanding of stakeholder needs and motivation

Year	Stage	Project Manager	Situation	Income
1999	Joondalup Stakeholders Group	PM-A	Small group gathering	N/A
2000	Wanneroo/	PM-A	Creating the basic group of	20.000 A$ from the

	Joondalup Regional Online Steering Committee +ECU		stakeholders, the "demonstration site" is put online by Joondalup Business Association	State Government
Mar 2001	NMCOA	PM-A	The NMCOA is created to be a separate financial and political body from stakeholders that can receive and manage founds	90,660 A$ from Federal Government (RAP) 108.000 A$ from the 2 cities and ECU
Feb 2002	IBC win contract	PM-A becomes PT consultant	Development of Portal	70.000 A$ for contract
May 2002		PM-B	PM-A resigns PM-B appointed TM appointed	92,000 A$ SBDC grant for TM
Aug 2002	Portal in test phase	PM-C	PM-B appointment withdrawn PM-C appointed TM resigns	
Dec 2002	Portal completed (6 months overdue) 60 users	PM-C	Soft launch of 2Cities.com	A$190 each
Feb 2003	Intended launch	PM-C	Delayed – new business plan developed	$50,000 additional revenue sought from 2 councils
June 2003	Crisis Meeting	PM-C	Threat of bankruptcy – stalemate between councils and Business associations - Revised business plan developed – PM-C retrenched	
Oct 2003	Marketing manager appointed	MM	Network found to be unusable – IBC take portal in-house	

Year	Stage	Project Manager	Situation	Income
Dec 2003	MM reports 3 new users	MM	2Cities put into abeyance until February 2004	Realistic accounts show balance of $1000
March	Appointment	MM	New Sales plan to be supported	Sales average 10 per

2004	of 2 Tele-marketers RFQ for re-view of IBC services		by PT TMs External consultant submits $11,000 proposal for evaluation	week
April 2004	MM resigns		Sales averaging 2 per week led to decision to offer MM commission only position	Board meeting called for dissolution of REM

*Table 2.*Project Development Stages

The initial business plan was almost wholly dependent on grant income which did not materialise and with unrealistic costs for REM users ($500 per annum as compared to a final fee of $199). The founding members did not realise the extent to which additional funding would be required nor the full extent of technical expertise which would be required to implement the portal. Project managers came and went (three over one year) and a training manager was appointed over six months before the implementation of the portal and resigned prior to the test period. The 2Cities budget had no provision for marketing or training costs and while the revised business plan now includes provision for marketing there is a completely unrealistic target of 6 new users per day signed by the marketing manager. Additional funds (through government grants or through voluntary contributions from the partners) must be obtained.

6. ISSUES AND LESSONS FOR FUTURE

The current status of 2Cities.com is that it commenced operation in December 2002 although the 'official' launch has not taken place and various 'take-over' bids are under discussion. To-date 159 businesses and 39 community groups are registered in the portal. However, less than half of these (78) are actually paying customers and there is no record of any successful trading activity.

Williams and Cothrel (2000) define an online community as groups of people engaging in many-to-many interactions and the motivation for the engagement is the shared interest in certain products. The idea behind such business-related communities is to adapt businesses to the culture of the internet by providing consumers with the ability to interact with each other in addition to the company (Armstrong and Hagel III, 1996). It is not required that members of such communities share beliefs or a feeling of belonging together, However Williams and Cothrel identify three activities which are central to the success of every online community: member development, asset management and community relations and these are examined in turn with respect to problems which have arisen within 2Cities.com.

6.1 Member Development

Communities need critical mass to remain active.The 2Cities business model adopted is one which is totally dependent on a critical mass of large corporate buyers. The portal, however, does not necessarily offer any advantages to these groups since the sellers, typically SMEs, are unlikely to be able to offer discounted prices for large orders. Promotion is essential to build the community but, in fact, 2Cities.com has no marketing budget.

6.1.1 Asset Management

Assets in an online community range from content; to alliances with other groups; to the knowledge and experience of experts, to the community infrastructure. The community coordinator needs to capture the information members need but 2Cities has two customer communities as a focus, the REM community and the social community. These two groups have very different needs from an online community, require different support and need different training. Content generation is required for each of the five types of e-commerce supported in the portal, each involving very different players but all required to adopt some basic standards. An on-going Project Manager is essential.

6.1.2 Community Relations

Interaction with other people is essential for successful creation of an active online community but requires online moderation and facilitation. The desired 'village community' of 2Cities.com will require constant moderation yet has to stimulate member generated content which will be seen to be of value to a very diverse community. There is an additional political dimension here since the two communities are in fact, quite competitive and do not normally view themselves as a single group.

Armstrong and Hagel III (1996) distinguish four types of community as communities of transaction, communities of interest, communities of fantasy and communities of relationship and argue that these are not mutually exclusive and further that communities would miss out on business opportunities if they do not cover all of them. However, managing the complexities of these relationships presents a real challenge to SMEs and the business groups associated with them and seems to be at the heart of the problems involved in 2Cities development. One solution may be to consider the community holistically as a virtual community.

7. VIRTUAL COMMUNITIES

Lee et al (2003), propose five stages of growth for a virtual community as:

1. Fundamental understanding of concepts, principals, definitions and models
2. Technology development for sustained growth
3. Protocols for applications development, relationship building and knowledge sharing
4. Evaluation of implementation and outcome assessments
5. Institutionalisation and enlargement of benefits.

These stages may well be appropriate for an integrated and IT active community with high levels of motivation to interact (Grewal et al, 2001) but need to be preceded by additional steps when small businesses are involved and the 'village' concept embraced. These include:

1. Developing real understanding of benefits from e-communities
2. Stimulating and nurturing motivation to actively participate
3. Education and training on IT and e-business for all users
4. Gaining commitment from all stakeholders
5. Realistic budgeting and hands on project management

As with many such IT ventures it is not just securing the technology but also developing the social interfaces and commitment to participate which will lead to virtual community development.

8. CONCLUSIONS

This paper describes an approach to developing an online regional marketplace associated with a community portal. While there is no dispute that real value can be obtained from online communities (Lueg, 2003) the factors which contribute to the success of such communities seem to be little understood by small players in the market. The case of 2Cities.com illustrates some of the problems and highlights the need for far more effective social management of all the implementation issues. The approach suggested here requires the adoption of a holistic virtual community model which can develop through a series of well defined and more importantly well managed stages.

There is a real need to develop e-markets to allow SMEs to capitalise on online trading but the marketplace must acquire a critical mass of players and must also offer a real alternative to large corporate buyers. 2Cities.com is an extremely ambitious project which is still in its infancy. The revised business plan includes provision for three new REM participants captured every half day over the next year. Time (and a very depleted budget) will prove whether this is a realistic proposition.

REFERENCES

Armstrong A. and Hagel III, J. (1996). The Real Value of On-Line Communities. Harvard Business Review, May-June, 134-141.

Bakos, J. Y. (1991). A strategic analysis of electronic marketplaces. MIS Quarterly, Vol. 15, 3, 295-310.

Banham, R. (2000). The B-to-B virtual bazaar. Journal of Accountancy, Vol 190(1), pp 26-30.

Bode, S. and Burn, J. M. (2001a). Website Design Consultants, Australian SMEs and Electronic Commerce Success Factors. International Journal of Business Studies, Vol, 9, No 1, 73-85.

Bode, S. and Burn, J. M. (2001b). Strategies for Consultancy Engagement for e-Business Development - a case analysis of Australian SMEs. In Burgess, S. (Ed). Managing Information Technology in Small Businesses: Challenges and Solutions. Idea Group Publishing.

Burn, J. M. and Spadaccini, A. (1999). On-Line Organisations - the hype,myths and realities. A Study of IT enabled communication in organisations in WA ACIS Conference, Wellington, New Zealand, Dec.

Burn, J. M. and Tetteh, E. (2001). A Framework for the Management of Global e-business in Small and Medium Sized Enterprises. In P. Palvia, P. Palvia and E.Roche (Eds), Global Information Technology and Electronic Commerce- issues for the new millenium, Ivy League Publishing.

Burn J. M. and Zanaboni, C. (2003) A Tale of 2Cities.com. PACIS, Adelaide, July

Carver, C. (1999). Building a Virtual Community for a Tele-Learning Environment. IEEE Communications. Vol. 37, 3, 114-118.

Choudhury, V., Hartzel, K. S., and Konsynski, B. R. (1998). Uses and Consequences of Electronic Markets: An Empirical Investigation in the Aircraft Parts Industry. MIS Quarterly, Vol. 22, 4, 471-507.

Clark, T.H., and Lee, H. G. (1999). Electronic Intermediaries: Trust Building and market Differentiation. Proceedings of the Thirty-second Annual Conference on System Sciences.

Cowan, D., Mayfield, C., Tompa, F. and Gasparini, W. (1998). New Roles for Community Networks. Communications of the ACM, Vol. 41, 4, 61-63.

DCITA (Department of Communications, Information Technology and the Arts). (2000). E-Commerce Beyond 2000. Commonwealth of Australia, Canberra.

Fariselli, P, Oughton, C., Picory, C. and Sugden, R. (1999). Electronic Commerce and the Future for SMEs in a global Market-Place: Networking and Public Policies. Small Business Economics, Vol. 12, 3, 261-176.

Grewal, R., Comer, J. M. and Mehta, R. (2001). An Investigation into the Antecedents of Organizational Participation in Business-to-Business Electronic Markets. Journal of Marketing, Vol. 65, 3, 17-34.

Jones Donald Strategic Partners (2000). Taking the plunge 2000, sink or swim? Small business attitudes to electronic commerce. National Office for the Information Economy: Commonwealth of Australia.

Kaplan, S. and Sawhney, M. (2000) E-Hubs: The New B2B Marketplace. Harvard Business Review, May/June, 97-103.

Kleindl, B. (2000). Competitive Dynamics and New Business Models for SMEs in the Virtual Marketplace. Journal of Development Entrepreneurship, Vol. 5, 1, 73-86.

Korchak, R. and R. Rodman, eBusiness adoption among US small manufacturers and the role of manufacturing extension. Economic Development Review, 2001. Vol. 17, 3, 20-25.

Lee, F., Vogel, D. and Limayem, M. (2003). Virtual Community Informatics: A Review and Research Agenda. JITTA: Journal of Information Theory and Application, Vol. 5, 1, 47-63.

Lucking-Reiley, D., and Spulber, D. F. (2000). Business-to-Business electronic commerce. Journal of Economic Perspectives, Vol. 15, 1, 55-68.

Levy, M. and Powell, P. (2003). Exploring SME Internet Adoption: Towards a Contingent Model. Electronic Markets, Vol. 13,2, 173-181.

Lueg, C. (2003). Knowledge Sharing in Online Communities and its Relevance to Knowledge Management in the e-Business Era. Int. J. Electronic Business, Vol. 1, 2, 140-151.

McAdam, R., The implementation of reengineering in SMEs: A grounded study. International Small Business Journal, 2000. Vol.18, 4, 29-45.

Mirani, R., and Lederer, A. L. (1998). An instrument for assessing the organizational benefits of IS Projects. Decision Sciences, Vol. 29, 4, 803-838.

OECD, (1998) A Borderless World – Realising the Potential of Global Electronic Commerce, Ottawa, Canada 7-9 October, Organisation for Economic Co-operation and Development.

OECD, (2000). Enhancing the competitiveness of SMEs in the global economy: strategies and policies. Proceedings of the Conference for Ministers responsible for SMEs andIndustry Ministers. Bologna, Italy.

Pacific Access (2001) Yellow Pages Business Index SME Survey of Computer technology and E-Commerce in Australian Small and Medium Businesses, July. [URL: www.corporate.pacificaccess.com.au]

Poon, S. and Swatman, P.M.C. (1997) Internet-based Small Business Communication: Seven Australian Cases, Electronic Markets, Vol. 7, 2, 15-22.

Said, A.J. (2000). Helping small firms trade effectively with the Internet. International Trade Forum, 2000. 3, 16-19.

Small Business Index (1998). Small Business Index: a survey of e-commerce in Australian small andmedium businesses. Melbourne: Yellow Pages

Standing, C. The Characteristics of Successful e-Marketplaces. in Pacific Asia Conference on Information Systems. 2001. Seoul, Korea.

Standing, C. Vasudavan, V. (1999). Internet Marketing Strategies used by Travel Agencies in Australia. Journal of Vacation Marketing, Vol. 6(1), pp. 21-32.

Swatman, P. (2000). Internet for SMEs: A new skill road? International Trade Forum, 2000(3): 22-24.

Tetteh, E. and Burn, J. M. (2001). Global Strategies for SMe-Business: applying the S-M-A-L-L framework. Journal of Logistics and Information Management, Vol 14, No 1 and 2, pp 171-180.

UNCTAD (2002) E-Commerce and Development Report, available at http://r0.unctad.org/ecommerce/ecommerce_en/edr02_en.htm.

Williams, R. L. and Cothrel, W. J. (2000). For-Smart Ways to Run Online Communities. Sloan Management Review, 41, 4, 81-91.

ANALYSIS OF A YIELD MANAGEMENT MODEL FOR ON DEMAND COMPUTING CENTERS

Yezekael Hayel[1], Laura Wynter[2] and Parijat Dube[2]
[1]INRIA/IRISA, [2]IBM T.J. Watson Research Center

Abstract: The concept of yield management for IT infrastructures, and in particular for *on demand* IT utilities was recently introduced in [17]. The present paper provides a detailed analysis of that model, both in simplified cases where an analytical analysis is possible, and numerically on larger problem instances, and confirms the significant revenue benefit that can accrue through use of yield management in an IT on demand operating environment.

Key words: Yield management, optimization, discrete choice model

1. INTRODUCTION

In [17], a model for performing yield management in the context of IT provisioning was presented. This model is especially valuable in the context of an on demand operating environment. On demand IT services allow users to arrive at will into an IT system, in which scheduled jobs have already reserved the resource. Many potential applications of this type of IT infrastructure exist and a few are already in operation.

One example of an on demand IT service that exists today is the case of dynamic off-loading of web content. When a customer, such as an online retailer, experiences very heavy web site traffic, that retailer may have its excess traffic automatically redirected to an off-loading service. The process is invisible to end-users of the retailer. The yield management system as described in [17] could be used by the off-loading service provider to allocate its own capacity optimally and profitably. Many other potential applications of this technology are on the horizon: application service providers may run software applications on their own cluster of servers and allow customers, for a fee, to use those applications remotely. Yield management in this case sets capacity allocations (server use, storage, and bandwidth) and multiple price points to offer to those customers, depending on the available resource level of the service provider, as well as the market demand. Similarly, computing centers, that rent processing capacity to customers, can operate more profitably and more efficiently through use of a system of yield management.

Yield management is the technique used by the airline reservation systems to set booking limits on seats at each price class. In an on demand operating environment, customers and jobs, or service requests, arrive at random. Whereas some of the IT system resources are pre-reserved, the real-time arrival of new customers introduces the possibility to accomplish any number of desired service objectives. The service objectives are achieved by the yield management modules by setting prices judiciously, as a function of the resource utilization and user demand levels.

For example, when spare capacity exists, introducing dramatically low prices serves to introduce new demand into the system. Yield management allows the provider to set the dramatically low prices without sacrificing profits. On the contrary, it was proved in [17] that, under certain conditions, as the number of price points increases, the revenue increases. When usage costs are increasing linearly or sublinearly in the number of users, as is generally the case, profits can be shown to increase monotonically as the number of price points increases as well, in spite of the fact that some price points can be set below cost. The key to the remarkable increase in revenue and profits is that the number of slots available at each price point is limited, and set optimally so as to maximize revenue, given the demand model and available resource level.

In this paper, we analyze the model introduced in [17], both analytically and numerically. The analytical study is carried out on a simplified version of the model with only price points and fixed job sojourn times; as such it provides a bound on what can be said about the full-scale model. The numerical study then illustrates the benefits that the approach and our model can provide and confirms the tractability of the yield management paradigm to the IT On Demand context.

While the literature on airline yield management is clearly of great relevance to our problem of yield management in on demand IT services, there are notable differences which lead to significantly high complexity in our setting. First and foremost, the service under consideration in IT on demand does not have a fixed duration nor does it occupy a predetermined percentage of the resource capacity. That is, an airline seat is occupied precisely for the duration of the flight, and the number of seats to sell on any flight is known in advance.

On the other hand, in On Demand IT utilities, the duration of a job depends upon the type of server upon which it is run, and the number of servers, if it is parallelizable; further, the number of servers it requires depends upon the type of servers that are used. In other words both the capacity needed and the time taken by a job are not simple, exogenous parameters in the compute On Demand yield management problem. Some features of this time variability can be observed in other sectors, such as hotellerie, restaurant yield management, and even golf course yield management (see, for example, [7] and [8], and other references by those authors). Nonetheless, the capacity and percentage of capacity occupied in these latter examples are still fixed and exogenous, as opposed to the setting with which we are faced.

Research work on the pricing of information and telecommunication services, such as the pricing strategies of internet service providers (ISPs) has traditionally considered some of these issues of job duration and capacity occupation through queuing formulae. The literature on that and related areas is quite vast and a thorough survey of it is not the focus of our work here, but a few relevant references are [4, 5, 6, 11, 12, 13, 15]. The difference between the decisions optimized in those and related work is the degree of segmentation. In the Internet pricing world, a single price per type of service is proposed. It is sometimes the case that multiple qualities of service (QoS) are discussed, but in that case, each QoS level has associated with it a single, fixed price. The number of such price levels is generally limited to three, for example, gold, silver, and bronze-level service. The yield management strategy takes customer segmentation to a much finer level, and does so through the incorporation of demand models.

In short, what makes this yield management approach to IT resource pricing and management so appealing is that it allows an IT provider to very tightly couple her IT resources to the demand. By so doing, the IT provider can substantially increase profit margins on the existing capacity, and furthermore modify the demand through targeted pricing/offering definition. As a by-product, the IT provider can accomplish other objectives, such as smoothing the demand over time, to avoid, for example, weekly peaks and excess spare capacity on the week-ends. Existing approaches to pricing IT resources that do not make use of this yield management approach do not have sufficient segmentation, in time or in the description of user demand, to accomplish these management objectives.

The structure of the paper is as follows. In Section 2, we propose and study an analytically tractable version of the model of [17] so as to gain qualitative insights on the nature of the problem. Section 3 contains a numerical study of the model. Finally, we conclude in Section 4.

2. THE MODEL

In this paper, we shall assume that the on demand service infrastructure is composed of a pool of homogeneous nodes (processing units) to allocate to different fee classes. The optimization problem that we will need to solve is then the following: in a particular time epoch (in this paper we consider only one), we would like to reserve the available resource for the different fee classes. The resource should be allocated so as to maximize expected provider profits, that is, expected revenue less expected costs, where expected provider revenue is related to the distributions of different customer arrival types, their preferences (in terms of service/price trade-offs) as well as their service requirements, and to the number of nodes assigned to each fee class, on each server type.

Fee classes are defined as follows: for an identical resource several different prices may coexist; each fee class then has a maximal number of users, and once that number is reached within the time period for that fee class, new requests are offered only the next higher level fee for that resource.

Resources are also defined in a broad way. While a server and storage are clearly aspects of the resource, the service-level (SLA) parameters are as well, such as availability, advance notice, penalties in case of non-satisfaction of service level by the provider, etc. The broad scope of the *resource* in this manner allows the price differentiation to become still finer-grained; that is, for an identical server/storage combination, different SL offerings create new sets of fee classes.

With respect to notation, T_c is the (here, deterministic) sojourn time of a job of class $c = 1... C$ in the system. The decision variables, denoted by n_k, represent the number of resource slots to reserve for price segment $k = 1... K$. Further, let $n = (n_k)$ be the vector of all n_ks, and N the total amount of resource; while this could be extended to heterogeneous resource types, here for notational simplicity, we make use of a single resource type, of which there are N units. In general, job sojourn time depends on the workload, or size, of the job, W, the number of slots allocated n_k, and the type of job, c. However, modeling explicitly that dependence leads to a non-convex feasible set, in that the sojourn time appears in the definition of the constraints. Therefore, in this paper, we have assumed the job sojourn time, T_c, to be externally provided.

The choice probability of a user with job class c accepting a slot of segment-type k is given in general by $P_k^c(W,n)$, but again for simplicity, we have suppressed dependency on the particular workload, and made use of a choice probability of the form $P_k^c(n)$. The probability of an arrival of job class c is given by G_c. Recall that we are considering here only one time epoch. The parameters r_k are the price points of the resource. By enumerating a wide range of such prices, the optimization model works by identifying those price segments which are most profitable to offer, given the characteristics of the available demand and resource levels.

As stated earlier, we consider, in this paper, a simplified model in which two different prices per node are offered, i.e. $r_1 \neq r_2$. Furthermore, we shall consider two different user, or job, classes, $c = 1,2$. Under these simplifications, we shall be able to examine the model analytically and obtain bounds on the decision variables. The simplified yield management for IT resource model can be expressed as:

$$\max_{n_1,n_2 \geq 0} F(n_1, n_2) = \sum_{c=1}^{C}\sum_{k=1}^{2} T_c r_k n_k P_k^c(n)\Gamma_c.$$
$$n_1 + n_2 \leq N$$

Alternatively, one can assume that the resource limits are *soft constraints* and include the possibility to surpass those limits, at a cost associated with having to make use of remote resources or to pay a penalty to the customers.

While these results cannot be extended in general to any number of parameters, they, along with the larger-scale numerical results, provide valuable insight into the nature of the problem under study.

To model the behavior of customers, or job requests, we introduce a *deterministic* discrete choice function That is, we use the normalized ratio of the utility of choice i to the sum of all choice utilities, that is, $\forall c$, and $\forall k$,

$$P_k^c(n) = \frac{1}{K-1}\left(1 - \frac{U_k^c(n_k)}{\sum_{j=1}^{K} U_j^c(n_j)}\right)$$

The first term normalizes the quantities $P_c^k(n)$ so that they sum to 1 for each customer class, c. The second term is expressed as 1— ratio, since the $U_c^k(n)$ are actually dis-utilities and hence decreasing in price and delay. With only two price segments, we have, for $c = 1, 2$,

$$P_1^c(n) = \frac{U_2^c(n_2)}{U_1^c(n_1) + U_2^c(n_2)} \quad \text{and} \quad P_2^c = \frac{U_1^c(n_1)}{U_1^c(n_1) + U_2^c(n_2)},$$

where the (dis-)utility functions are:

$$U_k^c(n_k) = \zeta_1 T_c r_k n_k + \zeta_2 T_c.$$

The parameters ζ_1 and ζ_2 are constants that define the price-time trade-offs, and render the utility U unitless. There are different ways to define these parameters, but we have chosen to use a single, deterministic, parameter vector for all customers. Recall also that T_c is a constant that depends only on job class. The utility function is thus linear in the decision variable, n_k.

Explicitly including the deterministic discrete choice model into the objective function for this two-price-segment model, we obtain:

$$\max_{n_1,n_2 \geq 0} F(n_1,n_2) = \sum_{c=1}^{C} \Gamma_c T_c \left(f(n_1,n_2) + g(n_1,n_2) \right) \tag{1.1}$$

$$n_1 + n_2 \leq N \tag{1.2}$$

with

$$f(n_1,n_2) = r_1 \frac{\zeta_1 r_2 n_1 n_2 + \zeta_2 n_1}{\zeta_1 r_1 n_1 + \zeta_1 r_2 n_2 + 2\zeta_2},$$

and

$$g(n_1,n_2) = r_2 \frac{\zeta_1 r_1 n_1 n_2 + \zeta_2 n_2}{\zeta_1 r_1 n_1 + \zeta_1 r_2 n_2 + 2\zeta_2},$$

As the revenue increases in the number of nodes reserved to all price segments, the inequality constraint expressed in (1.2) will be active. In this simplified setting, we have the following result.

Proposition 1 *The nonlinear yield management reservation problem of 1.1 has a unique maximum*

Proof: We shall seek a maximum of the objective function on the induced, linear subspace defined by the active capacity constraints. To do so, we shall define the Hessian of the objective function augmented by the Lagrange multipliers and capacity constraints; this Hessian matrix is sometimes referred to as the "bordered Hessian".

First, the Lagrangian function is :

$$L(n_1, n_2, \mu) = \sum_{c=1}^{C} \Gamma_c T_c.(f(n_1, n_2) + g(n_1, n_2)) - \mu G(n_1, n_2),$$

with Lagrange multiplier $\mu \in \Re_+$, and constraint function: $G(n_1,n_2) = n_1 + n_2 - N$.

Again, as mentioned, at optimality, the capacity constraint, $G(n_1,n_2) \leq 0$, will be active, hence $n_1 + n_2 = N$. After some manipulation of the Lagrangian, we obtain the following system:

$$\begin{cases} \frac{r_1 \sum_{c=1}^{C} \Gamma_c T_c (2\zeta_1^2 r_2^2 n_2^2 + 4\zeta_1 \zeta_2 r_2 n_2 + 2\zeta_2^2)}{(\zeta_1 r_1 n_1 + \zeta_1 r_2 n_2 + 2\zeta_2)^2} - \mu = 0, \\ \frac{r_2 \sum_{c=1}^{C} \Gamma_c T_c (2\zeta_1^2 r_1^2 n_1^2 + 4\zeta_1 \zeta_2 r_1 n_1 + 2\zeta_2^2)}{(\zeta_1 r_1 n_1 + \zeta_1 r_2 n_2 + 2\zeta_2)^2} - \mu = 0, \\ n_1 + n_2 = N, \end{cases}$$

from which we obtain:

$$\begin{cases} (\zeta_1 r_2 n_2 + \zeta_2)^2 - \left(\sqrt{\frac{\mu}{2r_1 \sum_{c=1}^{C} \Gamma_c T_c}} (\zeta_1 r_1 n_1 + \zeta_1 r_2 n_2 + 2\zeta_2) \right)^2 = 0, \\ (\zeta_1 r_1 n_1 + \zeta_2)^2 - \left(\sqrt{\frac{\mu}{2r_2 \sum_{c=1}^{C} \Gamma_c T_c}} (\zeta_1 r_1 n_1 + \zeta_1 r_2 n_2 + 2\zeta_2) \right)^2 = 0, \\ n_1 + n_2 = N. \end{cases}$$

Noting that each of the first two equations is a quadratic, we obtain four sets of equations. However, of those, only one has a feasible solution, which we shall show is the unique maximum. The solution is given by:

$$(n_1^*, n_2^*) = (N \frac{\sqrt{r_2}}{\sqrt{r_1} + \sqrt{r_2}} + \mathcal{H}, N \frac{\sqrt{r_1}}{\sqrt{r_1} + \sqrt{r_2}} - \mathcal{H}),$$

with $\mathcal{H} = \frac{\zeta_2}{\zeta_1 r_2} \frac{\sqrt{r_2}}{\sqrt{r_1}+\sqrt{r_2}} (1 - \sqrt{\frac{r_2}{r_1}})$. The optimal Lagrangian multiplier, μ^*, is then:

$$\mu^* = 2 \sum_{c=1}^{C} \Gamma_c T_c \frac{r_1 r_2}{(\sqrt{r_1} + \sqrt{r_2})^2}.$$

Additionally, as n_1^* and n_2^* are non-negative, we obtain two necessary conditions on the feasible range of prices, r_1 and r_2, for a solution:

$$r_1 \geq \frac{r_2}{(1+N\frac{\zeta_1 r_2}{\zeta_2})^2}, \tag{1.3}$$

$$r_1 \leq r_2(1+N\frac{\zeta_1 r_2}{\zeta_2})^2. \tag{1.4}$$

Thus, depending on the values of the problem constants, we can determine the range of prices for which a solution exists. Figure 1 illustrates this range for a capacity level $N = 10$, and for a range of a new parameter, ζ, which is defined as $\zeta = \zeta_1/\zeta_2$

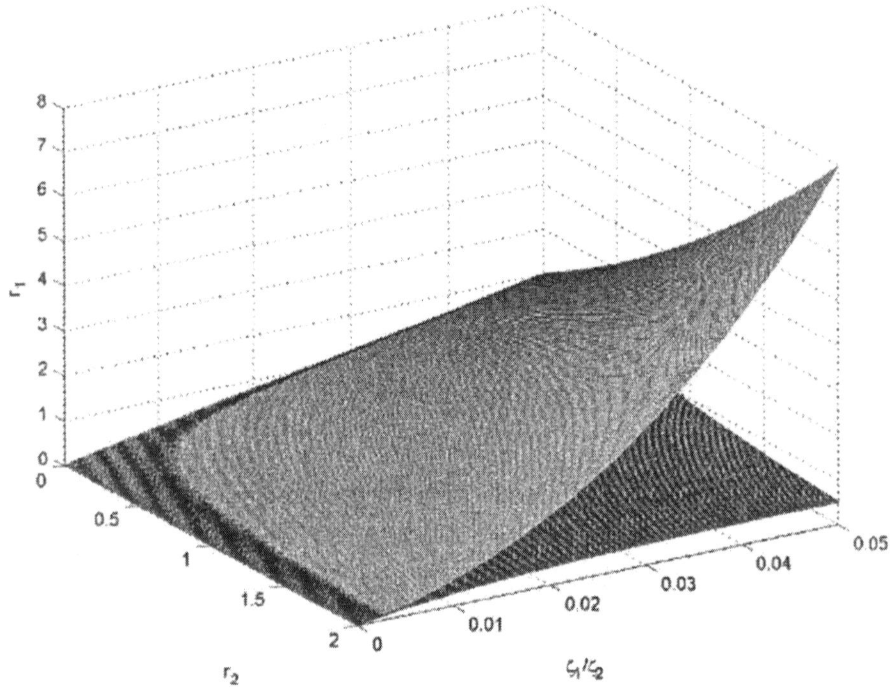

Figure 1. Existence area of the solution when N = 10

To prove that the solution we have found is indeed a maximum, we examine the second-order conditions for this constrained maximization problem. The Hessian of the Lagrange function is defined by:

$$\overline{D}(z) = \begin{pmatrix} 0 & G_{n_1} & G_{n_2} \\ G_{n_1} & L_{n_1n_1} & L_{n_1n_2} \\ G_{n_2} & L_{n_2n_1} & L_{n_2n_2} \end{pmatrix},$$

where $z := [\mu, n_1, n_2]$ We then must determine whether the Hessian of the Lagrangian function D, evaluated at the possible optimum, is negative semi-definite subject to the linear constraint $w'Dw \leq 0$ for all $w \in \Re^3$ satisfying $(\partial G/\partial z_i)(w_i) = 0$, where the index on z indicates the element of that vector, and similarly for w. This negative-definiteness condition implies that the principle minor determinants of the Hessian of the Lagrange function alternate in sign. In our two-variable, one constraint, setting, the second-order condition amounts to the 3×3 determinant (including the constraint) being *positive*. Note, from the alternating signs, that in a three-variable, one-constraint problem, the corresponding 4×4 determinant would need to be negative, etc…

The second derivatives of the Lagrangian function are:

$$L_{n_1n_1} = \frac{\partial^2 L}{\partial n_1^2}(n_1, n_2) = -\sum_{c=1}^{C} \Gamma_c T_c (2\zeta_1^2 r_1 r_2^2 n_2^2 + 4\zeta_1\zeta_2 r_1 r_2 n_2 + 2 r_1 \zeta_2^2) \frac{2\zeta_1 r_1}{(\zeta_1 r_1 n_1 + \zeta_1 r_2 n_2 + 2\zeta_2)^3},$$

$$|\overline{D}| = -G_{n_1}^2 L_{n_1n_1} + 2G_{n_1}G_{n_2}L_{n_1n_2} - G_{n_2}^2 L_{n_2n_2},$$

$L_{n_2n_2} = \frac{\partial^2 L}{\partial n_2^2}(n_1, n_2) = -\sum_{c=1}$ [illegible] $\frac{2\zeta_1 r_2}{(\zeta_1 r_1 n_1 + \zeta_1 r_2 n_2 + 2\zeta_2)^3},$

$$L_{n_1n_2} = \frac{\partial^2 L}{\partial n_1 n_2}(n_1, n_2) = \frac{\sum_{c=1}^{C} \Gamma_c T_c}{(\zeta_1 r_1 n_1 + \zeta_1 r_2 n_2 + 2\zeta_2)^3} [4\zeta_1^4 r_1^3 r_2^2 n_1^2 n_2 +$$
$$+ 4\zeta_1^4 r_1^2 r_2^3 n_1 n_2^2 + 16\zeta_1^3 \zeta_2 r_1^2 r_2^2 n_1 n_2 + 8\zeta_1^3 \zeta_2 r_1 r_2^3 n_2^2 +$$
$$+ 4\zeta^3 \zeta_2 r_1^3 r_2 n_1^2 + 8\zeta_1 \zeta_2^3 r_1 r_2 + 12\zeta_1^2 \zeta_2^2 r_1^2 r_2 n_1 + 12\zeta_1^2 \zeta_2^2 r_1 r_2^2 n_2]$$

The determinant of the Hessian is:

where $G_{n1} = G_{n2} = 1$. Thus we obtain that the determinant of D is indeed positive for all $n_1 \geq 0$ and $n_2 \geq 0$, and we conclude that (n_1^*, n_2^*) is indeed a maximum over the frontier.

3. YIELD MANAGEMENT FOR WEB TRANSACTION DATA

We apply our optimization model to web transaction data over an eight-day horizon. The data we have does not include job durations; therefore we consider all jobs to have unit duration (here, the time unit is one hour). The yield management reservation (YMR) system functions similarly when jobs have heterogeneous durations. The subscription works as follows: some users, not willing to pay high prices for service, subscribe only if they can obtain the service at an acceptable price level to them. If no such acceptable price is available (not offered, or the maximal quantity is attained) then those customers" go elsewhere". Other users with higher willingness-to-pay can still subscribe, until their threshold is reached, and so on. Therefore, depending upon the prices offered, and the available quantities of each, a different share of the market can be captured, and revenue will thus vary as well.

The objective of the YMR system is to determine which offerings to propose to customers, and the optimal quantity to propose of each offering, so as to maximize potential revenue. Here, we illustrate the output of the YMR system in terms of the optimal number of slots to propose at each of the price levels, and then compare the resulting revenue stream with the base-case, in which a single price per QoS is charged.

The transaction data represents the demand at each point of time. The YMR model allows for the possibility that a user does not accept any of the offerings proposed. In this series of examples, we have considered a single QoS level and multiple prices for that QoS, with the quantities of slots available at each price limited, by a number to be determined by the YMR. Possible price levels are determined in advance, with not necessarily all price levels open in the optimal solution; the possible set of price points are given in Table 3. On the left column of the table, we consider a variable number of price segments in each optimization run, from 1 single price (be it high, medium, or low) to 6 price points.

Table 1. Input data on the possible prices for each simulation, in which 1 to 6 price segments are offered to customers, in limited quantities

K max. number of price points avail.	Actual price levels normalized to vary in [0,1]
1, single low price	.2
1, single medium price	.6
1, single high price	1
2	.4 .8
3	.3 .6 .9
4	.2 .4 .6 .8
5	.2 .4 .6 .8 1
6	.2 .35 .5 .65 .8 .95

The first figure illustrates the optimal revenue over time when 2 to 6 price segments are made available to customers, in limited quantities. Note that the topmost curve is the total demand, not the revenue. The revenue accrued under each simulation (2 through 6 price segments on offer) is indicated in the lower series of curves. The larger numbers of price segments (5-6) clearly gives higher revenue during peak periods, whereas during periods of lower use, 2-3 price segments on offer is optimal.

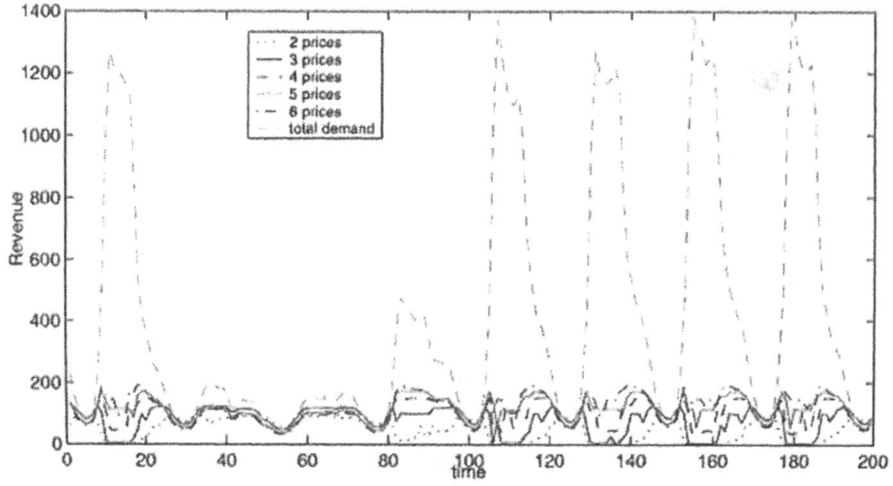

Figure 2. Revenue stream for different numbers of price segments on offer.

The highest curve gives the total demand over time, and serves only to illustrate the peaks and valleys.

Figure 3 summarizes the data of the first two figures for certain time periods, for increased clarity. In particular, we have chosen 5 time periods, with alternating peak flows and off-peak flows, to illustrate how the optimal number of price segments to offer varies.

The last set of figures (Figures 4 and 5) compares the revenue when only one price segment is offered (for three cases: a low, medium or high price) with a strategy of offering five price points (irrespective of the demand level).

Observe that the 5-price-segment offering is always superior to offering a single price, irrespective of whether a low, medium, or high single price is offered. Furthermore, from the above figures, we know that the YMR system would not suggest always proposing 5 price segments irrespective of the load level, but would allow further revenue increase by modulating the number of segments to offer with the demand level (less segments when demand is low, more when it is high).

Figures 5 illustrates the optimal numbers of slots to offer at each of those 5 price levels and demonstrates that the optimal number of price segments varies with the total demand, or load, in that the higher

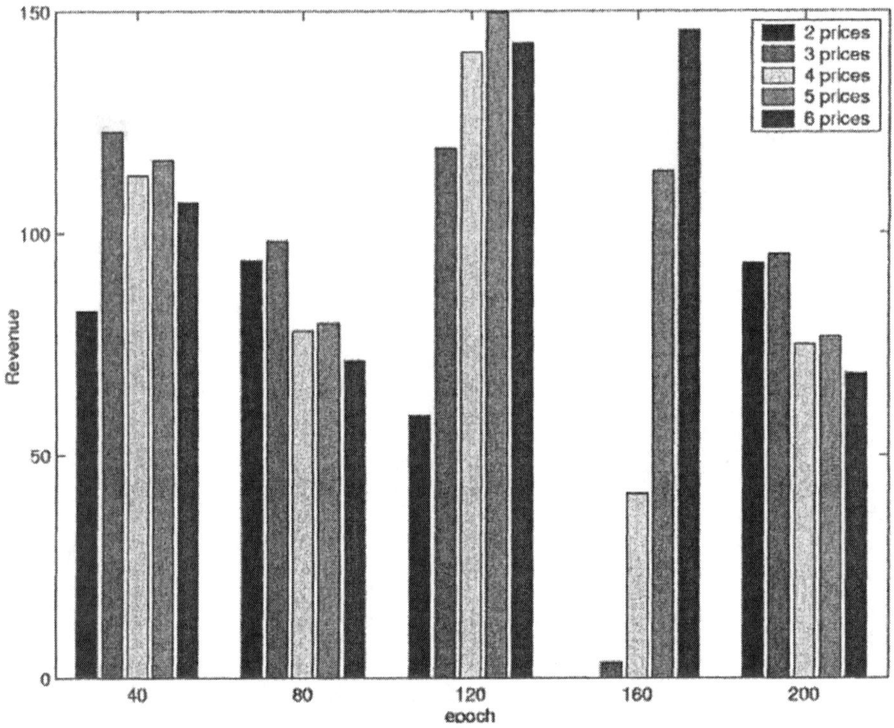

Figure 3. Optimal revenue for 5 diflferent time periods (periods oflf-peak(40), medium (80), peak (120), peak (160) and oflf-peak (200)) over the 5 diflferent YMR strategies (offering 2-6 price segments).

the demand, the higher the number of segments should be to maximize revenue. This implies furthermore that the YMR should be re-run as new and better demand data become available. Figure 5 shows the entire breakdown over the 8-day time horizon.

4. CONCLUSION

In this paper, we have presented a yield management model for *on demand* IT services such as e-commerce services, or data processing centers. We have provided an approach for determining an optimal reservation of resources in order to maximize expected revenue, as well as a detailed analytical analysis of the resulting optimization problem when the number of class of prices is small. Finally, we provide numerical results on time series data of web transactions that illustrate the impact of the approach on service provider revenue.

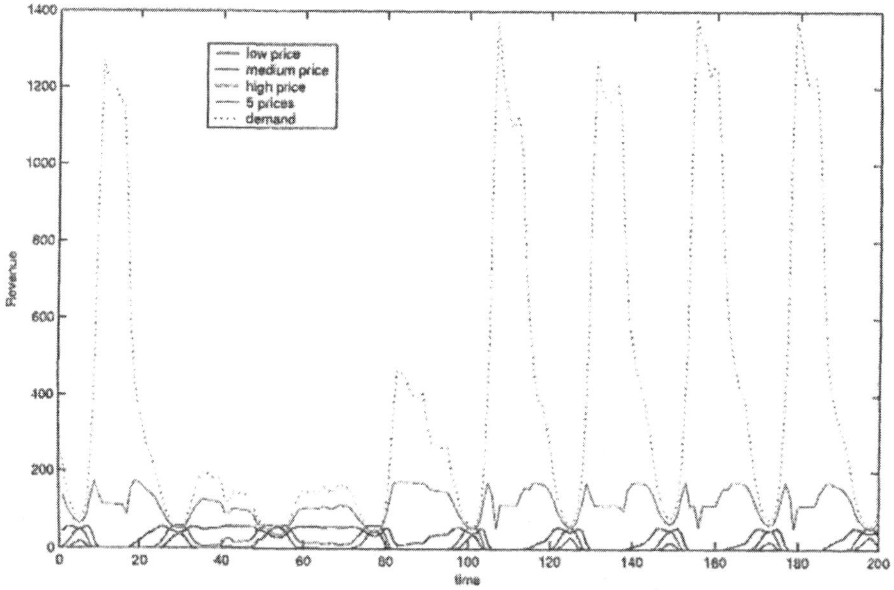

Figure 4. Comparison of YMR strategy of offering 5 price segments with a single-price offering, where the single price is either low, medium, or high

REFERENCES

[1] P.P. Belobaba, Airline yield management: an overview of seat inventory control. Transportation Science, 21, 63-73, 1987.

[2] M. Ben Akiva and S. Lerman Discrete choice Analysis: Theory and application to travel demand. MIT Press, Cambridge, 1985.

[3] P. Davis, Airline ties profitability yield to management, SIAM News, 27-5, 1994.

[4] R. El Azouzi, A. Altman, and L. Wynter, Telecommunications network equilibrium with price and quality-of-service charactersitics to appear in the Proceedings of the 18th International Teletraffic Conference (ITC), 2003.

[5] R. J. Gibbens and F. P. Kelly, Resource pricing and the evolution of congestion control, Automatica, 35(12), 1969-1985, 1999.

[6] A. Gupta, D. Stahl, and A. Whinston, The Economics of Network Management, Communications of the ACM, 42(5), 57-63, 1999.

[7] S.E. Kimes, D.I. Barrash and J.E. Alexander, Developing a restaurant revenue management strategy, Cornell Hotel and Restaurant Administration Quarterly, 40-5, 18-29, 1999.

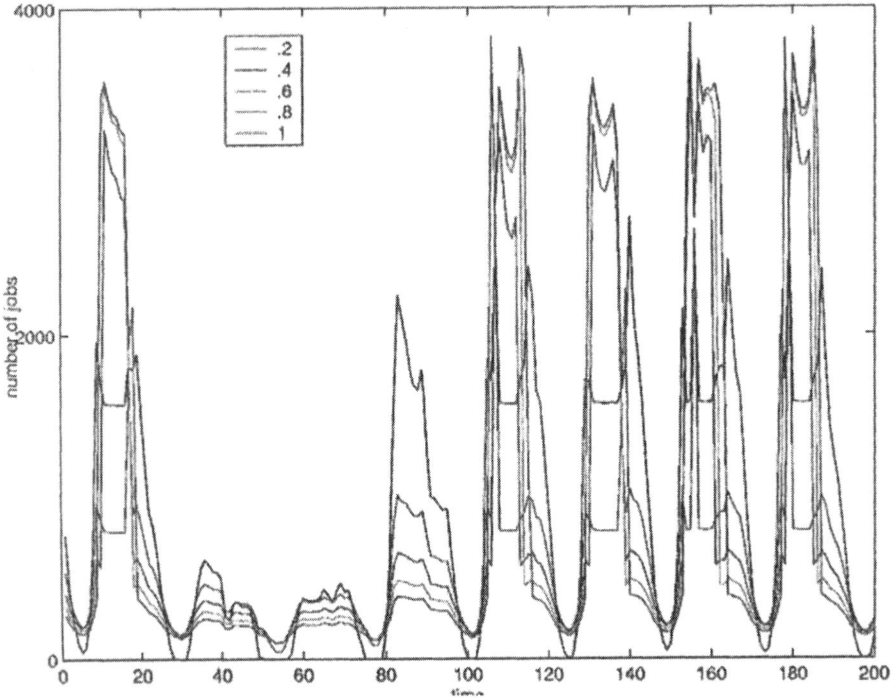

Figure 5. Number of slots to oflfer at each of the 5 prices segments over time.

[8] S.E. Kimes, *Revenue management on the links: applying yield management to the golf course,* Cornell Hotel and Restaurant Administration Quarterly, 41-1, 120-127, 2001.

[9] A.J. Kleywegt, *An optimal control problem of dynamic procing* Georgia Tech Research Report, 2001.

[10] K. Littlewood, *Forecasting and control of passengers* 12th AGI-FORS Symposium Proceedings, 95-128, 1972.

[11] Z. Liu, L. Wynter, and C. Xia, *Pricing information services in a competitive market: avoiding price wars* INRIA Research Report 4679. Available at www.inria.fr/rrrt/rr-4679.html. Also in proc. of 4th ACM conference on Electronic commerce, San Diego, CA, USA, June 2003

[12] J. Mackie-Mason and H. Varian *Pricing the Internet* in Public Access to the Internet, B. Kahn and J. Keller, (Eds.) Prentice Hall, Englewood Cliffs, 1995.

[13] A. Odlyzko, *Paris metro pricing for the Internet* in Proceedings of the ACM Conference on Electronic Commerce, 140-147, 1999.

VALUE CHAIN MANAGEMENT

THE SEVEN-STEP MODEL FOR E-GROCERY FULFILMENT

Martin Barnett and Paul Alexander
School of Management Information Systems, Edith Cowan Universit, Perth WA, Australia

Abstract: Online grocery shopping is a specialised subset of online shopping with difficulties all of its own. Most of these occur, not at the front end of customer ordering, but during the last mile: the home delivery process. A study of third party fulfilment in Australia has demonstrated the existence of an optimal seven-step model for linking the lowest possible delivery costs to a given customer density. Developed from a national case example, our model shows that as volume of deliveries increases, cost characteristics and activities fall within seven clearly bounded stages as business volumes increase. Where competition is centred around this component of grocery sales, e-grocers wishing to compete using a cost leadership strategy are likely to reduce their prices (to customers) to such levels. However, a survey of Australian e-Grocers indicates that some may be immune to this pressure, and therefore continue to pocket very significant profits derived from e-fulfilment.

Key words: e-Groceries, e-fulfilment, logistics, online retail, delivery, transport, marketing, last mile

1. INTRODUCTION

Business-to-consumer e-commerce stimulates fierce debate at all levels: from angel investors, through practitioners, to the earnest inhabitants of business schools and readers of IS journals. Nowhere are the battle lines between sceptics and believers in the retail revolution more definitely drawn than on the battlefield of e-grocery.

Online ordering complemented by home delivery for the grocery sector is perceived as particularly problematic. Compared with most other goods offered online, groceries have lower value to bulk ratios, present greater handling problems and have low margins.

Despite this the potential for interactive home grocery shopping attracts attention on two counts. Firstly, a significant proportion of household spending in developed countries goes through relatively few retail grocery stores, and secondly, a successful approach to this retail area serves as a model for other retail areas to follow suit. To date clear and accepted business models for success have yet to emerge.

Some studies conducted on the economics associated with online retailing fulfilment , take a macro and perhaps simplistic view of the situation. Evident in these cases is a tacit assumption that simple relationships exist between costs and volume/density of fulfilment, and that these hold during both commencement and routine operation of the business. This paper describes the costs associated with delivery services for a general fulfilment organisation attempting to address different customer densities, and demonstrates that for different densities and volumes, businesses need to be on different steps of a predictable cost model operate optimally.

e-Grocery operations provide a bellwether for Internet fulfilment operations in all fields. They are an extreme and sensitive system owing to their high bulk, perishability, high frequency and low intrinsic per-unit value, combined with customer expectations of delivery urgency, stringent and challenging timetabling, routing, storage, picking and packing methods, and health issues. This separates them from other online retailers focused on other consumer durables. In these lines, the above fulfilment factors may be mitigated by other aspects of the value proposition, and consequently greater versatility consequence.

In other words, the overall value of the purchase is not particularly high, hence the delivery cost may form a significant portion. This in turn makes the customer potentially sensitive to delivery prices.

Some studies have been conducted on the economics associated with e-tailing fulfilment in general (Schuster and Sporn 1998; Laseter, Houston et al.; Laseter, Houston et al.) and for e-grocers in particular, but these take a macro view. Their main simplification is a tacit assumption that simple linear relationships exist between costs and volume/density of deliveries. This paper reports on the costs associated with delivery services for a third-party fulfilment organisation (ie. not a specialist e-grocer), as it scaled its operations to meet increasing delivery volumes and different customer densities, and suggests that for different densities and volumes, one operates on different steps of a seven-step cost model.

We use as an example, this model applied to an Australian city of known density and grocery consumption. Its concentrated suburban spread makes this example readily applicable to other European cities, and local data may be input to yield area-specific predictions. On the basis of this, e-grocery businesses operating in Australia are examined to predict the viability of such operations.

2. RETAILING AND E-GROCERY MARKETS

Home shopping, particularly Internet shopping, is on the increase. For example, research group IMRG reports that online shopping in the UK grew 19 times faster than high street shopping in 2002, and doubled in value during the first six months of 2003 (to £4.75 billion) . In 2003 this continued as Internet shopping reached an all-time high in the UK in November - soaring 44% at an annual growth rate 12 times higher than the 3.6% reported for all retail sales by the British Retail Consortium. (Netimperative). These figures are particularly important for us as the UK has led the way in the development of grocery supply chain efficiency and Tesco is the most successful online grocer to date (Tesco Annual Report).

By any standards these increases are substantial, and they mean that more product than ever before is being sent to people's houses in vans. A similar growth rate is reported for the US by Forrester Research, which says first-half results for 2003 were worth about £61 billion compared with £45 billion the previous year. In 2005, US$118 billion worth of U.S. online retail spending will result in 2 billion deliveries, according to Jupiter Media Metrix, mainly by third party carriers (UPS, Federal Express and the U.S. Postal Service being major examples).

The retail grocery trade in developed countries has profound social and economic impact on the whole of society. It accounts for 30 to 50% of all retail spending on physical products, depending on income levels and definitions (Wileman and Jary 1997). As each person in a cash-based economy buys food, this puts retail grocers in a market class of their own. It has given rise to sophisticated networks of supermarket chains expanding by virtue of their advantages of economy of scale, buying power, brand marketing and cross marketing with loyalty and group promotion packages.

The emergence of larger retail operators has enabled the use of more efficient methods of distribution. Over time, wholesalers have more or less disappeared from many of the retail markets, with large retailers dealing directly with manufacturers. This trend has probably been greatest in the grocery retail market; between 1982 and 1992, retail turnover increased by 125 per cent whilst turnover from delivered wholesale trade increased by only 59 per cent.

The method of delivery has also changed enormously as retailers become more efficient. Before the emergence of multiple retailers, manufacturers or wholesalers made most deliveries to retailers. Such deliveries were of an assortment of products to individual retail outlets. Nowadays, manufacturers tend to deliver large amounts of a particular product in each delivery to a retailer's own centralised warehouse. The retailer has effectively internalised the wholesaling and much of the transportation function. Centralised warehousing leads to reduced stock levels, reduced delivery visits per store, reduction of necessary storage space in stores themselves, fewer incidents of running out of stocks and empty shelves in the outlet, and lower shrinkage rates.

3. FULFILMENT AND E-GROCERS

When delivering physical goods there are three key delivery and logistics drivers to business sustainability. These are sales concentration (the value of sales per square kilometre), population density and total population (Laseter, Houston et al.).

Population density and sales concentration set upper limits on revenue expectations for aspiring e-grocers; and based on the low overall population size and density, modest ones in most parts of Australia except perhaps Melbourne and Sydney. But the costs of delivering must also be considered in relation to this density.

There are many factors any e-grocer must consider in moving its online orders that last mile. The actual solution is set by the nature of the product and the customer expectations inherent in the business model for the e-grocer – speed required, range of deliveries, conditions of delivery, bundled services (eg. COD, signature on delivery, etc). These factors greatly affect the costs, and can significantly impact the overall profitability of the operator; indeed its very survival (Harty 2000; Bannister 2001; Colin 2001; Hoyt 2001; Mendelson 2001; Griffith 2002).

The e-grocery delivery model is extreme. It is driven by customer expectations, health regulations, and perishability factors, picking stringency issues, varying storage requirements of product, traditional alternatives, and potentially high delivery overheads (table 1).

Item	Notes
4-temperature vehicle	$200K capital cost + increased running costs
Complex pick & pack	Many items, temperature variation
Same-day delivery requirement	Customer expectations
Intelligent picking	Quality of produce, knowledge of fruit/veg, expiry dates

Table 1: Typical fulfilment requirements for an e-grocer

There is certainly no shortage of information on these aspects (eg. (Barsh, Crawford et al. 2000)), but for the most part they are associated with particular business models at a particular point in time (or with a particular goal). This has lead to the appearance of a plethora of fulfilment models, each of which can be successful in one situation and yet fail in another (Reynolds 2000; Colin 2001). But is it possible that these different models may be different aspects of the same one; each aspect being appropriate for a different phase of the business's operation, and the type of operation itself? Tacit in many explanations of delivery models is that any particular delivery model for an e-grocer is scalable for all densities and any customer volume. Evidence presented in this paper suggests this is not so. There are in fact, several discrete alternatives for delivery, which become appropriate for different volume and density conditions.

4. EVIDENCE OF A DEVELOPING COST INFRASTRUCTURE FROM A START-UP FULFILMENT ORGANISATION

Data provided by a third-party fulfilment operator, a large Australian National organisation (ANO) forms the basis for this model (ANO 2003). ANO is a long-established fulfilment, logistics, delivery and courier business which facilities other businesses as an alliance partner. It is uniquely placed to provide insight into costing and fulfilment processes for diverse industries.

Relevance of ANO's experience

ANO presented an unusual opportunity to study emerging fulfilment processes for several reasons.

a) Its large size, significant market share, high customer profile and well-developed sales/marketing/promotions infrastructure, and overall brand power, which allowed rapid acceptance of the services being offered.
b) The long term profit focus which reduced the pressures on achieving quick-hit successes at the expense of long term success strategies.
c) Rapid mobilisation due to an existing logistics capability, which allowed leverage across the whole delivery, pick/pack, cross-dock, and warehousing range of services.
d) ANO had the ability to change organisational structures/sizes rapidly in line with needs, through redeployment and secondment of key resources.
e) Significant budget was available to implement and acquire necessary resources.

f) Ongoing financial analysis was available, to assist with recommending new structures, infrastructures, capabilities and pricing/costing models.

The business goals

ANO sought to capitalise on existing infrastructure and profile to establish a presence in the emerging online retailer market as an extension to existing fulfilment that represented its core market. It recognised that online retailing will, not only attract new customers but also absorbing some from others. This led to the recognition that it needed to attract a share of this emerging channel to protect its existing market share.

ANO wanted to differentiate itself by being an early-entrant provider of specialist capabilities tailored for e-fulfilment.

The startup strategy

In developing a specific online retailing fulfilment service, ANO adopted an underpinning strategy of using existing capabilities to provide the service to rapidly turn "on" or "off" (from an e-fulfilment perspective) any delivery, logistics, warehouse, pick & pack, courier or regular delivery service at very short notice, with little barriers to setting up, and with few capital costs. This approach was taken to allow a dynamic e-fulfilment organisation to be piloted in the face of unpredictable market demand Additionally, the organisation took a strategic view of building this business, concentrating initially on developing accurate, cost-effective internal capabilities and attracting external markets rather than chasing early profits.

As the market becomes firm, ANO is building appropriate separate, bigger-scale but less dynamic, infrastructures, and attention is switching to profit.

To determine the most appropriate resources and capabilities at any point in the organisation's development of this business, analyses were undertaken which quantified:

- Direct per unit costs to deliver a particular capability;
- Basic resource availability from existing functions;
- Leverage through economies of scale (by combining e-fulfilment and existing fulfilment service volumes);
- Costs to scale up existing functions (rather than setting them up specifically);
- Fixed costs.

These analyses were undertaken prior to initiating the project as a whole, using projected market data. As this data firmed, and as the service grew from its inception, the analyses were repeated regularly and if necessary, a different approach was constructed at each step. The catalyst for this step was a combination of – changes in customer volume, customer density and/or resource capability/availability. Because the e-fulfilment service was sold quite discretely from other services, it was possible to monitor customer activity and continuously build a picture of alternative and optimal solutions based on these parameters.

Delivery Approach

Services offered to business customers included picking up from their premises, and delivery to another specified metropolitan location within 4 – 5 business hours. Thus, a morning pick-up would be delivered the same afternoon, while an afternoon delivery would be delivered the following morning. This schedule applied to a clearly defined region. Some (outer) parts of the metropolitan area were specifically excluded because of the low density of businesses. Any deliveries required outside the time or area constraints would be delivered by special means using ad hoc arrangements. These were "one-off" situations undertaken to support customer-service. Most customers were regular subscribers to the service, all with a standard pick-up point, but often multiple drop-off points.

Pickups and deliveries were undertaken (by contractors) in business hours. The delivery region was divided into four delivery "runs" (figure 1). Each run was a roughly defined "spoke", using a warehouse/loading bay as a common "hub". This was calculated as being the minimum to provide delivery guarantees (time and range) that had been set. A single delivery contractor would eventually service each of these runs. Though discrete, the actual route of the "run" varied each day depended on the exact address of both pickups and deliveries. Contractors utilised vans and planned their routes so all pickups and deliveries could be transacted with maximum efficiency.

Thus, contractors had a roughly fixed route which had to be navigated in a fixed time,

This structure imposed eventual maxima on the number of pickups and deliveries that could be undertaken by a single contractor. The actual number of deliveries was governed by transporting issues such as traffic conditions, parking availability, locating obscure addresses, and also the speed of the actual pickup and delivery process, itself a function of any added services (eg. obtaining a signature, collecting cash).

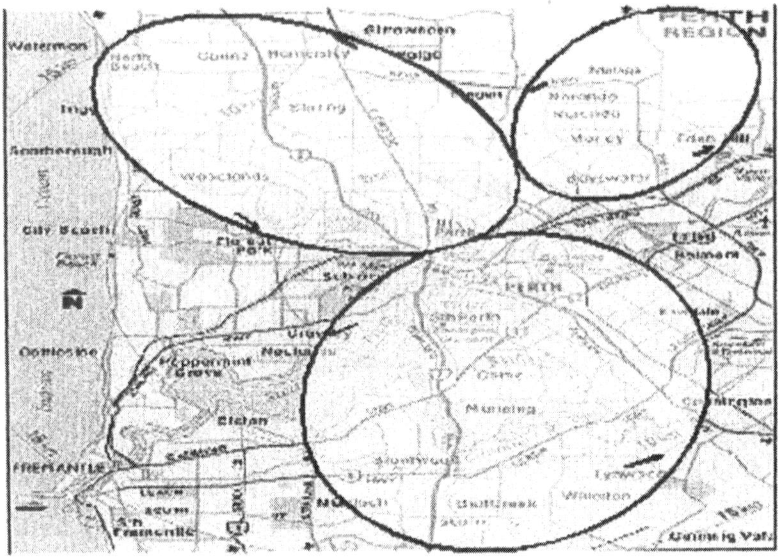

Figure 1. Structure of delivery routes

5. THE PHASES

Figure 2 shows the average parcel cost for given daily delivery volumes, calculated frequently, based on fixed and variable costs at any particular time. Whenever volume of deliveries increased, the costs were recalculated.

As can be seen, economies of scale appeared. However analysis revealed that the cost trend is not a linear or even a stepwise reduction of cost (often seen in cost verses volume plots), but consists of various different segments.

Seven discrete steps in evolving e-fulfilment capabilities were observed. At the time of completion of the observations, ANO had passed through three of them, and had identified and was preparing for the next stages.

We defined each step as "requiring a restructure of relevant business processes to adapt to evolving volume and cost conditions". So doing, at each phase ANO identified resource requirements, payment methods, and associated infrastructure requirements.

It also developed a Spreadsheet model to calculate cost and volume relationships for the particular phase being operated in. This model then served to monitor financial performance of the project. The mathematics for each phase was not complex but involved several variables – and different ones – for each phase.

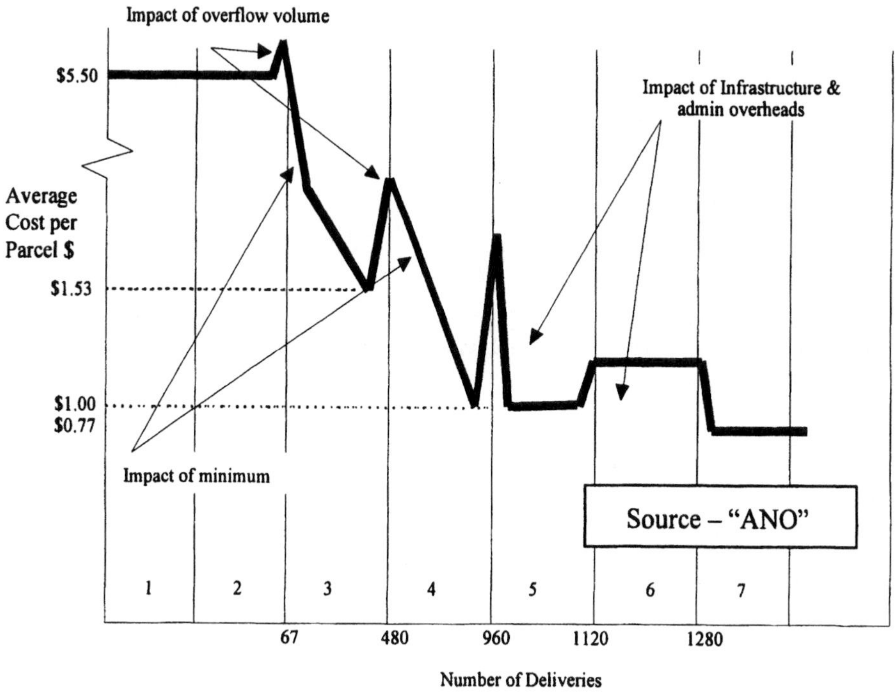

Figure 2: Cost characteristics of fulfilment implementation, showing approximate volume breaks.

It is valuable to include the mathematics here as it serves to explain the underlying driving mechanism.

Phase 1: Ad hoc delivery

As the first e-fulfilment orders were received, they were delivered via couriers, and by special arrangement with staff. Few systems and no cost or performance contracts were in place. Cost of delivery was dictated by normal courier/delivery costs and fixed at around $5.00 per delivery and less than 20Kg.

$$C_1 = c_o * V$$

where

C_1 = total daily costs, phase 1

c_o = commercial delivery cost per item, using ad hoc carriers

V = unit volume of deliveries

Phase 2: Low volume outsourced arms length arrangements

As a steady flow of orders built up, arrangements were made with contract service providers. The deliveries were pooled into regular contract services. Taxis were used when the other services were full or did not meet promised delivery timelines.

$$C_2 = (c_s * V_s) + (c_o * V_o)$$

where
C_2 = total daily costs, phase 2
c_s = commercial delivery cost per item, standard items
c_o = commercial delivery cost per item, overflow items
V_s = unit volume of deliveries, standard items
V_o = unit volume of deliveries, overflow items

Phase 3: Startup of defined delivery "runs"

When sufficient volumes justified it, basic routes were put into place, though they were not yet evolved into the 4 spokes of the final delivery pattern. These were based on a definable delivery run. They were resourced by contractors with their own general-purpose vehicles, who were offered a fixed daily fee. Thus, this phase built on the previous phase. Ad hoc (taxi) services were still used to meet specific overflow demands.

$$C_3 = C_2 + c_g + c_a$$

where
C_3 = total daily costs, phase 3.
C_2 = costs, phase 2
c_g = minimum payment guarentees to contractors (regardless of V)
c_a = emerging administration costs

Phase 4: Minimum Regional delivery runs with high-percentage regional coverage & low capital investment strategy

As volumes grew, the initial rounds were expanded and multiplied to provide delivery to guaranteed standards throughout a region. This required 4 rounds - the spokes.

During this period, minimum payment guarantees were still in place for delivery contractors. There was considerable attention placed on process efficiency, and aligning capabilities with customer promises during this phase. Also, all deliveries were handled by contractors, thus precluding the use of overflow or ad hoc services.

$$C_4 = (c_s * n_s) + C_{a2}$$

where
C_4 = total daily costs, phase 4
c_s = fixed daily costs per spoke
n_s = number of spokes
C_{a2} = increasing administration costs

Phase 5: Sophisticated regional delivery runs

As rounds began to fill, further analysis (now with significant numbers of transactions and substantial trend information) was undertaken to re-align and refine delivery rounds.

Particular attention was paid to parcel size (volume and weight), number of parcels per delivery and per round (ie. density of deliveries). Also during this period the intention (this phase has not yet occurred) is to reduce minimum payment guarantees and negotiate longer-term contracts at per-parcel rates reflecting higher volume and overall contractor revenue expectations.

Importantly, the building of a purpose-built infrastructure will begin. This calls for cross-dock, and loading/unloading facilities, management and administration staff.

$$C_5 = (c_{s2} * V_s) + C_{\text{admin}} + C_{assets}$$

where
C_5 = total daily costs, phase 5
C_{admin} = increased administration & booking costs
C_{assets} = costs of maintaining assets
c_{s2} = commercial delivery cost per item, renegotiated contracts
V_s = unit volume of deliveries, standard items

Phase 6: Growing regional delivery runs

As volumes increase, analysis by ANO indicates that emphasis should be placed on efficiently filling existing delivery runs and scaling up volume. Where one contractor had serviced each round, multiple contractors on some rounds will be required. Extra flexibility and cost effectiveness in deliveries will be the result.

Additionally, contractor payment emphasis will be shifted, from a "per-parcel" to a "per-delivery" basis, to better position the service for accepting business-to-business assignments, where multiple deliveries to single sites is expected.

$$C_6 = C_5 + C_2$$

where
C_6 = total daily costs, phase 6
C_5 = total daily costs, phase 5
C_2 = total daily costs, phase 2

Phase 7: Range-increasing capabilities

Once the operation was proven the major pressure was created by the potential to increase market; primarily based on offering similar services over a wider geographic range.

Analysis indicated this would be best accomplished through:

- alliances with other fulfilment/delivery services;
- joining of other regional e-fulfilment groups being set up in other states.

Financial implications have not been analysed for this stage, but ANO's analysts consider its approach to be to focus on more complex (sophisticated) administration structures, and online systems to automate and integrate processes. Economies of scale, and increased market penetration for national customers are seen as the main drivers to reach this stage.

The physical characteristics of these phases are summarised in Table 2

Cost Item	Phases						
	1	*2*	*3*	*4*	*5*	*6*	*7*
Ad hoc component (courier)	●	●	●				
Inhouse arms length contractor		●					
Guaranteed minimum volumes			●	●			
Committed in-house contractors			●	●	●	●	
Significant overflow expected				●	●		
Significant administration				●	●	●	●
Infrastructure (x-dock, systems, etc)						●	●
Specialised in-house contractors							●
Alliances							●

Table 2: Summary of features in each step

6. TRIGGERING THE STEPS

The model shows distinct phases, each with different cost and logistical characteristics. But these phases are not merely a recognition of these differences. They appear to be actively "triggered" by factors directly related to delivery volume.

Thus, each phase appears to be triggered by volume overload condition existing in the previous phase. This results in a rapidly increasing percentage of deliveries overflowing into a backup, high-cost service, and gives rise to a changed break-even cost structure that soon justifies increased resources required for the next phase.

Why this is so uncovers a fundamentally important aspect of e-fulfilment infrastructures: For any particular logistical, organisational and financial configuration of the service, there is a minimum and a maximum sustainable volume.

Another feature evident in this case is that the unit delivery cost is not optimal until the phase is almost completed. This is a function of overheads that are required to establish each stage. In the early stages, these take the form of minimum guarantees for contractors, but eventually include major infrastructure projects and administrative structures.

A phase appears to be cost-optimised just before overflow conditions increase unit costs and trigger the next phase.

7. IMPLICATIONS FOR NEW E-FULFILMENT OPERATIONS

ANO offers a rare insight into start-up delivery cost dynamics. The most appropriate costing, resourcing, service offerings, and infrastructure development is determined, then immediately implemented.

It is unlikely that all these stages can be shown to occur in other e-fulfilment start-up businesses. It is more likely that management determines a model, which then works sub-optimally until a break-even, or target volume/service level/service region is reached.

In other words, we contend that this case demonstrates a "best case" cost behaviour model, and that the costs it suggests will be the lowest that can be expected for a similarly resourced operation servicing (comparable to the Australian metropolitan) client base. In addition, since the structure and resourcing is quite orthodox, this we believe, has wide applicability to start-up e-fulfilment operations.

8. PRELIMINARY EVIDENCE ON PRICING STRUCTURES FOR AUSTRALIAN E-GROCERS

A short display of typical delivery charges for e-grocers in Australian cities is shown in Table 3. Based on discussions with ANO executives and research in progress into 40 Australian e-grocers, we believe this model is at work in most fulfilment operations.

ANO sees the logistics and fulfilment industry as a straightforward one, with relatively few fundamental methods of delivering the service. Warehouses, transport operations, courier operations and the like are operated similarly by competitors in the industry. Competitive advantage is occasionally achieved by a radical change to processes or services, but much more often by slight advantages in cost efficiencies, ability to leverage existing delivery networks and warehouses. Many industry costs are similar between competitors, set by local rental prices, award wage rates, and market-value courier (and other) resources; all shared by all competitors in a region. Supporting this scenario are the closely aligned prices and absence of raw discounting[29] that exists in the industry.

Our model describes costs in terms of these basic components, and so we consider it reasonable to apply it to the e-grocers' deliveries; at least at a macro level that can distinguish between, say, phase 1 and phase 3 operations. The only added complication for e-grocers appears to be the need to deal with perishability issues, which demand the use of special "4-temperature" delivery vehicles (that is, they carry product at frozen, chilled, room and oven temperature). Such vehicles cost approximately A$200,000, so place an immediate overhead cost on operations that must be factored into any cost calculations. Though we do not make these calculations in this paper, we observe (in table 3) that delivery charges for Australian e-grocers are often broken into separate charges for dry goods (without issues of perishability), and for perishables. We believe this reflects the differences in economics and infrastructure at work.

The study indicates also that the major Australian e-grocery suppliers are fulfilling at prices that cover even phase 1 costs, and apparently at a profitable level. (A more detailed examination of this data is under preparation for a forthcoming paper submitted to Bled 2004)

[29] But there is fierce competition nevertheless, and also much opportunity for discounting based on marginal prices charged for spare capacity – for example, of a truck delivering to a particular location.

That this is sustainable is indicated by the stability of these services, which have not been subjected to significant change in 3 years, and all players surveyed have been in existence for (at least) that length of time.

Supplier	Cities *=some areas	Delivery Charge ($A)	Delivery Charge (A$), Current (from web site)
Woolworths (Homeshop)	Syd *, Canb, Melb	$12.50 (min order $60)	$12.50 (min of $30)
Coles	Syd *, Melb *	$13.69 (min order $60)	$12.50 (2hr window), $9.95 (4hr window), no min orders-Syd, $9.95 (2hr)/$7.95 (4hr) Melb. Different product prices to normal grocery lines.
Greengrocer	Syd, Melb, some regions	$4.00 refrig (min order $25)	(Now through Woolworths) System under restructure following takeover
Shopfast	Syd – metro, central coast & Woolongong	$6.55, no min order	$5.95 to $10.95 depending on delivery time slot
Dewsons	Perth *	NA	$6.93 +6% (full delivery) 6% pickup $6.93 delivery only
Electrolley	Perth	NA	$5.95 (unrefrigerated) for selected items more than $30 per order, $13.65 otherwise. For refrigerated, $75 min. Min overall order=$30

Table 3: Delivery charges for significant Australian e-grocers (NineMSN 2003)

9. CONCLUSIONS & DIRECTIONS FOR FURTHER RESEARCH

The ANO case provides valuable insights into the dynamics of providing an e-fulfilment capability for online retailers. It supports the very strong relationship between customer density and cost of the "last mile" so often quoted by authors (Laseter and al; Laseter, Houston et al.). However, where there is an implied assumption that this relationship is somehow linear, or at least a continuous function based on static forces, ANO shows that several quite discrete phases occur as the operation responds to demand pressures.

The immediacy of response, and the readiness to adjust to needs without too much short-term sensitivity to cost (ANO was/is aiming at positioning for a dominant operation, so sees this as a pilot and, to some extent, an "experimental platform") is unusual in a business. More often, such organisations may not have the capabilities, resources, and/or the will to adapt and divert them.

But this does not mean that ANO's response and approach to e-fulfilment is different from other organisations. On the contrary, the services it is building are entirely orthodox. Indeed, the value of this study is that it provides transferable insight relevant to many other organisations.

Underpinning this, we believe there are four major drivers:

- the need to respond to immediate customer demand;
- the need to maintain this response at the lowest cost;
- the need to prepare for response to the next phase of anticipated customer demand, and;
- the desire to minimise risk at any point;

This creates a response pattern that consists of discrete steps which represent the organisation's need to establish structures and capabilities that last long enough to serve their purpose (to meet customer needs at the lowest cost), yet provide a relative degree of stability of processes and resources (to be manageable and practical). At each point, the organisation establishes the least-risk path of meeting these needs, which (in ANO's case) means making most use of direct cost options while delaying implementation of capital costs until trends indicate reduced risk.

Cost efficiency demands for deliveries, in turn, have lead to a push for maximum units of delivery to saturate a particular delivery run. This translates to a lower per-unit cost as volume increases. But saturation of the runs carries with it costs in the form of expensive overflow delivery processes. As this is not a cost efficient approach, it then serves as a catalyst to create a newer, more appropriate and cost efficient structure. However, once created, its (new) capabilities are underused, so driving up the per-unit delivery cost again.

Complicating this situation is the difference in cost dynamics in each phase. It is not just a matter of scaling particular costs up or down, and having the money in the bank to cover the situation. Costs are controlled by making decisions about how resources are allocated, and how payments are made to delivery resources. In different phases, it is necessary to switch from per-hour payments (to ensure availability of contractors) to per unit payments (to ensure minimisation of per unit costs) to per-delivery payments (to maximise potential revenue on a delivery run).

As volume increases, various administration and infrastructure tasks become significant and must be addressed. These are not as reversible as some of the contractor-related decisions. Building a cross-dock facility for instance, is an investment that is not easily reversed and must be justified by activity projections that are both favourable and reliable.

The ANO case also shows that there appears to be an appropriate response to delivery volumes, and with it a characteristic set of cost dynamics, and with those a minimum attainable per-unit delivery cost. We believe the services that ANO is building are driven directly by customer demands. This organisation's response is not radical, and we would expect similar approaches on providing these services from other industry entrants. The equations developed in this paper therefore can be transferred to other organisations.

We note that some organisations, particularly those extending from off-line to online operations, will telescope some of the steps together, for instance delaying the establishment of committed delivery resources. How they approach this will depend on the competition for reducing delivery price. Some customers may be insensitive to delivery price, for instance where there are few delivery alternatives or where the delivery price is only a small percentage of the price of the item being delivered. Where this occurs, it is possible to maintain the convenience of an ad hoc service.

However, where large grocers require a third party e-fulfilment service provider, we believe this model will operate.

For such organisations, we expect the phase transitions to continue until a continuously scalable operation has been reached. In the ANO case, this may represent a situation we would call Phase 8. Such a phase would be characterised by low, and relatively constant per-unit costs. This goal provides a major driver for the creation of large, wide-distribution organisations and may indicate strong pressure to create a few dominant e-fulfilment providers in the future of this market.

Using this model, it should be possible to estimate minimum achievable costs for any volume of units delivered. How many units can be delivered is based on the total delivery potential and the density. Total delivery potential sets the maximum rate of units delivered in a time period, while the delivery density influences the costs of delivering those units. Thus, Figure 2 can be used as a guide to establishing achievable costs, while facilitating planning for projected activity.

For Australian conditions, it suggests that potential delivery costs can vary from around \$5.50 in phase 1 to under \$0.75 for phase 7 operations. Ironically, Australia is not a densely populated country, with only two cities (Melbourne and Sydney) with high population densities. So, whether these volumes can be achieved equally across the nation is debatable in the short term. Exploring this aspect provides a direction for current research.

The material adduced shows that, despite fears that online ordering and home delivery would be a dead duck from the start, Australian e-grocers are delivering their goods and charging prices that allow them to completely cover the costs of a phase e-fulfilment model. Under these circumstances, it is certainly possible that these businesses are able to operate the e-fulfilment component of the business.

Integrating the data presented within Table 2 with that of Figure 2, we note that consumers are demonstrating willingness to pay the necessary additional cost for the selection of a home delivery channel

The limiting problems of scaling an interactive home shopping service do not necessarily arise from the "last mile" component. On the contrary, given reasonable urban density an increase in delivery volume enables dramatic reduction in cost-per-parcel.

The phased model indicates that to lower costs, competitive pressures have the potential to drive fulfilment operations associated with e-grocers to become more sophisticated in their operations – essentially driving them through stages two to six.

In terms of cost competition, margins for the groceries themselves are relatively lean, so we predict that when it comes, these battles will be fought on the delivery front, where there is still much fat. At potential least unit cost for a stage 6 operation, of around $0.77, the current prices being charged, of $5.50+ leave considerable room for downward pressures to impact delivery charges.

The ANO case describes the cost dynamics of a single startup fulfilment operation targeting e-businesses. In 2002, there were well over 40 e-grocers in Australia who must be using operations with similar characteristics (Ltd 2002), and many appear to have been in existence for 2 to 3 years, indicating some degree of stability in their pricing strategies and offerings. Almost all were offering customer deliveries integrated to their online product, and these deliveries were either performed as a function of the business or an outsourced supplier/partner. Without exception, delivery charges represented what we would call Phase 1 costs; that is, based on ad hoc delivery. We are interested in analysing the changing price structures as competition increases in such an environment. Indeed, there is some indication that the major bricks and mortar grocers are positioning to compete in the online channel, and the nature of their fulfilment operations and offerings will provide further insight into, and expansion of our model.

We note that net profit margins are not traditionally high in groceries (3% to 6% are commonly recognised net returns), and with current e-grocery delivery charges, a significant profit stream may well exist that is at least as significant as the margins from the groceries themselves. Under such conditions, we speculate that competitive e-grocery offerings may well be based on the delivery price and characteristics rather than the groceries. This will in turn influence the very nature of the e-grocery industry, impacting the players, their delivery performance, and perhaps the viability of the industry. Analysing Australian e-grocers as they respond to increasing competition, will elucidate this.

Our study has also highlighted the strong connection between customer density and the potential for efficacy of last mile deliveries. With Australia's highly urbanised population based in relatively isolated cities of different densities we have an opportunity to further examine the dynamics of this model. Using it, we can make predictions about e-grocers' fulfilment offerings in different cities, and so test the operation of the model more fully. Papers are in progress focussing in on both these areas.

REFERENCES

ANO (2003) Personal correspondence and discussions supplied and held under conditions of corporate and client confidentiality to Paul Alexander

Bannister, C. (2001). "Shopping simply by site." Retail World 54(5): 16.

Barsh, J., B. Crawford, et al. (2000). "How e-tailing can rise from the ashes." McKinsey Quarterly(Number 3, 2000): 98-109.

Bos, G. (1999). Virtual Supermarket Index. 1999.

Colin, J. (2001). The impact of e-commerce on transport. Joint OECD/ECMT Seminar, Paris.

Griffith, V. (2002). "Welcome to Tesco, your "glocal" superstore." Strategy+Business (www.strategy-business.com)?(?): ?

Harty, C. (2000). "Australia Post wins Coles contract." Retail World 53(23): 23.

Hogarth-Scott, S. and S. Parkinson (1994). "Barriers and stimuli to the use of information technology in retailing." International Review of Retail, Distribution and Consumer Research 4(3): 257-275.

Hoyt, D. (2001). "Tesco Delivers." Graduate School of Business, Standford University Case Number: EC-32.

IMRG (2003). IMRG e-Retail Sales Data Survey. 2003.

Laseter, T. and e. al The last mile to somewhere. Strategy+Business: 1-5.

Laseter, T., P. Houston, et al. The last mile to nowhere. Strategy+Business: 40-48.

Laseter, T., P. Houston, et al. (2000). The last mile to nowhere:Flaws and fallacies in Internet home delivery schemes. Strategy+Business, Booz Allen Hamilton Inc. 2003: 40-48.

Laseter, T., P. Houston, et al. (2001). The last mile to somewhere. Strategy+Business, Booz Allen Hamilton Inc. 2003: 29-34.

London Economics (1997). Competition in retailing. London, Office of Fair Trading.

Ltd, P. A. G. P. (2002). Australian e-Grocers Page, Professional Assignments Group Pty Ltd.

Mendelson, H. (2001). "Webvan: The new and improved milkman." Graduate School of Business, Standford University Case Number: EC-31.

Murphy, D. (2001). "When speed is king." Far Eastern Economic Review 164(7): 36.

NineMSN (2003). NineMSN Fact sheet & vendor sites, NineMSN.com. 2003.

Reynolds, J. (2000). "Supply chain, distribution and fulfilment." International Journal of Retail & Distribution Management 28(10): 417-444.

Schuster, A. and B. Sporn (1998). "Potential for online grocery shopping in the urban area of Vienna." Electronic Markets 8(2): 13-16.
Wileman and M. Jary (1997). Retail power plays: From trading to brand leadership. New York, Ney York University Press.

E-BUSINESS GOVERNANCE: A CO-EVOLUTIONARY APPROACH TO E-BUSINESS STRATEGY FORMULATION

Janice M. Burn and Colin G. Ash
School of Management Information Systems, Edith Cowan University, Perth, WA

Abstract: e-Business evolution is generally presented as a highly dynamic process where organisations focus on business transformation and the creation of the agile extended enterprise. What is not well understood however is how organisations can plan for this process and whether standard business strategy formulation approaches can apply in such a dynamic environment. The research presented in this paper resulted from a longitudinal analysis of e-business governance and implementation involving eleven international organisations over a four-year period using multiple interviews and extensive secondary data collection. Three separate research models were used to analyse different stages of e-business growth and the results of this multi-stage analysis consolidated into a staged model of e-business governance. This model identifies three different orientations of the business during the transformation process as Integration, Differentiation and Virtualisation and associated with these three different strategic formulation approaches which will align with e-business governance. These together provide for a co-evolutionary approach to e-governance.

1. THE CO-EVOLUTIONARY APPROACH TO STRATEGY

There are many existing theoretical approaches to strategy - designed strategy, emergent strategy, strategy as revolution, etc and yet few examples of organisations applying these well defined models to secure competitive advantage in an e-business environment of constant change. It may be argued that these frameworks are inappropriate and redundant in the post-net era. Beinhocker (1999) suggests that what is needed is a model of a world where innovation, change and uncertainty are the natural state of competitive engagement. Strategy may be associated with many contradictions and dilemmas as evidenced by the Red Queen effect (Kauffman, 1995). The Red Queen in Through the Looking Glass remarks "It takes all the running you can do to keep in the same place". In a system of co-evolution, when the predator learns to run faster, the prey starts to climb trees and then the predator develops alternative means of pursuit. Long term sustainable advantage is not possible without continual adaptation. A study of the performance of more than 400 organisations over thirty years reveals that companies find it difficult to maintain higher performance levels than their competitors for more than about five years at a time (Beinhocker, 1999). In this new sophisticated global e-marketplace advantage tends to be even more fleeting. (Burn and Hackney, 2000).

In a system of co-evolution, adaptation can be seen as the attempt to optimise systems riddled with conflicting constraints. It is therefore critical to reconcile opposing issues of tension, dilemmas or polarities. Traditional strategic approaches are incomplete since they over emphasise executives' abilities to forecast and predict in a highly competitive, high-velocity market and under emphasise the challenge of actually creating effective strategies. Given uncertain environments, strategies must also be robust and allow for the organisation to pursue a package of potentially conflicting issues at the same time (Hackney and Burn, 2001).

This process of evolutionary search is continuous but needs to be supported by a portfolio of strategic approaches, which reflect the orientation of the business at its stage of e-business development. Successful adaptation also implies co-evolution between the organisation and the strategy model. Not only must strategy models be adapted to fit the unique characteristics of an organisation but also organisations need to evolve to benefit from the lessons incorporated into the strategic model and so both the organisation and model continually change and learn.

This view is supported by Eisenhardt and Galunic (2000) who point out that the new roles of collaboration in e-Business are actually counter-intuitive and that collaboration does not naturally lead to synergy. Where synergies are achieved the managers have mastered the corporate strategic process of coevolving. These managers routinely change the web of collaborative links - everything from information exchanges to shared assets to multi-business strategies - among businesses. The result is a shifting web of relationships that exploits fresh opportunities for synergies and drops deteriorating ones, as shown in Table 1.

	Traditional Collaboration	Coevolution
Form of collaboration	Frozen links among static businesses	Shifting webs among evolving businesses
Objectives	Efficiency and economies of scale	Growth, agility, and economies of scope
Internal dynamics	Collaborate	Collaborate and compete
Focus	Content of collaboration	Content and number of collaborative links
Corporate role	Drive Collaboration	Set Collaborative Content
Business role	Execute collaboration	Drive/execute collaboration
Incentive	Varied	Self-interest, based on individual business unit performance
Business metrics	Performance against budget, preceding year, or sister-business performance	Performance against competitors in growth, share and profits

Table 1. Traditional Collaboration Versus Coevolution (after Eisenhardt and Galunic, 2000)

To be successful in this new climate, however, organisations have to learn new approaches to planning for collaborative systems and to manage e-business enabled cycles of innovation (Wheeler, 2002; Zahra and George, 2002). Few studies have explored the dynamics of e-business strategy and scant information is available on how to implement new paradigms successfully and how to ensure more effective e-business governance as a result (Damanpour, 2001; Kallio et al, 2002).

This paper reports on the findings from multiple case studies of e-business projects in ERP enabled organisations. Each organisation was investigated in a three-stage study over four years, using three theoretical models of e-business implementations to evaluate facilitators and inhibitors of success. The key findings from each case study were captured into a staged model for e-business governance and related to a dynamic strategic planning model that can be applied across all stages of growth of the extended enterprise.

2. STRATEGIC PLANNING FOR E-BUSINESS

Fahey et al (2001) state

"e-business embodies the most pervasive, disruptive, and disconcerting form of change: it leaves no aspect of managing organisations untouched, it challenges long-accepted business models, and organisation leaders have little to draw on from their past experience to manage its effects. In particular, its capacity to transform business processes is no longer in dispute. - - -Senior executives - thus confront a central challenge: How should they endeavour to capture, analyse, and project the transformational impact of e-business on their organisation's most critical or core processes?" (p.890).

Existing strategy models are unequal to this task (Riggins, 1999; Pant and Ravichandran,2001; Colman et al, 2001; Floris et al, 2001). Planning for such systems has to encompass capabilities for managing, measuring and evaluating organisational capabilities to create value across the network of alliances and hence requires evolutionary approaches which can be tailored to organisational needs at different stages of e-business growth (Wheeler, 2002; Ash and Burn, 2003). This whole process is referred to as e-Business governance. This includes an examination of assets, resources and competencies to align e-business strategies with corporate strategy and relate the outcomes to corporate productivity (Chang et al, 2003; Kallio et al, 2002).

In order to study this environment in detail the authors embarked on a longitudinal study of organisations implementing large-scale e-business applications based around Internet enabled ERP systems over a four-year period. The eleven organisations were visited three times during this period and a minimum of three interviewees participated on each visit. The structured interviews were focused on three separate models of e-business change to investigate different aspects of e-business governance and the results from these investigations brought together into a model for e-business governance. The use of three research models was specifically intended to give breadth to the study and allow the incorporation of a variety of strategic views, which informed the planning process.

3. THEORETICAL FRAMEWORK

Figure 1 illustrates e-business implementations from the perspective of three strategic theories: Virtual Organising, e-Business Change, and Benefits of B2B.

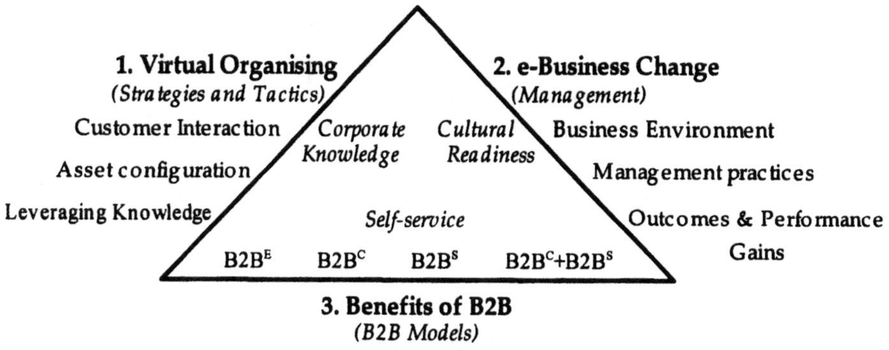

Figure1. Three views of e-business Implementations

1. Virtual Organising strategies provides a model of e-business evolution. Progress is along the three dimensions of customer interaction, asset configuration, and leveraging knowledge (Venkatraman and Henderson, 1998).
2. e-Business Change (eBC) is illustrated by a model in which progress is across eleven interrelated components based on research in the areas of organisational change, strategic management innovation, and information systems evaluation" (Guha et al, 1997).
3. Strategies for e-business relates to a model in which e-business activity is correlated against e-business benefits within a set of B2B models (Carlson, 1995). Benefits of B2B are illustrated by a two dimensional model where value returns are directly proportional to the level of integration of e-business activity.

Each model reflects a different strategic focus: organisational strategy, change management, strategies and e-business strategies. The final conceptual framework is described in terms of a dynamic strategy formulation model for e-business innovation. The approach is a co-evolutionary process between alliances where there is a continual review of alignment of the e-business transformation against business orientation. This is quite distinct from the 'one size fits all' approach of centralised planning and allows strategy to evolve with changing market conditions.

4. METHODOLOGY

The study was carried out over a four year period and followed a structured case study approach. This involved multiple interviews in eleven international organisations which were developing extended e-business applications based around their e-ERP systems as shown in Table 2. The research questions in association with the three models identified from the literature on the topic were used to develop a composite case-based method. These questions set the main research objectives to test three practitioner "theories-in-use" namely, benefits of e-business implementations derived from virtual organising through e-business change management.

The research questions are presented in order of increasing theoretical complexity as:

Q.1: What factors facilitate and inhibit success of e-business transformation?

Q.2: How do organisations maximise benefits from e-business implementations?

Q.3: Is there a pattern of effective strategies for e-business governance?

Data was gathered from three sources; primary, secondary and tertiary:

i. Primary data – from semi-structured interviews conducted November 1999, June 2000, and June 2001.Three separate interviewees were identified within each organisation and revisited across the study.

ii. Secondary data – from company documents collected or sent via e-mails.

iii. Tertiary data – from case research papers written by third party specialists.

iv.

Table 2: Target Organisations with Stages of data collection,

			Interviewed			Business Model:		
			1st	2nd	3rd			
#	Case	Industry	Nov-99	Jul-00	Jun-01	$B2B^S$	$B2B^C$	$B2B^E$
1	UBS	Banking	•	•	•			•
2	Biotech	Bio-technology	•	•	•	•		
3	UNICEF	Charity	•	•	•		B2C	
4a	Dell*	Computing	•	•			•]	
4b	LSI*	Electronics	-	•	•	[•		
5	Employ-Nation/1	Employment	•	•	•			•
6	Halliburton	Engineering	•	•	•			•
7	Burtelsmann	Media	•		•	•		
8	Statoil	Oil & Gas	•	•	•	•		
9	Novartis	Pharmaceutical	•		•			•
10a	Siemens**	Science/electric	Phone &	•	•	[•	•]	
10b	(FSC)	technology.	emails	(•)			(•)	
11	The Wine Society	Wine Retailing	•	•	•		B2C	

11 cases, across 11 industries, from Australia, Europe, Scandinavia, UK, USA (ordered by industry type)

* *Dell* and *LSI* represent a B2B twin case - supplier and customer

** *Siemens* represents the parent company of Fujitsu Siemens Computers (*FSC*) division.

Semi-structured interviews were used to collect the primary research data about the eleven case organisations. It should be noted that no formal coding techniques were used but "pattern matching" applied as a data analysis technique. Consistent with a hypothetico-deductive logic approach, the researchers searched for patterns in the empirical research which were consistent with the patterns suggested by the three theoretical propositions underpinned by the three research models (Sarker and Lee, 2003, Segev and Gebauer, 2001).

Much has been written about the case-study based approach to research. Depending on the type of research to be performed they may be classified as exploratory, descriptive, or explanatory and further, theoretical, evaluative, or associational (Yin, 1994). A combination of case study types can be incorporated into an overarching framework for theory validation and ultimately creation of new theory. Case-based strategies in research are widely used in case study methodology as well as in a number of qualitative methodologies, including grounded theory development, phenomenological research method, and psychotherapy process research (Edwards, 1998).

Lee (1987) identifies four corresponding problems with case study research as a lack of controllability, deductibility, replication, and generalisability. The latter two limitations stem largely from the lack of power to randomise. However, these problems are not insurmountable and can be overcome by quality of design. Drawing from Caroll et al. (1998) a range of research methods are designed into a composite structured method (case-based) to overcome these limitations.

5. THREE PHASES OF THE RESEARCH METHOD

Figure 3 diagrams the three types of case-based research methods: exploratory, descriptive, and explanatory. Importantly, it shows the interrelationships between them:

- Exploratory Phase 1 – pilot study. Carroll et al. (1998, p.66) provide "structured-case studies" for use in the pilot study to build initial conceptual foundations, with the focus on rigour and relevance. The elements of the structured-case studies method are embedded within a research cycle with multiple inputs for two iterations.
- Descriptive Phase 2 – main study uses three views of multiple case studies. Eisenhardt (1989, p.533) provides eight research activities as the "basics" of case work for theory testing of the three research models , using multiple case studies.

- Explanatory Phase 3 – holistic study. Klein and Myers (1998) offer the key principles for interpretive field research in the "Hermeneutic circle" as the interdependent meaning of the parts to understand the whole they form.

This triangulation of methods was applied across three views of e-business. A pilot case study of nine Australian organisations helped ground the theory of the study. This was followed by a three-stage study of eleven international cases within a diverse industry context. . Finally, synthesis of the findings of three research models of the main phase of this longitudinal multi-case study, was carried out between September 1999 and June 2001. A final conceptual framework was developed in terms of e-business transformation (eBT).

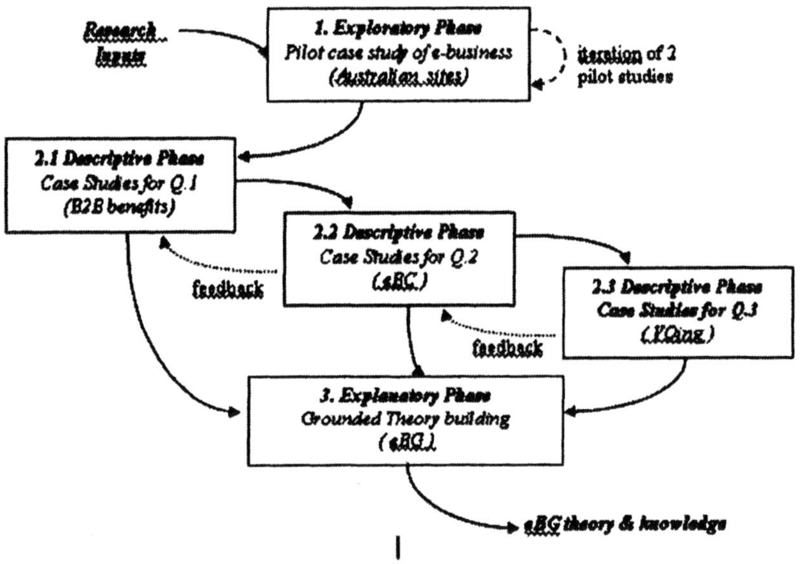

Figure 2: Composite Case-based Research Method

At each stage of the study the data collected from each set of interviews was analysed against the particular research model applied in that stage of the study. These results were used both to verify and extend the theoretical models used as a basis for the study. The full set of case material collected was used to verify all the strategic characteristics of e-business transformation and to develop a comprehensive e-business governance model.

6. E-BUSINESS GOVERNANCE MODEL

Once the three stages of the study were complete the findings were pulled together to identify whether different models of implementation reflected different stages of growth in e-business development. This supported a stage growth model with three identifiable strategic orientations governing e-business implementation

Stage 1 - Integration of technologies is critical for cost reductions and operating efficiencies along the supply chain (Coltman et al, 2001);

Stage 2 - Differentiation of products and services is critical for e-business market positioning through effective resourcing across multiple supply chains (Oliver et al, 2003; Chang et al, 2003);

Stage 3 - Demonstration of value propositions within an inter-organisational network to design and leverage multiple interdependent communities to create superior economic value across the virtual supply chain (Venkatraman and Henderson, 1998).

Table 3 represents a map of the issues distilled from the findings of this longitudinal three-stage study.

Table 3: Stages of e-Business Governance

	Stages of e-Business Governance (1999 -)	(2000 -)	(2001 -)
Business Dimensions	**Stage 1: Integration**	**Stage 2: Differentiation**	**Stage 3: Virtualisation and Realisation of Value**
Technology (virtual infrastructure)	* ICT ERP with e-Sales & e-Procurement applications.	Differential Resourcing ASP vs cost of ownership on the outsourcing spectrum	Innovative Technologies ERP and non-ERP networks for e-marketplaces
Products & Services (virtual experience)	e-Malls e-Mall integration and information exchange	* e-Branding Customisation vs standardisation, Brand identity & integrity	e-Communities Foster customer, supplier, and employee expertise. Emerging collaborative online communities
Business Models (virtual B2B interactions)	e-Commerce Integration B2B Integration of e-Sales & e-Procurement systems $B2B^C + B2B^S$	e-Positioning B2B positioning within a range open to private e-marketplaces	* e-Enterprise One2Many vs One2One Distinct focus of One2One partnerships

Examples	Remote experience of e-catalogues. More tasks, "group ware" skills for online communication.	Assemble and coordinate assets through effective use of online services	Business network to design and leverage interdependent e-communities. Dependent on relationships
	Dynamic planning focus across stages of organisational transformation		
Strategic focus	Self-service	Empowerment	Relationship building
Planning focus	Internal SCM	External SCM	Community Networks of SCM
Outcomes and Performance Gains	Improved operating efficiency (ROI)	Effective resourcing (QWL)	Virtual and economic value added (EVA)

* The diagonal cells(shaded) represent the critical stages of eBG and the arrows represent real organisational transformation with e-business

Table 3: Stages of e-Business Governance

These findings closely align with the strategic grid framework proposed by Riggins (1999) which identifies three different ways of generating value through electronic commerce as efficiency, effectiveness and strategic benefits. Whereas the EC value grid related to online storefronts only, this study shows that the model is similarly applicable to e-procurement and the extended value chain.

The results of the analysis can be mapped along the e-business stages of growth as: integration of e-business technologies for e-malls and B2B commerce, differentiation of products and services for e-business positioning, and virtualisation and the realisation of value propositions of the e-partnerships. The three shaded cells in the eBG model indicate the 'critical' elements that require a cultural shift for a real organisational transformation and represent distinct shifts in the orientation of the business. The other elements contribute to the organisation's competitive advantage.

7. CASE ANALYSIS FOR E-BUSINESS GOVERNANCE MODEL

STAGE 1: INTEGRATION

Technologies: e-ERP

The findings show that 'back-end' to 'front-end' enterprise application integration is essential to achieve savings and cost reduction. Integration of the system architecture is made possible through a variety of 'back-end', 'sell-side' and 'buy-side' systems; all 11 cases demonstrated this and the planning focus was directed towards internal efficiencies driven top-down. This represents the first 'cultural' shift where integration across different functions and processes promotes a mono-culture within the organisation.

Products and services: e-Malls

A number of cases developed their e-business systems to create integrated online sales systems offering a variety of products and services for example, Fujitsu Siemens Computers achieved integration of three groups' online sales systems. Again the focus was on efficiency and integration.

Business Models: e-Commerce B2B Integration

The integration of e-business models, $B2B^C$ with $B2B^S$ is essential to maximise efficiency gains from supporting technology infrastructure, so that people can get the job done efficiently. This extends the efficiency focus across the organisational supply chain and a typical example of this was Dell.

STAGE 2: DIFFERENTIATION

Technologies: Differential Outsourcing

The cases demonstrated a range of outsourcing options from total outsourcing (UNICEF) to partial (Fujitsu). This is the result of the organisation attempting to differentiate itself in the marketplace by focusing only on core business. While this shifts the strategic focus to an external supplier and may create additional strategic issues, it does not generally lead to extensive organisational culture change. It may well, however, create the need for extensive relationship management and failure to do this well as with UNICEF can result in a significant gap between strategic expectations and fulfillment (Levina and Ross,2003).

Products and services: e-Branding

It is at this stage that significant cultural change is experienced when organisations differentiate between brand identity and brand integrity, where 'e-branding' becomes a critical issue [30]. This requires all members of the organisation to look 'outside the box' and differentiate between corporate customers and end consumers. Bertlesmann, UNICEF, Wine Society, Dell and Fujitsu all experienced this shift as employees became empowered in their roles and participated meaningfully in the strategic process. .

Business Models: e-Positioning

At this stage the organisation repositions itself in the marketplace through e-services to the wider community. Biotech, Fujitsu, Dell and were all examples of successful differentiators through e-business. The tendency of these pioneers was to start with development of public relationship building and then shift to private relationship building between suppliers and buyers. This occurred very much at grass roots level throughout the organisation with all members embracing a 'community culture'.

STAGE 3: DEMONSTRATION OF VALUE PROPOSITIONS

Technologies: Innovative Technologies

The cases gave mixed evidence about the need to embrace advanced technologies but where this occurred it typically added value to the user communities. Halliburton's HR Intranet ERP system demonstrated a B2E value proposition. Their technology innovation was bottom-up driven and from both sides of B2E and B2G of the value chain. This bottom-up approach then provided a model for collaborative implementation of the system across the company's global e-ERP infrastructure.

Products and Services: e-Communities

A number of cases were actively exploiting e-communities through a collaborative planning approach. Statoil and UBS used Intranet employee self-service applications to develop a practice of industry-based e-communities. Dell has competence centres where customers can validate system design and configuration without disrupting their live computing network. The focus is very much on extending communities and bringing partners into the planning process.

Business Models: e-Enterprise Model

The final stage of the model is where federated planning applies and when the organisation undergoes a further cultural shift to manage multiple relationships across a global network. A pilot approach demonstrating a value proposition is shown in the One2One relationship formed by Dell and LSI. In the short term, it may be better to adopt e-commerce implementations (e-sales and e-procurement) with new customers and suppliers. This has the capability of persuading existing customers and suppliers that are more resistant to e-business change of the win-win value propositions.

Strategy Formulation model

The changing focus across the stages of the Strategic Formulation model is classified in Table 4, and each stage viewed as interdependent and supportive of each other. This is especially so in the area of *outcomes and performances objectives* where *efficiency* through employee self-service and *effectiveness* through empowerment in customer care is used to support *value adding* activities for sustained competitive advantage. Value includes complementary benefits realised for all network partners across the virtual supply chain. The interplay between strategy, e-business, change management and evaluation is crucial to the creation of dynamic capabilities and will enable organisations to gain sustainable competitive advantage (Zahra and George, 2002).

Table 4: Stages of e-Business Strategy Formulation Model

	Stage 1	Stage 2	Stage 3
Strategic focus	Self-service	Empowerment	Relationship building
Planning focus	Top-down Training Internal Organisation	Bottom-up Self-learning External Value chain community	Federated planning Value enhancement Collaboration chains Virtual networks
Outcomes and Performance Gains	Improved operating efficiency (ROI)	Effective resourcing (QWL)	Virtual and economic value added (EVA)

Key: Return on investment (ROI), Quality of working life (QWL)
Economic value added (EVA)

At stage one of the extended enterprise, the focus is very much internal with top-down planning and an emphasis on training employees to become proficient in self-service to improve operating efficiencies and increase returns on investment. The first shift comes when the enterprise extends its relationships across the full supply chain for products or services. At this stage, the focus is on empowerment and self-learning through bottom up planning within the organisation. There is also a realignment of business objectives to include external alliances across the supply chain. Finally, the focus will be directed towards re-engineering the supply chain though collaborative planning to gain value enhancement throughout the networked community. This occurs with a shift of business model towards the e-enterprise.

By taking a more holistic approach, executives can turn these stages of a company's transformation into the drivers of e-business excellence. So the central task for senior managers lies in understanding what drives operational excellence in the e-business realm, and then committing the necessary resources (structures, training, planning responsibilities) to the development of the drivers. To this end managers should assess the company's operations by looking at both the traditional and e-business measures.

The complete model for e-business strategy formulation (Table 4) can act as a comprehensive tool, for assisting managers in diagnosing the key facilitators and inhibitors of successful stages of e-business development. It is not seen as a prognostic tool. The case analyses confirmed that the more successful projects were found to have facilitators in all components of the eBG framework.

Some key enablers found through this study are highlighted below:

- Organisations attempting to change performance radically seem to require some "sense of urgency" in their business situation, which translates in turn into a compelling vision that is espoused throughout the organisation.
- An important ingredient in the right cultural mix for successful eBG is leadership from the top and initiatives from employees, together with an atmosphere of open communication, participation and committed cross-functional interactions.
- An organisation's "vision" for change must be embraced throughout all levels of the organisation, especially by those functional and middle-level managers affected by the eBG. To achieve this requires continuous articulation and communication of the value of reporting results and how each individual is contributing and accountable to the overall company's change effort. At this individual level, concern should be placed on how the e-business system will improve employee satisfaction and the quality of work life.

- Measurement is a means to success. A well-defined transparent management approach should include a documented methodology of change, use objective and quantified metrics showing the value of change, continuously communicate process metrics to senior management, and possess a well-documented rollout of the new e-business design.

8. CONCLUSIONS

This study of e-business governance was based around a triangulation of three independent research models: strategies for virtual organising, e-business change strategies and strategic benefits from B2B interaction. Each model exhibits attributes that have varying influences at different stages of e-business planning and implementation. The current findings are based on eleven case organisations which were investigated over a three year period, through semi-structured interviews.

The results from this study are drawn together into a staged model of e-business transformation and governance and a dynamic strategic formulation model for progress through a cycle of innovation. The model offers a foundational perspective of strategies, planning tactics and performance objectives for e-business implementations. This can be viewed as a co-evolutionary approach to governance in which improvement is measured along the three dimensions of integration, differentiation and virtualisation. Successful transition across each dimension will require an organisation to orient itself through three 'cultural shifts' towards the development of networks of innovation.

REFERENCES

Ash, C. and Burn, J. M. Strategic Framework for the Management of E-ERP Change. European Journal of Operations Research,46, (2), April, 2003, pp. 374-387.

Barua, A., Konana, P., Whinston, A. B. and Yin, F. Driving e-Business Excellence. Sloan Management Review, Fall, 2001, pp. 36-44.

Beinhocker, E. D. (1999). Robust Adaptive Strategies. Sloan Management Review, 40, 3, 95-106.

Burn, J. M. and Hackney, R. Strategies for I-Business Change in Virtual Markets: a co-evolutionary approach. International Journal of e-Business Strategy Management, Vol, 2, No. 2, (2000) 123-133.

Carlson, D.A. Harnessing the Flow of Knowledge. 1995. Retrieved April 20, 1998, from Ontogenics website: http://www.ontogenics.com/research/papers/default.htm

Carroll, J.M. Dawson, L.L. and Swatman, P.A. (1998) Using case studies to build theory: Structure and rigor, Proceedings of 9th Australasian Conference on Information Systems, ACIS98 (64-77), Sydney: UNSW

Chang, K, Jackson, J. and Grover, V. E-commerce and Corporate Strategy: an executive perspective. Information and Management, 40, 2003, pp.663-675.

Coltman, T., Devinney, T. M., Latukefu, A. and Migley, D. F. E-Business: revolution, Evolution, or Hype? California Management Review, 44, (1), 2001, pp. 57-89.

Damanpour F. E-Business e-Commerce Evolution: Perspective and Strategy. Managerial Finance, 27, (7), 2001, pp. 16-34.

Edwards, D.J.A. Types of case study work: A conceptual framework for case-based research, Journal of Humanistic Psychology, 38 (3), 1998, pp.36-70.

Eisenhardt, K. Building Theories from Case Study Research, Academy of Management Review, 14 (4), 1989, pp. 532-550.

Eisenhardt, K. E. and Galunic, D. C. (2000) Coevolving. At last, a Way to Make Synergies Work. Harvard Business Review Jan-Feb, 91-101.

Fahey, L., Srivastava, R. Sharon, J. S. and Smith, D. E. Linking e-Business and Operating Processes: The Role of Knowledge Management. IBM Systems Journal, 40, (4), 2001, pp. 889-908.

Floris, P. C.,Van Hooft. F. P. C. and Stegwee, R. A. E-Business Strategy: How to Benefit from a Hype. Logistics Information Management, 14 (1/2), 2001, pp.44-54.

Guha, S., Grover, V., Kettinger, W.J., & Teng, J.T.C. Business process change and organisational performance: Exploring an antecedent model. Journal of Management Information Systems, 14 (1), 1997, pp. 119-154.

Hackney R A & Burn J (2001) SPECS - Strategic Planning for E-Commerce Systems: towards a e-customer focus, International Journal of eBusiness Strategic Management, Vol 2, No 4, 281-291

Kalling, T. ERP Systems and the Strategic Management Processes that Lead to Competitive Advantage. Information Resources Management Journal, 16, (4), 2003, pp. 46-67.

Kallio, J., Saarinen, T. and Tinnila, M. Efficient Change Strategies. Business Process Management Journal, 8 (1), 2002, pp. 80-93.

Kauffman, S. A. (1995). Escaping the Red Queen Effect. The McKinsey Quarterly, 1, 118-129.

Klein, H.K., & Myers, M.D. A Set of Principles for Conducting and Evaluating Interpretive Field Studies in Information Systems, 1998, URL http://www.aukland.ac.nz/msis/isworld/MMeyers/Klein-Myers.htm, Accessed Feb 10, 1999.

Lee, A.S. A Scientific Methodology for MIS, MIS Quarterly, 13 (1), 1987, pp. 32-50.

Levina, N. and Ross, J. W. From the Vendor's perspective: Exploring the Value Proposition in Information Technology Outsourcing. MIS Quarterly, 27 (3), 2003, pp. 331-364.

Oliver, K., Chung, A. and Samanich, N. Beyond Utopia, The Realists Guide to Internet-enabled Supply Chain Management, Strategy+Business, 23, 2003, pp.1-10.

Pant, S. and Ravichandran, T. A Framework for Information Systems Planning for e-Business. Logistics Information Management. 14 (1/2), 2001, pp. 85-95.

Patel, N. Emergent Forms of IT Governance to Support Global e-Business Models. Journal of Information Technology Theory and Application. 4 (2), 2002, pp. 33-49.

Riggins, F. J. A Framework for Identifying Web-based Electronic Commerce Opportunities. Journal of Organisational Computing and Electronic Commerce, 9 (4), 1999, pp. 297-310

Robey, D., Ross, J. W. and Boudreau M. Learning to Implement Enterprise Systems: An Exporatory Study of the Dialectics of Change. Journal of Management Information Systems, 19 (1), 2002, pp. 17-46.

Sarker, S. and Lee, A. S. Using Positivist Case Research Methodology to Test Three Competing Theories-in-use of Business Process Redesign, Journal of Association of Information Systems (AIS) 2 (7), 2002, pp. 1-72.

Sarker, S. and Lee, A. S. Using a Case Study to Test the Role of Three Key Social Enablers in ERP Implementation. Information & Management, 40 (8), 2003, pp.813-830.

Segev, A. & Gebauer, J. B2B procurement and market transformation. Information Technology and Management, 2 (1), 2001, pp.242-260.

Venkatraman, N., & Henderson, J.C. Real strategies for virtual organising. Sloan Management Review, Fall, 1998, pp. 33-48.

Wheeler, B. C. NEBIC: A Dynamic Capabilities Theory for Assessing Net-Enablement. Information Systems Research, 13 (2), 2002, pp. 125 -146.

Yin, R. K. Case Study Research: Design and Methods, Sage, NewburyPark, CA.1994.

Zahra, S. A. and George, G. The Net-enabled business innovation Cycle and the Evolution of Dynamic Capabilities. Information Systems Research, 13 (2), 2002, pp.147-151.

INTER-ORGANISATIONAL COLLABORATIONS SUPPORTED BY E-CONTRACTS

Zoran Milosevic[1], Peter F. Linington[2], Simon Gibson[1], Sachin Kulkarni[1] and James Cole[1]
[1]Distributed Systems Technology Centre, The University of Queensland, Brisbane, QLD 4072, Australia; [2]University of Kent, Canterbury, Kent, CT2 7NF, UK.

Abstract: This paper presents a model for describing inter-organizational collaborations for e-commerce, e-government and e-business applications. The model, referred to as a community model, takes into account internal organizational rules and business policies as typically stated in business contracts that govern cross-collaborations. The model can support the development of a new generation of contract management systems that provide true inter-organizational collaboration capabilities to all parties involved in contract management. This includes contract monitoring features and dynamic updates to the processes and policies associated with contracts. We present a blueprint architecture for inter-organizational contract management and a contract language based on the community model. This language can be used to specialize this architecture for concrete collaborative structures and business processes.

Key words: Community Model, Contract Specification, Contract Monitoring, Business Contract Language

1. INTRODUCTON

Business contracts are the key governing mechanism for inter-organizational collaborations and they are increasingly taking a central role in e-commerce, e-business and e-government applications. This is driven mostly by business demands for more transparent, cost efficient and accountable processes and for the preservation of corporate knowledge associated with contract-related procedures and artifacts. As a result, there is a need for a new generation of contract management systems that go beyond the intra-enterprise contracting focus as typically supported by today's Enterprise Resource Planning (ERP) systems or even more frequently, by numerous spreadsheets or simple databases that many organizations use to record their contract information. Increasingly, organizations require new contract management capabilities to facilitate collaborative aspects in cross-organizational arrangements – to enable better insight into capabilities, activities and performance of their partners.

This paper presents our generic contract architecture solution for building a new generation of contract management systems. This solution makes use of Web Services to support the cross-organizational nature of collaborations and to integrate contract management services into the overall business processes between organizations. The solution consists of:

- a repository of contracts to provide access to contract related information such as start and end date of contract, the status of contracts, parties involved as well as relationships between contracts;
- a contract monitoring facility that performs checking of the fulfillment of obligations and compliance monitoring;
- a contract notification component that sends various contract notifications to the parties involved in contract management;
- other components and facilities to support contract negotiations, enforcement and also dynamic configurations of the system to reflect new business rules and structures

This architecture can be regarded as a blueprint architecture for contract management. Its full potential can be achieved by having a powerful contract language that is used to configure the architecture for a particular contract arrangement. In the paper we also present our Business Contract Language (BCL) developed to support such configuration. The BCL expresses the semantics of contracts although it can be applied to express many other enterprise policies and collaborative arrangements. Essentially, BCL is a domain specific language developed for the contracting domain and can be used to express concrete models for specific contracting environments. Our approach follows the model-driven development philosophy which is currently being proposed by the Object Management Group (OMG) Model-Driven Architecture (MDA).

The next section provides the description of the community model that provides a basis for describing cross-organizational collaborations. We then present our architectural model for cross-organizational contract management. This is followed by an overview of the business contract language that we developed to support contract monitoring capabilities and an example of a procurement related contract to illustrate this language. The paper concludes with a list of open issues and future research directions.

2. MODELLING OF INTER-ORGANIZATIONAL COLLABORATIONS

Web Services provide a way to integrate applications running across the Internet and are well suited to support cross-organizational interactions. However, collaborative arrangements require the capability to express the business rules and constraints of each enterprise and the rules/constraints of engagement with other enterprises – which is an abstraction layer above Web Services. These rules, be they organizational structure rules, business process rules or enterprise policies, together constitute an enterprise model for collaboration. With emerging tools that support model-driven development it will be increasingly possible to use such an enterprise model to generate collaborative applications that can run on top of any middleware infrastructure, including Web Services. The power of a model-driven approach derives from the ability to flexibly and efficiently add new business rules or modify existing ones.

In this paper we present one such enterprise model, a community model, which was developed based on the ODP standards[1,2]. The aim of this model is to capture, in an object based way, the organizational structure of the enterprise and the various localized constraints within it. The community is the basic element of specification, and so is the element used to capture common reusable patterns of constraints[3].

A community is a configuration of objects defined to express some common purpose or objective[1]. It is decoupled from the individual objects representing actors and resources in the distributed enterprise by the use of the role concept. A community defines constraints on the behaviour of the roles it declares, and in any instance of the community these various roles are each filled by particular objects. By forcing its member objects to honour the constraints defined for the roles they fill, the community progresses its objectives. A number of separate communities can be defined to capture different aspects of the community behaviour, so that a particular object might be fulfilling roles in a business process community, a security management community and an auditing community; the result is an enterprise with behaviour satisfying all the different aspects.

The behaviour defined for a community can include, but is not limited to, simple sequences of algorithmic steps. Much of the behaviour specification is concerned with defining the bounds of reasonable behaviour and expressing preferred choices within them. Because of this, many of the constraints are modal in nature, expressing permissions, prohibitions or obligations on the objects filling the roles, rather than giving a single acceptable sequence of actions.

In general, however, the definition of a community in terms of a set of roles allows great flexibility in deciding how the roles are to be filled, leading to considerable flexibility for the reuse of communities to express, for example, common contract elements. However, in some cases a community may also place additional constraints on how a role is to be filled. For example, a separation of duties concern may be expressed by prohibiting a pattern of role-filling in which two particular roles are filled by a single object.

In addition to the construction of business rules by the parallel composition of communities indicated above, there can be hierarchical composition, so that a single role in a high-level community is filled by an object that has resulted from the definition of some smaller-scale community. For example, a single role in confirming the correctness of a tender in some bidding process might, in detail, be filled by a community formed by a quality assurance team.

Another structuring technique in the modeling of inter-organizational processes is the definition of policies. The main idea here is to acknowledge the fact that the structures being defined are organic and evolving, and to distinguish between parts of the specification that are essential to the process being described, and so cannot be varied without effectively starting over again, and those parts that can be expected to vary, either by local choice or by a foreseen process of renegotiation. These circumscribed areas of variability are the policies associated with the enterprise communities. In an e-contracting environment, policies can be a very powerful tool for tailoring general contract behaviour to the specific circumstances in which the contract instance is to operate. A policy can be defined, for example, to indicate how the progress from stage to stage is to be signaled, or how various kinds of foreseeable violations, such as late payment, are to be acted upon.

Policies can also be defined to control the extent to which the structure of the contract can be allowed to evolve with time, indicating, for example, whether the way objects fill roles can be updated, or even whether the number of instances of some general kind of role can be increased or decreased to accommodate changing levels of interest, and if so whether there is a specific limit to ensure a sensible quorum for the activity.

The community specifications discussed here are templates, in the ODP sense, in that they are generally parameterised, and that they are used to create community instances by applying a set of instantiation rules derived from the context of the creation action; the term template is used in this paper to highlight the distinction from the more neutral term model.

A more detailed description of community model is described in our earlier paper[3] and also in our recent publication[4].

3. BLUEPRINT CONTRACT ARCHITECTURE

3.1 Extended Enterprise: role of contracts

Inter-organizational collaborations in the extended enterprise increasingly require tighter electronic links between organizations while preserving their individual processes and practices as an element of their competitiveness. This means that organizations are to be involved in cross-organisational business processes but the nature of such processes is different from the nature of internal business processes.

In the cross-organisational space the emphasis is on coordinating message exchanges sent between organizations that typically carry business documents, as shown in Figure 1. Messages can be created as a result of various events, such as actions of objects filling roles, deadlines events or arrival of other messages. Here, there is no centralized engine that coordinates message transfer – rather every organization implements its own decision logic about how to process incoming messages, what internal activity is to be carried out and where and when to send outgoing messages. There are several standardization activities that are attempting to define how Web Services can be used in the cross-organisational business process context such as BPEL[5]. We note that the focus of internal processes is primarily on the control flow and data flow between tasks in a business process.

Contracts are the key mechanisms to govern cross-organisational collaboration. From a legal point of view contracts state what obligations, permission, or prohibitions parties have in respect to each other and what actions are to be undertaken in cases of contract violation, either as a result of a contract breach or due to circumstances in which force majeure is applied.

The legal jargon in contracts can to some extent be mapped onto a number of more formalized modeling concepts which can be used to facilitate integration of the contracts with cross-organisational business processes and other enterprise systems. However, this mapping is a non-trivial problem and in this paper we present our solution for expressing contracts in terms of modeling concepts suitable for supporting automation in cross-organisational collaborations. These modeling concepts are based on the community model introduced in section 2, and can be grouped in three broad categories:

- expression of roles and their relationships as part of a contract; roles can then be included as part of the basic behavior concepts and policies listed below
- expressions of basic behaviour, e.g. a set of actions carried out by the parties filling the roles and being involved in business transactions and various styles of constraints on these actions including temporal constraints;
- expressions of policies such as obligations, permissions and prohibitions as refinement of basic behaviour; both policies and basic behaviour expressions use more primitive behaviour expressions such as states, events and event relationships

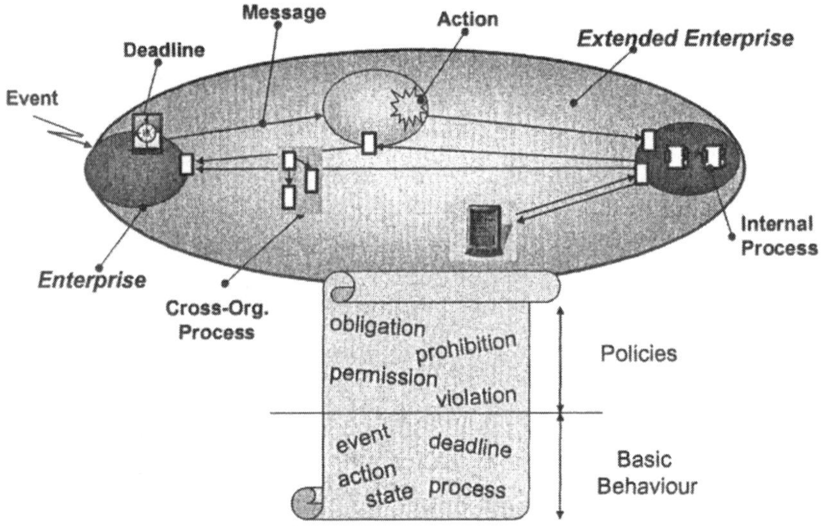

Figure 1. Contracts and cross-organisational interactions

The electronic representation of contract templates can be stored in appropriate repositories and it can be used either for accessing and navigating information related to a contract or for real-time monitoring of contract execution. The latter includes monitoring of events that are occurring (or not occurring) as part of business transactions carried out in the related enterprise systems, such as e-procurement, payment systems and so on.

3.2 Contract architecture components

To support the full contract life cycle and satisfy the most common contract management procedures we propose a minimum number of architectural components that can be deployed either within one or more collaborative organizations or as a stand-alone system. This Business Contract Architecture (BCA), originally proposed by Milosevic[6], consists of the following core components (see Figure 2).

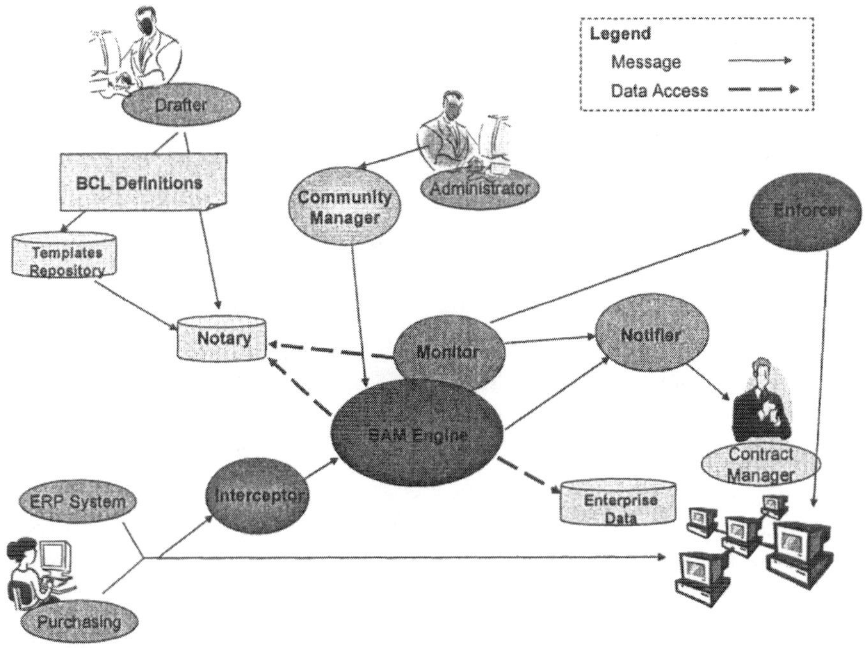

Figure 2. Business Contract Architecture blueprint

- A Contract Repository, which stores standard contract forms (or contract templates), and if necessary standard contract clauses that can be used as building blocks when drafting new contract templates; there are several deployment options for the Contract Repository role – it can be deployed within either or both of the trading partners or it can be owned by a trusted third-party authority;
- A Notary that stores evidence of agreed contract instances after a contract has been negotiated to prevent any of the parties repudiating it; this component can also store relationships between contracts as necessary;
- An Interceptor, whose purpose is to provide non-intrusive interception of specific messages exchanged between business parties so that they can be further processed for contract monitoring purposes; this is a plug-in component allowing integration with any enterprise system and will vary from one implementation to another, as it implements different message protocols;

- A Business Activity Monitoring (BAM) component, which facilitates the processing of events obtained from the interceptor, managing internal states related to the contract and access to various enterprise data needed for policy evaluation performed by the Contract Monitor component; we note that this component represents an extension of the original BCA in order to enable more powerful event-based monitoring capability;
- A Contract Monitor, that performs the evaluation of contract policies, to determine whether parties' obligations have been satisfied or whether there are violations to the contract; this component makes extensive use of the BAM component for event pattern and state processing; it then sends appropriate messages to the Notifier component mentioned below;
- A Contract Notifier, whose main task is to send notification messages (human readable format) to contract managers such as reminders about the tasks that need to be performed, warnings that some violation event may arise or alarms that a violation has already happened;
- A Contract Enforcer, which can perform some corrective measures such as preventing further transactions if some violation has been detected.

The architecture components above represent core functionality needed for most contract management processes. A contract architecture can also have additional components that can provide further value to the decision makers in the contracting processes such as:

- Contract mediator and arbitrator roles that can be used for discretionary contract enforcement capabilities[7]. The contract mediator essentially collects evidence of parties' behaviour according to the contract. In case of some dispute it can be used as an intermediary to assist the signatories to the contract in determining a future course of corrective actions to ensure contract compliant behaviour. A contract arbitrator can be used in conjunction with a contract mediator as a party that makes decisions about who is at fault (just as judges make their decisions) and whose decisions must be obeyed by a party determined to be at fault. These two roles are to be used as an alternative or in combination with the non-discretionary enforcement capabilities of a contract enforcer;
- A Contract negotiator, which is a role that facilitates negotiation between contracting parties, possibly as a third party mediator that might have access to business information of relevance for future contracts, and which is not accessible to either of the parties;
- A Contract validitor which can perform a range of activities to ensure that a contract that is being negotiated is valid; this can include checking consistency of contracts[8], or checking the competence aspect of a contract[9];

- A Contract performance repository, that stores various information of relevance to the performance of parties to the contract and that can be used when future contracts are to be negotiated;
- A Contract approval manager, which ensures that only parties with corresponding privileges can execute actions governed by a contract such as role-based or price-based purchase order issuance;
- A Community manager, which allows the contract administrator to make dynamic updates of roles, policies and other community model elements; these updates will need to be checked for their validity and approval by the contract monitor and BAM component.

Our architecture is easily configurable so that additional roles can be added as necessary.

Thus, BCA identifies the main components involved in contract creation, execution and monitoring, but it leaves great flexibility in the way responsibilities can be assigned to organizational units. For example, the trust model associated with the monitor will vary depending on whether there is first, second or third party monitoring. Similarly, the event management infrastructure may be associated with the participants or run by a trusted third party, and this will alter the way that events are analysed.

We note that in the inter-organizational setting these components can be integrated using Web Services technologies. For example, in our prototype the back-end system for Contract Repository and Notary are implemented using IBM Web Sphere platform and the front-end for manipulating and viewing data in the repositories is implemented using Microsoft's ASP.Net technology.

4. BUSINESS CONTRACT LANGUAGE CONCEPTS

The Business Contract Language (BCL) currently under development[4,10] is aimed at describing contract semantics for the purpose of automating contract management activities. Although BCL covers the structural aspects of contracts, describing their composition in terms of contract clauses and subclauses, in this paper we concentrate on the part of BCL that is concerned with support for the automation of contract monitoring during contract execution, i.e. after a contract is agreed and the fact stored in the Notary. This automation is aimed at supporting various contract management roles during a contract's lifetime in their activities and decision-making.

BCL is a domain language specifically developed to express contract conditions needed for contract monitoring and to some extent contract enforcement. BCL is a largely declarative language with a minimum number of imperative fragments. BCL interpreter is embedded as part of the BAM and contract monitor components of which implementation details are beyond the scope of this paper.

The BCL language concepts can be grouped in three categories as described next and shown in the figure below:

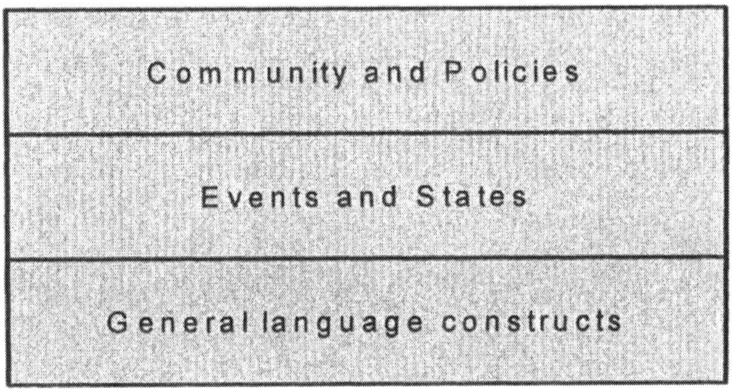

Figure 3. Business contract language modeling concepts

4.1 Community and Policies

BCL concepts related to communities and policies define organizational, basic behavioural and modal constraints that apply to inter-organisational interactions. Of all of the BCL concepts they are closest to the domain of contracting as they resemble natural language terms and expressions used in contracts.

Organizational constraints can be expressed using a community model that specifies the roles involved in a contract and their relationships, including hierarchical relationships (through the notion of a nested community or sub-community). The roles can represent organizations as part of their collaboration governed by a larger community, viz contract, or structures within organizations so that it is possible to model internal relationships as well. In order to support the notion of a contract template as a basis for the creation of the corresponding contract instances we introduce the concept of a community template and instantiation rules that specify condition for the creation of contract, as explained in the example below.

Basic behavioural interactions between roles in a contract express the ordering of their actions or steps in a business process carried out by the signatories in a contract. In BCL most basic behaviour constraints are expressed using event patterns as described in section 4.2. Similarly, policies apply to the roles involved specifying refinement of their behavior, in particular modal constraints such as obligations, rights, permissions, prohibitions, accountability, authorizations and so on. As with basic behaviour, policy conditions can be expressed in terms of event patterns.

The main purpose of this group of concepts is to define collaborative arrangements between parties. We note that, although community and policy aspects of the BCL language are developed for the contracting domain, they also have wider generality such as for example the description of internal policies within organizations.

As with other aspects of BCL, these language descriptions are stored in the Notary and will be used by the Contract Monitor and BAM engine to initiate contract monitoring activities.

4.2 Events and States

BCL concepts covering the definitions of Events and internal States are used to describe detailed behaviour constraints that are used as part of community and policy descriptions in the community model. These are fundamental behaviour concepts that can be used for most Business Activity Monitoring (BAM) applications, and are not related only to business contracts. This group includes concepts for the expression of:

- event patterns which are to be used to detect certain occurrences related to the contract either as a single event or as multiple events related to each other;
- internal states and their changes in response to the events;
- event types to be created when certain conditions have been matched, e.g. creation of contract violation or contract fulfilment events

The purpose of BCL's event and state concepts is to support real-time evaluation of the execution of basic behaviour and policies as stated in the contract with the aim of detecting contract violations or contract fulfillments.

In terms of states, this evaluation can, for example, consist of checking whether a certain internal state related to a contract has been reached, such as detecting whether the total number of cost-free withdrawals per month has reached its maximum.

In terms of events, the evaluation can also involve checking whether one or several events have occurred. In BCL an event represents an occurrence of a certain type. An event can be atomic or it can have a duration. In the case of multiple events the BCL provides a rich set of options for expressing relationships between events, namely event patterns. BCL provides a rich set of event pattern expressions and their full description is beyond the scope of this paper. We provide here some examples of event pattern expressions:

- Sequence of events - the event pattern is satisfied when all the events have occurred in the order specified in the sequence

- Disjunction of events - the event pattern is satisfied when either of the events have occurred
- Conjunction of Events - this pattern is satisfied when all the events have occurred
- Quorum – this pattern is satisfied when a specified number from the set of all events have occurred
- Event Causality - the event pattern is satisfied when the currently matched event is causally derived from a specific preceding event.

A special kind of event pattern is introduced to allow for the detection of certain conditions that need to be determined during some 'sliding' period of time. This event pattern is called a sliding Time Window event pattern. The time window is defined by the window's width, the specific condition that needs to be checked within that window (e.g. maximum number of PO requests issued per day), the expressions stating what to do when a condition is found or is not found, and if, appropriate, how to move the window forward.

The event pattern mechanism in BCL has many similarities to the specification of complex event processing[13]. Most of the event pattern language concepts are implemented as part of the BAM component. This component uses event subscription mechanism to listen for the events generated either by external system (through the Interceptor component) or internally from within BCA (e.g. timeout events). Some of the events would require further processing such as the evaluation of policies by the Monitor or creation of new events by an Event Condition Action mechanism. The flexibility of our design and implementation comes from the fact that the interceptor can subscribe to any events such as the events generated by sending and receiving of messages in the cross-organizational settings, either initiated by machines or by humans.

4.3 General language concepts

While the Communities, Policies and BAM aspects of BCL are used to express key concepts of the contracting domain we needed additional language constructs familiar in most programming languages to support assignment of mathematical or logical expressions to variables, control of loops, conditional constructs, and so on.

5. EXAMPLE: E-PROCURMENT SCENARIO

Consider a simple e-procurement scenario that focuses on a process around the issue of a purchase order (PO) and dispatch of the requested goods. A community template is defined to describe this cross-organisational behaviour involving purchaser and supplier roles, and this may be specified in an umbrella contract.

The contract clauses outline the following behaviour fragments:

- Purchaser is obliged to issue the PurchaseOrder whose integrity must be correct with regard to quantities and pricing.
- Once a PurchaseOrder is received then the goods must be dispatched within some number of days of receiving the purchase order.
- Payment must then follow within so many days of the goods being dispatched.
- If the total of the purchase order is above some threshold then the goods must also be insured.
- Once a cumulative total of purchase orders is reached some discount may then be applied.

This example has been kept simple for reasons of brevity. Realistically it should be extended to handle other likely possibilities such as partial payment and delivery, shipping problems and a plethora of other atypical but possible events and scenarios.

We first introduce a contract template that corresponds to this e-procurement umbrella contract. Since we have defined only a template then the actual values must be defined during some negotiation phase to create a contract instance. These values will include the roles involved, durations for dispatch and payment and thresholds for insurance and discounts. We provide a community instantiation rule that specifies the event which will trigger creation of a community instance. Note that we also define an activation rule to specify a condition after which this contract (i.e. community instance) may start to be monitored say for the purpose of checking whether the above policies are satisfied.

This example also involves the definition of a nested sub-community for each purchase order (PO) in order to handle monitoring for each individual PO instance separately. Note that the example also shows our policy expressions which follow the spirit of deontic constraints and that some policies are defined in the context of a main community and others as part of a sub-community. We also show how the internal states to the contract are expressed and updated in response to events. This example expressed in pseudo BCL syntax is included below.

```
CommunityTemplate: E-Procurement

 InitialisationSpecification:
                CreateE-ProcurementContractEvent

 ActivationSpecification: StartDate

 Role:  Purchaser
 Role:  Supplier
 Value: StartDate
 Value: DespatchThreshold
 Value: PaymentThreshold
 Value: InsuranceThreshold
 Value: DiscountThreshold
 Value: PurchaseOrderCumulativeTotal

 Policy: POverification
    Role:     Purchaser
    Modality: Obligation
    Condition: On POEvent verify content

 State: CumulativePoTotal
    InitialisationSpecification: 0
    CalculationExpression:
            POCumulativeTotal += POEvent.total

 --- Purchase order sub-community defined below -

 CommunityTemplate: PO
    InitialisationSpecification: POEvent

    ActivationSpecification: OnInitialisation
      EventPattern: GoodsDespatchDeadlineEvent
        GenerateOn:
                POEvent + DespatchThreshold DAYS

      Eventpattern: PaymentDeadlineEvent
        GenerateOn: GoodsDespatchEvent
                       + PaymentThreshold DAYS
```

```
Policy: GoodsDespatchWithinThresholdPeriod
  Role: Supplier
  Modality: Obligation
  Condition: GoodsDespatchEvent
        BEFORE GoodsDespatchDeadlineEvent

Policy: PaymentMadeWithinThresholdPeriod
 Role: Purchaser
 Modality: Obligation
 Condition: PaymentEvent
            BEFORE PaymentDeadlineEvent

Policy: GoodsInsuredOverValueThreshold
 Role: Supplier
 Modality: Obligation
 Condition:
   If PurchaseOrderEvent.total GREATERTHAN
      InsuranceThreshold
   Then Action (Insure Goods)

Policy: ApplyDiscountOverCumulativeTotal
 Role: Supplier
 Modality: Obligation
 Condition:
  IfPurchaseOrderCumulativeTotal GREATERTHAN
       DiscountThreshold
  Then
       Action (Apply discount to goods)
```

Note that this example only shows a small set of key BCL concepts and that a more detailed description of BCL features is presented elsewhere[4].

6. CONCLUSIONS AND FUTURE WORK

In this paper we have presented our solution to the problem of integrating contracts as part of cross-organizational collaborations. The solution consists of a generic architecture based on our earlier work[6], which can be tailored to specific contract situation by using Business Contract Language developed for contract domain. This architecture and this language used together facilitate fast deployment of enterprise contract management systems to fit specific organizational requirements. These systems are needed to support important collaborative processes as part of broader inter-organizational arrangements. In particular they support more effective and efficient activities of people responsible for contract management activities.

Our work on BCL adopts a similar approach to the early work of Lee [11] on electronic representation of contracts. Lee proposed a logic model for contracting by considering their temporal, deontic and performative aspects. BCL is developed from a different angle – the enterprise modeling considerations related to open distributed systems. Our approach, based on the ODP community concept [1,2] and inspired by deontic formalisms, gives prominence to the problem of defining enterprise policies as part of organizational structures. Further, we treat contracts as a group of related policies that regulate inter-organizational business activities and processes. In this respect we take a similar approach to that of van den Heuvel and Weigand[12], who developed a business contract specification language to link specifications of workflow systems.

In addition, we consider contracts as the main coordination mechanism for the extended enterprise and, considering possible non-compliance situations, we provide architectural solutions to the problem of monitoring the behaviour stipulated by a contract as firstly proposed in the BCA solution[6]. In addition, this monitoring makes use of sophisticated event processing machinery similar to that of Rapide language[13].

In near future we plan to test our solution in a pilot e-business, e-government or e-commerce environment. This would help us determine expressive power of the language and its acceptability by contract domain experts and practitioners. We also plan to explore the use of existing and emerging tools that support model-driven development to minimize the cost of language maintenance. Another alternative is to consider suitability of high level languages to implement BCL constructs. Finally, we expect that some of the BCL ideas can be used as part of OASIS legalXML e-contracts standardization[14].

ACKNOWLEDGEMENTS

The work reported in this paper has been funded in part by the Co-operative Research Centre for Enterprise Distributed Systems Technology (DSTC) through the Australian Federal Government's CRC Programme (Department of Industry, Science & Resources).

This project was supported by the Innovation Access Programme-International Science and Technology, an initiative of the Government's Innovation Statement, Backing Australia's Ability.

REFERENCES

1. ISO/IEC IS 10746-3, Open Distributed Processing Reference Model, Part 3, Architecture, ISO 1995
2. ISO/IEC IS 15414, Open Distributed Processing-Enterprise Language, 2002
3. P.F. Linington, Z. Milosevic and K. Raymond, Policies in Communities: Extending the ODP Enterprise Viewpoint, in Proc. 2nd International Workshop on Enterprise Distributed Object Computing (EDOC'98), San Diego, USA, November 1998.
4. P.F. Linington, Z. Milosevic, J. Cole, S. Gibson, S. Kulkarni, S. Neal, A unified behavioural model and a contract for extended enterprise, Data Knowledge and Engineering Journal, Elsevier Science, to appear.
5. Business Process Execution Language for Web Services, 1.1, May2003, http://www-106.ibm.com/developerworks/library/ws-bpel/
6. Z. Milosevic. Enterprise Aspects of Open Distributed Systems. PhD thesis, Computer Science Dept. The University of Queensland, October 1995
7. Z. Milosevic, A. Josang, T. Dimitrakos, M.A. Patton – Discretionary Enforcement of Electronic Contracts. Proc. EDOC '02. pp(s): 39 -50. IEEE CS 2002
8. Z. Milosevic, G.Dromey, On Expressing and Monitoring Behaviour in Contracts, EDOC2002 Conference, Lausanne, Switzerland
9. Z. Milosevic, D. Arnold, L. O'Connor - Inter-enterprise contract architecture for open distributed systems: Security requirements. Proc. of WET ICE'96 Workshop on Enterprise Security, Stanford, June 1996
10. S. Neal, J. Cole, P. F. Linington, Z. Milosevic, S. Gibson, S. Kulkarni, Identifying requirements for Business Contract Language: a Monitoring Perspective, IEEE EDOC2003 Conference Proceedings, to appear.
11. R. Lee, A Logic Model for Electronic Contracting, Decision Support Systems, 4, 27-44.
12. W-Jan van den Heuvel, H. Weigand, Cross-Organisational Workflow Integration using Contracts, Decision Support Systems, 33(3): p. 247-265
13. D. Luckham, The Power of Events, Addison-Wesley, 2002
14. OASIS LegalXMLTC http://www.oasis-open.org/committees/legalxml-econtracts/charter.php

E-BUSINESS MODELS

JOINT DEVELOPMENT OF NOVEL BUSINESS MODELS

Jukka Heikkilä[1], Marikka Heikkilä[2] and Jari Lehmonen[2]
[1]Department of Computer Science and Information Systems, University of Jyväskylä, P.O. Box 35 (Agora), FI-40014 FINLAND; [2]Information Technology Research Institute, University of Jyväskylä, P.O. Box 35 (Agora), FI-40014 FINLAND

Abstract: Changing competitive environment forces companies to innovate and renew their business models towards a more value-adding and customer-centric direction. Often, a prerequisite for this is that the companies are willing to combine their capabilities by co-operating and creating long-term strategic networks with each other. The formation of networks is a cyclical learning process, along which the infrastructure and strategies emerge incrementally through mutual adjustment.

We analyze such network formation process among three companies that are operating in separate but complementary industries. They are seeking to expand their service offering through the use of ICT. We reflect upon this development with the state-of-the-art research on the networked organizations and business models. It seems that business models are necessary and useful in depicting the areas of adjustments within and between the organizations in the networked setting.

Key words: e-business; business model; ICT; networked organization; knowledge creation; knowledge Sharing.

1. INTRODUCTION

The transformation to digital economy is a search for innovative interlinked, strategic business networks, e-powered commerce and interorganizational systems. The companies are forming firmer relationship with strategic partners, more often with a few chosen contractors which are given the responsibility for larger entities than before (as predicted by Clemons et al, 1993). The coordination of transactions is achieved through – instead of hierarchy or markets - the interaction and mutual obligation of the firms in the network (Powell, 1990).

For decades, the new ideas for technology enabled businesses were created by one party, which then appropriated the business benefits by obtaining required additional resources and capabilities to implement and learn innovations' potential (e.g. Cohen & Levinthal, 1990). Nowadays, the tendency of firms to focus on their core competencies and with increasing degree of outsourcing, have made the companies more dependent on each other's knowledge and capabilities (Soekijad & Andriessen, 2003; Powell, 2000; Dyer & Singh, 1998). As a result, also new business ideas seldom are feasible for a single company only, but require co-operation between multiple firms. This tendency is further leveraged due to technological complexity of new innovations (Hagedoorn and Duysters, 2002). As Powell, 2000 states it:

> "The boundaries of many firms have become so porous that to focus on boundaries means only to see trees in a forest of interorganizational relations. The core competence of a firm, to use the new argot, is based on knowledge production and building a sustainable advantage that can be leveraged across products and services, thus enmeshing firms in all manner of different relationships and markets that were traditionally called industries. Power, to be sure, remains crucial, but it is employed to enhance reach and access and to compete in high-speed learning races. These new innovations are inherently fragile because they are premised on obtaining deeper engagement and participation from "core" employees and more collaboration and mutual involvement among ostensible competitors. But employees toil in a context of greater labor market volatility and inter-firm cooperation coexists with rivalry among competing networks." (Powell, 2000, p. 5)

Hence, also the know-how required for the creation of new innovative business ideas is dispersed into multiple organizations. To large extent, innovation derives from knowledge exchange and learning between firms (Nooteboom, 2000), which is also reflected in their strategic intentions towards simultaneous competition and co-operation (Nalebuff & Brandenburger, 1996). All this - i.e., need for shared resources, and shared knowledge creation between partners, competitors and/or customers combined with favorable strategic intent and technical means - makes co-operation networks between firms in creation and realization of new business ideas a tempting option. The phenomenon is getting ever more topical with the advent of ICT-facilitated business models, as they are growingly based on the idea of fluent co-operation and information exchange between the parties (see e.g., Ciborra & Hanseth, 1998; Ciborra & Andreu, 2001).

Our discussion is related to the literature on business models (e.g. Osterwalder & Pigneur, 2002; Osterwalder, 2004; Faber et al, 2003; Bouwman, 2003; e-Factors, 2002), organizational learning (e.g. Cohen & Levinthal, 1990; Ciborra & Hanseth, 1998; Ciborra & Andreu, 2001; Andersen & Christensen, 2000) and strategic alliances (e.g. van de Ven, 1976; Powell, 1990; 2000; Kumar & van Dissel, 1996; Nalebuff & Brandenburger, 1996). Our viewpoint is closer to the infrastructural aspects of co-operation. This means that we look into the creation process of business model in a business network context, rather than on restructuring processes within an organization or within a supplier chain (e.g. Hammer, 1990), or on the strategy formulation process, or contractual issues. Unfortunately, previous literature has mainly focused on networks as given contexts for the organizations within them (Beugelsdijk et al., 2003). There are few studies on the initial formation of the network or creation of the joint business. Hence, the question arises how the companies come up with a business model that is feasible for each individual, independent company. In this article we focus on the necessary requirements for the joint business model. We claim that in order it to be acceptable to all parties, it should be in line with each of the participants business strategies and processes. This calls for a joint learning process at the network level, and parallel adjustments processes within each company.

In this paper we focus on creation of network business model by three independent business partners. We have a privilege to take actively part as researchers, probably also as conciliators and facilitators, in an establishment of this co-operation network. Despite the limited generalizability of our research, it offers a view on the outset of the cyclical evolution process of business network creation.

The article is organized as follows: In chapter 2 we will summarize the networked organizations concerns in global, ICT-enabled business. We illustrate the important aspects and emergent properties that have been found to affect formation of the business networks and organizational learning. This is to set the arena for discussion on business models, i.e., the creation of a joint business concept. Finally, we reflect upon the knowledge creation and sharing within the network, to sum up some of the findings for future research agenda.

2. WHY NETWORKED ORGANIZATIONS?

2.1 Networked organization forms

The institutional economics (Coase, 1937; Williamson, 1985; Alchian and Demsetz, 1972; Jensen and Mecklin, 1973; Picot et al, 1997) concerned with the boundaries of the firm, contracts between co-operating parties, and 'make or buy '–decisions, generally positions networks as an intermediate governance form between markets and hierarchies. Williamson (1985) claims that, in the case of high uncertainty and asset specificity, parties have an incentive to protect their investments by realignment of incentives, creation of a specialized governance structure, or introduction of trading regularities that signal continuity of intentions of the parties. Specifically, asset-specific products often involve a long process of development and adjustments for the supplier to meet the needs of the client. This calls for continuity that can be ascertained within hierarchy or in close co-operation (Malone et al, 1987; Kumar and VanDissel, 1996; Gulati and Singh, 1998). It seems that when technological complexity of the product or service is high the companies more often prefer co-operation instead of mergers and acquisitions. For instance Hagedoorn and Duysters (2002) suggest that these kinds of flexible forms of organizations are appropriate because new knowledge expires quickly and requires timely learning. They can also be more easility adapted to changes under uncertainty. Instead of prices or authority/routines co-operation netwoks rely more on relational communication, free will and trust, and aims at benefiting all its partners (Powell, 1990; Tsupari et al., 2001; Beugelsdijk, 2003). The form of co-operative relationship may vary from single business transactions to annual contracts or projects to strategic partnership.

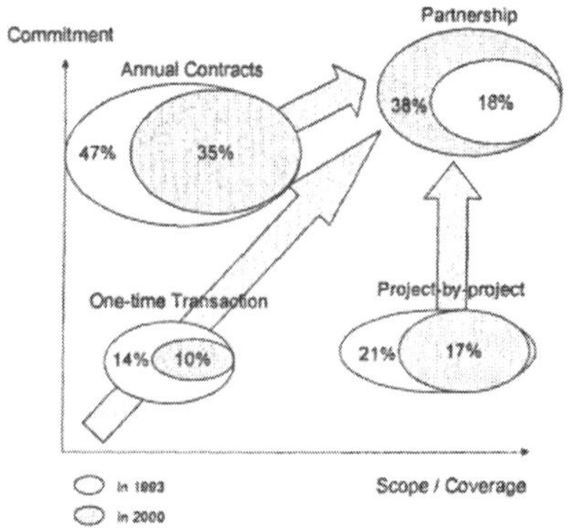

Figure 1. The evolution of manufacturing networks in Finland. (Tsupari et al., 2001)

It seems that various kinds of networks in business have become common also in reality, for example a study by Tsupari et al. (2001) shows that over two thirds of companies in manufacturing industry in Finland[30] are involved in networks to some extent. The tendency seems to be a move towards partnerships requiring higher levels of commitment and higher coverage of firms' operations (see figure 1. on the empirical results of the evolution of manufacturing networks in Finland).

Ultimately, the motivation for organizations to join a network is the attainment of goals that are unachievable by the organizations independently (as postulated by van de Ven, 1976). The firms may enter alliances in order to gain fast access to new technologies or new markets, or they may try to shape competition, or gain legitimacy (Powell, 1990; Nielsen, 2002). They may also share the costs of large investments, pool and spread risk, reduce the uncertainty, attain economies of scale or scope, etc. (Kumar and van Dissel, 1996). Traditionally the firms approach collaboration from a complementary or exploitation view; they seek for additional knowledge from other companies operating in similar or same domain. The aim is to find matching knowledge related capabilities that can be transferred, incorporated and appropriated in the assimilating firm (Nielsen, 2002; March, 1991). In this view, it is crucial that there is some similarity between the co-operating firms, for instance sameness of goals, services, staff skills, and clients (van de Ven, 1976), so that they can absorb the innovation within reasonable timeframe (Cohen & Levinthal, 1990). This timeframe can be further shortened by improving the absorptive capacity within a firm by accumulating the capacity in particular areas (ibid., p. 136). But this approach is vulnerable in fast changing, uncertain situations.

An alternative motivation to form a business network may be to explore on external problem, or opportunity in the overlapping domains of organizations (van de Ven, 1976). In such cases the need emerges out of an awareness, for example of changing need priorities, resource distribution channels, or power relationships in the environment (van de Ven, 1976). This explorative and synergistic view challenges the traditional complementary view especially in knowledge intensive environments (Nielsen, 2002; March, 1991). Whereas the traditional complementary view is concerned with increasing productivity through standardization, systematic costs reduction, and incremental improvement of existing technologies, skills and capabili-

[30] Tsupari et al. (2001) reports findings of a mail survey carried out 2001. The questionnaires were posted to 700 manufacturing firms in Finland. The response rate was around 52% (363), accounting for 40% of the total personnel and 60% of the total net sales in the manufacturing industry. It is worth noting that around 60%. of the products of manufacturing of metals and electronics is exported in 2002 (National Board of Customs, 2004).

ties, exploration, in turn, is about finding new opportunities for wealth creation through building new capabilities and innovation. Nielsen (2002) pictures synergistic knowledge networks as networks where new knowledge can be created among the participants as a synergy (and not simply the sum). For example experimental activities such as prototyping, experimenting and conceptual testing can be used to ensure rapid gain of knowledge. We would expect these networks to be more of static type: they aim at achieving long-term goals, for example, by forming longer-lasting relationships (Hoogeweegen et al, 1999). However, as these explorative networks are concerned with new, innovative matters, they are facing more uncertainty in their tasks and outcomes. In line with real-life observations of business process re-engineering projects, also many explorative networks may fail in achieving their objectives and break up after only a short trial period (see e.g. Sivadas & Dwyer, 2000).

To summarize, business networks are considered especially useful for the exchange of qualities or commodities whose value is difficult to evaluate, like know-how, technological capability, a particular method or style of production, or a spirit of innovation or experiments (Powell, 1990). This implies that knowledge related capabilities are of central concern in the formation of networks. Therefore, we will next discuss the knowledge related issues of business networks.

2.2 Business Networks as Arenas for Learning

The original rationale in developing business networks was to enhance company specific assets and seek complementary resources and capabilities from partnering firms. Because of the path dependent nature of the absorption process, van de Ven (1976) and Kumar & van Dissel (1996) pointed out that evolution of business network is an emergent and cyclical process over time. It simply takes time to build trust and learn to work together and adjust operation within the network: "The emergence and functioning of an IR (inter-organizational relationship), therefore, is a cyclical process of: need for resources – issue commitments – inter-agency communications to spread awareness and consensus – resource transactions – and structural adaptation and pattern maintenance over time" (van de Ven, 1976, p. 33).

This is well in line with the idea of absorptive capacity, too. Ability to recognize the value of new information and assimilate it is a function of level of prior knowledge. Prior knowledge enhances learning because events are recorded to memory by establishing linkages with pre-existing concepts. Absorptive capacity is, hence, history and path dependent (Cohen & Levinthal, 1990), which means that it will be built incrementally on the existing knowledge, and most likely nowadays on ICT-infrastructure. Some amount of redundancy or knowledge spillovers may be desirable to create cross-function absorptive capacity, which again makes organizations more capable of proacting (Cohen & Levinthal, 1990). Basically, the longer the capacity has evolved the higher it grows, and the more proactive the organization can become. Some recent studies suggest that the relationship may be more contingent on the knowledge and infrastructure interplay than suggested above. For example, Ciborra & Hanseth (1998) argue on the basis of longitudinal case studies that sometimes decentralized processes may speed up the adoption of new practices.

In addition to absorptive capacity Andersen and Christensen (2000) point out the importance of communicative capacity within the network. Their case study shows how poorly managed communication between firms may easily destroy long-standing and cumulative efforts of trust-building. Specifically diversity in culture, organization culture and strategy between the parties increases misunderstandings and difficulties to communicate (Andersen and Christensen, 2000). Communication capabilities can be, at least to some extent, be improved by establishing common experience and joint practices or developing a new jointly spoken language that facilitates cooperation (Ciborra & Andreu, 2001). Also, an independent intermediary or conciliator/moderator (for example university) may help in the dialogue between the parties for example by providing unbiased background information, and translating the message of one party so that it is understandable to the other companies that have different domain and 'language'.

However, as Ciborra & Andreu (2001) highlights a firm that is entering an alliance with another firm having its own knowledge management system and practices, may find its own internal knowledge management arrangements and resources "too rigid, 'closed' and incompatible". Thus, in addition to absorptive and communicative capabilities we need also development of synergistic knowledge networks and explorative knowledge creation (Nielsen 2002). Seeking business network as arenas for learning and linking capabilities into strategic intention we refer to the cyclic process described by Ciborra & Andreu (2001). In their learning ladder model for a single firm they picture learning with three loops. The lowest loop is about routinization of the knowledge. A second loop is about transformation of 'abstracts' and 'constructs' capabilities from existing work practices. These capabilities are more abstract than work practices, they are 'skills without a place'. The third strategic loop, in turn, is concerned about selection of core capabilities from the capabilities in the context of competitive environment and business mission of the firm. Ciborra and Andreu (2001) carry on by proposing that there is another source of competitive advantage stemming from the establishment of interfirm linkages, recombination of separate learning ladders, which in themselves can become a distinct source of relational quasi-rents. "Valuable know-how can be attained by mixing and transferring capabilities, by placing resources and routines in new contexts or by letting existing practices be molded by different capabilities in order to form new routines". Governance of this phenomenon is vital in securing compatibility, transferability and value generation.

3. BUSINESS MODELS – ARCHITECTURAL DESCRIPTIONS BETWEEN STRATEGY AND PROCESSES

3.1 Business models

Business models have recently been a topical issue especially in the field of electronic commerce. Since the end of 90's (Osterwalder, 2004) there has been a vivid research stream proposing differing definitions, lists of components, taxonomies, change methodologies and evaluation models for business models (e.g Timmers,1998; Amit & Zott, 2001; e-Factors, 2002; Osterwalder & Pigneur, 2002; Faber et al, 2003; Bouwman, 2003; Osterwalder, 2004). In essence, the topics discussed in the business model literature are not new: the components of business models have been recognized - at least to some extent - in business strategies and business planning for decades. But, the need for explicit analysis and description of the business model has become more evitable as the introduction of information and communication technology has enabled completely new ways of making business.

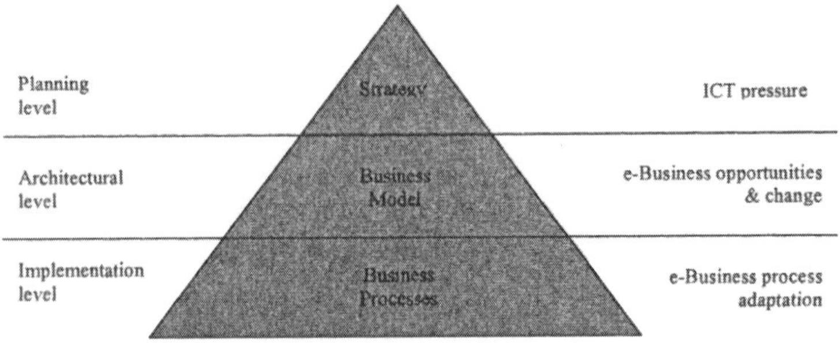

Figure 2. Business Logic Triangle (Osterwalder & Pigneur, 2002)

The general targets for the business actions are set in organizations strategy (see Figure 2). Business model mediates this organization strategy at an architectural level. It depicts how the business works, the general logic that creates the business value in relation with the organizations architecture/infrastructure. Thereby the business model, as a representation of the corporate strategy, is the starting point for planning operative business processes (e-Factors, 2002). Business model tells how the strategy is implemented by describing e.g. product offering, IT-infrastructure, financials customers and supplier relationships. Thus "the business model depicts the content, structure, and governance of transactions designed so as to create value through the exploitation of business opportunities" (Amit & Zott, 2001).

Osterwalder and Pigneur point out that in its essence, a business model consists of four interrelated components (see Figure 3.): *Product innovation* component defines what business the company is in, and the product innovation and the value proposition offered on the market; *Customer relationship* aspects consider who are the target customers, how the service is delivered to them and how to build the relationship; *Infrastructure management* component is about how to perform efficiently infrastructure and logistics issues, and *Financials* component includes the revenue and costs model (Osterwalder & Pigneur, 2002).

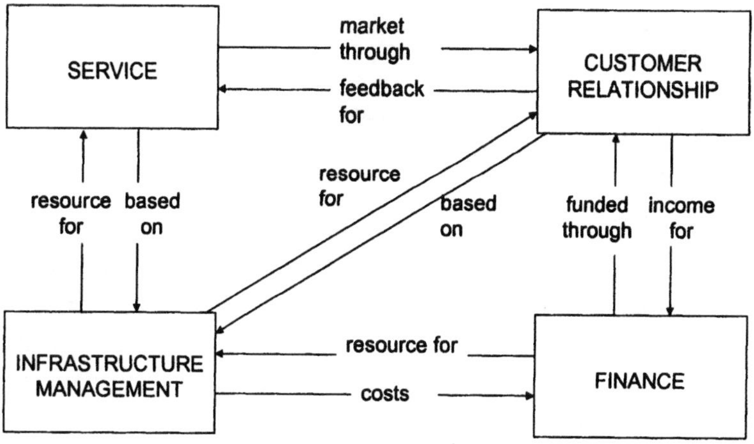

Figure 3. The four Components of Business Model Ontology (a simplified version of a figure by Osterwalder & Pigneur, 2002)

In general, a business model represents primarily a single organization view. In reality, it is always linked to an outer context (figure 4. eFactors, 2002). In the long run, business model is applied to new markets (x-axis, spatio-temporal dimension). The feasibility of the business model in global markets is even more dependent on external variables, such as consumer preferences, employee competence (individual level), industry specific standards and business codes of conduct (industry) as well as cultural aspects and market regulations (society). The framework presented in Fig. 4. presents the complex interactions of a business model levels, and our limited prevailing (endogenous) view on it in the gray-shaded area. This framework expands nicely the previous static presentation of a business model on a space-time continuum and it can be used in analyzing business context in different market areas.

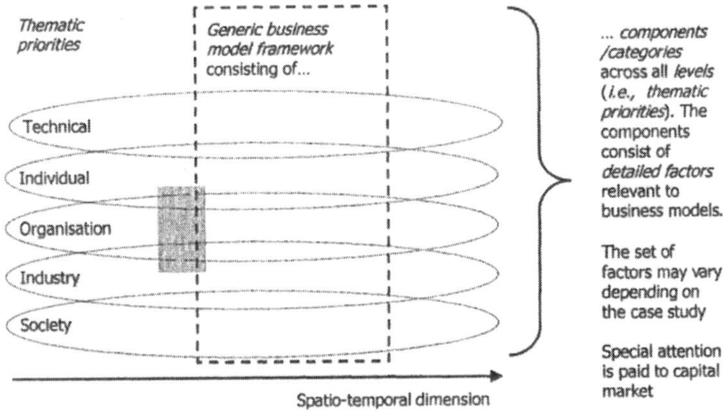

Figure 4. The eFactors framework (eFactors, 2002)

3.2 Interoperable networked business models on a compatible infrastructure?

So far the research on (e-)business models has concentrated mainly on analyzing offering and customer relationships (according to Hedman & Kalling, 2002) and limited effort is put on the profitability problems of infrastructure and operations (lower part of figure 3). However, Ciborra and Andreu (2001) point out that at infrastructure or resource level issues such as compatibility emerge almost immediately when setting up inter-organizational alliances. Many ERP- or legacy systems may actually hinder the data transfer within the network. Information structure might, on the other hand, act also as a carrier of formative context. Thus, inter-organizational systems are crucial, and can be considered as a planned and managed way to realize cooperation between organizations (e.g. Kumar & van Dissel, 1996).

An example of the qualitative change taking place in ICT-infrastructure towards e-business and partnerships is explored by Riihimaa and Ruohonen (2002)[31]. First, the internal operative information systems are updated or integrated (ERP Phase). Secondly, the emphasis is put on supply chain processes within the corporation and/or with suppliers (SCM). The third phase is generally about better integration of customer relations management systems to previously mentioned ERP- and SCM-systems (CRM). As a fourth phase emerges Knowledge Management -Phase (KM), which requires even more profound knowledge about customers, suppliers and partners. In KM phase a firm is aiming at partnerships, in which knowledge is shared with the help of ICT networks. In this stage it is also possible to create innovative methods for producing, distributing and developing products. Service is included in the product, for instance maintenance and updates are enhancing the length of the customer relationship. Riihimaa and Ruohonen claim that it is difficult, or even impossible, for a firm to enter KM phase without going through the first three phases. It should be carefully analyzed how – and to what extent – data between various information systems should to be exchanged between organizations.

The above discussion on ICT-infrastructure based articulated business models illustrate our approach to the empirical setting. The basic challenge of ICT-enabled co-operation is that there are multiple participants with their own background, interests, business contexts, and individual strategies aiming at different product/market areas with specific schedule and by utilizing their proprietary technology stack and knowledge.

To conclude: if we know relatively little about the infrastructure in one company business model context, what do we know about the infrastructure for business models of networks of companies? Not much, we are afraid.

4. THE CASE OF DEVELOPING GLOBAL SERVICE CONCEPTS

The motivation for this article arises from a practical case we are currently involved with: A consortium of three corporations (hereby called as A, B and C) and two research organizations. The consortium is focusing in primarily onto the clientele of the two consortium members (A and B). The

[31] Riihimaa and Ruohonen (2002) carried out 40 interviews in metal and electronics companies in Finland at the turn of the year 2001. Of the companies interviewed they categorized around 20% to being at ERP Phase, 50% at SCM Phase, 20% at CRM Phase, and 10% at KM Phase.

aim is to create joint ICT-supported business-to-business service offering of the three companies, thus enabling better response to customer needs. The researchers' role in the consortium is to aid in the process of communicating the needs and intentions of the parties to each other, and to help in forming an acceptable joint business model. This brings us to the discussion on strategies, business models and business processes. What sort of change in present domain, infrastructure, and revenue models of the consortium and also of each company we would need in order to succeed in co-operation? The consortium has to understand the differences in strategic intentions and 'paths' of the participating companies. Only against this backdrop it can formulate a network business model, which articulates the necessary changes, and facilitates communication and creation of shared understanding between the participants

4.1 Strategic intentions and 'paths' of the companies

Company A has become the leading supplier of capital goods on its own worldwide segment, and is generally considered also the technology leader in its field. It was company A that made the first move towards negotiations for establishing this consortium.

Figure 5. below is our interpretation of the changes of the company A on its way to present situation. The figure depicts the changes in its core competence, mode of co-operation and business network topology alongside with the evolution IS-architecture as they have emerged to support this evolution.

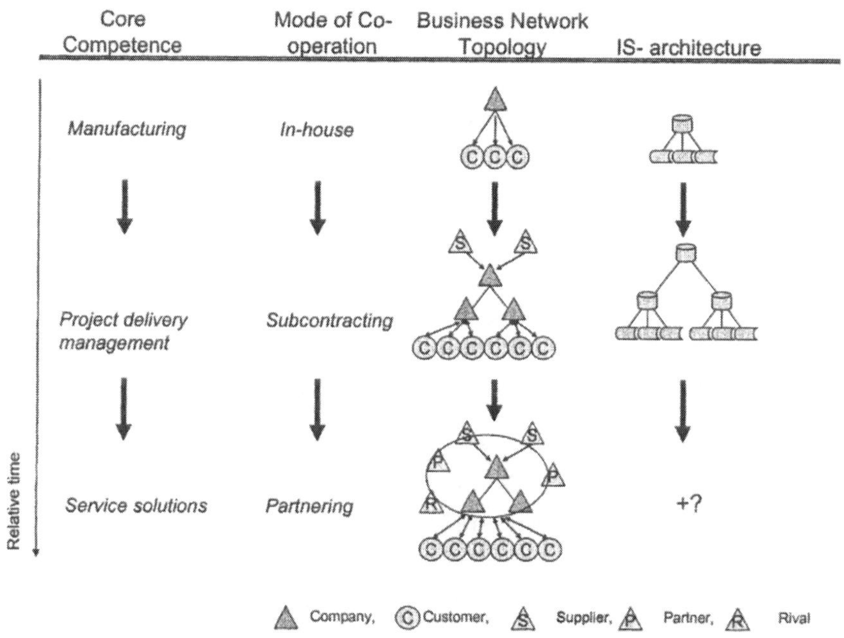

Figure 5. Evolution of core competences, mode of co-operation, business network topology and IS-architecture of Company A.

The change in the core competence can be divided in the three major eras during the last two decades. In the beginning the Company A sold, manufactured, and delivered capital (b-to-b) goods as components from the single company under the supervision of customer representatives (i.e., project consultants) around the world. Automation and IT companies supplied separately the computerized information systems, which were needed to operate, diagnose and maintain production and processes on customers' sites.

The shift from production towards customer orientation started with delivery project management. As the degree of integration of the separate components grew at the customers end, it became feasible and necessary to coordinate the delivery and design stages of the individual components more closely with partners before and during the delivery. This means that the whole final equipment including automation and supporting ICT systems were supplied to customers in close co-operation with subcontractors, and Company A took the role of a coordinator in the delivery project (i.e., Move-to-the-Middle, Clemons et al., 1993). At present, the extreme cases are turn-key projects, when the company takes a main contractor role for the whole project with all components including automation and ICT systems configuration. The industrial and technical evolution (especially the growth of complexity) has thus changed the core competence of the industry from manufacturing to project delivery management.

The next step in the evolution of core competence of Company A has been stated in its business strategy: it is expected to move towards customer oriented service. The final outcome of this development might mean that operation and maintenance of the customers' equipment may be outsourced to an alliance of company A with its partners. There are requirements to increase profitability and meet the tighter quality standards set out by the customers' clients, and environmental restrictions by the authorities. The possibilities emerge along with the advances in ICT, remote diagnostics, control and coordination systems; on the other hand there is constant pressure to cut costs.

This development has had its implications on the information systems of company A. In the early stages the ICT-architecture was rather simple (in relative terms): one company solution with functional application software, the purpose of which was primarily to coordinate the intra-company product design, and planning of production. In the second stage the architecture was enhanced with distributed work support and document management, especially in terms of creating a knowledge base on the installed base and its configuration. The last phase would require a lot of synchronization with clients, partners, and even from competitors information systems to meet the needs of profitable, high quality service offerings.

Company B, a software house, has been moving towards more customer centric strategy. Until now it has acquired the needed additional industry specific knowledge primarily by company acquisitions. Its clientele includes among others Company A and C, and also many customers of Company A. So they share the same clientele, and are partially competitors in some product groups. Company B has developed its ICT infra to support partnering mode of co-operation.

Company C, has been serving both A and B, plus some of their clients. They primarily search for markets for their value-added infrastructure services, both by expanding the existing clientele and by providing new services to and with the companies of the consortium.

In summary, in order to carry on with their espoused strategies, our consortium companies can not operate alone any more. First, they need each other to complement each others' services cost-efficiently. They also are likely to need capabilities, knowledge and innovations from outside their own competence. This development is paced by the growing tendency of the 'end' clients to outsource parts of their business, and on the increasing use of networks for creating, storing and accessing knowledge to share and appropriate information that can not be produced internally. As stated by Powell (1990): "By improving the spread of information, they sustain the conditions for further innovation by bringing together different logics and novel combinations of information." As we are talking about worldwide business, it would mean also expansion of the network, so that there are local companies working together with global companies.

As the companies have separate self-interested strategies, they should agree on 'rules' for co-operation and formulate a joint service concept that would articulate the objectives of the consortium set by corporate strategies. It calls for considerable amount of trust and openness between the companies. In our consortium the companies decided to ask for facilitation from an independent university.

We have been involved with these topics for the past two years, and the synthesis presented in article is based on a pre-study in 2002, and the following data from *MesoCompus*–research project, 2003-2004: As of writing, we have had seven workshops, four open discussion steering group meetings, around 40 one partner meetings, and 12 transcribed interviews with specialists on the topic in company A and B. The data has been supplemented also with four company A headquarters personnel meetings. The process is documented in a non-disclosed diary (Newbury, 2001) by the university party.

4.2 The Joint Development of Business Models

Transformation from manufacturing to anticipated full-service orientation with the help of ICT seems to be emerging also in our case consortium as postulated e.g., by Powell (2000). The problem is that the consortium companies are still hesitating how deep into a co-operation they should engage, what are its consequences to their businesses, and how to deal with the information infrastructure. Our understanding of the situation is that this calls for articulated business model, which can serve as a basis for learning from the other partners, as a starting point for proofs-of-concepts, to reveal the trustworthiness of the partners, and also to communicate the potential in their own organizations. As the companies are operating on a global scale, world-wide knowledge management and inter-organizational learning must be facilitated by interoperable or shared IOS systems supporting – at least partially – joint practices.

The separate organizations participating in the network have naturally each own business strategies for the present and the future. Especially, if the network is to produce new innovative services or products, the companies should encage in a process of creating a joint business model to match its and each companies strategies (see figure below, the topmost horizontal shade). This means that the parties are to agree on the value proposition offered on the market; the target customers and CRM related aspects, other infrastructure and logistics issues, timing, and the revenue sharing model (to name some of the crucial characteristics of the business model offering and segmentation). This aims at describing the strategy-business model - interface.

The above factors of business model are often uncertain and difficult to estimate in advance. For example, to be on the safe side, the partners are probably not willing to invest heavily in the beginning of the co-operation. Instead "As the trustworthiness of a potential partner is circumscribed in the beginning, firms do not commit large resources at one go, but engage in tit-for-tat games where trust gradually builds up and a growing proportion of resources are invested in the relationship, forming a set of ties between the firms." (Andersen and Christensen, 2000).

As a consequence, the network emerges incrementally through mutual adjustment, commitment, communication, and resource transactions (van de Ven, 1976; Andersen & Christensen, 2000). Moreover, especially in terms of information systems infrastructure the adjustment is an adaptive process depending on for instance organizations' histories, strategies, practices, hierarchies, cultures and infrastructure (Kumar & van Dissel, 1996). Whenever co-operation and especially exploration approach (March, 1991) is wished for, the organizations must commit into an uncertain joint effort of creating business model incrementally, most likely with a light infrastructure (Ciborra & Hanseth, 1998). We believe that this process requires extensive discussions and knowledge sharing between the participants. In these negotiations trustworthiness and alignment of motives of the parties can be validated.

We illustrate the creation of the joint business model as follows in Figure 6: The underlying blue triangle represents the business network's strategy, business model and processes (in a corresponding manner than in figure 2., Osterwalder & Pigneur, 2002) to meet the customer demand. It is constructed by adjusting the companies' own business logic triangles A, B, and C with the network level business model (e.g., Gemünden et al., 1996). The individual business models are to be adjusted in four ways: First, horizontally at the *strategy-business model* -interface between the companies, and horizontally at the operative *processes-business model* -interface between the companies. Thirdly, they can be used '*vertically' within each company* to align the strategies and processes to meet the challenges of co-operation. There is also an evident need for a fourth adjustment, namely to find new partners for the uncovered parts of the business model (the white spaces indicated by the arrows in the left and right at the business model –level).

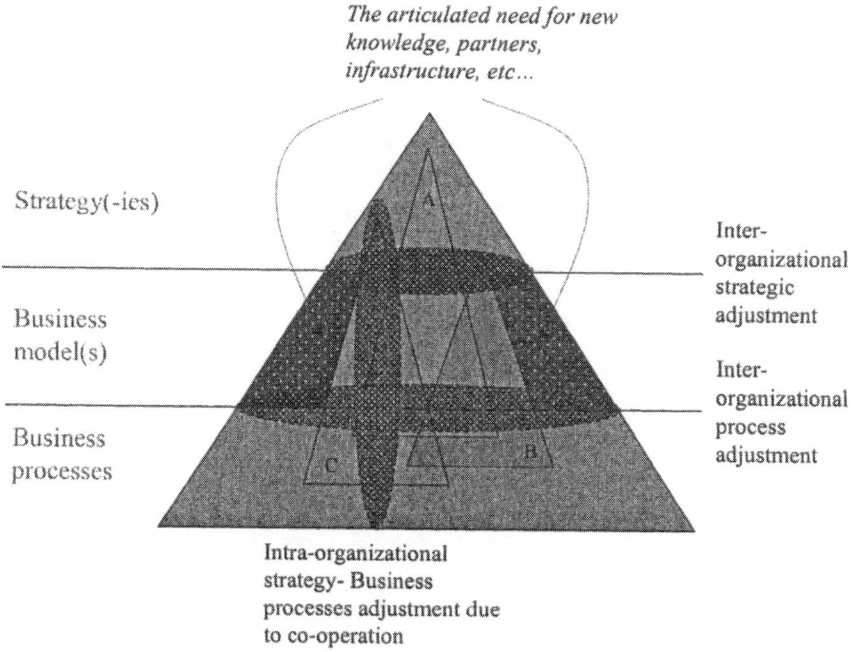

Figure 6. Joint development of network business model.

The **first adjustment**, between strategy and business model, is needed since individual strategies of participating companies are very unlikely to converge completely at network level. This is because the companies are specialized in their own fields (complementarity, van de Ven, 1976), and they are developing in the different pace towards co-operation. This means that if the companies are aiming at co-operation, they should be able to create a joint business model that is in line (Powell, 1990), or, sufficiently compatible with each company's own business strategy.

The **second adjustment**, between business model and operations, is needed to harmonize central operative processes between the companies of the network. As they even operate on different principles (or production types), there is an evident need to align at least some of the processes and ensure data compatibility. This will become even more important, when more companies join the network in the future. This is depicted in Figure 6. by letting individual business models to overlap on the processes-business model level. This overlap should cover the whole interface for interoperability reasons. This is important in our case, as the companies are looking for feasible ICT-enabled business model building upon their existing infrastructure and company specific ICT-architectures at a global scale.

The two adjustment processes mean that the business model is a necessary means of articulation of joint activities between the companies' strategies and processes. It utilizes parts of the compatible infrastructure(s) of the network parties. The boundaries between strategy and business model, and between actual processes and business model can serve as starting points in creating the joint business model. The **third adjustment** should also take place within each company between strategy and processes, which are reflected in individual business models to ensure the strategic fitting, absorption of innovations, and change management.

Fourthly, the model is also helpful in recognizing the needs for new resources, capabilities, and partners, etc., to fill in the gaps in capabilities and resources of current or proposed partners in network.

5. CONCLUSIONS

In this paper we present a conceptual framework for joint development of network business models. We have synthesized it for the purposes of an ongoing consortium aiming at developing a joint service offering relying on the extensive use of ICT. It relates the concepts of the absorptive capacity and adjustment of individual business models to the network's business model. This calls for matching the strategies and actual processes of each company with the joint business model. It points out vital adjustments processes that should be carried out in parallel to the sketching of components of a business model (in the sense of Osterwalder & Pigneur, 2002).

More specifically, in the establishment of *a joint business model* for networked, ICT enabled operations, each company should: Firstly, reflect upon the joint business model and adjust their individual strategies; Secondly, the same kind of adjustment (although more concrete) should be done between the joint business model and actual business processes of each company; Thirdly, the business model can be used 'vertically' within each company to align the strategies and processes to meet the challenges of co-operation and absorbing innovations; and fourthly, the model is also helpful in recognizing the needs for new resources, capabilities, partners, etc., to fill in the gaps in the capabilities and resources of current partners in fulfilling the product/service offering.

Whether this analytical framework will be of use to our consortium remains to be seen. Yet, by combining the research on learning and knowledge sharing between firms with expanded business model ontology for networks, we think it may be useful in directing and framing future research. For instance, we can immediately raise questions such as: Is there any recommended ways to carry out the four adjustments cycles pointed out in the framework? How should we manage knowledge in business networks? How they can be supported with ICT? How can we explicitly incorporate dynamics to the business models?

ACKNOWLEDGEMENTS

This research was financially supported by the Academy of Finland, National Development Agency and the participating companies. We thank the three anonymous reviewers for their invaluable comments in improving this article.

REFERENCES

Alchian A. and Demsetz H. (1972), "Production, Information Costs and Economic Organization", American Economic Review, 4, pp. 777-795.

Andersen P.H. and Christensen P.R. (2000). "Inter-partner learning in global supply chains: lessons from NOVO Nordisk", European Journal of Purchasing & Supply Management, 6 (2000), pp. 105-116.

Beugelsdijk S., Noorderhaven N. and Koen C. (2003) . "Organizational Culture, Alliance Capabilities and Social Capital", in the social capital workshop in Tilburg on March 27, 2003, 25 pages.

Bouwman H. (2003) "Designing metrics for business models describing Mobile services delivered by networked organisations", 16th Bled Electronic Commerce Conference eTransformation, Bled, Slovenia, June 9 - 11, 2003, 20 pages.

Ciborra C.U. and Andreu R. (2001). "Sharing knowledge across boundaries", Journal of Information Technology, Vol. 16, pp. 73-81.

Ciborra C.U. and Hanseth O. (1998). "Toward Contingency view of Infrastructure and Knowledge: An Explorative Study", Proceedings of the international conference on Information systems, Helsinki, Finland, 1998, pp. 263-272.

Clemons E., Reddi S. and Row M. (1993). "The impact of information technology on the organization of economic activity: The 'move to the middle' hypothesis", Journal of Management Information Systems, Fall 93, 10, 2, pp. 9-35.

Coase R. (1937), "The nature of the Firm", Economica, 4, Nov. 1937, pp. 386-405.

Cohen W. and Levinthal D. (1990). "Absorptive Capacity: A New Perspective on Learning and Innovation", Administrative Science Quarterly, 35, 1990, pp. 128-152.

Dyer J. and Singh H. (1998). "The relational view: Cooperative strategy and sources of inter-organizational competitive advantage", Academy of Management Review, 23, No 4, pp. 660-679.

eFactors (2002). "WP3: E-business Model Roadmap", Deliverable 3.1. of Information Systems Technologies e-Factors Thematic Network Report, IST-2001-24868.

Faber E., Ballon P., Bouwman H., Haaker T., Rietkerk O. and Steen M. (2003). "Designing business models for mobile ICT services", 16th Bled Electronic Commerce Conference eTransformation, Bled, Slovenia, June 9 - 11, 2003, 14pages.

Gemünden H.G., Ritter T., and Heyedebreck P., (1996). "Network configuration and innovation success: An empirical analysis in German high-tech industries", International Journal of Research in Marketing, Vol.13, pp. 449-462.
Gulati R. and Singh H. (1998), "The architecture of cooperation: Managing coordination costs and appropriation concerns in strategic alliances", Administrative Science Quarterly, Vol. 43, Issue 4, Dec 1998, pp. 781-814,.
Hammer M. (1990). "Reengineering work: Don't Automate, Obliterate", Harvard Business Review, July-August 1990, pp. 104-112.
Hedman J. and Kalling T. (2002). "Analysing e-business Models", in Monteiro J., Swatman P., Tavares L. (eds.) "Towards The Knowledge Society: eCommerce, eBusiness, and eGovernment", The Second IFIP Conference on E-Commerce, E-Business, E-Government (I3E 2002), October 7-9, 2002, Lisbon, Portugal, Kluwer 2002, pp. 259-270.
Hagedoorn J. and Duysters G. (2002), "External Sources of Innovative Capabilities: The Preferences for Strategic Alliances or Mergers and Acquisitions", Journal of Management Studies, vol. 39 (2), pp. 167-88.
Hoogeweegen M., Teunissen W., Vervest P. and Wagenaar R. (1999). "Modular Network Design: Using information and Communication Technology to Allocate Production Tasks in a Virtual Organization", Decision Sciences, Fall 1999, pp. 1073-1103.
Jensen M.C. and Meckling W.H. (1973), Theory of the Firm: Managerial behavior, agency costs and ownership structure, Journal of Financial Economics, Vol. 3 (Oct 1973), pp. 305-360.
Kumar K. and van Dissel H.G. (1996). "Sustainable collaboration. Managing conflict and cooperation in inter-organizational systems", MIS Quarterly, 1996, 20 (3), pp. 279-300
Malone T. Yates J. and Benjamin R. (1987), "Electronic Markets and Electronic Hierarchies", Communications of the ACM, 30, 6, pp. 484-497.
March J. (1991). "Exploration and exploitation in organizational learning", Organizational Science, Vol. 2, No. 1, February 1991, pp. 71-87.
Nalebuff B. and Brandenburger A. (1996). "Co-opetition", Profile Books, 1996, 288 pages.
Newbury D., (2001). "Diaries and Fieldnotes in the Research Process", Research Issues in Art Design and Media, Issue 1, (2001), The Research Training Initiative, University of Central England.
Nielsen B. (2002). "Synergies in Strategic Alliances: Motivation and Outcomes of Complementary and Synergistic Knowledge Networks", Journal of Knowledge Management Practices, Vol. 3, 2002, 26 pages.
Nooteboom B. (2000). "Learning by Interaction: Absorptive Capacity, Cognitive Distance and Governance", Journal of Management and Governance, 2000, 4, pp. 69–92.
Osterwalder (2004). "The Business Model Ontology: A Proposition in a Design Science Approach", Doctorate Thesis, l'Ecole des Hautes Etudes Commerciales de l'Université de Lausanne, 172 pages.
Osterwalder A. and Pigneur Y. (2002). "An e-Business model ontology for modelling e-Business". In the proceedings of the 15th Bled Conference on E-Commerce, Loebbecke et al. (eds.), 16-19 June 2002, Bled, Slovenia, 11 pages.
Picot A. Bortenlänger C. and Röhrl H. (1997). "Organization of Electronic Markets: Contributions from the New Institutional economics", The Information Society, Vol. 13, pp. 107-123.
Powell W.W. (1990). "Neither Markets nor Hierarchy: Network Forms of Organization", Research in Organizational Behavior, Vol 12, pp. 295-336.
Powell W.W. (2000). "The Capitalist Firm in the 21st Century: Emerging Patterns" in DiMaggio P., (ed.) (2003). "The Twenty-First-Century Firm: Changing Economic Organization in International Perspective", Princeton University Press, 275 pages

Riihimaa J. and Ruohonen M. (2002). "Sähköisestä kaupasta osaamisliiketoimintaan – Metalli- ja elektroniikkateollisuuden sähköisen liiketoiminnan strateginen suunta" (From eCommerce to Knowledge Based Business – The Strategic Directions of eBusiness in Metal and Electronics Industries) , Metalliteollisuuden Keskusliiton julkaisuja, 2002, 86 pages, in Finnish.

Sivadas E. and Dwyer R. (2000). "An Examination of Organizational Factors Influencing New Product Success in Internal and Alliance-Based Processes", Journal of Marketing, Vol. 64, pp. 31-49.

Timmers P. (1998). "Business Models for Electronic Markets", In Gadient, Yves; Schmid, Beat F.; Selz, Dorian: (eds.) Electronic Commerce in Europe. Electronic Markets, Vol. 8, No. 2, 07.98.

Tsupari P., Nissinen T. and Urrila P. (2001). "Kohti strategisia yritysverkkoja: Osaraportti I Teollisuuden verkottumisen yleiskatsaus" (Towards Strategic Enterprise Networks: Report I An Overview of the Networking in the Industry), Teollisuuden ja Työnantajain Keskusliiton julkaisuja, 2001, 42 pages, in Finnish.

van de Ven A.H. (1976). "On the Nature, Formation, and Maintenance of Relations Among Organizations", Academy of Management Review, 1976, pp. 24-34.

Williamson O.E. (1985). "The Economic Institutions of Capitalism; Firms, Markets, Relational Contracting", The Free Press, New York, 1985, 450 pages.

DRIVERS AND BARRIERS FOR E-BUSINESS: EVOLUTION OVER TIME AND COMPARISON BETWEEN SMEs AND LARGE COMPANIES

Dirk Deschoolmeester[1], Evelyne Vanpoucke[2] and Peter Willaert[3]
[1]Vlerick Leuven Gent Management School, Reep 1, 9000 Gent, Belgium, dirk.deschoolmeester@vlerick.be; [1]Faculty of Economics and Business Administration, Hoverniersberg 24, 9000 Gent, Belgium, dirk.deschoolmeester@ugent.be; [2]Vlerick Leuven Gent Management School, Reep 1, 9000 Gent, Belgium, evelyne.vanpoucke@vlerick.be; [3]Vlerick Leuven Gent Management School, Reep 1, 9000 Gent, Belgium, peter.willaert@vlerick.be

Abstract: The ups and downs of e-business investments are related to a hype cycle. This hype cycle strengthened the statement that companies are too willing to believe in the promises of the new Internet economy without really thinking about internet-ability. According to the data in this practice-oriented survey work, SMEs are more eager to follow the e-business hype cycle. We try to give some explanations for these differences in e-business between SMEs and large companies. This requires an examination of the planning, the drivers and the barriers for conducting business processes over a computer-mediated network. We found that larger companies are mainly driven by cost-cutting to implement e-business, while SMEs attach, next to cost-savings, high importance to cooperation between their suppliers and clients. Furthermore, we can observe that larger companies see more opportunities in translating their e-business strategy into a formal long-term plan. This explains perhaps why larger companies are less trend sensitive for investing in e-business than SMEs.

Key words: e-business hype cycle, IT investments, SME, CADIGA-rule, internet-ability

1. PURPOSE OF THE SURVEY

In order to collect the data to understand the e-business use and readiness of Belgian companies, four surveys have been conducted over a period of time (1999-2002). In this survey we assessed in the first place the current status of e-business in the companies. To investigate the process of organizing a business over a computer-mediated network, it was analyzed whether companies located in Belgium find it important to have a strategic e-business plan and whether these companies also have developed such a formal plan.

It was also thought to be useful to make a deeper study on the drivers for implementing Internet technologies and on the impediments or barriers hindering the adoption of Internet technologies for small and large companies.

Resistance, pressures and barriers for e-business were investigated and reclassified in 5 main categories. In order to identify the drivers for e-business, we asked for the expected organizational and strategic impact of e-business and its benefits. The drivers were classified based upon what the authors further define as the CADIGA framework (a further development and adaptation of Wiseman's work on strategy and IT, 1985, Figure 3). These themes were part of what has been called Internet-ability by the authors of this survey work and are also an important input for adoption stages models (Scupola, 2002).

After taking a closer look to the general evolution of e-business for all Belgian companies, a particular interest is paid in this practice-oriented survey work to whether small and medium sized companies show relevant differences in their Internet-use and -readiness compared with larger companies (criterion: total employment lower (SMEs) than 500 persons and higher (large companies) than 500 persons, European Parliament definition (OECD, 1999)). A comparative analysis of drivers and barriers in large companies and SMEs was also conducted.

Survey data of 235 companies, collected in the period 1999-2002 was used to investigate Internet-ability in Belgian companies. As well descriptive statistics, as explanatory statistical analysis were performed to test the reliability and validity of our findings.

2. E-BUSINESS FOLLOWS A HYPE-CYCLE

By looking at how many Belgian companies have a strategic e-business plan and how important it is to have one, we can see that e-business follows a hype cycle. During the early adoption stage, i.e. for this study in 1999, only 30% of the companies had an e-business plan. Since 2001 however, nearly 50% of the Belgian companies had already some sort of strategic e-business plan formally written down (Table 1). On the other hand, the study shows that slightly more than 50% of the Belgian companies do not have such a plan!

Table 1. Belgian companies holding a formal e-business plan (1999-2002)

% of companies with a strategic e-business plan (1999-2002)			
1999 (N=78)	2000 (N=56)	2001 (N=52)	2002 (N=49)
% of companies with a formal e-business plan	% of companies with a formal e-business plan	% of companies with a formal e-business plan	% of companies with a formal e-business plan
29%	33%	48%	47%

The importance that companies attach to a formal e-business plan (Figure 1) increased in the first two years and is in a later period followed by a decrease. In 2000, already 91% of the companies believed in the importance of having an e-business strategy. A similar increase in companies holding such a strategic e-business plan (Table 1) confirmed this statement. However, the belief that a formal plan is needed decreased after the year 2000. The reaction came later: since 2001 the amount of companies writing down an e-business plan felt slightly back. This increase followed by a decrease indicates that e-business follows a hype-cycle with a peak in 2000: when the hype was over, the urgent need to formally plan in several companies was apparently gone.

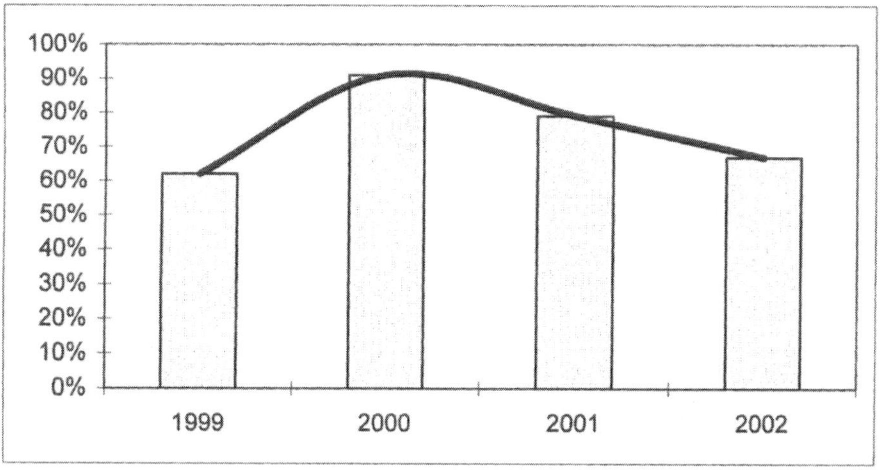

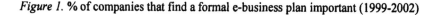

Figure 1. % of companies that find a formal e-business plan important (1999-2002)

If the results are split along the lines of company size, we can find that small and medium-sized companies show an emerging, especially widening lag in their formulation of an Internet strategy (Table 2, Figure 2).

Table 2. Companies holding a formal e-business plan (1999-2002)

	1999 (N=78) % with a formal e-com strategy	*2000 (N=56)* % with a formal e-com strategy	*2001 (N=52)* % with a formal e-com strategy	*2002 (N=49)* % with a formal e-com strategy
SMEs	26%	27%	37%	33%
Large enterprises	31%	36%	55%	68%

This widening gap can be better understood when asking companies' response on how important it is to have a formal e-business plan. The graph below shows that there exists a large gap between the perception on the importance of e-business plans for larger and smaller companies today. The lower interest and/or lower "Internet-ability" of SMEs are seen as the main reasons for this gap. Remarkable is again the peak in 2000, which can be explained by the hype around doing e-business in 2000 and by the fact that the falldowns in active interest are higher for SMEs than for larger companies.

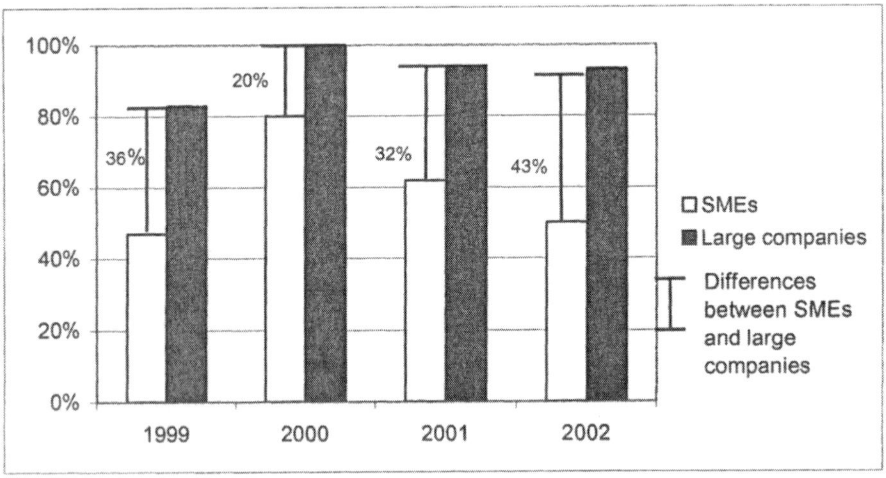

Figure 2. The importance of a formal e-business plan (1999-2002)

Since it can be assumed that the lack of explicit strategy formulation - being used as a guideline for future e-investments - poses one of the major barriers for the adoption and implementation of these Internet technologies, the relative lack of SMEs in formulating a strategic e-business plan can be considered as a major reason why SMEs are tending to lag behind in effectively implementing these more advanced technologies for information processing and communication. Large companies do not only provide a variety of e-applications such as catalogues, on-line surveys, ordertaking, marketing and procurement via the internet, they also use IT for processing the order-related transactions (ordertaking and payment) and providing customers with detailed information.

The European Commission claims that e-business in Europe is hampered by a lack of trust. Although 66% of small companies have Internet access in Europe, only 6% of these small European companies transact business online in real-time. (Jutla en Weatherbee, 2002) The same conclusion can be drawn for Belgian SMEs in this study: only 6% of the transaction processing is done by the Internet (Table 3).

Table 3. The use of Internet technologies in SMEs and large companies (2002)

Internet technologies for SMEs and large companies in 2002						
	Realized		Planned for within 1 year		Planned for later than 1 year	
E-applications (SME: N=30, Large: N=19)	SME	Large	SME	Large	SME	Large
Catalogue of products and services	79%	69%	21%	19%	0%	12%
On-line survey	50%	46%	29%	39%	21%	15%
Handling requests for proposals	52%	33%	16%	34%	32%	33%
Ordertaking and handling	45%	43%	25%	21%	30%	36%
Access to forums and newsgroups	24%	36%	38%	7%	38%	57%
After-sales-service	25%	50%	54%	14%	21%	29%
Prospecting and direct marketing	41%	43%	27%	28%	32%	29%
Co-managed inventory	18%	10%	9%	10%	73%	80%
Vendor-managed inventory (VMI)	20%	18%	10%	9%	70%	73%
E-procurement	25%	42%	25%	25%	50%	33%
Internet technologies that are more often used by large companies than by SMEs						
Transaction processing*	6%	33%	22%	17%	72%	50%
Search engines*	43%	77%	26%	11%	31%	11%
Access to FAQs*	38%	75%	29%	13%	33%	12%

(*) Significant difference between SMEs and large companies with a 85% confidence interval

3. STRATEGIC DRIVERS FOR E-BUSINESS

Besides the degree of formalization of the planning, this study was also interested in the motivations and arguments to invest in the Internet technologies. These drivers and barriers (infra) are important aspects in the adoption stages of SMEs. An example of such a stages model for SMEs is the PriceWaterhouseCoopers' model (1999). In a first stage, SMEs have certain perceptions of the opportunities and benefits (or so-called drivers) for e-commerce. In th ond stage, the SMEs try to develop their e-commerce capabilities based on the information from the first stage. Next, the companies experience a number of barriers in the realization process which they try to solve in the following stage. They look for governments or other stakeholders to help them to overcome these barriers. If they finally see the results, they go on with developing e-commerce capabilities. As we described here, this stages model indicates that drivers and barriers have important consequences in the adoption of e-commerce and e-business in SMEs. This is also the reason why we attach a lot of importance to these drivers and barriers for e-business.

Table 4 explains the strategic reasons companies quote for adopting e-business. In a study of 1999 (Deschoolmeester, ea.), only a minority of Belgian companies were convinced that the adoption of the most basic Internet technologies, e.g. an online catalogue of products, would cut costs. Internet was not only seen as a way to improve the bottom-line results of the company, but also as a way to improve collaboration and differentiation.

In this research, six reasons were retained why companies build an Internet business alongside their existing one: 1) cutting costs (C), 2) improving internal and/or external integration and cooperation (A), 3) differentiate from competitors (D), 4) using ICT to improve innovation and its related external replication (I), 5) improve the companies position for growth (G), or 6) agility for external changes (A). This rule of thumb (CADIGA-rule) points to strategic drivers that can be attained through the use of ICT (Figure 3). The model is an adaptation made by authors on the basis of ideas from Porter (1980) and more specifically Wiseman (1985). They give business management a list of motives for investing in ICT. Also other studies argue that amongst IT-investments in general, Internet technologies have the highest potential for value-creation through linking companies, its suppliers and customers in new and innovative ways (Armit, Zott, 2001).

Zhu et al. (2002) identify six significant e-business adoption predictors, which are comparable with those included in the CADIGA-rule. These six predictors are technology competence, firm scope, firm size, consumer readiness, competitive pressure and lack of trading partner readiness. Consumer and trading partner readiness reflect the drive for alliances, the competitive pressure explains the drive for differentiation, firm size is a predictor related to the growth reason, technological competence is represented by the innovation drive and finally firm scope reflects the urge for cutting costs.

Table 4. CADIGA-rule

CADIGA-rule for investing in IT*	
(C) CUTTING COSTS	A lot of companies implement an Enterprise Resource Planning (ERP) to obtain a more productive procurement- and production planning. In this way they can achieve smaller inventories of resources, work in process and finished products. They can also achieve a more optimal use of production-resources through efficient information processing, smaller teams of purchasers and production planners.
(A) ALLIANCES: Internal: integration External: cooperation	Integration between functional domains via central databases and the coordination of activities in an integrated process are made possible with the aid of ICT. In an extended enterprise, suppliers and customers can cooperate non-stop and in real-time thanks to the new ICT.
(D) DIFFERENTIATION FROM COMPETITORS	Via Internet Web browsing, the customer can place his order and buy a custom-made product. The cycle-time between sales-order and delivery can also be drastically reduced. Websites where these facilities are available can differentiate a company from its competitors who still follow the traditional way of selling.
(I) INFORMATION AND KNOWLEDGE / INNOVATION	Having the right kind of information, on the right time, available to the right kind of decision-makers, is an essential task of all information management. If wisdom and experience are added to information, one gets knowledge. Companies who create and share a lot of knowledge with the help if ICT and who have a learning mentality and sharing knowledge among personnel will be the star players of the future. If companies want to have an image of being technologically advanced, ICT is one of the best means to achieve this image of being innovative. Some customers and suppliers prefer working with companies who prove to have a knack for innovation.
(G) IMPROVE GROWTH POSITION	With the help of ICT, companies can grow in size, in the number of business activities or on a geographic scale. Besides quantitative growth this also entails qualitative growth whereby information is more accessible when needed, which will eventually empower personnel.
(A) AGILITY, FLEXIBILTY	To improve awareness on the role of ICT for the organization, higher level management has to question itself on a regular basis about the relationship between potential and obtained results in the past, current and future ICT project portfolio. When the external environment changes, adequate modification has to be made swiftly.

(*) Further developed and adapted by Dirk Deschoolmeester from Wiseman's work on strategy and IT (1985) and ideas from Porter (1985)

In 1999, cost-savings were seen as the main motivator for implementing Internet technologies, but cannot be the single reason for applying e-business. Improving alliances and flexibility are examples of other important drivers to implement these technologies in companies. By looking at the differences between small and large companies in 2002, one can see that the main driver for developing Internet technologies is not the same for SMEs as for large companies. While large companies are mainly motivated by the cost-saving aspect of Internet technologies (Figure 3), SMEs are in the first place driven to implement these technologies by the improvements in cooperation with their suppliers and clients (Figure 4). This is in contrast with findings in other research on SME drivers and barriers for e-business where costs are found to be a major concern (Levy, Powell, Yetton, 2003; Prananto, McKay and Marshall, 2003).

On the other hand our findings are also reflected in research of Zhu et al. (2002), which identified technology competence, firm scope and size, consumer readiness, and competitive pressure as being significant e-business adoption facilitators, while lack of trading partner readiness is a significant adoption inhibitor. Moreover this study confirms our results in claiming that in high e-business intensity countries, e-business is no longer a phenomenon dominated by large firms; as more and more firms engage in e-business, network effect works to the advantage of small firms. In this case these SMEs have more opportunities to form alliances.

Improved communication around the clock, administrative cost savings, increased efficiency and easiness to do business are the most important short-term drivers. Increased company visibility, market potential and a contribution to internationalization, on the other hand, are among the most important long-term indirect drivers (Poon, Swatman, 1999). In this study, we can conclude that SMEs and large companies focus mainly on short-term drivers.

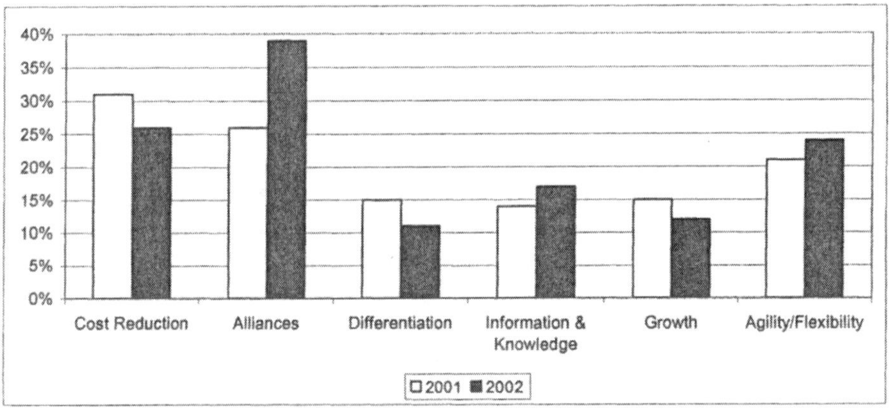

Figure 3. CADIGA-rule for Belgian SMEs (2001-2002)

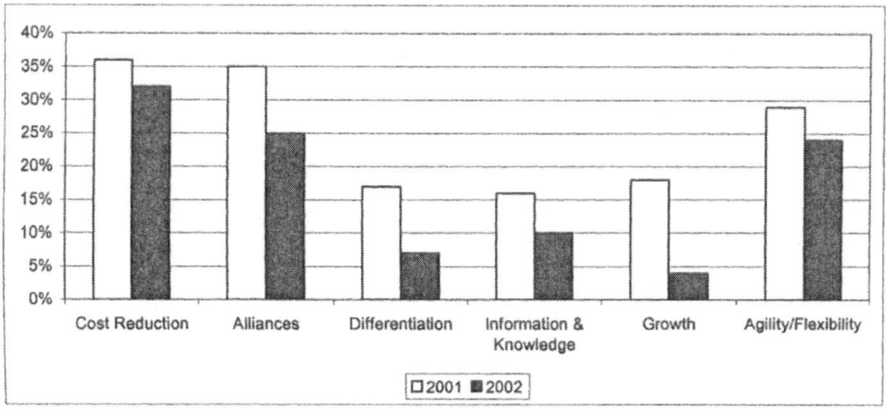

Figure 4. CADIGA-rule for large companies in Belgium (2001-2002)

While looking at the implementation of Internet technologies in SMEs and large companies, one can see some differences between SMEs and large companies in the CADIGA-rule concerning the specific application fields.

3.1 The CADIGA-rule: growth (G)

Some companies, especially the smaller ones, believe that Internet technologies give them opportunities to grow. The majority of large companies, on the other hand, do not often use Internet technologies for supporting growth opportunities in their company. These differences between large companies and SMEs in seeing e-business as a growth factor is situated mainly in the field of co-engineering of new products and handling requests for offers/proposals/information (Table 5). Other studies support this statement (Levy, Powell, Yetton, 2003).

Table 5. Significant differences in growth between SMEs and large companies according to their application yield

Benefits\Company size	Importance of the growth driver for implementing IT in small companies	Importance of the growth driver for implementing IT in large companies
Co-engineering of new products	25%	6%
Handling requests for offers/ Proposals/ Quotations	19%	0%

(*) Significant differences between SMEs and large companies: t-test with a confidence interval of 85%.

3.2 The CADIGA-rule: Flexibility (F)

Flexibility is another important item for both SMEs and large companies. Although the way to reach this flexibility through the use of Internet technologies is different for these two groups, SMEs see Internet technologies as a tool to improve the flexibility of marketing activities, i.e. the prospecting of customers and doing surveys, whereas large companies pay more attention to the flexibility of their inventories (Table 6).

Table 6. Significant differences in flexibility perceptions between SMEs and large companies according to their application yield (2002)

Benefits\Company size	Importance of the flexibility driver for implementing IT in small companies	Importance of the flexibility driver for implementing IT in large companies
On-line surveys	32%	6%
Co-managed inventory	8%	28%
Prospecting and direct marketing	15%	0%

(*) Significant differences between SMEs and large companies: t-test with a confidence interval of 95%.

3.3 The CADIGA-rule: Alliances (A)

A third important driver for IT is the creation of alliances. One can see that small companies expect that the development of new information technologies for customer service will improve their internal and external collaboration and cooperation. In other words, SMEs believe that Internet technologies will help them to streamline and to improve the supply chain (Table 7).

Table 7. Significant differences in the perception of cooperation and collaboration between SMEs and large companies according to their application yield (2002)

Benefits\Company size	Importance of the cooperation and collaboration driver for implementing IT in SMEs	Importance of the cooperation and collaboration driver for implementing IT in large companies
Handling requests for offers/Proposals/ Quotations	57%	22%
Offering access to FAQs	80%	50%
Provide customer service	89%	50%

(*) Significant differences between SMEs and large companies: t-test with a confidence interval of 85%.

3.4 The CADIGA-rule: Information and knowledge (I)

Another significant difference in the perception of information technologies between SMEs and large companies is that SMEs are convinced that using IT to develop catalogues or ordertaking processes offers large advantages in managing information and knowledge. Large companies do not share this believe (Table 8).

Table 8. Significant differences in the perception of "information and knowledge" between SMEs and large companies according to their application yield (2002)

Benefits\Company size	Importance of the information and knowledge driver for implementing IT in SMEs	Importance of the information and knowledge driver for implementing IT in large companies
Catalogue of products/ services	46%	17%
Ordertaking from customers	18%	0%

(*) Significant differences between SMEs and large companies: t-test with a confidence interval of 85%.

3.5 The CADIGA-rule: Costs (C) and Differentiation (D)

According to costs (C) and differentiation (D), there are no real differences between SMEs and large companies.

4. BARRIERS TO THE IMPLEMENTATION OF E-BUSINESS

Information technology managers experience different impediments in the adoption and/or the development process of e-business. We have measured the importance of 16 potential barriers, which can be categorized by a factor analysis into 5 main e-business obstructions: rules & standards, costs, safety & security, know-how & technology and lack of awareness. In 2002, costs and safety & security are seen as the most important barriers for the further implementation of e-business (Figure 5).

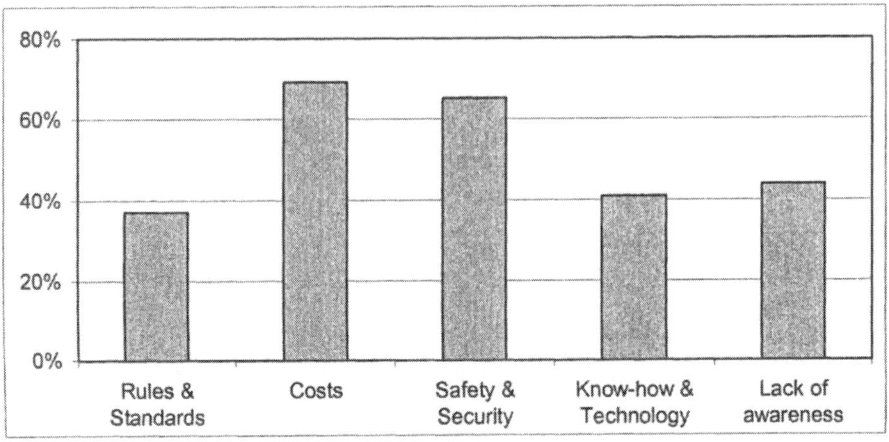

Figure 5. The five important barriers for e-business

The table below (Table 9) illustrates the evolution in the importance of the barriers. It is striking that, from 1999 until 2002, most barriers have been perceived to be less stringent. Some other barriers like security, privacy, lack of ready-to-use software, problematic integration with the existing business processes and cost barriers stayed at the same level. The general decrease of barriers for implementing Internet technologies shows that there is a positive development towards better competence for e-enabling business processes. Although barriers became less strong, we can see again that security and costs are perceived to have kept a rather high level of hindrance for companies implementing Internet technologies.

On one hand, these five factors form strong barriers for Belgian companies to implement e-business projects. On the other hand, they can also function as accelerators for competitors who are able to overcome these barriers. The reader can analyze the situation in more detail in the following table. Some variation in ups and downs might also be related to the well-know e-business hype cycle (supra).

Table 9. The importance of the 16 barriers (1999-2002)

	Importance of barriers				
	1999 (N=78) Very + Rather important barrier	2000 (N=56) Very + Rather important barrier	2001 (N=52) Very + Rather important barrier	2002 (N=49) Very + Rather important barrier	Changes (*)
Safety					
Security	82%	79%	84%	90%	=
Privacy (on payments)	86%	66%	65%	80%	=
Fear of cannibalizing / competing with your existing business	43%	38%	39%	24%	-
Know-how & technology					
Language	49%	29%	25%	17%	-
Lack of ready-to-use software solutions	65%	61%	68%	40%	=
Lack of internet technology know-how / Experience	66%	59%	50%	48%	-
Problematic integration with existing business processes	65%	75%	73%	58%	=
Lack of one-to-one marketing experience	68%	57%	42%	41%	-
Rules and standards					
Lack of government regulations	64%	45%	52%	11%	-
Legal issues / lack of regulation	79%	49%	63%	49%	-
Lack of industry standards	64%	56%	63%	50%	-
Costs					
Too high costs / Investments	78%	55%	69%	76%	=
Lack of internal budget / Funding	61%	46%	53%	62%	=
Awareness					
Lack of e-business awareness in my company	78%	48%	43%	43%	-
Lack of e-business strategy	73%	64%	61%	45%	-
Lack of internal top management support	57%	29%	33%	45%	-

(*) = means keeping at the same level ; - means becoming less strong

According to the figure below (Figure 6), there are some significant differences between SMEs and large companies in rating barriers. Large companies generally experience higher levels of impediments (74%) than SMEs (47%).

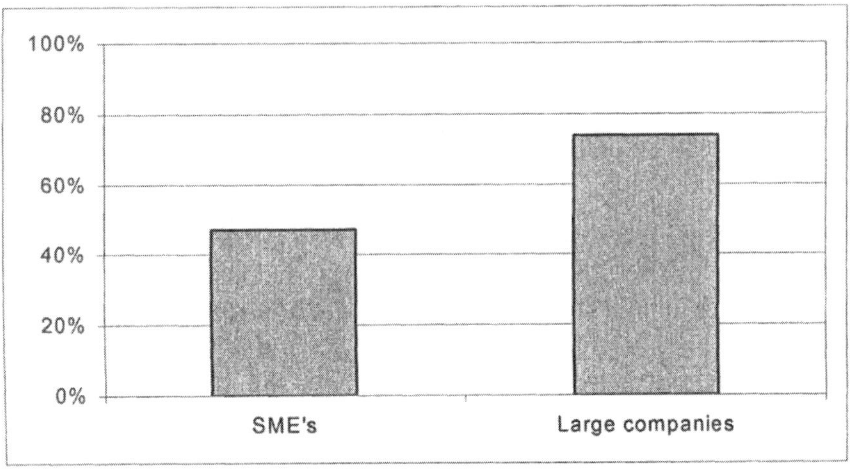

Figure 6. The importance of barriers for SMEs and large companies

The larger the enterprise, the more the aspects such as 'rules and standards' and 'lack of awareness' are seen as important barriers. This shows that the implementation of new Internet technologies are far more complex or this shows that large companies have a higher perception, consciousness and planning attitude in their companies than SMEs do in that respect. Since Internet technologies are expensive, costs and 'safety and security' represent the most important thresholds to develop and implement these technologies in SMEs. Compared to the barriers of large companies, some aspects, which are not mentioned in this study, are especially problematic for SMEs. Some of these barriers include lack of qualified personnel, risk of loss, partners' e-commerce readiness, lack of business models and legal issues (CommerceNet study, 2000).

From 1999 until 2002, we can see, on one hand, that the barriers became generally less important or at least stayed at about the same level for large companies. On the other hand, the perception of costs and safety factors as impediments for further investing in e-business seems to be increased in the perception of SME management (Table 10).

Table 10. The importance of barriers in SMEs and large companies (1999-2002)

	Importance of barriers									
	1999 Very + Rather important barrier		2000 Very + Rather important barrier		2001 Very + Rather important barrier		2002 Very + Rather important barrier		Changes	
	SME	**Large**	**SME**	**Large**	**SME**	**Large**	**SME**	**Large**	**SME**	**Large**
	N= 42	N= 36	N= 26	N= 30	N= 19	N= 33	N= 30	N= 19		
Safety										
Security	**73%**	**91%**	74%	82%	79%	88%	93%	83%	+	=
Privacy (on payments)	**78%**	**94%**	60%	71%	63%	66%	86%	72%	=	=
Fear of cannibalizing / competing with your existing business	**31%**	**55%**	**27%**	**50%**	**16%**	**52%**	24%	24%	-	-
Know-how & technology										
Language	50%	48%	27%	29%	26%	25%	21%	12%	-	-
Lack of ready-to-use software solutions	59%	71%	54%	68%	79%	61%	41%	39%	=	-
Lack of internet technology know-how / Experience	64%	68%	54%	61%	42%	55%	40%	61%	-	=
Problematic integration with existing business processes	56%	74%	65%	82%	**58%**	**82%**	57%	59%	=	=
Lack of one-to-one marketing experience	**60%**	**76%**	50%	64%	53%	63%	37%	47%	-	-
Rules and standards										
Lack of government regulations	63%	65%	35%	54%	44%	57%	48%	56%	=	-
Legal issues / lack of regulation	**73%**	**85%**	**38%**	**59%**	61%	63%	46%	53%	=	-
Lack of industry standards	63%	65%	50%	64%	63%	63%	48%	53%	=	-
Costs										
Too high costs / Investments	79%	77%	50%	61%	74%	67%	78%	72%	=	=
Lack of internal budget / Funding	56%	65%	56%	39%	56%	52%	64%	59%	+	=

continued

(*) = Means keeping at the same level ; - means becoming less strong

(*) The figures in bold show significant differences between SMEs and large companies: t-test with a confidence interval of 85%

	Importance of barriers									
	1999 Very + Rather important barrier		2000 Very + Rather important barrier		2001 Very + Rather important barrier		2002 Very + Rather important barrier		Changes	
	SME	Large	SME	Large	SME	Large	SME	Large	SME	Large
	N= 42	N= 36	N= 26	N= 30	N= 19	N= 33	N= 30	N= 19		
Awareness										
Lack of e-business awareness in my company	74%	83%	**35%**	**64%**	42%	55%	**29%**	**69%**	-	=
Lack of e-business strategy	72%	74%	62%	64%	68%	56%	39%	53%	-	=
Lack of internal top management support	49%	67%	27%	32%	32%	34%	**30%**	**67%**	-	=

(*) = Means keeping at the same level ; - means becoming less strong
(*) The figures in bold show significant differences between SMEs and large companies: t-test with a confidence interval of 85%

5. CONCLUSION

E-business shows -also in this series of surveys made in Belgium- a hype-cycle with a peak in 2000. This hype cycle strengthened our believe that companies were much too willing to believe in the promises of the new Internet economy without really thinking about Internet-ability.

In this survey work, first of all a longitudinal analysis of the e-business situation of Belgian companies is described (1999-2002); secondly a comparison of drivers and barriers for e-business adoption between large companies and SMEs was made (under 500 employees being an SME in a wider European context). Research showed that larger companies more often formalized their Internet technology objectives into an e-business plan than SMEs. This poor formalization explains why SMEs lag behind.

Internet technologies affect all processes of an organization: selling, finding partners, marketing, transfer documents, after-sales service, etc. But according to a report of the French Ministry of Economic Affairs, Finance and Industry few enterprises, large and smaller ones, are aware of all the opportunities the Internet has to offer. Moreover the 2004 e-readiness report of the Economist Intelligence Unit stated that Belgium is not yet completely ready for the internet-economy, with only a 17th place out of 60 countries over the world. The Internet is not something that can be neglected. Essential to the success of Internet-adoption, is the capacity of companies to adopt and innovate in order to face international competition.

The Public Governments have an important role to play in order to create a favorable context for Internet-adoption (especially for SMEs), elevate the barriers, and more importantly to integrate these necessary evolutions in their own organizations when they act as client, supplier or partner for other companies.

Business Schools, Universities, government agencies and various SME stakeholders can help to overcome this threshold and can advise, collaborate and provide services to build an environment for aggressive e-business adoption in SMEs (Jutla en Weatherbee, 2002). Coordination, particularly formal programs between government organizations and IT industry, is key to success (Economist Intelligence Unit, 2004). It is important that all stakeholders cooperate to develop proper e-governance for a region or a country in order to promote e-business activities and overcome the barriers to e-business adoption. Furthermore, SMEs have to create a multiple e-business approach to create a more holistic view. This holistic view can be created by business cases on e-business. This can also be boosted by Business Schools and Universities.

As far as the drivers concerned in this study, it is shown that whatever the size of these companies, interest in e-business is very much oriented towards obtaining cost-reduction in some of the major processes. It can be seen that other drivers, such as the improvement of customer service, but especially collaboration and cooperation are sometimes of greater importance. For some processes and some application fields, this study shows a widening gap between SMEs and large companies in the importance of e-business over time.

To have a more detailed view on the drivers and barriers that influence the Internet-ability, this study made an analysis about the differences between larger and smaller companies for a limited number of variables. We can conclude that larger companies are mainly driven by cost-savings to implement Internet technologies whereas SMEs are more driven by improving cooperation with suppliers and clients than by cost-cutting only. This is in contradiction to some other views on SMEs. Levy, Powell and Yetton see an e-business investment as either a driver for costs or as a driver for growth. Prananto, McKay and Marshall, on the other hand, believe that cost is the main barrier for SMEs' e-business initiatives. Another phenomenon is that barriers for e-business became less strong during the last four years. Only security and costs stayed large obstructions for e-business investments. This study shows that these barriers are higher in large companies than in SMEs. Furthermore, we can observe that larger companies attach more importance to e-business, see more opportunities in translating their e-business strategy into a formal plan and are less trend sensitive concerning e-business matters than SMEs.

The study however has to be careful with generalizing its findings since each year is based on a rather small sample of companies of both sizes. Further analysis on this Internet-ability concept and on studying drivers and barriers over time need to be done for a larger sample, before making any strong and final conclusion in this subject. Another remark is that this study does not measure the e-business capabilities that should be taken into account before investigating the drivers and barriers. We hope however that the material of this research might have an influence on the formulation of new hypotheses withheld in other studies on the subject of e-business adoption and implementation.

REFERENCES

Armit, R., Zott, C. (2001), 'Value creation in e-business', Strategic Management Journal, Jun/Jul 2001, Vol.22, Iss.6/7, pp.493-520.

CommerceNet Study (2000), 'Survey: Barriers to Electronic Commerce', <http://osiris.sund.ac.uk/~cs0pco/iec/CommerceNet2000SurveyBarrierstoEC.doc>

Deschoolmeester D. & Braet O. (2001), 'On the Five Mechanisms for Strategic IS Alignment', Proceedings of the 8th European Conference on Information Technology Evaluation, 17-18 September 2001, Oxford, London, pp.1-27.

Deschoolmeester D. & Kortleven C. (2001), 'Internet-ability - On the context & criteria influencing Internet attractiveness for organisations', EFMD (European Foundation for Management Development), Dublin, 12-14 Sep. 2001.

Economist Intelligence Unit, The 2004 e-readiness rankings, a white paper from the Economist Intelligence Unit in cooperation with IBM Institute for Business Value, http://www-5.ibm.com/services/uk/pdf/eiu_ereadiness_19april04.pdf

Jutla D., Weatherbee T. (2002), 'Supporting Clear: A Strategy for Small and Medium sized Enterprise Adoption of E-business practices in Atlantic Canada', IFIP World Computer Congress, June 9-11 2002, Copenhagen, Denmark, pp. 169-186.

Levy L., Powell P. and Yetton P. (2002), 'IS alignment in Small Firms: New Paths through the Maze', ECIS, June 16-21 2003, Napoli, Italy.

Ministère de l'Economie, des Finances et de l'Industrie, Ministère délégué à l'Industrie, Internet et Entreprise mirages et opportunités?, Pour un plan d'action, Contribution à l'analyse de l'économie de l'Internet, Rapport de la Mission conduite par Jean-Michel Yolin, 1 January 2004, http://www.telecom.gouv.fr/documents/yolin/1215mirage2004.pdf

OECD (1999), 'Business-to-Business E-commerce: Status Economic Impact and Policy Implications', OECD Working Paper, No.77.

Porter, Michael E. (1980) Competitive Strategy: Techniques for Analysing Industries and Competitors, New York: The Free Press.

Porter, Michael E., Millar, Victor E., (1985), How Information gives you competitive advantage, Harvard Business Review, July-August 1985, Vol.63, Iss. 4, Pg. 149, 12 pgs.

Prananto A., McKay J. and Marshall P. (2003), 'The spectrum of e-business maturity in Australian SMEs: A Multiple Case study approach to the applicability of the stages of growth for e-business model', ECIS, Napoli, Italy.

PriceWaterhouseCoopers (1999), 'SME E-commerce study, Asia Pacific Economic Cooperation (APEC), Final Report September 24.

Scupola A. (2002), 'Adoption of E-commerce in SMEs: Lessons from Stage Models', IFIP World Computer Congress, June 9-11 2002, Copenhagen, Denmark, pp. 291-308.

Wiseman, C. (1985), 'Strategy and Computers Information Systems as Competitive Weapons.', Dow Jones Irwin, London.

Wiseman, Charles, (1988), Strategic Information Systems: Trends and Challenges over the Next Decade, Information Management Review, Summer 1988, Vol. 4, Iss. 1, pg.9, 8 pgs.

Zhu Kevin, Kraemer Kenneth L. and Xu Sean (2002), A Cross-Country Study of Electronic Business Adoption Using the Technology-Organization-Environment Framework, Center for Research on Information Technology and Organizations (CRITO), University of California, Irvine, ICIS 2002 Best Paper, 15-18 December 2002, Barcelona.

PERCEIVED USEFULNESS AND EASE-OF-USE ITEMS IN B2C ELECTRONIC COMMERCE

Findings from an Analysis of Web-based Qualitative Data

Jonna Järveläinen
Turku Centre for Computer Science; Turku School of Economics and Business Administration
Lemminkäisenkatu 14 A., 5th floor
FIN - 20520 TURKU
tel. +358-2-4814 457
fax +358-2-2410 154
e-mail: jonna.jarvelainen@tukkk.fi

Abstract: The standard perceived usefulness and ease-of-use items of technology acceptance model were developed for organizational contexts, but they are also used in studies of consumer acceptance of electronic commerce. However, the terms used in the items are to some extent ambiguous. It is difficult to evaluate improvement in productivity, performance or effectiveness in purchasing products online. In this paper, items from a few recent electronic commerce studies applying technology acceptance model are summarised. Web-based qualitative data is analysed and the emerged features of electronic commerce that are important to consumers are compared with the measurement items from prior research. Finally, a combination of items based on the comparison is proposed. Consumers perceive the 24/7 accessibility of Web shopping site as useful, but this feature has not been measured in the prior studies reviewed here.

Key words: item, perceived usefulness, perceived ease-of-use, electronic commerce, consumer research

1. INTRODUCTION

How is a consumer's shopping performance improved by electronic commerce? Alternatively, how is a consumer's productivity increased when purchasing a book online or how is effectiveness enhanced when making an online travel reservation? Imagine a situation where searching for the product from online shopping sites would be time consuming but the actual purchasing process would be fast and the product would be cheaper online but, on the other hand, the delivery would bring the total cost higher than if the product had been bought from a traditional shop. Comparing improvement in shopping performance, productivity or effectiveness between effort and outcome would be difficult.

In online shopping surveys based on the technology acceptance model (TAM) consumers have been asked questions such as the examples presented above (e.g. Gefen, 2003; Gentry and Calantone, 2002; Liu et al., 2003). The occasional electronic commerce studies applying TAM have modified construct items to measure e.g. savings in time or money, ease-of-navigation, simplicity of placing an order etc.(Aladwani, 2002; Heijden, 2003; Heijden et al., 2003; Stylianou et al., 2003; Wang et al., 2003).

However, the variation of construct items seems to be as wide as the range of authors. A unified combination of items that does not compromise the spirit of TAM and uses familiar concepts for consumers has not been developed for business-to-consumer electronic commerce research. Understandable concepts are vital in rigorous research: construct validity is in danger if it does not measure up to the intended notion, which is the case when the subjects do not comprehend questions.

The objective of this paper is to propose constructs that could be used in measuring consumers' perceptions of usefulness and ease-of-use in business to consumer (b2c) electronic commerce. A comparison of items used in prior research and features of electronic commerce that consumers find important will be made to accomplish this. The data set of this paper is qualitative and consists of 1900 answers to open-ended questions from a Web survey implemented in February 2002.

The paper is organised as follows: First, the constructs used are reviewed by synthesising published consumer TAM studies in an electronic commerce context. After that, a qualitative data set is analysed to find electronic commerce features related to usefulness and ease-of-use from the consumer perspective. Finally, similarities and differences between the features that emerged from the data and items used in previous studies are discussed.

2. THEORY

The perceived usefulness and ease-of-use of a system are central concepts in the technology acceptance model. Perceived usefulness (PU) has been defined as a user's subjective perception of the ability of a computer to increase job performance when completing a task. Perceived ease-of-use

(PEOU) is a person's subjective perception of the effortlessness of a computer system, which affects the perceived usefulness and has therefore an indirect effect on a user's technology acceptance. (Davis, 1989; Davis et al., 1989; Venkatesh and Davis, 2000)

Table 1. Most common perceived usefulness items used in b2c electronic commerce studies.

Perceived usefulness item	Aladwani 2002	Devaraj, Fan and Kohli 2002	Gefen 2003	Gentry and Calantone 2002	Heijden et al. 2003	Liu et al. 2003	Stylianou et al. 2003	Wang et al. 2003
Using the system improves my performance in my job.			X			X	X	X
Using the system in my job increases my productivity.			X	X				
Using the system enhances my effectiveness in my job.	X	X	X			X		
I find the system useful in my job.	X	X	X	X	X	X		X
The website enables me to search and buy CDs/books faster.	X		X			X		
The website makes it easier to search for and purchase CDs/books.			X		X	X		X
Perceived ease-of-use item								
My interaction with the system is clear and understandable.		X	X		X	X		X
Interacting with the system does not require a lot of my mental effort.			X			X		
I find the system easy to use.		X	X	X	X			X
I find it easy to get the system to do what I want it to do.		X	X		X	X		
It is easy to become skilful at using the website.			X	X				X
Learning to operate the website is easy.			X	X	X	X		X
The website is flexible to interact with.			X		X	X		

The standard items of perceived usefulness and ease-of-use constructs have been used in several b2c electronic commerce studies; the most common items are presented in Table 1. However, since the questions have originally been developed for organisational context, the items used in consumer studies have been modified. The word "job" has been replaced with searching or buying, gathering information, navigating, etc. The word "system" has evolved into Web site, e-commerce, shop-bot, etc.

But how exactly does a Web site improve purchasing performance or e-commerce increase productivity? The Cambridge online dictionary defines performance as "how well a person, machine, etc. does a piece of work or an activity". Productivity refers to "the rate at which a company or country makes goods, usually judged in connection with the number of people and the amount of materials necessary to produce the goods". Effective is "successful or achieving the results that you want" and the derivative effectiveness is "how successfully the wanted results are achieved".

Performance, productivity and effectiveness are work-related concepts, however, they may be ambiguous to consumers since consumers and managers have different frames of references (El-Shinnawy and Markus, 1992). These terms are not clear and understandable to consumers, which may influence the validity of the instrument. The concepts should be adapted into a consumer context by using familiar terms, such as "getting the job done" or "saving money". An effort to translate items into consumer settings has been made in some electronic commerce studies applying TAM. Examples of these items are presented in Table 2.The items measure various actions: placing a purchasing order, cancelling an order and navigation. Control, quality of decision-making, saving money and time, interest of information, adding value, quality of navigation, increase of consumption, accomplishing more navigation as well as advantages and disadvantages are measured too.

Table 2. Additional non-standard items of PU and PEOU in b2c electronic commerce studies.

Study	Const	Item
Aladwani 2002	PU	Using this site would improve my ability to place a purchasing order.
		Using this site would enable me to cancel an order quickly and without hassles.
	PEOU	It is easy for me to place a purchasing order at this Web site.
		I find it easy to cancel a purchasing order at this Web site.
Devaraj et al. 2002	PU	Shopping online gives me greater control.
		Shopping online improves the quality of decision-making.
	PEOU	Overall, I believe that shopping online is easier.
Gentry and Calantone 2002	PU	Using shop-bots would save me money when buying books.
		Using shop-bots would save me time when buying books.
Heijden et al. 2003	PU	The online purchasing process on this website is fast.
Heijden 2003	PU	The information on the site is interesting to me.
		I find this a site that adds value.
	PEOU	It is easy to navigate around the site.
		I can quickly find the information that I need.

Study	Const	Item
		I think it is a user-friendly site.
Liu et al. 2003	PU	Using the e-commerce site with the standard user interface SUI improves the quality of the navigation I'm able to do.
		Using the e-commerce site with the SUI gives me greater control over my navigation.
		The e -commerce site with the SUI supports critical aspects of my navigation.
		Using the e-commerce site with the SUI increases my consumption.
		Using the e-commerce site with the SUI allows me to accomplish more navigation than would otherwise be possible.
	PEOU	I find the e-commerce site with the SUI cumbersome to use.
		Interacting with the e-commerce site with the SUI is often frustrating.
		It is easy for me to remember how to perform navigation using the e-commerce site with the SUI.
		I find it takes a lot of effort to become skilful at using the e-commerce site with the SUI
Stylianou et al. 2003	PU	E-commerce will be of benefit to me personally.
		The advantages of e-commerce to me will outweigh the disadvantages.
		Overall, using e-commerce will be advantageous to me.
	PEOU	I have the skills, capability and knowledge necessary to use e-commerce applications.

Moreover, there are various factors related to the usefulness in the literature. Ability to present rich information, accessibility, speed as well as inexpensive and easy purchases have often been mentioned as the main benefits of b2c electronic commerce (Leinbach and Brunn, 2001). Convenience has been defined as the speed of a process, ease of finding desired products, time savings, instant delivery, hassle-free shopping (Shim et al., 2001). The layout of a Web shopping site, organization features, ease of navigation and use are also convenience items (Lohse and Spiller, 1998). Burke (2002) discovered in his study that customers expected improvement in convenience so they that would be able to use one-click ordering, to browse their purchasing history and to be able to return defected items to a local retail store where they would also be delivered.

The ease of the purchasing process is a combination of perceived ease-of-use of a reliable system and the ability to get the desired product/price combination from the system. For example, Zeithaml, Parasuraman and Malhotra (2002) describe an e-SERVQUAL instrument for measuring e-service quality, which includes measures for efficiency and reliability. Efficiency-construct contains items concerning "the ability of the customers to get to the Web site, find their desired product and information associated with it, and check out with minimal effort". Reliability refers to the technical functioning of the site.

Park and Kim (2003) have measured for example user interface, product and service information quality, information satisfaction and relational benefit. User interface quality refers to the customer perception of convenience and user friendliness of a Web shopping site. Information quality measures relevancy, timeliness, sufficiency, understandability, consistency and playfulness of product or service information. Information satisfaction is defined as "emotional response to the experience provided by the overall information service" and relational benefit is associated with the benefits a customer gains from using the site.

To summarize, the terms used in standard perceived usefulness and ease-of-use constructs are not appropriate for electronic commerce consumer research. There are numerous candidates for adapted PU and PEOU items, and the following data analysis could assist in selecting the most suitable items for future b2c electronic commerce studies applying TAM.

3. THE RESEARCH BACKGROUND

The data used in this analysis is part of a Web survey conducted in February 2002, which has been reported in other papers (Järveläinen, 2003a; 2003b; 2003c). The overall research question of the study was: why do people who use the Internet for product information seeking not make their purchases online?

As the research question concerned online information seekers, the target population included both customers who had some online shopping experience and those who had none. A Web survey was therefore chosen as the data collection method. This setting omits the people who have not adopted Internet technology yet, since they do not have either means or motive for online shopping and consequently it would not be meaningful to include them in the target group.

The sample used in this study was based on the customers of a large passenger cruise company that sells products online. The company under study is one of the largest Finnish passenger cruise companies operating in the Baltic Sea, owned by a large European ferry operator. Its substantial market share (between Finland and Sweden approximately 50% and between Finland and Estonia roughly 20%) and its long reputable history make it a trustworthy company.

The customers have four purchasing channel choices: travel agency, company-owned ticketing agency, telephone and the company's interactive online booking system (since the products are in this case cruises the more appropriate word "booking" will be used hereafter). The online booking system is in real-time and the payment methods include a secure Internet banking payment solution, credit card or bill, the same as in the bookings made through the traditional channels.

In comparison with postal mail or telephone surveys, a Web survey is a more rapid and a cheaper way to collect a great amount of data. In addition, the data coding is easy and reliable as with any computer-supported data collection method. The disadvantages include for example a biased sample or biased results and counting the response rate. (Humphrey, 2000; Ilieva et al., 2002; Zhang, 1999)

Ensuring the validity of the respondents is not easy with Web surveys because of the anonymity of the respondents. To reach the target population and valid subjects, the Web survey was placed on the company's homepage and only visitors who had made a reservation with the company during the previous three months were requested to answer the questionnaire. The risk of a very biased sample was minimal since it was apparent that not every customer visiting the company's Web site had any online shopping experience because of low adoption rates of b2c electronic commerce globally, locally and among the customers of this company. An effort was made to eliminate multiple responses from the same respondent with 1) no-reward policy (O'Neil and Penrod, 2001), 2) a cookie that was saved in the respondent's computer under his own username (and so impeded answering more than once) and 3) a careful screening of responses to find exactly similar responses.

The data was collected between February 1st and 11th 2002. The total number of responses was 2,511, from which 2,479 were unique and valid. The respondents were compared demographically to the respondents of two previous Web surveys (from January 2000 and November 2001, 920 and 2,875 responses respectively), which collected data about the average visitor to the company's Web site and development suggestions for the Internet pages. In all three Web surveys, 58.5 per cent of the respondents were women; the majority of subjects were between 18 and 45 years of age. The majority of respondents lived in the greater Helsinki area and Western Finland where the departure ports are situated. In these respects, this survey's data seems to correspond with that of the other surveys.

Quite a high percentage, 92 per cent of the respondents, used the Internet daily or almost daily. In 2003 (Statistics Finland, 2003), 66 per cent of the Finnish people used the Internet and as a Web survey cannot reach the non-users, the high percentage is understandable. Over half of the respondents (51.5 per cent) had made the previous booking over the telephone and approximately one in four had visited a travel or ticketing agency. Merely 23.2 per cent of all respondents had made the previous booking online.

The mainly quantitative questionnaire also included a few open-ended questions. One of them was: "Why have you used or not used the online booking system? Are you going to use the online booking system in the future? Please explain why." Over 1,900 respondents answered this open-ended question. This qualitative data was too interesting to be ignored totally, since most of the answers were quite long and rich in information, as open-ended responses tend to be in online surveys (Gunter et al., 2002).

4. ANALYSIS AND RESULTS

In order to capture the essence of the large qualitative data set, the data had to be organized systematically. (Romano Jr. et al., 2003) describe a methodology for analyzing Web based qualitative data. The data codes were derived from the data itself as in grounded theory (Glaser and Strauss, 1967), because of the explorative nature of this study. The data was coded with a qualitative data analysis software package called QSR NVivo 1.3 and in the first phase, 19 categories emerged. Each response was coded into one or several categories.

Due to the extensive size of the data set the dichotomous coding was clustered with principal components analysis. Dichotomous data may be analysed with factor analysis if the underlying inter-item correlations are moderate, below 0.6 or 0.7 (Kim and Mueller, 1978). The largest correlations were between Online booking easy and Online booking quick with coefficient being 0.367. Approximately half of correlation coefficients were not statistically significant and nearly half of coefficients were below 0.2. In that sense, the data set meets the requirements. The results of the principal components analysis with Varimax rotation and Kaiser normalisation are presented in Table 3. The interpretation of components and descriptions of categories appear in Table 4. Approximately 50 % of variation was extracted with the analysis and seven factors emerged.

Table 3. Principal components analysis results.

	1	2	3	4	5	6	7	Extract
Online booking easy	0.728							0.579
Independent use of online booking system	0.519							0.291
Online booking system accessible 24 hours	0.588							0.352
Online booking quick	0.626							0.418
Offline when necessary	0.466							0.238
Offline booking easier		0.599						0.443
Product not available online		0.733						0.561
Offline booking cheaper		0.670						0.495
Satisfied with the system or online channel			0.707					0.515
Has tested the online booking system			0.634					0.453
Received an incentive when used the system			0.563					0.363
Distrust of the online channel				0.779				0.623
Conversation preference				0.727				0.599
Satisfied with traditional channel					0.795			0.649
Other reason					0.714			0.601
User interface of the online booking system complex						0.764		0.639
Experienced problems with the system						0.778		0.650
(Product related) information easier to get traditionally							0.608	0.396
Online booking slow							0.776	0.613
Eigenvalues	2.002	1.444	1.375	1.304	1.255	1.077	1.022	
Variance extraction	10.536	7.598	7.236	6.863	6.603	5.668	5.378	49.883

Table 4. The factors and data categories.

Higher category /factor	Lower category	Description
Trusts only the customer service	Conversation preference	Wants to communicate with a person or merely prefers offline booking.

Higher category /factor	Lower category	Description
	Distrust of the online channel	Distrusts the online channel itself or the security or his/her own skills with the online booking system (cannot be sure that he or she is able to get the intended booking e.g. correct booking).
Online booking useful	Ability to browse independently	Can check timetables, prices or availability independently at his or her own pace, or does not want to disturb customer service persons.
	Online booking easy	Perceives online booking as easy.
	Online booking quick	Considers online booking quick or quicker than offline booking or dislikes queuing on the phone.
	Online booking system accessible 24h	Online booking system accessible whenever most appropriate for customer, after call centre or agencies have closed.
	Offline when necessary	Usually prefers online booking system, but books the special arrangements offline.
Cheap and complex bookings easier offline	Offline booking cheaper	Knows or suspects that the products are cheaper offline or wants to ensure the cheapest product available or information about discounts and therefore books offline (e.g. discount cruises including bus transportation from home town).
	Offline booking easier	Perceives the booking (process or product) as complex or offline booking as easier or clearer than online, and therefore prefers traditional booking.
	Product not available online	Has e.g. a discount or gift voucher or a special cabin requirement, or a special service requirement for transportation, baby cot or pet, or a table reservation, none of which can be booked online.
Problematic or complex user interface	Experienced problems with the system	The online booking system has not been available, or has received an error message or there has been some other system related problem.
	User interface of the system complex	E.g. clicking back and forth through the stages in the user interface.
Tested, got incentive and satisfied with online channel	Tested the system	Either has tested or will test the system, possibly out of curiosity.
	Received an incentive when used the system	Perceived online booking as cheaper or received an incentive when he or she used the system (during a marketing campaign).
	Satisfied with the system or the Web	Used to or satisfied with online channel or system, or merely preferred online booking.
Satisfied with traditional customer service	Satisfied with traditional channel	Used to or satisfied with trustworthy expertise or friendly customer service in traditional channels.
	Other reason	Books always with the same person or is a regular customer, or has no knowledge of the online booking system.

Higher category /factor	Lower category	Description
Getting information and booking online is slow and difficult	(Product related) information easier to get traditionally	Has specific questions about entertainment, destination or wants extra information and considers information more easily available from traditional channel.
	Online booking slow	Perceives online booking as slow or slower than offline booking, e.g. because of having to click back and forth through the stages in the user interface or because of slow connection speed. Prefers to get immediate answers to his or her questions or to book last-minute cruises through traditional channels.

5. DISCUSSION

The objective of this paper was to propose constructs that could be used in measuring consumers' perceptions of usefulness and ease-of-use in electronic commerce. The items used in prior research were synthesised and features of online shopping that consumers find important were explored. The similarities and differences, summarised in Table 5, will be discussed here.

Three of the standard PU items were equivalent to data categories that emerged from the qualitative data. Additionally three analogous PU items were found from Table 2. There was no equivalent item for "Online booking system accessible 24 hours" in the standard or additional items. This is quite surprising since accessibility is one of the most beneficial features of the Internet (Lohse and Spiller, 1998).

Factors "Trusts only the customer service", "Cheap and complex bookings easier offline", "Problematic or complex user interface", "Getting information and booking online is slow and difficult" contained categories that referred to perceived ease-of-use of the traditional channels or perceived difficulty-of-use of the online booking system. It would be fruitful to also measure the ease-of-use of other channels in channel choice studies, but in technology acceptance studies these should be modified to focus on an online channel instead.

The first three PEOU categories related to a standard item: *I find it easy to get the system to do what I want it to do.* This item is derived from self-efficacy, which refers to the belief that one has the capability to perform a particular task (Chau, 2001), or computer self-efficacy, which is a belief in sone's ability to put computer technologies to use (Venkatesh and Davis, 1996). Instruments for measuring computer self-efficacy (Wang et al., 2003) and Internet self-efficacy (Hsu and Chiu, 2003) could also be used here.

The standard ease-of-use items are also mostly applicable in b2c electronic commerce research. However, the usefulness items may be ambiguous for consumers, and the proposed items below could be used instead.

Table 5. The data categories and equivalent items related to PU and PEOU constructs.

Data category	Const.	Equivalent item from published study
Online booking easy	PU	The Web site makes it easier to search for and purchase CDs/books.
Online booking quick	PU	The Web site enables me to search and buy CDs/books faster.
Online booking system accessible 24 hours	PU	
Independent use of online booking system	PU	Shopping online gives me greater control.
Offline booking cheaper	PU	Using shop-bots would save me money when buying books.
Online booking slow	PU	Using shop-bots would save me time when buying books.
Satisfied with the system or the Web	PU	I find the system useful in my job / The advantages of e-commerce to me will outweigh the disadvantages / I find this a site that adds value.
Distrust of the online channel	PEOU	I find it easy to get the system to do what I want it to do. Or I have the skills capability and knowledge necessary to use e-commerce applications.
Offline booking easier	PEOU	It is easy for me to place a purchasing order on this Web site.
(Product related) information easier to get traditionally	PEOU	I can quickly find the information that I need.
Experienced problems with the system	PEOU	Interacting with the e-commerce site with the SUI is often frustrating.
User interface of the system complex	PEOU	I find the e-commerce site with the SUI cumbersome to use
Online booking easy	PU	The Web site makes it easier to search for and purchase CDs/books.

Perceived usefulness

1. The Web site makes it easier to search for and purchase products.
2. The Web site enables me to search and buy products faster.
3. The Web site is useful since I can use it at any time suitable for me.
4. The Web site gives me greater control.
5. The Web site would save me money when purchasing products.
6. The Web site would save me time when purchasing products.
7. I find the Web site useful in purchasing products.

Perceived ease-of-use

1. I find it easy to get the Web site to do what I want it to do.
2. It is easy for me to place a purchasing order on this Web site.
3. I can quickly find the information that I need on this Web site.
4. Interacting with the Web site is often frustrating.
5. I find the Web site cumbersome to use
6. My interaction with the Web site is clear and understandable.
7. Interacting with the Web site does not require a lot mental effort.
8. It is easy to become skilful at using the Web site.
9. Learning to operate the Web site is easy.
10. The Web site is flexible to interact with.

6. LIMITATIONS AND FURTHER RESEARCH

There are some limitations to this study. The literature review was not exhaustive, but exemplifies some recent and representative TAM studies in a b2c electronic commerce context. Although the data coding was checked with randomly selected samples presented for coding to colleagues, the data set was too large to be checked thoroughly by two or more data coders. Therefore, some categories may have been overlooked although the author has carefully read the complete data set 4-5 times. The proposed items in the constructs presented above are merely suggestions. However, validation of the items is beyond the scope of this paper and remains to be carried out in future research projects.

REFERENCES

Aladwani, A. M., 2002, The development of two tools for measuring the easiness and usefulness of transactional Web sites, *European Journal of Information Systems*. 11 (3): 223-234.

Burke, R. R., 2002, Technology and the Customer Interface: What Consumers Want in the Physical and Virtual Store, *Journal of Academy of Marketing Science*. 30 (4): 411-432.

Chau, P. Y. K., 2001, Influence of computer attitude and self-efficacy on IT usage behavior, *Journal of Organizational and End User Computing*. 13 (1): 26.

Davis, F. D., 1989, Perceived Usefulness, Perceived Ease of Use and User Acceptance of Information Technology, *MIS Quarterly*. 13 (3): 319-340.

Davis, F. D., Bagozzi, R. P., and Warshaw, P. R., 1989, User Acceptance of Computer Technology: A Comparison of Two Theoretical Models, *Management Science*. 35 (8): 982-1003.

El-Shinnawy, M. M., and Markus, M. L., 1992, Media Richness Theory and New Electronic Communication Media: A Study of Voice Mail and Electronic Mail. A paper delivered at the International Conference on Information Systems, Dallas, Texas.

Gefen, D., 2003, TAM or just plain habit: A look at experienced online shoppers, *Journal of End User Computing.* 15 (3): 1-13.

Gentry, L., and Calantone, R., 2002, A comparison of three models to explain shop-bot use on the Web, *Psychology & Marketing.* 19 (11): 945-956.

Glaser, B. G., and Strauss, A. L., 1967, *The Discovery of Grounded Theory.* Aldine De Gruyter, New York.

Gunter, B., Nicholas, D., Huntington, P., and Williams, P., 2002, Online versus offline research: Implications for evaluating digital media, *Aslib Proceedings.* 54 (4): 229-239.

Heijden, H. v. d., 2003, Factors influencing the usage of Websites: The case of a generic portal in The Netherlands, *Information & Management.* 40 (6): 541-549.

Heijden, H. v. d., Verhagen, T., and Creemers, M., 2003, Understanding online purchase intentions: Contributions from technology and trust perspectives, *European Journal of Information Systems.* 12 (1): 41-48.

Hsu, M.-H., and Chiu, C.-M., 2003, Internet self-efficacy and electronic service acceptance, *Decision Support Systems.* (Article In Press - Available online at www.sciencedirect.com).

Humphrey, T., 2000, Does Internet research work?, *Journal of the Market Research Society.* 42 (1): 51-63.

Ilieva, J., Baron, S., and Healey, N. M., 2002, Online surveys in marketing research: pros and cons, *International Journal of Market Research.* 44 (3): 361-382.

Järveläinen, J., 2003a, Barrier to online bookings: Lack of Trust in Online Skills. A paper delivered at the 26th Information Systems Research Seminar in Scandinavia, Haikko Manor, Finland.

Järveläinen, J., 2003b, The Impact of Prior Online Shopping Experience on Future Purchasing Channel Choice. A paper delivered at the 11th European Conference on Information Systems, Naples, Italy.

Järveläinen, J., 2003c, Preferring Offline Bookings: An Empirical Study of Channel Choice Motives of Online Information Seekers. A paper delivered at the 16th Bled eCommerce Conference, Bled, Slovenia.

Kim, J.-O., and Mueller, C. W., 1978, *Factor Analysis: Statistical Methods and Practical Issues* Sage University Paper series on Quantitative Applications in the Social Sciences, 07-014. Sage Publications, Beverly Hills and London.

Leinbach, T. R., and Brunn, S. D., 2001, E-Commerce: Definitions, Dimensions and Constraints, in: *Worlds of E-Commerce: Economic, Geographical and Social Dimensions,* Thomas R. Leinbach and Stanley D. Brunn, ed., John Wiley & Sons Ltd., Chichester, England pp. xi-xviii.

Liu, S.-P., Tucker, D., Koh, C. E., and Kappelman, L., 2003, Stadard user interface in e-commerce sites, *Industrial Management & Data Systems.* 103 (8): 600-610.

Lohse, G. L., and Spiller, P., 1998, Electronic shopping, *Communications of the ACM.* 41 (7): 81-87.

O'Neil, K. M., and Penrod, S. D., 2001, Methodological variables in Web-based research that may affect results: Sample type, monetary incentives, and personal information, *Behavior Research Methods, Instruments, & Computers.* 33 (2): 226-233.

Park, C.-H., and Kim, Y.-G., 2003, Identyfying key factors affecting consumer purchase behavior in an online shopping context, *International Journal of Retail & Distribution Management.* 31 (1): 16-29.

Romano Jr., N. C., Donovan, C., Chen, H., and Nunamaker Jr., J. F., 2003, A methodology for analyzing Web-based qualitative data, *Journal of Management Information Systems.* 19 (4): 213-246.

Shim, S., Eastlick, M. A., Lotz, S., and Warrington, P., 2001, An online prepurchase intentions model: The role of intention to search, *Journal of Retailing.* 77 (3): 397-416.

Statistics Finland, 2003, *Tieto- ja viestintätekniikka jo osana arkea, mutta käytön yleistyminen on hidastunut (ICT is already a part of everyday life, but the generalization of usage is decelerating),* Statistics Finland, 18.12.2003, Accessed 9.1.2004, Available from http://www.stat.fi/tk/tp_tied/tiedotteet/v2003/915ttts.html.

Stylianou, A. C., Robbins, S. S., and Jackson, P., 2003, Perceptions and attitudes about eCommerce development in China: An exploratory study, *Journal of Global Information Management.* 11 (2): 31-47.

Wang, Y.-S., Wang, Y.-M., Lin, H.-H., and Tang, T.-I., 2003, Determinants of user acceptance of Internet banking: an empirical study, *International Journal of Service Industry Management.* 14 (5): 501-519.

Venkatesh, V., and Davis, F. D., 1996, A model of the antecedents of perceived ease of use: Development and test, *Decision Sciences.* 27 (3): 451-481.

Venkatesh, V., and Davis, F. D., 2000, A Theoretical Extension of the Technology Acceptance Model: Four Longitudinal Field Studies, *Management Science.* 46 (2): 186-204.

Zeithaml, V. A., Parasuraman, A., and Malhotra, A., 2002, Service Quality Delivery Through Web Sites: A Critical Review of Extant Knowledge, *Journal of the Academy of Marketing Science.* 30 (4): 362-375.

Zhang, Y., 1999, Using the Internet for Survey Research: A Case Study, *Journal of The American Society for Information Science.* 51 (1): 57-68.

Author Index

L

M

N

P

R

S

T

V

W

Z

Printed by Publishers' Graphics LLC